Enchanted Vagabonds

by
Dana Lamb

The Long Riders' Guild Press
www.thelongridersguild.com
ISBN No: 1-59048-080-5

To the Reader:

The editors and publishers of The Long Riders' Guild Press faced significant technical and financial difficulties in bringing this and the other titles in the Equestrian Travel Classics collection to the light of day.

Though the authors represented in this international series envisioned their stories being shared for generations to come, all too often that was not the case. Sadly, many of the books now being published by The Long Riders' Guild Press were discovered gracing the bookshelves of rare book dealers, adorned with princely prices that placed them out of financial reach of the common reader. The remainder were found lying neglected on the scrap heap of history, their once-proud stories forgotten, their once-glorious covers stained by the toil of time and a host of indifferent previous owners.

However The Long Riders' Guild Press passionately believes that this book, and its literary sisters, remain of global interest and importance. We stand committed, therefore, to bringing our readers the best copy of these classics at the most affordable price. The copy which you now hold may have small blemishes originating from the master text.

We apologize in advance for any defects of this nature.

*To
the many people,
officials and citizens of Mexico
and Central America, who gave
us a helping hand along the
way, and without whose kindly
assistance the trip could never
have been completed; to Captain Fischer, Captain Dobbs
and the crews of the* S.S. Mayan *and* Fisherman II; *to our
friends in the United States
Army and Navy who not only
co-operated with us at the beginning, but who made our
journey's end a delight to be
long remembered. Adios, amigos, que le vaya bien.*

*Illustrations
from Photographs Specially Made
by the Author During His
Sixteen-thousand-mile Journey
Recounted in*

ENCHANTED
VAGABONDS

by

DANA LAMB
in collaboration with
JUNE CLEVELAND

1. and 2. Two views of the *Vagabunda* in the process of construction. A sixteen-foot canvas vessel, it was a combination of sailboat, kyak, surfboat, and canoe.

3. The slopes of the volcano were honeycombed with fissures, the breeding-grounds for great colonies of cormorants.

4. We made camp on the beach, between the grave of a Chinese and a small hut made of whisky-cases.

5. We promptly grounded on a mudflat — but we did get some fine clams.

76. At Boca de Conejo. These giant cacti are said to grow at the rate of six inches in ten years.

7. With a piece of copper tubing and two five-gallon oil-cans salvaged from a wreck, we solve the fresh-water problem by distilling sea-water.

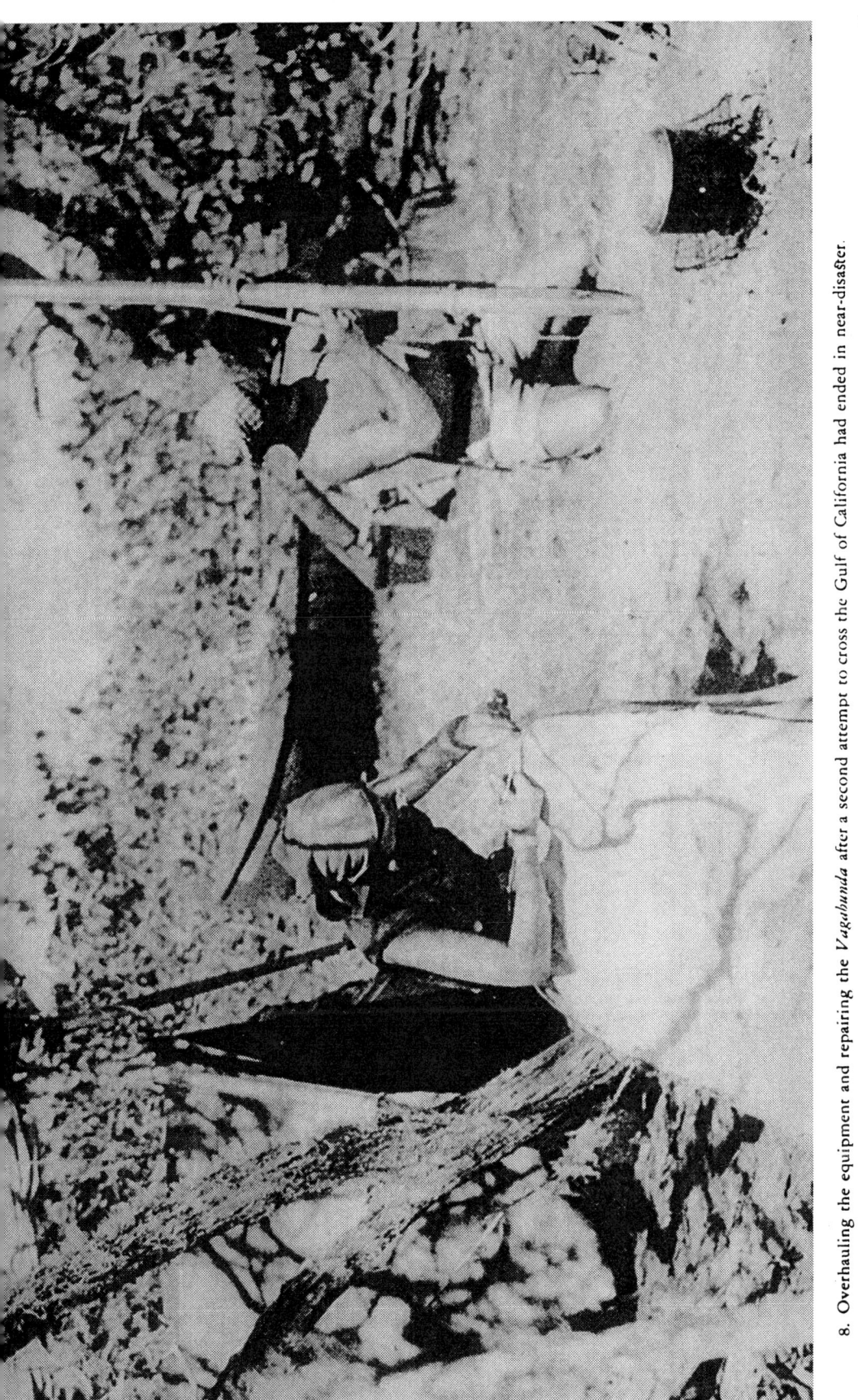

8. Overhauling the equipment and repairing the *Vagabunda* after a second attempt to cross the Gulf of California had ended in near-disaster.

9. An iguana, and to the left, my new machete with a three-and-a-half-foot blade and a bone handle carved into a serpent.

10. We make temporary camp and wait for the tide to turn.

11. Dinner at Wilderness Camp.

12. Ginger and Elena at Puerto Escondido. Elena was a blonde from an inland tribe.

13. With no further nonsense we shot two large alligators and three little ones.

14. Catching iguanas near Sacrificios Harbor.

15. Ginger arrayed in full Tehuana costume, wearing a necklace made of U. S. gold coins — about $400 worth.

16. Cortez' lighthouse at La Ventosa.

17. Doña Lupe (centre) and friends, in embroidered clothes of notable beauty.

18. Starting up the Coatzacoalcos River.

19. Fording a stream just before we reached the army's camp, where we found the enamelled pot and discarded equipment.

20. We decide to return Pussyfoot to the village. Note the slashes on her neck.

21. Ocelot, mountain lion, and jaguar skins.

22. Don Juan and Doña Facunda, Ginger and Dan.

23. Ginger in her Tarzan outfit—taken at Base Camp.

CONTENTS

I	Prelude to Adventure	1
II	Adventure Comes to Meet Us	6
III	Think Fast or Die	17
IV	Where the Tides Meet	32
V	*Los Coyotes*	37
VI	The Captain of the Guard Plays Poker	49
VII	Make Way for a School of Whales	53
VIII	Wreck at Boca de Conejo	57
IX	"The Damn Fools!"	63
X	Four to One Against Us	71
XI	Mexico's Untamed Indians	86
XII	The Jungle That's Not in the Guide Books	94
XIII	Jungle Idyll	107
XIV	Jungle Rhythm	123
XV	They Do It Differently in Hollywood	133
XVI	Jungle Gangsters	142
XVII	Jungle Fever	150
XVIII	Minor Misadventures	166
XIX	Country of Cortez	178
XX	Forbidden Land	215
XXI	Land of Primitive Men	248
XXII	The Second Portage	287

XXIII	Swamp Grass, Quicksand, and a Few Mareños	296
XXIV	Holiday in the *Cerrado*	325
XXV	Guatemala to Costa Rica	352
XXVI	Cocos Island—The Last Adventure	370
XXVII	The End of the Trail—Panama	410

MAPS

1.	From San Diego to Cedros Island	11
2.	Cape of Lower California	33
3.	Lower California	75
4.	From Mazatlan to Chamela Bay	99
5.	From Chamela to Escondido	135
6.	Mexico	145
7.	From Puerto Escondido to Salina Cruz	171
8.	Isthmus of Tehuantepec	220
9.	From Salina Cruz to Sacapulco Bar, Mexico	261
10.	From Sacapulco Bar to Champerico	335
11.	From Champerico to Panama	359
12.	North Portion of Cocos Island	375
13.	Cocos Island	389

ENCHANTED

VAGABONDS

Chapter One

PRELUDE TO ADVENTURE

"You can't take that young girl to Panama in any canoe. Why . . . the whole idea is ridiculous. We are here to stop you—if we have to get out an injunction!"

Wholly unprepared for this assault, I turned towards the speaker in amazement. She was a large, emphatic lady, with an imperative voice and manner, who had just come aboard the old square-rigger, *Star of India*, our headquarters in San Diego harbour during our last two weeks' preparation for our voyage down the west coasts of Mexico and Central America. The lady headed a committee of five—apparently self-appointed—guardians of my wife Ginger's welfare. All five women were complete strangers to both of us! Their attitude indicated that no man did right by any woman —unless he had to—and they were there to see that justice was done.

Red-faced and embarrassed, for the boat was full of people who had come to see us off, I feebly muttered some response about "Two years' intensive preparation for this voyage."

For this was the day! Our "Great Adventure" was about to begin.

During the hubbub, Ginger said nothing. How often since have I yearned to possess myself of that committee's power over Ginger!

We had dreamt about this day. Ginger and I had talked about adventuring ever since we were kids together. And I had wanted, as long as I could remember, to go to all those places marked "unexplored" that dotted the maps that I had hung upon the walls of my den, together with old flintlock pistols and rusty knives. I knew, from my reading and experience, about the perils of the sea and jungle—but nothing in my background had prepared me for committees. Had those doughty adventurers of the past, whose exploits had fired my imagination, had to run the gauntlet of committees? If so, they should have stated so plainly, and not—cravenly—kept still. Had Leander, and the redoubtable Halliburton, braved committees to swim the Hellespont? History remains silent.

Four of the five ladies were no doubt entitled to be addressed as "Madame Chairman," but the fifth was a demure soul who would never have aspired to that honour. She had apparently come "just for the ride." As the committee indignantly bustled away to get its injunction, she slowly followed. The last to go over the side, she turned round and grinned at me— I could have sworn that one eyelid faintly drooped!

We had intended to take our leave of San Diego that morning at seven —this was October 9, 1933. All the last-minute errands were done, our equipment packed and loaded in our boat, the *Vagabunda*. At last we were ready to leave the life we knew, to trust our lives and fortunes to our wits and to whatever vicissitudes the Fates had in store. In some ways it seemed an easy choice. The depression-ridden world was sunk in a morass of its own making. Like thousands of young men and women, we had come to maturity in such a world—and we were tired of it.

This jaunt off to the wilds was not the result of a sudden impulse, nor was it conceived as a stunt. To both of us a life of routine was distasteful, and we had always planned to avoid it. We like doing things for the fun of it rather than for necessity. We wanted to go alone, and to do this we had to have a little boat that two people could manage. A boat that could be beached along the harbourless coasts of Lower California, and sailed up the rivers of Central America. As a matter of fact, although we called our boat a canoe, it wasn't a canoe at all. The *Vagabunda* was a mongrel boat, a sort of cross between an Eskimo kayak, a surfboat, and a sailboat with a canoe.

Our initial preparations over a period of two years had been conducted rather quietly. Friends knew of our plans; and there had been no little talk as to the wisdom of our attempting to cut ourselves off from the life to which we were trained. Everybody believed that a lot of our fine romantic visions of "freedom and the good life" were but the yeasty ferments of adolescence. And perhaps they were. At any rate they made fine fireside conversation in our parlour in Santa Ana.

The public, however, had shown no special concern with our affairs.

Now enters the villain of the piece. On this last day the papers suddenly decided that we were news! They made a Roman holiday of what they were pleased to call "Puddle-jumping to Panama . . . Couple Take Honeymoon Cruise to Panama in a Canoe . . ." The fact that we were not a "honeymoon couple," but a staid old married pair of nearly a year's standing, didn't mean a thing to the press. Ginger protested violently at first, and then weakly gave up in disgust. The result of all this ballyhoo was most unfortunate. That last day the *Star of India* and ourselves were the reluctant hosts to hordes of newspaper people and curiosity seekers, as well as to our friends and relatives. The air was full of confusion, of contradictory statements, and all the other clamour that the press can so successfully arouse. But among our unknown and uninvited guests were two people whom we still remember with affection.

A little old man came aboard who asked to see us privately. He had brought us a present of an automatic pistol; and his disappointment and grief over our admission that we already had one touched us both. He was old and frail; and judging from his general appearance, the gun was a princely gift. When he said, "You two are doing what I've always wanted and never had the chance to do," we knew that that gun was more than a firearm to him. He was also a symbol to us, for he represented all those romantic spirits hiding beneath the shiny alpaca coats of their routined days the souls of Captain Kidd and Richard Coeur de Lion. What circumstances had chained him we never knew. Perhaps adventure to him had been a shining dream, not meant to be literally translated. And now he was too old. Nevertheless, he did so desperately want to be in some way a part of what, for him, was a dream come true. So he said he'd keep the gun and look at it often and think of us off in the jungle. Then we three cried a bit—and he went away.

The other visitor was a man who offered us his dog. When we explained the impossibility of maintaining a dog in our tiny boat, he insisted, "But, man, you can't go adventuring without a dog. You've *got* to have one!"

A funny business, this of people—the women who wanted to stop us; the men who wanted to aid us. Perhaps, in both cases, a transference of their own hopes and fears. The women's fears of the unknown rationalized into fear for my wife's safety. They represented Woman, the eternal conservator, who has most to lose through Man's restless spirit, and who tries unceasingly to mould it to her needs and uses. We've often wondered since if either of those two men could have been the committee's husband? It would explain much.

Almost all our visitors that afternoon brought some little gift. Since our cargo space was limited to one hundred and fifty pounds of dunnage, which had been carefully selected after countless eliminations, our frail craft was loaded to the gunwales with this additional cargo. So that when we put to sea late that afternoon, with the committee's injunction still unserved, the *Vagabunda* wallowed sluggishly in the quiet waters of San Diego harbour.

All that day, and for many days past, we had been keyed up to a high pitch of excitement. We had been far too busy to really analyse our feelings towards the trip, now fast becoming a reality in place of a rosy dream. Our weeks in San Diego had been spent in visits to the Naval Hospital for inoculations against tropical diseases, and to pick up what medical lore might be of use. We had gotten clearance papers, seamen's certificates; had done all the things that a ship's master, no matter what the size of his craft, must do in order to gain entry into foreign ports. Incidentally, the opposition to our plans had tended to obscure rather than to induce reflection. We just got mad, and stayed that way.

In our conversations with each other, we had talked of sailing the whole distance to Panama. But if we found the trip too difficult, or our craft unseaworthy, we meant to explore the coast of Lower California and the waters of the Gulf of California—and call it a day. This we carefully explained to the press.

So here we were. The excitement that had buoyed us up these many months, that had made us brush aside the fears of friends and ignore the warnings of sea captains and many another hard-bitten familiar of that barren coast—that first fine flush had lessened. Now for the first time we freely admitted a question. Could we do it? Human opposition had vanished with the shore line. There was nothing now to fight—except Nature. We couldn't vanquish elemental forces by talk; we well knew their notorious indifference to oral argument.

The lessening of the tension produced a feeling of chill and uncertainty. Through the fog rolling up the bay we could see the friendly lights of San Diego and the ships at anchor. Only the open sea and the fog ahead. Had we mistaken cocksureness for wisdom, in this attempt to pit ourselves against the treacherous sea and barren land to the south? Too tired and dispirited to go further, we decided to camp upon a sand spit in the outer harbour for the night. Do you remember how you felt when it began to get dark, the first time you ran away from home, when you were six? It was a little like that.

We beached the heavily laden canoe, and in silence began unloading her. The ground was soon strewn with all the well-meaning gifts our kind friends had pressed upon us. And it seemed that days instead of hours had elapsed since we said good-bye. We knew that the canoe could never be gotten out of the harbour unless we lightened her load, so we made a disposition of the gifts.

Now our invariable answer to the question, "What will you eat?" had been: We would dine like kings off Nature's bounty. That night, however, we somehow felt unequal to the test, so we made a dismal meal from a box of candy and similar oddments.

One of our chief immediate concerns was that some one who knew us would come along and see us sitting on that sand spit just outside the harbour, glumly munching nougat. It seemed—well, sort of funny, in view of all the build-up.

We knew that our depression was partly psychological, for after all we were not entire strangers to the life we were about to embrace. We had spent months—about two years—hardening our bodies, sleeping on the ground, and eating the coarse unpalatable food—chiefly corn and beans—that we knew we would have to subsist on once we left civilization. We were expert swimmers, good sailors, and first-rate marksmen. There were few contingencies, we believed, that we had not foreseen. Yet not so many months away from that sand spit we were to risk our lives for a can of condensed milk.

True, we had kidded ourselves and each other a bit about the hardening process. If on some jaunt we found the fishing poor, or felt disinclined to fish, we would "skip it just this once," and go up town and demolish a T-bone steak. If the place we had planned to land seemed rather craggy when we got there, we'd compromise on some nice soft beach.

We also had yet to learn to control our thoughts and discipline our minds in the face of real peril. We found—not many days away—that the thing most to be feared was fear . . . that physical danger and suffering could all be met, provided we were free to act. We learnt in those bleak outlands to which we were going that men more often die from fear of starvation and thirst than from lack of food and water.

At this precise point, however, we might have felt happier could we have planned a graceful retreat if a retreat became necessary. But the newspapers had practically demanded, come what might, that we go on to Panama. Alas, we were victims of the press. Furthermore, we had indiscreetly boasted a little. Now it seemed easier to face the perils ahead than the chorus of "I told you so's!" behind.

This, then, was the "Great Adventure."

Chapter Two

ADVENTURE COMES TO MEET US

WE COULD hear the cry of sea birds, and the pounding of the surf upon the perpendicular cliffs. The cries fell upon our ears like the ghostly wail of some far-off locomotive whistle heard at night. Such sounds produce a strange, nostalgic effect upon the human spirit that no words describe. We could see nothing; an eerie, two-dimensional world of sound and fog bounded our horizon.

For ten days we had been on this small island, one of the Coronados group, about ten miles south of San Diego. We had planned to make the islands our first stop-over on Mexican soil, though we had not intended to roost here indefinitely. The Coronados are volcanic rocks, without resources of any kind. An occasional lobster fisherman their only human visitor, the islands remain the unmolested property of the sea birds which nest upon their rocky ledges.

We had arrived here the day following our inglorious landing on the sand spit. It was to be the jumping-off place for Ensenada, sixty miles due south. The two weeks' food supply with which we had left San Diego seemed ample until we reached the Mexican mainland, for it was to be supplemented by the fish that abounded in these waters. That is, the fish abounded theoretically—when we tried to catch them, they became coy and elusive. Besides, we were in no fishing mood. To the front and the rear of us our fears volleyed and thundered. Fear of ridicule if we turned back, and in front of us . . . ? We were just plain scared. The trip had seemed so feasible—and so romantic—back in Santa Ana. But on the Coronados, it was somehow different.

Fortunately, our premonitions of danger were vague and ill-defined. We had no hint of the precise nature of the events ahead—and it was just as well. For it is time enough when the situation demands all one's physical and mental resources to meet it.

So we just sat, part of the time hemmed in by fog. But when the days were clear and we could have left, we wrote in our log anyway "unable to leave because of fog." The Coronados were in no way inspiring to amateur adventurers.

As I said, we were in no mood to fish, so when we discovered lobster traps belonging to some absentee owner, we just moved in and helped ourselves. Six fat, succulent lobsters had fallen before our hardy appetites when the owner of the trap hove in sight.

"How are you fixed for water?" he greeted us. Our canteens were nearly empty, and he promptly filled them. "And how would you like some lobsters?"

He insisted, over our protests, on leaving six! We were both red to the ears with shame and embarrassment. A pretty pass we'd come to, raiding other people's lobster pots! Galvanized into life by our collective guilty conscience, we began diving and soon wrenched twelve astonished lobsters from their hiding places underneath the rocks. These we placed in the generous fisherman's traps, hoping that his pleasure in finding such a catch on his next visit would equal ours when we discovered his traps.

The next day we got our nerve back, and paddled away from the Coronados bound for Ensenada. The weather looked right, and though there was not enough wind for sailing at the outset, we anticipated breezes that would enable us to sail part of the way and bring us into Todos Santos Bay sometime within the next twenty-four hours. A few miles out from the islands we met a fishing boat bound for the mainland, and asked the crew to report us "en route to Ensenada" with the approximate time of our arrival.

The *Vagabunda's* prow shot skyward over the back of a giant wave; white froth raced down the canvas deck and spurted over the gunwale. "Where are we?" Ginger stopped bailing long enough to make herself heard above the scream of the wind. The boat plunged through the crest and skidded down into the trough. Tons of water smashed against the thin mahogany hull of our cocky sixteen-footer.

I didn't answer, for I didn't know—it was anybody's guess. The tiny needle of the compass strapped to my wrist was whirling about with no regard for the magnetic north. We were possibly fifty, maybe sixty or a hundred miles off the coast of Baja California . . . and with a northeaster on our tail.

All day we had paddled under a brassy sky with no breath of wind stirring. Then suddenly, out of nowhere, sometime after nightfall, the storm had struck us. For ten hours the *Vagabunda* had been pulling herself out from under the cascades that boiled over her stern. A miracle! But she was still together.

When the *Vagabunda* wallowed in the troughs, Ginger would bail madly, while a mountain of furious water rushed down on us from behind. Then, as the wind caught the close-reefed sail and slammed us into the wave ahead, Ginger gripped the gunwale for dear life.

"The wind's easing . . ." Ginger, the incurable optimist, pointed to the sail. It was true; the wind was losing some of its fury.

During the next hour only an occasional gust of wind bore down on our craft with sufficient force to test the *Vagabunda's* seaworthiness. And a few hours later she was riding cumbersome swells with only the chop-chop of a mildly ruffled sea slapping her sides.

"Had enough?" I asked.

This was my way of reminding Ginger that she was at least partly responsible for this harebrained adventure. It would also forestall any complaint that her hair hung in pasty strings, or that her thin clothing was plastered coldly against her slender body.

But she did not answer.

Ginger and I had grown up together.

Not so many years before this day, she was the little pig-tailed pest who tried to muscle in on anything we fellows planned round the open fire on winter evenings. Soon she became the tomboy whose dirty fingers smudged the map of Cocos Island that hung in my den. She was the young amazon, as burnt and as sooty as the rest of us, whom I found on the fire line, after the smoke of four hundred acres of burnt-over California watershed had cleared away. It used to make me mad, too. For when there was some hazardous, and purely masculine, excitement afoot—such as chasing a fire truck—you could bet your last nickel that Virginia Bishop would somehow get wind of it, and probably be at the scene of action when you arrived. These things were vexing to the young male ego. Then one day, when she thought she was safe from interference, she undertook to ride a wild-eyed broncho, Grey Wolf, that I owned. I had expressly forbidden her to go near the horse, for he was dangerous. I got there just in time to pull her out from beneath his hoofs. But in that split second, when I heard his maddened squealing, and knew without question who it was he was attempting to kill, Ginger ceased to be "the girl who lived next door." . . . And so we were married.

It had been her suggestion in the first place that we take this canoe trip. We had built the *Vagabunda* together; had spent weeks modelling the mud form over which we laid the keel and bent the ribs, while old salts and helpful friends looked on and made suggestions.

Our canoe, when finished, weighed one hundred and fifty pounds, had a forty-two-inch beam, and a depth of twenty-four inches. She carried a fourteen-foot mast, and with the jib had a hundred square feet of sail. With the exception of a cockpit scarcely big enough for the two of us, she was decked over. Into her construction we had put everything we knew, or could find out, about a sailboat, a surfboat, a canoe, and a kayak. She was a sweet little ship, and with dreams of the open sea and adventure, we christened her the *Vagabunda*. We could have picked no better name, for a "vagabond" she surely was to the end of her life.

We started on our equipment as soon as she was finished. Since none of the outfitting companies could supply us with the type of equipment we thought necessary, we made our own. This was a problem that took considerable thought. The *Vagabunda* had a capacity of not more than five hundred pounds. Ginger and I, plus the sails, paddles, and lines, weighed three hundred and fifty pounds. That meant that we could carry only one hundred and fifty pounds of other gear, including food and clothing. The equipment offered for sale was entirely too cumbersome. The lightest tent with a canvas floor that we could buy weighed eight pounds. Our homemade, insect-proof tent weighed four. Four pounds less tent to carry enabled us to carry four pounds of something else, equally essential. The tent, sleeping bag, compact mess kit, and other gear were of our own manufacture. Into two strong, light, waterproof boxes, we stowed our food, guns, camera, films, first-aid kit, diaries, fishing gear, and repair outfit, together with the tent, sleeping bag and mess kit. Oh yes, and our cash resources as well: $4.20 carefully wrapped in a bit of oilskin.

So here we were, the three of us, somewhere off the coast of Baja California, and still going strong. I made the entry in the day's log: "Oct. 22. Position unknown. Northeaster struck us last night, and we had to run before it. This morning we are becalmed in a fog. Three gallons of water in canteens. Provisions for two more days." I put the log away in its waterproof box, and settled down to keep watch.

"Dan! Dan!"

Ginger was shaking me. Evidently I had dozed off.

"There's a ship out there!"

We could barely hear the muffled drumming of a powerful engine. A narrow grey bow crept stealthily out of the fog. I grabbed for the steering paddle. Ginger cupped her hands and was about to hail them, when something in the craft's strange outlines made me hesitate.

"Hold it!" I commanded.

"But, Dan, she'll get away. We ought to at least find out our position. Perhaps they'll even take us in to shore."

The outlines of the strange craft were becoming well-defined. Long, low, and rakish, every line indicated that she was built for speed. She was perhaps a hundred and eighty feet in length, and her hull was painted grey. But in spite of her colour and general appearance, we knew that she was not a United States Navy vessel, for she carried no identifying numerals upon her bow. Then I had an awful hunch . . . somewhere off this coast the notorious fleet of rum runners that supplied contraband liquor to nominally bone-dry America had its anchorage. It was no place for Ginger.

We heard a voice shout. The mysterious boat cut her engines. A figure dimmed by the haze, appeared at the rail. He stood there looking at us for several minutes. Then, quite distinctly, we heard him. "Hell's bells, It's a canoe!" Other figures joined him.

"Gimme those glasses!" a voice commanded. There was a moment of silence. Then, "I'll be damned! There's a woman in it!" This was followed by an explosion of profanity.

"A woman—a woman!" The way they kept repeating that one word sent a chill of apprehension up my spine. Ginger turned towards me, her face chalk-white.

"Get out the guns," I said.

I eased the boat round. With every ounce of strength, I began a chop stroke with the paddle. My hope—to lose ourselves in the fog.

"Hi, you . . . !" A voice like the bull of Bashan hailed us from the deck. The big grey vessel glided towards us with maddening ease.

Ginger, meanwhile, had slipped open the zipper that held the canvas well of the cockpit in place and protected the dunnage beneath the deck from water. I reached out for the Luger and the extra clips of ammunition. She held her .22 automatic in her lap.

"Come about there!" the voice from the boat ordered. "And you might be telling me what you're up to."

"This is the canoe *Vagabunda*," I replied. "We're en route from San Diego to Ensenada."

There was a chorus of shouts, quickly stopped by the man with the binoculars. "Bound for Ensenada, are you?" he asked incredulously. "Then you'd better turn about, you're heading for China."

"We would be obliged," I answered, "if you will report us safe when you make port." There was the sound of hearty laughter at this.

The boat was now close enough so that we could get a good look at its crew. Four were clean-cut young fellows, but the fifth was a large, hairy-armed brute in hip boots, wearing a slicker with the sleeves rolled back. He looked like nothing so much as Jack London's "Sea Wolf."

There was the rattle of glass. A window in the pilot house opened, and a young blond head popped out. "I say there," he shouted, "before you start for Mexico, you'd best come aboard for a cup of tea."

We waited expectantly for the cries of derision which should have greeted this remark, but the men on deck regarded us soberly.

"Thanks," I replied, "but if you'll give us our position, we'll be on our way."

"You'd best reconsider our invitation," the blond-headed pilot insisted. "As for your position, you're nearer Davy Jones's locker than any other place I know of. Furthermore, if you have any sense left, you'll come aboard—before we come and get you!"

We knew he meant it. Ginger turned to me and said quietly, "Since we can't get away, we'll have to take a chance. Let's go."

Without more ado, we shoved our side-arms into our belts, pulled our sweaters down over the gun butts, and swung alongside the stern of the other boat. Our blond-headed host was there to meet us—his boat so close

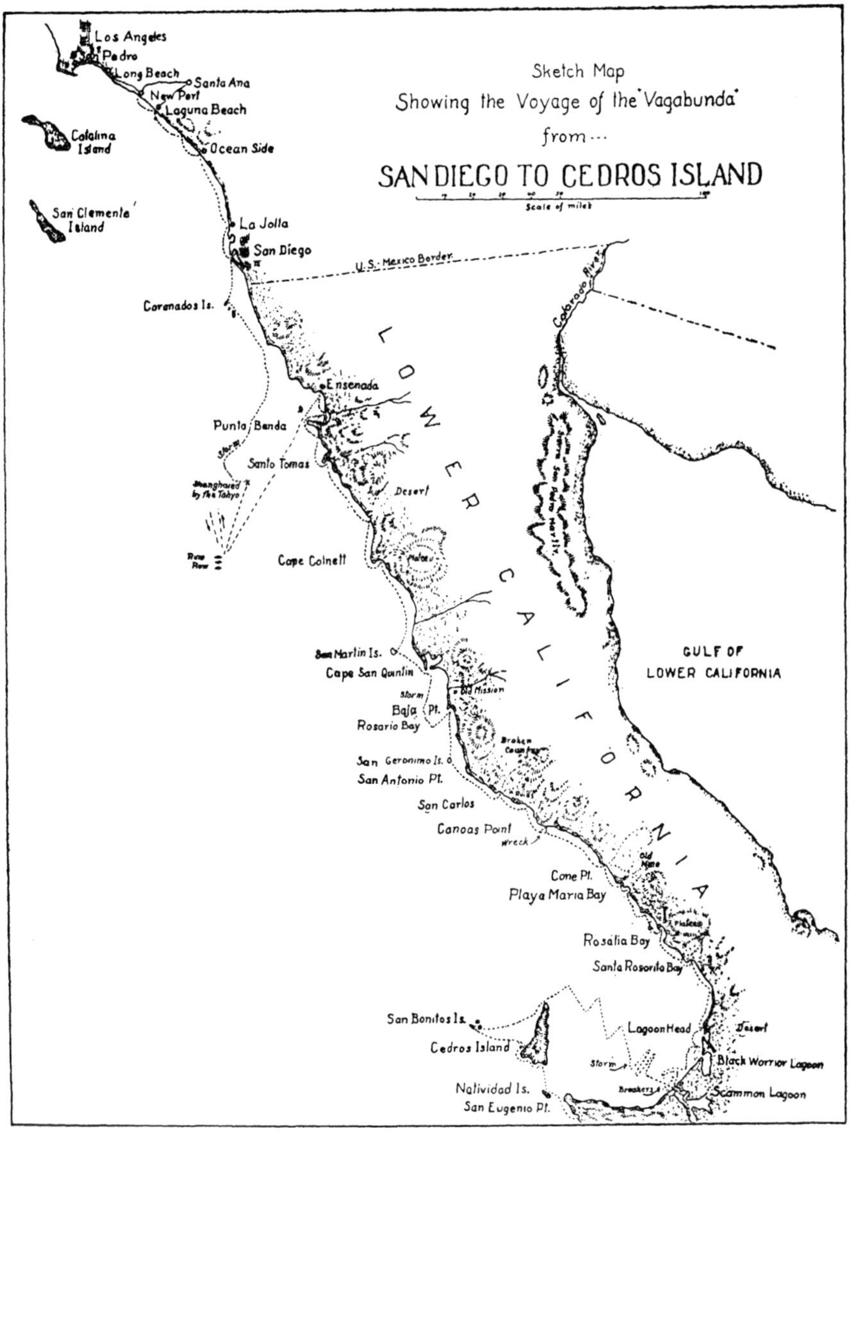
Sketch Map
Showing the Voyage of the "Vagabunda"
from...
SAN DIEGO TO CEDROS ISLAND
Scale of miles
Los Angeles
Pedro
Long Beach
Santa Ana
New Port
Laguna Beach
Catalina Island
Ocean Side
San Clemente Island
La Jolla
San Diego
U.S.-Mexico Border
Colorado River
Coronados Is.
LOWER CALIFORNIA
Ensenada
Punta Banda
Storm
Santo Tomas
Shanghaied by the Tokyo
Desert
Row Row
Cape Colnett
Plateau
San Martin Is.
Cape San Quintin
GULF OF LOWER CALIFORNIA
Storm
Old Mission
Baja Pt.
Rosario Bay
Broken Country
San Geronimo Is.
San Antonio Pt.
San Carlos
Canoas Point
Wreck
Old Mine
Cone Pt.
Playa Maria Bay
Plateau
Rosalia Bay
Santa Rosorito Bay
San Bonitos Is.
Lagoon Head
Desert
Cedros Island
Storm
Black Warrior Lagoon
Natividad Is.
Breakers
Scammon Lagoon
San Eugenio Pt.

to the water that he only needed to extend his hand in order to help us scramble aboard.

"I'm Captain Budge," he said. I introduced Ginger and myself. A few minutes later, the crew had the *Vagabunda* dragged on deck.

"Now, if you'll follow me we'll do our best to warm you and your lady up a bit," he said. Then he turned to the crew who stood by, staring. "Proceed at four knots—and keep a sharp lookout."

As the craft got under way, we marched along the steel deck and past the pilot house, through a very small hatch and down a steep stairway into a small, triangular galley jammed in the bow. The quarters were cramped but spotlessly clean. We sat down on opposite bunks that served as benches during the day. The Captain busied himself among the tea things.

"You Americans prefer milk and sugar in your tea, do you not?" he said in his pleasant English voice.

"We'll take it any way—just so it's hot," Ginger answered.

"Now tell me," said Budge, as we settled back, "just what in hell you think you're doing out in the middle of the Pacific in that cockleshell?"

"Why—er—a—we're going to Panama," I said, somewhat taken aback.

"You're going *where*!?" he demanded.

I repeated.

"In that funny little boat?"

I nodded.

The fog horn was blowing incessantly, and the sound seemed to irritate him. He kept looking towards the hatch. "Pardon me," he said finally, and started towards the stairway. "If they don't stop that damned racket, they'll have every damned cutter in the Pacific on our necks."

After he'd gone, we looked at each other. Well . . . what have we gotten ourselves into now? Something ought to be done . . . what? Will he put us ashore?

Budge returned.

"Captain, will you put us ashore at Ensenada?" I asked. "And by the way, what's the name of your boat?"

He looked at me oddly for a moment. "Oh, yes, this is the *Tahyo*, out of Vancouver," he answered, "but we haven't been home for some time."

The *Tahyo* was the most notorious rum runner on the Pacific coast.

He turned abruptly to Ginger. "Can you cook?"

"A little bit; why?"

"Do you suppose, while we're taking you in to shore, that you could bake a chocolate cake?" Ginger smiled, rather dubiously. "You see, we've been on this craft for over six months, and we haven't tasted a chocolate cake for all that time," he explained.

This was too much for Ginger. Somehow the two didn't fit together. "Rum runners . . . chocolate cake," she said in a dazed, wondering voice.

"Rum runners or not," said the Captain, "*we still want a chocolate cake!*"

It would have been no greater shock to have learnt that Captain Kidd's favourite tipple was malted milk—"vanilla flavour, please."

Ginger started hunting round the galley for the "makings." Budge started up on deck. I followed, with the idea of keeping an eye on the "Sea Wolf."

While on deck, looking over the lashings that the crew had put on the *Vagabunda*, I saw the "Sea Wolf," who answered to the name of "Big Bill," start towards the bow. He was headed for the galley—and Ginger was there—alone. I hunched my gun into a handier position, and started after him. His great hulk disappeared down the tiny hatchway.

And then—bedlam broke loose. The smashing of dishes mingled with the piercing screams of Ginger. I ran to the hatch with my gun drawn and looked down, and there was Bill, sitting on the floor with a blanket draped over his head. He had slipped going down the steep ladder, and reaching out for something to prevent his fall had grabbed a blanket that hung over one of the upper bunks. His huge feet skidding out across the floor had knocked the table loose from its moorings. There he sat in the midst of ruin, frantically pawing at the blanket. Ginger, who had taken refuge on the flour bin, seemed unable to make up her mind whether she was frightened or amused.

As Bill emerged from under the blanket, he grinned sheepishly and said, " 'Scuse me, but kin I lick the frostin' bowl?" So this was the "menace" to my domestic peace! Here I was prepared to rescue a lady in distress, and . . . hell! I put away the Luger, feeling very foolish. "Sea Wolf," indeed! I needed to curb my imagination.

After the crew had polished off the last crumb of Ginger's cake, Budge called us both up to the pilot house. "I've changed my mind about taking you to Ensenada. You're shanghaied," he said roughly.

"But Captain, you promised," I protested. All my fears came back.

"I've changed my mind," he said sternly. "Ginger, your job is to bake a chocolate cake for every meal. Dan, you're production superintendent." Then he grinned. "No joking, how would you like to spend a week with us ditching cutters? If you're out for adventure, here is your chance. But of course, it's dangerous."

Ginger and I nudged each other. This was right up our alley. Our impression of rum runners underwent an immediate change.

As a matter of fact, these men were not the roughnecks and hoodlums that the average person believed them to be. They were mostly ex-Navy men picked for their intelligence and ability to outwit the men aboard the United States revenue cutters. Their job was to pick up a load of liquor at "Rum Row"—a fleet of freighters anchored well out to sea off the Mexican coast—and then to carry this load up the coast and deliver it to the shore boats, who handled it from there on. The revenue cutters could not touch the "mother ships," which were on the high seas, well beyond the jurisdiction of the United States; nor could they prevent the "shuttle boats," such as the *Tahyo*, from contacting them, as long as they kept out of American territorial waters, for most of the boats engaged in the business were of foreign registry. But the cutters could, and sometimes did, capture the "shuttle boats," if they were found within the twelve-mile limit.

On our first run north, we were "cutterized" by a "six-bitter." To be "cutterized" means that a revenue cutter has attached itself to the "shuttle boat," to prevent it from contacting the shore boat. The rum runners catalogue the cutters as "two-bitters," which are the old type sub-chaser; "four-bitters," the new type revenue cutters; and "six-bitters," captured and converted high-speed rum runners. And being "cutterized" by a "six-bitter" was something to challenge the resource of these rum running crews.

We tried all the regular methods of ditching the cutter, but she was too speedy. Finally, about eleven o'clock that night, we shut down our engines and put out all the lights except the small riding light on the very short mast. The weather was hazy, and it looked as though there might be a heavy fog before morning. The cutter wasn't taking any chances on our remaining "put," however; she began circling us in a wide orbit, keeping her engines turning over, so she could get under way in a hurry, if we should decide to run for it. I was in the pilot house with Budge, showing him how to make a leather holster for his side-arm, when Big Bill came in.

"How would you like to take a look at the engine room?"

"Fine," I said, and followed him aft. I had been in lots of engine rooms in my time, but this was the cleanest and most efficient one that I had ever seen. A twelve-hundred-horse-power Diesel engine stood in the centre, her bright work sparkling in the light. On each side of this great engine Liberty airplane motors were set in tandem. The boat had three propellers.

"Dan, I've got a new idea," said Bill. "It's fishing—fishing for suckers." He grinned. "Want to lend a hand?" I nodded. He took down a long bamboo fishing pole, and sent me off to get Budge's flashlight. When I returned with the flashlight, he removed its bulb, and fastened it to the end of the fishpole. Then we ran wires from the bulb down to the end of the pole, where we connected them to the flashlight batteries. A small switch in the middle of the pole completed the arrangements. I was completely puzzled as to what he meant to do with the contraption. "Suckers?"

Then Bill went round the room collecting pipe fittings and weights. He cut a small hole in the top of a thirty-gallon oil drum, through which he dropped the weights. Together, we wrestled the big drum on deck. Bill took the fishpole, stuck it through the small opening in the drum, and lashed it securely into place. In response to my questions, all he would say was, "Wait." Off through the haze we could see the cutter, still circling warily.

Bill left me and went forward. When he came back with the crew we lifted the strange contraption into the water.

We waited in silence, watching the cutter until she came astern of us. "When I give the signal, snap the switch," Bill whispered. I leaned over the side, he raised his arm . . . at that precise moment the masthead light went out. On the fishpole's tip, the tiny flashlight bulb glowed. The *Tahyo's* decks began to vibrate as the big Diesel turned over.

In the pilot house, Ginger was steering the craft as we glided off into the night, leaving the revenue cutter going round and round our dummy masthead light!

"Hang on, everybody, we're off—and we're late." Budge stepped to the engine-room telegraph and shoved all three indicators "Full speed ahead." The *Tahyo* shuddered, settled low in the water, then, enveloped in spray, she raced through the night, taking us to some unknown destination.

A week later, we cautiously steamed in towards Todos Santos Bay and Ensenada.

Budge paid not the slightest attention to our suggestion that we be left off on the high seas, but steamed impudently right into the harbour. Soon the *Vagabunda* was over the side, and we were paddling away towards shore. Not even then did the *Tahyo* leave. She circled round us twice, tooting her whistle and ringing her bell, while the crew waved good-byes. This was too much for a revenue cutter standing by in the harbour, and it promptly gave chase; only to have the elusive *Tahyo* take to her heels and quickly disappear seaward in a cloud of foam.

When we sailed into Ensenada and presented our papers, we had plenty of explaining to do. The fishing boat had reported us as "en route to Ensenada," and when we failed to arrive we were given up as lost at sea. The very cutters that the *Tahyo* had been playing tag with had been searching for the wreckage of our canoe.

After this ordeal was over, we started out to face the desert coast of Baja California.

Chapter Three

THINK FAST OR DIE

OCEAN liners, sea-going yachts, fishing boats, and craft of all kinds pass daily the west coasts of Baja California, Mexico, and Central America, on their way to and from the great ports of the Pacific. Yet in the year 1933 the maps of these countries still had large areas marked "unexplored —unknown country." We used to wonder why. Surely countries with great mineral wealth, potential resources, with traditions of magnificent ancient civilizations had as much to offer the explorer as the bleak lands of Antarctica and Mongolia.

Perhaps the least known of all these vast stretches is Baja California. As you approach it from the sea it suggests a land arrested at some moment of its creation, some great, unfinished building whose outlines and foundations imply its builders' purpose and intent before an unforeseen contingency for ever prevented its completion. The huge backbone of the bleak Cordillera traverses its length, rising abruptly from the Pacific Ocean for its greater distance, terminating in the great ranges that parallel the Gulf of California. Between the coastal mountains and the Sierra de la Giganta and Sierra San Pedro Mártir ranges of the Gulf lie deserts, plateaus, and semi-arid valleys. Eroded gullies and arroyos, denuded of earth, support scant stands of mesquite, cacti and other desert growths. Here the struggle for life can be won only by the man who has stripped himself of every need except the most elemental. The peninsula's 58,000 square miles of windswept plateaus, deserts, and infrequent oases support a population of 93,000 people, most of whom live in scattered villages along its sea coasts, and near the American border. Its great interior ranges and mountain valleys are the unmolested home of the cougar and the condor. Torrential cloudbursts and cyclones occur at periodic intervals. Little wonder that much of it is still unexplored, even though it was discovered by Cortez in the sixteenth century, and its settlement attempted when New England was still a British colony. It has a wealth of minerals and precious stones; its waters abound in marine life, but Baja California, like Pandora's box, contains much beside blessings.

The Jesuits sought to tame the country's inhabitants, and the men-in-mail to exploit them; both failed. But when the Europeans withdrew, the hardy natives had all but disappeared—perhaps softened by European influence and diet. This land offers, in the true Darwinian sense, survival only to the fittest. It could well be an object lesson to our modern prophets of Utopia who are always screaming about some new dispensation that will take from men the need for unremitting effort. In a sense the Indians of Baja California are a case in point.

This then was the land which we had set ourselves to conquer. I mean conquer only in the sense that survival itself in such a land is a major conquest—not only of environment but of one's self.

The second day out from Ensenada, the blank checks which we had given Fortune, duly filled out by the fickle jade, began to be presented for payment. No piker, Fortune; she tried to take it all!

We had stopped at the Island of San Martin, an extinct volcano rising out of the sea, where we made camp on the beach, between a Chinaman's grave and a small hut made of whisky cases. Then we started out to see San Martin.

The slopes of the volcano were honeycombed with fissures, the breeding grounds for great colonies of cormorants, pelicans and other sea birds. We explored the large crater on the island's summit, and were making our way down the seaward side of the cone when we spied a small crater, in the centre of which yawned a black hole, the rocks round its edges burnt black. The crater looked as though it needed exploring—one of those things that seem a good idea at the time. We speculated as to whether the vent, through which hot gases and steam had escaped during the volcano's period of activity, would go clear to the main crater. We just had to know, so we hurried back to camp to secure a sixty-foot lariat and a couple of candles.

Returning to the crater, I made one end of the lariat fast round a big boulder near its edge. Then I lowered myself through the tiny opening. Ginger handed me the lighted candle, and I slid down the lariat to the floor of the cave, about ten feet below the surface. A large cavern extended in two directions from where I stood.

Ginger attempted the descent feet first; but as she had not the strength in her arms either to let herself down on the rope or to pull herself back up, she dangled helplessly, half in and half out the tiny opening. To help her, I knotted a stirrup hold in the rope about four feet above the ground, thinking that if I stood in it her feet could reach my shoulders. But just as I placed my foot in the stirrup, Ginger, with a shower of rocks and the rope, tumbled down on top of me. There was a crash and we were in darkness. Feeling round, I recovered the candle, lit it, and looked up. The big boulder, round which I had tied the lariat, had rolled down over the opening! We were trapped inside the volcano.

It sounds melodramatic beyond belief, but that was the simple fact. We dared not think about the implications of the situation, nor speculate about the possibilities of suffocation before we even had a chance to plan some method of escape.

"I wonder if we'll ever get out of this?" was all I could trust myself to say.

"There's only one way to find out, and that's to start looking right now, while the candles hold out," Ginger said quietly.

There were two passages. One appeared to lead upward; the other led down a rather steep declivity. The upward passage seemed the best bet. We began slowly moving over its rocky, uneven floor until we came to a place where it apparently terminated in an abrupt drop. I lowered the candle by a string and found another ledge about ten feet down. Working my way down over the edge I let myself down as far as possible and slid the rest of the way. Ginger followed, and we continued our search. Soon we arrived at an absolutely impassable place. The first candle was almost burnt out.

We retraced our steps to the slide. The descent to the lower level had been difficult, but the ascent almost had us licked. By using meagre handholds on one side, I managed to climb to where I could take hold of the upper ledge; then while I held on, Ginger scrambled up over my body and helped me up.

Back at the entrance, only one course remained—to follow the downward passage. One short hour of light . . . one small candle . . . one long chance . . .

I kept wondering as we crept along the passage, "Who will ever know what happened to us? Some one will find, sometime or other, that neat, orderly little camp, with the boat drawn up beside it—but what of us?" The only encouragement that we had was a faint draft of air upon our faces as we crept along.

Finally the candle was all but gone. I put the remaining scrap of wax on a rock. It seemed wise to use what little light remained so that we might see each other for what was probably the last time.

"I wouldn't mind so much . . . going on a fighting basis . . . but sort of crawling out—well . . . ? " Ginger managed a wan smile.

"There goes the light," I said. "Let's start crawling. Anything is better than this damned inactivity."

I led the way, round and over the huge boulders that blocked the dark passage. On and on we crawled; our hands and knees bruised and bleeding from the rough, slashing surfaces, our faces always turned towards that tiny bit of draft. Several times we came to sheer drop-offs. Tossing a rock in the darkness, we could hear it rattle far below in some dark cavern. This meant retracing that tortuous trail, inch by inch, until we found another passage. The blood pounded in our ears. We could hardly hear each other's voices. We became dizzy and lost all sense of direction.

We had spoken no word for a long time. My mouth was dry and sticky. I stopped and stood up, helping Ginger up beside me, and tried to speak, but the words came with difficulty. "Draft—stronger—somewhere," was all I could manage.

Ginger put her arm around my shoulders. "Look! light—up there." I raised my head—above us there were specks of light.

"Out!" I cried.

By a one-in-a-million chance, we had emerged through one of those tiny fissures that we had seen on our way up the slope. Exhausted, we lay down on the rocky ground, watching the stars through the cloud rifts.

In the grey light of dawn, we stumbled our way round the island and into camp. Ginger immediately got out the coffee pot. "Dan," she said, "next time we explore a cave like that one I'm going to wear knee-pads."

"Lady, you're lucky to have any knees left to put them on," I reminded her. "And by the way, I'll take my knee-pads now—in the form of flapjacks."

After we'd eaten breakfast, Ginger lifted the canteen and shook it. "Another pretty surprise. We're almost out of water."

I promised that after a good sleep, and another meal, we'd load the canoe, and go to the mainland and see if we couldn't find some.

The next morning, but little the worse for our experiences, we hoisted sail, and started down the coast looking for water.

We knew that water was scarce, but we had yet to learn just how scarce. Springs and wells that we had been told to look for had dried up or were just not there. Places marked on the map turned out to be non-existent. We would find an old adobe ruin or the long-abandoned relics of some commercial enterprise instead of the village or hacienda marked on the map. We began to have a sinking feeling. We could do without a lot of things but we had to have water.

We came at last to a little bay that was supposed to have a spring. The promise of water was sufficient reason for shooting the heavy surf. We landed and began looking for the spring, but to our great disappointment it was not there. On the north shore there was the wreck of a boat, and back in a little ravine, away from the beach, we found the remains of a pathetic attempt to build a shelter. Two shallow graves on a nearby knoll were further evidences of tragedy.

"Two graves," I said. "Wonder what happened to the third fellow? No one left to bury him—coyotes, maybe."

Looking carefully through the hut, we found several cans of food rusted and spoiled. It was evident that the shipwrecked crew had had food but no water.

Ginger sighed dolefully as I said, "We will have to think of some way to get water, even on this beach. Let's go out to the wreck and see what we can find."

The old derelict contained quite a bit of gear—even the engine was still in place. I salvaged a piece of copper tubing about two feet long. On the beach we found two five-gallon oil cans in fair condition. These cans litter the coasts from Alaska to Tierra del Fuego, I suppose. We found them everywhere. We carried our spoils back to camp and sat down and looked at them. Two five-gallon cans and a piece of tubing ought to spell "water," if we could find out how to fit those letters together. We had a fire and the Pacific ocean for additional material.

"Of course," speculated Ginger, "we could make a still if we had enough tubing for a coil to condense the steam—but we haven't."

I began to remember stories of other outfits who had made fresh water by distilling sea water, but all of them seemed to have had a terrible time doing it. Some sailors had told a woeful tale of being adrift on a disabled ship in the Atlantic for two years. They had made a little still, which they dared not leave day or night. One man spent all his time pouring cold water on the rifle barrel which they had used for a pipe, to cool it sufficiently to cause the steam to condense. We would have to think of a better solution than that.

"Damn!" I said. "We've spent two years training our bodies for this trip, but we've neglected the most important thing—how to think in terms of this coast. We've always taken water for granted. From now on there will be a lot of other things we can't take for granted too."

"Well, and why not? At home water comes from a tap. I've never had to think about water before," Ginger answered.

"But we both had physics and chemistry in college, and we ought to know how to make water, with that background," I argued.

"I know the formula, if that's any help," Ginger offered. "All I ever did in 'lab' was read the manual, follow instructions, and there it was. Besides, I wasn't sent to college to think. I was sent to learn what other people had found out. If I did that I got a good grade."

We sat round for half an hour drawing diagrams. Finally, as the result of our deliberations, I whittled two wooden plugs, drilled holes through them for tubing; dug two pits in the sand, built a fire in one, and put one can two-thirds full of sea water over it. In the other pit I put the empty tin, and on top of it the shipwrecked crew's rusted two-pound coffee can full of sea water. In places the rust had eaten through its sides so that a thin stream of water constantly dripped on the oil can and kept it cool. Soon the water was boiling and steam whistled round the plugs, whose fit was far from perfect. In about an hour I dismantled the still and picked up the can that had been empty. I was surprised at its weight. I poured some of the hot liquid into a cup and tasted it. It was perfectly sweet water.

"Whoops!" said Ginger. "A quart an hour—that will keep us going."

We kept the still going all day and by sundown we had both canteens full and enough water for Ginger to wash out a few clothes, though we had a sense of guilt in using water for washing where other men had died of thirst. Later we were forced to devise methods of obtaining water which made our first triumph seem like child's play.

The next morning we got off to an early start down the coast. Our course paralleled a barren shore whose cliffs were broken by an occasional arroyo filled with boulders. After some hours of sailing we began to watch for a place to land. A narrow little cove backed by greyish-brown boulders offered the best possibilities, so we picked up a swell and shot the breaker line. Before the canoe grounded I jumped out and right there got one of the surprises of my life. The brown boulders came to life and began moving towards the canoe. We had landed in a seal rookery. Dodging a herd of sea lions was a new experience, but we managed it without casualties on either side. The beach was uninhabitable, however, for a seal rookery does not smell like violets. Disappointed, we abandoned the cove and started out to sea once more.

Had we known that we would find no other landing that night and would have to fight a thunderstorm at sea into the bargain, we probably would not have been so fastidious and would have shared potluck with the seals, irrespective of their personal habits. As it was we spent the night fighting the worst storm in our experience.

Along towards morning Ginger said, "If we keep afloat in this storm I'll never be afraid of another. I thought the storms we fought while in training were bad enough."

"All your life," I said, "you've tagged me round looking for adventure. Now you've got it. How do you like it?"

"Just fine," she retorted, "only I'd prefer this kind of an adventure in daylight. It isn't what I thought it would be, with just an occasional flash of lightning to show you what you're doing. I've bailed out the Pacific ocean at least twice and my arms are so tired I think they're going to drop off."

Daylight revealed our situation. We were about ten miles off shore and had been blown past San Quíntin Bay where we had intended to land. We ate an unpalatable breakfast of tortillas soaked in salt water. The wind blew from first one direction and then another, and by noon we were still three miles off the beach.

Suddenly we heard a great commotion on the seaward side of us. It sounded like the roar of heavy surf. On the horizon the water was churned to white foam. The sound grew louder as the white foam moved steadily in our direction. We lowered the sail and cleared the decks for action. After the storm we were not particularly anxious for additional excitement. Now the foam was streaked with black. Soon we could see great shapes leaping high into the air and falling back into the water with such force that it was churned to spray.

"Dan, it's a school of porpoises and there must be thousands of them. Look! That white line must be at least two miles long."

We pointed the canoe round to meet the assault, hoping that they wouldn't run over us. For twenty minutes we watched the school go by. They dived and splashed round the boat, filling the cockpit with spray. They were five to eight feet long and so numerous that the water was black with them. Finally the last stragglers leapt and splashed by and we heaved sighs of relief.

With our minds on hot coffee and dry blankets we headed for the beach. We could see Baja Point and knew that on the other side of it would be Rosario Bay. There were other reasons besides the coffee for hurrying. The horizon was darkening in the west and the rising wind gave warning that another storm was on the way. We reefed sail and zoomed before the wind, just outside the breaker line and into Rosario Bay.

The surf was high and the shore was rocky—always matters for apprehension to us, since one injudicious landing could do a lot of damage to the *Vagabunda's* canvas bottom.

I took the sail down, lashed it on deck, fastened two long lines on to the sides and let them trail astern.

"What are those lines for?" Ginger wanted to know.

"Safety lines. If the canoe goes ashore too fast, we'll jump overboard, grab the lines and hold it back."

We paddled in near to the breakers, waited for a low wave, and with it shot in close to shore. Just before we reached the beach we both jumped out and grabbed the canoe. Ginger held the canoe in water about waist deep, while I unzipped the cockpit and carried the camp gear to the beach. As soon as the canoe was empty I took the paddles and the centreboard and laid them on the beach just above the high-water line. Then, with Ginger at one end and me at the other, we gently carried the canoe and laid it on the centreboard and paddles. This is the way we landed on almost every beach. In this manner we prevented the canoe from coming in contact with the rocks which would bruise the canvas and soon start a leak. During our three years of travel the bottom of the canoe never touched the beach except when we were unable to prevent it.

We had a camp routine which we maintained throughout the trip. After landing, I built a fire while Ginger got out her mess kit and started preparations for the meal. Then I set up the tent. If we were in the vicinity of game we both took a hike while the coffee water boiled and the fire made a bed of coals to cook on. If we were not in hunting country, I fished while she started cooking. We had agreed upon a division of duties, and by team work in handling the canoe and in making and breaking camp, we managed with a minimum of confusion.

On this particular evening, while Ginger made the long-awaited coffee I caught a mess of jack smelt. As I started to dig a hole in the sand to rinse them in, I made a discovery—clams. They were so closely packed that a few square feet of beach yielded twenty.

There was, in this wilderness, a sense of peace and freedom. We had ceased fretting over the future and what tomorrow would bring. We lived in a timeless world where each day was complete in itself and one accepted whatever it brought without cavilling.

The next morning we made an early start and after two spills managed to get out through the heavy surf. In the late afternoon we came to San Gerónimo Island where, after a fruitless search for a place to land, we finally tied the canoe in a kelp bed and spent the night. San Gerónimo is a great rock with a covering of ash, sand, and guano, surrounded by kelp beds and rocks. There I had the bad luck, while trying to land a big fish, to step on the gaff (a large hook on the end of a pole) and run the point about half an inch into my heel.

After leaving San Gerónimo Island we sailed on down to San Carlos Point, past barren, rocky beaches with high bluffs coming down to the water's edge. We landed near the point and found the wreck of a twenty-two-ton schooner, its name illegible. It had been wrecked, we thought, not more than six months prior to our landing. Its Diesel engines were still in good shape. The beach was strewn with wreckage: parts of old sailing vessels, timbers, cabin fittings, and weather-beaten life preservers. A careful search of the beach disclosed the camp of the shipwrecked crew, the remains of a fire and an old can with coffee grounds in it—but no evidence as to what had befallen the survivors.

We sat round the campfire that night discussing this country. Baja California was evidently a place where you thought fast or died.

There was so much to see and explore on this beach and in the back country that we stayed here several days. Although there was no fresh water, sea food was abundant and we lived well. I made a lobster pot out of driftwood and caught three. At low tide there were also mussels and clams.

My injured foot had begun to pain me, and from its appearance I knew that infection had set in. It had long been my conviction that an injured part of the body heals more quickly if it is used than if it is pampered. This may be contrary to medical opinion on the treatment of infections, but at least it worked in my case. In addition to keeping the wound clean I walked on it at every opportunity. This caused a constant drainage from the infected area and I believe hastened its healing.

In support of this theory we decided to take a walk into the back country, and the next morning scaled the high bluffs that rise almost from the water's edge. On the mesa above there were evidences of newly dug earth, marked with cairns. We speculated as to what might be buried there, but as a cursory examination yielded nothing, we abandoned the inquiry. As we walked inland we saw rich outcroppings of copper ore, quartz, and gypsum. After a considerable climb we came to another high mesa. Here was a big pile of coke, at least ten tons of it. From the coke pile a trail led further inland, and we assumed that at some time mining operations had been carried on near-by.

On our inland trips we frequently came across the relics of abandoned commercial enterprises. Whether their abandonment was always due to the unyielding nature of the land, or to the various political upheavals that have kept Mexico in turmoil for many years, it is hard to say. Doubtless, when men need to utilize the vast mineral, and other resources of Baja California, a way will be found to do so. In the meantime, only those men prepared to risk defeat and inured to hardships should attempt its exploitation. There are too many reminders of their predecessors' failures.

After we left San Carlos we sailed down the coast close to high bluffs of red volcanic rock and yellow sandstone. A strong northwest wind soon had us skimming along under double-reefed sail. Late in the afternoon we rounded Canoas Point and wet, cold and hungry, decided to share the beach with a large herd of sea lions. The seals were anything but pleased at our intrusion. One old bull who made his home in a battered metal lifeboat which was half submerged in the sand was particularly indignant. He remained in the boat barking insults both day and night. The wind was blowing a gale by now and, seals or no seals, we dared not put to sea again.

The wreck of the fishing boat *Welfarer* lay just off shore. On its seaward side in six-foot letters was the word "help" and an arrow pointing in the direction of a narrow canyon. In the canyon we found two shacks but no crew. On the beach were two battered lifeboats (now the homes of seals), lobster pots, potato crates, a woman's high-heeled slipper, ragged blue jeans, and a sailor's hat. There was something indescribably lonely and tragic about these beaches with their mute evidences of disaster. We found them often and they always left us with a feeling of desolation.

Along this section of the coast there was little to differentiate one day's routine from the next. The surf was always dangerously high, the landings uniformly difficult. The country behind the rocky beaches was, with few exceptions, cactus-covered desert. The scant vegetation was heavily armoured with daggerlike thorns to repel invaders. Its cell structure was cunningly contrived to retain and store every bit of moisture that could be extracted from the air or from the ground. A few birds made their homes in these cacti and we also saw occasional reptiles and rodents.

We were not able to do nearly so much exploring in the back country as we wished. The problems of food, water, and finding a place to land (and getting there after we found it) necessarily took up most of our time. Our dependence on the beaches for food cut down the radius of our operations away from it considerably. For like the life round us we were stripped to the fundamentals, not only in our way of living, but in our thinking as well. Survival meant cutting the cloth of our desires to fit the circumstances of our environment. Some one has said that "Civilization is a magnificent aggregation of the non-essentials." Baja California gave a new meaning and interpretation to the essentials. Here they often meant the least we could survive on, and it took unremitting effort to obtain them.

One of our most difficult adjustments was the regulation of our bodies' reaction to our diet. Used to having quantities of milk, butter, eggs, and other easily digested foods, our digestive juices seemed unable to cope with the problem of extracting nourishment from the coarsely ground corn and the low protein fish diet. At first we were always hungry, and we gained little satisfaction from our meals. Later on this discomfort passed away and our stomachs became hardy enough to have coped with shoe leather. In spite of the lack of variety in our diet we were in perfect health, and our outdoor life seemed to agree with us. We could see the increase in the size of our muscles, and our endurance had doubled. There was also a decided difference in our mental reactions to situations that would formerly have bothered and worried us.

After leaving Canoas Point our next port of call was Blanca Point. Here the surf was dangerously high—at least twenty feet. While we were waiting for the calm spell—that is, the low breaker in the series—a big sea caught us and we came in end over end. A sorrier looking pair of adventurers you never saw—bruised, our clothing torn, and covered with sand. The coyotes here were very troublesome; some of them were even bold enough to come right into camp.

A bit beyond the point lay the little bay of Playa Maria. The beach looked inviting and we stayed there several days. There were fine white sand dunes that offered a roller-coaster ride full of thrills—we slid on our stomachs—and there was also good swimming, fishing, and hunting.

Certainly the old saying, "When the tide is out, the table is set," applied to this beach. We ate abalones, mussels, clams, lobsters, crabs, and large jack smelt. A square yard of beach would yield a gunny sack full of the most succulent clams you ever tasted. We found fifteen pearls of various sizes and shapes in the mussels. On one of our hikes in the back country we found a deep canyon in which there were many quail, deer, and foxes. I had the good fortune to shoot a young deer and we had the welcome change of venison for supper. The balance of the meat we prepared to take with us by cutting it into strips and hanging it on crosspieces over the fire to dry. We always tried to build up a food reserve whenever possible from these infrequent windfalls. We killed nothing for sport, and never more than we could use. We often thanked our lucky stars that the "game hog," so prevalent among a certain class of Americans, had not preceded us.

From now on, travelling along the coast would be more difficult, if anything, and it was evident that the canoe was still too heavily loaded to ride out the storms that blow off these shores. Now that we were past the tenderfoot stage we felt that we could safely dispense with some of our extra equipment, such as a fire grate, extra tools, and so forth, so we left them on the beach when we sailed away.

The cliffs along this coast gave evidences of heavy mineralization. Their faces were streaked with iron and copper oxides, and quartz outcroppings of exceeding promise were plentiful. Ahead of us now lay Scammon's Lagoon, one of the most famous spots along the coast.

We reefed sail when we reached what we thought was the entrance to this extensive lagoon, and skimmed along just outside the breakers. The further we went, the further out to sea the breakers extended. We were three miles off shore and a creaming line of breakers whitened the entire distance between us and the coast. We realized that somehow we had passed the entrance. Turning round we tacked back, scanning the surf for a possible channel—there was not a break in the line of foaming water. I stood up in the canoe and it seemed to me that I could see a small area of calm water just inside the breaker line.

"I think there is a channel," I said to Ginger, "but we are going to have to shoot very heavy surf to enter it. How about giving up the idea of going to Scammon's?"

"No," she said positively, "not unless it can't be done. We've finished everything so far that we've started on this trip—it would set a bad precedent."

We unshipped the mast, and lashed down everything, including the paddles, which we fastened with lanyards long enough to give us the use of them.

We ran a line round the gunwales through the ring bolts, for hand holds in case we should spill. We trailed astern two lines about fifty yards long, so that if we turned over we could swim across the wake of the canoe, grab the lines and not lose it.

When everything was ready we headed in towards the breaker line and waited for the calm spell—there was none. Big seas were coming in our direction and we hastily tried to paddle out of the way. Too late—one caught us astern and lifting us high in the air, almost tossed us out as it carried us swiftly towards the shore.

Ginger, in the cockpit, was paddling first to one side and then the other in an attempt to keep the canoe from skidding sideways. But in spite of our desperate efforts the canoe rolled over on its side. I grabbed for the safety line on the gunwale, caught it with one hand and held it as the canoe rolled like a log towards the beach. With every roll I was either dragged down into the water or tossed into the air. Everytime I came up I looked frantically for Ginger. It was impossible to see anything behind me for the foam of the following sea was too high. My heart sank as I realized that somewhere in those breakers she had been washed off—at least two miles from shore. The only thing I could do was to try to stop this rolling and get the canoe back through the breakers to Ginger. I knew that if I worked my way back to the stern of the canoe and took hold of the trailing lines my body would act as a drag. Each time the canoe rolled over dragging me with it I thought my arms were being torn from their sockets. To work my way along the rolling canoe was the hardest thing I hope I am ever called upon to do, but finally I got back to the line and swung the stern end of the boat round to the breakers. As I began to crawl back along the line to the canoe, Ginger emerged from somewhere and climbed on deck. My relief was so great that I almost dropped the line. I got on board and heard Ginger say, "Thank God! I thought you were washed overboard. I've been almost frantic trying to think of some way to get back to you."

Each of us had been clinging to safety lines on opposite sides of the canoe!

The canoe had lost momentum, and though the breakers were still high they did no further damage. We had a difficult time, however, paddling through them to the quiet waters of the channel. Soon the shore line closed in on either side, and as we struck a current we knew that we were in the lagoon itself. We edged away from the breakers and, laying aside the paddle, I said, "Well, here we are!"

Ginger looked at me, her face contorting like a baby's as she started to cry. "What on earth is the matter now?" I asked.

"Oh, nothing, I'm just frightened," she sobbed.

"Afraid of what?" I asked. "We're safe now. It would be more natural to be afraid of something when it was happening, not when it is over."

"I'm frightened just the same, and I'm going to keep on crying whether you like it or not. When the thing I'm frightened of is happening I haven't time to cry—you can't blame me if I take time out now," she answered.

We spent over a week in Scammon's. The waters of the great lagoon are uncharted and there are many sand bars and islets along its length. It is visited from time to time by fishermen and turtle hunters, but we saw no signs of its present occupation by men. The channels of blue-green water twisted and turned. Great glistening dunes, reefs of clam shells, here and there the whitening bones of whales, a few scattered chollas and other grotesque cacti forms gave the landscape the strange and eerie aspect of some lost and primeval world. Its profound silences were accentuated by the shrill cries of sea birds and the ceaseless movement of water.

One morning we were ready once more to pit ourselves against the tremendous surf line at the bar. Again we had prepared the canoe for an emergency. The tide was going out fast and with the strong current we should be able to clear the entrance in a hurry. We dug in our paddles and headed into the crashing breaker line. As the bow of the canoe rose with the first comber, I shouted to Ginger, "Afraid?"

Without turning her head, she shouted back, "No."

The *Vagabunda* did a noble job as we forced her through each oncoming breaker with steady strokes. Many of the big seas washed completely over the canoe, filling the cockpit with water. When this happened, Ginger bailed out while I paddled, then we would paddle on together. It seemed that we would never get through that surf, even with the tide in our favour. Our muscles began to ache as though jabbed with white-hot irons. Sharp pains ran up our backbones, ending with miniature explosions in our skulls. The sight of open water at last encouraged us to put our final reserves of force behind the paddles, and soon we were out in the open sea. We rested before hoisting sail.

I hadn't realized the lateness of the hour until I got out my tiny compass to take our bearings. It was a little after noon and we were still a long way from our next destination, Cedros Island, which we had hoped to make by sundown. Whipped along by a considerable breeze, the *Vagabunda* dipped her lee rail under, making good time tacking a zigzag course towards the island. By three o'clock, however, the wind had increased so that while we were still making five knots, we were making so much leeway that we were only advancing half a mile an hour in the direction of our destination. We just tacked back and forth helplessly.

At sundown I was astonished to see that we had not gotten more than three miles outside the breaker line. The tide had turned, and we were getting nowhere. With the coming of nightfall the wind increased to almost gale force. We reefed the sail, and making poor time against the strong wind, bucked and bumped round in the darkness. Later Ginger's sharp eyes spied something ahead of us.

"Look! it's white," she cried.

At first I could distinguish nothing, then I saw a great mass of white about two hundred yards ahead of us. "Breakers!" I groaned. "Breakers in front and breakers behind. We can't go ahead, we can't go back. The tide's going out, too, and we're in shoal water. There's nothing to do but fight it out."

Breaker after breaker, each one larger than its predecessor, crashed down upon us as we dug in with our paddles and tried to ride them through. We paddled for our very lives. Blisters rose on our hands and broke, and soon the flesh was raw and bleeding. The paddles became sticky with the mixture of salt and blood. The cockpit was full of water, but we could spend no time in bailing now. It took all our efforts to keep the loggy canoe headed into the breakers. Wet and cold, our bodies aching so that it seemed they would break under the strain, we fought on hour after hour.

We had thought that we were completely exhausted with our initial effort in getting out through the bar of the lagoon, but now we learned what severe stress the body can stand when life depends upon it. Past the barriers that fatigue normally imposes on the will and body, there is another level of energy and another stopping point as well; then beyond that barrier lies a zone of action in which the will alone functions, and the beaten body responds with no counter suggestions of its own.

When Ginger began to falter in her stroke, I shouted, "One more stroke!" We chanted in unison, "One more stroke," hour after hour, all through the night.

Perhaps we continued to paddle long after the heavy seas had ceased, for the realization came very slowly to me that now there were only the high swells of the open ocean about us.

"We're out!" I croaked. "Let's rest."

I tried to lay my paddle down but my hand stuck to it. I was unable to relax my fingers from their grip. After a bit, while Ginger bailed out the cockpit, I managed to work them loose.

Soon we had the sail up and were making good time to our old destination, Cedros. We reached the island in the afternoon but were unable to find a place to land, so went on to a further group of islands, the San Benitos. The first camp we set up was anything but the neat, efficient job we prided ourselves on doing. After a bite to eat we turned in for twelve hours of drugged sleep—on our stomachs, since our backs were raw from wear and tear.

Our hands and bodies were in such a condition that it was impossible to continue until they had had a chance to heal, so we built a camp suitable for a stay of several weeks if necessary. The torture of setting up that camp on San Benitos is something that we are both going to remember.

There wasn't much we could do round camp but think and plan. Our hands were scabbed over, and the least use of our fingers would cause these crusts to break and bleed. Gathering firewood was a great trial. And Ginger must have suffered equally in cooking our meals.

Huge herds of sea lions and sea birds were the island's only inhabitants.

After a week's rest, thanks to the perfect condition of our bodies, we were able to put to sea once more.

Our sojourn did more than rest our bodies. It gave us a chance to summarize the advantages and disadvantages of our adventure. We realized more than ever the necessity for team work, quick thinking, and disregard of self, if we were to continue. If our personal safety came first at all times, then it was better to go home and do our adventuring vicariously. On the other hand, if we could gain some satisfaction from knowing that the aching muscles of today would become the efficient, tireless muscles of tomorrow, and that the mental disciplines imposed by hunger and thirst would eventually free us from concern with our bodies and appetites, we could take the chance that we knew the future held.

Our main objective from here on was Magdalena Bay—and by Christmas. That became our slogan: "Magdalena by Christmas."

We stopped for a day's exploration on San Pablo Point, south of Cedros Island. There was a legend that in the ruins of an old mission there, the padres had hidden a quantity of gold after the order for their expulsion from New Spain. I think they were given thirty-six hours in which to leave their missions, so that they would have no time in which to incite the Indians.

I had kept a careful record, begun when I wore knee pants, of all the "bonanzas" rumoured to be lying along this coast. Truth to tell, as I became older the possibility of finding these hoards seemed remote. Nevertheless, Ginger and I always looked for them if they were not too far off our route. It was something like hunting Easter eggs.

After considerable searching we found the ruin of the mission, a crumbling heap of adobe. I got out the map and found "where a cross marks the spot." The rock was there but the tree was long since gone. Ginger did the specified number of paces, which brought us to the point where the old mission tower had fallen. Beneath this rubbish was supposed to be the treasure. The sun was hot and we both looked with great disinterest at the cementlike adobe that stood between us and riches.

"Now that we know where it is we can come back some other time and get it," said Ginger.

I knew that we never would, but I said, "Yes, of course, we can come back later with shovels." That was part of the game. Then I marked on the map, "located."

We were both in high spirits as a light breeze filled our sails and bore us south towards Magdalena—and a heap of trouble.

Chapter Four

WHERE THE TIDES MEET

WE WERE paddling off Boca Las Animas. Shooting the heavy surf at the bar, we made a perfect landing in the smooth waters of the lagoon at the north entrance leading into Magdalena Bay proper. There are hundreds of miles of these lagoons, uncharted and unexplored, round the bay.

The land began to close in on both sides as we paddled along, observing the scenery. The intense green of the mangroves lining the shore contrasted with the purple haze of the desert behind them and the silvery blue waters of the lagoon in the foreground. It made a lovely, serene picture. How tranquil it seemed!

For years I had been telling Ginger, "It's a wonderful place; you'll love Magdalena Bay." I had made a trip aboard a Navy destroyer years before. For weeks we had been anticipating sailing in its quiet waters. I felt pretty good. Perhaps a trifle too complacent, but under the circumstances I felt we had a right to be. So far we had successfully met a lot of difficult and dangerous situations on the hundreds of miles of travel, afoot and afloat, that now lay behind us. Furthermore, we had made "Magdalena by Christmas."

"We won't have to worry about fighting rough water, riding out storms at sea, or landing through heavy surf for quite a while, Ginger," I said. "We're going to take it easy and——"

"Heaven knows, I *hope* you're right," she interrupted. "We could do with a little tranquillity—for a change."

She was tired, poor dear. Well, from now on, for a while, it would be different. We hoisted the sail to a light breeze and headed down the narrow lagoon toward Magdalena Bay, thirty miles to the south. We had some difficulty in following the channel because the tide was coming in and making the water muddy. Occasionally we'd strike a mudflat. Ginger would lift the centerboard and we'd sound with the paddles until we found deeper water. So we sailed along, singing and enjoying ourselves, though we both noticed that the water was beginning to be bumpy and to kick up little whitecaps.

"Dan, what's making the water so choppy? It's too light a breeze."

I never got that question answered; for suddenly, without further warning, the water round us went mad. Waves were running in every direction,

CAPE OF LOWER CALIFORNIA

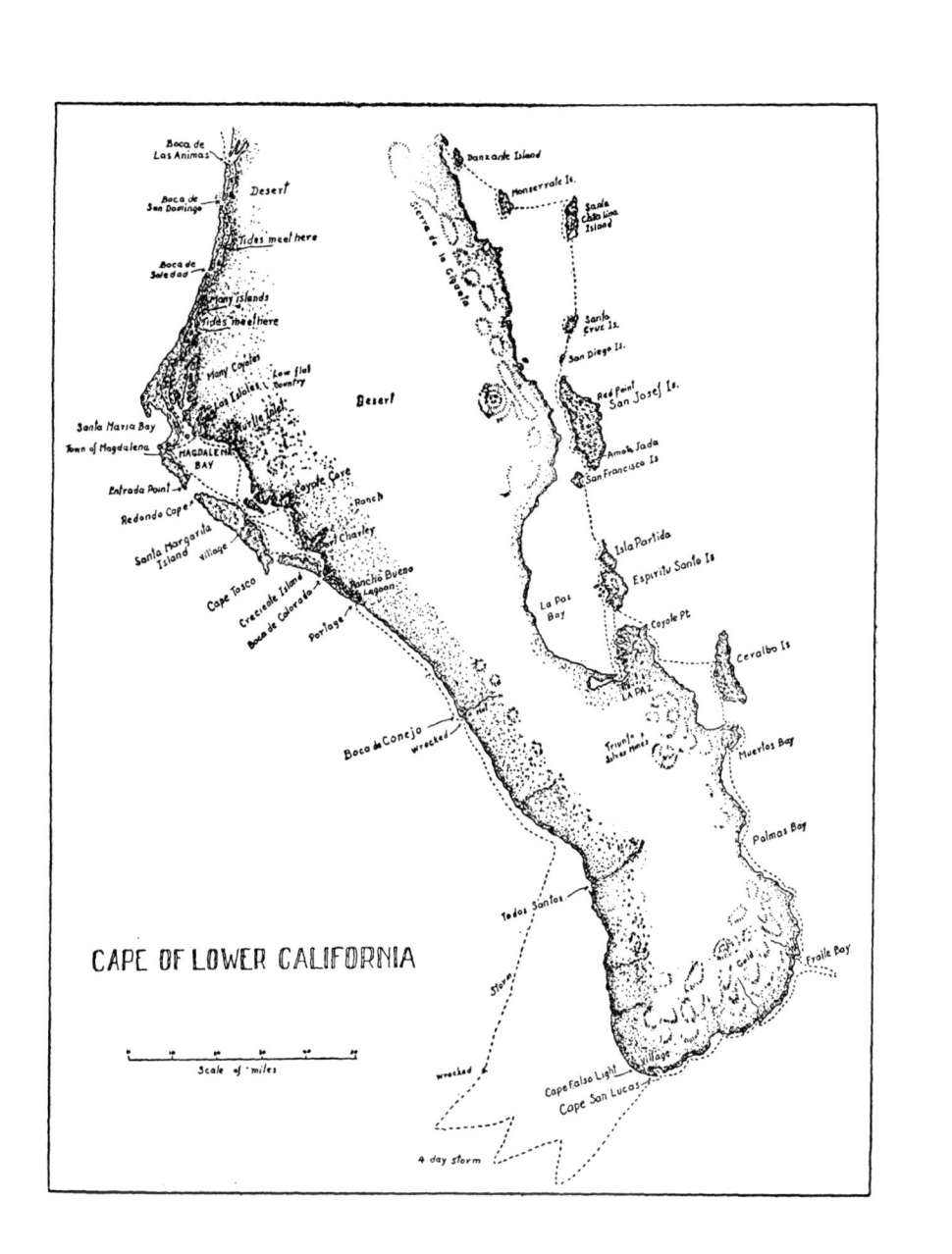

bumping into each other, sending spray high into the air. The canoe began bouncing like a cork. Scrambling to our feet, we hastily tried to get the sail down. Ginger stood up to untie the halyards; the canoe swerved crazily and she was flung overboard, as though a giant were playing crack-the-whip with the canoe.

I grabbed a paddle and held it towards her, hoping she could catch hold. The canoe whirled out of her reach. The next thing to do was to get the sail down and paddle towards her. I knew that no human being, no matter how expert a swimmer, could stay afloat in that furious sea for long. My fingers were all thumbs in my agitation. I finally untied the halyards and dropped the sail. This accomplished, I paddled towards Ginger for all I was worth. I could see her fighting desperately to keep afloat. For some reason I seemed to lose all sense of direction. The scenery round me was reeling drunkenly. As I redoubled my efforts to reach Ginger, it seemed that I was heading towards the sea. Then I'd turn towards the desert; but always in the direction of Ginger. What the *devil* was this, anyway? Then, I realized what was happening. We were being whirled in a great maelstrom—Ginger on one side of the vortex, and I on the other. This was the giant.

Ginger, in trying to swim towards the canoe, and I, in attempting to reach her, were being carried into the centre of the maelstrom. There followed a sickening shock when I realized fully that if she *did* swim into the centre of that seething vortex, she would be carried down by the suction. My heart stood still; my throat closed.

"Ginger! Ginger!" I shouted, "swim to one side so that I can meet you. Look out! Whirlpool!"

She did not hear me. Every faculty was concentrated on the one purpose of reaching the canoe quickly.

Then, as though the furies were not satisfied with this predicament, there came, their dorsal fins sharply cleaving the water, a new menace—sharks. The water seemed alive with them, all of them heading towards Ginger. She looked up, saw my face, my increased efforts with the paddles, and looked round—one horrified glance. Then she dug in with fear-driven strokes. But she was heading straight for the centre of the whirlpool—that equally fatal centre. Somehow, I must reach her before she hit that vortex.

Closer and closer we came to each other, running an awful impromptu race. Ginger, her face barely out of the water, had not as yet sensed the danger of that sucking centre. All she knew was the approaching danger of those deadly fins. She was beating me to the centre. I could see only her frightened, determined face.

Suddenly, the only thing that I could possibly do occurred to me. I jumped upright, grabbed the mast as high as I could, swung my weight outwards towards Ginger, and carried the mast with me. The mast and I hit the water at the same time, the end of the spar within Ginger's reach.

She lost no time in grabbing it. Near exhaustion, she pulled herself on to the capsized canoe.

After taking a few minutes to get our breath and to allow our emotions to subside, we crawled along the side of the overturned canoe to the mast and pulled it out of its socket. Putting our combined weight on the high side, we miraculously righted our craft as it gyrated madly in the very centre of the vortex. Despite the canoe's buoyancy, it looked as though we should most certainly be carried down by the tremendous pull. We fought with every ounce of our remaining strength, putting all we had behind each paddle stroke.

Then the whirlpool slowly subsided. The water became quiet except for sullen eddies, each going in a different direction.

"Well!" I exclaimed. "What a merry-go-round that was!"

These were the times when banalities saved us. We simply didn't dare show each other how frightened we had been. "Get back to normal just as soon as possible" had to be our rule on such a trip. The nervous reaction to the ordeal we had been through would set in soon enough.

Ginger, coughing up sea water, gasped, "Look at the chart and see if there isn't some explanation; there must be a reason."

We examined the document closely. Finally, in minute letters, we found the legend, "Where the tides meet." "That's it!" I said. "The tides coming in at each end of this narrow channel meet at this particular point. The currents hit each other in such a way that they form a giant whirlpool. After wearing themselves out, they continue on as usual."

"Let's make camp," Ginger suggested. "After all, my friend, I'm about ready for that rest and relaxation you promised me. A while back didn't I hear you say something about there being nothing to worry us? Can this be the 'restful place' you've talked so much about? It seems full of dynamite to me, but correct me if I'm wrong."

"Please skip it," I said.

Chapter Five

LOS COYOTES

Reaching shore on the seaward side of the lagoon, we lost no time in setting up camp. As usual, while Ginger started to prepare the meal, I began fishing. But for the first time on the whole trip there were no fish, not even a nibble. I prowled along the beach looking for clams, but the tide was in too far. Apparently Nature had closed her cupboard doors.

The next day things continued to go wrong. All morning the current was against us. In the afternoon when the current was with us, the wind was against us. By night we had made only fifteen miles.

The following day, however, we rounded Man o' War Cove, where the village of Magdalena lies, bleak, barren, wind-swept and desolate, perched precariously between the encroaching waters of the bay and the overhanging brown, rocky hills that pile up on its northern side.

As we pulled into the rickety little pier, we could see people running from one house to another, followed by flea-bitten dogs who paused to bark at us.

We wondered a bit at all this activity as we paddled up to the pier. Ginger started up its ladder—but sat down on deck a bit abruptly with a rotten ladder rung in her hand.

"What a place! What a reception!" she said disgustedly.

"This place hasn't changed a bit," I said happily. "Good old Magdalena." I noticed a pile of decaying timbers on the beach which, on my previous visit, had been a boatshed.

"I think," said Ginger with a slight hint of sarcasm in her voice, "I'd rather land on the beach, if you don't mind. *That*, at least, won't crumble the minute I step on it!"

Trooping to the beach to meet us, there came the men we had seen running from house to house. But what a difference! They were now elegantly attired in white uniforms, with Sam Browne belts and much gold braid.

"A dress reception," I said, as the officials came forward to examine our papers. We had great difficulty in concealing our merriment at the pompous air of officialdom that hung over the proceedings. With great solemnity we were given the freedom of the port and invited to the Port Captain's quarters.

On the way I whispered to Ginger that I hoped their houses held up better than their pier. After glancing at the porches, she murmured that she had her doubts.

Later, as we sat on the dilapidated porch of the customs house, I inquired about water.

"There is no water here," the official said. "We haul it from Santa Margarita Island, fourteen miles away."

"How many people live here? How do you make a living?" I asked.

"There are twenty-five families, including the port officials and the garrison of two privates and fifteen officers," he answered.

"Have you no industry; no commercial fishing?"

"No, Señor. We are officials."

"But what do you do to keep busy?"

He smiled. "Our main occupation," he said, "is *'toreadoring el viento'* " (dodging the wind).

Later we noticed that when the men ran from one house to another, they twisted their bodies sideways against the blasts of sand and wind.

After our papers were signed, I mentioned to the Port Captain that we intended going to Turtle Inlet to camp.

"It would never do!" he protested, and his face grew worried. "It is very dangerous, Señor. One of our men was attacked by coyotes there only last week. We hardly found enough of him to bury. Don't go there. We have had no rain here for eight years; the coyotes are starving; they are ravenous, and they will attack anything that hints of food."

I replied, "We have had coyotes all the way down the coast; we are not afraid of them. Can we find a water hole there?"

"There is no water," he answered in a deep, mournful tone. It was plain that he was both puzzled and incredulous. His expression revealed the question in his mind—why should we want to go to such a God-forsaken place?

These officials were appointed to their posts from Mexico City. Few of them ever left the confines of the village to go wandering in the barren back country during their term of office. That they thought we were lunatics was apparent.

We were determined, however, to get to Turtle Inlet, and despite the protestations of the Port Captain, we traded two fishhooks for enough water to fill our canteens, loaded the boat, and shoved off.

Since we had no money to spend in Magdalena, our reason for wanting to go to this inlet was not mysterious, at least not to us. It had the reputation for being the home of thousands of great green sea turtles. We wanted a barbecued turtle for our Christmas dinner. We had, according to our intentions, made Magdalena by Christmas. We were very pleased. It was an occasion for a double celebration.

Approaching the inlet, we came upon a low sand island. On the shore, about thirty feet from the water, were two huge sea turtles. "There's

Christmas dinner," I said. "Let's sneak up on them." Ginger's eyes sparkled as she nodded. Paddling carefully, scarcely daring to breathe for fear of frightening our quarry, we silently approached the unsuspecting turtles. We moored the canoe to a paddle stuck in the mud a few yards off shore. Slipping quietly overboard, we waded stealthily to the beach. The turtles, still unaware of our design, dozed placidly in the sun.

Since turtles found on land are captured by turning them over on their backs, we decided, after a whispered consultation, that Ginger was to tackle the nearest one on the right, while I made a run for the other. In our excitement it seemed to us that the turtles were becoming uneasy. What if they should make a dash for the water? We delayed no longer, but rushed upon our victims and turned over—empty shells!

"Everything in this damned bay has been contradictory," I fumed. "If we want to sail, there's no wind. If we want to paddle, the current's against us. The fish have moved away; and just when we think we're catching turtles, it turns out we're just collecting turtle shells. What kind of a place is this, anyway?"

Disappointed and disgusted, we turned the canoe again towards Turtle Inlet. As we entered the channel great swells came rolling in for no apparent reason. Since there is a strong tidal set in these lagoons, we found the current against us as well. We were at last forced to make camp on a desolate little sand beach at the entrance to the inlet, where thickets of thorny cacti grew almost to the water's edge. Grotesque in the gathering dusk, their arms seemed to reach out for us. We were tired, disappointed and a little lonely. Our minds flashed back to home. What was happening there? We could see the lights, the hurrying crowds, and, for a fleeting moment, feel the flush of expectancy that lies over the whole world at Christmas time. We decided it was best not to think about it.

Next day, with the tide, we paddled to the end of the inlet, about five miles, where we found a comfortable camp site on the edge of the desert. The shore was lined with coyote trails and some of the tracks were huge. After setting up camp I proceeded to scout round for food. Our bad luck of the previous day was still hounding us. No turtles; the fish wouldn't bite; but fortune finally favoured us with a few clams.

All that night we were annoyed by the prowling of coyotes. This was unusual, for they ordinarily kept away, yapping their defiance from a safe distance.

The third day was a repetition of the other two. No turtles; no fish; no rabbits—nothing. While we were hunting, starved-looking coyotes ran ahead of us about a hundred yards, yipping and barking. I doubted that we could have gotten to the game first if we had found any.

So Christmas dinner was clams. We had them all ways: clam chowder; steamed clams; fried clams; and for dessert, clams broiled crisp over live coals. We made a little Christmas tree from a desert shrub, and that evening as we sat by the fire we presented our gifts. Ginger had made me a handkerchief; and I presented her with a spoon I had carved from mesquite wood. Sometime after retiring I was awakened by coyotes sniffing round the grub box. I took a couple of pot shots at them and missed—but I did hit the grub box.

The morning after Christmas the bay was teeming with food. I came back to camp with the canoe loaded to the gunwales with a fine turtle (I had seen three), a nice mess of fish, and some oysters which I had found on the far side of the inlet growing on mangrove trees! They attach themselves to the tangled roots which protrude above the water at low tide.

Ginger shook her head. "This certainly is the Bay of Contradictions," she remarked as she surveyed my loot. "For our first Christmas dinner away from home, almost nothing; the day after, we dine sumptuously on turtle soup and— Say! Where did you get those oysters?" she demanded incredulously as she saw them for the first time.

"Oh, I picked them off trees; they grow on trees here, you know," I answered nonchalantly. She eyed me with a you-can't-fool-me look. "That's right," I added. "This is the Bay of Contradictions—you named it yourself. I suppose you aren't hungry today, either; and that's another contradiction."

"I could eat," she admitted, "but what are we going to do with all that food?"

"Eat all our shrivelled stomachs can hold now; dry what we'll need later; and use the balance for coyote bait, because I'm going to start on those devils."

That night I laid my coyote trap within clear view of the tent. I piled turtle meat in an open spot on the beach; tipped the equipment box at an angle in front of the tent's entrance, so that by placing my gun barrel upon it the bullet would pass about a foot off the ground, directly over the turtle meat, and I could shoot without using my gun sights. Before we turned in I unzipped the tent flap and pinned it back.

"Dan," Ginger said, while wriggling down into the sleeping bag, "I wish you wouldn't fool with those coyotes. I've heard their bites are poisonous; that they will cause infection—if not rabies. Please don't do it!"

I laughed. "And when does a coyote get close enough to a man to bite him? You know they're cowards."

"Well, how about that man from Magdalena? The coyotes evidently weren't afraid of him."

"I think that story is just hot air. Forget it now and go to sleep. I'm going to stand watch for a while and see if I can't pick off a few of these nuisances."

I lay awake a long time, listening. No coyotes came, and finally I dropped off to sleep. Hours later, something struck me in the face. "Ginger's having a nightmare," I thought, and reached over to put her flailing arms inside the sleeping bag. She was lying quietly. Wondering what could have hit me, I opened my eyes and stared into the darkness of the tent. My scalp began to tingle. I was looking point-blank into the snarling face of a huge coyote directly above my head.

I pulled my hand out of the sleeping bag to reach for my gun. At the movement the beast snapped at my hand, his teeth biting deep into my flesh. I grabbed his neck with both hands, trying to hold him away from my face. The battle was on! Ginger awoke, startled from her sleep, she said later, by his tail brushing across her face. There was no sound except the snarling of the coyote. As I tried to choke him, he kept tearing at my hands, his hindquarters bouncing all over the tiny pup tent.

Ginger finally crawled near enough to grab those powerful hind legs. There was no chance to get out of the sleeping bag, no chance to get the gun—I dared not release him long enough. He made repeated lunges for my face, which I had to protect from those dripping fangs at heavy cost to my hands, for he tore them to ribbons. With Ginger grimly holding on to his hindquarters, I managed to turn over on my stomach, which somewhat relieved the strain on my arms. This couldn't last much longer! But we would simply have to hang on somehow until the infuriated animal strangled to death. My hands by this time were in agony. Each time he lashed at me, I could feel his teeth sink deep into the flesh of my arms and wrists. He snarled and cried with pain and anger. Evidently I was not shutting off his wind as I had hoped.

"For the love of Mike, Ginger," I cried, "get something to tie round this devil's neck!"

Wedging her shoulders down over his still active legs, and hanging on to them with one hand, she reached for her belt. Somehow we managed to take a turn round the coyote's neck with the belt, cinching up on it. His struggles began to lessen, and I wriggled out of the sleeping bag far enough to throw him on his side. When I was on top instead of beneath him, Ginger handed me the Luger, and I pushed the beast far enough out of the tent to shoot him.

We crawled from the tent into the cold moonlight, looked at the dead coyote at our feet and at each other. Ginger's face was badly scratched and my hands were dripping blood.

"Something certainly caught up with us that time," sighed Ginger as she surveyed our wounds. "Well, we asked for it." She said nothing else, and I, too, remained silent as we both thought of the stories we had heard in Magdalena about what happened to men who were bitten by coyotes.

I finally broke the silence by saying, "I wonder if he had rabies? That demon must have had something to make him enter a human habitation. What do you think?"

She didn't answer my question, saying instead, "Let's get a fire going and look at your hands. It must be nearly dawn."

Since I was unable to use my hands, Ginger built the fire and surveyed the damage. The backs of both of my wrists and hands were torn to shreds, the flesh hanging from the edges of the cuts. We realized that I was staring a pretty messy death straight in the face. We dragged the dead animal over to the fire where I peeled back his lip. His teeth were blackened and discolored, flecked with foam and bits of decayed food.

"Well," I said, as calmly as I could, "he doesn't seem to have enjoyed the best of health."

Suddenly Ginger grabbed her largest cooking pot and, on her way to the beach, shouted, "Get the iodine and the permanganate of potash crystals. I know something that will either cure or kill you."

I got the things she asked for out of the first-aid kit, assuming that she meant to soak my hands in the solution. But I was soon to learn that her intentions were far, far worse than that; for she heaped more wood on the fire, set the pot of water over the flames, and poured in the iodine and the permanganate. When the water became lukewarm she announced her fiendish purpose. "I'm going to heat that pot of water. You're going to put your hands in that water and keep them there just as long as possible. The disinfectants will have a better chance to penetrate; the heat will draw out the poison." Then as though giving the signal for an execution she snapped, "Put them in!"

Resigned to my fate but hoping to talk her into less Draconian measures, I pleaded, "I know that drastic situations require equally drastic measures to combat them, but don't you think this is just a little too severe?"

Ginger was adamant. "In go your hands," she commanded. In they went—and right out again. What that iodine did to my poor hands! The pain was almost unbearable, but I decided I'd let them cook until they dropped off rather than die of rabies. Gradually the temperature of the water increased until steam rose in my face. I grew faint with pain. The fire burnt my arms and ankles while the water cooked my hands. Eventually Ginger was satisfied. "That's enough. I don't want you burnt as well as bitten."

When I took my mutilated hands from the almost boiling pot, they looked completely boiled, but the flesh was clean. With a small surgeon's scalpel we cut away the shreds of flesh, made a swab from a small stick and a piece of cotton and daubed the wounds with disinfectant. As the east greyed Ginger made a pot of coffee. We were far too upset to concern ourselves with eating. Both of us were shaking as though with ague. We discussed our situation.

"We're going to need water, firewood, food and bandages—or some way to wash and sterilize the bandages we have," I said. "I think Santa Margarita Island is our best bet."

"Yes, since there are natives there to aid us," Ginger agreed. "We'd better sail over right now."

We loaded the canoe and started off towards Santa Margarita Island and the only fresh water in the vicinity. This time Ginger played skipper, and she had no small task. The wind was against us, the tide was against us, and Ginger made poor time with the paddle. Sunset found us only as far as the entrance to the inlet. We camped for the night. Next morning, however, a fair breeze sprang up which carried us half-way across the bay. Then it suddenly died and left us at the mercy of the swift currents again. Great swells began to pile up and small seas to break round us. We were on a shoal spot, and Ginger had a tough time handling the canoe alone in those breakers. Each time we went over a wave, it dumped us down on the mud of the shoal with a resounding thud, almost breaking the canoe apart. Then, as quickly as it had died, the wind came up again and Ginger hoisted sail. The nearer we came to the island, the harder the wind blew. As we rounded the little sand spit that forms the harbour, a sudden gust almost capsized us.

As we pulled into the little pier, natives came to help us unload and to beach the canoe on high ground. The leader introduced himself as José, and gave us the use of a vacant cabin. He made polite inquiries about my bandaged hands and nodded his head in understanding at my reply, "They are sore." The natives helped Ginger carry our gear up to the little cabin. José invited us to have supper at his house. Members of his family were sympathetic when they saw my bandaged hands. But they asked no questions and I volunteered no information. The evening passed pleasantly.

Taking leave of our hosts, we went to the cabin assigned to us. We soon found out why it was unoccupied. Thousands of fleas and bedbugs had claimed it for their own. Well, they could have it. We set up our tent inside the cabin, remembering that we had killed one hundred and sixty-eight (we counted them) fleas we had found in our sleeping bag after similar hospitality at Santo Tomas.

Early next morning José came round to offer us a thirty-gallon oil drum which had been converted into a sort of cookstove. He also brought wood. While he was there I began to dress my hands. Shocked at the sight of the torn flesh, he exclaimed, *"Dios! Que passon!?"*

"Coyote bit me a couple nights ago over on the mainland," I answered, trying to minimize the accident.

"Los coyotes!" he breathed in horror, backing towards the door, fear and dread plainly evident in every line of his face.

He left, but soon returned bringing his family, who in turn brought small gifts of food. During their short visit they asked several times, anxiously, if we were their good friends. We assured José and his family that we were most certainly their good friends; that we more than appreciated all they were doing for us.

Later that day I saw José going from hut to hut. Plainly he was worried about something. I wondered what it was.

Then, one by one, the villagers came to see us, each one bringing a small gift of dried fish and turtle meat, small quantities of coffee or firewood (which is at a premium on the island). One old woman brought a piece of candle to light our hut. Each and every one of them, like José, asked anxiously if we were *"buen amigos,"* and to be assured over and over that we were indeed *buen amigos*. We were both puzzled and amused. These people differed little from the other natives we had met along this stretch of coast, most of whom had been kind and hospitable to us; but this was something else again. There was a very definite point to this reiterated, anxious query, "Are you our friends?"

We went for a stroll among the huts. Everywhere we were greeted with an effusive show of friendship and the persistent inquiries regarding the warmth of our friendship for the villagers. Since we could think of nothing we had done to deserve this lush display of friendship, we were more puzzled than ever.

The next afternoon, while Ginger was visiting José's family, trying to improve her Spanish, and I was strolling along the beach, José approached me. "Señor," he said, "I must ask you a question. It is—how shall I say it—a very personal question."

"Why not; are we not *buen amigos?*" I questioned in reply.

"This is difficult to explain and I am afraid you will take offense," José countered.

"Nothing you could say would offend me, José. Need I remind you again that we are friends?"

"Señor, may I walk along the beach with you?"

Once out of hearing of the village, José turned to me with a pathetic expression and said, "Are you *very sure* that we are friends? Are you sure that nothing I could say would make you angry with me?"

It seemed to me that since that question had been asked of me a million times, by now my answers should have carried some conviction. I was losing both my patience and my temper; and if it were not so obvious that something of great importance (to him) was about to occur, I should have permitted my feelings a little leeway. But I held my tongue.

Finally, he looked up with pleading, eloquent eyes and said, "Señor, *El Coyote* has bitten you. When the dark of the moon come, you will *go mad*. Like *El Coyote*, you will go crazy and bite all your enemies; maybe you will even bite your wife!"

"Yes," I admitted, "I know that coyote bites are serious; that is why we came to you for help. What makes you think that I will bite the Señora, José?"

"I do not know, Señor, why it is so, but when a man is bitten by *El Coyote* he bites his enemy, and sometimes bites his wife. Perhaps"—and José's face brightened—"he does not know that she is not his enemy."

"There's a lot in what you say, José," I replied. "Some men have great difficulty in making up their minds."

"We will do anything we can for you," he said, "but we do not want you to go mad here and bite your enemies."

"But, José, I have no enemies here; no one to bite except the Señora."

"There is another thing," he muttered, "but if I ask you, you will surely be angry. Please, Señor, do not be angry if I ask this of you, will you?"

"No, a thousand times no!" I promised. "Go ahead."

"I am afraid," he confessed. "Señor, when the dark of the moon comes, may we tie your hands and feet? Sometimes people as sick as you are going to be—even bite their friends!"

"That's a good idea, José," I said. "If you want to do that, there won't be any hard feelings."

"Maybe if *I* tie you, you'll be angry." Then his eyes lighted. "Señor, I have the great idea! We will let your wife tie you!"

"That's not such a good idea, José," I demurred. "I might bite the Señora first, and then she'd be mad too."

However, José seemed greatly relieved that I was willing to be tied and carried the good news back to the village.

The next day the people again filled our hut with food. We protested, telling them it was not necessary to deprive themselves of much needed food to make us presents. They insisted that they did it "from the heart." With this, we ceased protesting. Further refusals might alarm them, and that was one thing that we were most anxious to avoid.

On the following day—the day before the dark of the moon—the village was strangely silent. No children played in front of the huts. One old man began to oil an antiquated shotgun. Other men appeared wearing great knives in their belts. As the day wore on tension increased, and we began to feel uneasy, too. Conversation with the people who came to visit us became forced and strained. Natives, we knew, were kind and charming people so long as they had mastery over their fears, but, like panic-stricken mobs at home, once those fears took possession of them they got entirely out of hand. Night approached. José appeared. His eyes were sad, but his manner was determined. He fingered a rope.

"I am afraid—I am afraid to do this," he said. "But, Señor, I must—I must do it." His voice rose.

I soothed him. "If you think it will quiet the people, we will take our canoe and spend the night on Crescente Island. Surely then your people will be safe."

He showed his yellow teeth in a broad grin and said in a relieved voice, "That would be wonderful, Señor!"

But during the afternoon a strong wind had come up, and by now was blowing a gale too strong for the *Vagabunda* to weather with Ginger as the sole crew. When I told José our predicament he was silent for a long time. Then he said, "I will take you over in my sailboat. We will leave you there. I will get Lazaro and Pedro to help me handle the boat."

Lazaro was a big, husky *marinero* (sailor), with a deep machete scar across one cheek. He looked very tough. Pedro, José's son, was another big, husky Indian, who liked to be called "boss."

José's wife, Rosa, promised to look after Ginger while I was in exile. Solemnly we loaded the thirty-foot boat with our sleeping bag, and some food cooked by the native women. As the sun sank the wind filled the patched sails and we were off. The little village looked almost beautiful in the glow of the sun's last rays. Lazaro took the tiller. José stood far up in the bow, his rusty shotgun by his side; Pedro, fingering his machete, lounged on the underdeck.

As I stood in the tiny cockpit, I said to myself, "You're in a bad spot now, Dan Lamb." And I kept wondering if there could be any possible truth in the natives' stories. I had found, to my sorrow, that there frequently was. Perhaps I'd soon be having a fine time running around Crescente Island all by myself, baying at the moon—when there was a moon to bay at. Maybe I could find a coyote to bite. I kept thinking, "I'll bet this bunch of monkeys will be glad to be rid of me." I tried to bolster up my flagging spirits by thinking about the ridiculous nature of the situation, because I didn't feel funny. Ginger was constantly on my mind. What was to become of her, if— But I didn't dare think of that.

The old bay fooled us again. Half-way across, the wind died completely. We drifted at the mercy of the strong currents which began to sweep down into the great expanse of water forming the northern portion of Magdalena Bay. Lazaro scowled at the sky. Pedro grew fidgety and nervous. José, on the bow, wrinkled his face in deep concern. Though I could see that they were getting in an ugly mood, I could hardly keep from chuckling. It was their turn now. They were willing enough to dump me on a desert island and go home. Now the three of them were marooned with me, and me a potential madman! They would have been far better off in the village. "This is going to be funny before the night is over," I said to myself.

About seven o'clock it grew chillier; I shivered and gave way to a robust sneeze. The sound electrified them. Pedro, machete in his hand, jumped to his feet; José grabbed his gun and raised it, ready for action.

"What's the matter, José?" I asked. "Something wrong?"

"No," he grunted, setting his shotgun back against the mast.

Lazaro still held his place at the tiller, although we were only moving with the current. We waited, all of us in tense, moody silence. The boat rolled easily to the swells, and the slap-slap of the water against her sides was the only sound. But the situation didn't seem so funny to me now as it had only a moment before. "Suppose the joke is on me? These men are jittery and nervous. They really believe that I am about to go mad. Why not shoot, and be rid of me? From their point of view, such a course is both logical and justified. They can say what they like tomorrow, and who can contradict them?" I shivered again. The silence was becoming oppressive and dangerous; I decided it was time to talk.

"How about a bite to eat, José?" I asked.

The food was in the tiny cockpit where I was standing. I called to Lazaro to come and get it since my hands were still too sore for me to play mess boy to the others. He squirmed uneasily and eyed Pedro, who still played with that machete of his as if he were trying to make up his mind as to what he ought to do with it. Neither man moved. "Come on, my good friends," I said. "I cannot go mad, as you know, until midnight; and it is still three hours before that time."

Then Lazaro inched himself forward and dropped his long legs over the cockpit edge, feeling with his feet for the bundle of tortillas, his eyes never leaving my face. His feet found the bundle. As a cormorant dives for fish, he swooped down upon it and bounded back on deck, like a released steel spring. Rolling a piece of fish in a tortilla for each of us, he passed them around with nervous care. We munched the food in silence. There was a touch of hysteria in the air and it was beginning to affect me. "What if I should start—but this was nonsense!" Then I had an idea.

"José, my friend, are you afraid?" I asked.

"Yes, my friend," he admitted, "I think I am afraid."

"Have you a hatch for this cockpit?" He nodded affirmatively. "Then you can put the hatch on and hold me prisoner until morning when the danger will have passed."

As he grabbed for the hatch, he said, "Oh, my friend, this is a wonderful idea!"

I ducked my head just in time as the hatch slipped into place. I could hear them battening it down, and then came sounds as though they were all trying to sit on top of it. I spread out the sleeping bag and promptly went to sleep.

The next morning I was awakened by the careening of the boat as a brisk wind was taking us back to Santa Margarita. In response to my pounding, José lifted off the hatch. I grinned up at the weary, bleary-eyed features of my hosts; and pointing to the bag of tortillas, suggested that we eat. They were shivering with cold, hunger, and the weariness of their all-night vigil.

"My friend, do you still feel all right?" José asked anxiously.

"I have not gone mad yet, as you can see."

"Then you cannot go mad until tonight at midnight," he said in a relieved voice.

"Good heavens!" I thought. "How long will this continue? I wonder just how long the 'dark of the moon' lasts in these parts?" But I decided to ask no questions.

The entire village met us on our return, with gifts as usual.

That night José appeared, bringing his coil of rope. He tied my hands and feet, most careful not to hurt my injured hands. After he had left, Ginger untied the ropes and we went to sleep, retying them in the morning before José's arrival, so that it seemed to him that I was as he had left me the night before. This comedy went on for several nights; and then one morning José announced with beaming face, "Señor, I think that you will no longer want to bite your enemies now. Perhaps"—he seemed doubtful—"you will still want to bite the Señora; who knows?"

After breakfast, we noticed unusual animation among the villagers. Children played as usual. Women ran back and forth from hut to hut. Lazaro came to offer his congratulations.

"What's going on?" I asked.

"Señor, we are going to have a fiesta now that you are well!"

"It's going to be a three-way celebration, Lazaro," I said. "You are going to celebrate because I didn't bite you; the Señora will make fiesta because I didn't bite her; and I will make fiesta because my hands are healing nicely—and because I didn't die!"

Chapter Six

THE CAPTAIN OF THE GUARD PLAYS POKER

WE STAYED several weeks longer to give my hands a chance to heal. During the period of waiting, we tried to show the natives how to do little things that might be of use to them. We also improved our Spanish. In the abandoned cannery I found tools and scrap iron with which I taught the natives how to make fishhooks and other small gear. The natives here are not mechanical, but once shown how, they can copy an article fairly well. Ginger showed the women how to make some of the foods we had evolved from the produce of the country, that they might have more variety with the same material.

After my hands had healed sufficiently to be of some use, we made our planned cruise round Magdalena Bay, with the same luck which had pursued us since we had first entered it. On our return to Santa Margarita, the natives welcomed us like long-lost brothers and we moved back into our old flea-ridden hut. Since being bitten by the coyote I had been unable to keep my log or diaries. I now built a little table and started to work on the accounts of the last weeks.

We were sitting in our hut writing one day when a troop of natives, accompanied by a *celador* of the *aduana* (minor customs official) came knocking on our door.

"Señor and Señora Lamb, these are my orders: you are to accompany me back to Magdalena," he said. Questioning brought no further enlightenment; he "did not know."

"Dan, perhaps a telegram—the folks. We'd better leave at once," Ginger said.

Upon our arrival at Magdalena we were greeted by the usual officials dressed in their whites and gold braid. But they were not cordial—decidedly not. Nevertheless, we were ushered into the office of a scowling Port Captain with considerable ceremony.

All pretence of courtesy ended at the door. "Señor," he said abruptly, "I am ordering the arrest of yourself and the Señora for violating the hospitality of Mexico—you are spies!"

The announcement so dumbfounded us that we giggled. We sobered, however, as two guards ranged themselves on each side of us, and we noticed the .45 automatics that swung from their belts. Another order sent men to the *Vagabunda*, where they searched every parcel and every cranny.

They returned and presented the Captain with our log book and diaries which, knowing no English, they could not read. This was fortunate, for we had made several references to the port and its officials that would not be regarded as complimentary.

Then the questions began. He wanted to know "what kind of work" we were doing.

"We, as you know, *Señor Capitán*, are travellers and explorers. We do no other work," I told him.

"Do not think to fool me, Señor," he answered. "You *are* engaged in some kind of work." We only could reiterate our denial. He began warming up to his rôle of inquisitor; his scowl deepened, his manner became more pontifical. You could see that he was enjoying himself immensely. Already he was anticipating the smiles of his superiors in Mexico City for his clever and audacious unmasking of "gringo spies." He felt himself to be a made man—it oozed from every pore. "Why should any one want to go to Turtle Inlet unless that person's work consisted in spying on Magdalena Bay?" he queried triumphantly.

"Nuts!" I retorted in English, then added in Spanish, "There is nothing there to spy on; nothing but desert, mangroves, and muddy water."

"Exactly," he said grandly. "That is why I am convinced that you are both spies. In the name of the Mexican Government I hereby place you under arrest."

Thinking it over, I could hardly blame the fellow. From his point of view nothing we had said made sense. He dispatched a messenger to summon the Captain of the Guard. When this personage appeared, we could have sworn that he came straight from Hollywood. He had the long drooping mustachios, the hard glint in his eye, that are a director's dream of Pancho Villa. However, he was short and roly-poly, and his seamed brown face looked as though it might break into a smile at any moment. He instructed us to follow him, and as we marched away, footsteps behind made us look back. The two armed guards were close upon our heels.

We followed the Captain down the beach which served as the street, and following his example, dodged in between the buildings to get away from the force of the wind. He finally guided us into a dark hallway and up a flight of stairs—in imminent danger of collapse. The door was opened by a young and handsome girl who had the perfect oval features and blue-black hair of a Spaniard. "My wife," he announced. "This is my house. Here I will hold you prisoners."

The room we stepped into was barren of furniture and the floor, like the stairs, threatened momentarily to break through. We were ushered into a little living room in which there were several chairs, a bed, and a table. Shells formed elaborate designs upon the walls and were set round the walls on crude shelves. On the table was a well-thumbed deck of playing cards.

By now the Captain had dropped some of his formality. He turned to me and asked, "Señor, do you know how to play poker?"

"*Capitán*, I know the game," I replied, grinning.

He smiled and his seamed face broke into a pattern of wrinkles. "Ah, Señor, I hoped you played poker; that is why I brought you to my house." He immediately began taking off his Sam Browne belt and was soon peeled down to his shirt-sleeves.

"I believe," he said, "that your period of captivity will be extremely pleasant for both of us. Let us hope that it may continue. Maria," he called, "fix us something to eat."

While Ginger and Maria bustled round getting supper, the Captain sat down across the table from me and dealt a hand of cards. After one or two rounds, he said, "I am very fortunate. Few in this place know how to play this game." I rather doubted the wisdom of his use of the word "fortunate," for it seemed to me that unless he began to play better poker, and at once, his point of view might change. Then a dinner of tortillas and pounded and fried dried fish was served. During the meal I asked the Captain why we were being held.

"Señor, they think you are making a map of Magdalena Bay, and they want to get in touch with Mexico City to find out what to do with you. They have sent a telegram to *El Presidente*."

"And how long will it take for an answer?" I questioned.

"Who can say?" he replied. "It might take a day or two; perhaps much longer. It depends upon what *El Presidente* is doing when the telegram arrives. Have you seen our gaol, Señor?" I replied in the negative. "Ah, it is just as well, perhaps: it is not a pleasant place. We have had no prisoners for a year or more and my pigs have been using it. It would be most distasteful to the Señora. I think it would be better for me to hold you both prisoners here in my house where you and I can play poker. Which do you prefer, Señor?"

"We would rather stay here," I said meekly.

The Captain beamed. "I think we shall make very good friends. We shall play poker—the women shall cook. Ah, we shall have one happy party."

The Captain and I continued our poker playing until the small hours of the morning. Ginger and I finally got to sleep on the floor, as the house boasted no guest beds.

The next morning we were taken before the Port Captain for further questioning. Eventually he dismissed us and I went back to the poker game. Several days went by. Each day started off with the Captain shuffling his well-worn deck. He also continued to lose steadily and happily since I spent the proceeds of his bad luck on *tequila*. After a "spot" or two of the fiery liquid, neither of us cared who won or lost. It was just one "happy party."

The Captain continued to marvel at the niceties of "gringo poker." **He** watched me closely as I dealt the cards. He thought my success was due to my "delicate touch"—or so he said.

Eventually I began to wonder just how energetically the Captain, or any one else, was trying to establish our innocence. True, he told us every day how passionately he proclaimed our guiltlessness to the *Capitán del Puerto*; but he seemed singularly untroubled by his continued failure to secure our release. So, after supper one night, I made the Captain this proposition:

"*Capitán*, how would you like to learn to play poker as the gringos play it? Would you be interested in finding out how this is done?"

He broke into smiles. "But surely, Señor. Oh, there are so many things I do not know about poker that I am *most* eager to learn."

"All right," I said, "I'll teach you if you will help *me*. As you know, my *Capitán*, we are most anxious to continue our travels in your charming country. Due to a slight misunderstanding, we have had to trespass greatly upon your hospitality. I am sure, however, that if you, personally, would use your prestige with the *Capitán del Puerto*, he would release us." From the expression on his face I knew I had smelt a rat, for he seemed slightly reluctant to put his "prestige" to the test. I hastily continued, "Very well; let us play five hands just to prove the superiority or inferiority of gringo poker against all other systems of poker. If you win all five hands, I will then show you, without further obligation on your part, all that I know about gringo poker. If, on the other hand, you cannot win all five hands, then I shall show you how to play the game—but only when we are released."

"Yes, that is a most fair proposition," he agreed.

I dealt the cards. I had picked up here and there quite a few of the finer points of dealing. I had never had occasion to use them—but I *knew* them. The Captain's cards, while good, mind you, were not . . . conclusively so. He was both philosophical and resigned about it; a philosophy slightly tinged, I began to feel, with a growing scepticism regarding gringo poker . . . but as the game progressed an appreciation of its speculative possibilities dawned on the Captain, for after the fifth and final game he sighed rather woefully, "Ah, Señor, I wish that I, too, might have—how shall I say it? Yes, the Señor's 'delicate touch' with cards. Then I could win from any man in Baja California."

The next day we saw little of the Captain. About four o'clock he returned to his quarters and announced that we were free to leave. So we accompanied him to the Port Captain's office, where that dignitary, with effusive apologies, formally released us. But we were not allowed to leave Magdalena until I had instructed the Captain of the Guard in the finer points of gringo poker.

Later we learnt that his accomplishments, following my tutelage, had not proved of unalloyed benefit. There were rumours of a shooting scrape over his phenomenal luck!

Chapter Seven

MAKE WAY FOR A SCHOOL OF WHALES!

THE next day we returned to Santa Margarita, where our native friends held a fiesta for us which made our leave-taking the following morning doubly hard. The women clung to Ginger, while the men tried to persuade us to make our permanent home with them. We missed saying good-bye to José and Lazaro, who were off in the sailboat. At last we broke away and started paddling towards Cabo Tosco, the southernmost point of the island. Half-way, we met José and Lazaro who were lounging comfortably on deck beneath their idly flapping sail.

"Where are you going, José?" I called. They were going to Cabo Tosco to get *tijeretas'* eggs, he said. "That's where we're going, too," I called back.

"Come aboard, Señor, and wait until the wind rises," he suggested, "and then we can all go together."

"But we can paddle there in a couple of hours," I answered. "When you arrive, we will have food ready and waiting for you."

"Why are you in such a hurry, Señor?" he asked. "Surely there is no one waiting for you there. The wind will blow after while," he added philosophically.

But we paddled off, leaving them shaking their heads. "Strange people, why do they hurry?" we could almost hear them say—to which we could have given no intelligent answer.

As we neared the southern tip of the island, we came upon a great school of sharks. Some of them came so near the *Vagabunda* that they almost touched its fragile sides. One huge fellow rolled up under the canoe, nearly capsizing us. "He's trying to tip us over so he can get a square meal!" I said excitedly.

"The natives say that when sharks are particularly hungry they do attack small boats, and I think we'd better make tracks for a less crowded spot," Ginger answered.

We hastily paddled close inshore, continuing on in about a foot of water. The man-eaters kept pace with us just outside the shallow water, until we finally arrived at the tiny cove that was our destination.

The fish were running and the air was filled with man-of-war or frigate birds, called by the natives *tijereta*, although we have heard them called *tijerilla* and *tijera*. All three names are derived from the Spanish word for scissors, because when in flight the bird's forked tail opens and closes like a pair of scissors. These birds are great fishers, but oddly enough, they can neither land nor rise from water. Instead, they skim down close to it, seize a fish in their long, hooked beaks, and fly off without wetting a feather.

A small breeze had sprung up, roughening the water; and while we were watching, one of the birds dived after a fish and was knocked over by a whitecap. Then an amazing thing occurred. Other *tijeretas*, fishing nearby, dropped everything and flew to his aid. They hovered in the air a moment, and then, as though executing a long planned and trained manœuvre, swooped down upon the bird struggling in the water. Each member of the life-saving crew gripped some part of its body in their strong beaks, and rising in the air carried the rescued *tijereta* with them. When high enough, they released him, whereupon he shook out his feathers and coasted to a nearby mangrove tree to dry out.

We noticed that while some of the *tijeretas* were expert in securing fish, others, not so dextrous, stole from the more successful birds. They make their nests in the tops of the mangroves, and lay only one egg at a time. If this egg is taken, the female lays another. While she is off fishing, the male bird incubates the egg. Securing the eggs is easy, but unpleasant, because generations of birds have covered the trees with feathers and guano. They are so tame that sometimes they have to be pushed from the nest; and while you rob it, they circle round screaming insults and threats.

We placed the pilfered eggs in a kettle of water. If they sank, they were fresh; if they floated, incubation had already begun and we put them back in the nest. José came ashore just as we were replacing some. He grinned as he watched us. "The Señor makes more work, but then it makes more eggs, to make more work for the Señor," he laughed.

Boiled *tijereta* eggs make a good meal. They are larger than a hen's egg and have a flavour all their own; but they can be cooked in most of the same ways.

After trying to dissuade us from going further down the coast, José moaned when he learnt that we were going out by the bar at Cabo Tosco. "Oh, you can't do that," he said. "We never go out by the bar at this time of year, the breakers are too high. Further south is Boca Colorado, where we can sometimes get out. You cross this channel to Crescente Island and continue up the bay until you come to Boca Colorado."

The next morning we started off. The tide was going out and we were paddling at an angle, upstream, to offset the strong current. Breakers crashed heavily on the bar. A third of the way across the narrow channel we saw to the north what looked like great puffs of smoke. We thought at first that it might be the American battle fleet at practice; they used to come to these waters, we knew. "But there's no noise, no boom," said Ginger.

"And now that I think of it, I don't believe the fleet comes here any more," I answered.

Make Way for a School of Whales!

Big black puffs shot up from the water, hung an instant, then disappeared. Sometimes four or five appeared at once. The colour changed from black to grey and then to white vapour as they steadily came our way. "Dan," gasped Ginger, "that's a school of whales!" It was too late by this time to do anything about it; we were half-way across the channel and fighting a swift current. "Whales are supposed to be afraid of noise," she continued. "Do you suppose we could make enough to stop them until we reach the other side of the channel? If they try to go out while we're trying to cross, there isn't going to be much room for us."

"No, there isn't going to be much room," I agreed looking round at the channel, which at this point was only about a hundred and fifty yards wide. "If those whales decide to come through here, we're going to be in a traffic jam."

When they were within fifty yards of us we began making all the noise we could. And were we in a frame of mind to make it! I thought, "The water's full of sharks, and if a whale brought its huge tail down on the canoe or came up beneath us, what would happen?" I shivered; it was an appalling speculation. So we filled the air with shouts and gunshots, and pounded on the canoe. Our idea of noise differed apparently from a whale's idea of what it was afraid of, for they came charging down upon us without hesitation. One big fellow broke water just in front of the canoe. As he emerged, he blew a high geyser, most of which landed on us. With his great tail smacking the water, he dived, showering the cockpit.

This was our first close-up of these gargantuans—the largest animals ever to inhabit the earth, so the zoologists say. We had often seen them from a distance, but a whale a mile away and a whale as a next-door neighbour . . . well, it is different. Fifty or sixty feet long, and weighing many tons, yet they seemed as sportive as kittens. When they came to the surface, they spouted clouds of vapour through a nostril placed high on their heads, and looked for all the world like submarines coming up from a dive. Remaining a moment to fill their great lungs with air, they dived silently, their huge tails smacking the water. It was a breath-taking sight . . . ten feet away . . . in a canvas canoe!

As we watched them the canoe rose with a lurch, lifted completely out of the water. On each side of us there was a huge expanse of mottled grey and white, with big barnacles clinging to it. We were riding topside of Moby Dick!

"Dan! Dan!" Ginger screamed. "We're on a whale's back!"

"You're telling me!" I yelled back.

"What do we do now?"

"Nothing!" I said. "The whale does it. Hang on tight."

The canoe executed a series of sickening skids as it lay half over on its side. I suppose we were just another barnacle to that whale, but he looked like the *Queen Mary* to us! Then the canoe started to volplane, and pitched violently into the water. The whale's great tail—it seemed twenty feet across—hovered over us . . . and then came down. The canoe bounced into the air and we catapulted into the channel. We took one look round; the water had its usual quota of sharks, which with the breakers on the bar gave us an added incentive in our race towards the canoe. Breathless, we climbed aboard; but where in heaven's name were the paddles? Then I spotted them drifting forty feet away. The current was rapidly carrying us towards the crashing breakers. I had to get those paddles!

"I'm going to take a chance," I told Ginger. And tying one end of the harpoon line round me, while Ginger hung on to the other, I dived overboard. I secured one paddle, but meanwhile the canoe drifted rapidly towards the surf, so I let the other paddle go and climbed aboard. With the rescued paddle I managed to recover the other one. We then headed for the sand spit we had left that morning, for both of us had had all the excitement that we needed in any one day.

"Well," said Ginger after we had landed, "that's another one for Ripley. Nobody in the world will believe that story; and if we ever *do* get back home, I shall certainly hesitate to tell it."

The next morning, without further incident, we crossed the channel and continued down to Boca Colorado. Here we found a phenomenon characteristic of this section of Magdalena Bay—everything was red! The bushes and mangrove trees; the sea water, great patches of it—all were unmistakably red. No doubt some minute marine organism causes the strange coloration. The name, Boca Colorado, means Red Mouth or Opening. I remembered that on some of the early maps of California, the Gulf of California is called the "Vermilion Sea." It seemed probable that we should find similar phenomena in the Gulf.

The breakers here were worse than at Cabo Tosco, and we were unable to get out through the surf. We tried another lagoon and promptly grounded on a mudflat. Finally we sledded the canoe across slippery mud, and after heartbreaking work, portaged the canoe and the equipment over mountains of sand dunes to the ocean. By the time this job was completed we were completely exhausted, but we made up our minds that we were going to leave this damned bay—and soon! With our food supply almost gone, with only one gallon of water left, we put to sea next morning—glad to be deep-sea sailors once more.

Chapter Eight

WRECK AT BOCA DE CONEJO

THE relief that we felt in being at sea again, after our experiences in Magdalena Bay, stayed with us the early part of the first day's cruising. We talked, as we watched the rocky, precipitous shore line glide by, of those other sea adventurers who had passed these coasts long before us; of Drake and the *Golden Hind*, Cabrillo, Portola, Cortez; Yankee clippers en route for the New Eldorado; the old-time whalers and their daring crews—all the storied figures of the past whose names are California. We could almost see the stately galleons of Spain searching for the Seven Cities of Cibola; running with the rape of Montezuma's altars, the treasures of Atahualpha's "Temple of the Sun"; pursued by ships whose mastheads flew the flag of Britain—or a nameless flag of black.

Then the weather changed and our preoccupations returned to the present. About three o'clock in the afternoon the horizon to the south turned black and the wind came in chilly, spiteful gusts. Large swells began to roll in. Ginger, shivering with cold, urged, "Don't you think we'd better try to land? That's a real storm coming up."

"It *is* a real storm," I agreed, "but I don't know about landing. Look at that surf. But we might find a place beyond that little point."

From the chart we identified the place as Boca de Conejo, but found, instead of the sheltered bay that we had hoped for, merely a straight coastline such as we had been following. Boca de Conejo was only a small beach, bounded by towering cliffs, and pounded by heavy surf. However, there was the storm bearing down upon us; we had to land. So we prepared to shoot the surf—cruising about seventy-five yards off the beach. This was our usual procedure when landing through heavy surf. We'd first lash down the sailing gear, and then ride outside the breaker line for twenty minutes or longer, observing the way the swells broke and counting the number of high and low breakers. They always run in series. Then we'd try to shoot inshore with the low breaker.

By now we were about fifty yards offshore, and there seemed to be a fair chance of getting in without a spill. A chill wind was blowing, but we had stripped to swimming shorts and sweaters—just in case. Our attention had been focussed so intently inshore, watching the surf, that we were startled to feel the canoe rise suddenly on a great swell, then drop abruptly, a sensation similar to that caused by the swift descent of an express elevator. Hastily looking seaward we saw another great green monster bearing down on us; it grew mountainous as it approached, and the crest was dangerously sharp.

"Give her hell," I shouted to Ginger. "We've got to get out of the way before it breaks."

We paddled madly to get into deeper water, but before we could get out of its way, we had climbed the side of the great crest, balanced for an age-long second on its peak—and then the sea rolled out from beneath us. We were safe. Out to sea, however, we could see another, larger swell, its great height more terrifying than the last, its crest racing down upon us. Again we paddled furiously to get beyond the breaking point, getting further and further away from the beach. By now we were fully a hundred yards offshore. "Dan!" shouted Ginger. "Breakers just *can't* break this far from shore, or in water this deep!" A note of panic was in her voice as the monstrous wave continued to race towards us.

"Look out! Here it comes!" I yelled, as the huge sea towered above us.

The nose of the canoe rose in the swell until it was almost over our heads from where we sat in the cockpit. Ginger looked up, and over the roar of the water I heard her yell, "It's forty feet high!"

Almost before we knew what was happening we were turning over backwards—looping the loop—inside the crest of the breaker. I froze on to the stern, while Ginger's knuckles were white as she grimly hung on to the sides of the cockpit. The canoe stood straight up on its stern. Over our heads we could see the breaker's white crest, slowly, relentlessly curling over us. Then the huge sea crashed, and the canoe pitched over backwards —end over end—in the churning surf.

As I shot forward into the water, I could feel the canoe scrape along my back, then I was free of it. I remember being twisted and turned, pounded and tossed about like a chip in that powerful surge. It seemed hours before I came to the surface, but when my head finally broke the water I could see our canoe inshore with Ginger still in it.

"What shall I do?" she shouted.

"Get out and swim ashore," I yelled back, wondering why she asked.

"I can't," she cried, "I'm pinned in the cockpit."

Then I saw why. The sail had slipped its lashings and now lay across the cockpit with only Ginger's head sticking to one side of it. Just then another breaker came along, and I was rolled and tossed in the surf. Coming to the surface once more I saw the canoe rolling over sideways with Ginger still in it. Again I sank in water that was almost foam; again I came up, this time to see that Ginger was free and swimming inshore. Almost too exhausted to breathe, I let the breakers carry me towards shore, where they were also carrying the canoe. Finally, we both dragged ourselves up on the beach.

Ginger's first words were, "Where's your sweater?"

"I don't know," I answered vaguely. "I had it on when the breaker struck, but it's gone now."

"Well, I'm not surprised," she said. "Every time I saw you, you were performing contortions that probably gave you no time to think of sweaters."

We were both bruised and badly skinned from being scraped across the ocean floor, but when the canoe came in we managed to drag it far up on the beach. We collected the paddles and other gear as it washed in—but we never saw the sweater again. In the intervals, we stood laughing at our perfect three-point landing, for each of us, including the canoe, had landed on a different point along the little beach. But as we sat down on the sand, now that it was over, we began to tremble. Ginger's face was white and drawn—and mine, too, I suspect. She began to cry. We both always suffered a nervous reaction after a particularly dangerous bit of excitement, but it affected us differently. I'd swear, and Ginger would cry—and we'd both shiver. So we huddled together and shivered for awhile, trying to dig the sand out of our eyes and ears.

The next morning, refreshed by a good night's sleep, which we sorely needed, we took a good look at the canoe.

"It's bad enough," I reported in reply to Ginger's hopeful query. "Four broken ribs, a portion of the siding caved in, and the canvas is ripped along the keel."

"What do we do now—or are we permanently marooned?" was her next question. For the moment I did not know. "Just a little question of lumber, canvas, glue, and paint," she said mournfully. "Apparently that's *all* we need to get us off this God-forsaken beach." She laughed—but without merriment.

"Oh, you think that's funny, do you? Wait and see; we'll get out of here," I said. "In the meantime, how would you like to take a hike up the canyon?"

We started off, picking our way among the big boulders that lined the dry wash. A few stunted mesquite grew among the rocks and big cardón cacti stood everywhere. Many of these cacti had been uprooted by the wind and lay bleaching in the sun. Half-way up, the arroyo widened out and we struck what seemed to be a trail. Then abruptly ahead of us, in a desolate clearing between the high cliffs, stood a hut and a few sheds.

The hut was a tiny structure made from the big cardónes we had seen in the arroyo. Their pulpy, thorny outside covering, rotted away by the elements, left porous, spongelike trunks, which were set vertically into the ground to form the hut's sides. The wide-eaved roof was made from palm thatch. On the ground, near the hut, a cowhide was pegged out to dry. Round a circular stone fireplace were grouped three huge vertebrae that had once belonged to a preposterously large whale. On rawhide lines, strung between cardónes, strips of meat were drying in the sun. Off to one side were ramshackle sheds made from the same materials as the hut.

Peeping round a corner of the hut, we saw a child, a little brown boy of seven or eight. He was practically naked, but he came readily, though a trifle shyly, at Ginger's call, and as readily answered her questions. His father was gone, he said, but his mother, who was ill, was at home.

"I think I'll go in, and find out if there's anything I can do for her," Ginger said, hurrying off.

I continued talking to the child. Where had his father gone? "Off trying to kill a steer, that we may eat," the child answered. His father had once had many cattle, but the cattle were now starving because the drought had left no food for them. He had formerly killed game to feed his family, but now he had no bullets.

"No tortillas?" I questioned.

"No," he said. Pointing to the leathery black strips on the rawhide line, "Nothing but that."

He told me that it had not rained "for a very long time." In fact, he had never seen rain!

A half-dozen starved-looking chickens scratched dispiritedly round the yard. His papa was saving them, he said, in case he should not be able to kill a beef some day. Where did they get their water from? He took me over to a well. It contained a cloudy, brackish-looking liquid which the child assured me was water.

Then Ginger came out of the hut.

"Very sick?" I asked.

"Well, she's had a baby, and at the moment she isn't very robust. They are having a hard time. They have a gun but no bullets. He can't even kill one of his own half-starved cattle unless one wanders in the yard looking for water. The gun is a .22; can't we spare a few shells for it?"

We left some shells, a bit of tobacco, and some other odds and ends that we carried in our pockets, and started back towards the beach.

"What was in the hut?" I asked.

"A bunk covered with palm thatch and rawhide, a table, a stove built on a wooden platform covered with mud and rocks, a couple of saddles in one corner, and an olla—that's all."

"I'm afraid there isn't much that we can do for them, Ginger. We're in rather a spot ourselves, you know."

"I know that too," she answered, "but just the same I'm sorry for them. I wish we could do something."

I stopped to examine some stunted trees growing in the arroyo, and then cut them down with my bolo knife. "Ribs for the canoe," I explained. "We're also going to try to harpoon a couple of sharks today."

"What are the sharks for?" Ginger asked curiously.

"Paint and patches," I replied.

We caught two medium-sized sharks, removed their huge livers, sliced them and set them on a slanting rock. The hot sun rendered out the oil, which dripped into a kettle placed beneath. After we had obtained sufficient oil, we left it in the sun, stirring it occasionally until it became thick and viscous as the moisture evaporated.

The next morning, while we were pounding smooth some talc and ochre which I had dug out of the cliffs to use in making the body of the paint, the absent *Indio* for whom we had left the ammunition appeared. His face beamed with pleasure as he thanked us profusely for the presents we had left. He was an attractive man of medium stature, with large, golden-brown eyes and skin, and black hair of an almost silky texture. His strong white teeth flashed when he smiled. He had also brought a gift "for the kind Señora," he said, and proffered Ginger—one little, wizened egg!

We gravely accepted his gift, and thanked him heartily, knowing how much it meant in his circumstances. In the afternoon he returned with two rabbits which he had shot. These were also "due to the kindness of the Señora." He would now kill some rabbits for himself, he said. We were deeply touched and grateful for the fresh food. We should have liked to refuse them because of his greater necessity; but we knew that he would have been offended and hurt. We also accepted an invitation to visit his hut that evening.

We took along a little of our precious coffee, and a few grains of corn and beans that we had brought from Santa Margarita. "Perhaps he can plant the corn and beans near his well," Ginger suggested optimistically.

The family were waiting for us in the yard where a cheerful fire blazed. We sat down on the joints of whale vertebrae and talked about the absence of rain. I asked, "Why don't you kill your cattle if they are dying; cure the meat, and sell their hides?"

"Señor, I cannot butcher cattle unless I pay the government a tax of two and one half pesos each for their hides. I kill an occasional animal for my own use, and as long as I do not try to sell the hide I am not bothered—because they do not know." He played with his baby girl and gently rocked her as he talked. Yes, he would most certainly try to make a garden with the seeds, he said, and thanked us for bringing them.

I pointed to the wide cracks in the hut where the crooked trunks had left spaces big enough to put an arm through. "Is it not cold when the wind blows?" I asked.

"*Si*, it is sometimes cold," he agreed, "but the air is good for you; it makes you strong."

Thus we spent the evening, talking and singing songs. On our way back to the beach, Ginger said, "Amazing people! How do they manage to keep so cheerful with just nothing?"

"Well, suppose they weren't so cheerful," I countered, "would they be any better off? They still enjoy just being alive; they enjoy each other—and they can even afford to be generous. I've seen people worse off, with more."

We spent days thereafter collecting materials with which to patch the canoe. The work went slowly because we had to search for food as well as distil fresh water each day. The country offered so little in the way of game that we had to subsist mainly on seafoods.

Since we had no canvas with which to patch the *Vagabunda's* torn bottom, we caught two small sharks with hand lines and skinned them. After a partial drying, I soaked them in shark oil to soften them and keep them from curling. On the rocks at low tide we found an owl shell that secreted a kind of glue. This little shell fish is exposed to the sun at low tide, and uses this sticky secretion to keep the moisture in, so it will not cook in its own shell. It made an excellent adhesive for the fish-skin patches.

Then our Indian friend managed to kill a beef, and presented us with a generous portion. Some of this we salted and cured for a reserve ration to use on the journey down to Cape San Lucas.

The second week we replaced the broken ribs with the new hand-hewn substitutes, fitted new siding on the canoe, and glued the fish-skin patches on the hull. After that we gave her a coat of shark-oil paint of a nondescript colour.

Just before we were ready to leave, Ginger gave the Indian woman one of her sun suits to remake into a dress for the baby. I gave the man a small shovel and a few other things, including a flashlight, explaining the advantages of hunting deer at night with the aid of a light. His pleasure in these trifles was so great, and his thanks so extravagant, that we felt embarrassed.

Finally the *Vagabunda* was loaded for sea duty. We were anxious to be off. Ginger had taken her accustomed place in the cockpit. I was standing ready to shove off; we were just waiting for a chance to go through the surf. Ginger turned and looked at me. There was a question in her eyes. "Yes, let's unload," I said. Simultaneously, we had had a hunch that this was not an auspicious time for sailing, even though it was a beautiful calm morning and we had no particular reason for being apprehensive. We occasionally had these hunches, and experience had taught us that it was better not to disregard them. We sat round wondering what was going to happen until three o'clock, when the "reason" arrived. A violent storm blew up, almost without warning, from the south. By five o'clock it had blown itself out. But what a blow it was while it lasted! It was probably a good thing that we hadn't been caught in it at sea.

The following day was clear and calm. We reloaded and shot the heavy surf—just missing a spill—and headed toward Cape San Lucas, the tip of Baja California.

Chapter Nine

"THE DAMN FOOLS!"

"It's getting late," I said. "How about looking round for a place to land? We can go on to San Lucas in the morning."

"I'd so much rather sail on all night, Dan, than attempt another landing on one of these beaches. I've had about enough," Ginger said decisively.

"Well, let's run in and take a peek anyway," I suggested. "I have a feeling that we ought to try to land if we can."

We ran inshore. The surf certainly looked ugly. It was extremely doubtful if we could execute even a "three-point landing" there.

"No wonder the fellows in the Hydrographic Bureau were so sceptical when we offered to make maps and take soundings for them," I commented.

"Well, *they* hadn't been able to. Why should they think we could?" Ginger reminded me.

We had a bite to eat, and Ginger, deciding to take a little rest, got out the sleeping bag. By sailing all night, we could easily make the village of San Lucas by morning, and I could manage the boat alone for awhile.

Ginger would wake up every now and then to ask, "How's it going?"

"Okay, but it's getting rough," I'd answer.

By nine o'clock the wind had increased so that handling the canoe—we were quartering the waves—became difficult. The pitching of the boat made sleep impossible. Ginger got up and began to stow things away, lashing everything down, including the paddles. We reefed the sail, but still couldn't battle the waves, so we ran with them. This took us directly away from land.

"A sea anchor," I speculated, "would at least hold back the canoe enough to keep us from going so far from shore."

We proceeded to make one, using Ginger's sweater, our shirts—anything that would form a drag. I tied the bundle to the harpoon line and trailed it astern. This helped some, but as the wind increased the seas became so high that they washed completely over the canoe, filling the cockpit and almost tearing our anchor loose. Despite continual bailing, the cockpit was full of water, and we were soon reduced to trying to keep afloat. It became a nightmare. In the darkness we could see the great white crests of the seas as they rushed down upon us. Above the gale, I could hear Ginger shout, "Oh, if we can just weather this one!"

"This sea anchor idea isn't so hot," I yelled back. "We've got to keep on top of the waves; it's too much to expect the boat to go through them." I tried to pull the anchor in, but it was too heavy—I couldn't budge it. "I'll have to cut the line," I shouted. And cut I did, saying good-bye to our shirts and the one remaining sweater.

We double-reefed the sail, but even this was hazardous. When the canoe dropped into the trough of the waves, the sail went slack from lack of wind; she rode the crests, the gale filled it and carried us along at a dizzy pace, as though we were riding a surfboard. Every now and then a bigger sea would catch us, washing over the canoe and nearly tearing the sail from the mast. It took every ounce of my strength on the steering paddle to keep the huge swells from rolling the canoe over sideways.

The storm increased in fury. The roar of the wind and waves sounded like the boom of cannon in our ears. We were rapidly being blown out to sea. One thought was constantly with us both: what if we should be carried past the Cape—into that waste of water? In pitch darkness we continued our battle to keep afloat. The icy seas that charged down upon us and the wind whining through the rigging chilled us to the bone; the spray pelted our shivering bodies like shot.

Then it came! A great black mountain of water, coming full speed ahead, rose behind us. I shouted to Ginger to hang on, and saw her wriggle herself more firmly into the cockpit. My arms were already so tired that I wondered if I had strength enough left to steer the canoe through this catastrophe. Then the wind struck just as the towering pile of water poured down on us. The canoe rose in mid-air, and down we went into the trough, the canoe turning over and over—both of us hanging on for dear life. I was torn loose and washed free by the powerful surge of water. The last I saw of Ginger, she was still hanging on to the gunwales inside the cockpit. When I came up I could see the shiny bottom of the canoe—but no Ginger. I started swimming madly towards it. Just as I reached it, she pulled herself up from the other side. The mast had broken off, and the sail and rigging were wrapped round the canoe, partly pinning her down. How she managed to free herself and crawl out from under is more than she or I will ever know!

I had neither time nor strength to shout directions. Both of us knew that we had to get the canoe freed of the fouled rigging before we could right it. Each time a wave struck us, it rolled us over and over as we worked frantically to clear the wreckage. I was afraid that the jagged end of the broken mast would puncture the side of the canoe. We finally freed the tangled rigging, righted the canoe, and climbed back in. I tied the painter to the wreckage of the sail, letting it drift astern where it acted as an impromptu sea anchor.

The remainder of the night seems like a bad dream. I remember tying the long heavy fishline to the painter to ease the shock of the heavy seas. The sail and broken mast made a better sea anchor than the clothing, for the mast kept it afloat. When it seemed best to ride the waves, we payed out the fishline, and pulled the anchor in between heavy seas. This probably saved our lives.

At dawn the wind abated. Soon we were riding in comparative calm. The sun came up, giving us encouragement. We pulled in the soggy mass that had once been the rigging, and in about two hours constructed a small jury sail from what was left of the mast and canvas. With these emergency repairs we attempted to set a course in the direction of land. Nothing but the turbulent ocean was visible, and the wind was still strong enough to cause concern.

We ate the doughy, brine-soaked mass that had once been food. We had water in a canteen in the stern of the boat, but we didn't dare unzip the cockpit. Unless the hull were punctured or the canvas well of the cockpit removed, the boat was unsinkable. We preferred to keep it that way. Any one of the big seas still breaking over us occasionally could sink the *Vagabunda* once the water-tight canvas of that cockpit covering was off. By sundown we were still out of sight of land; but during a brief lull we had hurriedly opened the cockpit, snatched the canteen, and closed the canvas well again without shipping water, so we were no longer thirsty.

We sailed all that day and through the following night, but morning found us still out of sight of land. The wind died down completely. We were unable to make headway except with the paddles. The chilling winds of the night before had given way to the blistering heat of a tropic sun. All day long we sweated at the paddles through a heaving, glassy sea. Towards sundown Ginger, pointing to a hazy blue speck on the far horizon, said she thought she could see land. Again the wind sprang up, blowing another gale in the wrong direction, and once more we were obliged to fight the raging seas until dawn. Daylight found us out of sight of land, freakishly becalmed under a pitiless sun. This day, too, we spent labouring at the paddles; and before the wind started up, we got in close enough to see quite clearly the mountains of Baja California. But if this fresh wind continued to blow us southward, it would take us past Cape San Lucas and into the path of the tropical hurricane—the treacherous "chubasco" of the Gulf of California.

I wondered dully just what we'd do if that happened. Neither one of us could take any more; we had had little sleep since leaving Boca de Conejo; our carefully rationed food supply, and water were gone; our tongues so swollen that speech was difficult. Salt-encrusted, blistered, and burnt to a crisp, we could hardly move. But throughout a third long night, we were blown further from land. Somehow we marshalled enough strength to make a little headway against the contrary winds, tapping once again that storehouse of reserve energy that lies beyond the purely physical.

"We ought to be able to see the lighthouse on Cape Falso unless we've been blown too far out to sea," Ginger managed to whisper. "I continually think that I do see lights, but my judgment's not to be trusted—I'm too all-in." She finally curled up in the cockpit, in three inches of water, and slept like a baby.

I kept watch for the light, but my tired eyes refused to focus; everything within my field of vision was doubled. I saw two masts on the canoe, that crossed and recrossed as I tried to fix my eyes upon the distant horizon. I knew that the lighthouse threw a powerful beam, and I should be able to see it. During the storm I had lashed myself to the stern of the canoe, so that the heavy seas could not sweep me off; and only the ropes now kept me from falling off through sheer weariness.

Then I began having hallucinations; things began to appear in front of me. A glass of water balanced itself on the bow of the canoe; packages and packages of my favourite cigarettes, with heaps of dry matches were beside it. I would have traded my right leg for either one. I dreamt of dry blankets, and cups and cups of hot coffee. I knew that heaven was a place where you could lie down. Later I was home in my den in Santa Ana, looking at maps of Mexico and Central America—maps on which I had placed tiny cross-marks. One cross stood out clearly; it marked Cape San Lucas, where there was supposed to be a treasure cache. Now I was back in the canoe, with a big cross wavering first to one side and then the other of the mast, while I babbled wildly, "Where is that damned light!?"

Some time after midnight the wind died down. I untied my lashings to ease the pain, and tried to paddle. It was no use; I was too all-in. Then I was sure that I saw a light—a faint beam through the haze—but my eyes still reported strange things. I'd look down at the cockpit, shake my head and swear, trying to clear my foggy brain and vision. Nevertheless, each time I looked up, instead of seeing one light, I'd see two, one above the other. This further confused me, because previously when my eyes went out of focus, the two images stayed on a horizontal plane; now the two lights were perpendicular. In desperation I wakened Ginger. "Is there a light over there?" I pleaded.

"Yes, there are two lights," she confirmed.

"No, no! There can't be—we're both going crazy. There's only one lighthouse. Look again."

Ginger calmly reaffirmed, "There are two lights—one is a bit higher than the other."

"If there are two lights, look at the lower one and see if it is flashing," I insisted.

She concentrated for several minutes and then announced, "The lower light flashes, but the one above is steady."

"It's no use," I groaned; "we've both gone crazy. It's too hazy to see anyway."

Ginger sat quietly watching the lights. The sky seemed to clear a bit, nd she turned to me excitedly. "Why, of course; the upper light is the noon."

"Yes, but the lower light, can you see that?" I again demanded.

"That's the lighthouse; I can see it flashing."

We cheered feebly. I dropped into the cockpit beside Ginger. Off in the darkness I could now see the reassuring flash of Cape Falso light. I propped my head on my hands to keep my face out of the water, and we both went sound asleep.

We were awakened by the heat of the sun beating on our unprotected faces. Greatly refreshed by our sleep, we gazed hungrily at the blue-grey mountains that were Baja California. Never had a sight been so welcome. Ginger said she had awakened for a few minutes at sunrise and had watched the sun tint the mountains with delicate pastels of rose, amethystine, and opal.

Not a breath of wind disturbed the turquoise mirror of the sea as we reached over the side and splashed cool water on our faces. Then we began to paddle in the direction of Cape Falso. In the late forenoon the outline of Cape San Lucas became clearly visible. Between the two we could see little sandy beaches with the smallest of wavelets breaking on their shores. I wanted to pick out a nice soft beach, land, distil some water—and sleep for a week; but Ginger wouldn't hear of it. She said she had a "hunch," and that she wanted to go on to the village of San Lucas.

I didn't like the idea for various reasons. The paramount objection was that we were a mess! A sorrier-looking pair of adventurers never turned up anywhere. It wasn't my idea to be seen encrusted with salt, bleary-eyed, burnt and blistered by the wind and sun, and with a four-days-old beard. We were supposed to be doing this for fun, and it outraged my vanity to be seen looking like a castaway. The fact that this trip was not always unalloyed romance was my secret and I had no intention of sharing it with the villagers and officials of San Lucas.

Ginger, as usual, won the argument. I paddled shoreward, while she got into her shore clothes. Then she took the paddle, while I made some improvements on myself. Our mouths were swollen and our tongues felt like fur-covered balls, but Ginger nevertheless had the ill grace to laugh as I attempted to shave myself in the bobbing canoe with nothing but salt water and a dull razor. Finally the job was done, and I got into my shore clothes just as we rounded the beautiful rock with its famous archway, that forms the west point of San Lucas Bay. The Cape ends in a great sandstone slab, set on edge, that rises sheer from the ocean. Twin pinnacles of rock, called Los Frailes, rise several hundred feet into the air from this bastion. They have been eroded by the elements until they are needle-fine, and form an archway of surpassing beauty and impressiveness.

Then a sight greeted us that thrilled us clear to our toes. Lying in the bay was a great black yacht, flying the Stars and Stripes. The big ship was famous in Pacific waters, where her owner, an American multi-millionaire, spends most of his time. We were well acquainted with the much publicized name painted on the bow.

"Dan, Dan, aren't you glad we came, now! Just think! On that boat there's white bread—butter—cheese—coffee with cream in it, and ——"

"And ham," I broke in, "and cigarettes, and water, and clean white towels and shaving soap—and nice, clean, scrubbed Americans to talk to. Whee!"

"They're putting off a boat, Dan," she cried.

A shore launch, her brightwork glistening in the sun, was coming towards us. In it were white-coated sailors, and several figures in tropical "whites" and Panama hats lounged in the stern. We waited expectantly for them to hail us. All the way down the coast wherever we had landed, the Mexican people had been most kind to us. News of our coming had generally preceded us, and we were welcomed with open arms. Now our own people were coming to meet us. As the launch came abreast of the canoe, most of its occupants rose and peered at us curiously. Instead of the anticipated greeting, this is what we heard: "I wonder who they are?" "You know, the couple sailing down the coast to Panama." Then the lounging figure in the stern—whose face, name, and product is familiar to millions of his fellow-Americans—turned and surveyed us disdainfully. "The damned fools!" he snapped . . . and the launch sped on.

Ginger and I sat and looked at each other in shocked silence. Gone was all our elation. I thought to myself, "Why, damn him! An ignorant Indian wouldn't have the ill grace to do anything so crude—and most certainly not to a woman. I'd like to wring his neck." I remembered the *Indio*, and his pitiful gift of that one poor little egg! I swallowed to choke down my wrath.

"Never mind," said Ginger calmly. "I'll bet we're having a lot more fun than he is."

Then we saw another boat in the harbour flying the American flag. A very unpretentious boat compared to the great sea-going yacht. By now, however, I didn't think I cared to see any more Americans; I'd take Indians, thank you—and like it! But just then a little skiff with an outboard motor, carrying two men and a woman, came towards us. They circled round us, getting closer in, all the while staring curiously. We could hardly blame them for that, for we were sorry-looking sights, in spite of all our efforts to fix ourselves up. They came closer, and a man hailed us. "Are you—do you speak English?"

"Sure," I croaked. "We're from California."

"So are we," he replied. "But what are you doing here in a little boat like that?"

"We just came down the coast," I answered.

"Oh, yes. Why, I know who you are! We've been hearing about you . . ."

"Look as though you'd been having some rough weather," the other man said.

"A storm," I replied. "We're ready to enter port now."

"We'll follow you in," said the man who had spoken first. "But you look . . . isn't there something we can do for you?"

"If you have any water aboard your boat," I replied eagerly. "We sure could—well, we haven't had any for two days."

We must have looked like apparitions, for they just stared at us for a few moments. "Better stop by our boat," said the first man; and the skiff started off.

We stopped just long enough to wet our parched throats so that we could at least talk to the port officials. Then we went ashore to make the necessary official entry before doing anything else. As the canoe grounded, the Port Captain stepped forward to help Ginger on to the beach. She had crawled forward along the bow on her hands and knees to avoid wetting her shoes. He extended his hand; she stepped down on the sand, and immediately collapsed in the Captain's arms. He stood there holding her clumsily, his face a study in perplexity. What did one do with a "Gringa" who fainted? Nothing in his book of rules had prepared him for such a contingency.

"That's all right," I said. "Just let her rest on the sand a moment. We're a little . . ." I just managed to keep on my own feet, but I was doubtful how long I could remain upright. In a few minutes Ginger came to, and we were able to continue on to the Captain's office under our own power.

After officially entering port, we left for the little yacht *Valkyrien* (out of San Pedro, California), where we had been invited to spend a few days. Our kind hostess was a trained nurse, and after giving us a half glass of lemonade and a half sandwich apiece, she led us to a bunk where we turned in for a short but sound sleep. At sundown she brought us more lemonade. Then we went out to sit on deck. Emil, our host, announced that the Port Captain had invited all of us to come ashore for dinner.

On the beach all San Lucas had assembled to greet us. Big fires blazed; white tablecloths were spread on the sand, where a real Baja California feast awaited our arrival. The natives had prepared broiled quail seasoned with a sauce of wine, lemon juice, olive oil, and chillis. This is a dish to intrigue the palate of a gourmet. There were many varieties of vegetables from the village garden—big, red, luscious tomatoes; squashes, melons, potatoes, and different kinds of baked roots. A huge platter of potato salad had been contributed by the *Valkyrien*—this and many other typical American dishes that we had not even thought of in months.

The soft strumming of guitars, the sounds of laughter and conversation went on round us as we sat munching the crisp quail and other savory dishes. Silhouetted against the dancing firelight along the white beach were little groups of men and women. Overhead was the great luminous moon of the tropics. Across the harbour where the great yacht lay, outlined in shining pin-pricks of light, we could hear the faint moaning of a saxophone. Ginger smiled at me; we were having a party, too.

It was such a big fiesta that I finally asked the manager of a small fish cannery what other event, besides our arrival, was being celebrated. "Nothing," he beamed; "no reason except that my people and I, and our good friends aboard the *Valkyrien*, thought you might enjoy a little fiesta. So have a good time, enjoy yourselves, *buen amigos*."

We spent the night aboard the *Valkyrien*, and the next afternoon began repairs on the canoe. All our gear was so soggy and wet that we wondered how we had escaped foundering under the added weight. The foreman of the cannery loaned us two carpenters to help with the mast and rigging. With their assistance the *Vagabunda* was quickly repaired.

On the third day we were ready to resume our voyage round the tip of Lower California and into the Gulf of California towards La Paz. Our friends aboard the *Valkyrien* offered us canned goods, which we could not take because of their weight. But we did gratefully accept some American white navy beans and rice. We pulled out of San Lucas with our grub box and canteens full.

Waving a final farewell, we turned and headed towards the great Sea of Cortez, the Gulf of California.

Chapter Ten

FOUR TO ONE AGAINST US

THE imaginary line of the tropic of Cancer crosses the tip of Baja California just above the Cape. We noticed a decided change in the vegetation after crossing it. On the gulf side of the peninsula there were many small green coves studded with palm trees. These were in marked contrast to the arid, barren, cactus-covered arroyos on the seaward side. There was plenty of fresh water, the seas were calm, and a safe landing could be made almost anywhere. We took our time and enjoyed the first easy sailing we had had on the trip.

One thing that did cause us considerable concern, however, was the number of great manta rays. They are a type of giant ray fish similar to the common sting ray found along the coasts of the United States. Some of them are at least twenty feet wide. The Spanish name "manta" means "blanket." These huge "blanket" fish would swim with just the tips of their flippers showing above the water, and they sometimes came so close to the canoe that they startled us. Fortunately they appeared rather sluggish and indifferent to us and we soon got used to them.

Being constitutionally unable to enjoy tranquillity for any length of time, I said to Ginger on the third day of our trip round the Cape, "Don't you think it would be fun to harpoon one of these babies and let him take us for a ride?"

"It would sound better if we knew just what one of them would do," she demurred.

"We can easily find out."

I rigged the heavy anchor line to the harpoon and waited patiently for a giant ray to come within striking distance of where I stood in the bow. Ginger was paddling from the stern. Several small rays passed unmolested —we wanted a big one. Soon a great dark shape glided in front of the canoe and I lunged the harpoon into tons of fish. The ray, taken by surprise, gave a spurt of speed, the harpoon line grew taut as I snubbed it to the figurehead on the bow. Our joy ride was short lived, for the line soon grew slack. The ray had turned and was coming directly towards us. Almost before we knew it, he was underneath the canoe and beating it savagely with his powerful flippers. We bounced round like a cork in a washing machine. The spray became so thick that we could see nothing, and besides it took all our efforts not to be thrown into the water. I took the Luger and Ginger the killing lance and we prepared to dispatch the ray without further ado. The ray had other plans. Nothing that we did made the slightest impression on his thick hide—he just kept beating the canoe as though it were a drum. Each time his great flippers smacked it I could hear the splintering of its frail siding. I tried to shove him out from under the canoe with the paddle but I might as well have saved my strength. Then, with a splash and a surge that almost turned the canoe on its beam end, the ray changed his tactics and started off up the gulf. We skimmed the water at a rate of speed that threw a spray ten feet on each side of us.

We took positions in the stern and sat back to enjoy the free ride, but shortly, instead of continuing up the gulf the ray turned and headed for the ocean. "If we aren't going to China on this cruise, we'd better stop him," said Ginger. "I hope you're satisfied—now that you know what a manta ray will do."

I crept along the bow to have another try at dispatching the ray, and began pulling in the harpoon line and passing it back to Ginger so that she could lend a hand in the tugging. As the ray came into view we both began firing. The line grew slack again and we knew that he had turned. We were ready to meet his rush this time, and managed several thrusts with the lance and a couple of shots in the head.

At last we knew we had succeeded, for the great shape began to sink, and with it the canoe, bow end first. I grabbed the line and carried it to the stern to balance the weight. The canoe began to ride so low that I prepared to cut the line and lose it and the indispensable harpoon. This would have been a serious loss, since it was one of our most important tools for securing food. Suddenly the canoe bobbed up as though the line had parted under the strain or the harpoon had pulled out. We were relieved to find that the latter had happened.

Ginger sat down on deck and mopped her forehead. "How about finding another manta to tow us back to shore?" I asked.

"No, thanks!" she answered. "We've had enough for today. It might be a good idea, though, to go ashore and see what he did to the canoe. From the sound of the splintering, we'll probably have enough to keep us busy for awhile."

We swung the canoe round and started for shore. The tussle with the ray had taken us out about two miles, and for the first time we had an opportunity to see the tip of Baja California. It is a magnificent and impressive sight. Behind the bold rocky headland of the Cape rise purple peaks, and beyond lie the mysterious mountains of Triunfo, sprawled round the base of a great peak that stands in their midst like a giant's thumb. Nature here has accomplished what man has failed to do—she has gained a foothold. Deep canyons of vivid green gash the mountains' otherwise barren and precipitous slopes. The sight was one to excite the imagination, and we found ourselves putting more force behind our paddle strokes as we glided towards the grey headland. We landed in a beautiful bay called Los Frailles, and proceeded at once to examine the canoe. It had received a marcel; its sides were wavy where the siding had caved in between the ribs. But the damage was not so severe as we feared, and since the mahogany was not completely broken, we decided not to make repairs at this time.

I was tired of our exclusive fish diet, and wanted to go hunting for deer in the green, palm-lined canyon that opened up just back of the beach. Here was fresh water and the ground was carpeted with grass and flowers. Small game was everywhere and coveys of quail and turtle doves broke cover at my passing. I found no deer, but saw many tracks. The canyon was a decided contrast to the arid, inhospitable coast we had left behind.

Ginger wasn't interested in hunting, because she had read glowing accounts of the fishing in these waters, so I left her trying her luck in a fisherman's paradise. The waters were teeming with beautiful and brilliantly coloured fish of every variety and size. They could easily be seen swimming over the white sands.

The next day we paddled leisurely along the shore, stopping to examine each interesting cove. We could land anywhere. This is certainly the canoeist's and fisherman's Valhalla; it has everything. Fish of all kinds leapt and glided by us. Giant rays swam close to the boat as though daring us to harpoon them. Ginger shivered every time I even motioned towards one.

In many canyons we could see thatched native huts set in among the palms. The highly mineralized formations of many of the canyon walls added colourful background.

Late in the afternoon we found a beautiful camp in Muertos Bay, where an old pier extended out a little distance from shore. The beach was strewn with timbers, old iron, and other evidences of the time when silver from the mines of Triunfo was shipped from this port.

After setting up camp, we hiked up the canyon which lay behind the beach and came to an old Spanish ranch house. It seemed to be deserted but as we drew nearer an old man came to meet us. He apologized for not being able to ask us to eat with him, but he had no food, he said. His cattle had died during the dry years and now he had nothing to sell. Though the ground was fertile and there was evidence of water, he had no garden. Yes, the waters were full of fish, he agreed, but his sons could seldom catch edible fish—only sharks. The deer were too wild, one could not get close enough to shoot. This was odd, for to us they seemed to be starving in a land of plenty.

I returned to our camp and got two of our homemade jigs (fishhooks with bone shanks), and on the way back to the old man met his son arriving home empty-handed. I instructed him in the use of the jig and took him fishing in our canoe. We soon had a large catch of dolphin, bonito, and mackerel. Then I suggested that we go hunting. Ginger, the young Mexican boy, and I set off up the canyon, and an hour later returned with a good-sized buck. The old man thanked us fervently.

These people were cattle raisers, and, like our one-crop farmers at home, felt that with the failure of their efforts in this direction, nothing remained but to starve. Accustomed as we had become to rustling up a meal wherever we found ourselves, this was an amazing spectacle: that men could so quickly lose their ingenuity, once they became wedded to the idea that life itself depended upon having something to sell to the other fellow.

"I'd certainly like to have that place," I said to Ginger as we trudged back to camp. "There's a gold mine there for a young, energetic man. It would make the best headquarters for fishermen on the Pacific. Comfortable cabins could be built at low cost. Fruits and vegetables could be easily grown. Horses could be bought cheaply and furnished for trips inland. Also small boats with outboard motors. The sun shines every day, the climate is perfect, and there are no pests. Chambers of Commerce from one end of California to the other would be ravished by the white beach. And the water is always just right for swimming."

Ginger laughed at my enthusiasm, but agreed that some day perhaps, when we were tired of roaming, we might come back and do that very thing.

We put out of Muertos Bay the next morning soon after sunrise, and by ten o'clock were sailing between Ceralbo Island and the mainland. We had a treasure location for Ceralbo. "The third cove from the end," read our little notebook.

The island looked extremely interesting. Sixteen miles long and about four miles wide, its steep volcanic peaks reared over two thousand feet in the air. We skirted its shores looking for our pirate cove, passed bluff headlands and shingle beaches. Then the third little bay opened before us, with a fine sand beach backed by a dense growth of trees.

After lunch, armed with our treasure map and guns, we started up the canyon, which was filled to its mouth with great boulders and scrubby brush. A quarter of a mile brought us to where the canyon narrowed down. Here the trees were larger, and on one of them we saw peculiar markings that must have been cut there many years ago. They were in the form of a double cross and had two perpendicular lines on the side. Our map indicated that the gold was buried at the northeast corner of a large rectangular boulder set on the face of the north side of the cliff. Examining trees nearby, we found another one marked with a perpendicular line and three lines cut at an angle across it, and a single line standing alone. Eagerly we began looking at other trees and finally found a third one with a perpendicular line crossed by four lines at an angle, and three slanting lines cut beside it. We lined up the three trees and found that they formed a perfect triangle. A re-examination showed that the markings pointed north and indicated

Sketch Map of
LOWER CALIFORNIA
Showing the voyage of the Vagabunda
Scale of miles
CALIFORNIA
San Diego
Coronados Islands
Ensenada
Santo Tomas
Old Mine
Desert
Cape Colnett
San Felipe Bay
Old Mission
San Martin I.
Cape San Quintin
Storm
Rosario Bay
San Geronimo
Desert
Red Bluff
Copper Mine
Canoas Pt.
San Juan Desert
Blanca Pt.
Placer Mine
Playa Maria
Santa Rosalia
San Benito Is.
Cedros Is.
Lagoon Hd.
Block Warrior
Turtle Bay
Scammon Lagoon
Placer
San Hepolito
Ballenas Bay
Flat Sandy Country
Juanico Bay
Boca de Los Animas
Boca de Soledad
Desert
Magdalena Bay
Boca de Conejo wrecked
Gold
Cape Falso
Cape San Lucas
6 day Storm
BAJA CALIFORNIA
MEXICO
State of SONORA
Tiburon Island
Seris Indians
Kino Bay
Palms
GUAYMAS
Tortuga
San Marcos
Los Algodones
Yaqui Indians
Punta Rosa
Santa Barbara Bay
Carmen Is
Ahome
State of SINALOA
San Josef
Espiritu Santo Is
Ceralbo Is
LA PAZ
MAZATLAN

a group of huge boulders. "No one would bury anything in this boulder patch," I said.

"Let's look anyway," Ginger suggested.

We started peering round and beneath the boulders. Then Ginger called excitedly, "Here's another marking." It was cut deep in the stone and looked very old—a single slanting cross with two straight lines beside it.

"X marks the spot, but there is no way for us to dig under those boulders," I said.

"Well, we know where it is now, so let's go on up the canyon and see what else we can find."

We soon came upon an old, deep-worn trail that had not been used in many years. In some places it was completely washed away, and in others covered with landslides, but it led eventually to the head of the canyon. Tracks indicated that goats were now the only users of the trail. From the head of the canyon we followed a zigzag path up the mountain, and at last stood on top of the ridge. From where we were the trail branched off in two directions, north and south. We chose the northern route and followed it for a mile to where it led out on a big promontory which commanded a magnificent view of the waters below.

"Here's where the pirates camped!" I exclaimed. "See how the boulders are laid in rows. They must have formed the base of a building at least fifty feet square." The ground around was covered with broken sea shells for a considerable distance.

Now the trail led down the hill and evidently into the canyon that entered the next bay north of our camp. We decided to investigate that canyon tomorrow.

We returned to the trees and made a rough sketch map of the place, then hiked back to camp in time for a swim before dark.

The next morning we sailed into the next bay and made camp. This canyon was wider and more heavily wooded than the other. On a little mesa to one side we found the remains of a considerable settlement. The adobe dwellings had washed down into piles of dried mud, but there was still a well-constructed masonry well, which was dry.

We followed a once well-used trail inland. It wound high up into the canyon and to another mesa on which stood the ruins of what appeared to be an ancient fortification. Here the ground was also covered with shells. There were several deep holes round the old wall where some one had been digging. A corner of the thick wall had been taken down and now a huge pit yawned there.

Dreaming about buried treasure and digging for it are two very different things. While the charts give implicit directions as to how to find the landmarks, the landmarks, if found, are seldom conclusive evidence that the treasure is there. Assuming the landmarks are there, then the only thing that remains to be settled is just where to dig—you generally have a choice of about an acre. I personally have always entertained a doubt as to why any one who knew the location of a hoard would make duplicate maps and pass them round. Probably the way to have the most fun would be to get a good metal locator, and each time the indicator gives the signal —dig. It may be that only a rusty shovel or a bit of anchor chain will come to light, but you will have had the fun of discovering something hidden— as well as blisters on your hands.

We returned to camp for a closer inspection of the beach. Fastened to a large rock on the north side of the bay, we found an old rusted iron ring, such as is used in mooring ships. There is small doubt but that the buccaneers made good use of these little-known places. By our campfire that night, we could almost see them swaggering by, on mischief bent.

The farther we travelled from the Cape, the sparser the vegetation became, indicating a lessening of rainfall. It was still more luxuriant than on the seaward side, but by no means as lush as it had been nearer the Cape. We were drawing near the principal seaport and capital of the lower part of Baja California, La Paz.

We approached La Paz through a narrow channel, flanked on one side by bare, brown, gutted-looking hills with no sign of human habitation; then we saw the white beach where La Paz lies. We pulled up at a little pier jutting out from a low masonry wall built long ago by the Spaniards.

A glum, sullen-looking crowd of people awaited us. We were so used to the gay welcoming committees that usually met the *Vagabunda* that we looked at each other in astonishment.

"What on earth do you suppose is the matter?" Ginger asked.

We would soon find out, for now the Port Captain was coming towards us. His face wore a sour expression as he shouldered his way unceremoniously through the crowd. Gruffly, and with a complete absence of all the usual courtesies, he ordered us to follow him to his office. He led us through a lane of scowling faces, glanced over our papers briefly, made the usual entries and then curtly bade us good-bye. Not a word of welcome —just good-bye.

"Wait a minute," I said. "What's wrong? Why do all of you act as though we were bringing bad news?"

"Because you *are* bad news," he said savagely. "Yes, you are distinctly bad news. Why, I bet fifty pesos myself that you couldn't get here. When word came overland that you were going to try to sail round the Cape, I and all my people bet four to one that you would never arrive in La Paz."

After a moment I found my tongue. "With whom did you bet?"

"The officials of Magdalena," he replied. "They were most anxious to bet. I bet with the Captain of the Guard, who wanted to bet one hundred pesos."

"Oh, he did, did he?" Trust *El Capitán* to think of some way to recoup his poker losses.

Then I had a bright idea. Why, I asked the Port Captain, didn't he bet with the people of Guaymas that we couldn't cross the Gulf? I told him that I was sure that we had a fair chance, and perhaps the people would jump at the odds when they learnt that we were attempting to cross in a sixteen-foot canoe.

His eyes glistened and he laughed. "My friend, you have the good idea. Welcome to La Paz."

La Paz is an altogether charming town, and we thoroughly enjoyed our stay. It was at one time one of the great pearling centres of the world. The famous blue, black, and green pearls, which are the delight of connoisseurs, are found in this area. Also, it was once the headquarters of a pirate fleet. There is a breeze which comes up regularly every afternoon, called "Cromwell's Wind." A famous old-time buccaneer of these parts, Cromwell, would take his ships out in the Bay of La Paz, hoist all sail, and wait for the wind. When it came it would carry his ships out into the Gulf at a brisk speed, and he was thus able to overtake and capture any ships that were becalmed offshore.

We spent some time in and round La Paz, studying the possibilities of various commercial enterprises, since this is practically virgin territory. We were particularly interested in ways and means of making La Paz available to tourists.

La Paz, in our opinion, has a provocative charm for the North American visitor found in no other place in Baja California. There is a peculiar blending of the past and present that carries one backward and forward in time. A few great houses line its streets, cheek-by-jowl with the adobe huts of pre-Conquest Mexico. Automobiles rush about in its narrow rutted streets, while patient *Indios* plod in their wake, their immemorial burdens carried on their heads. Mexican and Chinese shopkeepers stand in the doorways of their tiny establishments. Slow-paced and leisured, the life of La Paz flows on as it has since the men-in-mail raised the standards of Spain in its streets, and the dark-robed padres converted the Indios in its now ruined mission compound. Trees shade its streets, flowers brighten its gardens, coco-nut palms line its shores, and in its sheltered harbour fleets of little down-at-the-heel boats ride quietly at anchor. We liked La Paz.

One day we sailed out into the harbour and waited for "Cromwell's Wind" to pick us up and carry us into the "Vermilion Sea," the Gulf of California. We must have failed to follow Cromwell's course, however, for the stiff breeze promptly landed us on a mud flat. Small waves picked us up and carried us a little distance, only to smack us down once more upon the flat. We wondered how long the *Vagabunda's* canvas bottom would stand the rough treatment, as we hopped, skipped, and jumped our way to deep water.

That night we came to Espíritu Santo Island and made camp in a beautiful little landlocked harbour. This island, too, was once the stronghold of the boys who flew the "Jolly Roger."

Next day, while skirting along the coast of the island, we entered a narrow channel between sheer cliffs and found ourselves in another hidden bay. Great iron mooring rings were fastened to the rocks. In the canyon back of the beach we came to a trail about ten feet wide and followed it until we reached a great hole, thirty feet square and forty feet deep. We could find no explanation for it unless it had been made by some enthusiastic treasure seeker. We kept on up the canyon and came at last to a great cave approximately one hundred feet long, twenty feet wide, and thirty feet high. At its mouth the ground was covered with shells and charcoal. Inside were many evidences of habitation, some ancient and some modern. There were broken arrow heads and bits of flint that may have been tools, and a very large, ancient, rusted padlock. At the back of the cave was a deep hole. From this cave the trail led on for about two miles up the ridge to the top of the island, then down an incline to the edge of a perpendicular cliff. On the ridge we found large stone mounds and the ground was thickly strewn with shells. Further north we came to a dry lake. A heavy stone wall ran along one side of its shore and the shore line was fringed with dead trees and many large stumps. On the west side we found the ruin of a six-cornered building. The trail over which we had come was apparently the only approach to this lake, for sheer cliffs bounded it in other directions. It was a site that a corporal's guard could hold against an army.

During our stay in the Gulf we made numerous exploratory trips among its many islands. On several we found caves blackened by fire, huge piles of shells, bits of pottery and stone implements made by prehistoric men, as well as evidences of later habitation. We were unable to supply the answers to the riddles propounded by the relics, and they were many. These islands should prove a profitable source of information to the anthropologist and the archaeologist.

The sea near Espíritu Santo was full of many varieties of marine life which we had never seen before. The most interesting to us was a peculiar little spiked fish which we called the "balloon fish." If it was poked or played with it would inflate itself with water until it was perfectly round, and in this condition it was entirely helpless. We tossed one variety, whose spines were short, back and forth like footballs. Another type, whose spines were long and sharp, we gave a wide berth.

The time had now arrived for us to make a decision as to the future course of our travels. The trip so far had been difficult and dangerous at times for both of us. It was the accepted thing for a man to seek adventure in dangerous ways, if he chose to do so, but to take a young girl along on such an enterprise was to invite public wrath. I had often wondered if it was not best for us to go home.

If our original plan of going down the west coast of Mexico was adhered to, it meant crossing the Gulf of California. This is considered a perilous undertaking even by men versed in the Gulf's treacherous moods and equipped with more suitable sea-going craft than ours. We had never before, voluntarily, left sight of land.

There was also the question of how much Ginger was missing the comforts and amenities of home. So one night I asked her, "What do you say—shall we continue up the Gulf to the Colorado River, and then go back home?"

"What makes you ask that question?"

I gave her the reasons that were uppermost in my mind.

She laughed. "That sounds funny coming from you. What's a neck for if not to risk? Besides, I'm having a good time, aren't you?"

Apparently the insidious bug of adventure had bitten her, as it had bitten me years ago when, little more than a kid, I ran away from home with my buddy and spent two years tramping over Asia, Africa, and the Mediterranean countries on a joint capital of thirty dollars.

So for several weeks we continued up the Gulf, cruising among the many islands that line its mountaingirt shores. The mighty Sierra de la Giganta (the Mountains of the Giantess) rise precipitously from the water's edge—great towering cliffs, harsh eroded valleys, in a land of silence, empty of vegetation. The islands of the Gulf are volcanic uplifts, supporting a family or two where there are springs, but for the most part, barren of all life. Even the sea birds avoid these rocks. Great manta rays, sharks, jewfish, swordfish, porpoises, and whales pass silently to and fro in their endless quest for food, accompanied by an occasional pearler or small freighter bound for the gypsum mines of San Marcos, the copper mines of Santa Rosalia, or Guaymas on the mainland. These silent voyagers only emphasize the loneliness and emptiness of the great "Sea of Cortez." In this infinitude of waste and water, man and his works are but the substance of shadows.

Along the west coast of San Jose Island we made one of our loveliest cruises. The colouring of the cliffs there is comparable to painted canyons and deserts of Arizona and New Mexico; in addition, a turquoise sea provides a mirror of splendid contrasts. Reds, dusky blues, greens, yellows, ochres, whites, and tans blaze across their sheer faces. The results of ancient disturbances are seen in the sedimentary deposits, upended and lying diagonally along the precipices.

The fish in these waters are also colourful. There are orange, blue, rust, and greenish-purple starfish, and fan clams, whose iridescent shells are fully twenty inches long. These clams are called *hachas*, meaning ax, by the natives. The big muscle is eaten and tastes like scallops; the rest of the meat, which is trimmed with an orange and black ruffle, is too rich to eat but makes a delicious soup.

It is sometimes necessary to use extreme understatements in order not to be judged a liar. Neither Ginger nor I have any desire to work up reputations as Munchausens, yet our friends look at us in unbelief when we give a literal account of something we saw or experienced.

One day while fishing I saw a huge mollusk clinging to a rock in about three feet of water, its shell wide open. It looked like a giant clam and might be good to eat. I was using the sharp-pointed killing lance at the time, and thrusting it in the clam, tried to cut the big muscle that hinged its shell. The clam promptly closed upon the lance, and no amount of tugging or twisting could extricate it, until darkness forced me to abandon the job for the time being. The next morning I tried to pry the clam off its rock, so that it could be dragged to the beach and the lance retrieved, but I couldn't budge it. Eventually Ginger and I, tugging and pulling together, did extract the lance—but we didn't get the clam. We won't tell you how big that clam was, but don't entirely disbelieve the next deep-sea diver who tells you of the risks involved in stepping in one.

As the time drew near for us to cross the Gulf, we became more apprehensive. There is an unpredictability about the Gulf and its moods which can be appreciated only upon close acquaintance. We began to understand more fully why every activity along its coasts is undertaken with the proviso—if the Gulf be willing. We were told of tornadoes that sweep up its waters, destroying everything before them. These are for the most part seasonal storms of short duration but of terrifying intensity, and are given the name "chubascos." They spring up without warning, and during the time of year in which they prevail small boats never venture far from land. Larger boats cancel sailing dates at the slightest hint of a "chubasco" in the offing. We were becoming impatient—perhaps because we were afraid, for the longer we waited the more hazardous it seemed.

Finally, on a day when everything seemed auspicious, we began the hazardous venture of crossing the Gulf to Guaymas on the mainland, a hundred miles away. The surface of the water was a burnished mirror. In its tranquil depths we could see the white sands far below and the ceaseless passage of a multitude of living forms. We were only a few miles off shore when dark wisps of clouds began to form in the southeast. The air became humid and a small flock of sea birds ceased their fishing and flew back towards their rookery. An oppressive feeling, a peculiar nervous tension, sent us hurrying shoreward with the birds, and not a moment too soon, as a "chubasco" swept up the Gulf, the *Vagabunda* running before it. We managed to beach the canoe and pull it up on high ground before the full force of the storm struck. Mountains of water propelled by an eighty-mile gale roared past our haven.

This is without question one of the most terrifying phenomena in nature. Safe in the lee of the island, it could do us no harm, but its capacity for destruction left us breathless and shaking.

Ginger was an accomplished cook and performed near-miracles in broiling, frying, baking, sautéing, and French frying fish and other sea foods. Considering her limited resources in both food and materials and her lack of knowledge when she left home, the results which she obtained were little short of marvellous. Nevertheless, the tough and leathery tortilla which of necessity was our only breadstuff had become a trifle monotonous.

One day, as Ginger made up a batch of them, I suggested, "Why don't you toast those leathery things? When they are cold they taste like shoe soles."

"No," Ginger said positively. "A tortilla is a tortilla, and if you do anything else to it, it's not a tortilla. They are supposed to be large and tough enough to roll your food in."

We had been eating an unrelieved diet of fish, tortillas, and an occasional mess of beans and rice. A change of any sort was desirable. Tortillas, which are the basic foodstuff throughout Mexico, are made from unleavened ground corn, which is first boiled in lime or lye water to remove the husks (as hominy is prepared) and then pounded and made into thin flat cakes, which are cooked on hot rocks or in an iron skillet. When freshly cooked they are quite palatable, but when a day or so old, they resemble nothing so much as a piece of leather, and are about as tough.

As usual, the tortillas this day were large and tough, and Ginger made a stack of them big enough to last us on our journey across the Gulf. Then, as the morning was fine, we made a second attempt to reach Guaymas. We had nice sailing all day, and although the wind was light we made good time. By nightfall we were at least twenty miles offshore. We had a bite to eat and settled down in the cockpit for the night. Sailing along in quiet waters silvered by a great white moon, I played the harmonica and Ginger sang.

Our idyll was rudely interrupted by a jarring crash that sent the canoe careening to one side. Scrambling on to the bow, I found that we had run into a half-submerged log that now held the canoe in the grip of its gnarled branches. I freed the canoe, but once on deck again, I could distinctly hear the gurgle of water. I unzipped the cockpit, pulled out the dunnage bag, and wriggled under the tiny deck to the bow. Feeling round in the darkness, I found that a snag on the log had poked a hole in the canvas bottom. Water was coming in fast. We had ten minutes at the most before the canoe would sink. Something must be done right now.

I shouted to Ginger, "Throw in the tortillas!"

Without question she obeyed me. I grabbed the stack, and one after another placed them in and over the hole. When I had used them all I wedged the rest of the dunnage over the patch. It was a gamble, but a poor patch was better than none, and strange as it seems the gluey mass held until we reached the island we had left that morning.

We carried the canoe up on the beach, and while Ginger prepared some breakfast I looked at the damage. The hole was about two inches in diameter. Although it had been easy to place the tortillas between the siding and the ribs over the hole, getting them off was another matter. Water-soaked, they had welded together into a regular rubber plug which it took a half hour's hard labour to remove.

Towards evening a native dugout came gliding into the cove. Three natives beached their craft and approached our camp. The elder was a man of about sixty; the two younger men were his sons. They were pearl divers, working their way along the islands. When we told them that we were attempting to cross the Gulf, and the circumstances of our two failures, the old man had a lot to say. We were forcing our luck; we were too impatient; we were demanding, not accepting. He was a veritable storehouse of knowledge and a philosopher as well.

We told him also of our failures in goat hunting. He explained that since each herd has a sentinel which stands upon a point overlooking the surrounding country, you cannot approach the herd except from behind and above the sentinel. Otherwise the sentinel sees you and gives the signal.

He told us how to hunt turtles at night by paddling quietly along until we heard their breathing, then to wait. When the turtle emerged for another breath it could be quickly speared.

His most interesting information was in regard to the natives of Tiburon Island—the Seris, members of an ancient race with strange powers and knowledge. We had heard many tales of the place, which lies near the upper end of the Gulf, and meant to go there if it was at all possible.

He talked to us long and earnestly about waiting for the propitious time to embark upon a venture. "Impatience," he said, "destroys your judgment and defeats your purpose. My children, wait and go *with* God, since you cannot go without Him. Wait without impatience for the time which is best for you. Only men who seek to know are given the truth. Foolish men and men blinded by their own vanity disbelieve this, but great men are not ashamed to seek the wisdom and guidance of forces greater than themselves. Do not court failure by refusing to listen— remember that you are a creature of time and governed by it."

The Indian's face exuded the patience and wisdom of which he talked, and his eyes were infinitely wise. There was a kind of goodness about him that there was no discounting. Ginger was much impressed, both by the man and by his counsel. When he rose to leave, he said to her, "Remember, my child, that you are young and pretty now, and if you want to, you can always stay that way. The years are not heavy on one who has youth in his spirit and kindness in his heart, and who seeks to use his life to improve his character."

Long after he had gone we sat round the campfire and talked over what he had said. He had put his finger on our besetting sin—impatience, and we agreed that it was not well to attempt the hazardous crossing a third time until we felt an inner sense of certainty as to the outcome.

The next day, after mending the canoe, we sailed along the rugged coast, past Ildefonso Island and on towards Concepción Point. Near the island we came upon one of those strange red patches of sea water that looked as though it had been dyed with the blood of the sea monsters that swam nearby. The true explanation is doubtless far less romantic. We could find no landing for the canoe at Concepción, and decided to unload only what we needed for supper, anchor out from shore, and sleep in the canoe. Early next morning we would go on to Tortuga Island and from there attempt to cross the Gulf.

We went to sleep in the canoe as we had planned but were awakened by something bumping against its side. My first thought was that the anchor line had parted and we were against the rocks, but this theory was dispelled when we sat up and found ourselves in exactly the same place where we had gone to sleep. Then we saw the phosphorescent trail of great shapes darting round in the water. The creatures were too big to be seals. What, then? I got out the harpoon, but decided against attacking such huge prey at night. I tied one end of the anchor line to the killing lance, so that if necessary we could spear but the lance could be quickly withdrawn. Soon one of the creatures darted too close to the canoe for comfort and I jabbed at it. They were huge sharks, and as we lanced one after the other, more kept coming, attracted by the blood. The water was a carnage, for the uninjured turned on their injured fellows and tore them to pieces. The water was alive with them, and because of the phosphorescence it looked like a fireworks display. For awhile I thought we would be tipped over. Some tried to bite the canoe and succeeded in scratching off quite a bit of paint. We were glad when daylight came.

The next day we pulled up in the lee of Tortuga Island just before dark, found no landing, and again slept in the canoe.

We started out the following morning in a green-and-gold dawn. Somehow we felt that this time we could cross the Gulf in safety. We sailed and paddled all day. Sometimes the placid waters of the Gulf were whipped up into short choppy seas that wet us to the skin. Again the sail hung idly in a dead calm. The afternoon of the second day we sighted the low-lying mainland, and only then did we realize the strain we had been under. Our feeling was one of relief more than triumph, but we had succeeded in the almost impossible—we had crossed the Gulf of California in a canoe.

Chapter Eleven

MEXICO'S UNTAMED INDIANS

WHEN we first discussed our probable ports of call, we had no particular intention of going to Tiburon. But the incessant warnings about not going to Tiburon, and the dire predictions of what would happen to us if we *did* go there, finally decided us. Señor Ortiz Rubio, former president of Mexico, whom we met in San Diego, warned us that "not even a Mexican gunboat is safe near Tiburon." This statement seemed a design to scare us rather than a record of fact. What could unarmed primitives, no matter how savage, do against steel and high explosives?

Much has been written about the savage Seris Indians, who, after centuries of warfare with the Spanish and Mexican governments, were at last rounded up and driven from their homes in the State of Sonora to a bitter exile on the bleak, waterless wastes of Tiburon. They are reputed to file their teeth into sharp points; to be cannibals; to shoot poisoned arrows from ambush; and to have a bitter and undying enmity towards all whites. We were told tales of fishermen who, after landing on the Island, never left it. Prospectors, anthropologists, archaeologists—and particularly authors—are others who arouse the Seris' ire. It is said they have a temple of authors' skulls.

To reach Tiburon, we left Guaymas one morning before sunrise and started up the Gulf. We both agreed that, irrespective of our success, the magnificent scenery along the coast was well worth the trip. Its colours and formations were superb. Brilliant Chinese-lacquer reds blazed across the mountains of Sonora; delicate orchid and mauve were blended with the sharper blues and greens and the subtly toned browns and pastel greys of the desert. Sunrise and sunset left us breathless.

Then against the flaming backdrop of a Sonoran dawn, we saw the rugged outline of Tiburon. Indescribably bleak, barren and desolate, it rose from the water—an ugly excrescence, sinister and oppressive in a world of sunlight.

As we approached the island, I began making an assortment of fishhooks to give to the Seris. In all our travels we found nothing that coast or island natives needed or prized so highly as fishhooks. Then Ginger suggested that we might troll as we went along, and pass the fish out to the Indians. That seemed a good idea, so we put out the lines. Soon the cockpit was full of fish. Tiburon now lay before us. It had an air of waiting—for death perhaps. Back from the beach stood a few miserable brush shelters. A weather-beaten dugout was drawn up on shore. There was not an Indian in sight. This was not a good sign, for unfriendly natives always keep under cover until you make the first move.

We cautiously edged the canoe inshore; our every sense alert for the showers of poisoned arrows and other warlike manifestations we had been told to expect. Then in a clump of bushes we saw the black thatched head of a Seri, and could soon pick out several others where they squatted motionless. I asked Ginger to hold up a fish and make signs for them to come and get it. She did so with many friendly gestures and appropriate comments in Spanish. I doubted if her motions depicting the dove of peace would be of any particular interest to the Seris, for unquestionably they were better acquainted with fish. One of them came out from the bushes and began to shuffle towards the canoe—a dejected figure with the slouch of a whipped dog.

He spoke no Spanish, and we communicated our desire that he take the fish by smiles and gestures. When he finally comprehended, he accepted the fish and walked stolidly back into the brush, where we could hear a rapid discussion going on in an unfamiliar tongue. They must have decided that we meant no harm, for in a few minutes Seris surrounded the canoe, each one patiently waiting for his fish. One man spoke a little Spanish. We told him who we were; that we were making a trip up the Gulf, and would continue on our journey that afternoon. He told us that their chief was away visiting a few of the tribe who still lived on the mainland.

Then he said, "Are you writers—do you make marks on paper?" We promptly disclaimed any such ability. He gave a grunt of satisfaction. "We don't like writers. They come here and treat us as though we were strange beasts. This poor place is our home—the only home that we have left. To be here at all is bad enough, but to be treated insolently in one's home by strangers—that makes my people very angry." We nodded agreement, meanwhile wondering where and when the Seris had made the acquaintance of the writing fraternity.

"Tell us something about your people," I urged. He nodded agreeably, and began to talk in very poor Spanish which I translate freely.

"We were once a great people—a proud race—who owned vast fields of corn on the mainland. Most of Sonora was ours. Then came white men, who drove us from our fields; and when we fought back, more men came with guns, until finally we were driven back to the Gulf. But they were still not content. Eventually they made us come to this poor place. Here there is hardly enough water to drink, and none for the raising of crops. The land is worthless, even if water could be had. Our people have been forced for many years to live on fish. Our only clothing and blankets we make from pelicans' skins. We are bitter against those who have done these things to us, for now we are doomed; our race is going to die. Our women will no longer bear children to suffer what we have suffered."

He talked on, apparently glad of a sympathetic white ear into which to pour his troubles. Soon, we were walking towards a little row of huts, miserable makeshifts built of brush and driftwood, and so low that it was impossible for a man of average height to stand upright in them. Such shelters would be poor protection against the heavy rains and chilling winds that sweep up the Gulf.

But in spite of their poor diet and inadequate shelter, the Seris still have fair physiques. They are tall and well-proportioned, with wiry muscles; and look as though at one time they might have been a highly developed people. Some of those we saw were clad in clothing that they had probably begged from the crews of visiting fishing boats.

Traces of civilization lay here and there. One hut had an old battered washtub, another a tin cup. The chief's hut boasted two five-gallon oil cans, and a few other odds and ends probably given to him by the fishermen.

We soon took our leave of the Seris and returned to the canoe, too depressed to want to remain longer. Putting to sea at once, we spent the night in an isolated cove. Although the visit to Tiburon had not been the highly coloured, romantic adventure that we had been led to expect, it was nevertheless an experience worth having—to discover, not more than three hundred and fifty miles from San Diego as the crow flies, savages living in conditions as primitive as these.

One day after our return home, I picked up a copy of "Modern Treasure Hunters" by Harold T. Wilkins, and glancing through it saw a reference to the Seris, which explains, I think, their attitude towards authors. Mr. Wilkins says:

"It is on record that a French authoress, Madame Titayana, the Italian colonel Masturzi, and a lone hermit, the American, John Thompson—who has lived for many years on a small island in the Gulf of California, landed on the island in 1930. When they approached its shores, the wild Seris lined the wooded banks, brandishing bows and poisoned arrows, with very hefty spears. Madame is said to have sung them a Spanish ditty, which so charmed that a landing was permitted, and even a movie camera was used. However, the three foreigners took care not to outstay their welcome, but quitted Tiburon's shores eight days after landing."*

The Seris are apparently fonder of fish than of Madame's singing, for they brandished no bows at us, and we saw no sign of a "hefty spear." Four years after Mr. Wilkins' tourists had reported their findings, not only had the Seris ceased to "brandish bows and poisoned arrows" at passersby, but the "wooded banks" of Tiburon had also disappeared!

Back in Guaymas, we decided to give the canoe a thorough overhauling,

* From *Modern Buried Treasure Hunters* by Harold T. Wilkins. Published by E. P. Dutton & Co., Inc. Printed by permission of the publishers.

so I got a job with a fish company that enabled us to buy some badly needed canvas and paint.

Guaymas is entirely landlocked, which gives it a wonderful harbour but also shuts out any vagrant breeze that might cool things off. While we were there the sun was almost directly overhead; and a thirty-foot pole cast a shadow only a few inches long at noon. During the day the rocks on the hillsides absorb the blistering heat, which they give off at night—as do the thick-walled adobe houses. Consequently there is little change in temperature. At midnight we have walked beside an adobe building and felt its heat four feet away.

Miramar Beach, a ten-minute ride from Guaymas, is the town's playground, for it is always ten degrees cooler there than in the city. On Saturday night Guaymas goes dancing in its little pavillion, but strictly along "class" lines. The *mestizos*, mixed bloods, the "second class," dance until midnight. After that, the whites, the "first class," take over. The *Indios*, the "third class," look on. The classes never mix, for if a man who belongs to the "first class" associates with the "second class" socially, he automatically becomes déclassé with his own group. Americans on first coming into the country are assumed to belong to the "first class," but they, too, are subject to the rules. If they are seen to associate with the other two classes, they immediately become social "untouchables" in the eyes of the ruling caste.

We went to visit one of the *los correctos* families of Guaymas, the "first class." Seen from the street, their single-storey house was unpretentious. Its front wall met the sidewalk, and there was nothing in the heavy door and shuttered windows to give the passerby any indication of the owner's status. Our knock on the door was answered by one of the daughters of the house, who cordially escorted us into the formal entrance hall. After the blazing sun outside, the profusion of potted palms and ferns gave the darkened room a sense of restful coolness. The young girl went off to announce our arrival to members of her family, and we looked round at our surroundings. The hall opened into a long roofed-over veranda, the living room, which was open on one side to the walled-in patio. Heavy blinds were drawn on its open side to keep out the heat. The room, fully sixty feet long, was furnished with wicker and leather hand-tooled furniture. Several cabinets contained fine porcelains, and various objets d'art. A beautiful antique chest of carved wood stood to one side of the room. The furnishings and their arrangement indicated taste as well as wealth.

Our hostess entered, and made us welcome in beautiful, soft Spanish. She immediately drew the blinds so that we might see out into the patio. In the lovely garden ablaze with flowers, a tiny boy was gleefully trying to catch goldfish in a pond resplendent with water lilies. A maid entered with cooling glasses of lemonade and papayas.

However, not all the *los correctos* live in such comfortable circumstances.

Wars, revolutions, and time have swept away most of their resources. Few of them are able to maintain more than the simplest establishment. The homes of the poorer classes range from mud huts to decrepit adobes.

People in Guaymas are very friendly, greeting every passer-by with "Adios"—except during the siesta hour, which is from one to three o'clock in the afternoon. Then if the impatient gringo demands goods or services, he is received with anything but cordiality. All the stores are shuttered, and hell and high water won't open them.

A few weeks after our visit to Tiburon, with the *Vagabunda* decked out in a new coat of paint and looking as spruce as the day she was launched, we paddled out of Guaymas and headed south along a barren desert coast. It was the country of the fierce Yaqui Indians.

Both of us were happy to be on our way again. The bright sunshine, the blue waters of the Gulf, the sense of mystery communicated by a strange land and its unpredictable people—all these combined to exhilarate us.

Near Los Algodones Point, we ran into a school of blue jellyfish. As far as we could see, the water was alive with them. Their colour varied from the palest azure to a sapphire as deep as the sea on a sunny day. Their delicate, transparent, bell-shaped bodies, fringed with waving tentacles, moved slowly while they searched the water for their prey. We soon found that their fragile tentacles packed a potent sting that left a red welt on our skins wherever they touched us; that is, while they remained in the water—out of water they were harmless, and could be picked up and handled.

As yet we had seen no Yaquis. Just what would happen when we did was a matter for speculation. We had been warned many times about them. They were an unpredictable people, we were told, fierce in their likes and dislikes. They harassed the few American ranchers on the outskirts of their territory; they continually caused the Mexican government trouble; and like the Seris, their hatred of whites was proverbial. The parent stock from which the great Aztec civilization of the Valley of Mexico sprang, these people interested us tremendously; we were anxious to meet them, and at the same time apprehensive. For it was evident that the same qualities that had made them a thorn in the side of government since the time of the Conquest had under more fortuitous conditions made them great. The miracle of a magnificent, indigenous American civilization that had flowered in the short span of four hundred years from a rude, barbaric people had been no accident—the human stuff had been there. What of the present Indians? Were they the degenerate descendants of a once potent stock; or were they valuable human material going to waste because of their conquerors' stupid and inept handling?

One day we came into Santa Barbara Bay, where we planned to make camp just east of Santa Rosa Point. Here the country was a little greener than any we had seen since leaving Guaymas. This stretch of coast is low, sandy and barren, with occasional bays and lagoons to break its monotony. Offshore there are a few sand islands. While we were busy setting up camp, we were surprised to see a solitary figure standing close by, who seemed to have materialized out of thin air. His tall, clean-cut figure was clothed in patches. No trace of the original garment remained, just patches superimposed on still other patches. A Yaqui! As immobile as though cast in bronze, he silently surveyed us; and we became as silent and still as he. It was our move, but I didn't know what to do. I pulled up the equipment box, and said, *"Sientese, Señor."* He made no response to my invitation to be seated, but stood as silent and immobile as before. Opening the fishing kit, I selected four fishhooks and handed them to him. He tucked them away with a broad grin.

Within a few minutes our visitors had increased to four. They came as silently as the first one; shrouded in soundless invisibility one moment, they appeared out of the ether the next, as though they were jinn. It seemed wise to explain immediately to them who we were, where we were going, and why. I followed up the explanation by asking their permission to camp. The Indian who had first arrived said briefly, *"Una dia, no mas!"* ("One day, no more!") They started to leave, but I called them back and gave each one a few fishhooks and a bit of line. We spent the night wondering what the outcome would be, now that we had met the Yaquis.

The following morning, we had breakfast over and the canoe loaded and ready to go before sunrise—mute testimony to our state of mind. Nor had we slept too soundly. Among our possessions there were many things that the Yaquis could make good use of—the canoe, fishing gear, harpoon, guns and ammunition—things that would spell munificent riches to a people as poor as these Indians seemed to be. Furthermore, there was precious little we could do to stop them if they chose to attack, for they had guns, and knew how to use them. And if their reputation was to be believed, they welcomed nothing so much as a good fight.

When everything had been packed, so that we could leave at a moment's notice, we decided to wait for the Indians and find out what they had in mind. We hadn't long to wait, for in a few minutes yesterday's quartet appeared, accompanied by an older, better-dressed Yaqui, who offered us a freshly killed rabbit, and some dried shrimps. "You stop here this day," he said in fairly good Spanish.

We immediately built a fire, broiled the rabbit, shelled the shrimps, and made a big pot of coffee. While we sat eating the old man put us through the third degree. Just why were we here? What did we want? I answered that we were here to learn something about the country and its people; and we also hoped to be of service to them as we travelled through their country.

This must have been a new approach, for the old fellow warmed up at once and treated us as kindred spirits—which to a certain extent we were. Indians are fine people; and the white man who takes the trouble to know them, and to treat them decently, is invariably well rewarded for his pains. The old chief launched into the story of the Yaquis. They were a strong, proud race, he said. But the Spaniards, when they came into the country, instead of recognizing their pride and trying to understand them, did nothing but mistreat them and steal their lands. So the Yaquis struck back. Furthermore, they intended to keep right on retaliating for any bad treatment. His people were good, the Indian insisted; friendly to those who were friendly to them; but they had no intention of being treated like dogs. His hatred of the white oppressors and the governments who had tried to crush the Yaquis was mirrored in his face as he talked. We sympathized with him, and I gave him some fishing gear.

Then I asked his permission to hunt and fish in Yaqui territory; this pleased him immensely. "We give you permission gladly, Señor," he replied, and went on to say that few people recognized the Indians' rights to the game on their lands. The deserts of Sonora and Sinoloa were poor places at best—game was scarce—and then to have people kill for sport the animals that the Indians needed for food . . . well, the Yaquis wouldn't stand for it. They had as much proprietary rights over the rabbits, deer, and shrimps as a rancher had over his cattle and grain fields. Whereupon he invited us to spend the day with them shrimping in the lagoon.

Now that we were friends, the Indians exhibited an entirely different behaviour. They laughed, talked, and were exceedingly boisterous, and treated each other with a rough-and-ready good humour. Then as we went about the business of shrimping, they were about as stolid as a bunch of high-school boys on their way to a football match.

The Yaqui is tall, slender, well-knit, and wiry. His face, with its high cheek-bones, proud aquiline nose, mobile mouth, and square jaw, indicates intelligence, humour, and great personal courage. There is nothing languid about these Indians. Indeed, their high spirits would need to be held in check by careful and adroit handling if they were to be subdued at all. We gathered that they went on an occasional rampage just for the fun of it.

That night we had dinner together, and we all did a great deal of laughing. On parting, the old chief made the statement that we were very, very strange white people: the only ones he had ever met who understood the Yaqui. We were the Yaquis' friends, and he would send word along the coast to treat us well. He was as good as his word, for we never received anything but kindness from these Indians wherever we met them.

We slept like tops that night. No longer did the Damoclean sword of fear hang over our heads. The next morning when we sailed away, we saw their brush shelters down the beach, only a short distance from where we had camped.

A final word about these very primitive Indians. They eat burro meat in preference to beef; permit no racial intermixture by marriages outside the tribe; and practise a religion that is best described as a thin veneer of Catholicism overlaying their ancient pagan worship. In the last quarter-century they have become slightly more tractable than they were. During Porfirio Diaz' régime the government fought them constantly; and they hastened to join forces with Francisco Madero to drive the old dictator out. Then they discovered that they could hold a hand in the great game of Mexican politics. Today some of the best fighters in the regular Mexican army are Yaquis. It is possible that some day in the distant future, as in the past, these Indians may play a part in creating a great indigenous culture for America. The heirs of Montezuma still live—and the future may be theirs.

Chapter Twelve

THE JUNGLE THAT'S NOT IN THE GUIDE BOOKS

MAZATLAN is almost on the tropic of Cancer, and at Cape San Lucas we noticed a marked change in the vegetation. The sparse growths of the north gave way to the prodigal verdure of the south. We entered the tropics with the keenest anticipation.

The past months had worked wonders in our physical condition. Despite our loss in weight due to the long hard hours at the paddles under a blistering sun, and the slim rations, we were in perfect health. Our muscles were hard and tireless, and there was a distinct difference in our sensory and mental reactions. Our hearing had become so acute that the snapping of a twig would bring us out of a sound sleep, whereas at home an alarm clock had failed to waken us. Constant scanning of the horizon had exercised our eye muscles and improved our sight. We had developed a precision in the co-ordination of our eyes and mind that we particularly noticed; they worked in unison. We saw instantly the entire picture of anything, with a minuteness of detail which at first surprised us. Our sense of smell improved. In the city the confusion of smells makes it impossible to distinguish any one odour clearly, but in the clean air we could soon differentiate between the scents of animals and discover a fresh water hole a mile away, if the wind was right. Our sense of taste was sharpened also, possibly due to the lack of complicated seasonings. The various sea foods of our daily diet took on decidedly different flavours.

After leaving Mazatlan, we paddled south through the lagoon country, thoroughly enjoying the sight of the lush green vegetation after the long sojourn along the desert coast. We passed fields of sugar cane, the thatched roofs of native villages, and dense tropic jungle. There was a price to pay for all this beauty though. Thousands of mosquitoes swarmed round us. Tiny, almost invisible gnats, called *jenjenes*, stung us, leaving red welts on our skins.

The first night out of Mazatlan—our first night in the jungle—we began to discover what these pests can do to you. About midnight we were routed out of a sound sleep to discover that we were not alone. Scrambling out of the tent, we fanned the embers of the fire into flame and proceeded to investigate. A colony of ants had found a tiny hole in the bottom of the tent, and had moved in bag and baggage—hundreds of them.

In the morning we crawled out of the tent to be greeted by clouds of

The Jungle That's Not in the Guide Books 95

assorted insects. We built a smudge fire, and tried to hide behind the barricade of smoke. No use. We could keep out the bombers, but the pursuit ships didn't mind the smoke screen a bit. Furthermore, it in no way discouraged the ants, who seemed to prefer their meat seasoned with smoke.

We decided that we'd rather brave the perils of the deep, so while Ginger made breakfast I went to collect coco-nuts to take with us. The refreshing milk would quench our thirst as we paddled under a blazing sun. I picked up my bolo knife and started to hack my way through the undergrowth towards the palms. The knife, with its twelve-inch blade, was much handier round camp than an ax, but for cutting through tropical underbrush it was little good. Each time that I slashed at the branches, I was showered with bugs. Finally I dropped the knife and frantically pawed with both hands at my neck. I must have looked funny, for Ginger, watching me, laughed. Then I grabbed my foot; fighting the bugs, I had overlooked the knife and had stepped on it, cutting a tiny slice out of my heel.

In the meantime, Ginger's laughter had turned to ejaculations of horror. I rushed over to the campfire where she stood as though made of stone. "What's the matter?"

"Look!" she answered, pointing to the ground. Two scorpions were crawling out of the dead wood she had just placed on the fire.

"Grab a stick and kill them," I said crossly as I limped off. I was going to climb a tree and get those coco-nuts if it killed me. I reached a tree and started up. When my legs and stomach began to burn, I looked down and saw that the bole of the tree was covered with ants. Then I was mad; everything seemed to be conspiring to thwart me in getting those nuts. To cap it all, when I reached the top I discovered that in my excitement I had failed to bring the knife! Exasperated at my stupidity, I began wrenching the nuts off with my hands; but as I reached for a particularly large cluster, I almost fell out of the tree in horror—a great hairy tarantula was crawling down the bole and heading straight for me. I started going places. The palm's spikes pointed upwards, and I wanted to go in the opposite direction—fast. The result was a massacre.

I must have looked a pretty sight as I limped into camp, covered with scratches, cuts, dirt, and bugs. The only thing I didn't bring was the tarantula.

"For the love of Mike, who's been clawing you?" Ginger demanded.

I told my story.

"Well," she said as she proceeded to disinfect my wounds, "it's evident that the tarantula had the better punch."

While we sat eating breakfast in the smudge which burnt our eyes—though the bugs just loved it—I said, "It seems that we're just babes in the wood after all. We've got a lot to learn. Let's pack up and get out of here." So we beat an inglorious retreat from what we had once regarded as our promised land.

Paddling down a tropic lagoon, we discovered, was quite different from paddling down the coast. Here the wind was shut off and not a breath of air stirred. The humidity, coupled with a sun that almost seared our toughened skins, soon had us stewing. We were bathed in perspiration and round our necks swarmed clouds of mosquitoes. Where were our story-book tropics? I began to suspect that their most enthusiastic delineators had limned their charms from an air-conditioned flat in Manhattan.

As we paddled along we were both preoccupied with the problems presented by this new challenge to our ingenuity. The mosquitoes and *jenjenes* were greatest in number at sunrise and sunset. We decided to circumvent them by having our supper early, retiring to the tent until after sundown when their numbers decreased, and by staying in bed until after sunrise. The problem of ants and other crawlers we could meet by building a brush fire over the proposed camp site, and then scraping the ashes into a ring round it. We doubted that even the toughest ant would run the gauntlet of hot ashes.

That night we put our new system into effect. The bugs were eliminated. The night was so hot, however, that even without the bugs to annoy us it was almost impossible to sleep. It was like an oven inside the sleeping bag, so we slept on top of it. The canvas was soon wet with sweat.

I had just dozed off when a rustling sound outside the tent brought me to my feet.

"What do you hear?" Ginger whispered.

"That's what I'm going to find out," I whispered back as I unzipped the tent flap.

Just as I stepped outside something grabbed my foot. I jumped about two feet in the air to land on something else that crunched as I hit it. One more leap found me beside the remnants of the fire, whose hot ashes burnt the soles of my feet.

"Close the tent, and stand by with the gun—we're invaded!" I yelled.

"Invaded by what?"

"I don't know, but they look like scorpions or spiders."

The tent was zipped shut in a hurry, for Ginger, braver than most people about so many things, has a mortal fear of spiders, no matter how small or harmless.

Not having nerve enough to reach for the woodpile, I took the crossbar off the fireplace to use as fuel. Then when I had fanned the coals to flame, I looked round. The camp was literally alive with strange creatures whose great orange bodies were carried on blue legs. I looked at them a full minute before I could identify them—giant land crabs, quite harmless, but often present at night. When we awoke at daylight there was not a crab in sight.

After breakfast, we loaded the canoe and headed south. Coming to a small inlet, we stopped to inspect it and found its shallow water full of sting rays, whose long tails were armed with barbs that could inflict a nasty wound on the feet of the unwary. In shoal water we found a great many shrimps and prawns, which we used for bait to catch a large mess of fish for our lunch. We tied them over the stern of the canoe, trailing them behind in the water to keep them fresh, and then went on down the lagoon.

There was a distinct thrill in paddling along the quiet blue water, listening to the sounds of jungle life that went on round us. Stately herons fished in the shallows. Silvery cascades of spray hung an instant in the still air in the wake of leaping fish. Overhead parrots bustled past in pairs. An odd thing, but we never saw a single parrot—always in pairs or even-numbered groups.

As we gazed about us at this new world of sound and life and movement, the canoe stopped with a jerk, and then moved rapidly backward. Turning hastily round, we saw that a large shark had tried to get himself an unearned meal by stealing the fish trailing astern. I grabbed the killing lance and gave him a vicious jab in the gills, expecting him to loose his hold and swim off. But he refused. He hung on to the fish, turning over and over. Each time his white belly came up I jabbed him again, literally cutting him to pieces. He died at last, hanging on to our fish. With my sheath knife I cut the fish off just above his jaws. There was not enough for a meal. We could well imagine what it would mean to have one of those killers grab a man's leg.

That night by the light of the campfire I wrote in my diary: "The *animalitos*, as insects are called by the natives, are with us again tonight. Ants, land crabs, *jenjenes*, and many others whose names we do not know, thousands of them, are crawling or flying round—each one of them intent on getting a meal. Some of them subsist on foliage; some of them, like the ants, are scavengers; others are parasites and bloodsuckers. We must study and understand this complexity of life if we are to survive. We had no adequate comprehension of its extravagant abundance or its exceeding cheapness in this land. The country is beautiful, but we do not understand it, and are afraid to explore it on foot. We only see what faces the lagoon, and have not yet ventured ten feet into the undergrowth. Tonight we could find no cleared spot to set up camp, so we undertook to clear a site. The first log we moved unearthed a nest of scorpions. Then a centipede crawled over Ginger's foot. Ants dropped from the tangled foliage above, and ants crawled out from the decayed humus below. We are both a mass of welts from insect bites; and as I write this I am still being bitten.

"Off in the jungle today we could see the homes of some of these minute jungle folk. Great mud balls, built by the *comején*, which is similar to our termite. The stately castles of the cutter ant; and the brush-covered mansions of other intelligent and voracious insects whose acquaintance we have not yet made. It's going to be a tremendous task to know these tiny creatures, their method of existence, their likes and dislikes; and above all, to learn how to avoid them as we tramp through the undergrowth. I am wondering as I write, just how many of the authors whose jungle stories I used to read ever saw the jungle. If so, why did they so flagrantly omit the bugs!"

The next day we paddled on down the lagoon, and the day after arrived at Boca Tintexo, which opens into the ocean. It was a difficult channel to negotiate, but our first taste of the jungle had not been too attractive and we were glad to face the open sea.

To acclimatize ourselves gradually to the humid tropic heat, we spent the following fortnight in leisurely sailing down the coast—most of the time close inshore—until we arrived at Banderas Bay, where we decided to make camp on the beautiful north shore, between the bay's blue waters and the jungle.

While we were busy setting up camp, we saw three natives coming down the beach, swinging long machetes. In appearance they were strikingly different from any natives we had yet seen. They were dressed in loose pyjama-like pants, with the sides crossed over and tied in back, and the legs tightly bound at the ankles. A loose slip-on shirt was held in place by a broad, bright sash, knotted at the side. They wore flat-crowned hats with broad brims, set squarely on their heads; and on their feet, heavy *huaraches*, with the heel and toe built up like a Chinese shoe. A pouch hanging from the sash completed their costume. Their features were oriental, with round faces, high cheek-bones, flat, broad noses, and slightly slanted eyes.

They came walking into camp with friendly gesture, and asked us who we were, where we were going, and where we were from. I told them that we were going to Panama. They had never heard of Panama, or in fact any place outside the limits of their own country.

I examined one of their machetes, a beautiful weapon, with a blade about three and a half feet long, its bone handle carved into a serpent. Then I handed my bolo knife to one native, and inquired what he thought about that kind of a knife in the jungle.

"It won't do," he answered, "it's too short."

How would he like to do a little trading? I suggested. We had discarded so much of our extra equipment that we had little left to dicker with except the fishhooks and needles that we always carried. I laid out an assortment of them and we started bartering. The natives were not too impressed. Finally Ginger said, "I've been putting one over on you; I have an extra lighter hidden away in my ditty bag—perhaps we can trade that."

She got out the shiny lighter, filled it with some of our remaining gasolene, and showed them how it worked. This turned the trick—the machete was ours.

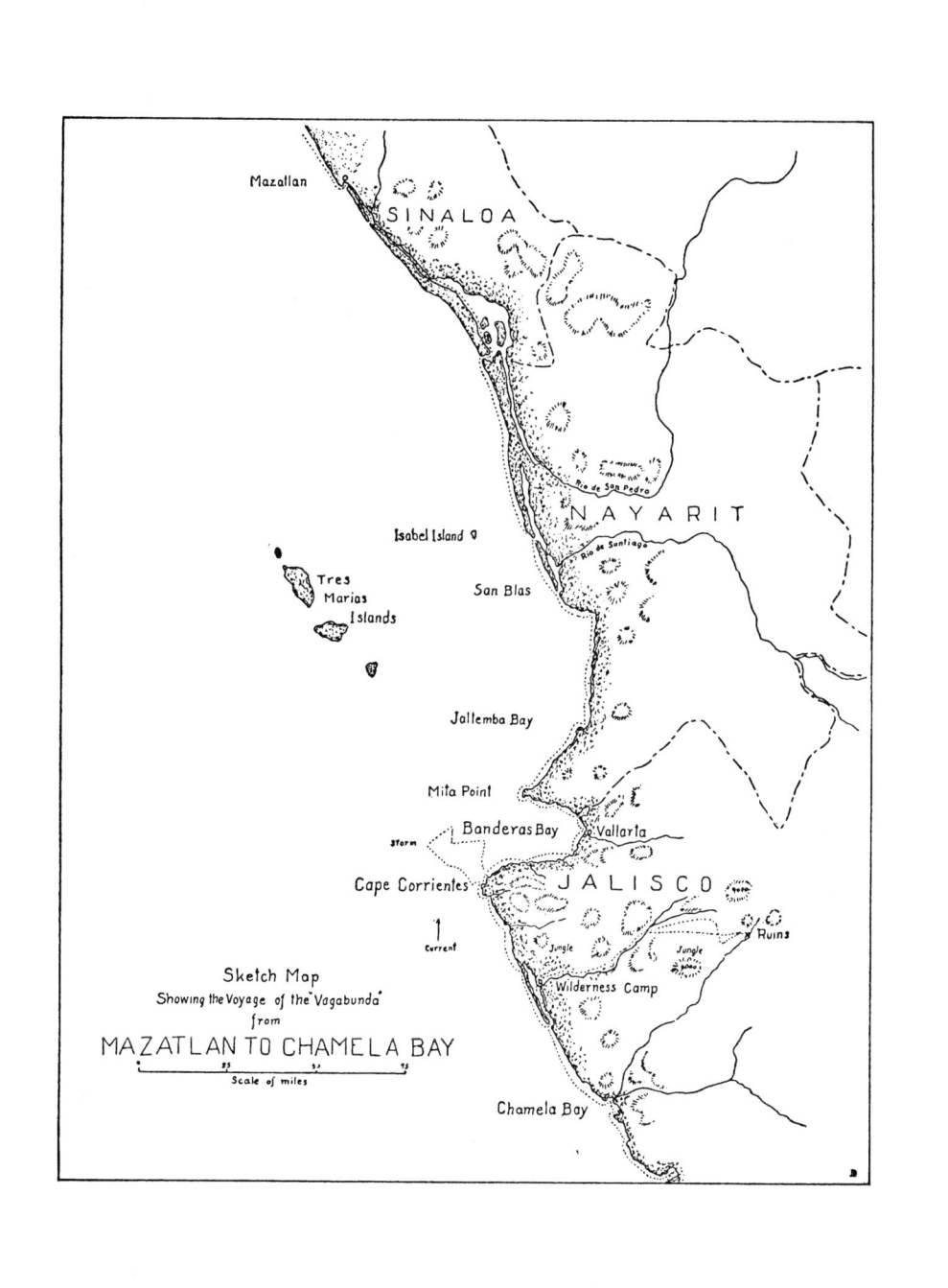

The Jungle That's Not in the Guide Books

They stayed with us until dark, asking many questions and exhibiting great curiosity over our equipment. They were Huicholes, they told us, and lived near the Piginto River.

Then we had our turn asking questions; and we asked innumerable ones, particularly about the insects. We took notes as they talked. When they came to a recital of an insect that crawled in under the toenails to lay its eggs; I held up my foot. We had noticed peculiar wartlike protuberances between our toes and nails. The natives gave one look. "*Nigua*," they said, and one man reached for his machete.

"What are you going to do with that?" I asked.

"Cut out the *nigua*, of course."

"Not with that machete, you aren't," I replied, hastily withdrawing my extended foot. "If there's any cutting to be done, I'll do it. You just show me how."

I went over to the first-aid kit and got out the surgeon's knife, whose shiny blade filled them with admiration. As I took it out of its oiled wrappings, I explained to them that it was a knife made especially for cutting flesh.

Picking out a large lump on the side of my toe, I carefully followed instructions and cut the top off. There under the skin lay revealed a round white sac about the size of a pea. The natives said that it must be removed without breaking—it was full of eggs. Using the tweezers, I worked the sac loose and pulled it out. Ginger daubed the big hole with iodine.

"Are there any more *animalitos* that make sores?" I asked.

"*Si*," a native answered. "There is one much worse, whose name is *talaje*. A little grey one, who when he bites leaves a blister. Round that blister a purple bruise forms. If you are very careful and do not break the blister, it will heal before very long; but if you break the blister, it makes an open running sore that takes a very long time to heal. Sometimes people bitten by *talajes* die."

We spent the evening removing *niguas*, and next day limped round camp on pretty sore feet. The following day we were able to sail over to the little village of Vallarta. The village, built on a hill, seems to be standing on end as you approach it from the sea. We landed on its pebbly beach, and a crowd of husky natives, as usual, immediately took hold of the *Vagabunda*. We always had a difficult time explaining to natives that the canoe could not be dragged up on the beach as could one of their heavy dugouts. But once they got the idea they were always very careful.

The Port Captain soon appeared and examined our papers. When we told him that we were going to Panama his face took on a look of great concern. "This is a very bad time of the year," he said, "for the rainy season starts in about two weeks. No small boats travel along this coast during the stormy season; and I, as Port Captain, cannot permit you to put out to sea."

I began to argue that there surely must be some calm days between storms. During the rainy weather we could camp on the beach. But he shook his head. "Señor," he said, "these squalls come up with great violence and suddenly. You have no warning. It is best not to attempt to travel at all. Even our canoes do not venture out during this season."

Ginger turned to me and said in English, "They seem to have a deep-rooted respect for these rainy seasons. You'd better listen."

I then tried to persuade him by promising that if he would clear the ship we would go down the coast a little way and camp there. He also refused to listen to that argument.

"Señor, I have told you that you cannot go. This section of the coast is very bad. There is nothing but the jungle, and in it are tigers. There are no people, for even the natives go to higher ground at this season. You had better make up your mind to stay with us until after the rains."

"But we have no money," I protested. "Here we cannot eat. Down the coast we can hunt and fish."

He was adamant. "Look!" pointing to the overcast horizon, "there is the forerunner of the rains."

We were in despair. We couldn't leave the port without permission; and there was no way to eat if we were forced to remain. Finally, in my most eloquent Spanish, I explained our predicament. Would he let us go not farther than one week's distance from Vallarta if I solemnly promised we would stay there during the entire rainy season? Wearily he shrugged an assent.

"Very well," it seemed to say, "let these foolish gringos go to their destruction; I've done my best." And he had.

We made the rounds of the few native stores, trading fishhooks for some things that we needed. Again we loaded the canoe, and started down along the coast, sailing close to the shore.

This was one of the most spectacular and beautiful sections of coast that we had cruised along since leaving the Gulf of California. High cliffs made an amphitheatre of the blue and brown waters of Banderas Bay. Patches of red water dotted its expanse; little streams rushing out of the jungle emptied into it. Most astonishing, however, were the snakes, swimming everywhere.

Towards sundown we came to the mouth of the Ylapo River. As we pulled towards shore, we saw that the water was full of these snakes—bright green, with yellowish-orange bellies. In places they were knotted up in bunches. I offered up a prayer of gratitude that there was no heavy surf here, for the *Vagabunda's* prow seemed to cleave a passage through snakes. My thankfulness was a bit premature. Just then a small wave caught us on the stern, the canoe skidded sideways, and for no particular reason tipped us out into the nicest collection of snakes and stinging jellyfish you ever saw. We swam to shore so fast that we hardly got wet, and turned round to see what kind of mixture we had come through just in time to see the wind carry the canoe, and all that we owned, rapidly down the beach. I started after it, willing to risk anything to retain our sole earthly possession, and retrieved it at the cost of a few stings from the jellyfish.

While Ginger prepared the supper, I went out into the water and captured a snake to examine it. Instead of the fangs we were led to expect, its mouth was lined with very small, sharp teeth. I don't think the bite is poisonous, but it is probably painful.

A strange phenomenon occurs along this coast, near the mouth of the Ylapo River. The bay at this point is extremely deep, over one hundred fathoms (six hundred feet) within a few hundred feet of the shore. The currents, coming round Cape Corrientes, seem to spill into this submarine canyon, and as they emerge, to bring with them many strange creatures from the ocean's greater depths. As we hiked along the beach, we found the carcasses of many odd marine animals which we knew were not from surface waters. The Indians of this locality tell many weird tales of these marine monsters.

The following morning we left at daylight for Cape Corrientes. While sailing through the calm waters of the bay, the water beside the canoe suddenly burst into spray. A great manta ray, at least twenty feet across, leapt into the air, turned over completely, and came down with a mighty splash that showered us with spume. A moment later it jumped again, but this time it was far enough away so that we could watch it without being frightened to death. One of these rays was caught in the Gulf during our stay there. It weighed *three tons*! Except for the whales, they are the biggest marine creatures in these waters.

As we rounded the high cliffs of the Cape, we saw a lighthouse half-way up the steep slope. This bit of man's handiwork made the untouched wilderness about it, if anything, more striking.

We had started to round the Cape about 11 A.M. The wind shifted to north-east; and while we seemed to be making good time, the strong currents that gave the Cape its name (Corrientes means currents) bore against the wind and prevented us from making any headway. The wind grew stronger, and we had a hunch to go ashore and try again when it fell a bit.

As we changed the course and started shoreward our hearts sank; for instead of approaching, the shore line receded—we were being carried out to sea. The tide, the current, and the wind were against us. By three o'clock that afternoon we were ten miles off the Cape.

Ginger sighed as she got out the dry rations, and prepared the canoe for a night of rough sailing. In one respect it was not as unpleasant as similar experiences further north had been, for the wind and spray were warm. The sky, with the exception of an occasional cloud bank, was not alarming. But the Cape Corrientes light flashed her eye at us from increasing distances—as though waving farewell.

At 12 p.m. the wind shifted, and blew from the north-west. We were running before, riding high swells, with a nasty cross chop. It was my turn to be on watch, and Ginger had settled down in the cockpit to sleep. Every time she dozed off, however, we'd ship a sea that would slap her awake. At two o'clock in the morning, she said drowsily, "There's something wiggling round in this cockpit." Then she yelled, "It's a snake!"

In her haste to get on deck, she almost overturned the canoe. I lifted my feet out of the cockpit in a hurry, too. The moon was hidden behind clouds and it was pitch dark. The canoe bucked like a bronco; and Ginger, perched on deck, made it even more unwieldy. I hated to feel round with my bare hands, for by now I imagined that each wave breaking over us unloaded more snakes in the cockpit. There was a chance that the snake might be scooped up with the bailing can. I peered hopefully at each canful, but no snake rewarded my straining gaze. How long will this keep up? I wondered, as I tried to keep my equilibrium on the pitching deck and bail at the same time. At last a pale moon came through a rift in the clouds and by its light I could see the elusive snake in the forward end of the cockpit. Reaching down, I grabbed by the end the tail was on (I hoped!), and flung it overboard.

At 4 a.m. the wind increased in strength, and we began to gain on the light. An ominous sound from shoreward made me scan the horizon. A white mass of foam came into view; and I hastily changed the course and headed out to sea again to avoid the tide rip that was churning the water. These tide rips are of frequent occurrence in this area, and it is best to give them a wide berth.

The next morning the wind died and we were left under a blazing sun far out to sea. We paddled all day in sweltering heat, the sweat stinging our eyes and streaming off our bodies. In the afternoon a little breeze came up, but it was gusty and did not do much good. At sundown we were still five miles offshore, and the breeze had increased. We were blown this way and that, without apparently making headway in any direction. Then rain fell in torrents; thunder roared in our ears, and the heavens blazed with lightning. The Corrientes light blinked off in the distance. At 9 p.m. a gust of wind from the south struck us, jibbed the sail over, and almost upset the canoe. We reefed and double-reefed the sail, but it was impossible either to sail or paddle.

"We'd better ride this out with a sea anchor," I yelled, "or we'll be swamped."

Ginger made repeated attempts to open the cockpit and secure a line with which to rig the anchor; but each time she was defeated by the big seas that crashed down upon us, filling the cockpit and momentarily threat-

The Jungle That's Not in the Guide Books

ening to wash us overboard. These seas were not the mountainous, heavy, relatively slow-moving seas that we had battled in the north. They were short and high, and came rushing down with the speed of bullets. We finally decided upon a desperate expedient—we would use our life line from around the gunwales to make the anchor. Without the line, a heavy sea might wash us overboard, and that meant almost certain death, but it was the only thing under the circumstances that we could do.

Then, as suddenly as it had come up, the wind died down. We had just launched the sail overside, tied to the life line. Tensed and ready to meet the adversary, there was nothing to fight. We sat and looked at each other. It was like bracing yourself to bear the shock of an explosion, and hearing only the faint fizzle of the fuse. This was a perfect example of the unpredictability of tropic weather.

The chop went down soon after the wind abated. As the east greyed, we dragged in our waterlogged sail and hoisted it; and with a light breeze from the north helping us we started shoreward. We had been blown out to sea for a considerable distance, and it was late in the afternoon before we were near enough to the coast to look for a place to land. Our muscles were cramped and tired from long confinement in the tiny cockpit, and the lack of food and rest had made us weary beyond words. Now there seemed no place to make a landing. As far as we could see, great seas were breaking everywhere upon the beaches. We carefully watched the breakers, hoping to observe a lull. There was none.

"It's no use waiting," I said. "We've got to head in and take a chance. Wedge yourself in the cockpit, so that if we bounce round you won't be thrown out. If we do spill, go out the seaward side, so the canoe won't hit you on the head, as it did the last time."

Ginger shivered and turned a white face towards me.

"Afraid?" I asked.

"No," she answered, "but I'm tired, and I don't know whether I have strength enough to paddle through those big breakers."

We paddled in close to where the seas were breaking, and followed on the heels of a breaker that had just crashed, digging in with the paddles for all we were worth. Then we got one of the major surprises of the entire trip. As quietly as though we were landing on the shore of a lake, the *Vagabunda* ground her nose in the sand and stopped! We looked at each other in amazement. Ginger crawled up on the bow of the canoe and stepped to the beach, where she sat down suddenly.

"How did that happen?" she asked, still unbelieving.

We set up camp. Then while Ginger started the cooking fire, I took both guns—Ginger's automatic in case I should sight small game, and the Luger in the event of a tiger—and my new machete, and hacked my way towards a group of palms I had seen from the sea. Cutting through the last string of brush to the palm grove, I came upon a beautiful blue lagoon. I gazed in wonder. Tired and hungry as I was, I forgot everything else for the moment. This was the "Promised Land." A little fresh-water stream ran into the lagoon, and across it tall coco palms lined a white sand beach. Ducks floated in the water. Great blue herons, snowy egrets, sandpipers, and shore birds were everywhere. Parrots, and other birds with gorgeous plumage whose names I did not know, flew overhead. Fish made rainbow arcs of colour as they leapt and splashed. It was a scene whose beauty made me doubt the evidence of my own eyes. I needed confirmation and turned back to camp.

Ginger looked up in surprise. "I thought you went out to hunt."

"I forgot about that," I answered. "Come, I've found the most beautiful place in the world."

"Don't you want to eat first?" she protested. "You're so tired you're seeing things."

Reluctant and unbelieving, Ginger followed me. We soon stood together looking at the fairylike landscape across the lagoon. "Yes," she said, "that's the place we've been dreaming of. We can make camp there during the rainy season, and build a thatched hut among those palms. That site should please even the Port Captain of Vallarta."

The tortillas and scraps of dried fish tasted like ambrosia that night as, in our excitement, we talked with our mouths full.

The lagoon was parallel to the sea, so in the morning we loaded the canoe and started down the coast to find an entrance from the ocean. When we discovered it shortly, we shot the breakers at its mouth and were soon in quiet waters. But the tide was going out. Since there was little point in fighting the current, we looked round for a temporary camp site.

Chapter Thirteen

JUNGLE IDYLL

WE FOUND a little clearing, where we decided to pitch a temporary camp. We were both busy arranging our equipment when Ginger stopped. "What's that, Dan?"

It was the sound of a paddle against the side of a dugout. Since we knew nothing about the natives along this stretch of coast, I said, "Better have the guns handy."

Carrying our guns, we stole through the brush to the beach. A lone native was coming across the lagoon. We watched him as he paddled towards our beached canoe. About twenty yards from the water's edge, he stopped and scanned the shore line carefully. I stepped out into the open and beckoned to him. As the dugout grounded, I lifted its prow and dragged it further up on the beach. He stepped out, grinning.

He was a big, broad-shouldered young fellow, well-proportioned and very dark-skinned. Apparently he had been as apprehensive as I had been. We were so relieved that we just stood and grinned at each other. I think we became friends at that moment. Then his face sobered.

"*Quinina?*" he asked.

"What's the matter? Are you sick?"

"No," he said. "My friend has *paludismo*."

"Oh, your friend has malaria. Where is your friend? We will give him quinine."

"He is in our camp on the lagoon."

"How many natives are in this lagoon?"

"Just the two of us. The others go to the mountains at this time of year. This is the rainy season, you know."

"Why are you two here?"

"We are wanderers, we are vagabonds," he answered.

I pointed to the lettering on the canoe, *Vagabunda*. He stared uncomprehendingly at the name he had just given himself. "We, too, are vagabonds," I said.

Whether tribal differences or inclination had caused his wanderings, I did not ask.

"Come up to our camp," I invited. "We will eat and drink hot coffee, and then I will give you some quinine for your friend."

We sat round the fire talking. He said that he and his friend were

Aztecos, a tribe related to the ancient Aztecs. Although he spoke a mixture of his native tongue and very poor Spanish, we managed surprisingly well. He asked our names and we told him. Then we asked him his name. It was unpronounceable to both of us.

"We'll probably see a lot of these two if we stay on the lagoon," I said to Ginger. "What shall we call him?"

"Since we seem to be following in the footsteps of Robinson Crusoe, let's do what he did. What day is this?"

"My diary says Thursday."

"We'll call him 'Thursday' then," she decided.

I told him we were going to call him "Thursday." He grinned agreeably.

When I opened the equipment box to get the quinine, his eyes widened at the unfamiliar things. He was particularly interested in my automatic, and after putting on the safety catch, I handed it to him. He examined it cautiously. Apparently he had never seen one.

"Is that quinine?" he asked as I handed him a one-ounce package of the drug. He was unfamiliar with it in dry bulk.

"Yes," I said, and told him in detail how to administer it. As he couldn't quite comprehend, I suggested that he bring his friend to us and that we would give him the quinine.

"You will remain while I am gone?" he questioned. I promised.

After he had gone, Ginger said, "Well, I knew there would *have* to be something here. It was too good to be true. Wonder what kind of a boomerang they'll turn out to be?"

"Thursday looks pretty good," I replied. "Besides we'll be two miles away when we get to our permanent camp. Don't worry yet."

The next morning while we were eating breakfast, we heard the swish of a paddle. "Hurrah," I cried. "Here comes Thursday bringing Friday. We're going Crusoe one better."

"*Manda!*" shouted Thursday from the dugout.

"*Hola!*" I shouted back.

Thursday strode into camp with an almost regal bearing, followed by the sick man. Friday was the smaller of the two men, though of equally fine physique. He looked very sick, and had a blanket wrapped round his head and shoulders. I made a place for him on the equipment box, and had him sit down close to the fire. Thursday tried to tell us the sick man's name; and when I told him that we had decided to call his friend Friday, something about the name amused him. He broke into laughter. Our hearts warmed to the men. I looked at Ginger. She smiled. From then on I knew it would be all right.

I mixed a stiff dose of quinine; Ginger brought a cup of coffee to wash it down with. "This is raw quinine; it tastes bitter, but it will help you," I said, handing him the stuff. He took the cup gingerly and peered doubtfully at the milky liquid. *"Toma!"* (drink it) I urged. He drained the cup without further hesitation, making a wry face and reaching blindly for the coffee. He looked at me with an agonized expression. We sympathized, for the quinine was awful stuff to take. "You're going to feel better right away," I assured him. He smiled.

We had breakfast together, and during the meal the men gave us much valuable information about the surrounding country.

After breakfast we started packing for the trip up the lagoon. Thursday watched us. "You are leaving?" he asked. I nodded. "Where are you going?"

I turned to Ginger and said to her in English. "They'll find out that we are only going up the lagoon. I think we'd better tell them. How do they seem to you?"

"They seem like fine fellows. Yes, I think it's all right to tell them where we're going."

"Listen," I said to Thursday, "we're going up the lagoon to build a camp where we're going to stay during the rainy season."

His face wreathed in smiles. "May we come along? We are very strong and we can help you. We like you very much."

Ginger straightened up from her packing and looked at Thursday. He seemed to know that the decision rested with her. He just looked at her, his great, eager brown eyes watching her face. Friday sat by the fire and grinned. She was weakening—I could see it.

I laughed. "It's all right. You can come. The Señora likes you."

Both men leapt to their feet and gave us the *abrazo*, the familiar greeting used only between friends. They placed their arms round our shoulders and patted our backs. Indians do not do these things unless they like you; they are never friendly "for business reasons."

Now that their official status had been established, Thursday rushed round and helped us pack. The sick man sat by the fire and smiled. The canoe was quickly loaded, and we were soon paddling up the lagoon. Thursday sang songs, perhaps of his tribe, in a sweet, mellow voice. The sick man, wrapped in his blanket, lay on the bottom of the dugout.

We landed about noon at the palm grove we had first seen from across the lagoon. Tall, graceful palms grew on a white sand beach beside a little stream. Vividly coloured ferns and flowers lined its banks and hung from the trees. Birds and butterflies of every hue of the rainbow flew among the foliage. It was—well, I can't describe it. The brilliant, flaming splendour of a tropical forest can only be suggested. It assaults your eyes with colour and your ears with sound. The air is heavy with the sweet, overpowering perfumes of flowers, and the musty odour of decay. Everywhere there is life. Taken altogether, it is tremendous.

We immediately set to work clearing the ground and burning the fallen branches. Plans for a house took shape. Ginger had a bright idea. "There are four palm trees here that almost form a square. Why not a tree house? Don't you think that would be fun?" I called Thursday over and told him our plan. He nodded, and started off through the brush.

As soon as the ground was cleared I made a bed for Friday, who was still too sick to take part in the activity. While Ginger and I set up camp we could hear, off in the distance, the ring of Thursday's machete. "Wonder what he's up to?" I said.

"He's probably cutting trees for the house we said we were going to build," laughed Ginger.

We spent the rest of the day working. During preparations for the evening meal, Thursday came staggering into camp carrying a great pole. He dropped it and headed for the jungle again. By the time supper was ready he had brought in three more.

After supper we sat talking by the fire. Overhead the moon threw a silvery light on the midnight blue of the lagoon. The palms made soft rustling sounds in the light breeze. The firelight threw dancing silhouettes of shadow on the white sand.

Now for the other side of the picture. While we talked mosquitoes and gnats flew in our mouths. Giant moths danced round the flame. Ants crawled up our legs, sending little jabs of fire through us as they bit. We knew that there were tarantulas, spiders, and scorpions within hailing distance; and at any moment one or all of them might stroll in, fly in, or drop down on us. To this day, we are both scarred with the bites of innumerable tropic insects.

As the fire died down the Indians strolled over to their dugout to sleep. We noticed that their equipment was limited and of the simplest kind. Two hand-woven blankets, a few earthen pots, a spear, and their two razor-sharp machetes seemed to be all they had.

The following day was a long hard one. Friday, much better, brought in big bundles of *bejuco*, a tough tree-growing vine. With this vine we lashed the floor stringers to the trees about six feet above the ground. We flattened off the top surface of the floor logs with our machetes, and set them in place, lashing them down also. By sundown the floor of the hut was finished. It was about twelve feet square.

The next day was spent getting material for the roof and sides. For the siding we cut young shoots a few inches in diameter. I had started towards a group of shoots that seemed to be exactly the thing I wanted, when Friday called, "No, no, do not go near those trees."

"Why not?" I said. "They look all right to me." I proceeded towards the shoots. Friday just smiled. I gave a good whack with my machete, let out one blood-curdling yell, and ran for the creek. The creek wasn't deep enough, so I bounced out of the little pool and ran for the lagoon.

Ginger came running. "What in heaven's name has happened?"

"If you want to find out," I answered as I came to the surface, "go to that tree where I dropped my machete and shake it. Red-hot coals will drop down on you, stinger end first."

Friday came splashing across the creek and stood grinning at me. "Why in hell didn't you tell me it was *that* kind of a tree?" I asked wrathfully.

"Now you will always remember *that* kind of a tree very well," he said. "I suggested that you stay away from that tree, but you are very stubborn about some things, Danielito. Such trees are always bad. We who live in the jungle never go near them."

"I'll detour a mile round one of those bomb throwers, the next time I see one," I promised. This was my introduction to a tropic scourge, red ants, which inhabit only a particular kind of tree—at least in southern Mexico.

A word here seems in order about the natives' attitude towards giving advice. They frequently suggest that certain things are not wise for you to do. Sometimes this information is in the form of a legend or parable. But if you, an outlander, argue or persist, they waste no time in persuasion. "Very well," they say, "let the foolish one find out for himself—then he will always remember." The tropics in general, and the Indians in particular, have no use for the "wise guy."

I crawled sheepishly out of the lagoon, retrieved my machete, and the rest of the day tagged along in Friday's footsteps, sincerely grateful for any bit of information he felt inclined to offer.

In the afternoon it became hot and sultry, and the sweat rolled off us. I said jokingly to Friday, "How about running uptown for some lemonade?"

"Ah, *limonada*," he said. "Sure, I go." He started off into the jungle. I called after him that I was joking, but he kept on going.

I had not meant to send him off on a wild-goose chase, and I wondered uneasily where he'd gone. But in about fifteen minutes he returned, carrying several long sprays of an unfamiliar plant, with bright red, thick-skinned flowers. "*Haymaca*," (perhaps Jamaica?) he announced proudly. Without another word he borrowed one of Ginger's kettles, and started for the creek. He put the flowers to soak in the pot with a little fresh water, mashed and bruised them, and then filled the kettle with water. We sampled his concoction gingerly, and afterwards drank it to the last drop. It was the best lemonade we'd ever tasted.

The following morning both Indians were missing, and their dugout as well. While we were starting the breakfast fire, and wondering just why and where they had gone, they came paddling up to the tiny beach. Friday held a sizable string of fish, and Thursday escorted a huge sea turtle. "We need food," they said. "After breakfast we will go into the jungle and get more." During Ginger's preparations for breakfast, they butchered the turtle, cut the meat into long strips, and hung them on a drying rack which they made.

After breakfast, with our guns and foraging sacks, we followed them upstream. Soon Thursday stopped, called us, and pointed to a pool ahead. Strange little creatures were crawling round on the bottom. We looked closely and recognized them as a species of crawfish. "When we have no turtle or fish to eat, he is very good," he said.

I pointed to some watercress growing along the bank, asking them if it was good to eat. "Yes," said Friday, "but for that we should have clams."

We went further up the creek, the Indians peering into the underbrush as we went along. Finally they climbed up on the bank and cut their way to a small bush about twenty feet from where we stood. After clearing a space round the bush, they quickly dug up several roots that looked something like giant sweet potatoes, although they were longer, knobbier, and much rougher. Thursday held them up, "*Yuca*, very good to eat." The name he gave them sounded very much like the name, yucca, which we give to a desert plant, but these were entirely different. The Indians could not explain to us just what kind of a plant it was, but insisted that the roots were *muy sabroso*—very savoury. We put them in our sacks and started off again.

A little later we found some big mango trees and feasted on their delicious fruit. A tree-ripened mango tastes very different, we discovered, from the fruits picked green and carried to market by the natives. We had eaten the latter in Vallarta and had not liked them. Some of these we also put in the sack for use in camp.

In a swampier section of the jungle, we found a great bed of plants that looked like cat-tails. The Indians waded in and pulled them up by the roots, which resembled giant onions. They trimmed the tops, and these, too, were stowed away. Then we began circling back towards the creek.

A grove of bananas grew near the banks. I started searching for ripe fruit. "There are no ripe ones," Thursday said. "The monkeys eat them. You have to pick them while they are green and they will ripen later in camp." The bananas were tiny miniatures in comparison to the cultivated variety with which we were familiar. We picked several bunches.

Back in camp again, we set to work upon the roof, which, under the natives' tutelage, turned out to be a simpler job than I had anticipated. However, by nightfall our hands were sore and blistered from the rough *bejuco* with which we made the lashings.

At last the hut was completed. It was well-built, attractive, and comfortable. Inside were a fireplace, a bunk, a table, two benches, and a cookstove.

For our first meal in the new house, Ginger prepared an elaborate menu. She lined a cooking pot with boiled, mashed *yuca* roots, filled it with well-seasoned turtle meat, added bamboo shoots, and baked it in her tiny oven.

There was in addition fish broiled with coco-nuts, mango salad, banana pudding, and coffee.

When the meal was ready Ginger called the boys, but they would not enter the hut. Arguments and persuasion were of no avail. They insisted on building their own shelter and doing their own cooking. We felt rather hurt until Thursday, with his ready grin, enlightened us. "Two people under one roof, yes; three people—" he shook his head vigorously.

That night we all sat round a fire outside the hut and made fiesta, a sort of house-warming. We sang together, for the Indians had taught us some of their songs. The music echoed and re-echoed across the lagoon, and back into the jungle.

In the midst of the festivity, we heard a low rumble. Thursday, proudly using the slang we had taught him, said with the utmost gravity, "The thunder god is going 'haywire'—soon we will be 'all-wet.'" He looked at us for approval. We laughed hilariously at this unexpected demonstration of our pupil's cleverness. Then we began to collect what gear was outside, and headed for the hut. The boys piled extra branches and fairly heavy logs on their lean-to, and got under cover.

This was the first real storm of the rainy season, and it was a honey! The thunderclaps seemed to shake the earth, the lightning blazed across the sky; the rain fell with a thudding violence that I was sure would cave the roof in, but not a drop came through the palm thatching.

We built a fire in the fireplace and sat round enjoying the situation. We were safe and protected from the elements for the first time in many months. We knew what pounding rain meant when riding out a storm at sea in a little, unprotected boat.

"I've never been so happy in my life," Ginger confided.

"Then you're not missing all the things you had and could do at home?" I asked.

"No. And when I stop to think of it, there isn't much to regret. We take risks, but who doesn't? Remember the newspapers with those screaming headlines? 'Couple Commit Suicide' . . . 'Crazed Man Murders Six' . . . 'Airplane Crashes' . . . 'War Threatens Peace of Europe' . . . 'Ten Killed in Week-End Accidents, Motorists Warned to Be Careful' . . . Nothing will be different when we get home. Skirts may be longer or shorter, automobiles will have new gadgets, the greatest actor or actress will have Hollywood agog—for two weeks; there will be a new political 'crisis,' just like the old one. Otherwise it won't be a bit different—wait and see."

We sat in silence for a while. "Remember how we used to pop corn on rainy nights at home? Wish we had some."

"How about trying the native corn?" Ginger suggested. She got out the field corn, parched it in the frying pan, buttered it with turtle oil, and sprinkled salt over it. It was hard to chew, but tasted good, and we thoroughly enjoyed it.

There are times when the individual loses his concept of himself as a unique creation; when he finds himself caught up and merged in the flow of life round him; when he knows that the thunder, the rain, all life and the human spirit, are of the same substance—manifestations of universal energy whose parts can never be independent of the whole. Perhaps the Indian we met in the Gulf of California had been trying to tell us this when he said, ". . . wait and go *with* God, since you cannot go without him." Something of this the jungle was teaching us, and we were particularly conscious of it that night, as we sat listening to the rain beating on the roof, and heard the voice of Thursday's "thunder god."

"Dan, I don't feel as though I'd ever want to go back to the old way of living," Ginger said after a long silence. "We have everything that we need here, and we're as happy as any two people in the world have a right to be."

"Come now, aren't you becoming a bit sentimental over the simple life? How about those parties and dances you used to enjoy so much? How about a good movie?"

"Oh, you're movie enough." She started to laugh. "For instance, your performance yesterday. You took off with such a beautiful jackknife dive, then changed your mind in mid-air, and . . ."

"You would, too, and you wouldn't think it was so funny, if you'd seen a shark as big as I did, just where I was going to land.

"I've got an idea!" I went on. "How about building a platform on that big palm that overhangs the lagoon? We can weave a long *bejuco* rope to climb up with, and dive from there."

"Or we can dam the creek; then we'd have a fresh water swimming pool about twenty feet across and eight feet deep. Of course," she added, "it wouldn't be so much fun for you—you'd miss playing hide and seek with sharks."

This started an enthusiastic discussion of a series of projects. A beautiful spot near the creek could be converted into a park with benches underneath the trees. We'd plant a botanical garden there; dam the pool below it and stock it with fish and shellfish, and have an aquarium.

A big grove of bamboo near-by would furnish us with material for a variety of household necessities—cups, a salt shaker, vases, and containers. Receptacles for storing turtle oil could be made by boring a small hole in one end of the larger sections of bamboo, where it divides at the joints, and sealing the hole with a plug. This would enable us to keep a fairly large supply of clean, sweet cooking oil on hand.

We needed tableware, spoons, and forks. These could be carved from ebony. Two big turtle shells would make an adequate dish pan and an excellent soup tureen. Smaller shells could be used for soup spoons. The

Jungle Idyll

list of things grew as we talked: a potato masher for the *yuca* roots, floor mats woven from long palm fibres, charcoal sketches on bark, framed in driftwood, to hang on the walls.

In the following days, whenever the weather permitted, the Indians and I went on long foraging expeditions into the jungle to get food and the materials for these things. Gradually our plans materialized.

"Ginger," I said one day, "the house is finished, our work is done, and we've more food than we can eat in a week. How about putting on a party? We'll help you."

"Well," she said doubtfully, "I might be induced, if we had some mayonnaise—I'm tired of French dressing."

"You wouldn't care for a chocolate 'malt'—or any other little thing growing round here—would you?" We laughed. The idea of being "tired" of any kind of dressing after the lean diets we'd grown accustomed to, was funny. "Hop to it," I said, "while we go foraging."

Thursday, machete in hand, started off for the jungle. Friday and I headed towards the lagoon, where we found a great many big shrimps in a little inlet. Then, following turtle tracks to the nests, dug in the sand, we collected fifty eggs. Turtle eggs are white, round, and about the size of a golf ball, and are covered with tough membrane instead of a shell. On a bar, we discovered some sizable clams, similar to the Pismo clam that we have in California.

Friday kept his eyes on the jungle as we paddled towards camp. "More eggs," he announced, pointing to a tree.

"We couldn't eat the eggs we have now in a week," I protested.

"But those eggs are different. Perhaps the Señora would like them," he answered. We climbed the mangrove trees and found that our old friends, the *tijeretas*, had been busy. Friday was right; the Señora would like them—"mayonnaise."

Then Friday discovered some bees, caught one and held it in his cupped hand. I wondered what he meant to do with it as he walked towards the beach, where he released it, closely watching its flight. Going over to the canoe, he picked up a *tijereta* egg and broke it in half, dumping its contents into the stream. Then he caught a second bee, imprisoning it between the two halves of the shell. We got into the canoe and paddled about three hundred yards upstream in the direction taken by the first bee. There he released the second one and watched it head for the jungle. "Let us follow the bee, and we will have *buco*, too," he said. We hacked our way to the bee tree. "We need smoke. Have you a fire?" he asked.

I felt in my pocket. "No," I replied. "I left my lighter in camp." Friday had also failed to bring his flint. "Well, we'll have to think of some other way to make a fire." I started looking round for materials with which to make a fire block. Friday watched me dubiously.

I cut a section about a foot long from a good-sized dead limb, split it in half, and cut a slab ten inches long, four inches wide, and an inch and a half thick from one portion of it. From the other piece I fashioned a stick a foot long and an inch wide, and rounded it at both ends. A slender green limb fitted with a raw-hide lashing made a good enough bow. With my pocketknife I cut a little hole in the bone handle of my machete, and dug out a similar hollow in the base block. Giving the string a half turn round the pointed stick, I placed one end in the base block and the other end in the hole in the machete handle. As I began sawing back and forth on the bow, the spindle turned round and round. After a hole about an eighth of an inch deep had been drilled in the block, I cut a V-shaped notch in it that led to the centre of the burnt hole. A wad of dry palm-leaf fibre was placed beneath the fire block for tinder. I began spinning the stick rapidly. Soon smoke poured out of the little hole. When the V-shaped notch was filled with the ground, scorched fibres, I picked up the block and the palm-leaf wad, and blew off the cooler embers on top, leaving in the centre a tiny coal. This was placed on the tinder, and carefully fanned into flame.

Friday, who had been watching this procedure in open-mouthed amazement, began to grin. "Now we'll get *buco*," he announced.

It's best not to go into the details of all that we said, while trying to get that tree down and the bees smoked out. Eventually we wound up in the canoe, badly stung, but with a considerable quantity of well-smoked honey. We stopped long enough to plaster mud upon our stings before going back to camp.

"Mud fights?" asked Ginger as we turned up, bedraggled and dirty.

Silently, I handed over the honey for her inspection. But Thursday had provided us with competition. "He's brought back wild limes, tiny wild oranges, bananas, avocados, papayas, guavas—he even found some wild tobacco," she told us.

Towards evening we sat down to our banquet. We had turtle soup with bamboo sprouts, seasoned with wild onion; broiled filets of smelt, basted with lime juice and turtle oil; fried bananas; barbecued turtle breast with gravy; shrimp salad with avocado and egg sauce; *yuca* roots which were first boiled until they were soft, then mashed and mixed with fresh coco-nut, and wrapped in leaves and baked. There was also guava jelly; *yuca*, mashed and fried into thin patties for bread; a drink made from papayas and the red flowers. For dessert we had banana and coco-nut *empanadas*, a filled tart made from uncooked tortilla dough, fried in hot grease. It looks and tastes something like a turnover.

After we'd polished off this meal, we were too lazy to build a fire, so the four of us sauntered over to the little park where we sat down to enjoy the moonlight. The jungle was giving its nightly concert. We heard the piercing scream of a jaguar.

"I'm going to get that fellow some day," I said to Ginger. "Each night he comes closer and closer. I saw his tracks the other day. His pads must be six inches across. He's probably the reason why there are no deer here."

"If you're going after jaguar with that Luger, you'll have a pretty job on your hands," she replied.

"I don't see why," I defended. "I've brought down some big deer with it—why not a jaguar?"

"All right, but I'm going to be there to back you up."

"A lot of good you'll do, with that twenty-two of yours. You'll just sting him—and make him good and mad. Hunting jaguar is a man's job."

"If you're going jaguar hunting, *I'm* going jaguar hunting, and that's all there is to it," she insisted.

The Indians rolled sleepy eyes towards us; we were talking in English. "Ginger wants to go tiger hunting," I explained. They both sat up, no longer sleepy. It began to look as though we were all going tiger hunting. Friday began a detailed description of the native method of hunting jaguars.

Suddenly both men ceased talking. They seemed to be listening intently. "What's the matter?" I asked. Thursday held up his hand for silence, and continued listening, a withdrawn look on his face.

He turned to Friday. "The *Oojah*," he whispered, his eyes darting to the jungle back of us.

"Oojah?" I questioned.

"*Espiritu*" (Spirits), he explained.

"Does *Oojah* mean *espiritu* in your language?" He nodded.

There came to our ears a low, deep booming—so faint that we could barely hear it, but it was there. "Tell me about it," I urged. "What is it? Where does it come from?"

"It is the spirits of the great leaders"—he rolled his eyes, hesitated—"from the great city of the dead."

A thrill of eagerness shot through me, for I had heard natives talk before of this legendary city. "What kind of a city is it?" I asked Thursday.

The Indians exchanged worried glances. "I am afraid to tell you, Señor. You are white, and . . ." He stopped. This was the first time, since we had become well acquainted, that either of the men had called me anything but "Danielito." I didn't particularly like the sound of "Señor," for I knew that a barrier had risen between us.

"Go on," I urged.

"I am afraid to tell you, because if anything in that city is disturbed, it means the death of all my people."

"Thursday, you know I won't do anything to harm your people, don't you?"

"Yes," he said. "We trust *you*, but you might tell some one else. The North Americans might hear of it. They dig up the graves of our dead and scatter their bones. They destroy our sacred symbols. Even now they are digging in many places."

"But don't you understand," I explained, "that they dig them up to preserve them—to put them in safe places? The North Americans are trying to discover something about these people—who they were; where they came from. How can they know unless they dig? In years to come all these things will be destroyed by time. You know how the jungle and the rains ruin everything, don't you?"

He sat long in silence. Then he said in a tremulous voice, "Those people lived in that city longer ago than I have any word for. They were wise, and they were very good to us. They were kinder in every way than those white men who came across the sea long after them. Those people built to withstand time, and their dead and their history have remained undisclosed—and will remain so—until *they* choose to disclose it. They sleep, but they shall wake again. No one has any right to meddle with their dead. My people only seek to protect that which *they* placed in *our* keeping. We shall continue to protect it.

"I have talked with men who have travelled in your country,—who have been to that very city* from which you come, Señor. They say your houses are built of flimsy materials that will not last; and that you think only of the present and never of the future. When night comes to your people, nothing will remain—nothing of yourselves—and nothing of our people, if we let you take their things with you. No! We will never let you take them!" His voice rose. "It is our heritage, for our future—when dawn shall come for us again!"

We sat in stunned silence, hardly believing our ears. Where was the good-natured, child-like semi-savage of only a moment ago? This man was a different being.

"If you will tell us about this city," I said, "I will promise never to disturb it; and I will never disclose its location to any one else as long as I live. I make you this promise as one good friend to another."

"It is far away," he said. "You travel up this stream to its head, then over a ridge to the south. There you come to another stream, and then you climb to a great mesa. It is many, many miles inland, and far from any living man. A great temple to the Great Power stands upon a hill. There are big houses in the valley. The dead sleep upon a hillside where Guardian Spirits watch over them, and all that belongs to them. There they shall sleep until the dawn comes again, and the Spirits chant the ceremonies that shall waken them."

The Indians rose, and as they turned to go, Thursday said cryptically, "It is better to be poorly laid down, than well seated, Señor. *Buenos noches*, Señora." They disappeared into the night.

After the Indians had left us, we sat hand in hand for a long time, gazing out over the shadowy lagoon. The moon sank low before we finally returned to the hut.

* Los Angeles.

Jungle Idyll

The next morning the spell was broken, and all that the Indians had told us, remained only as part of the night.

After breakfast, Friday jerked his head towards the jungle. I grabbed my machete, strapped on my gun, and followed him. He led the way to a part where I had never been before, and stopped beneath an unfamiliar tree. Odd round fruit that looked like gourds grew close to the trunk. "*Jícara*, to make tiger calls," he explained. We collected a number of them and returned to camp.

Ginger eyed the gourdlike objects eagerly. "Fine!" she exclaimed. "We can make a lot of things we need with these."

I objected, "You can't have these gourds to play with—they're tiger calls."

"You only think all of them are going to be tiger calls. Some of them are going to be soap dishes and other things."

"Soap dishes?"

"Why do you think I've been saving and leaching ashes, if not to make soap with?"

So Ginger got her share of the *jícaras*, and Friday went to work on the big ones we had salvaged for our tiger calls. He cut off a third of a gourd and carefully scraped out the inside of the remainder. In the bottom he cut a small hole. Then he took a three-foot piece of light fishline which I gave him, knotted one end, and slipped the line through the hole. I laughed. He was making an old-fashioned ticktack, such as I had used to annoy the neighbours with on Halloween. The string he resined with the pitchpine which the Indians use for flares while hunting turtles at night. By cupping one hand over the open part of the gourd and rubbing his fingers along the resined string he produced first the plaintive voice of a kitten, then the low, menacing growl of a tiger. I was looking nervously over my shoulder before he finished playing with the thing. We made two of these contraptions and hung them in the sun to dry.

The rest of the day was spent in domestic activities. Thursday and I collected coco-nuts, which we split in half and set in the sun to dry. Later on the dried coco-nut meat could be rendered into fats for cooking and soap-making.

When we returned, we found Ginger and Friday digging in the creek. "Mining?" I asked.

"No," said Ginger, "we're making a bath tub. Of course you are both looking for a job."

We denied it vigorously, but she put us to work excavating the creek bed and building a dam.

Very late in the afternoon, Thursday and I headed off into the jungle. We followed a trail alongside the creek to a large clearing shaded by giant trees. The soil was packed down by the trampling of animals, and along the creek bank we found the spoor of a big cat. Selecting a large tree near the edge of the clearing, we laid cut logs against the trunk to form a shelter. Thursday explained that we would hide inside this shelter at night and then "call" the tiger.

We came back to one of Ginger's tropical banquets, and after eating, sat round waiting for the proper time to go tiger hunting. Both Indians were dubious about our guns. They said in resigned voices, intended for our ears, that undoubtedly they would have to come to our rescue with their machetes.

About nine o'clock we made our way through the jungle, took our places in the blind, and settled down to wait. It was not easy. The dark jungle seemed alive with sound and movement. Red ants invaded our shelter, crawled up our legs, and bit us in unexpected places.

Then off in the distance we heard the faint scream of a cat. Thursday picked up the tiger call. We almost jumped out of our skins at the blood-curdling sounds he produced; the howl of a jaguar rose and fell in the night. Ginger shivered and drew closer to me. I grasped the Luger tighter, and rearranged the extra clips in my left hand for quick reloading. Out of the jungle came the answering call. Thursday replied with the plaintive, enticing voice of a female in the mating season. Back came a note of excited, inquisitive interest. The big cat was circling wide, but his call came closer and closer. We were shaking like leaves. Soon he was behind us.

The jungle noises ceased as the jaguar drew near. We, too, sat in silence, waiting for the next rasping note, trying to determine his position by the sound. Puzzled by the human scent, he continued to circle. Round and round us he went, each time drawing nearer. In his bewilderment, he began to answer Thursday's enticements with a snarl that sent shivers up our backs. Now, it seemed, he must be right beside us. We could hear the pat-pat of his feet and the cracking of twigs.

Thursday emitted a low plaintive note, barely audible. Suddenly tense, he whispered, "*Ya viene!*" ("Here he comes!") Our straining ears could hear nothing. I tried to focus my attention in the direction of his last call, then a twig snapped in the opposite direction; and I turned in time to see his great body charging straight at us. I jabbed the pistol in his direction and fired. My bullet hit a log of the barricade. The staccato of Ginger's twenty-two mingled with the roar of the Luger.

Thursday grabbed my arm. "*Ya se fué*," ("He's gone") he said.

"Won't he come back?"

"No," he answered. "That tiger will never answer a tiger call again. He's different from people, Danielito. If he gets fooled once, he never gets fooled the second time by the same thing."

"Then let's go back to camp and have some coffee," I suggested.

But even after several cups of hot, strong coffee, our nerves were still jittery. "I was never so scared in all my life," exclaimed Ginger, who still looked frightened.

"He sure was a mad cat," I said.

"Surely," Thursday laughed, "that was not surprising. He was of an expectancy, and for him, too, the evening was a failure. Suppose you went to find a Señora, and instead you found a tiger—well, wouldn't *you* be provoked a little, Danielito? At any rate," he finished, "that cat will go a long way off now, and then the deer will come. Hunting will soon be good again."

The next day we finished the swimming pool, and started on Ginger's rock garden.

That night after supper, the Indians were strangely silent. "What is wrong?" I asked.

"Tomorrow we go," answered Thursday.

"Oh, you don't want to go yet," I protested. "Why, the rainy season lasts two months longer. We're just getting settled. We are good friends. Think of all the fun we are having together."

Thursday stood looking down, shoving pebbles round with his toes. "No," he insisted, "tomorrow we must go. Perhaps, who knows, we can come back next month."

No amount of persuasion could change their minds. They kept stubbornly repeating, "We must go."

Both men had appeared contented and carefree, until about a half hour before Thursday had announced their departure. Even the jungle had seemed quieter than usual, as they sat silent and preoccupied before the fire. Occasionally one of the Indians had lifted his head and peered intently towards the jungle. Then they had both listened, looking with queer, sidelong glances off into the darkness.

Since it was obvious that nothing would change their minds, I said, "Before you go I want to give you something. Is there anything that either of you would particularly like?"

Neither man answered. They stood embarrassed and silent, giving us both, odd, smiling glances.

"Could we spare that heavy hunting knife of ours?" I asked Ginger in English.

"I think so," she agreed. "We seldom use it in this country, and it is heavy."

I went into the hut and selected some things that I thought they would like and would find useful; the hunting knife, with its hand-tooled leather sheath; a variety of fishhooks, and a light fishline; and, remembering the delight that had flashed over Thursday's face whenever he used my cigarette lighter, I threw in my spare. A snapshot of the two of us in the canoe topped the little pile, which I tied up in one of our bandannas.

I walked over to their dugout, and placed the bundle in the bow. "There is a little *recuerdo* (remembrance) for you, but you must not open it until you are on your way, to wherever you are going."

The rest of the evening was rather sad. The Indians obviously hated to leave as much as we hated to see them go. However, they seemed to have no choice.

Late that night we gave each other the "familiar parting" and went silently to bed. When we awoke next morning they were gone, and we never saw them again.

Chapter Fourteen

JUNGLE RHYTHM

OF COURSE Thursday's story was too fantastic to be believed in its entirety, but how much of it was true? We were discussing "the great dead city" for the twentieth time since the Indians' departure. Unable to forget it, we re-examined the story from every angle. "We only seek to protect that which *they* placed in *our* keeping." Did that mean that the present-day Indians were descendants of slaves or peoples subject to those old pyramid builders, and perhaps of a different racial stock? If one could only get at the facts behind the mists of legend. "They sleep but they shall wake again." Where had they gotten the idea of death and resurrection? Was this a borrowing from Catholicism or did the pre-Conquest peoples of America have a similar belief?

After some consideration I said to Ginger, "How would you like to go and see this place?"

She protested. "It might be dangerous. So far we've only gotten into trouble by disregarding the natives' advice. Remember Magdalena Bay."

"Listen," I argued, "if we'd followed 'advice,' we'd be in Santa Ana right now. Sure, I got bit by a coyote; people get bit by going to zoos, too. We didn't promise not to go to their city. We promised not to disturb anything if we did go, or to disclose its location to any one else. I don't see why we shouldn't go if we want to."

"How long do you think it would take us to get there?" I knew from the feeble fight she was putting up that she was not really opposed to the plan. She merely wanted to be assured that it was a good idea.

"We don't care how long it takes," I answered. "It might take two weeks or a month. We have plenty of time. Now that we've learnt to forage for our food in the jungle, all we need to carry is our hiking gear and guns; and surely, we can manage that much of a load."

"I want to go as much as you do," she answered, "but I wonder if we know enough about the jungle yet to attempt this kind of a trip."

"Well, if we try it and find that we can't make it, we can always turn back," I said.

"Then let's go. I've really wanted to explore this ruined city ever since we first heard of it."

There were a great many things to be done in camp before we could leave. Food for the trail, toasted tortillas, *yuca* roots, dried meat, fish and shrimps, had to be prepared. Then it was necessary to build bug traps round the base of the coco-nut trees to keep the ants from raiding the place while we were gone.

Four days later everything seemed to be in order as we took one last look round. The canoe was safely stored under the hut and a heavy door had been lashed to the hut's entrance to keep the animals out.

We were dressed in khaki shirts, blue jeans, and tennis shoes, with bandanna handkerchiefs tied round our heads. Ginger carried her twenty-two automatic and her light hunting knife; and in her knapsack, which weighed about thirty pounds, she carried part of the rations. Her pockets were stuffed with articles from the first-aid kit, ammunition—and her powder box! I carried the Luger, plenty of ammunition and clips, the camera, and my big machete, in addition to my pack which weighed sixty pounds. In the pack were the sleeping bag and tent, part of our mess kit, the films, and the balance of the food.

After a short distance I discovered that it was impossible to hack a way through the jungle with the heavy knapsack on my back. "This idea isn't going to work," I said. "My shoulders are already raw from the straps." We stopped and I began unpacking the knapsack.

"What are you going to do?" asked Ginger.

"Make a horseshoe pack out of the tent. We'll leave the knapsack with the food in it here, and I'll come back and get it from wherever we stop for the night." Ginger protested that would mean that I'd have to double back all the way. "But there's nothing else to do. It's next to impossible to cut through this heavy growth and carry that knapsack at the same time. The pack interferes with my use of the machete, and if we try to force our way through without cutting, we'll be covered with bugs."

I made a horseshoe pack by laying out the tent, putting at each end the things I wanted to carry, then rolling it loosely and tying the ends, which I lashed together. It fitted snugly over my shoulders, leaving my right arm free to do the cutting.

After this change in travelling style, our progress became much easier. Soon we were in beautiful country. Great elephant-eared ferns grew higher than our heads. Innumerable vines laced and festooned the giant trees, and formed an aerial passage, high above the jungle floor, for groups of monkeys and other tree-dwellers. Gorgeous orchids, strange flowering plants, and trees grew everywhere. Had it not been for the insects it would have been a perfect Eden.

I began to itch and my legs felt as though they were on fire. Unshouldering my pack, I pulled up my pants' leg. My leg was almost black with millions of minute insects that looked like midget ticks. Ginger was covered with them, too. We decided to take a bath in the creek and see if that wouldn't rid us of them. But while they were not hard to wash off our bodies, they had a way of lodging themselves in the fabric and between the seams in our clothes. Once there, they almost defied us to come and get them.

Finding there were very few of them above the knees, I decided to make shorts out of the blue jeans. After cutting off one pants' leg above the knee with my pocketknife, I hesitated. What would Ginger say? Too late now, the other had to come off, too.

"Oh, Dan, your only pair of pants!" she wailed when she saw me.

"Pants—hell! These are shorts," I answered.

"You mean to go through the jungle in shorts?" she questioned unbelievingly.

"Why not? The natives do. Every time the boys went into the jungle they pulled their pants' legs up as high as they could. We're cutting the trail all the way, and the only things we come in contact with are the things we step on. Why don't you cut yours off, too?"

She did, and we continued on more comfortably, giving a wide berth to the trees we had learned to avoid, and picking the easiest way through the underbrush. Towards evening we found an open space beside a stream, where we decided to stop for the night. While Ginger began the supper preparations, I went back to pick up the knapsack. To my surprise we had travelled only a short distance; it had seemed like miles as we cut through.

Returning to camp, I found Ginger sitting in the middle of the clearing with her gun in her hand. She looked up with relief. "I'm glad you're back. This place is alive with more strange noises—animals—or something."

"Don't worry," I said. "We'll build a big fire and put the tent up, and we'll keep our guns handy—just in case."

That first night in the jungle, sleep was long in coming and difficult. Time and again we sat up, wide awake, our guns in our hands, tense and waiting—but nothing happened.

Morning found us tired and a little groggy from lack of rest. We broke camp, packed the large mess kettle with food, and left it hanging on a limb with our knapsacks. It was tough going as we cut our way upstream. Sometimes we came to fairly clear spots, where for a couple of hundred yards or so travelling would be easy.

In the afternoon the jungle became absolutely silent. Then off in the distance, we heard thunder. "Let's find some shelter, Dan," urged Ginger. Ahead we saw a big tree, and cut our way to it as the storm broke. It was poor protection, however, for the broad leaves acted as funnels. Water poured down the bole and on to us. We decided to go on regardless of the rain. It would at least keep some of the bugs washed off; and since it was warm, it would be more refreshing than uncomfortable.

At last we came to the headwaters of the stream. Here the canyon narrowed down to a deep, dark ravine, and to go further on up the gorge looked difficult. "Want to make camp by this stream, or climb the canyon side to the ridge and take a chance on finding another stream by night?" I asked Ginger.

"I'd rather try the ridge," she answered. "This place is so dark and mysterious I'm sure I could never go to sleep."

Leaving the gloomy and oppressive ravine, we climbed up the canyon to the ridge above. It was red adobe mud, and we slipped and fell so often that we soon looked like Indians in full war paint. I wondered how much longer I could continue to cut the heavy undergrowth on the slippery adobe without falling on my machete. The law of averages might be a million to one in my favour, but sooner or later I was due for some nasty consequences if I fell on that wicked four-foot blade. Most of the way we climbed on our hands and knees, taking a devious course round huge rocks, cutting and slashing through the dense growth. Eventually we reached the crest of the ridge.

The ground was fairly clear, and after the ascent, it seemed like strolling down a boulevard at home. The luxuriant jungle gave way to sparse growths of *ocote*, or pitch pine. The ridge sloped gradually to the high mountains of the interior, and we could see no canyon like the one we had been told to look for. There seemed to be only a succession of steep ridges. At sundown we were still on the hogback, far from water. We had brought none with us, and only a small quantity of food. I was thankful that we at least had the pup tent and that I didn't have to go back after the knapsack. Tackling the ridge twice in one day would have been a little too much.

"We can forage," said Ginger, "though for what, I don't know. Pine trees, no water, and I haven't even seen a bird on this ridge. We have enough food for supper, and tomorrow we will surely find the canyon the boys told us to look for."

We got a little water by spreading the tent under bushes and shaking the branches, then draining the water off into the kettle.

All the next day we walked along the ridge, and still no water. Every half mile, or so it seemed, there were new difficulties.

In one place the ridge was blocked for over a mile by a great maze of spider webs. In the centre of each web was a huge, brilliantly coloured spider. We cut long sticks and beat a passage through them. In other places large patches of bushes with dagger-like thorns forced us to detour down the side of the ridge, where we slipped and clawed for footholds along the steep faces of the cliffs. Towards evening the ridge flattened out and we found ourselves on the edge of a great plateau, densely wooded and covered with a heavy growth of razor-edged grass.

We stopped and debated our course—whether to plunge into the tiger grass and take a chance on reaching a stream, or make camp on the edge of it and continue on in the morning when we could at least see. Our tongues were beginning to swell. Two dry camps in succession held no appeal for us.

Jungle Rhythm

"Hell!" I said. "Let's start whacking through this stuff. If we can't get through we will just have to roost in a tree until morning."

"Listen, I think I hear ——"

I heard it too and then we could both smell it—water! It was somewhere to the left of us.

Cutting to the left, we came to a little stream. Our first impulse was to lie down and lap it up, but we merely filled our mouths with water until the swelling of our tongues was reduced.

Ginger started a fire while I took her twenty-two and went to look for something to fill our very empty stomachs. As I stumbled up the stream bed in the almost pitch-black night, I wondered just what kind of a damn fool I was. Even if I did see something to shoot at, I couldn't see the sights on the gun well enough to get a bead on it. Everything except the night prowlers had bedded down for the night or gone to roost. "Roost"—now that might be a good idea.

Looking up at the great trees, I could dimly make out the outlines of their branches against the sky. "Now," I thought, "if I could just find a bird." I stumbled along, peering intently at each tree within my field of vision. Finally I did see a bulge. I worked my way under the tree and tried to line up the sights. I couldn't even see them, let alone draw a bead.

Before we had started on our trip we had spent six months training ourselves to fire blind, and I had been fairly good in practice. So far, however, I had had no occasion to prove my ability.

I pointed the gun as accurately as I could and pulled the trigger. There was a faint squawk. Well, at least it was a bird. I fired again, with the same result. The gnawing hunger in my stomach steadied my nerves and my resolution. I would get that bird. I closed my eyes tightly, hoping to enlarge the pupils so that they could absorb sufficient light to line up the sights. On the twentieth count I opened my eyes, aimed and fired. The bird tumbled down.

Picking my way to where it had fallen, I found I'd bagged—it could as easily have been an owl or a buzzard—a wild turkey. I let out a war whoop and started for camp. Ginger met me halfway with the big Luger in her hand.

"Why were you yelling? I thought a tiger had jumped on you," she cried.

"No," I said, trying to act as if turkeys had been our daily portion for days past, "I just got a turkey."

While we were broiling the bird Ginger got up from the ground and stood listening.

"What do you hear?" I whispered.

"Drums!" she whispered back.

Again the jungle was silenced by that strange throbbing rhythm. You felt it even more than you heard it. It was like a nerve beat. It seemed to permeate the air. We were never entirely able to dismiss the effect of this vibration upon our minds and bodies, for we were to hear it many, many times in the months to come. We can offer no explanation as to what it was, where it came from, or who produced it. We called it drums for want of another name, but we do not know.

Ginger moved uneasily about the fire. I realized that her nerves were on edge. I sat down and tried to reason away her fears and my own. Self-preservation was our first concern, but we had not come this far by being afraid of what might happen. We had not crippled our efficiency by being afraid of possible storms at sea, so why fear the unforeseen in the jungle? Our only salvation lay in studying the jungle, in adapting ourselves to it and learning to understand it. We would have to become an integral part of the life of the country. Life was hazardous whether we were driving in heavy traffic, riding out a storm at sea, or camping in tropical forests.

We both felt better after this and began to think of the immediate physical problem of hunger.

"Won't this turkey ever get done?" Ginger complained.

"I'm so hungry that I could eat five turkeys as big as that one," I told her, "but here's an idea."

I split some of the pitch-pine wood into thin strips and bound them together with grass and lit one end. With this improvised torch we started up the creek. It wasn't a very good light, but by its aid we managed to pick up a dozen crawfish.

The banquet we finally sat down to seemed fit for a king. The mysterious jungle was still round us, but we had lost the sense of menace. We sat by the fire contentedly until big raindrops drove us to the comparative comfort of the pup tent for a sound night's rest—the first since leaving the lagoon.

All the next day we cut our way along the stream bed, which led us at length to a wide valley densely covered with jungle growth.

Our camp that night was by the stream. The next morning we started up a long, narrow, cliff-flanked canyon. It was difficult going. Late that afternoon a great tree-covered plateau opened out before us. Except for the heavy vines, it was like an immense park, an entirely different kind of country from any that we had yet seen.

Towards sundown we climbed a small solitary hill off to the left, to see if we could get an idea of the surrounding country. It was the first opportunity we had had, since reaching the plateau, to get above the level of the plain. Our hopes of finding any ruins were scant. The directions had been too vague and indefinite.

There was nothing to be seen from the hill but the great plateau below us, which seemed an unbroken sea of green. We started back down its steep slope, for it was late and we had not yet secured food for supper nor found a camp site.

"Don't you think it's rather odd that this one little hill should rise so abruptly from a level plain?" Ginger asked.

I had been thinking the same thing, as I peered through the thick growth at its slanting sides. I stopped and began to reconnoitre.

"Holy Smoke! Look, Ginger. This isn't a hill at all—it's a pyramid. The sides of it are flat and it forms an almost perfect rectangle." I was considerably excited.

"It is shaped like a pyramid, but it's all covered up with dirt," said Ginger doubtfully.

"Naturally," I answered. "It has been here so long that the humus deposited on it has simply covered it up. We'll explore the whole place tomorrow. 'The great city' must be somewhere nearby."

The next morning we climbed to the top of the pyramid again to get our bearings well in mind, and then started out on a circle round the plateau. On the southern arc of the circle we encountered nothing of interest. Noon found us back by the stream again, about two miles from where we had camped the previous night.

During our morning trek we found a great variety of fruits and berries. Some of them were unfamiliar to us, but we sampled them anyway. Our experience with unknown fruits had shown us that, while there are no sign posts to tell you which are edible, there are a number of indications which, if heeded, will keep you out of trouble. All edible berries have a pleasant taste and smell. We ate sparingly of the unfamiliar things until we had a chance to observe their effects. The results are seldom drastic. A bad taste in your mouth, hiccups, or a mild interior disturbance tells the story. By such experiments we found a variety of new foods.

Since we were not hungry, we stayed by the stream only long enough to wash off the morning's accumulation of insects and grime, then started on the circle to the north. It had begun to rain, but by now we regarded rain as more of a help than a hindrance, so we kept on going.

After we had gone only a short distance, perhaps half a mile, we came upon great mounds and what looked like the remains of an ancient wall thickly overlaid with vines and humus.

Eagerly we started slashing our way towards them, then stopped and stared at each other. The jungle round us had begun to throb again with that mysterious vibration. Under the circumstances, it almost froze our blood. We racked our brains for some natural cause of the phenomenon. We both agreed that it lacked the sharp explosive quality of thunder.

"Could it be the roar of the ocean against the sounding boards of those limestone cliffs?" asked Ginger.

"I don't think so," I answered. "If it were, we should hear it constantly. This sound is intermittent."

We had seen no evidences of recent human habitation, no man-made trails. There simply wasn't any explanation. We hesitated and then went on.

Parts of the ancient walls surrounding the city were still in place. They were cut from hard limestone blocks of considerable size, fitted and set together without mortar. The walls became higher and formed extensive rectangles as we neared the centre of the city.

We tried to determine the nature of the carvings on many of the stones, but they were so weathered that one could only guess at what the bas-reliefs had been originally.

The great mounds were everywhere, but so thickly overgrown with vines that it was difficult to do more than observe them from a distance. Occasionally we came to what appeared to be an entrance, so choked with fallen stones and debris that we made no attempt to penetrate it.

"Listen, Dan."

I stopped.

"It sounds like chanting," Ginger said.

"But there are no ——"

"Yes," she said, "I know that, too. Let's go on."

An ancient roadway led to the base of a great hill just north of the city. The road soon became too difficult to follow so we abandoned it and took a zigzag course through the ruins. This finally brought us to the base of the great hill.

We began the ascent. As we neared the top we could see the walls of a great temple. Out on the point of the hill facing east, was what seemed to be a limestone sacrificial altar. It was of cut stone about eight feet long and five feet wide, and clean and free from debris of any kind. Don't ask us why. We don't know.

We stood silently looking down on the scene below us for a long time. The slanting rays of the sun had turned the jungle-covered mounds into a checkerboard of light and shadow. We felt alien, small and insignificant beside these evidences of ruined grandeur and magnificence. I shivered, but I did not want to go.

"I would like to stay here all night and build a fire on that altar stone," I said.

"Do you think we dare?" Ginger was anxious and did not try to conceal it. "I have had a definite feeling all day that some one is watching us. Suppose they see a fire on that stone? It would be a beacon for miles round. And suppose *they* don't like it?"

"Well, suppose they are watching us," I contended. "They know that we have touched nothing and that we have respected their feelings about this place. There can be no greater harm in staying here than anywhere else."

She raised no further objections. We set up camp and gathered materials for a fire, which throughout the night blazed upon the great altar stone.

The effect of such an experience is indescribable. We seemed to have brushed aside time's limitations. The past and present were telescoped. The mind was able to recapture images as though it were not subject to the restrictions of space and matter. I do not tell you that we saw with our physical eyes, or heard with our finite ears, these evocations of the past. It was rather an awareness not dependent upon either of these usual instruments of sense perception.

We sat utterly still. The silence was broken only by the sharp staccato of the fire's explosions; then, far off, insistent, vibrant, that rhythmic monotone.

"*Oojah*," I whispered. "Do you hear it?"

Ginger nodded.

We began talking in low tones of these prehistoric peoples, and of the magnificence of their achievements. With no beasts of burden they had evolved architectural masterpieces in stone. With none of the scientific aids of which we are so proud, they became expert astronomers. They were mathematicians, skilled craftsmen, artists in metals, weaving, pottery, and wood and stone carving.

Expert agronomists, they discovered and developed corn, cacao, potatoes, beans, peanuts, melons, squashes, tobacco, and hemp. We owe to them such drugs and spices as quinine, cocaine, vanilla, and innumerable other things which they had cultivated and bred for so long that countless varieties had been developed years before the first white man ever set foot in the Western World.

They were skilled in the use of medicines and were competent doctors, surgeons, and dentists.

They built roads out of asphalt, as we do, and knew how to vulcanize rubber. They had an exact calendar and a written language when our ancestors were painting themselves blue and wearing ox horns on their heads.

"Does any one know where they came from—just who they were?" Ginger asked.

"Not for certain," I answered. "There are many theories, but few proofs. Anthropologists say that they came from Asia by crossing the Bering Sea. That doesn't account for the sculptured stone elephants found in Panama, though. The man who made those elephants had seen one. Many of the Indians we have seen on this trip look like Egyptians or Polynesians, instead of like Mongols, as they would if they were northern Asiatics."

"Is there enough evidence to prove that they came from Europe or Africa?"

"No," I said, "there isn't. They would have understood the principle of the wheel, which they apparently did not use, and they would in all likelihood have brought plants and animals with them which are indigenous to Africa and Europe. The Spaniards found neither.

"There is another story at which scientists scoff, but it could account for the fact that they brought nothing from the Old World with them. That is the legend of the lost continents in the Pacific and the Atlantic—Mu and Atlantis. Atlantis was supposedly destroyed by some great convulsion of nature. No one, under such circumstances, would delay long enough to collect seeds or bring livestock."

We wondered what clues to that mystery the jungle concealed. Were those ancient men and women who had stood before this very altar Aztec or Toltec, Indian or non-Indian, or representatives of races now unknown to man? Where had they come from—why did they go? What had Thursday meant when he said, "Which *they* had placed in *our* keeping?"

These are questions yet to be answered, but not by us.

The next morning we left the hill and started back in the direction from which we had come. No one approached us, nor were we in any way molested, but we still had the feeling that we were being watched.

The trip back to our base camp was a repetition of our trip coming in, except that our shoes had worn out, and the rains had made the slopes so slippery that most of the time we slid, sitting down and using our feet for brakes. Late in the afternoon of the third day, dog-tired and covered with cuts and bruises, we limped into camp. It was a mess. Despite our precautions, ants and small animals had gotten into everything.

Chapter Fifteen

THEY DO IT DIFFERENTLY IN HOLLYWOOD

WE HAD seen many motion picture versions, and had read stories of alligator hunting. Consequently we felt that we knew how to go about the business. There were, according to these authorities, several methods of attack. The most highly recommended, as I remember it, was to fasten a stick, sharpened at both ends, on to a long handle, forming a T-square. With this in your hand, you quietly approached the unsuspecting alligator, who dropped its jaw—no doubt in amazement—at sight of you. Seizing this opportunity, you thrust the sharpened stick down the alligator's throat; whereupon the animal shut its jaws, thereby pinning them together—and you had your alligator! Nice work.

In case this method did not appeal to your sense of sportsmanship, Hollywood gave you an alternative. The second procedure differed from the first, in that you immediately jumped upon the alligator's back, and firmly grasping each jaw, pried its mouth open—holding the jaws well apart—until a confederate had time to shove a log between its teeth. The alligator, unaware of the significance of this manœuvre, obligingly clamped its jaws upon the log—and you had your alligator! There was, of course, the less spectacular method of shooting them, but judging from the pictured versions this was seldom done in Hollywood.

We paddled slowly and quietly up the lagoon, but each alligator we sighted slid into the water before we could draw our guns. In the pictures, we had seen canoes paddling down lagoons with alligators swarming round them. These alligators must have lacked the fearlessness of the Hollywood variety, because we couldn't get within one hundred yards of them. Huge ones sunned themselves on the banks, but invariably disappeared into the water at our approach. I got one shot at a big fellow sleeping on a bank, but apparently did him no damage, for he too slid into the water to rejoin his friends.

At this point the lagoon narrowed down to a small channel choked with fallen logs. Here an alligator was swimming under water. I grabbed the harpoon, and scrambling to the bow, launched it with all my force. The shaft bobbed sideways, then shot up the lagoon, cutting the water so fast it fairly sang. The line grew taut with a jerk that nearly took the canoe out from under me. I catapulted down on top of Ginger, reaching out in all directions for hand and toe holds.

While we were untangling ourselves, the line went slack. I bounced back to the bow and began pulling it in. Then things began to happen. A great tail flashed through the air, slapped the canoe just once—and we were in the water swimming madly to retrieve it. I reached up to grasp the gunwale, but the canoe was jerked out of my fingers and went skimming merrily up the lagoon, towed by the drunkenly waving harpoon shaft. Weighted down by our gun belts, we shipped a lot of dirty lagoon water before we finally reached the shore, to find the canoe nowhere in sight.

"A fine pair of alligator hunters we've turned out to be!" I said disgustedly. "They certainly do these things better in Hollywood, or maybe that 'gator doesn't know the rules. He not only dumps us, but steals the canoe as well. We'd better get it back before he decides to chew it into kindling wood."

"Yes, and the fun starts from now on," Ginger remarked. "It ought to be a picnic going through this place barefoot." For our *huaraches* were in the canoe.

We ploughed through the dense growth, scrambling over, under, and round fallen trees, weaving through thick growths of palm. It was impossible to hurry. We had to scan the ground at every step; or take the chance of being bitten by a snake, centipede, or scorpion. At every opportunity we worked down to the water's edge, hoping for a sight of the canoe. Finally we sighted her, lodged among the branches of a fallen tree on the far side of the lagoon.

"Now we are in a mess!" I said, surveying the hundred yards of muddy water that separated us from the canoe. "I'll have to swim for it."

"You'll do no such thing, Dan Lamb. I won't let you. I've no desire to become a widow."

Ahead and behind us the lagoon widened out. With its many branches, the distance was at least fifty miles by way of the ocean to the other side. My machete, as well as our *huaraches*, was in the canoe. With the machete, we might have cut logs and built a raft; without it there was no choice. I took off my gun belt and handed it to Ginger. "Take the Luger and shoot round me while I swim across. That will discourage any alligators hanging round."

"I'm not sure that I'm a good enough shot with your gun. I haven't used it enough," she objected.

"That's all right," I assured her. "Just keep your nerve and a steady hand. Place your shots on each side of me, but *please* don't place them behind me, because they're liable to ricochet."

Before taking off, I climbed as far out as I could get on a branch hanging over the water. "A steady hand; and remember, I'm not an alligator." Then I dived.

This is one way to break all existing swimming records. Ginger pep-

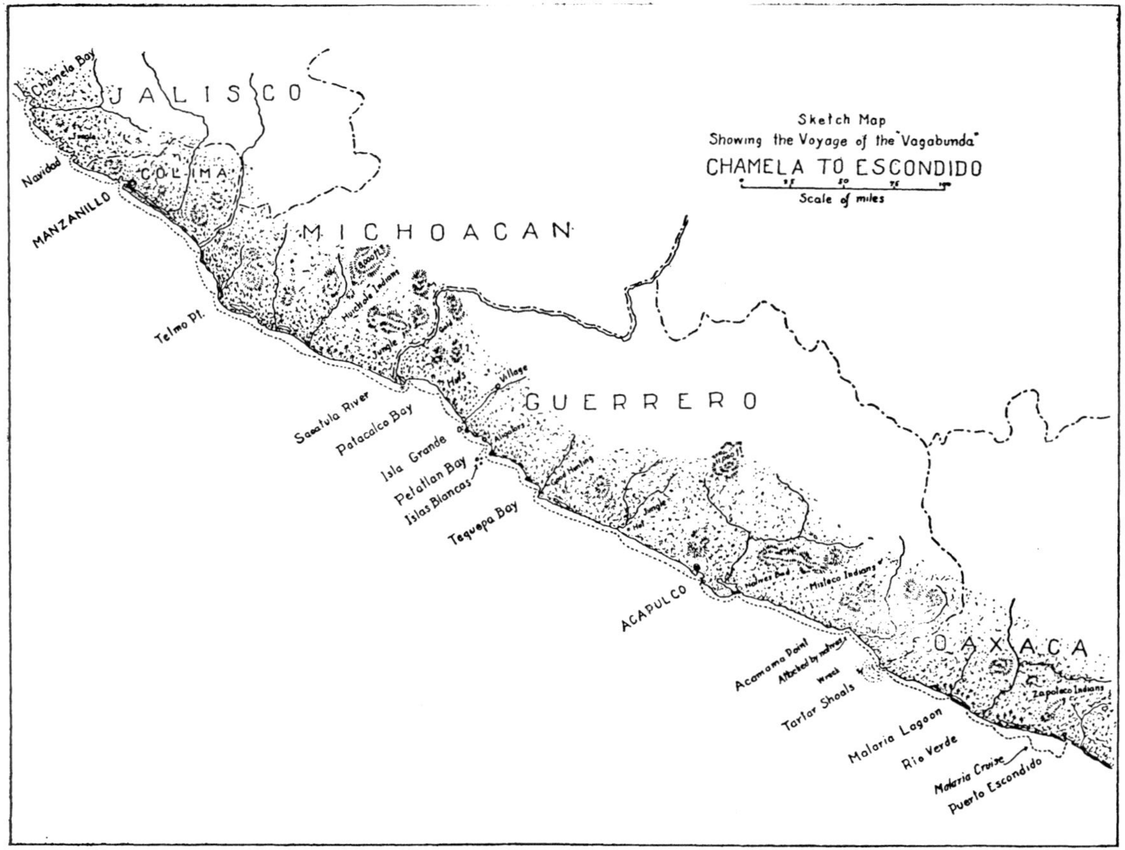
Sketch Map
Showing the Voyage of the "Vagabunda"
CHAMELA TO ESCONDIDO
Scale of miles
JALISCO
COLIMA
MICHOACAN
GUERRERO
OAXACA
Chamela Bay
Navidad
MANZANILLO
Telmo Pt.
Sacatula River
Petacalco Bay
Isla Grande
Petatlan Bay
Islas Blancas
Tequepa Bay
ACAPULCO
Acamama Point
Tartar Shoals
Malaria Lagoon
Rio Verde
Malaria Cruise
Puerto Escondido

pered the water with slugs, while I made for the canoe. Something smacked my sore leg as I pulled myself up on deck. Pushing the canoe out from the entangling branches, I gave the harpoon line on the bow a vicious yank. There was a violent commotion among the fallen logs, where the alligator had become entangled; but I had no gun with which to deliver a coup de grâce. I pulled in on the line until I was close to him. His huge jaws came out of the water with a snap that made me back away in a hurry. Tying the harpoon line to a tree instead of the bow, I paddled over to Ginger.

Our clips and guns reloaded, we again approached the thoroughly angered alligator. Another tug on the line brought frantic splashings as we both pumped lead into the swirling water. A great tail lashed out, and then all was silent. Further tugging on the line brought no response. With extreme caution, we pulled over to the bobbing harpoon shaft. Gun in hand, I reached over and wiggled it. It was loose—the alligator had got away. While I untangled the line from the branches, we expressed our opinions of people who knew how alligator hunting should be done. We had lost our faith in Hollywood.

On our way back to camp we shot two ducks and an iguana. In camp, land crabs by the hundreds were swarming over everything. Ginger picked up a stick but I stopped her before she had a chance to kill one. Dead land crabs would attract scores of hermit crabs and ants as well. We built a fire and tried to discourage them with blazing faggots. They were completely indifferent and continued their search for food. Now and then one would nip us on the foot.

"What on earth are we going to do?" asked Ginger. "There's no percentage in playing ring-around-a-rosy any longer."

I agreed, but reminded her that if we moved the camp, the crabs would undoubtedly move with us. My suggestion was that we go down to the canoe and sit in it. We could build a fire on the wet sand and cook our supper. I would place a pile of wood within reach of the canoe so that later we could feed the fire without leaving it. This procedure gave us a short respite but before we'd finished eating the second invasion began. So we set the grub box on deck and retreated to the cockpit.

After supper we got out the charts and studied them. The stretch of coast before us was unattractive. With the exception of Tequepa Bay, one day's travel away, there was no shelter between our present position and Acapulco—and it was rumoured that the port authorities there were not too friendly towards penniless gringos. Ginger, however, said she had a hunch that we would have no trouble there.

"*Quien sabe?*" I answered. "What worries me is getting there. It's one hundred and fifty miles the way we travel, and the stormy weather isn't over yet. It says in the Pilot Guide, 'Boat landing along this stretch of coast is almost impossible as there is always a heavy surf.'"

"In the meantime," Ginger suggested, "since we have an easy day's sailing tomorrow, we might as well sing while we're marooned." As I reached for the corroded harmonica, I asked her what she meant by "marooned." "Oh, a bit of wood and canvas completely surrounded by crabs," she answered. "Let's sing them a song; they might like to dance."

We sang "Red River Valley" to an orchestral accompaniment of booming surf, and the swish-swish of the waves upon the sand. An occasional high soprano note from the jungle told us that a near-by jaguar had joined the "community sing."

The next morning we sailed down to Tequepa Bay. It was a grand day for sailing, with just enough wind to make the *Vagabunda* prick up her ears. We skipped along outside the breaker line, admiring the beauty of the steep sand banks, the waving coco palms, and the jungle-covered hills in the background.

In the late afternoon we came to a small island called Morro de las Animas, and stopped there for two days to prepare food and distil water for the long jump ahead. We left the island in a dead calm, and sweated at the paddles until noon. When we stopped to rest and eat, we were disappointed at the small progress we had made. During the meal a small breeze came up, but the horizon to the south did not look too good. We hoisted sail and went on, making very poor time. Watching the mountain peaks inshore, I discovered that we were barely advancing. Ginger took the news calmly.

"What of it? We aren't going any place, so who cares?" She got out her sewing and settled back in the cockpit.

I wanted to turn back and make the attempt on another day, for I felt uneasy, and didn't like the look of the horizon.

"Nonsense!" said Ginger. "We're just as well off here as we'd be with those land crabs. Sit down and play your harmonica and quit fussing. You're always becoming upset over horizons."

I knew a good comeback to that. What about the time I'd wanted to land, and she had insisted upon sailing all night? But there was no use in starting a quarrel. Damn women anyway! One minute they were all for you; the next they were more interested in sewing than in getting to Acapulco. I got out my notebook and began to read. When I had finished Ginger looked up and smiled. "I'm sorry that I'm cross today. If you want to turn back, it's all right with me."

I answered sulkily that we'd keep right on. It was a twenty-four-hour run in any event, and with luck, we might find a landing tomorrow. To dissipate my growing irritation, I picked up the paddle and bent over it, hoping by work to avoid further argument. "So this is adventuring," I thought, as the sweat streamed off my body, making a little puddle where I perched on deck. Ginger just sat and sewed.

"Can't you change the course a little, so I'll be in the shade?" she asked.

"Anything you say," I answered. "We, as you've reminded me, aren't getting any place anyway, so it doesn't matter which way I steer."

When the sun touched the horizon the wind stopped altogether. "Now what?" I asked.

"It's time to eat. You might as well lower the sail," Ginger said.

"You don't seem very interested in the weather, do you? Well, if this calm means what I think it means, you're going to be a lot more interested before morning, my friend. You'd better tuck your sewing where it won't get wet."

"I've got good reasons for sewing," Ginger retorted. "When you feel like biting some one it's best to keep busy. We haven't been out of each other's sight for a whole year. Most of that time we've been pretty cheerful whether we felt like it or not. Don't you think it would be a good idea to have a first-rate scrap and get it out of our systems?"

"Sure!" I agreed. "Let's sit here and say nasty things. Or how about a good fight in the water?—at least it would wash the sweat off."

Ginger dived overboard and I followed her. "You asked for it!" she said as she shoved me under.

We had a royal battle. As I dived deep to grab her feet, I saw below me a dark shape that gradually turned to white. I clawed the surface. "Sharks!" We both raced for the canoe.

"Beat you," said Ginger, climbing aboard a split second ahead of me, "I feel a lot better."

"Because you're out of the water?"

"Not entirely for that reason. Mostly because I needed a good fight. How would you like to eat?" she replied.

We ate dried turtle meat while we discussed the peculiar problem of human temperament, and what to do about it—the perfectly natural irritations that long and enforced intimacy produced. After that we laughed together at the scowling horizon. Ginger looked at it speculatively. "It might be a good idea to put some turtle meat in our pockets, just in case we daren't open the cockpit," she suggested.

I asked her to roll me a cigarette out of the wild tobacco that we called "dynamite." "The more I smoke these things the more inclined I am to quit smoking entirely," I said, as the smoke curled everywhere except at the mouthpiece.

A blast of wind from the south warned us to reef the sail. The *Vagabunda* turned from shore, her gunwale dipping under water as she gathered speed and headed out to sea. We asked for it; and we certainly got it, speeding in a jerky, splashing sprint towards the ominous blackness off shore. Ginger curled up in the cockpit. "I'm not saying a thing," she said.

While she tried to sleep, I wrestled with my usual problem: how to keep out of the breakers inshore, yet not tack so far out to sea that the current caught us. The sky was so overcast that I couldn't find a star to go by. The wind had changed, but I couldn't be sure which way, or how much. I set sail for the inshore tack, still trying to get directions, and keeping an eye out for the breaker line.

The ground swell was heavy, and suddenly a great sea crashed right in front of the canoe. Then I knew that we were in the breakers. I put my weight on the paddle to swing the canoe round, while Ginger jumped up to the halyards to lower the flapping sail. A dark shape loomed up ahead of us, capped by a glowing line of phosphorescence. A thousand tons of snarling, hissing water cast itself at the canoe. The bow shot skyward. It knocked Ginger back against me. I would have gone overboard except that her weight pinned my feet in the cockpit. Floundering flat on my back, I tried to hold on to the paddle, expecting momentarily to feel the canoe crash back in a somersault. Then air replaced the pounding, swirling, glowing water, and I knew that by some bit of luck we had managed to get through.

For an interminable length of time we fought in the breakers. The boom slipped its lashings, knocking me on the head. The cockpit was full of water. I fully believed that we had reached the end of our earthly rope. But meeting each onslaught as best we could, we somehow managed to get the canoe out into the comparative safety of the wind-swept sea.

Ginger set her paddle down and felt for the bailing can. "It's gone," she said mournfully.

"Just luck that we didn't lose everything," I retorted.

We were equally responsible for our present fix—I for misjudging the direction of the wind, Ginger for her earlier indifference to the weather. Now we were both washed out. Ginger sat on the stern, worn out and shivering, while I tried to work on the sail. The boom had broken loose from the swivel joint at the mast, and the grummets of the sail had ripped loose from the mast's sides. We pulled the canvas cockpit bag up on deck, and drained out the water. I found a bit of fishline to repair the sail, and we were off once more, running close hauled at an angle off the coast.

I felt in my pocket for the turtle meat. It had been washed away, so I got another piece out of the grub box. Ginger curled up again in the cockpit, while I stayed on deck. Soon she was asleep undisturbed by the occasional wave that washed over her. I settled down to the business of sailing, hoping the morning star would soon make its appearance.

About daylight Ginger began to toss and moan. "Oh!" she said as she wakened, "I've had the most horrible dream—the zipper on the cockpit broke. Dan, if that ever happens, and water gets into the canoe during one of these storms, we'll be on the bottom before we know it!"

During breakfast, we discussed ways and means of preventing the natives from opening and closing the cockpit. Everywhere we went it was one of their special pleasures, and it was nearly worn out. After the meal, I turned in, while Ginger skippered. About two o'clock I woke up to find that she had hoisted sail and was making fair time down the coast. Then she slept until sundown, when I wakened her. The wind had increased, and it looked like another night at sea unless we picked up the Acapulco light soon. Ginger said she didn't care as long as we *kept* at sea. "You've nothing to worry about," I said. "By the looks of the weather, we'll be out of sight of land by morning."

The evening meal consisted of more turtle meat, flat tasting water, and a discussion of the paradisaical delights of T-bone steak, coffee with cream in it, and chocolate malted milks. The turtle meat, we reminded each other, was adventuring.

I got out the harmonica and began to play an old sea chanty. The wind dropped and the sail hung slack. On the far horizon we could see the light at Acapulco, blinking at us in derision. Nothing to do but paddle. We paddled until midnight. At 2 A.M., while I was contemplating the light that refused to come closer, Ginger, who had been asleep, woke up with the announcement that we were going to have a storm. I sent her back to sleep, telling her that I would waken her when it came. I paddled on, wondering if the skin was really worn off my backbone—or merely wearing thin.

Then the wind came up. We unreefed the sail, and tried to beat the storm. Quivering, leaping, bounding, we dashed on, with the storm at our heels. Soon we could faintly see the islets off the entrance to Acapulco harbour. As we steered towards the entrance, I saw a bay south of the harbour, and headed for it. We were in no condition to meet the officials of Acapulco.

Marques Bay opened its sheltering arms to us as the *Vagabunda* skidded round the headland into calm water and to the sand beach that lay beyond. Curiously enough we slept on our stomachs that night. On awakening, we were not pretty sights. Our hair hung in white strings, and we were crusted with salt from head to toe. We soaked our tired bodies in the warm, shallow water, then swam awhile to relieve our cramped muscles. Dry clothes and hot coffee made us feel still better. Lying in the shade of the tent and resting, we discussed Acapulco. Here, we could manage, but over there . . . ?

"It would be fun, if—" said Ginger a bit wistfully.

Acapulco is one of the most beautiful ports in Mexico, and I knew what she was thinking. "Yes, it would be fun—if we had a peso or two to spend for civilized food," I answered.

We gazed in the direction of the town, and thought about all the things a town could mean: bread and butter, ice cream, canned milk, a few yards of bright coloured cloth to make a new dress for Ginger. "If—?" But we were adventurers, we told ourselves; out to live off the country; to make the jungle feed and clothe us. Anyway, we said, Acapulco was a tourist port; people wore white uniforms and pith helmets. We bragged a little; we didn't need civilization. We got out the charts and looked at them. The country ahead seemed interesting. If we could get past Tartar Shoals without any trouble, we should have easy sailing from there to Salina Cruz.

Chapter Sixteen

JUNGLE GANGSTERS

WE WERE preparing breakfast the next morning when a boat manned by men in white uniforms put out across the bay and headed in our direction. That meant only one thing—customs men. To be found camping here before officially entering the port, meant trouble. The canoe, partially loaded, rode at anchor near-by. We hastily piled the rest of our equipment, our uneaten breakfast, the pot of coffee, the grub box, and ourselves into it, and started to skirt the shore. The boat changed its course and came after us, with three men straining at its oars.

"Better hoist sail, they're gaining on us," I said to Ginger, while I bent to the paddles. It was a close race as we skimmed out of the little bay and rounded Diamante Point. Away from its shelter, the breeze kicked us along. The men began to shout at us, but although we heard their voices the words were unintelligible. Soon we were on the open sea and speeding down the coast—our pursuers left far behind.

We laughed as we ate breakfast. This was fun. If our luck continued, one day we should get to the place of our childhood dreams—Cocos Island, and then perhaps to Panama.

Close to shore the reddish water was full of sea life. Sharks swam by, little green and orange snakes wriggled out of our path, great sea turtles floated lazily on the surface, and a school of dolphins acted as our escort. I remembered an old saying of the sea, "If a dolphin follows your boat it will be a safe passage." I dangled a rope end in the water and a big fellow came up to see if it was good to eat.

Dolphins, to us, are the most beautiful fish in the sea. Their streamlined bodies are swift and graceful. They have a chameleon-like ability to change their colour, turning from green to blue or brown, or to yellow and brown stripes, their fighting colours. The two fins on each side of the head and the long sail fin which extends nearly the full length of the back are a bright phosphorescent blue. Their young they herded under the canoe while the larger fish swam in guard formation on all sides of them. Every so often the young dolphins became annoyed by this excessive care and attempted to show their independence by swimming out from under the canoe. They were promptly rounded up and shooed back. An occasional shark, hopeful of seizing a wayward young dolphin, ventured too close to the escort, whereupon the big fish changed to their fighting colours and drove him off. They are vicious fighters. They stayed with us even when a stiff breeze made it difficult for the little fellows to keep up, and their antics kept the long hours of sailing from becoming tiresome.

We travelled all that day and night with just enough wind for nice sailing. Throughout the night, one of us stood watch while the other slept. Before daylight we heard the sound of breakers and hove to until daylight. Ginger wakened me at dawn. A long line of breakers extended out to sea, where they broke upon a rocky point ahead.

The dolphins had deserted us. Meanwhile, the wind had increased so that sailing became difficult and it seemed best to land. Paddling round the point we came to a rough, inhospitable beach, backed by sparse, scraggly trees. Unattractive as it appeared, it was the only landing in sight, and better than the now heavy seas. We paddled close inshore. Ginger held the canoe outside the breaker line while I swam to the beach and prepared a runway of driftwood, so that the canoe would have something to land on besides rocks.

After landing safely and unloading the canoe, we looked round. On a patch of sand there were footprints! Something about them made us uneasy and apprehensive. That there were no other signs of habitation was not strange, since this was a most unlikely spot for natives.

We pitched camp under the scrawny trees, and ate a meal of dry rations from our small store. There were neither fish nor clams in this desolate spot. "What's wrong with this coffee?" I asked.

"Weak, but you'd better like it. It's the last you'll have until we find some more wild coffee trees," replied Ginger.

The country round our camp site looked so unfriendly that we wondered why the natives or any one else would choose it as a place to live. Then we heard wild turkeys calling and decided to go hunting. Striking out across the rocky point we were again impressed with a sense of desolation. A rude cross set up among the rocks marked either a grave or a ceremonial ground. We circled back into the growth. It was the height of the dry season and we made so much noise walking on the dry leaves that we frightened off all the game. "Dan," Ginger said, "if the wind isn't too strong, I have a hunch that we had better get out of here."

I had the same feeling. In fact, this was the first place that I had ever definitely disliked. It felt dangerous, but I couldn't have told you why.

We were walking along looking at the ocean, by now a mass of wind-torn whitecaps, when we sighted camp. We had just a glimpse of running figures before they ducked into the brush. We hurried on. One glance told us they had stolen our paddles, harpoon, and fishing gear—our most indispensable items!

"They would have taken everything if those boxes hadn't been locked," I said, as I filled my clips with extra ammunition. "Stay here and guard camp; I'm going after them."

I started off with Ginger calling after me to be careful. I was seeing red. This was the first time anything had been stolen. As silently as possible I followed the dim trail that led over a ridge. Coming out on a little hogback I scanned the trail ahead, but there was no sign of natives. I ran down the incline and up the next rise. There on the trail were three natives carrying our gear.

I shouted for them to stop. Startled, they turned round and then made gestures of defiance while I hurled insults at them in Spanish. As they started to run I pulled the trigger. The Luger kicked and chattered in my hand. I threw in a second clip, pumped it dry, and threw in a third clip, firing as I ran towards them.

The paddles and harpoon lay in the trail, but the fishing gear had disappeared along with the natives. Only a red spot of blood shimmered on a leaf to show that they had been there. They had gone in different directions. I picked up the gear and started for camp. As I was coming down the last slope, the bushes moved and I shot into them. Out charged a cow, as frightened as I was.

Ginger came running to meet me, gun in hand. She had heard the sound of the Luger and come to join the fray. "How many were shooting?" she asked.

When I told her that I had fired all twenty-four shots and only nicked one native and frightened a cow, she made no comment. I said that we would put to sea at once.

"But we can't," she protested. "Look at that ocean. A storm is coming up and the wind is getting stronger every minute."

Between the boiling ocean and the natives, who had no doubt gone to their village with a wild tale of an unprovoked attack made upon them by gringos, we were in a pretty mess. Especially if they belonged to a tribe of mixed bloods (Indian and Negro) who inhabited this section of the coast and bore a bad reputation with both Indians and Mexicans.

"Do you think they will come back?" asked Ginger. "I'm frightened."

"If they do they will bring the village with them," I answered. "But let's have supper first and then plan the next move."

After the meal we got out cans of ammunition, turned the canoe parallel to the beach, blocked it up with sand, and covered the cockpit with canvas. Then we set the tent about thirty feet away so that any one in the canoe would have an unobstructed view of the beach. Close beside the tent we built a fire. The night was cloudy, but if the stiff wind blew the clouds by there would be moonlight.

"Let's get going," I whispered. Leaving the fire, now a bed of glowing embers, we crawled into the tent. We moved round, then lay quiet for about ten minutes.

"Follow me and don't make a sound," I cautioned Ginger, as we stole quietly out of the tent and towards the water. We detoured round the

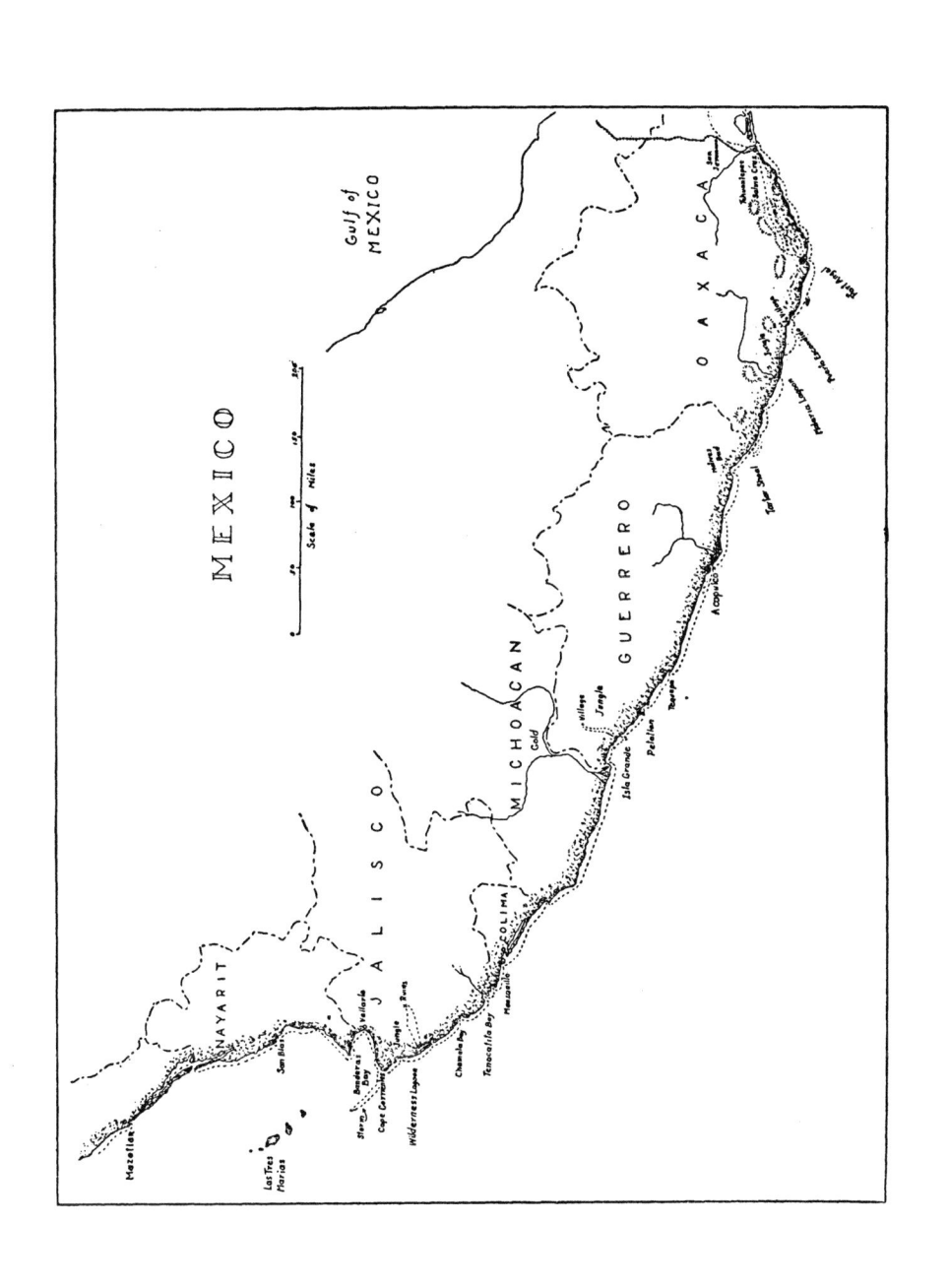

canoe and came up behind it. The wind was slapping the canvas covering as I removed a rock from the cockpit, and motioning Ginger in, crawled in beside her. I was sure that no native waiting in the darkness could have seen us enter the canoe, because the whipping, flapping canvas was continually in motion. If they were watching the tent they would assume that we were still in it.

"I hope this idea works," I whispered, as I pried the lids off quart cans of ammunition. "Got all your clips full?" She nodded. "Then lay them out where you can reach them instantly, and be careful not to get any sand in them—apt to jam your gun. If we have to shoot, place your shots and fire carefully. When your clips are empty, start to reload my clips. I'll time my firing so you can keep up with me. We will stand two-hour watches. I'll take the first two hours while you sleep. If the wind goes down we will load up and put out to sea."

Ginger stretched out in the cockpit for about ten minutes. Then she sat up beside me, loading and unloading clips, so that she could do it rapidly when the necessity arose, and to occupy her mind while we were waiting.

I watched the brush behind the shore. The wind had grown stronger and moaned and sang through the branches of the trees behind the beach. The clouds drifting across the face of the moon threw weird moving shadows against the rocks. Flurries of sand resembled ghostly running figures. I examined my gun again. Its grip was wet with sweat. I tried taking aim at objects on the beach, and cursed myself every time the gun trembled. Ginger asked me what I saw and why I muttered. "Nothing," I answered. "I'm just swearing at myself for being frightened."

The minutes dragged on. Everything on the beach seemed to come alive. Even logs began to crawl round. I watched every dark moving object, tensing every time the brush was whipped aside by the wind and a tree trunk came into view. Then I remembered that it was not dark figures that needed watching. Natives wore white clothes. I was now certain that there were more white objects moving round than black. My muscles ached from their long tension and my eyes began to burn.

"Dan," Ginger whispered, "I'm tired of loading clips. I've loaded them at least a hundred times and can do it quickly. Stretch out and I'll keep watch for a while."

Sleep was impossible, but I rested for a while, listening to the roar of the surf and the wind. Then Ginger tugged at my arm. "I see something!"

I grabbed the Luger and sat up, straining my eyes at the spot to which she pointed. There was nothing except moonlight shining on a tree trunk. The wind seemed to be easing a little and I began to hope that we could soon sail off. I knew that if the natives I had fired on should by some remote chance belong to one of the older tribes of pure-blood Indians, we had nothing to fear. Indians accept what happens to them as a natural result of their misdeeds without complaining. But if they belonged to the mixed tribes they would be bent on revenge.

Ginger again curled up in the cockpit while I watched the shadows along the beach. My eyes focussed on a moving blotch of white. It advanced and another blotch seemed to join it. Was this a trick of the moonlight, too? Then they moved again. I shook Ginger. "Take it easy," I whispered. "Watch the beach to the left and I'll take the right."

A figure, running low, darted out of the brush and headed for the tent, stopped, moved closer, and stopped again. Even the wind seemed to hesitate. A spurt of flame blotted out the figure. The tent shivered with the impact of the charge. One after another the white clad figures ran by, firing at the tent as they ran. We had to stop those flashes and those running figures. "Let 'em have it," I said.

The Luger jumped as it barked in my hand, followed by the high staccato of Ginger's twenty-two. I loaded the second clip. Again the roar of the Luger drowned out all other sounds. The spurts of flame against the dark background provided the only targets. Three clips, four clips. I drove the last clip home and covered Ginger's section while she reloaded the empty ones. My remembrance from then on is of Ginger shoving full clips into my hand, the blinding glare and the roar of the Luger, and the sharp pain of a burn as my hand slipped too far up on the barrel while reloading. Every moving object on the beach got a spray of lead. We sprayed the brush up and down the beach, pausing only to reload. Finally there were no more spurts of flame from the beach. We stopped firing.

"They've gone. Are you hurt?" I asked.

"No," she said, "but I burn all over from the hot shells in the cockpit. I'm sitting on about forty of them."

The ammunition was getting low in the cans. Our gun barrels were scorching hot. The wind had lost its force, and we felt that it was high time to be getting out of there. Ginger got behind the equipment box on the beach, and covered the shore while I got the tent down. Hurriedly we dragged the canoe down to the water's edge, firing every now and then into the brush as we worked. The fast action relieved the tension and we broke all records for speedy loading. Ginger held the canoe while I stowed the gear away. Each time I went back to shore I fully expected to find a dozen natives waiting for me.

We skidded the canoe into the water, loaded the last bit of equipment aboard, zipped the cockpit shut, and paddled madly to meet the oncoming surf, heedless of the breakers ahead. About two miles offshore, the inevitable reaction set in and soon we were too exhausted to go further. We took off our wet clothes and piled into the sleeping bag to rest until daylight. Ginger fell asleep immediately, but at first I could only doze, sitting up at intervals to scan the sea for an approaching canoe.

The sun was high when I awakened. Ginger was still sleeping. Little

beads of perspiration were standing on her forehead. I shook her gently.
"No, no," she mumbled, "I don't want to get up."

"It's getting late," I urged.

"No, I'm afraid. I don't want to wake up. Please let me alone."

Her face looked drawn and haggard. I dipped my hands in water and laid them on her forehead soothingly while I talked to her, telling her that she could go back to sleep just as soon as we had straightened out the packing and were started down the coast. The nervous reaction had left us both badly shaken.

Unzipping the cockpit revealed two or three inches of water in the bottom of the boat. I shivered as I stared at two small holes that let in a trickle of water each time the canoe rolled. The bullets had passed directly between us. A hurried examination showed that they were the extent of our damage, and I plugged them with little pieces of cloth. We arranged our equipment and hoisted sail.

A light breeze sped us along as we spent the balance of the morning taking our guns apart and giving them a thorough cleaning.

Ginger got out the *Pilot Guide* to find a landing for the night and read, "Tartar Shoals, off Maldonado, constitute the greatest menace to navigation on this portion of the coast. The shoals extend four miles offshore. Heavy breakers, strong currents, with frequent tide rips, cut the sea into treacherous chops, in which no small boat can live. The heaviest tide rips occur off the seaward extremity of the shoals." We tried to figure this one out in advance. It was too late in the day to attempt to get round the shoals. The surf was too high to attempt a landing elsewhere. The only chance was to try to find a channel through the shoals and to reach a small bight (a small bay between two headlands) which the chart showed to be under Maldonado Point. Our chance of doing this was remote, and I knew it.

Chapter Seventeen

JUNGLE FEVER

As we sailed along the coast towards the bight mentioned in the *Pilot Guide,* we could see the rocks of Tartar Shoals ahead, with big seas crashing all round them. The canoe was ready for any emergency, with a life line rigged round the gunwales, and a knotted line trailing astern for additional safety.

We discussed the nature of our fears as we paddled along. Neither one of us was actually afraid of bodily pain or death. One was a part of living and the other was inevitable. Our presence here proved our conscious acceptance of both facts. But beneath the level of consciousness was another self whose sole preoccupation was with living. It scented danger to the organism it inhabited; it grew panicky at the thought of extinction; it repeatedly warned us of things we would otherwise be unaware of.

Now as we drew nearer the shoals, the hiss and rumble of the seas breaking upon them became terrific. The scattered rocks that formed them extended seaward for a distance of four miles, and for the most part they were hidden. We shuddered at the fate of any hapless vessel caught among these agents of destruction. There was the possibility, however, that there might be an opening through them, and we scanned the vista ahead for signs of calmer water. Further inshore the water seemed less turbulent, and we carefully and cautiously worked our way towards it. Here the noise was deafening, for the breakers were on both sides of the narrow channel. It was impossible to gauge its depth, because of the churned-up sand, consequently we eyed each rolling sea with suspicion as we felt our way along. Headway was slow and difficult for we were going against a strong current. An hour, two hours passed, and then the way seemed blocked. Although we were weary from lack of sleep and exhausted from the strain of the previous night's ordeal, this obstacle had to be met in some way. If we turned back, it would be dark long before we reached the opening of the channel we had come through. And if we did reach it, where could we land? There was only one answer; we had to go on. Somewhere ahead of us lay the little bight of Maldonado—and safety.

The swells rising under us became sharper. Apparently we were getting into shallow water. Ginger stood up on deck to see if she could see the opening ahead. I warned her to be careful but the warning came too late.

Jungle Fever

A sea slapped the canoe, sweeping it out from under her feet. She catapulted into the water with a splash. With quick strokes I headed the canoe round, and paddled to the spot where she had gone down. The inevitable dorsal fin appeared. Her head came above the water and she started to smile. "Sharks," I yelled, and if there is any word in the marine vocabulary that can instigate faster action, I'd like to know what it is.

Ginger tumbled on deck as the shark hit the side of the canoe with such force that we felt the siding splinter. Several other fins appeared as by telepathic communication. They were fine company for a trip through a narrow channel in treacherous shoal water. Ginger reported open water ahead, and we waited, hoping for a lull in the breakers.

We finally paddled through to a narrow strip of open water that stretched between the nearest shoal and the rock-strewn beach. It was getting dark, but we were still some distance from the bight. Since we were making such poor time with the paddles, I suggested that we hoist sail, even though I knew that if a sea should hit us it would undoubtedly land us on the rocks. As we scooted along towards our destination, darkness overtook us. From then on our only guide was the phosphorescent breakers. Soon the surf in the bight loomed up ahead of us and we lowered sail. A small sea picked us up and left us on the sand. We stepped ashore with audible sighs of relief but without enough ambition to set up camp.

Ginger reported that there was nothing left to cook except some scraps of turtle meat, and that none too fragrant. Dismally we went to sleep in the canoe, wondering if we had put enough distance between ourselves and last night's camp.

The next morning we started off through the intricate three-mile passage between the shore and the shoals. We wanted very much to stay and do some hunting and fishing, but discretion told us to sail south. Distance was the best method of coping with revengeful natives. Our spirits rose as we faced open water and hoisted our sail to a spanking breeze. Tartar Shoals were behind us!

The water was alive with fish, and Ginger, though tired, caught and cleaned a mess of them and put them on the deck to dry. We knew that ahead of us was a big lagoon where we could undoubtedly replenish our exhausted food supply and find fresh water. The chart gave its name as Alotengo Lagoon, into which the Tecogame River empties.

We had sighted small villages earlier in the day, but as we neared the lagoon our hopes rose, for there were neither villages nor natives in sight. The country back of the beach was well wooded and looked green and inviting.

After shooting the breakers we found ourselves in the calm waters of the lagoon. We picked out a site, but without waiting to set up camp took our guns and started off in search of food. The turtle meat had made any variation in the diet a matter for immediate and enthusiastic consideration. Within a short distance from the beach Ginger bagged a wild turkey.

After banqueting on broiled wild turkey, palm hearts (the tender bud which grows at the top of the palm tree), and coco-nut meat and milk, we turned in for the first good sleep in a long time.

I woke in the morning feeling dazed and listless. The sun was high. My face and arms itched. I looked round. Mosquitoes were everywhere. Just then one of them lit on my arm, and as I slapped at it I noticed that, unlike other mosquitoes, it stood on its head as it bit. This, as I had heard, was one of the distinguishing marks of the mosquito that injects the malarial parasite through its salivary glands. I woke Ginger.

"What's the matter?" she asked.

"Anopheles—malarial mosquitoes—all over the place," I said. "Better take some quinine."

"Oh, Dan, and it's all my fault. I forgot to mend the tent. Look, it's full of bullet holes. We haven't much quinine either, have we?"

We spent a day half-heartedly securing food, although game was plentiful. At sundown the mosquitoes drove us to the shelter of the now mended tent.

The next morning we woke with headaches and at once built a smoky fire to discourage the mosquitoes that swarmed towards us as we emerged from the tent. Neither of us was hungry. After drinking some coco-nut milk and taking a stiff shot of quinine, we sat in the smoke and held our heads.

"This place gives me the jitters. It's the silence and the continual hum of the mosquitoes. Let's go," Ginger suggested.

Her skin hurt, she said, and felt "touchy." I know my bones and head ached as we paddled on up the lagoon. At its upper entrance we found a clean sand barrier that looked as though it might be fairly free from mosquitoes, so we decided to camp there.

"Perhaps those mosquitoes aren't malarial after all," Ginger said hopefully. "They don't carry malaria unless they bite some one who has it, and there are no natives here."

I was sorry to disillusion her, but she would have to know some time. "There was a dugout beached across the river from where we were hunting yesterday."

That afternoon while we were preparing food for the next jump, Ginger complained of being cold. I rolled her up in the sleeping bag and took her temperature. Then I was certain—102°—malaria. While making broth for supper, I too began to shiver. We drank the broth and crawled into the sleeping bag, trying vainly to get warm.

I knew that we would have to leave the first thing in the morning for Salina Cruz, two hundred miles away, and a doctor, but I did not want Ginger to know just how slim our chances were of ever getting there.

Jungle Fever

We had very little quinine, and we needed five grains each, every two hours. Though Acapulco was nearer, Tartar Shoals stood between us, and I knew that, with the wind against us and no place to land, we could never make it.

At daylight we got up feeling stiff and groggy. I broke camp while Ginger fixed some more broth. Then came the task of portaging the equipment across the soft sand. We tried rolling the canoe, but the roller stuck repeatedly and I'd have to lift the canoe while Ginger freed the roller and replaced it. Halfway across the barrier we were exhausted, but doggedly kept at it. It was afternoon before we stood beside our equipment on the beach and watched the heavy surf.

"Do you think we can make it?" Ginger's voice sounded weak and far away.

"We've got to."

Just to load the canoe took all the endurance we had. The strong current along the shore kept carrying the boat down the beach, so after every load I'd help Ginger work it back to where the equipment lay. Great waves, which in crashing threw spray thirty feet in the air, added to the hopelessness of the situation. The load finally in, we considered resting but agreed that we must get on to Salina Cruz without further delay.

We started, trying to gauge the lull and to paddle through the breakers while it lasted. Then, halfway out, big seas began to roll over us, filling the cockpit. We were soon wet with spray and shivering with chills. As an unusually big roller approached I tried to backwater, but it was too late. We were swept up in the curl of the sea, and crashed over backwards, the canoe on top of us. Churned and pounded, with sand filling our eyes, noses, and mouths, we finally rose to the surface and swam for shore, to sink on the sand half-dazed.

After great effort we managed to collect the canoe and our sailing gear from the water. And by now we needed no further persuasion that it was best to wait for the seas to become calmer.

Burning with fever, we spent a miserable afternoon and night. At daylight Ginger's fever was 103° and mine 102°. There were two hundred miles of storm-tossed sea between us and the nearest aid. Without a permanent camp and a supply of food, we couldn't manage alone. No matter how much quinine we took the mosquitoes would reinfect us if we stayed in the lagoon. Whatever seemed best to do must be done at once, before the ravages of fever made us completely helpless.

Shortly after daylight we made a second attempt to put to sea. The surf was fairly calm now, but it was difficult for Ginger, in her weakened condition, to hold the canoe against the surge while I loaded. The boat broke away from her time after time, and I would have to drop my load and stagger to help her catch it. The thing seemed possessed of devils.

At last we were loaded. Ginger lay covered with a piece of canvas in the cockpit, while I paddled. Well out from shore, I arranged the sleeping bag for her, hoisted sail, and with a light breeze from the south-east we started down the coast. At noon the breeze died altogether.

I have little recollection of what followed, though I was apparently able to write down the events in the log.

I quote:

"Dec. 17. Tried to rouse Ginger to take some food—seems in stupor. Gave her quinine. Tried paddling, couldn't keep it up. Very sore all over. Gave up, doubled up in cockpit. Dozed off until 2 P.M. when light breeze came up offshore. Making fair time. Ginger has severe chills. Covered her with tent and canvas. Very difficult handling paddle, as arms sore. No landing. Think we're off Minzio Point. 7 P.M. Just breeze enough to offset current. 10 P.M. Wind died, situation looks hopeless. Can't stay awake much longer. Almost fell over side. Moved Ginger and sat in the cockpit. Not enough room to stretch out.

"Dec. 18, 2 A.M. Wakened by a bad attack of chills. Nothing to wrap up in. Tried to keep warm by paddling, can't make paddle work. Hear breakers but can't determine direction. 3 A.M. Wind from the south. Flapping of sail woke me. Canoe rising to heavy swell. Either too close to breaker line or due for storm. Seems best to tack out to sea. 4 A.M. Sea choppy, difficult time handling canoe. Trying to head into waves so spray won't wet Ginger, can't manage it. Will try rigging piece of canvas over cockpit, using paddle for a ridge pole. Hoisting sail to try to beat way against the wind. Soaked and very cold. Just woke up from doze to find canoe heading into heavy breakers, now heading for sea. 5 A.M. Canoe almost turned over. Can't seem to sail into wind. Difficult to stay awake and great pain in back and shoulders. Had idea of turning back to Acapulco but can't seem to remember how far it is from present position. 6 A.M. Wind stronger. Horizon to south black. Three miles offshore. Danger we are in seems to have cleared my head somewhat. Judging from chills must have malignant type malaria. Wind now too strong to sail. 7 A.M. Woke up Ginger. Tried to tell her the situation. She's too sick to care. No landing in sight. Ahead is reef. Almost lost sail when wind struck us. Wind too strong, can't last much longer. Must rouse Ginger. We will have to take risk of cracking up on rocks rather than trying to ride out storm. Got Ginger out of bag. She understands and said 'shore.' 8 A.M. Waiting for lull. Afraid there won't be any. Tried to tell Ginger to get ready to jump and swim ashore. She just keeps turning her face and trying to smile, don't think she comprehends, Here we go."

As we dashed in towards the rocks under reefed sail, a small channel opened up before us. I headed the canoe towards it. Rocks and shore line flashed by. A huge swell picked us up and the next thing I remember we were on the shore in a heap. As in a dream I saw the canoe, her sail flapping, safe beside me on the sand. In the cockpit Ginger sat up and looked round.

Jungle Fever

She could no longer manage a smile. I pulled the canvas from round her and spread it out on the dry sand further up the beach, then lifted her from the cockpit and staggered off, my knees buckling under me. Before I reached the canvas we went down in a heap. Wet, half conscious, covered with sand, and shaking with chills, we lay where we had fallen.

I have no recollection of how much time elapsed, but I seemed to hear some one shouting, "Get up and fight, you fool!" I didn't want to fight, I didn't care. For Ginger, yes, but for myself I only wanted to be let alone. When I could no longer ignore that insistent summons, I staggered to my feet, then fell and crawled over to the canvas, which I dragged down and wrapped round Ginger. The wind tore at the silent roll as I stood looking at it. There was something so final and conclusive about that inert bundle, the end of life and movement and laughter; it filled me with fear and rage. By God, I would do something! I cursed my impotence and screamed defiance at the elements, which seemed to scream back, "You can't do it!" I would do it.

Above us, a black sky merged with a sable sea, around us towering funereal cliffs united with the jungle. My mood matched the blackness and the desolation as I stormed down to the canoe, dragged out the sleeping bag and tent and carried them up to the beach to roll them round Ginger. I then unloaded the canoe, staggering and falling and cursing my weakness each time I stumbled, and eventually dragged it to where it formed a windbreak for Ginger. That accomplished, I started looking for some dry wood, which I found under an overhanging rock.

Many times I tried to start a fire, but the wind would blow it out each time the tinder ignited. In my fevered state the elements became personified for me, as they were for Stone Age men. I sat up and shouted to the wind, "I'll build this fire in spite of you!"

With that I threw open the grub box, got out Ginger's largest kettle, and filled it with tinder and wood. Then, carrying it, I climbed into the canoe and under the deck. "Now blow *this* fire out." The fire kindled in the kettle. When the smoke became unbearable I carefully worked the live coals out on to the sand, and piled on more wood. I made a windbreak of the sail to shield the fire, set up the tent, and moved Ginger into it. As I worked the squall struck in all its fury. I remember shouting, "You can't lick us now. Ginger's in bed, we have a fire, and water and food."

The rain fell in torrents. The wind tried to tear down the shelter and whip out the fire. I gave Ginger quinine and soup, and tried to tell her that we had beaten the storm. But she shook her head, too sick to understand.

I lay down, dozed, got up, gave Ginger quinine and soup and lay down again—all through the rest of the day and the night. Ginger needed quinine most, so I took half doses as our supply dwindled. The thermometer readings seemed fantastic—103°—104°. She lay in a coma.

Some time during the night the storm abated. When the sun had warmed the sand, I dragged Ginger out of the tent and laid her on the canvas. Then in some fashion I loaded the canoe. I remember dragging the boxes because I couldn't lift them. The tide must have come in as I worked for the boat was beached when I started, yet it was afloat when I aroused Ginger. I don't know how she got in. I remember trying to lift her and being unable to do so.

Nor have I any recollection of the next two days.

Opening my eyes, I stared down at the water sloshing round in the cockpit. Ginger lay huddled under the canvas. I started to reach for her to see if she were still alive and discovered that I was lashed to the stern of the canoe. My body was chafed and raw where the ropes had bit into it. The deck was crusted with salt and the sail hung partly in the water. We had apparently been through a terrible storm. I undid my lashings and pulled the canvas from Ginger's face. She was unconscious but still breathing.

I looked towards shore, but couldn't see it. On the seaward side were tall cliffs. Then I knew that we were sailing in the wrong direction, so turned the canoe around and hoisted sail. I tried to call Ginger but could make no sound. Realizing that we had probably been without water for a long time, I got out the canteen and dripped some of its contents on Ginger's parched lips. She aroused herself sufficiently to take a few sips.

From time to time I gave her more water in small quantities.

We passed high brown cliffs and came to the entrance of a small bay. As we rounded the point I discovered a few native huts. I had no idea where we were, but here were people. I shouted the good news to Ginger. The excitement helped clear my head. Common sense told me not to land in the village, so I picked a spot about one hundred yards from the last hut. Dusky figures came running to meet us. A dozen hands reached for the canoe.

A huge broad-shouldered negro lifted Ginger and started to carry her away. "No, no," I shouted. A dozen voices protested. "We have malaria, *colentura, paludisimo*. We have a house, we must stay here on the beach."

As long as we remained in our insect-proof tent, there was little likelihood of our being bitten by mosquitoes, who in turn would most certainly infect the natives. It was important to make them comprehend this.

Piloto, the big negro, seemed to understand. I got out the sleeping bag and carried it near the trees on the edge of the beach. There Piloto laid Ginger down and a half-dozen native women dropped to their knees beside her.

The natives were Huichole Indians. Piloto appeared to be the only negro in the village. He was infinitely helpful and seemed to understand what I wanted done without words. Taking command, he had a camp site cleared

Jungle Fever

at a sufficient distance from the village and gave the arguing natives orders as to where to set the tent and how. I was too dazed to be of any use.

While I sat on the equipment box, two buxom old ladies worked over Ginger, washing her, getting her into dry clothes, and putting her to bed. After that they boiled food for us. Then they stood over me and picked at my wet clothes. I must go to bed at once, they insisted. Piloto wiped warm wet rags over my body and followed that with a brisk rubbing with rough dry cloths. When I had wriggled into a strange-looking suit of light, clean clothes, I crawled into the bag beside Ginger.

Curious snatches of conversation came to me before I dozed off.

"They are white and from the West. They came in a small boat with a figurehead upon its bow. It is said that from the West they will come." The voices droned on, the language a mixture of Spanish and native.

"*Pobrecita Señora, medicina.*" A fat old woman was on her hands and knees, peering at us and holding in her hand a *jícara* of some steaming liquid.

I helped Ginger to a sitting position, and we took turns drinking the medicine, which tasted like a sweetish corn concoction. Then another *jícara* was passed in; this had the bitterness of gall. I gagged as it burned all the way down, then panted for breath. "Drink it, drink it," the old woman insisted. I took another gulp and held it to Ginger's lips. She coughed and sputtered as I had, but did manage to swallow some of it. I drained the rest. Soon I became warm and comfortable. Outside it was dark, there were faint sounds of people getting dinner, the crackling of fires and the far-off hum of voices.

A strange, withered face, with eyes that seemed to glow, looked into the tent. "Listen, my children, sleep, my children, but listen." I nudged Ginger, but she was in a coma and barely breathing. The voice repeated, "Sleep, but listen." The face withdrew and I closed the tent.

I lay there and tried to assemble my thoughts, but could arrange them in no coherent pattern. Like will-o'-the-wisps the events of the last few days entered and receded from my consciousness. The face of the negro Piloto, with its uncanny look of awareness, and the gentle, quiet faces of the Indian women seemed thrown upon the walls of the little tent, as on a screen. All I knew for certain was that order had somehow superseded chaos. I sighed—I was too sick—and then I must have slept.

I awoke and listened. Now it seemed that the hallucinations were auditory. Strange sounds were filling the tent and I was conscious of a soothing, floating sensation. The hard ground on which we lay seemed soft as eiderdown. This startled me. I sat up. Could this be death? Now the sounds became more definite, a rhythmic rise and fall of a single note, a chant that came from directly outside the tent. Then I saw a flickering of light through the thin canvas, and reached over cautiously to open the flap. Kneeling in the sand before a tall lighted taper, was the old woman who had called us her children. She was swaying back and forth as she chanted, so intent that my movements did not disturb her. Quietly I crawled back into the bag and drifted off, with the strange rhythm of the chant rocking me to sleep.

Later on I awoke again, feeling quiet and peaceful. My first thought was of Ginger. I bent over her. Though burning with fever, she breathed slowly and evenly. I looked out of the tent again. The old woman was still there, her taper burned almost to the ground, still chanting her age-old song of healing.

About sunrise the sound of singing awakened us both. The old woman was gone now, but there was a procession of natives on their way to the beach. As they walked they sang to the rising sun, and they continued their song while they busied themselves about our fire.

I spoke to Ginger. She smiled. She was very weak, but miraculously better.

"Hello, in there."

I almost jumped out of my skin. Some one speaking English! For an instant I was tongue-tied. "Hello, I'll be right out."

"No," the voice said, "stay where you are. I have brought quinine, but you must have some hot *atole* first." (*Atole* in this village was a purée soup made from boiled wild rice.)

A Pennsylvania Dutchman! I wriggled out of the sleeping bag and looked for the white man. "Where has he gone?" I stammered in Spanish.

"Who, me?" I stared in wonder at the pleasant dark-faced speaker. His clothes were tattered and his face streaked with dirt. He was as obviously a Mexican as he was obviously not an American. But I could have sworn to that accent.

"Excuse my appearance, but I have ridden all night to bring you quinine. Get back into bed, the *atole* will soon be ready. I will sit here by the tent," he said.

Too dumbfounded for speech, I said nothing.

"Are you surprised that I speak English?" he asked. "I grew up in Pennsylvania—my foster father was a missionary—but I came back to my own people. I live on a plantation some distance inland. A native runner brought me word that you were here. I brought herbs from the high country and some quinine."

I told him that the natives had given us medicine. What it was I did not know, but it was more effectual than quinine.

"Ah, yes, the Wise Woman," he nodded. "She has great knowledge and I recommend her treatment."

"Why did she sit outside our tent and chant all night? Do you know?" I asked.

"Yes," he answered. "But do you mind if I do not speak English? It is so long since I have used the language that I speak it awkwardly."

"By all means speak Spanish."

"The natives have many reasons for chanting to cure illness. It keeps away the evil spirits. It soothes the mind of the listener, and makes it easier for the good spirits to effect a cure. And it is also a prayer. This is hard to explain to any one who does not have the native point of view. If you have strength to listen, I believe that I can explain. This 'evil spirit' is not a demon, but a part of your spirit, the part of you that is always preoccupied with yourself. When you are ill that spirit takes possession of you and you become fearful; and when you are fearful, you cannot become well. By listening to the chant, even if you sleep the mind is occupied. The fear of being alone is banished by the voice as well. But I will not talk further. Here comes your food."

The Wise Woman now appeared with an escort carrying steaming bowls of *atole*. I stepped aside while one of the women went into the tent, and propping Ginger's head on her capacious bosom, fed her the soup and a large dose of the bitter brew. The escort filled the bowls again and handed them to me.

"That medicine is good for you," said the man. "It is strong, but so is the fever. I have had malaria, and I know. Now we will go and let you sleep."

At noon I took Ginger's temperature. It was $103\frac{1}{2}°$, and my own was $104°$.

The fever dulled our senses, and I have little recollection of the next weeks, except that I awoke one morning bathed in sweat. Ginger's fever broke the next day. For several weeks longer we were listless and weak. During all this time we had constant care. Each night at sundown the Wise Woman, sitting before her candle, would start her night-long chant. Each day began with the sound of singing voices.

It was a full two months before we were strong enough to travel, and in that time we came to understand and admire these people. Their homes were open to us. They lent us horses for short trips into the interior. We attended innumerable parties and fiestas. We took long walks along the beach in the moonlight, accompanied by the entire village. They serenaded us by the hour before our campfire.

The name of the village was Puerto Escondido, which means "hidden." Though it was very small, it boasted a maritime official named Constantino, a quiet soft-spoken man with a superb sense of humour. His wife Elena was a handsome blonde from an inland tribe. There were often blondes among the Indians, she said. Whether this was due to some admixture of Spanish blood, I do not know. Her four-year-old precocious daughter, Rosita, was as dark as Constantino.

Since Constantino's family was typical of this village it might interest the reader to learn how they lived.

In Elena and Constantino's home were two elderly aunts, Maria and Concha. Most Mexican families have one or more old persons living with them, for Indians unfailingly care for and respect their aged members. And no one is ever left alone. In the event of the break-up of a home, the survivor is taken into another family, not necessarily related, where he is treated with kindness. There is never any question as to his welcome. He performs such tasks as are within his ability; but if he is unable to do anything, it doesn't matter. Nothing would seem more repellent or inhuman to an Indian than an "Old People's Home." We tried to explain that our people must work hard to provide for their old age, but this met with incomprehension. "Señor," I was asked, "have they no friends?"

The two aunts were remarkable old ladies, with a vigour that belied their wrinkled faces. Both were jolly, plump, and energetic. Maria attacked the *metate* with the *mano* (this word meaning "hand" is the local name for grinding stone) with a fury that used to make us wonder how she could fail to break it. While it looks easy, the odd rolling motion used in grinding corn is both hard work and difficult to master. Another fascinating occupation was to watch Concha deftly pat and cook the tortillas that Maria ground. Both women wore the long full skirt and overblouse and *rebosa* which constitute the usual costume of Indian women.

The house was made of saplings tied with vines and covered with a thatched palm roof. In one corner of the kitchen was the altar stove, built of mud and rocks and topped with stones set in a triangle to hold the earthen pots. The *metate* was placed on a forked upright near-by, with another forked stick below it on which hung the receptacle to catch the *masa* (ground corn). A three-forked upright held the water *olla*. A table, several stools, and some earthen pots completed the equipment. Hammocks were used to sleep in because of the humidity and they made comfortable beds, we found, once one became accustomed to them.

The main diet of these people consists of fish, tortillas, beans, and rice, augmented by turtles, turtle eggs (considered a rare delicacy), venison, and once in a while beef, although we could never discover where it came from. They also eat coco-nuts, pineapples, mangos, and a fruit which looks like a green orange, but tastes like a very poor combination of grapefruit, lime, and orange. It has almost no juice and very little flavour. Other articles used are *panela* (native sugar), coffee, and tobacco.

They never vary the traditional way of doing things. For instance, Ginger noticed that they never put salt in the uncooked tortilla dough but salted them as they ate them. She showed them how we season food. There was no reason why they shouldn't do it that way, they said—they had just never thought of it. Then Ginger tried out other culinary innovations. She mixed ground barbecued meat and black boiled beans into the uncooked *masa*, patted the mixture into tortillas and cooked them. The result was surprisingly good.

She also laboured mightily explaining the niceties of sanitation. With great difficulty and arm waving she painted for them a graphic picture of the horror of germs, the danger inherent in an unglazed, unboiled *olla*. She poured boiling water over everything, explaining what a good idea it would be to use ashes boiled in water to clean the *metate* and other cooking implements. We were careful to suggest nothing for which they lacked the equipment.

As a matter of fact the huts are by no means as unsanitary as one might suspect. The lime water in which the corn is boiled before grinding is sprinkled on the floors. This helps to sterilize the ground and keep out crawling pests. The people are very clean about their persons too. At least once a day, usually between eight and nine in the morning, or at five in the afternoon, all of them go for a swim in a little sheltered cove.

Ginger taught the women different embroidery stitches which looked very pretty on their hand-woven cloth (Elena became especially adept in the use of the cross stitch). She also taught them how to make a French seam, and the flat seam stitched on both sides so that their clothes would not come apart so easily. The proper way of patching a garment—with the edges turned under and stitched twice, and the patch larger than the hole—was new to them also.

I taught the men and boys various games; how to make sling shots, bows and arrows (these Indians had never used them), and some tricks of carving. And with Ginger's aid, I made a doll for Rosita. The child's dark little face would beam, as she proudly and tenderly rocked it.

Among the older men and boys I organized a life-saving crew, taught them artificial respiration, first aid, and the use of the tourniquet. They were especially interested in learning to make bone fishing jigs, and in ways of making fire other than with flint and steel.

In their treatment of social misfits these Indians are particularly humane. During one of our first visits to Elena's kitchen we saw a beautiful woman working on the *metate*. Her hair was fine and long, and her eyes were large and shaded by thick lashes. She looked like a Madonna. But as she arose from the *metate* and turned to leave the room, we got the surprise of our lives. From the rear we could see that our beautiful lady was wearing rolled-up blue jean overalls! Her costume, front view, had consisted of a woman's blouse, a long full apron, and a string of beads and earrings.

At the first opportunity I asked Constantino about this. He said, "He does not feel what he seems to be. He dresses as he wishes he were. That is all right, because we know the truth, and in this way he is happy too."

We saw transvestites frequently in isolated communities, where they are happy and useful. The villagers' attitude is one of tolerance, kindness, and watchfulness. Maria and Concha kept a sharp eye on Paula, who was not permitted to stray, unescorted, too far from the hearth. Paula's interests were distinctly feminine, and since he was strong, the women's burden of carrying water, wood, and the heavy bundles of washing to and from the river was considerably lightened. His voice was particularly melodious and pleasant and he always sang at his work, which he did well and painstakingly.

In the more "civilized" communities these people are taken away and put on a penal island, where they live a miserable existence with other convicts. But here they have found their proper niche, and lead a happy and morally decent existence. They are made to wear clothes proper to their sex, but otherwise they can deck themselves out as they please, and so are able to make the adjustments necessary to their mental and emotional well-being.

The Wise Woman, or the Little Old One, as she was sometimes called, was the repository of all the ancient lore. The office descends from mother to daughter and carries with it considerable prestige. These Wise People are highly secretive about the nature of their remedies, but are undoubtedly well-versed in herbal lore and other matters. One of the remedies for common ailments is a leaf similar to the mulberry leaf. These leaves, pounded, make an efficacious poultice when applied to a wound or sore.

A tea brewed from various dried leaves is given for stomach disorders; though we never used it, it seemed to work wonders with the natives.

The infusion for malaria, on the other hand, we had ample opportunity to sample and it most assuredly works. Consisting of various dried leaves put into cold water and thoroughly boiled, it is the most villainous concoction ever invented, but I'd take it tomorrow in preference to quinine if the need arose.

A small bush with a yellow flower which we saw growing wild is called the "rheumatism bush," and the natives and many Mexicans swear by it. Its leaves are brewed green and are said to lose their potency when dried.

The uses of poisons are known, particularly poisons deadly to animals and not to humans There is a weed growing in profusion which the natives pound on a stone until it becomes a pulp. This they throw into pools or still water where there are fish. The fish immediately die, but since the natives eat them the poison is evidently not injurious to human beings.

Notwithstanding all the care, courtesy, and consideration that our friends in Puerto Escondido gave us, we wanted very much to get to Salina Cruz. It is the biggest seaport on the west coast of Mexico, and there we could procure some of the food we needed to build up our run-down bodies. The mere mention of milk, eggs, ice cream, puddings, and fresh tomatoes made little shivers of delight run up our spines. Also we wanted to gossip with Americans, talk English again before we forgot how; and we wanted to experience the pride of seeing our canoe alongside the big ships from all over the world.

The day came at last, and before our departure Puerto Escondido put on its grandest fiesta. All our friends were present: the acting Port Captain with his famous pink shirt, Constantino and his family, Carlos from up country, Don Juan who owned the only boat in the village that was not a dugout, Señor One-eye, the town character, and many others—and of course Piloto.

Piloto, who was the village leader in everything, had put on a shirt in honour of his rôle as master of ceremonies. When everyone had assembled he announced that he had composed a song to us. Then he struck up a theme on his guitar and his friends joined in. The song was called "*Marinera Valiente*" (Valiant Sailor Lass). It told in great detail about the brave girl who sailed in a little boat from far-away California to Panama, and how she stopped at their village to warm their hearts with her smile. It was just as sentimental as the Spanish language and Piloto could make it. I looked at Ginger, whose eyes streamed with tears.

Carlos, who had left Pennsylvania principally because he had been looked down upon for his dark colour, immediately felt called upon to make some disparaging remarks about Piloto's singing. He wanted to show us that he knew how these matters were regarded in the States, I suspect. I reminded him that we were not in Pennsylvania, and that Piloto had waited on us hand and foot for two months. If my feelings were not outraged by Piloto's balladry, I asked, why should Carlos mind? He still grumbled, until I emphatically told him that since Piloto's colour had been no bar to our accepting his services, neither Ginger nor myself had any intention of drawing the colour line at this late date and spoiling his big moment. That big West Indian Negro had been a good friend to us both and we were proud of his friendship.

The fiesta lasted until midnight, then we moved the canoe and equipment close to the water so that we could leave at daylight. While we were making up our bed several natives came carrying blankets and *pavillones* (light covering to keep out mosquitoes), prepared to sleep on the sand close to the canoe. Soon a group of women laden with food put in appearance, and shortly fires were lighted. No one slept. Instead, we all sat round the fire talking until the morning star rose over the hill and the women began to prepare breakfast.

The *Vagabunda* was heavily laden with gifts and we were heavy-hearted as we took off. On the shore our many friends stood shouting until we were out of sight, "*Adios, amigos, que le vaya bien.*" ("God go with you, my friends, may you go well.")

We cannot help thinking how much of value may lie here for the patient researcher. These Huicholes, for instance, are famous throughout Mexico for their medicinal lore and are frequently called upon to treat people of the highest position who know the benefits of scientific medicine. There might be something of value here for the pharmacologist.

The research worker who hopes to be successful with Indians, however, will not go traipsing into their villages at the head of a retinue, flanked by interpreters, and set up his little court in the jungle. Nor will he hale the Indians before him as before a Congressional committee. They will only laugh, and mislead him as they have his predecessors. In many villages he will be lucky if he is not shot at sight. They won't wait to find out whether he is a scientist, a philanthropist, or a soldier of fortune. And they won't care.

Indians are highly intuitive as to people's motives; they are proud, sensitive, and independent. The white man's ill-concealed feeling of superiority is apparent to them immediately, and since they do not feel inferior, they hate him for it. They know he is passing judgment upon their way of living, which is based upon concepts of which he knows nothing. The following incident is a case in point.

One night when we were first able to be about, we were invited to dinner at Constantino's house. As Elena served the dinner, she said in a voice full of mockery, "Of course we are *very poor*. Isn't it too bad we have so little?" Both Ginger and I looked at her in astonishment, for Indians do not apologize for lack of anything, and the fare was more than bountiful. Questioning brought out the fact that a little prior to our visit a yachting party had come ashore, and strolling through the village had commented in Spanish on the natives' poverty.

Since Indians do not have the white man's pathological obsession with things, he is not only deeply offended by our attitude—he thinks us crazy as well. His values are ethical and aesthetic. Our factual and material values impress him not at all.

White men among Indians often pry in a silly and indiscreet manner into matters of the gravest import to them—customs and religion. This causes trouble. Men who should know better, carelessly or curiously handle what they are pleased to call the Indian's idols. As a matter of fact these symbols have no more idolatrous significance than has the Eucharist for a Christian.

The Indian's conversational trick of discussing natural phenomena in animistic terms is another stumbling block to the white man's comprehension of Indian psychology. To give an example of their manner of speech:

Ginger was sewing after dark one night with the aid of a lighted wick floating in coco-nut oil. Concha saw her and exclaimed, "You mustn't do that! Don't you know that if you sew after dark, the spirit of the needle will pierce your eyes?" That was the Indian way of saying that your eyes will hurt you if you sew by a poor light.

Another time, Ginger with the other women had been washing clothes in the river. Afterwards she started to iron with a heated flat rock. "No, no, you must not iron the same day that you wash," said Maria. "The spirit of the rock will hurt your head and you will sneeze." In other words, you will contract a cold in the head or at least a headache from the rapid shift in temperature. In an Indian household, I might add, the cook never washes the dishes, which Ginger says is good news.

Indians, where they have had the good fortune to escape the contaminating effects of white civilization, are highly ethical in their human relationships—indeed, that one thing has contributed more than any other to their spoliation by the whites. An Indian would scorn to do for personal gain the things that are the very bone and sinew of commercial civilizations. They are chaste and moral to a degree that should bring the blush of shame to the cheeks of those who seek to "civilize," "convert," or "exploit" them as savages. Indian men are frequently forced to deal summarily with white men because of their casual attitude toward Indian women.

Everywhere we went, wherever we had a chance to talk with them at length, we found them not only holding to the tradition of a past greatness, but believing profoundly in their future greatness.

There is a crying need for white men, who ask nothing for themselves, to go among these people and patiently teach and patiently learn. Much may reward such a seeker. It is not improbable that there are men living in Central America today who can read the great calendar stone of the Aztecs and the Mayans and who know where invaluable source material relating to these nations lies hidden; men who know the secrets of medicinal plants and nature lore. The investigator, however, will have to cast his lot with the Indians, eat their food, live in huts as they do, and not concern himself overmuch with the gold that lies in their hills and rivers.

Chapter Eighteen

MINOR MISADVENTURES

OUR muscles, weak after our long convalescence, ached from the unaccustomed strain of the first day's paddling as we headed down the coast towards Salina Cruz. We were more than relieved to find ourselves near Puerto Angel in the late afternoon. The little town, as we approached it, seemed to be a lovely place set well back in a deep cove banked on both sides by high cliffs.

The officials came to meet us as we pulled into the beach. A rotund, jovial Port Captain with a Charlie Chaplin moustache, looked over our papers hurriedly and pronounced them in order. We asked him where we might change our clothes and he suggested the *bodega* (warehouse) just off the beach. As we started off with our shore clothes bag, he called us back and said it was not safe to leave our canoe unguarded. A large crowd of natives had gathered about the boat and were tapping it and pulling at the equipment lashed to the deck. Sensing our uncertainty, he called two of his men and put them in charge of the canoe. We followed him to the warehouse, which was merely a shed on stilts. Behind bags of coffee we changed into our good clothes, and upon emerging were met by the Factor (shipping agent) and the Captain.

"Won't you sit down?" invited the Captain, pointing to a cement bench at the edge of the beach. They made a few polite inquiries about our voyage. We answered them and the conversation languished. Ginger inquired as to their wives and families, but this, contrary to past experience brought uninterested response.

Here we were, all dressed up and nothing to do. Badly spoiled in the native villages, we had grown accustomed to the idea that our appearance ought to call forth some interest. It certainly didn't in Puerto Angel. We told the Captain that we should like to stay all night and he directed us to a place that rented rooms. When we learnt that the price for one night's lodging was five pesos ($2.00), we decided to sleep in the canoe and cook supper on the beach.

With the aid of several natives we pulled the canoe under the warehouse, where we had head room beneath the pilings. It was the only place that we could find.

I had gotten the Captain's permission to build a fire on the beach, but when I began to get the paraphernalia ready for Ginger, the young sports from the village insisted on sticking their noses into everything. I zipped the cockpit shut in disgust. Gangs of small boys, despite the protests of the Port Captain's aide, threw sand on the canoe and generally acted badly. We decided to go for a walk in the hope that they would go home in the meantime.

After a walk through the village with its few adobe houses and thatched huts, we returned to the canoe. Most of the young men and boys had left. I collected driftwood and built a fire, whereupon they promptly returned. Ginger was having a tough time trying to cook in her best dress without soiling it. They poked fun at her toasting tortillas, they tossed sand at our food—wishing audibly that they had nerve enough to toss sand into it. They wrestled on the beach and made loud remarks intended for our ears. Used to the grave, courteous Indians, we could have wrung these offscourings' necks.

An automobile raced into town and slid to a stop close to the beach. A man in European clothes with a notebook and pencil in his hands sprinted towards us. I groaned. "A newspaper reporter." He threw rapid-fire questions at us and showed us clippings from Mexico City papers describing us as "intrepid, gallant adventurers, facing impossible hardships." Ginger squirmed uneasily, the fire went out, and the tortillas grew cold. He left with as much flurry as he had come. Soon high-pitched, elegant Spanish drifted down to us from the Port Captain's office.

We returned to our dinner preparations, to be interrupted this time by a minor port official. "The Captain wishes to see you," he beamed.

"What now?" I muttered to Ginger.

"I will guard the canoe while you are gone," he said.

We plodded up the sand to the Captain's office, Ginger patting her hair into place and powdering her nose as we went. The Captain greeted us with greater cordiality than before and invited us to dinner. The dinner was excellent and we spent a pleasant evening. As we rose to go he suggested that since he had a spare room we should spend the night as his guests. We declined, on the plea of an early start and the necessity of guarding the canoe.

"I will immediately send a telegram to Salina Cruz and tell them that you are coming, so that when you arrive, they will know who you are," he said, with emphasis on the last six words. He was anxious to do anything that he possibly could, he said.

"It makes a lot of difference who people think you are—in some places," I commented to Ginger, as we walked back to camp. "If Mexico City notices us we are big shots in Puerto Angel."

"Don't forget, either," she answered, "that we'd be thrown out of a lot of places if they even suspected that Mexico City had ever heard of us. The Indians aren't interested in Mexico City's pets. Self-interest has something to do with it, you know."

Our "watch dog" was dozing, his back against the canoe. He bade us a sleepy good night and departed. Immediately a group of young bucks put in appearance. Ginger sighed with exasperation, as she took off her shore dress behind the canvas I held round her. We put the canvas over the cockpit and settled down, but not to sleep. The rowdy boys threw sand and small rocks on the hull of the canoe. Ginger muttered, "Civilization certainly doesn't agree with these people."

Our molesters took heart at our silence and grew so annoying that finally we could stand it no longer. "Come on, let's get out of here," I said.

While coming in across the bay I had seen a little graveyard. If I knew my Mexicans, they would hesitate a long while before following us there. Ginger smiled as we paddled across the bay and beached our canoe near the rows of white crosses. We were soon as quiet as our silent companions.

As we pulled out of the bay in the morning we fell to discussing the old question of what benefit our kind of civilization confers upon a people alien to it. The people of Puerto Angel had contacts with the outside world—telephones, the telegraph, roads, a considerable business in shipping, more gadgets than the people of Puerto Escondido had ever heard of, much less possessed. Was the net result in favor of Puerto Angel? We thought not. Puerto Escondido still believed in the traditional culture and values of its Indian heritage. No one there could ever be lonely or hungry or feel shut out in any way because he had no money, or suffer a nervous breakdown because the competitive pace was too stiff for him. He was never idle, as were the peons in Puerto Angel, and his heart couldn't be broken because "industry didn't need him." We both passionately hoped that nothing would ever interfere with the busy, happy, socially useful, communal life of Puerto Escondido, and other places like it.

We spent a pleasant day sailing past little coves, sand beaches, and high cliffs. At times we paddled so close to the rocks that we could reach out and touch them. We landed several times simply for the novelty of being able to do so without shooting heavy surf.

Late in the afternoon we put in at Sacrificios Harbor, and camped in a tiny cove on the north side. After our months of constant association with people the solitude was pleasant, and we stayed over a day for fishing, swimming, and hiking. There were more iguanas here than at any place along the coast.

We sailed leisurely along the beautiful mainland for several hours. The canoe drifted while we dived for shells or stopped to fish. It was hard to believe that we were entering the Gulf of Tehuantepec. It is said to be the most dangerous section along the Pacific coast. Even the great ocean liners shape their courses to avoid its treacherous northers, or hug the coast line less than half a mile from shore in search of some lee against the wind. We consulted the *Pilot Guide,* which said, "These northers sweep across the Isthmus of Tehuantepec from the Gulf of Mexico. Here the wind blows all the year round. The violent northers of the Gulf of Mexico frequently cross the Isthmus through the opening between the Mexican and Guatemala mountains, and blow in sharp squalls. These heavy blasts, which have the local name of 'Tehuantepecers,' blow with great violence from north to north-north-east, raising a very short high sea, and are felt two hundred miles off the coast. They are not indicated by the barometer." This was, indeed, something to think about.

In the afternoon we came to a nice little island lying about three hundred and fifty yards offshore. It is called Cacaluta on the charts, and behind it lies a rather steep but fine sand beach. A canyon opening almost from the water's edge promised game and fresh water. We secured our gear as usual and paddled in behind the island for a landing. "This," I announced, "is going to be easy. Wish all our landings were like this." A small swell picked us up and carried us in. The *Vagabunda's* nose dug into the soft sand, though, owing to the steepness of the beach, her stern was in fairly deep water. As we stepped out a large, frisky swell stole up behind us, picked up the stern, and none too gently brought it down on our heads. We crawled out painfully bruised.

We soon discovered that we had landed in a dry river bed. Up the sandy ravine were a lot of tracks, similar to, but narrower than a turtle's, with a zigzag line between them—as though the creature had pulled a stick behind it. They were alligator tracks, and from the number of the markings we knew that there were many of them. Just back of the beach we found a small lagoon. The only camping place seemed to be where we had landed.

After dinner we circled the lagoon into the back country, hoping to find fresh running water. The whole country was dry. All the wild life seemed to be concentrated on that little lagoon. Walking was slow because every fifty feet we had to stop and pick off the ticks. Each bush and twig was alive with them. In addition to the ticks, mosquitoes, gnats, *jenjenes, mosco cabezones*, and horseflies had picked this spot in which to spend the dry season.

On our way back to the beach we cut in close to the head of the lagoon. Here there was a deep pool with a large tree growing out across it. At the sound of our approach a dozen alligators slid down its steep banks and hid in the water. It occurred to me that it might be fun to lasso an alligator and really get a good look at a live one. I suggested to Ginger that we return in the morning and see what we could do.

We followed the lagoon back to camp and were surprised at the number of alligators concentrated at that point. The rains for several seasons had apparently been negligible, and they had all come down from up the river.

After dark the jungle set up a noise which is like nothing else in the world. The bellowing of the alligators mingled with the screams of a tiger and the crashing of brush, as either pursuer or pursued ran by. There is nothing pastoral about these jungles.

The next morning, armed with a lariat, harpoon, and killing lance, we started up the lagoon. Alligator hunters may have a technique, but we never mastered it. We stalked one after another only to have them slip into the water when we were still a considerable distance away. We gave it up and went back to camp, but our defeat irked us. We decided to try a different method—to go in after the alligator. Authorities say they have underwater caves, but we couldn't find any. We couldn't even see an alligator, though we could see the ripples as they swam round in the shallow water.

We cut long poles and swished round in the shallows, on the theory that the alligator might bite the pole. I kept my harpoon handy. Jabbing with the poles at each step, we came at last to the pool. Here it seemed we had corralled the entire colony. They were constantly in motion, but as they stayed underneath the water it was hopeless to attempt to lasso one. If I wanted an alligator it was apparent that I would have to harpoon it. My plan was to climb the tree that overhung the pool and make my cast from there. Ginger was doubtful about the success of this manœuvre and said that I would only chase the alligators out of the pool. "Not," I said, "if you will stand at the other end and keep them from going out."

"And what's to prevent them from taking a little nip? That wouldn't be so hard with a mouth like a steam shovel. No thank you, Mr. Lamb."

I did induce her, however, to stand on one side and slap the water with her pole in an effort to keep the alligators in the pool.

It was ticklish work climbing the tree, but at last I got fairly well out on a limb that overhung the centre of the pool. The next thing was to find a good throwing position, and I cautiously began worming my way towards a couple of branches that formed a brace. There seemed to be plenty of alligators in the pool below, for each time a twig bent or a bit of bark fell, it caused a great commotion. Ginger, meanwhile, was slapping the water and admonishing me to be careful and not fall off the limb.

I had reached my objective and was getting into position to throw the harpoon, when I heard something crack and Ginger scream. My perch began to sink slowly towards the water. I tried to work my way back to safety but a snag interrupted my progress, and again the limb cracked. Every movement I made resulted in a crack. This slow torture soon ended. The limb gave way with a crash. I plummeted into the pool and hit the water swimming. It seemed to my excited imagination that a thousand gaping jaws were open to receive me as I clawed my way up the bank. I looked round to see how many alligators were following me but they were all going in every direction except the one that I had chosen. I could hear them crashing in the brush.

As we started back to camp with my gun full of mud and my person

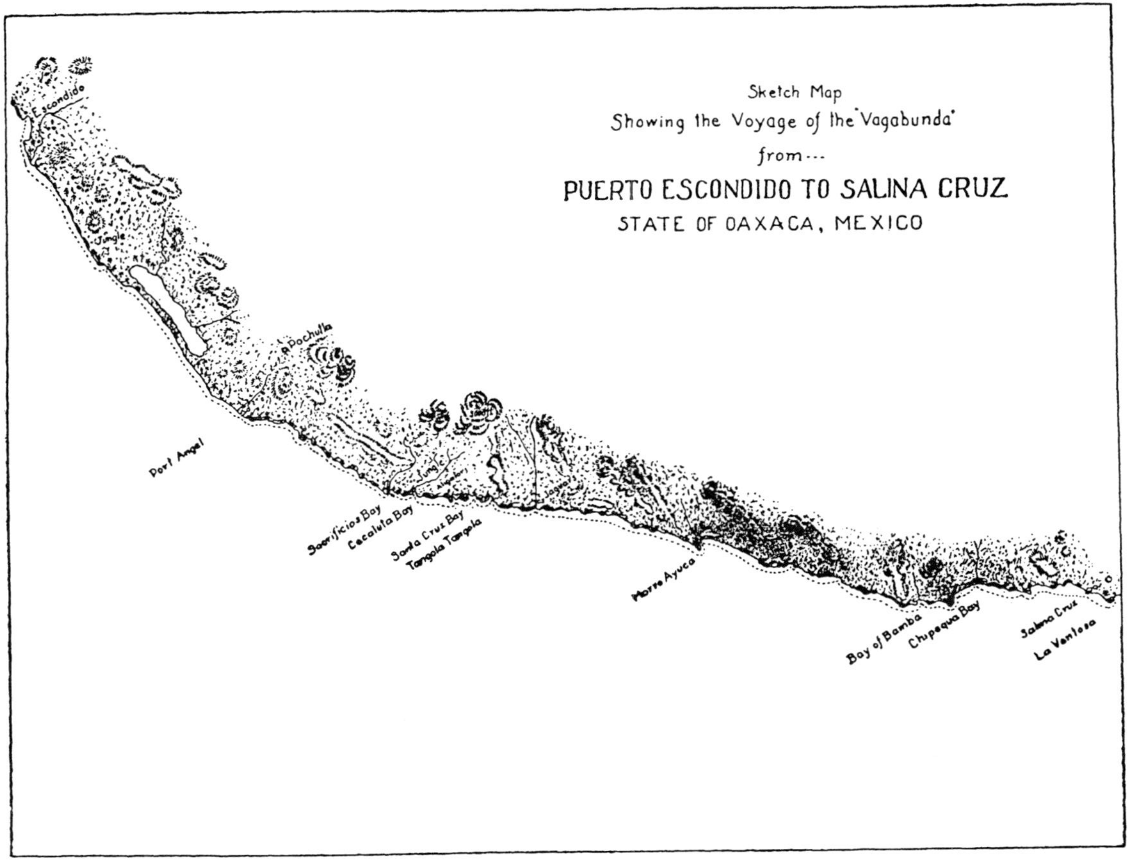
Sketch Map
Showing the Voyage of the "Vagabunda"
from...
PUERTO ESCONDIDO TO SALINA CRUZ
STATE OF OAXACA, MEXICO
Escondido
Jungle
R. Pochulla
Port Angel
Sacrificios Bay
Cacaluta Bay
Santa Cruz Bay
Tangola Tangola
Morro Ayuca
Bay of Bamba
Chipequa Bay
Salina Cruz
La Ventosa

covered with it, Ginger began to laugh hysterically. I demanded to know what seemed so funny. "Oh, everything," she gasped. "The alligators beating you out of the pool—and you—trying to swim in three feet of water—and there were only four of them—and they were just as frightened as you were——"

The next morning, with no further nonsense, we shot two large alligators. The rest of the day was spent preparing their hides, which, because of their thickness and toughness, would make good sandals.

Down the coast the following day we came to a deep little bay called Puerto Guatulco. As there was a village at the head of the bay, we about faced and went down a little further to a place called Tangolunda. Seeing no sign of natives, we landed on a smooth beach on the south side of a great cliff which jutted out into the tiny bay.

A cursory examination of the back country showed it to be swampy and almost impenetrable, so we returned to camp. Two natives were standing by the canoe, handling our equipment and fishing gear. This was an immediate warning, for a native will rarely examine anything without first asking permission. I started towards them with Ginger following. She was wearing shorts, and deciding it was better not to appear before them in such scanty garb, she returned to camp.

They were unpleasant-looking customers with shifty eyes and proffered an indolent greeting in Spanish. I started to return their greeting, then changed my mind, and nodded my head, grinning. "Do you speak Spanish?" one of them asked.

I shook my head and said, "No sabe." This expression leaves little doubt in a native's mind about one's ability to speak Spanish. *No se* is correct. "No sabe" is similar to "I doesn't know" in English.

"I would like to buy this spear. How much do you want for it?" one of them asked. They winked at each other when I made no reply.

"He wants just two bullets," said one of them. "Just two bullets."

"No," said the other. "He wants *one* bullet, because I want the lady."

I could have killed them on the spot, but I made no reply. They watched me narrowly, waiting to see what I would do. Then they looked at each other, tossed the equipment back on deck, and without further words sauntered off towards the cliff. As long as they were in sight, I walked slowly back to camp. When they had passed from view, we hurriedly packed everything, and Ginger stood guard while I carried the equipment to the canoe.

We pushed off, paddling as fast as we could and looking back every few strokes towards the beach. Then we saw them running out of the brush south of where our camp had been. They had circled back through the dense undergrowth and had come out on the opposite side with the clear intention of ambushing us.

I ducked and reached for my gun as Ginger warned, "They're going to shoot!" One fellow was taking careful aim with his rifle. Smoke blotted out his figure, and a bullet whined overhead.

We opened up on the pair of them at the same moment, emptying our clips, and from then on there was nothing to shoot at. After refilling our clips we went back to the paddles and were soon in the heavy chop of the ocean, which gave every indication that a storm was on its way.

Rather than ride out a storm all night we hoisted sail and headed back for Puerto Guatulco. Dirty weather struck us before we were half-way, and we fought through the chop until 9 P.M., when we entered the shelter of the bay.

No lights gleamed from the village and it was too dark to attempt a landing, so we pulled in under the shelter of a small point and dropped our tiny anchor. We could see nothing, and it was impossible to know how far from shore we were. Heavy swells coming in rocked the boat violently.

Throughout the tedious night we took turns keeping watch, but sunrise brought little comfort. Our anchorage was precarious; black rocks thrust their jagged heads out of the water round us; and the storm still raged outside. Why we weren't crushed upon them during the night remains a mystery.

The country ahead looked hungry—just as hungry as we were, for we had not eaten since noon of the previous day. As we worked our way closer inshore, we could see no signs of life round the village. That in itself was not reassuring. No dogs barked, no donkeys brayed, not one rooster crowed at the rising sun.

Ginger objected to landing. "What do you want to do?" she asked. "Get shot at?" So I left her in the canoe with the sail up and ready for a quick retreat, while I cautiously waded towards the beach.

My trigger finger felt jumpy as I tied the stern line to a boulder and approached the nearest hut. Peeking warily into doorways, I saw that their interiors presented the same desolation that prevailed outside. The houses had not been occupied for several months at least, and marauding animals had wrought havoc with what few possessions the natives had left behind.

After beaching the canoe, we started out to find what story this deserted village had to tell. It was beautifully situated, and had at one time housed at least two hundred people. A fertile valley lay behind it and there was nothing to account for its desertion, unless, as Ginger suggested, an epidemic had killed off the villagers. The tiny graveyard did not confirm the theory. There were many graves but none of them was very recent.

A wide path led from the village to the back country. Following that we came to an old well of Spanish masonry. Only a little water remained at the bottom. This was undoubtedly the reason why the natives had left their village. There was enough for our use, however, and we walked back to get our five-gallon still cans and the lariat.

Back at the well I lowered myself by means of the lariat, and cleaned the debris from the little pool. Ginger let the can down and after the water had settled I filled it. I scrambled up the mossy sides of the old well and when I reached the top, started pulling the heavy can up after me. As I leaned over the brink to grab it the improvised handle pulled loose and the can went hurtling to the bottom. We looked at each other in dismay. It was smashed beyond repair.

Going down again, I filled the second can, making the line fast, not only to the bail, but round the can as well. Back at the beach it was so depressing that we went to the outer extremity of the bay, where we found a little canyon, before setting up camp.

While Ginger got breakfast, I fastened the heavy can securely to a crossbar over the fire, where twenty minutes boiling would kill whatever germs were in it.

In the afternoon we went hunting. The next day would be our wedding anniversary, and Ginger felt that it called for an especially nice meal. All day I had been trying vainly to think of something I might give her for a present. I had wanted to make her a bag from alligator skins, but they were not yet sufficiently cured. One small turkey was the result of our afternoon's tramp and we broiled it for supper.

Afterwards we sailed out in the canoe to have a look at the ocean. It was still raging, so we reluctantly returned to camp. The tide had gone out, and because of the rocks we could not beach the canoe. As we manœuvred for a safe anchorage, Ginger slipped on the wet deck and sprawled on her face, almost going over the side. A black object flashed over her shoulder and into the water. She grabbed for her holster but the gun was gone.

I attached a fishline to a heavy sinker and dropped it as near to the spot as possible. With this as a marker I dived for the gun, but the heavy surge kicked up so much sand that I could see nothing. It was soon too dark to continue, so I abandoned the search until the next day. Ginger sobbed herself to sleep.

We were up at daylight, and while she prepared breakfast I went out to cut a forked stick to use as a scraper in hunting for the gun. I reached in my pocket for my knife, and let out a yell. It, too, was gone.

Our anniversary was a dismal day. I dived until I was exhausted, rested awhile, and then dived again. Ginger did her best to hide how much she felt the loss of her gun. It had been my first anniversary gift to her and she was attached to it for that reason as well as for its usefulness.

Before darkness fell, I went out to have one more try. The incoming tide had washed a lot of the sand away, and here and there black spots were visible. I swam from one to another, and finally, just as I was about to abandon the search, my hand closed on the twenty-two.

I wrapped it up in leaves and tied it with fibre. By my place at supper lay a small package wrapped in leaves, tied with grass, and decorated with coco fibre. We unwrapped our packages together. Mine was the lost pocket knife.

The norther held us up for four days. The second day we ran out of water and had to distil it from sea water without the use of our second can. By splitting a sapling and taking out the pith, then wrapping it tightly with vines, we managed to make a second pipe of sorts. This and our original copper tubing I attached to our canteens, using the five-gallon can as the "steamer." Wrapping the canteens in bits of wet clothing, we kept them cool enough for the steam to condense. At first the makeshift wooden pipe lost more steam than passed through it, but as its fibres swelled it worked fairly well. The water tasted woody but was not too unpalatable. Under the circumstances we were not fussy.

We finally got away from that miserable little beach, but we fought heavy weather day and night. In our anxiety to reach Salina Cruz we passed up one or two fair landings, hoping to keep on until we reached the Bay of Bamba. There we intended to stop long enough to replenish our water and food.

Sailing became increasingly difficult. Short high seas, fifteen feet high and only twenty feet from crest to crest, had the canoe standing on her bow or stern practically all the time. As we entered the Bay of Bamba the wind increased. The canoe was taking such a beating that we could see her bend, and could occasionally hear the splintering of wood. It took two hours to make the half-mile to the beach. While landing in the small but powerful surf, the canoe was picked up by a breaker and I was thrown off the stern. This time, as the canoe rolled on top of me, I got a badly wrenched knee. The canoe had five broken ribs, splintered siding, and a cracked gunwale.

The wind was blowing so hard that it was impossible to set up camp. We pulled the canoe high on the beach, piled the equipment in the lee of it, arranged a canvas shelter over the cockpit, and tried to sleep. The deafening roar of the wind made it difficult. Sometime during the night the canoe seemed to drop into a pit where it careened over on its side. I was sure that a violent earthquake had rocked us. An investigation showed that the wind had blown the sand out from round the canoe, leaving it on a sort of pedestal; then had blown the canoe off the pedestal and into the hole.

We had to remain here for six days. Part of the time it was impossible to hunt, and almost impossible to gather firewood, to build a fire, or even stand up. We nearly starved. Game could be found only in the densest undergrowth, where it took shelter from the wind. The air was filled with particles of sand which cut our faces. Out to sea we could see large freighters fighting their way close to shore, but the spray was so heavy that they were merely blurred outlines.

Finally the norther blew itself out and we set to work repairing the canoe. One morning while we were thus engaged we found ourselves surrounded by a band of natives. They were of the mixed nomadic breeds found along this section of the coast. One of the men had his foot bandaged in a filthy rag. There were too many of them to fight, and as they carried rifles it seemed expedient to deflect their purpose, before their intentions had time to crystallize. I immediately walked over, and with a big smile, gave the "familiar greeting" to the man with the injured foot, announcing in the same breath that I was a doctor. I asked to see his foot, which with evident relief he unwrapped at once for my inspection. He had stepped on a thorn, part of which was still in the nasty, suppurating wound. I removed it, cleansed and disinfected the wound, packed it with a bit of clean gauze soaked in permanganate, and bound it with a clean rag. Then I gave him a dose of raw quinine. Its vicious taste convinced him of its efficacy. He stepped on his doctored foot gingerly, and was all smiles. Ginger made them coffee, and that sealed the bargain. They lived near-by for the two days that we remained. They not only caused no trouble but were very friendly. The injured man was leader of the group, and with his support we could doubtless have remained indefinitely. They came down to see us off and seemed to feel real regret at our departure.

From here on we had fair sailing down the coast to Salina Cruz.

Chapter Nineteen

THE COUNTRY OF CORTEZ

IT WAS the hour before dawn, but not even the rough cold seas breaking over us in the darkness could chill our enthusiasm. We were waiting impatiently just outside the breakwater of the outer harbour for the sun to show us Salina Cruz. Not because we had heard that it was the greatest Mexican port on the Pacific, had it become so important to us. During our flight from the malaria-infested lagoon, Salina Cruz had spelled safety. Back in Puerto Escondido, to our fever-ridden minds it had meant ice, clean white beds, milk, everything that civilization represents to sick and frightened people away from home. Now it meant American ships, American food, and contact with our own people. It would be, we hoped, something like finding the *Valkyrien* at San Lucas.

So we waited impatiently, while the sun came over a cloud bank in the east, and the black mountains took on the colours of early morning. It was still too dark to distinguish objects clearly, but we strained our eyes in an attempt to see the masts of ships above the long line of warehouses that came slowly into view. As we pointed the *Vagabunda's* nose between the two great breakwaters, we sighed happily.

Now the port was bathed in the brilliant light of a tropical sunrise, but we simply sat and stared—unwilling to believe our eyes. Not a ship was in sight. The immense concrete docks with their long lines of warehouses were crumbling and deserted. Sections of their corrugated roofs, ripped loose by the destructive northers, hung flapping in the stiff breeze. Where vessels had sailed between the arms of the breakwaters, angry seas now pounded upon a sand bar. Not even the tiny *Vagabunda* could enter. The drawbridge between the inner and outer harbours was suspended half open. Behind it, the port of Salina Cruz lay dead.

Reluctantly we swung the *Vagabunda's* bow towards the rocky coast ahead. Half unbelieving, we could hardly drag our eyes away from that colossal ruin. Even the great steel beacon on the end of the breakwater looked as if it were about to fall into the sea. We asked each other what could have happened. Modern capital seeks to protect its own, and those silent buildings, those giant cranes and docks, represented an investment of millions. Later we learned the reasons for that failure.

The opening of the Panama Canal was partially responsible for the death of Salina Cruz. We were told that in 1912 Salina Cruz was considered the most difficult port in the world through which to clear ships. Every ship that entered port was a signal for a fight between erratic port officials and angry captains, who were fined by the former on the slightest pretext. It took a great deal more money than the amount necessary to pay for unloading and transshipping cargo, and the usual port fees, to clear a ship from Salina Cruz. Parts of cargoes were lost or stolen while they were being shuttled across the Isthmus by the railroad which connected Salina Cruz with Puerto Mexico on the east coast. In the scramble to determine whose cargo should clear first, there were more than hints of intrigue by representatives of the great maritime powers. The drama of graft, theft, and intrigue ended with the opening of the Canal. No, Salina Cruz was not entirely the innocent victim of progress.

We sighed, as cold, wet, hungry, and a little sad, we bent our heads to the shower of spray and sailed by.

"Well, where do we go from here?" asked Ginger wearily, as she got out the *Pilot Guide*. Shielding it from the spray with her body, she turned to a description of the coast south of Salina Cruz. She read, "La Ventosa Bay, to the northward and eastward of the Point, is about two miles wide and but little over one half-mile in extent. Landing here is difficult even in the best of weather."

"Let's try La Ventosa," I said. "We ought to stop somewhere for repairs before we tackle the rest of the Gulf. If we can't make La Ventosa, we'll have to go on to Champerico, Guatemala."

As we headed into the teeth of the wind, we saw high up on the headland that formed the point a small, square masonry tower. According to the *Pilot Guide*, it had been built by Cortez, the first lighthouse on the west coast of North America. "Well," said Ginger, as she gazed at the sturdy stone tower, "if Cortez could land here, we can."

I laughed, for the idea of any one duplicating the feats of the redoubtable Conquistador was funny.

Beating our way against the strong blasts of wind, we ran at last into the little bay of La Ventosa. Back from its beach was a small warehouse and a pier whose seaward end terminated in dry sand, for the bay was filling in. Several natives appeared and waved us to the proper landing place.

Shooting the light surf, we were met by a group of bare-to-the-waist, smiling fishermen, who helped us unload and carry the canoe to the beach. "Where is your Port Captain?" I asked. "We wish to enter port."

"He will be here shortly, when he has changed into his uniform," one of them answered.

Our group of friendly hosts increased by two's and three's, while we waited for the Port Captain. Without the pomposity so frequently assumed by his fellows in other ports, he looked over our papers and pronounced them in good order. He was not the Port Captain, he said, as he instructed us to follow him to the warehouse. In the little room which served as an office, he stepped to an old-fashioned telephone which was nailed to the wall, and began to crank it vigorously.

After much cranking and hammering on the battered box, he got his number. "Ah, *mi Capitán*," he announced, "a ship has arrived . . . yes, her papers are in order. . . . No, *Capitán*, she cannot anchor in that location. . . . But *Capitán*, that is impossible. . . ." He became so excited and talked so rapidly that we could scarcely follow his staccato Spanish. We heard him reiterate over and over, "Yes, it is a ship, but a little ship . . . yes, it has all the papers, but she cannot anchor in the bay. . . . Look, *Capitán*," he wailed at last in desperation as he pointed the receiver towards the beach, "here it comes now . . . two men are carrying it across the sand. Yes, it is the *Vagabunda*. . . . That is right, the Señor and the Señora Lamb." He hung up the phone and beamed at us. "*El Capitán del Puerto* is coming to meet you. Until then I am at your service."

The thing we wanted to do most was to change into our shore clothes before greeting "*El Capitán*." Mexicans, like other people, are impressed by clothes, and it always raised our social status to be correctly attired when meeting them. This was particularly true in Ginger's case, as they were by no means used to young ladies in shorts.

The official offered us the use of his office, with apologies that there was nothing better. We grabbed our shore clothes bag, barred the door of the little office, and pulled off our wet clothes.

Ginger's anguished wail filled the room, as she surveyed her one and only dress. We had shipped considerable water in our battle with the norther and some of it had found its way through the mast seat into the cockpit. Our good clothes had received just enough of a soaking to stamp the flowers from Ginger's blue print dress upon my white pants and shirt. We finally laughed off our chagrin and donned the streaked garments anyway.

As we stepped out of the little office, the crowd eyed us curiously. I explained our plight, to the sound of much laughter. A kind-faced old woman stepped up to Ginger, and placing her arms round her shoulders, said, "It is also our custom to give flowers—but not to white pants. Come, let us go to my house and we will see what can be done about it."

She introduced herself as Doña Facunda, and as we made our way up a winding road to a group of huts we were met and cordially greeted by her husband, Don Juan.

Their house was large, for in addition to the main room which was fifty feet square, there were three semi-detached anterooms. One was used as a kitchen during the rainy season, one as a store room, and the third as a spare room. They were built of the same materials and in the same manner as the other native structures throughout the area. The roofs were well thatched and wide-eaved to shed the rain, and were supported by poles.

The sides of the hut were of lattice work. The furnishings were simple. The main room housed the altar, stove, metate, olla, a handhewn table and benches, and several hammocks. The hard earthen floors were freshly swept and everything looked clean and neat. We were more than glad to accept Doña Facunda's and Don Juan's invitation to stay with them while in La Ventosa.

While Ginger and Doña Facunda discussed ways and means of bleaching my pants, provided they could be gotten off me long enough, Don Juan and I talked over the problem of repairing the canoe and equipment. He suggested that we could secure the use of the warehouse for our operations.

Our deliberations were interrupted by the rattle and bang of an antiquated Ford truck, which, together with many voices, announced the arrival of a large delegation from Salina Cruz. The truck, loaded to capacity with all the leading citizens and officials who could crowd into it, had bumped its way over the three miles of dusty road that separated the two communities.

My decorated pants were again the subject of much good-natured raillery. The Port Captain later confessed that he had prepared an impressive address of welcome, but had become speechless at sight of my pants.

Neither Doña Facunda nor Don Juan took any part in the festivities after the arrival of the others, but busied themselves in preparing coffee for the crowd. Our host and hostess were Zapotec Indians, the others, Mexicans of the official and commercial classes; and there was a distinct barrier between the two.

The Port Captain took complete charge of the arrangements. We must all go to Salina Cruz, he announced. Our equipment had been brought into the spare room by the fishermen, and we retired to select the things that we had learned from past experience to take with us. Since we frequently made unplanned detours on the trip, we always took along our mess kit, tent, guns, camera and films, rough clothes, machetes, diaries, and credentials. The rest of the equipment we carefully packed into the box and locked.

Don Juan and I left the party long enough to go to the warehouse, where we placed the canoe upon crosspieces in one corner, and stacked the paddles, harpoon, and sail on deck. Don Juan was mystified by these extensive preparations. "You are going away for a long time?" he asked.

"I don't think so," I replied, "but if we are not back in a few days, I hope you will take good care of our things."

"*Sí, Señor*," he replied. "Do not worry, I will take good care of everything."

Returning to the hut, we found the visitors from Salina Cruz anxious to depart. They eyed very curiously, our packsack with its two machetes strapped to the outside, but they asked no questions.

As we rattled off in the crowded truck towards Salina Cruz, we gazed with interest at the low, flat country that had been Cortez' domain. This was the State of Oaxaca, which a grateful sovereign had given him with the title of Marquess of the Valley of Oaxaca, and here he had made his home. The landscape was dotted with odd-looking trees, whose great trunks were out of all proportion to their height. They were devoid of leaves but on the tip of each little branch was a bright yellow flower. Inland were the peaks of the continental divide, and seaward the low, barren hills shut off all view of the ocean.

After three miles of bumping along a flat dusty road, we came up over a little rise and there below us lay Salina Cruz. The streets, with their rows of great empty houses, were deserted except for an occasional oxcart or a lone pedestrian. In the port's heyday, the wide, well-laid-out streets must have been impressive. Now the wind had undermined the paving and traffic was possible only where the drifting sand covered the jagged, sagging paving blocks. The once ornamental street lights had become pieces of rusted iron, their foundation blocks laid bare by the destructive winds. We rattled past the great railroad terminal, where formerly twenty trains a day had arrived from Puerto Mexico, and an equal number had left for the Atlantic seaport. We came to a final stop before the once famous Guasti Hotel where the few inhabitants of Salina Cruz now made their headquarters.

As we stepped inside, we were met by a Chinese who ushered us into the dining room. Here, gathered in our honour, were other important residents of Salina Cruz. Among them were the *Jefe de Aduana* (chief of the custom house), the Generalissimo of the garrison, the manager of the cable office, the *Presidente Municipal*, and others.

The meal that was placed before us rivalled anything that we had dreamed of. It consisted of soup, a salad of green vegetables, four meat courses with vegetables, broiled fish, stuffed peppers, and other delicious dishes. Let no one be misled by the tamale and chile con carne of commerce into thinking that they represent the Mexican cuisine—they emphatically do not. In addition to these foods, we ate quantities of cheese, and drank milk, coffee with cream, and cold beer. The dessert course found us stuffed like boas and unable even to taste the papaya and other fruits.

Immediately after dinner most of our hosts excused themselves for the siesta hour. During the meal we had become especially friendly with the chief of the cable office, who now invited us to his house. He had been studying English, which he spoke fairly well, and was glad of an opportunity to use it. He also politely suggested that it might be well for me to don a pair of his pants while my own were being bleached. This seemed like a good idea, and they were promptly dispatched to a washerwoman for treatment, while we enjoyed a good siesta.

The evening brought with it more food, which almost wrecked us, for we were unaccustomed to such gargantuan meals. The conversation during the evening turned to Tehuantepec and the Tehuana Indians. We sat listening avidly to the glowing accounts of the beautiful city and its interesting inhabitants. When they urged us by all means to see it, we had already made up our minds to go.

We had tried our luck at gold mining in the little creeks and rivers as we came down the coast, and had collected several ounces of the metal. I sold the gold that night, and at four-thirty the next morning we were sitting with Señor Jiminez, our host and escort, in the first-class compartment of the train bound for Tehuantepec.

The first-class compartment, which was placed at the end of the train, differed from the second-class accommodation only in having wicker-covered seats. Besides ourselves and Señor Jiminez there was only one other first-class passenger. I nudged Ginger, "Wouldn't you like to ride in front with the People?" She grinned as we made our way to the car ahead. It, too, was only partially filled, since most of the second-class passengers were still on the station platform. We craned our necks out of the windows to watch them. Though it was not yet daylight, and in spite of the fact that many of them had journeyed long distances carrying heavy burdens, they laughed and chattered together like magpies. Some of them carried big wicker baskets full of fresh or dried fish on their heads; others carried huge bundles of tortillas, corn, and garden produce to be sold in Tehuantepec; still others carried live chickens tied by the feet. A shrill blast of the whistle sent them scurrying to the train where they all tried to squeeze through the doors at once, or pass their chickens and bundles through the windows to friends inside. They scrambled and fell over each other in their race for seats, reminding us of a group of school children starting off on a picnic. The train, without further warning, jerked and wheezed out of the station.

Every seat was filled with passengers and their huge hand-woven baskets. They were all most friendly as we walked through the train exchanging greetings with them. Every little while the train stopped at some *rancherio* where more passengers got on.

The ten-mile trip took two hours. The country looked flat and uninteresting from the train windows. Its brushy expanse was broken occasionally by the cleared fields of some small farm. The few way stations were in almost complete ruin.

The Indians were sufficiently interesting, however, to make the trip seem anything but tedious. They were Zapotecs and a more picturesque crowd would be difficult to find. All of the women were dressed in long flowing skirts with elaborately ruffled flounces. Their blouses were sleeveless, with round necks and three yellow stripes coming down over the shoulders and forming a square at the waist line. They were good-looking, pleasant people and we liked them at once.

Suddenly a buzz of excitement ran through the train and when, upon inquiry, we found that we were about to enter Tehuantepec, we hastened back to our compartment. Our host eyed us disapprovingly and tactfully intimated that it was not wise for first-class people to associate with second-class people. This little homily was delivered more in sorrow than in anger, but it was intended to let us know precisely how upper-class Mexicans felt about natives—you couldn't be on terms of social equality with both. However, the present President of Mexico, Cárdenas, is a Tarascan Indian, and the time will come when the Indians will play a more dominant rôle in the southern republic.

The train now moved slowly among the thickly massed thatched huts which carpeted the beautiful valley, and along the winding Tehuantepec River. The train stopped, but none of the passengers moved. This was not the city, we were informed, but one of the seven *barrios* into which the city of Tehuantepec is divided. The main part of the city lies across the river. There we were in a different land. Everywhere were dense tropical gardens. On both sides of the track, hemming in the station, were papaya, mango, banana, coco-nut, *zapote*, and many other trees. Crowds of gaily dressed natives awaited the train, laughing, talking and calling out greetings to the passengers. Above the din I called to Ginger, "This is the place we have been looking for." She was unable to hear me and her face was a question mark, so I yelled louder, "This is the place. Look at them. Everyone is smiling, at seven o'clock in the morning, too."

Gradually the noise subsided as the people started towards town in a procession. Even our host entered into the spirit of the thing as he took each of us by an arm. The three of us fell in line behind a plump Tehuana woman. The spirit of merriment was so contagious that we laughed and joked as we jostled our way into Tehuantepec.

Both Ginger and I were all eyes as we made our way down the street towards the market. It was a scene of dazzling colour. Well-constructed buildings, painted in bright hues and made of plaster, mason work, and adobe, with tile roofs, lined the streets. Flowers filled every patio. In every nook and corner where a plant could grow, they bloomed. Tehuantepec should be called "The City of Flowers."

Now we turned our attention to the gorgeously attired Tehuana Indian women whom we met in increasing numbers. Their clothes had embroidered flower designs in bright colours, in addition to the three stripes down the shoulders and across the waist, which seems to be a tribal distinction. The Tehuanas are a branch of the great Zapotecan tribe which dominates southern Mexico. Immaculate white lace ruffles edged their full skirts and they occasionally wore the *huipil*, the distinctive white headdress of the Tehuana women. They carried themselves with dignity and grace. They were simply magnificent. If they did not wear the headdress, they had bright-coloured ribbons entwined in their hair, and some wore coronets of flowers.

The market itself was a great building without sides, its roof supported by pillars. Our Zapotecan acquaintances of the train found themselves places here and, uncovering their wares, set up shop.

We sauntered through a lane of venders to an eating establishment which occupied one of the booths. Here we seated ourselves at a tiny table, while the barefoot proprietress bustled round a charcoal stove made from a five-gallon oil can. She soon brought our breakfast of fried eggs, *empanadas de frijoles* (a tortilla folded over a filling of beans and then fried), and some very black coffee.

During the meal we listened intently to the people round us, but we seldom heard a familiar word. They used the Spanish names for things that had been introduced by Europeans, such as glass, table cloth, buckets, and similar objects, but otherwise retained their native speech. To our ears it sounded much like Chinese. We picked up a few words from the old lady who served our breakfast, such as the Zapotecan word for water, *nisa* (pronounced neesah). The language is not written and one can only guess at the spelling.

Very few men were in evidence, and in answer to our inquiries we were told that they were in the fields. Tehuana women are emancipated in the good old suffragist meaning of the word. They handle all the money, do all the buying and selling, and manage their homes and persons to suit themselves. As one of them explained, "Men do not understand business. It is better that they produce the things for us to sell."

After breakfast Señor Jiminez guided us round town and introduced us to the various officials and other people of importance. The winding streets made us walk long distances to reach relatively near-by places. The twelve thousand inhabitants live in seven *barrios*, or wards. These different sections have separate communal interests, such as fiestas and religious ceremonies. This happy circumstance makes it possible for the festive Tehuanas to attend a party every night if they are so inclined, since one is almost certain to find some sort of celebration going on in one of the seven *barrios*.

The summit of the brush-covered hill which rises almost from the centre of town is crowned by a small chapel. From this vantage point the view of the surrounding country was superb. A brilliant mosaic of flower-filled patios, winding river, emerald fields, multi-coloured tile roofs, and, in the far distance, mountains of misted pearl spread round and below us.

The scene gave us a clearer perception of the people who had been moulded by this environment. Their gaily-coloured garments, their bright-hued handicrafts in the market place, their mobile, laughing faces were but a reflection of the beauty of the river and mountain, the flowers and fields. Their quiet, unhurried movements, their spontaneous gaiety, reflected the languors of a tropic sun.

There were fresh flowers on the steps of the little chapel, but it, as well as the great cathedral in the centre of the town, was closed. This was true of almost all the Catholic churches during our sojourn in Mexico. Nominally Catholic, the native religion is a strange fusion of primitive superstition and church dogma. The Indians are innately and incurably religious. The government's contention that the Church's moral leadership was subordinated to its desire for political control led to the closing of the churches. The reaction of the people to this policy had its parallel when the United States passed the eighteenth amendment. Deprived of their churches, they built altars in their homes. Priests, ousted from their easy living, either abandoned their vocation or became earnest propagandists for the Faith. No longer a privileged caste, they threw in their lot with the natives. This has had a powerful effect upon the naturally religious Indian, who feels that now, for the first time, his church understands his problems and his needs.

We spent much time with the Indians during our two years in Mexico, and it is our belief that Catholicism is stronger among them now than at any other time since the Conquest. If it is to last, however, it will have to retain most of its present complexion, for the Indian will not submit again to the old tyranny.

Señor Jiminez took us to the home of one of his Tehuana friends. Big doors opened into a high-walled patio that fronted the street, and flower-bordered paths led to the house. The house was built in an L, with a high wall surrounding the two open sides. The long, tile-covered porch was gaily decked with hammocks. Inside the rooms were furnished with wicker and leather, which, with a profusion of ferns and flowers, gave the house an atmosphere of simplicity and coolness.

Our hostess, Doña Lupe, with her two daughters, Conchita and Maria, greeted us graciously. We were comfortably established in hammocks and served a *refresco* of limeade, a delicious cooling drink made from the wild lime. The wild, tree-ripened lime has a flavour and an aroma not found in the green-picked limes which are shipped to the United States.

Luncheon consisted of green salad, cheese, and enchiladas made with the soft white native cheese. As we sat and talked at the luncheon table we felt that we were having a rare and barely hoped for opportunity to become acquainted with these people and their way of living.

Maria, who had been looking at my pants quite steadily for some time, could no longer control her laughter. "But I can't help it," she laughed, "each of them is so reminiscent of the other." The laundress at Salina Cruz had laboured in vain, for the blue flowers were still apparent. Ginger's dress had not fared too well in the exchange either. We knew we must look ridiculous, and laughed with the rest.

Later in the afternoon the women took Ginger, and, with much giggling, closed the door of the bedroom behind them.

Our host, who had returned from the city, escorted me to a secluded place and produced a pair of local trousers which looked like white pyjama pants. I put them on, and with a broad blue sash round my waist felt much more comfortable than I had. My original pants were sent to the washerwoman with instructions that they were to be bleached.

As I sat talking with the men, a young woman dressed in native costume entered the room—a friend of the house, I assumed, after glancing at her casually. Then she grinned, and I looked at her again. It was Ginger arrayed in full Tehuana costume, which she wore as though to the manner born. The full blue skirt was heavily embroidered with flowers, and the starched white lace ruffle, about eight inches wide, just cleared the ground when she walked. From beneath it one had a glimpse of bare brown feet. Her round-necked red blouse was embroidered both front and back, and had the three yellow stripes across the shoulders and the waist. Round her head was a bright scarf, and a flower was tucked over her ear. Doña Lupe regretfully explained that she could not lend her the *huipil*, the distinctive white headdress, since this was a religious symbol, the right to wear it passing from mother to daughter, and not extending to outsiders. The *huipil* symbolizes the dress of the Sacred Christ Child, the Señora told us. And it actually is a dress. The full, pleated skirt forms a frame for the face, while the rest of the garment is draped over the back of the head.

Ginger looked very natural and at ease as she laughed and talked with the other women. Though our hair and eyes were lighter, our skins were as brown as theirs. Our knowledge of the country, the idiomatic Spanish that we used, and the insight we had gained into the psychology of native peoples all helped us to fit ourselves into the life at Tehuantepec.

Maria and Conchita, anxious to exhibit their new "Tehuana" friend among their old acquaintances, insisted that we go for a walk with them. We started, the girls and Ginger ahead, the men following. With elaborate ceremonies, Ginger was introduced to each friend that they met. Once they stopped, and with much laughter transferred Ginger's flower from above the right ear to the left, where theirs were worn. This puzzled me, but Ginger explained later that they were palming her off as an unmarried woman. A flower worn over the left ear indicates that the girl is unmarried; if worn on the right, married.

We strolled round the plaza and along tree-shaded streets until it was time to return to the house, where Doña Lupe had the evening meal waiting: hot *pan dulce*, a sweet bread similar to coffee cake; tortillas toasted with a relish-spread, cheese, hot coffee, and fresh pineapple. Afterwards everyone congregated on the porch, where they lounged in hammocks and laughed and gossiped in the musical clipped Spanish of the Tehuanas.

We talked of the town, and how happy everyone seemed to be. They were by far the happiest people we had seen in Mexico. Doña Lupe smiled as she said, "How could we be otherwise? We live surrounded by flowers." It was not entirely that, we knew; but it was the combination of a people with a flair for gracious living, and an environment that matched their needs.

Then they began to question us about our trip. We told them of our many adventures and of our desire to explore the unknown sections of Mexico and Central America. At that our host said something that made us sit up like bird dogs on the scent.

"Have you ever heard," he asked, "of the mountainous territory to the south of the Isthmus of Tehuantepec, which some of our people call the 'Forbidden Land'?" When we disclaimed knowledge of it he continued, "It is said that all those who enter it meet death. We do not know if this is true, but strange things certainly do happen to those people who attempt to penetrate this area. There is a man in Tehuantepec lying on his deathbed now, who only last week entered this country in search of lost cattle."

"What happened to him? Why is he dying?" I asked.

"Nothing really happened, Señor, in the ordinary sense. Nevertheless, the man is dying. You see, one of the beliefs concerning this place is that it is a Spirit Land, where the soul goes after death. Many people also believe that at the time of approaching death, the spirit of a dead friend or relative appears before the person who is about to die. The old spirit comes to act as guide and counsellor to the new spirit starting upon its unfamiliar journey to the land beyond life. This is the belief of the man who is now dying. He is sure that as he entered this country to search for his cattle, he was met by the spirit of a long dead friend. They talked together for a while, then his friend disappeared. This visitation was a summons, so he came back home and prepared himself for death."

"Would it be possible," I asked, "for us to visit this dying man?"

"Why, yes, we know the family very well," he answered. "Tomorrow we will go to see him."

This story so stirred our curiosity that we asked many questions about this "Forbidden Land." We were told other superstitions concerning it, and given some of the reasons why Indians of their own accord do not penetrate the high, mountainous plateaus of Mexico and Central America. The primary reason is that the land is of no use to them. An agricultural people, they are only interested in land of sufficient fertility and with sufficient water to grow crops. Having established themselves in country suited to their purpose, they see no reason for leaving it and seldom do so. The only natives who will go into the back country are the hardy *chicleros*, the native chicle hunters, in search of the *chicozapote* or sapodilla tree, from whose sap chewing gum is made. Used to the hardships and hazards of their difficult occupation, the *chicleros* nevertheless refuse to enter the Forbidden Land, although they travel for long distances into other sections of the back country equally difficult to penetrate. They, too, believe that it is menaced.

The Country of Cortez

Were there any evidences, other than native superstitions, to support the belief that this was a dangerous and difficult land to enter, we asked.

"Yes," replied our host, "there are." He then told us the story of a Mexican army that sometime after the Revolution of 1910, under the leadership of Feliz Diaz, revolted in Vera Cruz and was forced to retreat from the town of Matias Romero (formerly Rincon Antonio), which is located on the railroad about a third of the way across the Isthmus of Tehuantepec. Diaz,* leading an army of several thousand men, attempted to cross the "forbidden" area and reach the State of Chiapas to the south of it, where he hoped to contact the railroad which runs between San Jeronimo on the Isthmus and Guatemala City. This would have enabled him either to combine his troops with other units of the revolting army in Chiapas, or escape to Guatemala if the Government troops were victorious there as in Oaxaca. What happened to the army was a mystery, but it was known that it did enter the territory after leaving Matias Romero. Only three survivors, Diaz and two of his aides, were ever seen again. Some months later they appeared at the little town of Niltepec, about forty miles south of Tehuantepec. Sick, delirious, and half-crazed from their experiences, they were never able to give a coherent account of what had taken place.

"What do *you* think could have happened?" I asked our informant. "Are there sufficient numbers of warlike Indians living in this country to annihilate a modern army? If an epidemic had broken out among them, surely some of those men, unless the entire army was ambushed, could have safely reached some of the little towns along the railroad."

"There are no Indians living there, Señor," he answered. "And for your other questions, I do not know." His shrug was more expressive than any words.

I turned to Ginger and said in English, "It looks as though it might be a long time before we get back to Salina Cruz. Just how will we break the news to Señor Jiminez?"

"Oh, he won't mind," said Ginger. "Let's follow Diaz' trail and see what happened to that army."

When we announced our purpose to the people round us, the air became blue with protests. "But, my good friends, that is impossible. You will die. No one has ever entered that country and lived. You must not think of such a thing."

Our friend from Salina Cruz, Señor Jiminez, also attempted to dissuade us. "Surely you have seen enough. Why not settle in Tehuantepec for a while? There is plenty of land, and you can live in peace and happiness.

---

* Gruening's *Mexico and Its Heritage* states that General Diaz led a revolt, but that he was captured and taken to Mexico City. In all probability this "Diaz army" was a part of the revolting troops, but under different leadership, and in the passage of time the natives became confused as to who the leader actually was. Also, Diaz is a common name, and might have been the commander's name as well as the General's.

Travelling as you do is both dangerous and full of hardships. Certainly there can be no pleasure in that."

We tried to explain to them why we liked to do adventurous things, how we hoped to spend our lives in exploring unknown places. But it was little use. We had been none too successful in explaining to our own people in a language with which we were familiar. Certainly our Spanish was woefully inadequate to the task. We gave up.

Bedtime having arrived, canvas cots were placed near the windows in the various rooms. It would be impossible to sleep on mattresses in this country, because it is necessary to have the air circulate freely round one's body in order to keep cool. A mattress would soon become a wet, soggy mass. Only hammocks or cots are practical.

The next morning, dressed in native costume, we started out to see more of the town. In the market place we noticed a number of American tourists who had arrived on the preceding night's train from the east coast. One of the women looked at Ginger* and said to her companion, "Don't you feel sorry for these barefoot women? What poverty-stricken lives they must lead, not to be able to afford a pair of shoes!"

The women were dressed in what we assumed was the height of fashion at home. Their high-crowned, brimless hats, worn high on their heads, looked like dunce caps. They were girdled and brassiered within an inch of their lives. High-heeled shoes made them teeter unsteadily on the uneven ground. Hot and uncomfortable, their make-up streaked and runny, they consoled themselves by feeling sorry for the natives. It tickled our sense of humour to walk beside them, undistinguishable from the natives, and listen to their comments. Things were either "terribly picturesque" or they were simply not up to home standards. There was no comprehension of the differences the tropics impose upon a people's way of life, no appreciation of a culture alien to their own. We were alternately amused and indignant. The majestic, free-moving Tehuana women watched them through veiled, enigmatic eyes.

There was an American in Tehuantepec, however, whom we were most anxious to meet, a man who had made his home here for twenty years, and had successfully managed one of the largest ranches on the Isthmus. We found him in his lovely patio, contentedly swinging in a hammock. His bright blue eyes twinkled as he got up to meet us. A man past middle age, life had dealt gently with him. He had come to the Isthmus many years before to spend his vacation—he had never returned to the United States. Retired now from active business, he lived in his fine, spacious home among the flowers, with his beautiful Tehuana wife and daughters.

He ordered hammocks swung for us, and served us cool drinks made from papaya, while he graciously answered some of our many questions

---

* Ginger was wearing three gold necklaces and two arm bands, lent to her by the girls, made from United States $20.00 gold pieces—worth about $800.

regarding the Isthmus and the territory to the south of it. While he knew nothing at first hand of the territory, since all of his activities had been confined to the Isthmus itself, he confirmed the fact that natives never penetrate any difficult region unless they have good reason to do so. He had never heard of a "Forbidden Land," but knew of large unexplored areas to the south, particularly in the State of Chiapas.

Leaving the cool retreat of his patio, we went to call upon the man who was dying. Our host led us to a distant part of the town, west of the large hill rising from the centre of the city. In this *barrio* the streets were narrow and lined with thatched huts. It had its own plaza, church, *mercado*, and stores. On its outskirts we stopped at a well-constructed hut. A sad-faced old woman invited us to enter.

On one side of the hut was an altar on which tall candles burnt. On the other side was a cot with candles burning at its foot. A young man lay there, and though his face gave no evidence of sickness, his withdrawn eyes were looking on death. His mother quietly said that preparations were being made for his funeral.

I seated myself by his bedside and took his pulse and temperature, which were normal. There was apparently nothing organically wrong with him. He told us, in a matter-of-fact voice, about the visitation of his dead friend. It seemed incredible to us that a man who was otherwise in perfect health could will himself to die because of a superstitious belief. I attempted to point out the absurdity to him, but my efforts were useless. He shook his head and smiled. What could I know, his smile seemed to say, about such matters? I wondered. Nothing, perhaps. It may be that the soul always determines when it is ready to free itself from its fleshy envelope. Our belief in the causal relationships between life and death may not be *a priori* to the facts.

As we took our leave of the sad household he smiled again and thanked us for coming. Out in the bright sunlight, the thing we had witnessed became even less comprehensible. Nothing in our racial consciousness could aid us in understanding this passive acceptance of man's greatest fear— death.

The funeral was held at three o'clock* the following day. The man who was about to die witnessed the first half of his own funeral, but died before the ceremonies were concluded at four-thirty.

It had been our original intention to return to Salina Cruz after spending a day or two in Tehuantepec. But after hearing more stories about the country to the south of us, we went instead to Matias Romero. Here we met an American mining man who knew a great deal about the Forbidden Land. He was preparing to go on a prospecting trip into the interior and invited us to go along. Nothing would have suited us better, but there were certain difficulties. We were without passports or tourist cards. Our

---

* Three o'clock was the hour he had predicted as the time of his own death.

ship's papers allowed us the freedom of the ports, but did not permit us to visit inland cities. This was already worrying the chief of customs in Salina Cruz, who had allowed us to go to Tehuantepec. When we failed to return as we had promised, he sent orders for us to come to Salina Cruz at once or he would lose his job and we would be arrested. Back in Salina Cruz, there was no way of obtaining tourist cards unless we went to Puerto Angel, as the port was closed. This meant battling the northers if we went by canoe, or riding muleback overland. We chose the latter. Two weeks later we were back in Salina Cruz sadder and wiser about mules, but the proud possessors of tourist cards, which permitted us to go into the interior and remain for six months.

Returning to Matias Romero, we assisted our American mining acquaintance to assemble his outfit, then started off one night while the town lay in darkness, so that no one would know we had gone until it was too late to follow us. This prospecting trip was not successful, however, and we were soon back in Matias Romero, footloose and on our own.

The wisest thing to do, we decided, was to make a preliminary trip round the borders of the Forbidden Land. In this way we could pick up valuable information from the natives, study the country and its special problems, and gain some idea of its extent.

With small packs on our backs holding our best clothes, the camera and films, guns, notebooks, and so on, we started one morning for Guigoaxo. A cart road led us through a beautiful well-wooded country and past many small fields where the *rancheros* were busily preparing the land for the corn which was to be planted as soon as the rains started. Almost the only tool we saw in use was the machete, which serves every purpose from plough to paring knife.

On the road we met groups of natives bound for the railroad towns. Some of them carried heavy burdens on their heads, others drove small burros loaded with produce. Each group would stop, ask after our health and where we were going, smile and pass on. We replied to each individual greeting with the customary *buenos dias*. This is the custom of the country and no one is ever so hurried that he omits it.

When late in the afternoon we arrived at the little village of Guigoaxo, we were immediately made welcome. Most of these villages, we learned, have a thatched hut which is maintained as a guest house. There is also a small kitchen set up under a thatched roof and ready for the use of travellers. When not occupied by travellers the guest house serves as a meeting place for the village elders.

We were pleasantly surprised at the extreme hospitality of these people, for within a few minutes after our arrival we were tendered several invitations to supper. In reply to our questions about the territory, however, our hosts had little to say. It was a bad country—no one ever went there.

The following morning we took the trail to the next village, Los Flores, and found ourselves in the territory of the Guichicovis, a people similar in appearance to the Tehuanas, although they dress differently. The women wear wrap-around skirts of a striped material and a very short jacket-like blouse which exposes several inches of bare skin above the waist line. Their skin is darker than that of the Zapotecs, but they have the same fine features. Many of those we saw, especially the women, were disfigured by peculiar purple blotches on the surface of the skin which looked like birth marks.

Temperamentally the Guichicovis lack the spontaneity and good humour of the Tehuanas, also their industriousness. They are more superstitious and the stories they told us of the Forbidden Land were full of fabulous beasts. In this country, they said, were great mosquitoes whose bite caused blindness, winged monsters that drained the blood from your body, feathered serpents that flew among the trees. There were animals with tusks that would attack in herds, and a huge beast called the *anteburro*. Strange things, too, floated down the Coatzacoalcos River. And in all it was a land of fearsome wonders.

We left the village next day, disappointed that we had gained so little definite information, and travelled on to Mogone, whose inhabitants, also Guichicovis, differed little from the people of Los Flores.

Maps are almost worthless as aids to travelling in this part of Mexico. Towns called by a Spanish name on the map retain their pre-Conquest names among the natives. Most of the smaller villages throughout the State of Oaxaca have two names. When, worn out from a long day's hike, you arrive at the place you have marked on the map, it often turns out to be a figment of the mapmaker's imagination, or the fork in a stream, or the site of some ancient hacienda. It is seldom the village you hoped to find.

We travelled for several weeks along the northern boundary of this area as we made our way across the Isthmus. Sometimes we were able to go for short distances by muleback or oxcart; but mainly we travelled afoot, our course paralleling the railroad until we reached Puerto Mexico, the Atlantic terminus of the Trans-Isthmian railway. This port, unlike Salina Cruz, is still very active, since it is the only shipping point for the entire Isthmus of Tehuantepec.

Fresh from the back country with its friendly manners, we would occasionally call out a greeting as we sauntered down the streets of Puerto Mexico dressed in our best clothes. But instead of the answering smile and *buenos dias* of the countryside, the passer-by would turn and stare at us. It did make us feel lonesome.

In search of further information, we called upon one of the geologists for the Aguila Oil Company, an old-time resident of the tropics. But he knew nothing about any so-called Forbidden Land. His manner was gruff and it was evident that he thought us the moonstruck victims of romantic nonsense. It was also evident that he had no intention of being a party to any ill-conceived scheme. Hoping that he might take us more seriously, we told him something of our trip down the coast. The recital made him a little less contemptuous, but no more inclined to be helpful than before. Finally I said, "We're sorry you can't give us any information, for we are really serious about entering this area, and we had hoped that you might have something of value to tell us before we started in."

"Forget it!" he replied. "That's a bad country, and it's certainly no place to take a young woman. Why, I've sent seasoned geologists in there to look for oil, and in every case they've gotten themselves into some kind of trouble. And you can bet my old-timers weren't stopped by any banshees either. No one, so far as I know, has ever been into the interior. Mountains, jungles, rivers, and bugs stop 'em—the country's impassable. Parties of archaeologists have been down there too, attempting to get in. They've had no luck, and if they can't, don't you think it is foolish for you to try it? No one really knows anything about the country. Of course we hear stories from time to time of its being a 'forbidden land' or other bunk of a similar nature. One of the stories is that on some high plateau—no one knows just where—a remnant of the ancient Mayan civilization still exists. People are supposed to have retreated during the Conquest from Yucatan, and to have established a city in some inaccessible place. Their descendants are reputed to kill any one who approaches. It is highly improbable, but I don't know. I do know, however, that enough people who have tried to go into that country have never come back, to make anything possible."

"Well, have you any idea of the extent of this unknown territory?" I asked.

"No, I haven't. I do know that the northeastern section of Oaxaca, part of the states of Chiapas, Tabasco, and Campeche have never been explored. Apparently it's all high mountain country, and practically impassable. So you'd better just forget it and think up something else to do."

After we had left him, Ginger grinned. "Our looks are against us." Certainly our appearance was not impressive. Our clothes had seemed good enough in the villages, but contrasted with the smart, well-dressed people round us, we must have cut pretty sad-looking figures.

Walking down the main street we looked in the store windows at all the things we had done without for so long. Smart light clothes suitable for the tropics; powders, creams, shaving lotions, dozens of little personal comforts; shining tins of canned milk, peaches, cigarettes, and other things for which there had been no satisfactory substitutes. The displays of good food made us hungry so we decided to eat in one of the small restaurants. The price of the meal, however—a peso apiece—sent us almost running from the place. We could live for a week on a peso—and we hadn't many of them. The price of a room for the night, we were told upon inquiry, was three pesos. This decided us. Puerto Mexico was no place for us.

Back in the station master's little house where we had left our packs, we changed into our hiking clothes. Then, still undecided as to what course to follow, we walked over to the docks and sat down to watch the small boats plying about the bay. We were both confused and depressed by the noise and alien atmosphere. Ginger began to fidget. "Let's get going. We'd better get out of town before dark," she urged.

Along the docks we stopped to talk with some natives who were working beside their cargo canoes. They seemed to be friendly fellows from up-country, along the Coatzacoalcos River, and were preparing to make their way back home after having brought down a load of fruit and coco-nuts. They were full of stories about the river and the surrounding country. In their village, they said, there was a man who had made a trip into the back country and knew all about it. We should most certainly talk to this man. Almost before we knew it we had agreed to go with them.

"If you had told me half an hour ago," said Ginger as we pushed off from the bank, "that within the hour we would be sitting in a canoe headed up the Coatzacoalcos River, I'd have stated definitely that you were crazy."

Our companions were six river Indians, and differed noticeably in their physical structure from the other Indians we had met. Through centuries of paddling their heavy dugouts along tropical rivers, and never walking if they can help it, river Indians have developed enormous shoulders and arms which are out of all proportion to their slender hips and spindly legs. They are by no means beautiful otherwise. Their straight black hair grows from the crown of their heads in all directions like a Chinese coolie's hat; their small black eyes seem to be always squinting; their noses are sharp and their mouths thin-lipped.

The rancher at whose home we stopped for the night would not hear of our preparing our own supper, but insisted that we have our meal with him. It was a good meal too: chicken *mole*, fried rice, and tortillas.

We slept in one of the dugouts. There were three of them, each twenty feet long by three feet wide, and hewn from one piece of wood. The next morning we were wakened before daylight when the canoe began to rock violently. I sat up and began to grope round for a paddle. "Get up, my friend, the morning comes," laughed one of the boatmen, giving the canoe another rock.

"The only thing I don't like about Mexico," Ginger complained, "is that you are always getting up in the middle of the night."

"I'll teach you to squawk," I said, and picking her up I threw her over the side of the dugout. I was just getting ready to join her when she pushed the canoe out from under me and I hit the water with a splash. A good fight was just getting under way, when the Indians began shouting to us to come out of the water.

"It is always bad to go into the river before daylight," one of them admonished us. "The River Spirit will pull you down to the bottom."

I was puzzled for a moment, then I understood. "Oh, yes, everything is hungry just before daylight. We will not tempt the River Spirit again."

"Come," said our host of the night before, "we are hungry too."

As we followed him to his little hut, I warned Ginger: "Don't forget another thing. The mud banks along a river that runs through dozens of villages are not apt to be too clean. We must be unusually careful not to get scratched while we are on the river."

Our breakfast of tortillas and black coffee was quickly disposed of and we were gliding along the grey river close to its black banks. The air was milky with moisture, and everything was wet. The muted, early-morning noises of the jungle mingled with the soft sounds of water. Shrouds of pearly mist heightened the sense of mystery—the illusion of travelling in a world without substance or form, a world still unready for the advent of three-dimensional beings. Now long shafts of flaming light streaked over the horizon as night withdrew, and the jungle greeted its lord, the Sun.

We paddled through green aisles splashed with colour, under a brilliant panoply of flowering trees whose trunks leaned out over the river's steep banks. Our eyes were dazzled by the myriad hues that blended into a prismatic arc as far as one could see up the river. There were orchids and other exotic flowering growths whose shadings varied from white and palest cream to flaming orange; from delicate pastel pinks and mauves to deep-toned scarlet and imperial purple. The scene was like a page from some mediaeval manuscript.

Wherever possible along the shaded, winding course, we paddled single file. Not a breath of wind stirred the palm fronds, and the scent of flowers became almost overpowering as the day advanced. Sometimes the steep banks gave way to low-lying swamps with innumerable channels leading to and from the river. Here the odour of rotting vegetation in the steamy, flower-scented atmosphere was stifling.

Finally Ginger's strokes began to lag and she lay down in the bottom of the dugout to rest. My arms and shoulders were tired, too, and the gruelling pace set by the natives began to get my wind. As the sun circled higher and shade became scarce, I began to fudge a little in my strokes, and wish that I hadn't started this paddling business in the first place. But since there were four of us in our canoe and only two oarsmen in each of the other canoes, it seemed only fair that I should do my share.

The natives seemed tireless, as hour after hour they pushed their heavy dugouts forward with steady, rhythmic strokes. I marvelled at the play of muscles under their sweating bare backs, at the ever-changing pattern of sinewy cords that laced and interlaced the broad shoulders and arms. This was not the endurance built up on a knowledge of vitamins and physical-culture routines. Corn and beans and dried meat and fish and plenty of sweating at the paddles had produced these bodies.

We passed a settlement and a larger town, neither of which seemed to interest the natives; I had long since lost all interest in the river. As I was wondering just how much longer I could take it, the head canoe swung into the river bank. Through the dense trees we could see the thatched roof of a hut. When we arrived the natives from the other canoes had already disappeared up the trail that led to it. I suggested a swim before going up to the house, but our coxswain vetoed that as "very, very bad. One must not cool off too quickly."

It was noon. The sultry heat wrapped us in a blanket of wet steam, and we were very hungry. There were no indications, however, that any one intended to eat. The owner of the hut remained in his hammock in smiling silence, and the natives sauntered off along little paths that led into the jungle growths. Then one of the boys came back sucking on a mango. The light dawned on us. We lost no time in following the trail that led to a great mango tree. Two of the boys were seated at the base with a big pile of the fruit in front of them. The mangoes round the base of the tree had been badly crushed, but we managed to salvage a number of sound ones which had fallen but a short distance and lay on the outer edge. There is nothing more thirst-quenching on a hot, sultry day than a good, juicy, tree-ripened mango. Something like a peach, it is solid, luscious, and slightly acid. Incidentally, there is no dainty way to eat a mango. You just eat it.

We next paid our respects to a coco-nut grove. Some of the boys had preceded us and left a stack of the green nuts on the ground. It takes some skill and experience to know when to pick and how to prepare coco-nuts for special uses. They are best for drinking when the shell is still rather soft, and only a slight film of meat has formed on the inside. The coco-nut's green outer husk is sliced off with a machete to where the shell is visible. Then with a single quick, deft stroke a portion of the shell is cut off, leaving an opening about an inch in diameter. The trick is to slice off this portion without spilling the milk—which is not as easy as it sounds. The milk is delicious and refreshing.

The meal finished, we went down to the river to wash up. The boys had already returned to their canoes and were unloading the purchases they had made in Puerto Mexico and spreading them out in the sun to dry. We looked the assortment over, since we were interested in knowing what they considered worth the long, hard trip. There were several machetes, strips of bright-coloured cloth, bags of rice and beans, cans of powder and shot, several bags of nails wrapped in burlap, their town clothes, and a few miscellaneous items. We could understand everything but the nails. These, we discovered upon inquiry, were used for trading in the back country—which didn't seem so strange upon reflection. There could hardly be found a more convenient form of malleable iron from which to make spears, fishhooks or knife blades. We were to learn later that the back-country people also use them, chopped into short lengths, for their old muzzle-loading shotguns.

Following the example of the natives, we brought out our own gear for an airing. This is a very necessary precaution in humid, hot country, otherwise mould and rust soon destroy leather, cloth, and metal. Each article of equipment must be gone over at least once a day, and at times guns and metal objects must be oiled twice a day. To omit this tedious task is to invite ruin and sometimes disaster. A neglected gun, for instance, may mean your life. This is one of many reasons why it is wiser not to carry equipment that you can't care for properly, and so save yourself an enormous amount of energy. After a difficult day on the trail or at the paddle it is no small matter to spend an hour or two carefully cleaning guns, sharpening knives, or going over the tent and sleeping bag inch by inch to make sure that no rent will let in a horde of ants or mosquitoes before morning.

When we had finished spreading our things out in the sun I hoped that a swim might be in order, but again the natives said, "*Mala*" (bad). They motioned towards the hut. "It is now siesta time."

Ginger and I stretched out in the hammocks swung between the stanchions of the hut and tried to sleep, but it was quite useless, due to hordes of voracious insects. I sat up and tried to think of something to do besides play host to our tormentors. Then I noticed that all the other hammocks were in motion. The natives were swinging them by pulling on small cords attached to the eaves, or by shoving the ground with the foot occasionally.

"Live and learn," said Ginger drowsily.

The motion of the hammock served two purposes: it created a cooling current of air, and the bugs no longer bothered us. We swung lazily until the sun completed its midday arc. Then the boys bestirred themselves and began preparations for another grind at the paddles. After all our gear was carefully stowed in the canoe and covered with palm branches, Ginger and I dived into the cool water of the river, but the natives would not follow us.

"Don't you ever swim?" we asked.

Oh, yes, they replied, but not with clothes on, as we did. Wearing wet clothes would be very uncomfortable. We assured them that we were used to it and didn't mind. This interested them, and they were curious to know if all our women wore shorts when travelling. That depended on where the women were going, we said. Their own women wore long skirts which they tied round their waists when travelling on the water, but they often got them wet and it took a long time to dry them out. Shorts would be much better, they thought.

Ginger wanted to know of what material their women made their clothes.

"Long ago they used to spin their thread from the fibre of the cotton tree and weave it into beautiful cloth, but now they seldom weave because they like store cloth better—the colours are more pleasing."

During a lively conversation that kept up most of the afternoon, they told us many little things about their village, but we were unable to learn the name of the tribe to which they belonged. It sounded like Hindustani as they pronounced it, and meant River People. Their Spanish was fairly good, but they gave it an odd, clipped accent.

Soon after dark we arrived at the small village where we were to spend the night. Several scantily clad natives came running to meet us, but beat a hasty retreat at the sight of Ginger. Younger children, not so modest, came down to the dugouts and watched us curiously.

The canoes moored, we followed the natives to the village, which consisted of about twenty huts set round a small compound. The thatched roofs were steeper than in other villages we had visited, indicating a heavier rainfall. Many of the men were clad, as were our boatmen when travelling, only in a breechcloth. Some of the older women were bare to the waist, but most of the younger women wore short jackets in addition to wrap-around skirts.

Our party now split up. The men spent the night with friends or relatives, while we accompanied our helmsman to one of the larger huts of the village. Here arrangements differed slightly from other native dwellings we had seen. The cooking was done directly on the floor instead of on a raised mud platform, the pots being supported by large stones. There was in addition a very low slab table, several low three-legged stools, a number of hammocks, and the ever-present *metate*.

Ginger helped the women prepare supper, a simple meal of dried fish broiled over the coals, black coffee, and thick, biscuit-like tortillas; then it was time to retire. In this country the natives' day begins when the stars are still bright in the sky, for no man who can help it exposes himself to the merciless sun of midday. As I started to sling our hammocks between the stanchions, I saw a snake crawl out from the thatching on the roof and slither along a crossbeam. I called our host's attention to it, but he smiled. "He is our pet, and we have two more." Everyone kept them, he explained, not only in their huts to destroy cockroaches and other troublesome insects, but in the fields as well, to help exterminate the rats and mice which devoured the crops. They were quite harmless to people, and we might pet this one if we liked. But we did not choose to pet it.

The next night we were in uninhabited territory, and so made our camp on a knoll above the river. This was the first opportunity we had had to see how these natives prepared their food when on the trail. They allowed a big fire to burn down to a bed of coals, and after dusting off the coals they laid on strips of dried meat, which they frequently turned. The coffee was made in a small clay olla placed over the coals. When this was ready, tortillas were toasted, and the meal was served. Dried meat when prepared in this manner, and eaten in combination with the crude brown sugar which the natives call *panela*, is very palatable.

The following day we arrived at the natives' home village of Suchilapan, which is near the head of navigation of the Coatzacoalcos River. The old man whom we had come to see had very little to offer in the way of new or definite information regarding the so-called Forbidden Land. In the main, he simply reiterated the stories we had already heard. We did learn, however, that there were several small villages further up the river; so when our friends the boatmen offered us the loan of a small dugout, paddles, and poles for navigating the shallower water, we accepted and started off on a further quest for information.

Paddling the dugout up the misty river was not difficult, but poling it over the shallows demanded an expertness which we had yet to master. It had looked easy when the natives manipulated the poles, but our amateurish efforts caused the canoe to skid broadside to the swift current. We were forced to abandon the poles and resort to paddles. By sundown we had made very little progress.

The second day, late in the afternoon, we reached a small village and found that we were in different tribal territory. The natives were somewhat less friendly and more reserved than the other Isthmian tribes we had met, but we were welcomed in broken Spanish by the headman and offered the hospitality of his home.

This was territory of the Chimas, said our host. It bounded a large portion of the Forbidden Land, which was just across the river, but his people never crossed. As we approached the village we had seen evidences of trees cut on the opposite side, and I asked him about that. He explained. During high water his people paddled to the partly submerged trees and cut them while still in the canoes. If a tree fell into the water, they dragged it to their own side of the river, but if it fell on land they left it there. This land, he assured us, had for many many years belonged to an ancient tribe. It was a "Land of Spirits," spirits who forbade any one to enter, and it was full of remarkable animals. At time of high water, strange objects such as carved pieces of wood and magic *jícaras*, which would not let any one touch them, came floating past the village. As he talked on the Indian grew excited and lapsed more and more into his native tongue, so that it became increasingly difficult to follow him. Before I lost the thread of his discourse entirely, however, I caught fragments of a story about a great city somewhere in the high mountains occupied by a people different from other Indians.

We had heard from many tribes this legend of a people who had emigrated long ago into the high mountain country. Not every tribe knew the story, but those who did seldom varied its essential details. It was known to widely separated groups who had no intercourse with each other. Whether it was based on some migration taking place during the Conquest, or before, it was never possible for us to determine. Sometimes the people were said to be still living, in other versions their spirits now guarded the land. The persistence of the story is basis for believing it to be founded on fact. But since the Indian has no time sense, it might as easily have happened a thousand years ago as four hundred.

The Chimas told us that there was another village further up the river, but it was not possible to reach it by water, since many rapids and great falls barred the way.

The next morning we started forth in hopes that we might make the next village, but we travelled all day without seeing any signs of natives. The river narrowed as we progressed, and the current became much swifter. The country round us grew wilder, and the flowering vegetation more profuse and colourful. The trees were literally festooned with magnificent orchids. An oppressive silence hung over the jungle, however, that began to get on our nerves. This was coupled with a peculiar sense of apprehension, a feeling of foreboding, that could easily have accounted for the effect the country had on the imaginative and superstitious natives.

Not succeeding in our efforts to find a camping place in the late afternoon, we cleared a little space on the river bank large enough for the cooking fire, and slept in the canoe.

It was difficult to make headway against the swift current and the next day's travel brought us not much farther upstream. But now we could hear the roar of water and knew that we had come to the end of the trail. Progress on foot would be next to impossible through the tangled undergrowth, so we reluctantly turned back downstream. Two days later we returned the canoe to its owners in Suchilipan.

From Suchilipan, on the advice of natives, we travelled by oxcart to the little railroad junction of Santa Lucrecia, a day's journey away, and on arriving there found two young Americans also preparing to enter the unexplored country. They had just come from the States and were full of enthusiasm for the venture. At the little hotel where they were staying they proudly showed us their equipment: a substantial tent with heavy canvas floor, an eight-pound sleeping bag apiece, and an air mattress. There were in addition innumerable small items, some of which we had originally planned on taking, and some that we had taken and discarded.

When we told them of our plans to enter the territory they immediately asked to see our equipment. "There it is," I said, and pointed to the two small packsacks Ginger and I had been carrying.

The leader exploded. "Why, man, you can't travel in that country with what you've got there! It can't be done. We're old-timers at this game, and we know."

"That's all we have," I replied. "The clothes we are wearing are what we call our shore clothes. In our knapsacks we have our shorts, which we wear when travelling alone. We also carry native clothes to wear in the villages. These, together with our pup tent, sleeping bag, hunting knife, guns and ammunition, camera and films, part of our mess kit, a little food, and our machetes, complete the equipment."

"Listen, mister, you can't travel in jungle country wearing shorts. The bugs would eat you alive. You've got to wear hiking boots, breeches, and a heavy shirt to protect yourself. You'd better learn how to take care of yourselves in this jungle before you travel in it."

"Well," Ginger said in a meek voice, "we spent two years in training before we left home and we've spent two years in travelling to get here. Of course we're not authorities on the finer points of travelling through jungles, but we've been on the outskirts of them ever since leaving Mazatlan."

Our ideas differed so much from theirs that there was little we could say to each other on the subject. I did ask them, since their equipment appeared new and unused, if they had tried it out to be sure it worked perfectly and would serve the purpose for which it was intended, but they seemed to think that an unnecessary precaution. For food, they had worked out a perfectly balanced diet of dehydrated rations, they informed us. It was neatly packed in numerous small containers.

"Are you going alone or are you taking native guides?" I asked.

They were going alone, since natives seemed afraid to go into the country. We wished them a successful journey and departed.

From Santa Lucrecia we went on to the little town of Tolosita, and while there heard that the two men had started out but had got no farther than the borders of the territory before they had to be rescued by a party of natives. They had been found wandering, sick and half crazed by the heat and insects. One had been sent to the nearest hospital and was now in a critical condition. This sad state of affairs was in all likelihood due to the fact that they had attempted their trek without waiting to become acclimatized, and were too heavily loaded to withstand the gruelling labour of breaking trail.

In Tolosita we were the guests of a young Spaniard who had a contract to furnish a lumber company with twelve million feet of hardwood. The hundred natives he employed as lumbermen worked for several weeks and then went on strike for more pay. When he met their demands and increased their pay from one to two pesos a day, they went on strike for three pesos; and the lumber which he had already paid them to cut was still lying in the forest. He had no money left with which to pay increased wages and no one would lend him any more for fear the natives would go on strike again before the logs could be brought to the railroad. In the meantime, the natives had taken their oxcarts over the roads he had built and were cutting up his timber for railroad ties, for which they received twenty-five cents apiece. An industrious native, by working long hours, could get out about three a day. Our host's main concern was not the timber they were taking, but the fact that their heavy oxcarts were cutting up the roads so badly that it would soon be impossible for him to get heavy tractors over them to haul out his logs.

In desperation he decided to go to Matias Romero, where he had hopes of raising more money, and invited us to go with him. We accepted. While we three were waiting at the station the labourers put in an appearance, their idea being to prevent him from leaving. Only by carefully explaining that he was going to secure more money was he allowed to board the train.

In Matias Romero we went to the house of a shrewd Arab merchant who, after hearing our friend's difficulties, sat down and began to figure; and soon proved that at three pesos per day per man it would cost more to ship the lumber to the mill than he would get for it. By paying one peso wages, he could make enough profit to run a small-gauge railroad into the timber country, and build a business that would employ a thousand men. By paying two pesos, he could fulfil his original contract and break even.

The young Spaniard decided that he had had enough, and did not even bother to go back to Tolosita for his belongings. Instead, he invited us to go with him to San Jeronimo to witness one of the biggest fiestas of the year, the *Cinco de Mayo*, the Fifth of May.

It is not our intention to attempt an analysis of the almost continuous conflict between capital and labour in Mexico during the last twenty years. Much has been written by able commentators on the subject, to which we could add little. But it is worth stressing that part of the difficulty has been due to the inept way in which foreigners have handled the natives. People being as they are, tact and diplomacy often succeed where force would only add to the provocation.

On the way to San Jeronimo we stopped off at Chivela, the railroad station for what was once one of the largest ranches on the Isthmus. This was the property which had been so successfully managed by the American whom we had visited in Tehuantepec. He had been, we learned, the only man who had held the job and survived it. His six predecessors had either been murdered or driven out of the country. This state of affairs had been brought about partly through revolutionary activities and partly by the estate administrators themselves. One of his first acts had been to open and tie back the great iron gates in the high walls that protected the ranch house. Then he invited any one who had a grievance to come in and present it to him. When peons arrived bent on murder if the administrator failed to meet their demands, the deputation was sure to be greeted with soft words, a friendly welcome, and a glass of beer. Sometimes a *marimba* was brought in and the festivities continued until the would-be assassins had forgotten the purpose of their visit. It became a bi-monthly institution at Chivela for the *rancheros* to come from all over the great estate to make fiesta at the hacienda. And so the work went on without interruption for many years until the American retired. The owner then attempted to run it himself, and another shooting took place. Eventually the government divided it into small farms, and parcelled it out among the peons. Some of them promptly moved into town and as promptly squandered their property. Others attempted to farm their allotments. A few banded together and decided to pool their interests and hire a manager, but found that his salary would leave them little profit. Now the vast property was quickly reverting to the jungle. It apparently takes more than a formula in Mexico, as elsewhere, to achieve social justice. Possessions in themselves have no value without the ability to use them.

We had the good fortune to meet in San Jeronimo an American naturalist who spent part of each year on the Isthmus. He had, like ourselves, come for the celebration, and since he knew much of the history of the people, we listened with interest to what he had to say. "I think they are the happiest people in the world," he remarked as we watched the gaily dressed throng pass by. "I often wonder how far they would have advanced had the discovery of America been postponed, say, for a hundred years or so. Perhaps by that time the Old World would have progressed enough to appreciate the great culture that the Conquistadors so ruthlessly destroyed. Spain received no lasting benefit from her cruel exploitation of these people; in all likelihood she hastened her downfall—historical proof that easy money never benefits its possessor long."

"What do you know about the high mountain country?" I asked. "We're planning to penetrate the so-called Forbidden Country to the south of here as soon as the fiesta is over."

"I'm afraid," he answered, "that you are going to have very little luck. For the past fifty years archaeologists have attempted to get into that country and run down a story that has cropped up persistently ever since the first Mayan ruins were discovered. In the year 1842 a Spanish padre told an explorer, John L. Stephens, of a city that existed in the State of Chiapas—at least that was its approximate location. Here the old pre-Columbian civilization still lived, undisturbed by the influences that had destroyed it elsewhere. The padre asserted that it was on the other side of the great sierra, about four days' journey on the road to Mexico City. He had heard the story years before in the village of Chajul, where he was told that from the topmost ridge of the sierra this city could be seen. The padre was young then and he had climbed to the summit of a tall peak. From there he looked down upon a large plain extending to the north, and saw in the distance the gleaming white turrets of a great city. Since the padre's day no white man had ever looked upon this city. The inhabitants, so said the Indians of Chajul, spoke the Mayan tongue, were aware that strangers had conquered and ruled the surrounding country, and without hesitation killed any white man that entered their territory."

"Well, that *is* a story!" we exclaimed.

The naturalist was, I suspect, somewhat amused at our brashness in attempting the trip in the face of so many failures. We told him why we thought we had better chances to succeed than larger expeditions. They had the problem of feeding many men, while we lived off the country. We were used to the hot, humid climate and we had adopted a psychological attitude towards the jungle; instead of fighting it, we accepted its way of life.

We then discussed our plans for witnessing the ceremonies to be held on the morrow. The naturalist had intended to wear his European clothes and watch from the sidelines, but when we told him that we were going to join in the fun in native dress he decided that he, too, would be a participant instead of an onlooker.

Undoubtedly the fact that we wore native clothes, did our share of the work, and took part in the general life of the villagers was the principal reason why we were so successful in getting about the country, and were so warmly received everywhere. This, perhaps more than our good will, helped to dispel the Indians' ingrained suspicion of the whites. Even so, they were frequently reluctant to discuss certain subjects with us. Sometimes they engaged in amusing subterfuge. Two or more of them would discuss a topic just within earshot of us. Then if we overheard their conversation—and they intended we should—no one was directly responsible.

The celebration in San Jeronimo lasted for several days, and we three, gaily attired in Tehuana clothes, took part in the dances and processions that began in the morning and ended late at night. Each afternoon the festivities were suspended during the siesta hour, but the cool of evening found the throng again promenading the plaza, listening to the band, greeting friends from out of town, eating and drinking at the many little tables where piping hot tortillas, enchiladas, chicken, fried rice, barbecued meat, and many other good things could be had at a trifling cost. The women in their colourful costumes looked like animated flowers, and many of them added to the brilliance of the scene by carrying painted gourds full of fruit and flowers.

Here was no commercialized carnival sponsored by the local chamber of commerce. This was the spontaneous expression of a people's joy in living. These fiestas have been held since the earliest times, and much of the ritual that marks them does service not only for the commemoration of political events or honours the saints of Christendom but the pagan gods of Mexico as well—for they are not forgotten.

The crowning event of the last evening was to be a bullfight. The bull, however, was not a flesh-and-blood creation. A man carrying a wooden framework suddenly appeared, at sight of whom the crowd scattered in all directions. Then another man lighted a fuse, and the fire-works bull, for such it was, began spurting Roman candles. Carrying the wildly erupting bull, the man now plunged into the hilarious throng, charging one group of onlookers, then another. It seemed to be an honour to carry the bull, and as soon as one man became exhausted, a second was ready to take his place. When we were charged in our turn we raced ahead with the others, since had we hesitated our clothing would most likely have been scorched. In an effort to speed up Ginger, who was hampered by her long skirts, I took one of her arms while the naturalist seized the other. So intent were we upon the bull at our heels that we failed to see a low-banked pool ahead until we were almost upon it. Our friend swerved in in a last minute effort to avoid it. I stopped abruptly. And between us, we managed to pitch Ginger into the pool.

At last the fiesta was over. Tired and bedraggled as we were, we wouldn't have missed it for anything, and our American friend had had a grand time too. But now we had to think and plan for our trip. We had hoped to induce a native or two to accompany us, but our overtures were invariably met with a blank stare and a silent refusal. This was true whether we approached natives born on the Isthmus or those who had come there from other parts of Mexico. If we went alone it might be difficult to get out of the country in the event of trouble, but there seemed no other way. It was a choice of going alone and taking a chance, or giving up the venture.

Our friends among the natives offered us horses and other aids. We decided at last to accept an old horse, with the understanding that if the country became too difficult we would either turn it loose or leave it at one of the villages en route. With the horse to carry a month's supply of food—dried meat, corn, native brown sugar, rice, beans, coffee, salt, and a little tobacco—we could scout round the borders of the country and harden ourselves before taking the trail of Diaz' army into the territory. No one could give us any information as to how far the trail led; only that it passed through certain towns.

Our equipment consisted of one change of native clothes, our shorts, an extra pair of native sandals apiece, the tent, sleeping bag, mess kit, guns and ammunition, camera and films, small first-aid kit containing permanganate of potash, iodine and quinine, one hunting knife, two machetes and a carborundum sharpening stone, the sixty-foot lariat, government maps of the states of Chiapas and Oaxaca, our notebooks and pencils, a razor, a pair of scissors, and Ginger's powder box.

When the final preparations were completed we divided the load between our two knapsacks and swung them across the packsaddle of our dilapidated old horse, whom we promptly christened "Pussyfoot." We left town one morning before daylight, and picked out a road leading in the general direction of our objective. Our friends were loath to say good-bye, for they never expected to see us again.

A little distance down the road we fell in with a party of natives returning home after the fiesta, and journeyed with them to the little village of

Puente. But it was not until we reached the village of Pandopan several days later that we had the sense of having left civilization behind.

We had been warned that the people of Pandopan were outlaws, and it was with no slight trepidation that we approached the silent village. No curious natives came running to meet us as we trudged boldly in; only the cur dogs barked and snarled at our heels. Making our way to the open-sided hut that served as a market place, we took the packsaddle from Pussyfoot's tired back. Still no one approached us, until a naked boy ran out from one of the huts. Ginger held out her arms to him and he came to her as confidently as he would to his mother. With the little fellow in her arms she walked to the hut, and in about two minutes she was in deep discussion with his mother. The spell was broken. Soon natives came trooping from their hiding places, and after returning my familiar greeting they sat on the ground and we talked together. Ginger meanwhile remained in the hut in animated conversation with the child's mother, whose name was Francisca. The father, Jorge, now came forward and invited me to enter his house and meet his family. Jorge and Francisca were the village leaders. Having once made friends with them, there was no further social problem in Pandopan.

The hut was furnished much like other Indian dwellings except that the tables and stools were very small, about the size a child would use to play house with. There seemed no explanation for them—only that the people preferred them so.

After supper we sat outside and talked to the other villagers. One old lady asked if it rained where we came from. We said yes, and that it was also cold. They knew cold only as a means of comparison. Food that was not hot off the fire was cold. There was no way to make them understand the word in terms of weather, for the *tierra caliente* has only two seasons, wet and dry.

The Indians' faces grew grave when we told them of our plan to continue on to the village of La Tunita. "Those up-country people are very bad and your lives will be in danger," they solemnly assured us.

Despite their dire warnings, we left the next morning, and after travelling through difficult country reached the village above. "What! You have come from the village below?" the natives asked in amazement. Oh, the people below were very bad, as were the people in the village beyond. They themselves, however, were a kind, peaceful people. This story was repeated without variation in each village we came to until we reached Tarifa.

The inhabitants of Tarifa belonged to another tribe, and there were slight differences in their appearance and in their huts to set them apart from the Indians we had seen earlier. They were a more gracious people. As the headman greeted us he led us to a large thatched hut in the centre of the village intended for the use of travellers. "This," he said, "is your home. You are very welcome."

It was always our custom when entering a strange village to make a tour of the huts and exchange greetings with the occupants. In Tarifa we began the rounds as usual, stopping to compliment the mothers of large families on their offspring (just like the politicians at home before election) then passing on to the next hut. Our reception in this village was different, however. At each hut we were invited to enter and a little fruit or dried meat was presented to us with a good wish. We finally reached the home of an old lady who had nothing to give but flowers from her garden. By this time our arms were loaded with gifts, and I said as I laid them down on the table, "We are strangers in your country and do not know your customs, but it does not seem right for us to accept your gifts since we have nothing to give you in return."

She smiled. "Señor, we believe that it is better to give than to receive. When you leave here, if you see a little child who might like a banana, give him one, it will make him happy. If you meet some one who might enjoy flowers, then give the flowers. Thus two people will receive gifts, for you will be happy in the giving and happiness is the greatest of gifts."

We followed her advice, and passed out our gifts as fast as we received them. In the end we had one banana left apiece, but we had the sense of having shared in a concept of human living that is all too uncommon. Here was a people who literally lived a commandment to which most of the world renders lip service only.

That evening, as the villagers gathered in the guest house, we asked them more about their custom of giving, and how it worked. Weren't some people lazy and didn't they take advantage of the ones who produced? Not very long, was the answer. Each able-bodied person in the village followed some gainful trade or produced some useful thing. They were pottery makers, weavers, carpenters, farmers, or hunters. Their prestige was based upon how much they could produce for the common welfare of the group. The leaders were the people who could give the most. Those who were lazy were looked down upon by the community. Such people either left the village or mended their ways. Based upon their needs and desires, the standard of living in this village was high. Everyone had more than enough.

Here, as in many other villages, the children were taught their parents' means of livelihood, and their education began as soon as they could walk. Little boys went proudly with their fathers to the fields to scrape the *milpa* with their tiny machetes, helping him plant corn. At an early age they become amazingly proficient and able to take care of themselves. This does not mean that any hardship is imposed upon the child, for Mexican children are probably the happiest in the world. Their parents regard creation and production as play, and so do they. They seem to have as much fun helping with the crops or patting a bit of clay into an olla as our children do in playing hide and seek.

Little girls take great pride in being able to help their mothers. Ginger told me of a four-year-old who, when she was given a small flat rock about the shape of a *metate*, painstakingly searched for a "hand" rock, and finding one, put five or six grains of corn on her *metate* and began to grind them. A six-year-old girl asked her mother if she couldn't help her make tortillas. Too small to reach the grinding stone, she dragged a stool over to the *metate* and went about the work in a business-like manner. She was immensely pleased with herself. She was doing something useful too. When she had ground enough corn she carefully patted out a tortilla. Its edges cracked and she remade it. Again it failed to suit her, and again she worked it over until at last she achieved a perfect flat round disk. This took time and patience.

Tiny girls, half as tall as their palm brooms, sweep out the hut and yard thoroughly. Boys and girls both carry water in their little ollas to fill the large stationary olla kept in the hut. They do, according to their ability and size, such work as their elders perform.

At the age of puberty, generally about eleven or twelve years, the girls are separated from the boys, and from then on their training is intensified. Their shy courtships are carried on under the watchful eyes of the girl's parents, with perhaps a little more freedom during fiestas.* Marriage is by mutual consent of the contracting parties and their families. Unsuitable matches are nipped in the bud before they become serious. If a romance is allowed to progress to the point where a marriage is considered, parental consent is always obtained. Then after an exchange of gifts, the ceremonies are arranged.

The entire village now takes a hand in the approaching nuptials. The men go with their oxcarts into the jungle to secure materials for the new home. The women busy themselves round their pots, preparing food for the fiesta which will start with the hut's construction. The building completed, no one may cross the threshold of the unfurnished hut until the bashful couple are shoved through the doorway. Then a woven mat, the *petate*, on which Indians are born and die, is thrown after them, and they are left alone together. Usually they are serenaded throughout the night with love songs to the accompaniment of marimbas or guitars.

The next morning the village scans the faces of the couple to determine if the match has been successful. If so, the furnishings for the hut are

* The dances held during these fiestas are primarily for the purpose of choosing a mate by scent. The Indians believe that since everything in nature has an odour, human odour is most important; they believe that it reveals sickness, fear, hate, and love, and indicates sexual affinity. This belief plays an important part in their lives. They say that mates chosen by scent always form lasting unions. Frequently you will hear, "I chose him (or her) because he smelled good." A girl who is attracted by a man will sometimes induce the Wise One to place some article that she has worn in or near his bed. Wives sometimes do this if their husbands show signs of coldness towards them.

brought in, and a housewarming follows. But if they are not pleased with each other (which rarely happens) the girl returns to her home and the boy leaves the village. Divorce after the second night is unheard of in the outlying villages. In the event of death the survivor seldom marries a second time. A widow is ordinarily taken into some other family. A man usually packs up his belongings and moves elsewhere.

Authorities differ widely in their interpretations of the customs, religion, and traditions of Mexican tribes. This is partly because an observer frequently translates Indian behaviour into terms of his own social order or psychology. The early Spanish commentators tried to find parallels between sixteenth-century European culture and the culture of the New World. They talked of "emperors" and "empires," and any one who knows Indians knows that such concepts are alien to them. Each tribe has a leader, but his office is not hereditary; he is elevated to his position by reason of his superior attributes and his ability to solve the group's problems. He leads the religious ceremonies and other communal activities, and though he is accorded respect by other members of the tribal unit, his word is far from law. An American business executive (even a minor one) is the recipient of more kotowing than all the tribal chiefs of Mexico. There is no place in the communal organization of an Indian village for the individualist. The survival of the group depends upon the harmonious working together of its members, upon a subordination of the parts to the whole. The result is an absence of friction, and freedom from the necessity of continually asserting one's self. The clash of personalities which seems inevitable to social intercourse among our people has no counterpart there. If, as occasionally happens, an Indian talks too much about himself or boasts unduly, he is given a wide berth by the others.

The Indian sees very little point in discussing his beliefs or way of living. Fundamentally a realist, he accepts things as they are or as they appear to him. Things or beliefs are valuable because they are useful or beautiful. The modern Indian has undoubtedly degenerated culturally in recent years, but, particularly in those communities under the old tribal organization, his formula of living is based upon a fairly sound premise. Much of what is called his magic is not magic at all; white men have consistently misused the term. The Old One or the Wise One, or whatever the tribe calls its practitioner, is usually a good psychologist; his teachings and prescriptions have a great deal of sense and considerable therapeutic value behind them. But like all good showmen, the practitioner knows the value of making simple things sound mysterious.

Most Indians are monotheists, believing in one God, who often employs agents. We discussed the purpose of human sacrifice with one old shaman, and found his attitude interesting. There is no evidence that sacrifice is still practised, but the reasons he gave for it were logical. To begin with, the Indian neither fears death nor troubles himself over-much about a phenomenon which is universal. Hence to him it is not something to be unduly avoided. He believes in a personal immortality, and death in a good cause, particularly if it benefits the tribe, is an honour. In the past, in times of war or drought, when all other appeals had failed, it seemed logical to send a personal representative to stress the urgency of the people's need. A warrior of renown or a beautiful woman of stainless reputation was chosen. Such a one after death could surely plead for immediate assistance more effectively than could an earth-bound mortal. God works through agents, why not men? The shaman asked us if we believed that God sent the *santos* and the gentle Jesus to men, and if we did, why then was it strange that Indians sent messengers to Him?

It frequently seems to the casual observer that native superstitions and religion are inextricably mixed. Most superstitions have nothing to do with religion. They are, as I have explained earlier, metaphorical ways of expressing natural phenomena or relationships between cause and effect. One day after a hot and difficult march we pulled into a small village. The horse was dog-tired and sweaty, and I immediately started to remove the saddle. An Indian stopped me. "No, no, you must not do that. You must wait or an evil spirit will jump on your horse and ride him to his death." He was telling us that it was dangerous to let a sweaty horse cool off too fast. In the high altitudes it is often fatal.

Dangerous roads are possessed of evil spirits after dark. They in all likelihood are, for the traveller is apt to break his neck if he essays some of them at night.

As we continued on towards the mountain country the maps became more unreliable—if such a thing could be. A river supposed to empty into the Pacific drained into the Atlantic. A village marked on one river was on another river across the continental divide.

The villagers everywhere we stopped tried to dissuade us from going farther. Stories of the outlaw and bandit tribes who inhabited the area ahead became more lurid. Our route now lay over a high divide and up a canyon or valley to the north, where we were supposed to pick up the trail of Diaz's army. It took us two days of difficult travel over a succession of high ridges before we finally dropped down into the valley. This was the reputed home of the bandits, and our progress became slower as we carefully detoured round likely places for an ambush.

After several tortuous miles we came suddenly upon a well-worn trail and followed it in the direction of the river, since any settlement would be there. But after another mile or so the shadows began to lengthen, so we decided to stop for the night in a little clearing.

While we were setting up camp, three natives carrying guns came towards us. We immediately prepared ourselves for battle by dropping prone behind our knapsacks. Then as the Indians continued to approach with no sign of harmful intent, we got up feeling rather silly.

We gave them the usual explanation of our presence in the country and invited them to have a cup of coffee, expressing regret that we had nothing to offer them to eat since we had not yet secured permission to hunt in their territory. One of the men smiled at this and said in poor Spanish, "I am pleased that you recognize that this is our land."

It occurred to me then that he was probably the chief, for he was completely dressed in a hand-woven pyjama suit common to headmen, while the other two wore only pants. They were tough-looking customers and had little to say. As we sat and sipped our coffee and looked at each other, the headman broke the silence. "You have travelled in many countries?"

"Yes," I said. "Many countries."

"And do they have spirits in other countries?"

This gave us something to talk about, and we told of our long and intimate contact with spirits, and of our trip down the coast. But the ocean was incomprehensible to him, so I turned to the subject of guns. All three of them had been looking at our side arms with unconcealed interest, and we were curious to examine their old muzzle-loaders. They were of ancient vintage. How they ever found their way into this country was something to ponder over.

As I looked at his gun, an eager expression came over the chief's face. "Are you, too, aware of it?" he asked.

"Wha—? Oh, yes, yes," I answered, wondering what he meant.

"Then perhaps you can do something about it," he said handing me the weapon.

I examined the rusty old piece more closely and handed it back to him. He looked disappointed. "But, Señor," he pleaded, "can't you do something about it?"

I looked questioningly at Ginger, but she shook her head. We had no clue as to what he wanted us to do. "Tell me more about it, my friend," I urged.

"The spirit," he said excitedly, then grabbed his gun and pointed to the barrel. "He sits right here, astraddle, and every time I fire the gun he jumps on the bullet and steers it to one side so that it will not hit anything."

Here was the break we had been looking for. "But what have you done, my friend, to deserve such a spirit in your gun?" I asked. "Have you killed people? Many guns have spirits, but most of them are good spirits like the spirit in my gun." I drew the heavy Luger from its holster. His eyes widened as he looked at its complicated mechanism. "This gun," I continued, "has a good spirit. It will not allow any one but me to shoot it. If any one else should steal this gun, it immediately kills the one who takes it. Take it, see if the spirit will allow you to fire the gun."

The old fellow eagerly accepted the Luger and turned it over and over in his hands admiringly. "Go ahead," I prompted, "see if you can shoot it." He held the gun at arm's length and covering his face with his free hand squeezed the trigger—nothing happened. The safety catch was on. His face was a study in bewilderment as he pulled the trigger intermittently. We prayed that he wouldn't inadvertently slip the catch, because there was no knowing just where the bullet would fly. Tapping the Luger's intricate mechanism with his forefinger, he wanted to know what all the little pieces were for.

"This is a strange gun," I answered. "It keeps on firing until it hits the object aimed at." Since he had never seen an automatic it was safe to endow it with magic properties which he might think extended to its owners.

"Perhaps you can do something about the evil spirit in my gun," he said hopefully.

I agreed that perhaps I could but that it would help if he would make me a promise that neither he nor his people would use a gun to kill a human being. I added that it would be too bad if evil spirits took possession of all the guns in the village. He was prompt to promise and invited us to visit his village the following day.

With that they took their leave and I set to work on the old muzzle-loader, which the chief insisted on leaving behind. It had probably never been cleaned since coming into his possession. The barrel was caked with rust. I made a ramrod out of a sapling and gave it a thorough overhauling.

While we were eating breakfast the next morning the chief, escorted by several of his tribe, put in an appearance. He received the gun with exclamations of pleasure at my assurance that it now had a "good spirit." After breakfast we followed them back to the village. Late that afternoon, the chief, who had gone hunting, reappeared lugging a good-sized deer. This was the first kill he had made in months, and he was overjoyed—as I was at the success of my magical gifts.

The deer was taken to the open shed that served as a market, and several men helped the chief to butcher and distribute the meat to all comers. In the end the chief had the poorest piece left for himself. Curious as to why he had not retained a better portion, I questioned him. He grinned. "Tomorrow, Señor, some one else may kill a deer, and then perhaps I shall get the best piece. It is best to give the best, that makes everyone happy. This will do for today."

We had been told that this village was the last outpost before entering the unexplored area, and that Diaz's army had passed through it. Since we did not want the natives to know that we planned to go further, we replied to their questions by telling them that we were following the river a few miles and were then returning to the village below. They warned us not to go more than two miles beyond their village. An army had once tried to pass that way and the spirits had destroyed them. The women cried on Ginger's neck, moaning, "Oh, the poor Señora. Be careful and do not go farther."

When we started off, Pussyfoot was groaning under the load of food they had insisted on giving us.

The native trail continued on for about two miles and then disappeared. A fence we found across the narrow valley had been built to keep cattle from straying into the Forbidden Land. We took down a section of it, let Pussyfoot through, and then replaced the bars.

Well, here we were. Now what? Ahead of us lay the land of mystery.

Chapter Twenty

THE FORBIDDEN LAND

As we trudged up the valley, cutting our way through the dense growth, we were both preoccupied with the probable nature of the danger that gave this land its evil reputation. Discounting the interference of supernatural agencies, there still remained plenty of likely reasons why this country had so successfully resisted man's invasion. True, the land was mountainous, but this was not unusual in Mexico. Unless one believed the legend of inhabited Mayan cities, there seemed no human agency to fear. Three things remained: poisonous plants, deadly insects, or some endemic of the country. One of these three had killed an army. But which one? Round the night fires in a dozen little villages, we had listened to strange stories of an enchanted lake, magic gourds, fearsome beasts; to tales of vengeful spirits that guarded this land well. Although we had heard nothing concrete of which to be afraid, these stories created, against all reason, a state of mind in which the very atmosphere was surcharged with an ominous quality. We were more affected than we liked to admit by the genuine fear that this country inspired in the natives.

The jungle, in itself frightening to many people, we had grown to like. While it was full of physical discomfort, it had nevertheless an inexhaustible fascination. There was an excitement, a sense of uncertainty, in travelling through it, a continual challenge to the spirit of adventure. We had worked out a philosophy regarding it and ourselves that perhaps gave us a certain detachment from the purely personal considerations of bodily pain which is an inescapable concomitant to jungle travel. We had accepted the fact that the jungle can't be fought. It imposes a necessity for compromise, a yielding and an adaptability to its humours, that makes men hate or love it.

All that day and the next we cut through the heavy growth of the canyon, following the trail of the army. Many of the trees were covered with the scars of their machete marks, but there was nothing to indicate that they had encountered any difficulty beyond that inherent in entering the jungle at all.

Late that afternoon, however, our bodies began to sting as if a thousand needles were being jabbed into us. With one accord we started cutting our way to the water. Unstrapping our gun belts, we hurriedly jumped into the pool. Our bodies were covered with *pinolillos*, those tiny, biting curses of the jungle. We scrubbed them off with pads of moss before they had a chance to dig in, and immediately took off our native clothes and put on shorts. The horse's legs were also covered with them, so we gave her a scrubbing in the pool. Since the tiny ticks burrow into the seams of clothing, it was evident that men in shoes, breeches, and leggings must have suffered tortures from them.

That night, while setting up camp, we found the ground covered with *conchudos*, a larger and equally painful tick. For us the solution was simple; we burnt off the camp site and set up the bug-proof tent; but poor old Pussyfoot had no relief from their torment throughout the night. In the morning we spent over an hour picking them off her. There were hundreds of them in her ears, which were raw and bleeding by the time we had pulled the last one out. We daubed them with a solution of permanganate, and continued on up the canyon.

High cliffs closed in on either side of us. It was necessary to cross and recross the stream to find a place wide enough to get through. The horse suffered more than we did, for although we unloaded her pack and carried it ourselves, the stream bed was so deep and so filled with boulders that she had difficulty in making the fords. By noon she was so exhausted that we picked a fairly clear place near the stream and made camp. The canyon opened out here, and just behind us was a large flat shaded by great trees. As I led Pussyfoot back into the flat, looking for a place for her to forage, I saw a shiny object sticking up out of the humus. It was a battered enamelled pot. I called excitedly to Ginger, for I knew this was possible evidence that the army had camped here. Together we unearthed pieces of old army cots, rusted rifle barrels whose stocks had almost completely rotted away, battered kettles, and other bits of rusted and decomposed army equipment. We spent the rest of the day trying to decipher the fate of the men who had left these things behind them.

The next morning I found Pussyfoot with her head bowed almost to the ground. There were several deep gashes on both sides of her neck. The hair below them was matted with dried blood, and they looked as though they had been cut with a very sharp knife. The poor horse was so weak from loss of blood that she stumbled repeatedly as I led her back to camp, and I knew that it was not possible to take her any farther into a country infested with vampire bats. Contrary to general opinion, these bats are not bloodsuckers, but they lap up the blood which runs freely from the incisions which they make with their sharp teeth. The only thing to do was to take Pussyfoot back to the last village that we had come through and leave her. The fence would have prevented her from reaching the village without us, and if we turned her loose on the other side of it without putting in an appearance ourselves, the natives would either start looking for us, or send out word that we were lost. So we escorted Pussyfoot back to the village, taking four days to make the trip and return.

The Forbidden Land

Travelling up the canyon now became difficult. Each of us carried a heavy pack, and we had to cut every foot of the way if we travelled along the river's banks. If we waded in the stream, we had to fight a swift current as well as climb over the huge boulders which filled its bed. All along the way we continued to find evidences of the men who had preceded us. Numbers of blazed trees indicated that at least a considerable number of them had come this far. Then one day we came across the last traces that we were to find.

For several miles their trail had been growing fainter. Finally we lost it completely. We stopped to reconnoitre. A short distance behind us there was a large open cave in the face of the limestone cliff, and we made our way back to it. Its roof was blackened by the smoke of many campfires. Digging round in the humus near the entrance yielded bits of every conceivable thing that an army would carry. The equipment was so thickly scattered about that every square foot of ground gave up something. The men had thrown away their machetes, the one indispensable tool in the jungle. There were parts of rifles, cooking gear, buttons from clothes, but not a solitary clue to what had become of the men themselves. Nor did we ever find any—but we think we know.

We decided to make camp on their old site and see if anything would throw further light on their tragedy. For it was evident that the army's wild rout had been caused by something. Men in the jungle do not throw away their machetes, their guns, their clothing for no reason, particularly men who are native to the country. We doubted that they had been attacked by wild Indians, for the Indians would surely have salvaged the guns and machetes. Certainly starvation or lack of water had not been the cause, for the jungle was full of foodstuffs with which some of them at least would have been familiar, while the river was only a stone's throw. True, the place was alive with *pinolillos* and *conchudos*, but we were beginning to develop a certain immunity to their poison, and it hardly seemed likely that they had suddenly finished off several hundred men. The thing that puzzled us most was why they had not turned back. The trail which they had cut in would still have been fresh, and they were no more than a week's journey from the village where we had taken Pussyfoot. The possibility of some swift and deadly epidemic remained, or some unknown scourge—something as deadly to men as the vampire bats were to animals. Like the beaches along the coast of Baja California where we had come across the camp sites of shipwrecked crews, this place filled us with a sense of desolation which we did our best to fight off. At last, tired, depressed, and no nearer the solution of the mystery than when we arrived, we went to sleep in our bug-proof tent.

When I awoke my whole body felt as if, to use a familiar expression, it had "gone to sleep." It was numb and tingly all over, as though the circulation had been impeded. My head felt as if it were stuffed with cotton.

The feeling was much the same as the aftereffects of an anaesthetic. I lay still for a while trying to determine what could be the matter with me. When I finally unzipped the tent flaps and staggered out I could hardly use my legs; they felt like unwieldy clubs. Something was decidedly wrong, and I wakened Ginger. She rolled over on her stomach and crawled out of the tent. I stared at her body in amazement and horror. From the expression on her face I knew that I must be in a similar condition. With a sickening shock I realized what had happened to us. We stared at each other for a long minute and then uttered the one word, *"talaje."* The most deadly insect in the jungle had bitten us. The natives regarded it as a catastrophe of the first magnitude to be bitten once by a *talaje*—and we were covered with their bites. The possible dangers of our condition made a malarial attack alone in the jungle seem about as important as a light case of the *grippe* at home. Minutes passed before we could collect our scattered wits. I crawled back into the tent and examined the sleeping bag, which was fairly alive with the little grey insects. In one corner of the tent was a small tear in the canvas floor. Somehow, some way, we had snagged the tent during the previous day's travelling, and the *talajes* had found their way in.

The *talaje* is a small grey insect which travels only at night, and is found only in certain sections of the country. It is believed that they live in humus or rotten wood. Occasionally they are found in native huts. Flesh-eaters, they are reputed to travel great distances following the scent of human beings. Before the *talaje* bites its host it injects under the skin an anaesthetic powerful enough to numb the flesh for an hour or two. Then it injects another chemical which dissolves the flesh upon which the insect feeds. When it is through feeding, blood fills the little cavity beneath the skin, forming a blister. Within a short time a black bruise forms round the blister as the poison works its way out through the capillaries of the skin. If the skin is broken a running sore develops which lasts for several months, and since it is liable to infection it is frequently fatal. If the blister is not broken new flesh forms in the cavity in about a week. Then the sore scabs over and dries up.

Now we knew what had happened to the army, but death for ourselves seemed a pretty stiff price to pay for finding out. We carefully picked our way down to the creek and as carefully washed the remaining *talajes* from our clothes and bodies, for one careless move might break a blister. Then we sat on a rock with our feet in the water and tried to plan. It was almost impossible to think coherently because of the toxic conditions of our bodies and the pain of the wounds, now that the anaesthetic was beginning to wear off.

"Dan," Ginger said, "we've got to get out of this country somehow, but how are we going to do it?"

"I don't know," I replied. "We can't carry our packs, or even wear our gun belts without breaking some of these blisters. Even our feet are blis-

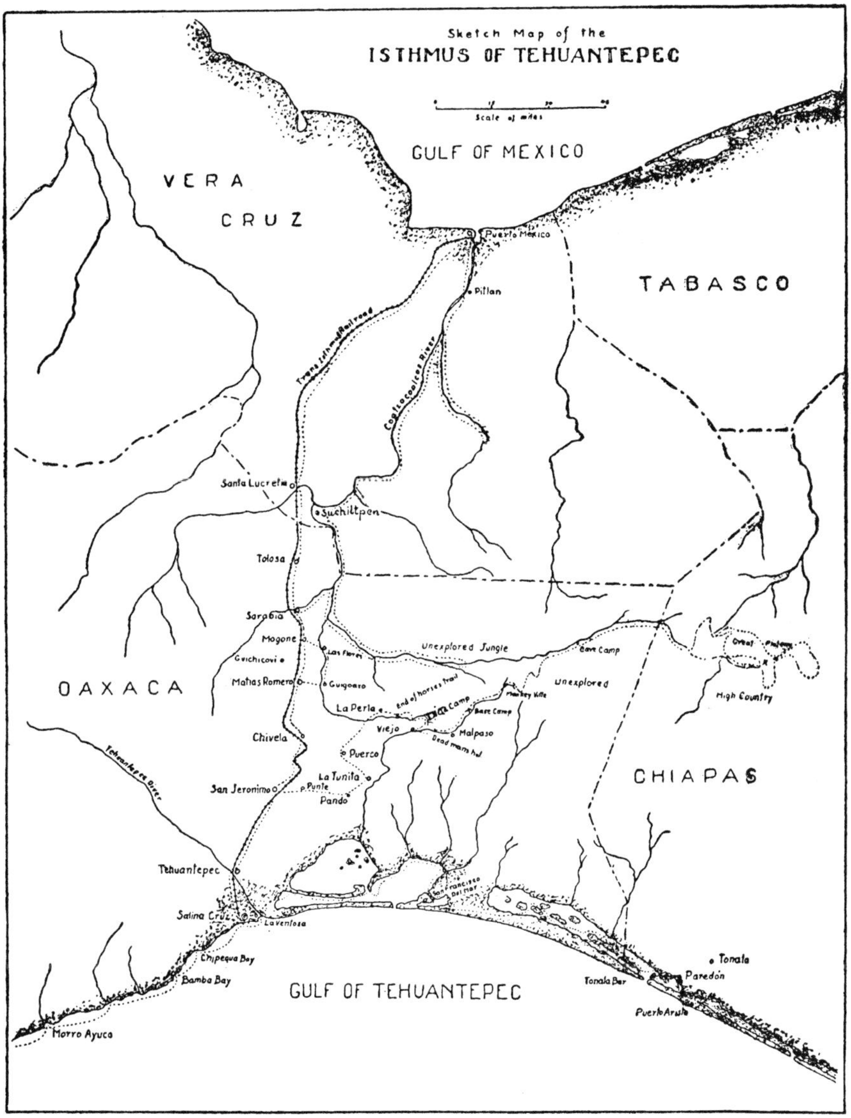

Sketch Map of the
ISTHMUS OF TEHUANTEPEC
Scale of miles
GULF OF MEXICO
VERA
CRUZ
TABASCO
Puerto Mexico
Pitlan
Coatzacoalcos River
Santa Lucretia
Suchiltpen
Tolosa
Sarabia
Mogone
Guichicovi
Matias Romero
Las Flores
Unexplored Jungle
Cave Camp
Unexplored
Base Camp
La Perla
Viejo
Malpaso
Chivela
Puerco
La Tunita
San Jeronimo
Pando
OAXACA
CHIAPAS
High Country
Tehuantepec
Salina Cruz
La Ventosa
Chipequa Bay
Bamba Bay
Morro Ayuco
GULF OF TEHUANTEPEC
Tonala Bar
Tonala
Paredon

tered, and we don't dare put on sandals—let alone hike. It's a hard week's travelling back to the village."

Then Ginger said something that gave us an idea as we turned over in our befuddled minds the few possibilities for action. "We've got to stay here until these bites heal, but we can't stay in that camp. Oh, if we could only find an island."

We started off upstream in search of an island, but our progress was painfully slow. Each move had to be calculated in advance, so as not to brush against anything that might break a blister, and each movement made us wince with pain. Our nervous systems were so dulled by the poison that our arms and legs responded poorly to our efforts to use them, and our heads seemed three times larger than normal. We continued the search, however, until further progress became impossible; the way was blocked by falls.

Discouraged by our failure, we made our way back to camp. The first thing that had to be done was to rid the tent and sleeping bag of the *talajes*. Ginger pulled the sleeping bag down to the creek and began to search them out and kill them, while I got the tent down to the water. Afterwards we built a fire and made some coffee. Neither of us had any appetite for food. As we sipped the coffee in silence, both of us preoccupied with our problem, I was filled with admiration for Ginger's courage, for she had never once complained. This heartened me as well, for the situation was going to call for all the self-denial and determination that we had. We should have to guard not only ourselves but each other as well against any possible chance of breaking a blister. If either one of us should stumble or slip against a rough surface, or even a twig, our chance of survival would be almost hopeless. The resultant running sores were focal points for infection.

Ginger set down her cup and gazed at the widening rings of purple that were forming round each bite. "It's a funny thing," she said, "how our fears shift from one thing to another. In the beginning I worried over what would happen if one of us should break a leg—that seemed to be the worst thing that could happen. If we survive this ordeal I'll never be afraid of anything again."

"Yes," I agreed, "we are so busy being afraid of what may happen that we seldom think about the real danger. From now on let's forget what will happen to us if—? Let's go downstream; there may be some place there we can find."

Our search downstream was rewarded. A large, flat rock extending well out into the water could easily be coverted into an island by a little digging on the mainland side. But there was another problem. Could we erect the tent on it to protect ourselves against the innumerable flying insects? It seemed possible that by taking our time and working slowly, we could build a platform of limbs and palm branches on which to set it.

All day we worked at the task of finding and transporting the necessary materials. We had to watch every movement, weigh every step. Our heads pounded and ached until it seemed that our eyes would pop out of their sockets. Our bodies were bathed in perspiration, which in turn caused an intolerable itching. The purple bruises were now about three-quarters of an inch in diameter, and almost covered us. By sundown we had accomplished our purpose and had erected the mended tent on a small palm-covered platform where we would be safe from insects.

Days of careful, methodical, and tortured existence followed. One of us always kept guard while the other slept, watching every movement of the sleeper, that he might not break a blister by tossing, turning, or scratching. We relieved the tedium by laughing at the restraints and compulsions of the situation—"every little movement" was so fraught with meaning, that we didn't dare even to slap at a mosquito.

Our diet during the first period of our convalescence was composed of the reserve rations that we had brought along. We ate nothing but boiled rice, corn, and beans. But as the poison left our systems we became ravenously hungry for fresh meat, and hunted for wild turkey, wild chicken, and doves. There were no other animals in the canyon, since they cannot survive in *talaje* country.

The blisters gradually dried and healed. They left scabs which remained for some time longer, but we were able to travel in about two weeks. The last few days before our departure we spent preparing food for the trail ahead. On one of the ridges above the canyon I had shot a deer, and this gave us a much needed supply of dried meat.

We left that last fateful camp of Diaz's army with a new attitude. Our egotism was left behind, together with a goodly supply of over-confidence and self-assurance. Man may be lord of all he surveys in some places—but he isn't in the jungle. It is easy to see why races that have successfully maintained themselves in the equatorial jungles have never been individualists in the Western meaning of the term. Only men who are group-conscious can survive.

Two days' journey from the *talaje* camp brought us to the headwaters of the stream we had been following. We climbed the high ridge to the west and dropped down into a great valley. Fresh machete marks which must have been made within a period of six months filled us with curiosity. Carefully we followed the trail through the thick growth, looking for the stumps and blaze marks on the trees. But there was one thing about those blaze marks that filled us with astonishment—they all *faced the trail*! We looked at each other in amazement. We were following the trail of a greenhorn! But how had he come this far? An experienced traveller would have blazed the tree on both sides so that the blazes could be seen going up or coming down the trail. "And have you noticed how all the machete marks slant the same way?" Ginger observed. "Whoever went up the trail did not return this way."

We were certain that it had been made by a white man because it led directly through stinging bushes that any native would have avoided. Our interest heightened as we followed this amateur's trail. Late in the afternoon it brought us to an extensive flat and to the banks of a river where we found a small thatched shelter. We approached it cautiously, but it was silent and deserted. We threw off our packs and prowled round, trying to read the story.

It had been constructed during the present dry season by some one only slightly familiar with the jungle, for it was so close to the water's edge that it would have been carried away by high water. The thatching came all the way to the ground. No native would have done this, for it gave crawling things an opportunity to get into the thatching and drop on the occupant. The builder had some knowledge of jungle animals, however, for heavy tiger bars guarded both ends. We stepped inside. It was plainly the camp of a white man. He had built a rough wooden bunk in one corner. Pieces of equipment lay scattered on the floor—a rusty knife, fork, spoon, enamelled plate, what was left of a pair of blankets, and a worn out pair of hobnailed boots.

Then we made a momentous discovery. In a mildewed pack under the bunk were a few cans of food. All of them were rusted through with the exception of one can of milk, which, though rusted all over, was still intact. This was a bonanza of the first order—the occasion for a fiesta. We decided to have it the following day, and in the meantime to clean out the hut, erect our tent in it, and see if we could find out more about its missing occupant.

As we cleaned the hut we examined every little clue that might show who the man was, why he had come here, and what had become of him. It was evident that he had not died near the hut, for his gun and machete were missing. After we had the place in order, we had a light meal and turned in, for we were very tired.

About midnight I wakened out of a sound sleep, startled by something, but by what I did not know. I immediately woke Ginger, and together we listened. The only sound was the beat of heavy rain upon the thatching. There was nothing unusual in that, for this was the beginning of the rainy season. Nevertheless, something was decidedly wrong. We got up, dressed, and built a fire. My uneasy feeling persisted although there was no logical explanation for it; so we strapped on our gun belts, stuffed our pockets with extra ammunition, and went out in the rain to look round. The only result was a good soaking.

As I built up the fire to dry out our wet clothing, Ginger also became uneasy. "I've got a hunch," she said, "that we had better pack up and get out of here."

That made it unanimous, and we began collecting our things. While we were taking the tent down, we heard a roar from up the river, followed by the sound of falling trees. Then we knew—the crest of the first flood of the rainy season was on its way. We hastily gathered up what gear we could carry, and stumbled along in the darkness towards a little hill that rose about fifty yards behind the hut. When we returned for the balance of the equipment, six inches of water swirled round the shelter.

At last we stood in the rain on the little hill with all our possessions beside us, listening to the roar of the water and the thunderous crashing of the great trees. We both shivered a little as we thought of our near escape. "Well, we at least have a can of milk," Ginger said philosophically.

"Did you bring it?" I asked.

"Why, no," she replied. "I thought I saw you pick it up."

We had failed to bring our precious can of milk! Together we started off down the hill. Half-way to the hut the water was already knee-deep; it was obvious that we couldn't reach it on foot. I was determined to have one last try for it, however, so telling Ginger to wait for me, I went back to the hill and secured the sixty-foot lariat. Working our way from tree to tree, we reached the little clearing round the hut. The angry waters were tearing its thatch away, but it still stood. I tied one end of the lariat round my waist while Ginger fastened the other end to a stout sapling. At first she protested vigorously, telling me that I would be drowned, but she was tying the line round the tree as she talked. She wanted that can of milk as much as I did.

Throwing my weight against the swirling water, I worked upstream, seeking what little shelter the trees offered. A sharp tug on the rope soon indicated that I had reached the end of the line. With a silent prayer that the rope would be long enough, I swung out in an arc towards the hut. The water knocked me off my feet, and I just managed to grab one of the tiger bars. The hut shook uneasily as I reached inside and groped round in the bunk for the can. My hand closed round its rusted surface, and I had only time to turn and shout to Ginger to pull on the line before the shelter gave way and whirled off down the stream. I hung on to the can as the rush of water washed me into the undergrowth at the edge of the clearing, where I managed to regain my footing. While Ginger tugged on the rope, I worked my way along by pulling on the bushes. Even with her help it was all I could do to work my way against the strong current to where she stood in water almost to her armpits. Together we fought the storm and regained the safety of the hillside.

As we sat in the rain, trying to catch our breath, Ginger said, "I wonder sometimes if we have good sense. Here we are, a hundred miles from nowhere, and we risk our necks for a can of milk. It sounds foolish."

"Well, men risk their necks for gold," I said defensively, "and right now I would rather have this can of milk, wouldn't you?"

A fire seemed highly desirable at this point, so we began to scout round for firewood. Very quickly we found that we were not the only occupants of the little hill. All the small walking and crawling things in the valley were sharing it with us. It was anything but pleasant to feel round in the darkness for wood, but at last we found a small log, and cutting off a section of it, dragged it back to camp. We made a shelter of the tent and, crawling under it, set about the task of chopping in the dark without cutting off our fingers. Everything was too saturated for us to light a fire in the usual way, so we made a fireblock. The wet wood was trimmed off the outside of the log to its dry centre. Then while Ginger made a spindle and bow, I fashioned the friction block, and scraped enough wood fibre for tinder. Soon we were sitting round a cheerful fire and beginning to enjoy ourselves.

At daylight we found a more comfortable camp site upstream. There we dried out our bedraggled equipment, and prepared a banquet with the can of milk for the pièce de résistance. The menu was broiled breast of turkey, turkey stew, and cream flavoured with coffee.

For three more days we toiled up this canyon, crossing and recrossing the swollen river. There were many moments of suspense as we made our way along precipitous rock ledges, or climbed the steep mountain sides when falls and rapids made progress below impossible. This was virgin country, for there were no indications that any one had ever been here before. On the fourth day we arrived at a parklike flat shaded by giant trees. Long vines trailed along the ground from the branches overhead, and birds with gorgeous plumage flew among the foliage. The scene resembled an exotic motion-picture setting for "Tarzan of the Apes."

The thought must have occurred to Ginger the moment she saw it, for she dropped her pack and ran across the clearing shouting, "I'm Tarzan!" She grabbed one of the trailing lianas and took off in a beautiful apeman swing. The result of this manœuvre in no way resembled Johnny Weismuller's dashing progress from tree to tree. There was a crackling of dead wood as she landed in a heap with the vine coiled over her head. I howled with laughter at her expression of disgust as she crawled out from beneath the tangled debris. "I never did like Tarzan, anyway," she sputtered.

Though the place proved disappointing as a practice ground for apeman activities, it was an ideal base camp. We spent ten days here building a substantial shelter, well above the high-water mark of the river, and preparing food for our journey into the interior. There was an enchantment about the place that grew with each day. Great banyan and Leche Maria trees spread canopied branches overhead. Fern palms and many varieties of broad leaved plants edged the clearing on three sides. On the open side the river flowed through a lane of fantastic tropic vegetation. The jungle and the river formed an amphitheatre of green against whose sombre background the brilliant flowers, birds, and butterflies stood out in high relief.

When the hut was completed we fastened over the door with much ceremony a carved sign reading, "Base Camp." The next thing was to secure the food supply. We smoked and dried venison and turkey, and collected and prepared wild coffee, *yuca* roots, and nuts from the *coquito* palm.

This palm is probably man's best friend in the higher jungle country. It is a small tree with a slender bole which grows only in shaded sections, and is well protected by thorns. The nuts hang in small, thorny clusters among the lower branches and are about the size of walnuts. The meat tastes like a coco-nut and is very oily. The creamy white blossoms, which grow in compact clusters, resemble broccoli and are good to eat. The heart of the palm is also edible and tastes like cabbage. The nuts are dried and the oil is rendered out for cooking. Its branches make excellent thatching for huts.

"Base Camp" was to be a store house for our extra rations, filled with enough corn, beans, and rice to see us out of the country in the event of an accident or illness. By making horseshoe packs out of the tent and sleeping bag, we could also leave one of the knapsacks behind. In this we left our native clothes, extra sandals, travelling papers, exposed films, and enough food for an emergency. To prevent animals and insects from reaching the stores, we took one of Ginger's kettle chains and suspended it in the smoke of the fire until it was covered with creosote. Then we hung the packsack from one of the rafters with it. As an added precaution we kept a smudge fire burning when we were not using the hut, until even the thatching had a liberal coating of creosote.

In addition to these physical preparations, we gave careful thought to the nature of the country before us. This territory could not be traversed in the leisurely fashion of the men who walk, clad in full tropical regalia through the parklike avenues of motion picture sets. There were no trails except game trails, and these were so low that one had to bend almost double to negotiate them. The ground was thickly covered with rotting debris and undergrowth, the home of crawling pests. In order to cut a path through this solid mass of vegetation, the machete must be razor-keen. A dull blade jars the growth overhead, and sends cascades of stinging insects down one's neck. Each plant has a method of protection that can spell disaster to the unwary.

Neither is the physical labour of swinging a machete hour after hour anything to discount. There is a technique to this. Two slashes cut off the growth just above the ground. Then two more strokes, high above the head and as far in front as you can reach, drop the whole tangled mass of vegetation into the trail below. The dense wall of green prevents your kicking this aside, so it is necessary to walk over it. As a result your feet seldom touch the ground. Frequent stops must be made at regular intervals to pick off the accumulation of insects which seem well supplied with grappling hooks.

In addition, there are hundreds of varieties of fungus growths, moulds, bacteria, and parasites. Some are harmful, others are not; but they all play a definite part in the scheme of things. Many have specialized functions which lay the ground work for the whole vast, intricate panorama of jungle life. The termites ceaselessly clean up fallen trees and pave the way for new growth. Some of them are aided by minute living organisms. One species of termite eats the wood, which is re-eaten by a protozoa which lives in the termite's stomach. The termite does not subsist on the original wood pulp but on the excretions of the protozoa. The soil is in turn fertilized by the excrement of the termite.

Another little insect which assists the termite bores in underneath the bark of the fallen tree and there deposits its eggs with the spores of a tiny fungus growth. By the time the eggs have hatched, the fungus, which grows in the form of minute asparagus, is well established. The fungus feeds upon the cells of the wood, and the young insects feed upon the asparagus, much as a cow would feed upon alfalfa.

We wondered what would happen if the delicate equilibrium between the forces of growth and destruction were thrown out of balance in any way. Besides the multiplicity of living forms round us we felt small and insignificant. Our only chance of being able to enjoy the jungle's prodigality and splendour depended upon our ability to fit ourselves into its complicated life pattern. This was as much a mental operation as it was a physical adaptation. Since bodily comfort was out of the question, its importance had to be discounted. It was possible, by an effort of will, not to think continuously of our bruises, abrasions, and bites. Otherwise the jungle would soon have made us both into hypochondriacs.

One of the things that we found reinforced our morale was our personal appearance. Ever since leaving the *talaje* camp we had been in constant pain and had grown careless. Ginger had let her hair grow down over her forehead as a protection against insects, and I had let my whiskers grow for the same reason. We decided to make a right-about face. From then on, we both groomed ourselves to the limits of our slender resources. The result was an increased sense of well-being which more than repaid us for the effort.

One night shortly before we left "Base Camp" Ginger said, "Dan, I wonder if we aren't going to have a difficult time fitting into civilization when we return home? If it's all right with you, I'd like to go back for a couple of months after we have finished our trip. If we don't like it we can start out again."

In a sense I was also curious, but I felt that I knew what the answer would be. Men who have left cities for any length of time are seldom happy in them again.

At last we were off, after making a careful last minute recheck of all our supplies and equipment. Ahead of us loomed a great canyon, and we set our course in its direction. Once on the trail, we fought for every inch of ground that we gained. The south-east course of the river led us for days through a mighty gorge flanked by sheer limestone cliffs. Then it changed its direction and turned at a sharp right angle to plough through a great crevasse—a fault line in a schist formation—emerging to follow again its channel along the base of towering limestone escarpments. Tributary rivers plunged over the cliffs in vertical, breath-taking cataracts into deep pools cut out of the solid rock of the river bed below. The roar of the water echoed back and forth between the gigantic sounding boards of the canyon's walls until our ears were deafened.

Progress up the canyon was slow and difficult. There were days when we advanced only a mile or two, although we travelled many miles to gain that slight distance. Falls blocked our way in many places and we were forced to scale the slippery, water-worn surfaces that flanked them by constructing ladders of long poles lashed together with tough vines. At other times it was necessary to climb the steep sides of the canyon. Going up was not so difficult as coming down. To get back to the canyon floor we braided long ropes of *bejuco*, fastened them to trees or round a rock on the canyon's rim, and lowered ourselves over the cliffs that formed its sides. Where the overhanging walls enclosed deep pools, we constructed rafts from saplings lashed together with vines, and poled ourselves past the barrier. Some nights we spent in caves. Other nights we slept among huge piles of boulders. Our bodies became battered and bruised from rough treatment.

But the satisfaction we achieved was worth the price. Each handicap that we were able to overcome represented more than a physical triumph over environment. Without question we gained a certain psychological freedom that widened the radius of our ability to act—a release from the self-imposed limitations of fear and doubt.

At last we emerged upon a second flat or mesa. It was not as large as the one at "Base Camp," but it more than made up in colour and variety what it lacked in size. Here, owing to the higher elevation, the bird and insect life, as well as the vegetation, differed from that below. The flowering plants, and notably the insects, were of brilliant and more vivid hues. Even the mosquitoes were a bright gun-metal blue.

Unfortunately we are not entomologists, and can describe only in non-technical terms the appearance of some of these extraordinary insects. Many of them may be unknown to science, for we saw them only in the highlands. There was one, perhaps an inch in length, shaped like a shield, whose back had an intricate design in powder blue and orange. Another, which we called the "Gold Bug," was an ovoid about an inch and a quarter long. It was like an iridescent jewel, with opalescent tints superimposed upon a background of glittering copperish gold. There was a long, slender, joined insect of a beautiful, translucent grass-green, which made its home among grasses so similar in construction to itself that it was almost impossible to detect its presence unless it moved. It was not more than a quarter of an inch in diameter, but it was four inches long! One bug, which lived among fallen leaves, hopped instead of walked. Since it looked exactly like a fallen leaf in shape, colour, and size, it could be detected only by accident. Grasshoppers were gaily dressed in green, red and black, and brown and red. An insect similar to a grasshopper in its general appearance, although fully two inches long, had a dark brown body and wings, and under wings of fine, transparent, veined red. There were insects that looked like bits of fallen bark. As a general rule, all of them blended perfectly with their environment.

The butterflies were miracles of protective colouration as well as beauty. And the orchids, not to be outdone, resembled butterflies. The most gorgeous of the butterflies dwelt in the deeper jungle. It was an ultramarine blue with a delicate Persian-like scrollwork on the underside of its wings. There were black butterflies with tailed hind wings, which seemed to be made of cut black velvet trimmed with red. There were white, apple-green, gold, orange, yellow, and blue butterflies, and others in all combinations of these colours.

There was so much that was new to us that we hiked round a bit before we made camp on a beautiful site near the river. It was time for supper and while Ginger collected twigs for a fire, I went out to gather larger wood. I had gone a short distance when I heard the sound of a breaking limb, and turned in time to see Ginger whirl and draw her gun. I reached for the Luger and peered into the underbrush. "What's the matter?" I called.

"Some one just hit me on the head," she answered. "I thought a native had sneaked up behind me."

Just as I finished assuring her that she must have been mistaken, another stick hurtled through the air and landed at her feet. We looked up into the trees and into the face of a spider monkey who was swinging by his tail and grimacing at us. In our relief, we teased the little fellow by making faces and jabbering at him. The monkey, however, didn't like our mockery, and began to emit ear-splitting shrieks as he jumped up and down on a limb, showering us with twigs, leaves, and branches. In a moment monkeys from far and near took up his refrain. The jungle reverberated with their angry cries. Suddenly they began to converge on our camp site from all directions, rushing to the defence of their brother. We were unfamiliar with the habits of spider monkeys or we would have been more cautious. As it was, they sprayed us thoroughly before we could seek the safety of the river. We took a good scrubdown in the stream, and decided to call the place "Monkeyville," although Ginger held out quite a while for

"Rainville" (which was a pretty way of saying it). We discovered, however, that if we left the monkeys alone they behaved decently.

We constructed another thatched hut in "Monkeyville" and collected more food for the trail. A preliminary survey indicated that the route ahead would be even more difficult to negotiate. In hopes of finding an easier passage into the interior, we climbed to the summit of a great peak. From this vantage point we discovered that the whole country was laid out in a series of great stairsteps, set at an angle. Some of the cliffs on the face of the steps appeared to be a thousand feet high. There was no route open to us except the canyon, however. For our next goal, we decided on a great limestone half-dome in the far distance. Beyond the dome the appearance of the country seemed to change.

Four days of travelling brought us to the base of the dome. We made camp near its foot on the opposite side of the river. As we explored the territory near-by we came to the entrance of a limestone cave. Since caves had always been our special weakness we decided to investigate this one. Upon a ridge we secured some pitch pine for torches. We split the wood into strips about four feet long and bound them together. One such torch will last over half an hour. Armed with as many as we could carry, we set out to explore the cavern.

None of the caves we had seen during our trip had prepared us for the beauty of this one. We spent several hours on our first visit wandering in the great room near its entrance, gazing at the fantastic forms and colourations. The torches flickered upon the glistening surfaces of the gigantic stalactites that hung from its ceiling. The years that went into the creation of the great stalagmites rising from its floor stunned the imagination.

On our next visit, loaded with armfuls of torches, we started out to explore its labyrinthine passages. One great room opened into another, equally dazzling in the variety and beauty of its formations. There were enormous altars, glittering icebergs, Chinese pagodas, alabaster urns, pipe organs no building made by man could house, and crystal chandeliers weighing tons, whose diamond facets shimmered in the light. We soon realized that it would take weeks to survey the cavern more than casually, so we decided to retrace our steps. It was round noon when we began the return journey, which we estimated would take about two hours. Hunger speeded our footsteps as we went along. As hours passed and no glimmer of light revealed the entrance, it was obvious that somewhere we had turned in the wrong direction, but when? Had the mistake occurred at the outset? It was also obvious that the seepage of water which had deposited the lime on the stalactites for at least one hundred and fifty million years had in all probability undermined an area many square miles in extent.

The only thing to do was to follow the pitch pine droppings back to the place from which we had started the return journey, and to leave other markers as we went along, so that we would not follow this passage a second time. We hoped that once back at the starting-point we could follow the droppings that we had left as we came in. There were enough torches left to last for about ten hours. It was one of the longest days either of us ever spent, but luck at last rewarded our efforts. We reached the entrance about midnight, and once again drew deep breaths of fresh air.

Back in camp and hungry as bears, we sat round the fire enjoying some toasted jerky and parched *yuca* roots. Ginger said speculatively, "I'll bet there's gold in that cave."

"Sure there is," I agreed jokingly. "Maybe a million or two."

She wanted to do a little panning, however, so the next morning we went back armed with our frying pan, plenty of torches, and a cup to carry the gold in. Neither of us took the matter seriously, and jested about the business as we filled the pan with gravel and settled ourselves near one of the many pools in the floor. As we worked the gravel off we were amazed at the amount of black sand in the pan. Amazed, however, does not do justice to our feelings when we saw by the aid of the torchlight the glistening yellow metal that hung back in the bottom of the pan. "It *must* be iron pyrites," I said. "There couldn't be that much gold in one little pan of gravel."

We scraped the metal into the cup and continued panning for several hours. Then we carried the results of our efforts out into the daylight. There was no mistake about it. It was gold! Yet somehow the discovery didn't excite us as it might have under different circumstances. We had done without money for so long that it had lost most of its importance. Not until that moment, perhaps, were we conscious of what this country had done to us. To live in it we had had to discard old values and acquire others. The fascination and mystery of the country itself overshadowed and minimized the discovery of gold.

That night round the fire we discussed the situation. Did we want to abandon the trip and become miners? If so, we ought to make up our minds to do it properly. It was slow, tedious work to extract the metal by using our mess-kit pans for gold pans. The thing to do was to cut timber, construct a sluice box, and build a drag to haul the gravel to the stream. It would preclude doing anything else for a long time, except hunt for food. The only thing we needed money for in the near future was to buy our passage home from Panama—if we ever got there. So we decided to continue with the mess-kit pan until we had at least that much gold. Later on, after the present trip was over, we could always return and engage in serious mining if we wanted to.

Our lives for the next two weeks became a routine of foraging, cooking, cutting pitch pine, and panning. Each afternoon we emerged from our treasure cave covered from head to toe with the soot of the torches. We relieved the monotony by a race to see who could find the biggest nugget first. Ginger walked off with the honours by finding a nugget as big as her thumbnail. We often stopped to examine some particularly lovely piece of gold. The cave itself was limestone, but on one side the schist cut into it. The gold we were panning had apparently been washed directly out of the formation, and had never been rolled or carried any distance by water. Ginger found a beautiful piece that resembled German script. I discovered one in the form of a pointing hand.

One day Ginger said, "If you think we have enough money to pay our passage home, let's quit and go exploring. From now on we can consider ourselves millionaires anyway. We've got a bank full of gold and I'd like to see any one try and find it."

So we stopped, buried what metal we had, and drew a complicated map of its location. After a week to replenish our food supply we were again ready to be off.

If the road to "Monkeyville" had seemed arduous and difficult while we toiled over it, in retrospect it became an ideal highway. For the country above the dome was broken and upended, and the river followed a tortuous course through the gigantic strata of broken limestone and schist. In places the schist was shot through with quartz stringers; in others the formation was broken by hard rock. From the many evidences of mineral wealth, it would have been a prospector's paradise.

We clawed and scrambled up the canyon for four days. Then the way became impassable. The canyon narrowed down to a deep gorge through which the water roared and tumbled. We spent two days trying to find a way over the cliffs to the north, before we abandoned the idea. Only a human fly could have found toe holds on their sheer vertical faces. A ridge to the south offered a possible route past the unscalable limestone barriers and we followed along its crest into higher country.

Now we travelled along a succession of pine-covered ridges. There was little game and we lived on our meagre supply of corn and beans. Unable to find any streams, we secured our water by spreading out the tent to catch the rain—when it rained. When it failed to rain, we shook the dew from the undergrowth and bushes on to the tent. This was vile-tasting stuff but it was wet.

Three days of hard climbing brought us at last to the summit of a high peak. The panorama which spread out below and before us was breathtaking. To the east we could see for the first time the high plateau that we were attempting to reach. Great waterfalls tumbled down the sheer cliffs that formed its sides. Between us and that gigantic butte lay a torn, twisted country that looked as though no man could defy its impregnability. It seemed absolutely impassable. But if there was ever a place to which a remnant of a conquered race might go to seek sanctuary, that plateau was assuredly the spot.

We sat on a huge granite boulder and gazed long and speculatively at those badlands through which we would have to find a way. Ginger sighed as she said, "I don't see how we can do it. But how the place matches the stories about it! It's certainly 'forbidding' enough."

There seemed only one thing to do, and that was to go ahead and trust to our luck and ingenuity to see us through. We did exactly that. Bareheaded and almost bare-skinned—for our clothes were threadbare—we toiled across the rocky ground. The tropic sun beat down unmercifully, burning our skins a deep mahogany. The rarefied atmosphere at that high altitude had us gasping for breath. The small amount of food and water that we consumed fell far short of supplying our overtaxed bodies. Though our feet were tough and calloused, the sharp flintlike rocks cut into our flesh through the holes in our native sandals. To complete our ruin, the thorny bushes tore away our few remnants of clothes. Under these conditions travelling became impossible, and we began to look for a place where we could rest a while and repair the damage.

We finally worked our way across a great limestone stairstep towards the rim of a deep canyon. Below, a cascading stream was surrounded by lush tropic vegetation. After a tedious day of lowering ourselves down precipitous cliffs and scrambling along dangerously narrow ledges, we reached bottom. Here the jungle's cupboard was wide open. Game was plentiful. Wild fruits and edible plants grew everywhere. We named the place "Paradise Valley."

After a day's rest we put up a shelter and replenished our supply of food and clothing. A word seems in order here about foraging in the jungle. Notwithstanding the plenitude of material, this is not altogether simple. Had we been forced to secure food in Paradise Valley at the outset of our trip we should probably have starved to death. Fruits, nuts, and berries do not grow in plain sight on every bush. Most of them are hidden, or grow in inaccessible places. It is seldom advisable to climb trees, for they are alive with ants. But a forked stick fastened to a long pole, or a sharpened boomerang will knock the fruit down. There is stiff competition among the birds and monkeys for the ripened fruit, so it must be picked before it attracts their attention, and allowed to ripen in camp. In hunting it is safe to say that ten animals see you for every one that you see. The odds are always against the hunter, owing to the animal's keener sense of hearing, sight, and smell. Securing food in the jungle soon banishes from your mind the idea that the world owes you a living. Here, as elsewhere, the ratio of return is about equal to the amount of industry and energy you are willing to spend. You can starve, or live in comparative luxury.

Three deer supplied us with meat, which we cut into thin strips and hung over racks near a smoky fire to dry. The hides we buried in the damp earth, allowing them to rot just enough so that the hair could be easily scraped off. Rendering out the marrow of the leg bones gave us a gun oil which, in our opinion, is far superior to any commercial product available The sinews and intestines were cleaned and cured to use as lashings.

While the hides were curing, we collected large quantities of *coquito* palm nuts, dyewood, and various barks that contained tannic acid; also gum from the pitch pines and the fruit and roots that we needed for food. Then Ginger busied herself drying and preparing the *yuca* roots, guavas, wild figs, *zapotes*, and a little berry similar to the elderberry, while I tanned the hides.

The hides were first trimmed, then given a good scraping to remove any fat and membrane adhering to the inside, as well as to remove the hair from the outside. Then they were dipped alternately in strong solutions made from dyewood and bark, and finally rubbed with a mixture of ashes and clay. This is not the best method of tanning hides, but it does well enough when one is in a hurry. This process completed, the hides were placed in the sun and saturated with a dressing made from *coquito* oil, resin, and deer fat. This was the tedious part of the job and required hours of rubbing, but when it was finished the hides were soft and pliable and quite waterproof.

Now the camp was turned into a tailor shop. Ginger cut and fitted a short skirt for herself and I made a pair of shorts. When the pieces were cut and ready to sew, we placed the seams side by side and cut a series of small holes directly opposite each other all the way down the seam. The pieces were then laced together with thongs made from the left-over scraps of leather. It is possible to cut a thong six or eight feet long from a small piece of leather by starting to cut it at the outside edge, cutting round and round towards the centre to form a spiral. Our footwear was easy to make, being merely a flat piece cut to fit the foot, and fitted with lashings to tie round the heel and over the toe.

Our work was finally finished, and we were eager to push on. But the only way open to us lay up the canyon, for we could not scale the cliffs, even though we had come down them. For two days we travelled pleasantly along the banks of the stream, until the thousand-foot canyon walls began to close in to form a narrow gorge. We hunted in vain for a way over these walls to the pine ridge above. Although it filled us with misgiving, there was nothing to do but tackle the gorge.

The river seemed to be jealous of every foot of space between its great stone ramparts. We hugged the face of the cliffs to avoid being swept off our feet by the swift current. Sometimes the way led us through little caves made by old watercourses, sometimes over huge boulders, where we slipped and slid over the mossy, water-worn surfaces.

The afternoon of the second day found us at the end of the gorge, in a box canyon with a narrow opening through which the river plunged in a great cataract. The overhanging walls seemed about to topple down on us. We scanned them carefully for any possible means of egress. To one side a

The Forbidden Land

high waterfall tumbled down into a deep pool. The formation near the top was broken into ledges. That gave us an idea, and we retraced our steps down the canyon to see if there was a ledge that we could climb to, and from which we might reach the broken formation. Finding a narrow ledge that might be negotiated with extreme caution, we worked our way along the cliff in the direction of the waterfall. When we reached a position above the pool we were astonished to see what looked like a hewn pathway cut into the face of the rock which led to the top of the falls. Whether it had been cut by the river during the ages when the canyon was in the process of formation, or made by men, it was impossible to tell. But after all our difficult climbing it looked like an easy ascent. I said to Ginger, as I stepped on it, "It's going to be a cinch to reach the top now."

Then for no reason at all I slipped, lost my balance, and plunged down into the pool some twenty feet below. Weighted down by my pack and gun belt, I was being carried swiftly towards the rapids at the foot of the pool when Ginger threw me one end of the lariat. With her aid I managed to scramble to safety.

We spread out the sodden contents of my pack on some boulders to dry, and again started up the trail. Although the way was not difficult we took no chances this time, and carefully helped each other over the rough spots. Nearing the top of the falls, we heard an angry warning hiss. Somewhere on the ledge, just above our heads, a rattler lay concealed. I tried to dislodge the snake by shooting at it, but the bullets ricocheted harmlessly off the intervening ledge. We retreated to hold council. This was the only possible course to the Great Plateau—by now we referred to it in capitals—and the hour was late and there was no place to camp in the gorge. What to do?

I swam across the upper end of the pool, my purpose being to shoot the rattler from the other side. However, it was not possible to get high enough to see it. Abandoning the idea of leaving the gorge, that night we built a fire on a boulder where Ginger prepared supper. Since there was no place to set the tent up, we picked out the biggest, softest, flattest rock to sleep on.

Night came swiftly in the gloomy canyon, bringing with it an almost overpowering sense of imminent danger. We sat round the fire and talked of the long series of coincidences that had blocked our progress in this Forbidden Land. If the Indians' Guardian Spirits had actually existed, they could hardly have done a better job of trying to keep us out. True, we had survived the *talajes*, the flood, the cliffs, and a lot of other things, but could we indefinitely continue to do so? Even the snake on the ledge began to assume an illogical importance. I undoubtedly had tumbled into the pool because I had been careless and overconfident. The *talajes* had bitten us because we had not been careful enough to avoid tearing the tent. Each incident had been the result of our own failure or foolhardiness. Nevertheless, we were unable wholly to overcome the impact of the country's history. Throughout the night we frequently wakened, to sit up and talk about what lay over that barrier of limestone guarded by the rattler.

The next morning we cautiously approached the place where the snake had been, but no warning rattle greeted us. I tossed a small rock into the alcove where it had been lodged. There was no answering hiss. The way was clear.

A wide valley which opened out above the falls seemed to offer fair opportunities for travelling, at least for a few miles. We tramped along until nearly noon, when the appearance of the sky heralded a coming storm. As the thunderheads began piling up, we made camp near a small side stream. Insects swarmed about us in clouds, as they always do before a midday tropical storm. Directly it begins to rain they take shelter beneath the leaves, but their idea seems to be to make hay while the sun shines, and their onslaughts on other animals are particularly vicious at this time. We retreated to the shelter of the tent to eat our meal.

The cloud formations that precede a storm in these highlands are most spectacular. They are great, piled-up, towerlike structures, their undersides inky black, their upper portions snow-white. Sometimes towards evening the white cloud masses are brilliantly coloured by the sun's rays. The clouds release their moisture without any preliminary drizzle. Just before the solid sheets of water descend, the jungle becomes silent—and then comes the deluge. Within a few minutes little streams become torrents. All other sounds are blotted out by the roar of the water.

The next day we marched along the valley until we came to a fork in the stream. Since it was necessary to avoid the swollen watercourses, we started up the ridge that divided them at the fork. Two days of hard climbing along its crest brought us to where we could at last obtain a clear view of the Great Plateau. The country ahead was rumpled and broken as though a giant's hand had crumpled it. But with the coming of the rains our last chance to retreat had been cut off. No one could travel up those canyons or along the stream beds until the next dry season.

Several days of travel over the wet, uneven terrain finally brought us to the sheer cliffs that formed the base of the plateau. There was no way that we could see to scale them. Our food supply was almost exhausted, for there had been no game along the arid, rocky pine ridges that we had come across. The only thing to do was to search along the foot of the cliffs for some way up.

After two days of hunting, we found a cleavage in the rock wall that looked as though at one time it had been a watercourse. It seemed to be a fault in the formation that had been widened by erosion. It might formerly have been a cave which had collapsed, for its floor was littered with big limestone blocks. There was some water, but it was not a stream. It would run along for perhaps fifty feet, to disappear into one of the many depressions in the stream bed, where it ran underground. Sometimes we were unable to see the sky because of the overhanging walls from which big stalactites hung. In many places there were caverns high above our heads, possibly eroded by the wind.

The passage was an altogether strange and eerie place. We were more than glad to be done with it when we finally emerged on the plateau itself.

We stood on the rim of a great basin, bounded on three sides by jagged peaks. It spread out like a many-coloured carpet, a hundred brilliant hues woven into its background of rain-washed green. Each detail of far-off peak and vivid flowering tree was sharply etched in the clear mountain air. It was the loveliest place we had seen on earth.

How much of our reaction to the surroundings was based upon the stories we had heard about it, is hard to say. Had we stumbled upon it accidentally, knowing nothing of its legendary import, we should probably have been aware only of its unusual beauty. But as it was, the very air seemed pregnant with mystery. Unconsciously we lowered our voices, or lapsed into silence, while cutting our way through the gloom of the thick undergrowth. The place had an aura—born of our imagination perhaps—of things unseen, but seeing. We had a sense of being trespassers, who might be rudely shown the door. It was uncanny, and we did our best to dismiss the haunted feeling that the place evoked, and for which there was no basis in fact.

The undergrowth became sparser after perhaps a mile. Great trees began forming a canopy overhead. Then off to the right we glimpsed a sight that stopped us. Three immense, vine-covered, pyramidal mounds stood like sentinals under blankets of green foliage. When we reached the first one I began to cut away the tangled vines preparatory to scraping off the humus so that we could determine whether the pyramids were made of cut stones. Suddenly we were aware of the absolute silence that had fallen over the jungle. All the usual small sounds had ceased. I stopped, and we looked at each other; then simultaneously we backed away from the pyramid and stood motionless, listening. But there was nothing. A silence so profound gripped the jungle that we could hear the blood pounding in our ears. It was as though we had been plunged into a void—some vacuum, insulated against all sound waves. Ginger shivered apprehensively. "Dan, let's wait until we become better acquainted with this place before we begin digging into things," she urged.

I agreed. But I was certainly puzzled about what was happening to us. Either we were becoming the victims of self-induced hallucinations, or there *was* some external factor in operation of which we knew nothing. I have no explanations to offer for this phenomenon, or for what happened later. I am not a metaphysician, nor do I believe in the supernatural; but there are plenty of things in this country to give pause to even a hard-headed realist. We decided to wait.

A game trail seemed to lead towards the centre of the plateau, and we hoped to a stream. It was late afternoon and time to think about a place in which to set up camp.

Our journey was interrupted by a wide black line which moved slowly across the trail—an army of black ants on the march. When we cautiously approached the line, a company of warrior ants who were flanking the main body of marchers, swarmed out to meet us. We beat a hasty retreat. It was impossible, even with a good running start, to jump over them. They were fascinating to watch and we spent over an hour observing the well-organized, compact body of marchers.

These ants are probably the most intelligent insects in the jungle. Before the colony migrates, an advance detail of engineers goes ahead to clear the way, build bridges, and scout the trail. When the ants are on the march, a company of warriors, led by a captain, heads the column; behind them, flanked by other fighting ants, march the carriers in orderly procession. Leaders are distributed among the carriers, their job being to keep the burden bearers in order, and to help them over difficult places. If one of the heavily laden carriers becomes stalled, its leader immediately runs up to assist it over the difficulty. If at times the carrier seems to lag, the leader urges it along by giving it a nip on its hindquarters. In the centre of the column, well protected by warriors with immense jaws, march the royalty—the queen and her drones.

The ants vary in size according to their duties. The warriors have large heads with great jaws. The cutters, whose work consists of climbing trees and sheering off the foliage, are equipped with long, scissor-like jaws. The carriers have small heads and strong, stout legs. There were also a number of smaller ants who were probably domestic servants, and who took care of the storage and preservation of food in the castle. The leaders or captains were well-proportioned ants of a lighter colour than the various groups of workers. Their job is purely executive—they just boss.

Much as we hated to interrupt their progress, we had to be on our way. Nowhere, though we looked up and down the trail, was it possible to cross. Each time that we approached too near to the army, we were driven back by the warriors. Fire was the only thing that would stop them. We built one of long sticks and tossed the faggots in a line across the column, so that they formed a burning bridge. Thousand of ants swarmed round the blazing sticks, but the heat kept them back. By moving quickly, and stepping directly upon the burning sticks, we managed to make a flying dash across the bewildered army. But for all our strategy and fast foot work, we picked up a few ants en route who inflicted painful stings.

Before evening we arrived at the banks of a little stream, and following its course, found a beautiful camp site. Great trees and feathery palms shaded a white sand beach beside the water. Here we planned to build a

The Forbidden Land

hut near a deep pool that offered an ideal place to bathe. There was a dreamlike quality about the little beach that charmed us both.

Experts by now at erecting thatched huts, we built a good substantial shelter, well off the ground, and guarded the entrance with heavy tiger bars. In one corner we built a raised platform, padded it well with palm leaves, and set up the tent on it. These precautions, we felt, should discourage *talajes*, tigers, or any other jungle menace.

As soon as we had time to become acquainted with our surroundings, we found an abundance of food. Besides several varieties of palms, there were guavas, avocados, plums, figs, breadfruit, *yuca* roots, and wild coffee. In addition to the common birds, such as mountain pigeon, wild chickens, turkey, and *pavo*, there were numbers of edible birds that we had never seen before.

The trees harboured their usual quotas of chattering spider monkeys, parrots, parrakeets, and other gorgeously dressed birds. It seemed to us that there were more varieties here than anywhere else.

After completing the hut, we cut trails to various points on the plateau, so that we could hunt without disturbing the birds and animals round the camp. While cutting up the creek about a mile away, we came upon huge, three-toed tracks in the sand. The round imprints were about the size of a dinner plate. The tracks were so deep that the animal who had made them must have weighed nearly a ton at least. We recalled the tall tales we had heard from the natives about strange beasts that inhabited the Spirit Land. Could this be a confirmation of one of those yarns?

Its spoor led us into a clump of *coquito* palms, where the animal had stopped to eat some of the nuts. We were relieved to find that it was a vegetarian, but its size still alarmed us, for the large branches it had stepped on were crushed and forced into the soil. The tracks finally came out on a well-beaten trail, which in turn led into a canebrake. There we stopped, for the trail now became a low tunnel in the thickly meshed cane.

"This doesn't look so good," I said.

We had a choice of going into the tunnel, or waiting for the animal to come out. We decided to wait. After an hour we became impatient. Was it never going to come out? "What do you say . . . shall we go in a little ways?"

Ginger said she was game if I was. So we checked over the extra clips of ammunition, got out the guns, and crawled through the entrance. The dark tunnel was not an attractive place to be caught in. It was very low in proportion to its width of about five feet. The animal which used the passage was approximately the same size, for the cane was worn smooth and polished from its passing. The ground was as hard-packed as cement. A bend in the tunnel cut off the view a short distance from the entrance. We decided to crawl to the bend, but after rounding it we were no better off, since another turn still obstructed the view. Screwing up our courage, we crawled a little further, wondering what we'd do if we heard the animal coming towards us. Finally the tunnel opened out into a clearing in the centre of the brake. On the far side stood the animal we had come to see.

A pair of small, sleepy eyes peered at us from the head of a moth-eaten burro. He looked like a hog whose metamorphosis into an elephant has been arrested halfway. A forlorn, abortive attempt to grow a trunk hung down over its mouth. Its high hindquarters sloped forward to low shoulders. Nature had certainly been confused in her purpose when she designed that monstrosity.

I carefully aimed the Luger. In case it decided to charge I'd get it first. Ginger tugged at my elbow. "Don't shoot, Dan; that funny face looks just like the burro we had at Escondido."

So we sat on our haunches and stared, and the strange beast stared back at us. But it seemed best to leave before it changed its peaceful intentions. We backed slowly into the tunnel, and then turned and ran as fast as we could on all fours. We weren't taking any chances on how fast that two-thousand-pound monstrosity could run. Out through the entrance we dashed full speed ahead, and kept on going until we reached a large tree. We peered out from behind it to see if we were being pursued, but the animal had apparently considered us beneath its notice and remained in the clearing.

On the way back to camp we decided to call it "Molly," in memory of the old burro we had liked so well in Puerto Escondido. Molly, we found out later, was not a survival from the age of dinosaurs. We had made the acquaintance of the Central American tapir. It was fortunate for Molly that we were unacquainted with the bad reputation that the director of the San Diego Zoo gave to tapirs, for he came right into camp on numerous occasions, and even ate the washing off the clothes line!

The next day, in the hope of discovering its source, we followed the stream to where it entered a canyon between low hills. There we left it and began cutting a way towards the top of the hills. Within a short distance of the stream we came upon an ancient roadway that led up the canyon. Parts of it were visible, but in many places it was completely eroded, and in others covered by small land slides. It was about ten feet wide, and well paved with large cobblestones. We were thrilled with the possibilities it suggested. It obviously connected that part of the plateau where we had seen the first three mounds with perhaps a higher mesa which lay beyond the intervening hills. We decided to turn back and see where the road came from before going ahead and finding out where it led. But to our great disappointment we soon lost it entirely. The ground was so thickly covered with humus that nothing could be seen.

The worst thunderstorm that we had ever experienced occurred that night. The thunder shook the hut, and the lightning was almost continuous. The periods of light far exceeded the periods of darkness. It seemed unlikely that the thatched roof could stand up under the terrific pounding of the rain. We could hear the crashing of great trees as the forest giants went down before the lightning.

The next day we set off to find out where the road went. This time we continued in the direction of the hills. The country was difficult to travel over and we lost the road several times. Finally it led us to a high mesa. Climbing a hill to reconnoitre, we found that the land lay in the shape of an hourglass, with the stream which separated its upper and lower portions forming the narrow neck. Each mesa was between four and five miles across. But there was nothing else to be observed from the hill except the sea of green jungle.

On the way back to camp I shot a deer. We dragged it into camp and skinned it. After cutting off a portion of meat for supper, I hung the balance high on a limb, and put the skin away to tan. About midnight we were awakened by the sound of snarling. Not one, but several jaguars had come into camp after the meat. A pot shot at one of them in no way discouraged them. All the rest of the night we heard the animals prowling round. In the morning I found that they had eaten practically all the deer.

We began a systematic search of our own part of the plateau by following game paths wherever possible. The dense undergrowth prevented us from seeing objects more than a few feet distant from the trail. We did find a large, level area covered with mounds, but so thickly overgrown with vines that we made no effort to explore it. There were also evidences of buildings in other localities. One of the strangest things we observed was an occasional open space in the midst of the jungle, where nothing grew. Since the prolific growths can seemingly find a foothold anywhere, these barren spots near the old building sites always added a touch of mystery.

One day while circling back to camp from one of these expeditions, we heard the squealing of what we thought was a herd of *jaboli*, a small Central American wild pig that usually runs in gangs of twenty or more. I shot a small one, and then heard a bellow, not of *jaboli*, but of wild boars. I had apparently shot a young boar—my mistake. We made for the nearest tree. While I was helping Ginger up, the herd charged. My hands were full of Ginger, and it was impossible to draw my gun. Before I had a chance to pull myself up, one of the infuriated animals slashed at my right leg. Another caught or hooked my sandal with its tusk and almost dragged me down. Ginger above was frantically trying to tell me something, but because of the thunder below I could not understand her. I managed to get up on a limb, and then I knew! We had picked a thorn tree. Also it was full of ants. We trimmed off the thorns as best we could, and settled ourselves for a nice long wait. The boars were raising bedlam, and we knew that they would be unlikely to leave in a hurry. We managed to get into good shooting positions, but they were hard targets to hit as they dashed madly about. Each time we wounded one the rest of the herd went crazy. They repeatedly charged the base of the tree, and this gave us our best shots. Finally as darkness fell the remnants of the herd left. We were a long way from camp, and I climbed down the tree with the idea of getting a flare to light us home. But the boars were not far off and I hurriedly rejoined Ginger. Then we thought we heard tigers, which gave us something else to think about. They would surely be attracted by the dead animals, and there was nothing pleasant in the prospect of staying in the tree all night with two or three big cats below. I broke off some dead branches, dropped down, and built a fire with them close to the base of the tree. Then we collected material for torches, lit them and started home. The wood was not suitable for flares and they went out continually as we felt our way through the dark forest. Each time this happened, we were sure that the boars would charge. Eventually we arrived safely in camp, to spend the rest of the evening picking out the thorns.

After my leg healed, we prepared enough food to last us for several days, and started out to explore the upper mesa. During the period of my convalescence, we had made new clothes from deer skin, and new sandals from the tough leather of the boars' hides. We now felt equal to the task of scaling the high peaks that bounded the plateau. From those heights we hoped to gain an accurate knowledge of the surrounding country. Travelling at first was very difficult, for our new shoes were so slippery that it was hard to maintain a foothold on the grass-covered slopes of the ridges.

The second day we entered a high mountain valley completely surrounded by cliffs on three sides. The ascent could be made only by traversing a narrow ledge that ran along the face of the rock wall. The valley was an ideal retreat, since it could be easily protected against attack. There were many caves at the bottom of the cliffs, with fire-blackened earth at their entrances. A narrow passageway led upward to another small flat, where there were several other caves with fire-blackened floors. We decided to spend the night in one of them, but we first had to eject its tenant, a small boa.

The next morning we carefully examined the caves, unearthing among the debris bits of pottery, stone chips, and arrowheads. Judging from the size of the fragments, the cave dwellers must have used huge, unglazed pottery ollas for the storage of grain and water. The shards were so weathered, however, that it was impossible to determine whether they had ever been decorated. The people had probably used obsidian for their cutting tools, for there were many fragments of the flintlike volcanic glass among the shards. The remains of a stone wall, which partially closed the entrance to one of the caves, indicated that they had been used as permanent dwelling places. We had no tools for digging, and it was our policy never to disturb anything needlessly, but we wondered what a thorough sifting of the earth on the cave floors might disclose. They had evidently been occupied over a long period.

Our next objective was the highest peak on the plateau. Here, we really had hopes of being able to map the surrounding country, to pick out the logical sites of ancient cities, and to map possible routes in and out.

Our government charts of the region told us that we were in the neighbourhood of the continental divide. But not until we reached the summit of the highest peak had we any idea of the magnificence of what we were about to see. To the east, the blue-grey line where the Atlantic met the horizon. On the west, the vast expanse of jungle merged into the faint haze of the Pacific. Now we realized how Balboa must have felt when he stood upon the peak in Darien. It was as though one stood on the top of the world. Off to the south a great expanse of unknown land, of high peaks and emerald valleys, spread out as far as the eye could see.

We followed a stream to where part of it entered a cave. A half mile or so beyond we came to a large basin, now overgrown with tiger grass, that at one time had been a lake. We speculated as to whether this could be the Enchanted Lake of which the natives had so often told us.

Cutting a trail to the upper end of the dry lake, we had skirted its boundaries for about a mile when we noticed that the ground was broken by little hummocks. They spread out in all directions, giving the otherwise level ground a wavelike contour. We had at last come to the site of the old city. Then we saw the pyramids. There were seven of them, arranged in the form of a huge triangle. At the apex, facing east, stood the largest of the group. All seven were so placed that from any angle the eye could always see three in an equidistant straight line. They were approximately one hundred feet wide across their bases and about fifty feet high; and of course were completely overgrown with vines and other jungle growths. There was one very odd thing about them, however, which, if it was a coincidence, was still unusual. We had found no *chico zapote* trees on the plateau; but in the north-east corner of each pyramid there was one of these trees growing—and they were huge. There were no others near-by.

Now comes the purely fantastic side of the story. The reader can give it whatever interpretation he chooses. We have no ideas on the subject, and only relate the incidents as they occurred because they are an integral part of our experience. There may not be the slightest causal relationship between the various episodes and our attempt to dig into the mounds, but they were, at least to us, sufficient deterrents. We agreed to let somebody else dig.

After our discovery of the pyramids we planned to stay in their vicinity for several days and see what else we might find. Having decided to make camp near the river, we were returning to it along a game trail in the late afternoon. We were about to cross a large log on the trail, when just ahead of it we saw a tiger. To see one at all in the daytime surprised us, since they are nocturnal prowlers. I took the Luger out of the holster, expecting every minute that the beast would disappear into the brush. To our amazement he kept right on coming towards us, in a crouching position. I was too dumbfounded to realize what was happening until Ginger cried, "Shoot! Quick!" I emptied the Luger at it, and still the beast kept coming. Ginger dropped it with a finishing shot to the head—on the log not ten feet away. Two bullets had gone clear through its chest, and three into its head. It measured eight feet long from tip to tip. We skinned it and went on to the river, where we made camp. Both of us were so excited that we lost our appetites, and could hardly eat our supper.

The next day we went back to the pyramids, where we dug away the thick deposit of humus down to the surfacing. The stones were laid in a uniform manner, but not with the precision that characterized the ruins we had visited while at Wilderness Camp. There is no hard limestone in the immediate vicinity of the plateau, and no attempt had been made to cut the soft native rock into finished blocks. The pyramids gave the impression of having been rather hastily constructed, or else they were built prior to the great age of Mayan architecture. Judging from the size of the trees growing on their summits, and the depth of the humus, the city had been abandoned for many hundreds of years.

We prowled round the ruins for several days, but it was hard to penetrate the tangled, gloomy undergrowth. To tell the truth, we were not happy about doing it. Perhaps our subconscious minds played us tricks, but we were certain that at times we heard the peculiar vibration or rhythm that we called "drums." We finally decided to return to the thatched hut on the lower mesa.

Several days later, while hunting on the lower mesa, we again came to the three pyramids that we had seen on first entering the plateau. To the left of the trail that we had originally made was a second city. There were many mounds and broken walls; and at its upper end we located the roadway which connected the upper and lower mesas. The only notable difference between the two sites was that here the ruins were not so deeply imbedded in vegetation. Nevertheless, the task of clearing away the jungle growth from the ruins in this fertile country would be far greater than it is further north in Yucatan. The rainfall here is heavier than on the peninsula of Yucatan, and with that is combined the difference between the scanty soil of the great limestone reef that forms the peninsula and the luxuriant soil of the plateau.

One tale told us by the natives aroused our curiosity more than any other. They said that here, concealed in a great vault, and guarded by the spirits of the Mayan chiefs, were to be found the historical records of the Mayan people. These records covered a very long period, according to the natives' story, and gave a detailed account of the history, migrations, and learning, not only of the Mayas, but of other early American peoples as well.

It is possible that this story may not be as fantastic as it sounds. After Bishop Diego de Landa burnt the Mayan books in Yucatan—in an excess of pious zeal—he began to have some doubts as to how history might regard his fanaticism. It is said that after his return to Yucatan from a visit to Spain, he tried, without success, to induce the Mayan priests to reassemble from other sources some of the priceless manuscripts that the Spaniards had so wantonly destroyed. The burnt documents, according to the holy Father, dealt with medicine, astronomy, geology, and the chronological history of the Mayas and other peoples. The story is that the priests were angry, and not only failed to produce any further records, but concealed them, so that today there exist in all the world only three known specimens of Mayan learning: the manuscripts called the Dresden Codex, Peresianus Codex, and the Tro-Cortesianus Codex. De Landa naïvely relates that the destruction of the Mayan Library caused the people "great pain . . . we burnt them all, which they took most grievously." Well, a lot of crimes have been committed in the name of religion, but few things have ever caused a greater pain to intelligent people than De Landa's stupidity.

One day, while scouting along the cliffs on the western side of the plateau, we came upon a pile of huge limestone blocks, weighing at least a ton each. At one time they appeared to have formed a great plaque, thirty to forty feet wide, on the face of the cliff. Behind the rocks was what seemed to us to be the sealed entrance to a cave. This was a highly provocative speculation, so we started to clear away the rubble. We worked until nearly sundown at the slow task, and then returned to camp, planning to go back early the next day and continue the excavation.

We were very excited by the possibilities of the cave—if it was a cave—and what it might contain. It was certain that no one had gone to the immense labour of arranging those stones unless the place had some very special significance. While we were talking, I suddenly experienced a severe pain in my left ankle. I had no recollection of having been bitten, or of having had any other accident that would cause such immediate and excruciating pain. By ten o'clock that night my foot was badly swollen. At eleven o'clock it was swollen to above the knee. The focal point of the pain was on the inside of the foot about an inch below the ankle bone. By midnight the entire limb was almost three times its normal size, and the foot was black and very hard. We tried hot packs but that only seemed to increase the pain; and of course there was no way of applying cold packs. Ginger said that I was delirious part of the night. The next day its condition was worse.

The following quotations from the diary of September, 1935, perhaps give a more graphic picture of the situation than any attempt at a description.

"Sept. 2. Rain all day. If foot doesn't get better will have to operate. Running high temperature, unable to eat. Ginger is very much worried. It may be a blood clot. If so, will have to open artery. Can tie on either side of clot and drain. If that doesn't work will have to take leg off at knee, but must have sun first to kill mould and germs. Not even a little scratch will heal in a long stretch of rainy weather such as we are having. Am praying for sun."

"Sept. 4. Still raining. Streams up, so there's no chance to get out of here. Examined surgical kit, mould everywhere, knives have sweated in waterproof wrappings, and are badly rusted. Will have to operate soon, for foot is getting worse. But flesh is still alive, does not dent. Feel in pretty bad shape."

"Sept. 5. Raining. Had chills all night and awoke with high fever. Temperature 103 this morning. Took thirty grains of quinine. At noon temperature 104. Ginger says delirious all afternoon, but feel better this evening."

"Sept. 6. High fever all day. Rational now, but Ginger says raved all day."

"Sept. 7. Fever broke last night at midnight. Felt sharp pain in foot, and during delirium pounded it with my fist. Then had piercing pain in my chest. Unable to breathe—lungs felt cramped. Ginger says in stupor rest of night. This morning feel better."

I had become ill on August 31, 1935, and it took until the middle of September for me to get back into my stride. But one bit of bad luck followed another, and though we stayed in the territory for another month, most of the time was spent in recuperating from one near fatality after another. A jaguar scratched me up. When my wounds had healed, we had simultaneous attacks of tropical fever. We finally decided that it was time to go.

Our decision was probably hastened by the fact that we always experienced some personal disaster each time that we dug into anything. Neither one of us is superstitious, but the country's reputation did not induce optimism or undue assurance. Then, too, we had had plenty of first hand experience with which to back up reports of its potential dangers. There seemed little use in further tempting Providence.

There are several possible explanations as to why the present-day Indians regard this country with such awesome reverence. Some of them seem to tie in with what we observed and with the legends. Whether the Mayan migration to this plateau preceded the Conquest, and was due to civil strife among themselves, or to invasions from the north, or whether it took place after the Conquest in an attempt to escape the Spanish aggressors, is a point that we have no means of settling. But the immigrants were probably few in number, and magnified the natural hazards of the country in an effort to frighten the less cultured tribes surrounding them into leaving them alone. Otherwise, the stories that we heard from so many sources would in all likelihood have died out long ago.

Then there is another possibility. The cities may have had some religious significance, and may have been considered holy places. The present-day Indians frequently refer to the area as "the home of the chiefs." This might mean that the priest-kings of the Mayas made some special use of it. Once or twice we heard it called "the home of the chiefs of the mountains and valleys." The ancient Mayas called the four principal rulers of the world, who were the gods of the earth, of agriculture, of the forests and animals, and the benefactors of man, "Lords of the Mountain-Valley." No place could be a more fitting home for them than the plateau. The caves might also indicate that it had been so considered since the earliest times. These, of course, are only speculations on our part. For beyond the fact that we discovered that the plateau had once been occupied, we knew very little more about it when we left than when we entered it.

It took less time to get out of the country than it had to come in, for we knew the general direction in which to travel. But descending the cliffs was harder than climbing up them. The best route seemed to be the one we had used on entering. We stopped at the various camps along the way to pick up our clothes and equipment, and to collect our buried gold. In spite of all our precautions, most of the food was spoiled and our clothes were mouldy. Also our exposed films had sweated, and in consequence were ruined.

After a month's travel we arrived in Matias Romero. There we hunted up the Arab merchant whom we had met on our previous visit. He bought the gold, and gave us the wherewithal to go on a spending spree—but he didn't tell us that gold was now worth $35.00 the ounce. We bought films, ammunition, five hundred fishhooks, two dozen packages of needles, and blue jeans and two native shirts for ourselves. Then we began to eat and drink everything in sight, which shortly resulted in our feeling liverish. Before leaving Matias Romero we replenished our store of rice, corn, beans, flour, coffee, salt, tobacco, and so on, since prices were cheaper here than in Salina Cruz.

Then, since it was just a month before Christmas, we separated to do a little private shopping. That finished, we took the train for Salina Cruz. It was nearly seven months since we had left Don Juan and Doña Facunda in La Ventosa, to be gone "perhaps two or three days."

Chapter Twenty-one

THE LAND OF PRIMITIVE MEN

OUR friends in Salina Cruz gave us a hearty welcome, and loaned us the dilapidated Ford truck to drive to La Ventosa. There the entire population rushed out to greet us as we rattled over its uneven streets to the hut of Don Juan and Doña Facunda. That kindly old couple met us with tears in their eyes, for they, like many others, had long since given us up for dead.

All the people who could crowd into the many hammocks Don Juan swung between the posts of his hut, came to hear the story of our adventures in the Forbidden Land. We answered their questions as well and as briefly as we could, for we were anxious to go to the *bodega* and find out how the *Vagabunda* had fared in our absence.

Don Juan accompanied us to the warehouse where we carefully examined the canoe and other stored equipment. Except for the sand which covered them, everything was in as good condition as when we left. This was welcome news, for it meant that we could resume our voyage down the Gulf of Tehuantepec at an early date.

Upon our return to Don Juan's house we found that a truck load of people from Salina Cruz had arrived in the interim. Preparations for a fiesta were in full swing. Towards evening the company sat down to a Mexican banquet prepared in the traditional manner. The principal dishes were barbecued lamb, chicken *mole*, broiled fish, and bean *empanadas*. But there were many other dishes from the kitchens of the village housewives who prided themselves upon some specialty. Doña Facunda had made her famous sauce of chili, onion, and tomato, spiced with garlic, *ajonjoli* seeds, and pickled peppers.

It was a grand party, but it did not occur to us that it was solely in our honour—for the natives make fiesta several times a week—until towards the end of the meal, when Don Juan arose and proposed a toast: "To those who have just returned and are about to depart, we wish you luck and a good voyage." Outside the hut a howling norther whipped gusts of sand through the reed lattice work. Not far away the storm-tossed waters of the gulf sounded an ominous note of danger. Inside, the gaiety became a trifle forced, although we laughed and joked and talked about everything but the wind.

It came my turn to reply to Don Juan's toast. *"Al viento,"* I said. "We hope the wind handles us with soft hands, for it is with fear and a sincere respect for its dangers that we face the Gulf of Tehuantepec. We do not want you to think that we are brave, for we are not. Soon we will be leaving for Champerico, Guatemala, and we will arrive there even if we have to carry the canoe along the beach. But we are leaving the warmth of your friendship with regret, and we hope that some day we may be fortunate enough to return to you."

There were several reasons for our departure at this season, although it was the most dangerous time of year for sailing in the gulf. Our tourist cards, permitting us a six-months residence in Mexico, had long since expired; and our continued presence, without official permission, would eventually cause trouble and embarrassment to our friends among the port officials, who had no authority to allow us to remain. Besides this, there was our natural desire to see what lay along the coast ahead.

As though to answer an unspoken challenge, the wind rose to a crescendo of fury. It whined through the doorway, and shook the sturdy hut with violence. The hour grew late, but our friends, who seemed to think that they were leaving us to our doom, were reluctant to bring the party to a close. Finally Don Juan asked, "And when will you depart, my friends?"

"When the norther subsides," I replied.

"Very well, then," he said, "let us all plan to meet again when that happens."

The party broke up, people taking their leave, one by one, until only we four remained. Doña Facunda and Ginger seated themselves by the fire, while Don Juan asked me to accompany him to the beach to make sure that the canoes were safe. Sometimes the norther would blow the sand out from under them until it formed a pit in which the canoes sank out of sight as the sand drifted over them.

As we walked together down towards the beach, the hard-driven sand stung our legs and burnt our faces. After Juan found the canoes to be in good order, he suggested that we sit down for a talk in the lee of the warehouse. Except for the wind it was a beautiful cloudless night. The constellation of the Southern Cross gleamed above us, and the stars seemed very near to earth. But Don Juan's face was grave and troubled. After a long silence I said, "What is it, Juan? Why are you worried?"

"I am thinking of many strange things," he replied. "You are not afraid of death?"

"Not particularly," I answered. "There isn't much use in being afraid. Why make life miserable by worrying over what can't be avoided. Why do you ask, Juan?"

"It is only that I wish to understand," he answered. "You know, of course, that you will meet death if you attempt to cross the gulf. Such a thing is impossible in a little boat."

"Yes," I admitted, "it seems impossible, but so do many things until some one does them. We may be forced to give up the idea, but first we must try. Soon we should have three days of calm weather, and that will give us time to reach Champerico. If we do not have three days of calm, of course we shall fail."

The old Indian silently contemplated the stars for a long time, and then he asked, "Do you believe in the heaven and hell that the Christian priests talk about? Do you think that the Great Power punishes men with fire or rewards them with golden crowns and everlasting life because they believe or disbelieve in Him?"

"I really don't know, Juan," I answered. "We are also taught these things, but I don't know."

"I cannot understand the priests," he continued. "They talk so much about what comes after life—and how can they know? And so little about how to live, of which men should know much. Perhaps it would be better to think more about how we can be good and useful men on earth and trust the Great Power to make the right plans for us later. I do not think He will punish us then for what we do now, more than we punish ourselves while we live. A good man knows the things that are right because they make him happy, and no man can injure others and find this happiness for himself alone. These are the things we were taught to believe by our own great teachers of the past, and for the Indian the old ways are best."

"Who taught you about the Great Power, Juan?"

"My father," he replied. "But my people first learnt of these things long ago when the Zapotecs were strong and powerful. A great teacher, whose bearded face was white, came to us from the East. This man taught us to do many things of which we knew nothing before his coming. He ruled over many tribes in turn and each of them called him by a different name. This man taught us to be unselfish, and to worship the Great Power; and while he ruled over us the tribe prospered. Then he departed in a little boat, but he promised that some day he would return to us. Long, long after he had gone, the Spaniards came. At first we thought that they, too, might be great and good teachers. We knew that this was not so when they tried to destroy all that he had taught. Our books, our temples, all these things perished. Then we were forced to build temples to their gods with the stones of our old altars. They rewarded our kindness with cruelty. Now we use their churches, pray before their altars, and listen to the words of their priests, but when we pray, we pray to our ancient god. Sometimes they know this, but what can they do?"

I could not help thinking as Juan told me his version of the great mythological hero, Quetzalcoatl, who according to Indian tradition ruled over the Toltecs, Mayas, and Zapotecs in turn, of the painful contrast between that "bearded man whose face was white," and the men who came after. Perhaps the great priest-king-teacher, whose memory is still venerated in a thousand little villages throughout Mexico, is only a folk myth, but I do not think so. Quetzalcoatl, as the Indians portray him, is an altogether attractive figure, who taught them agriculture, astronomy, and the use of metals; who gave them a calendar, taught them to write, and instructed them in the arts. If he has no historical reality, he is still a finer creation of the primitive mind than many a deity of more sophisticated peoples.

"Do all your people worship the Great Power, Juan?" I questioned.

"No," he answered. "Some of the mountain people worship the sun because he gives light and heat, and makes the crops grow. And because there must be two of everything, they also worship the moon, his queen. But my own people realize that the sun, the moon, the earth, and the stars are ruled by a still greater One."

"Juan, I am glad that you know," I said, "that the sun is only one of many heavenly bodies. Do you see that little star?" I pointed to a bright star overhead. "That little speck is many times as big as our sun, and much farther away. If the Great Power were to put His hand over it, its light would continue to shine on earth for millions of years. The light that you see left that star long before the coming of your great teacher."

He gazed at the twinkling point of light for a long time, as he tried to comprehend the distances of stellar space. Then he turned to me and said with glowing eyes, "Perhaps the Great Power will permit me to go there some day after I die and start life all over again."

"Who knows?" I said. "Perhaps you may. At any rate, Juan, I like your faith, for it has made your people kind and considerate."

"Danielito," he said hesitantly, "would you like to go back to the house and burn a candle with me?"

"Yes," I answered, "I should like to very much."

Ginger and Doña Facunda were still talking before the fire when we came in. The four of us went to the altar, where Don Juan lit a candle, and asked for the Great Power's protection for his dear friends. Ginger and I felt that if any one had a right to invoke the Deity's aid in our behalf it was surely that good and humble Indian.

We retired, but not to sleep, for the fleas bit into us unmercifully. After one abortive attempt to rid ourselves of their attentions by swinging our hammocks four feet off the ground—in the naïve belief that no flea could jump that far—we were finally forced to swing them just under the roof beams, where we could only reach them ourselves by standing on benches. This was too much for the Olympic champions below, and we were at last able to sleep in peace.

The norther awoke us at daylight, and while the women were busy round the breakfast fire, I went down to the beach to have a look at the gulf. Its waters were whipped to a froth, and great clouds of spray were being whirled out to sea as though they were in the grip of a cyclone. Sharp gusts picked up sand on the beach and hurled it high on the sand hills to the south. It was not an encouraging picture, and I returned to the hut wondering what our chances really were.

While we were eating breakfast, the local shipping agent, Jimenez, stopped his galloping Ford at the door to announce the appointment of a new Port Captain at Salina Cruz, who would have to sign our clearance papers before we could leave La Ventosa. This was sure to be a long-drawn-out negotiation with a new man, and we proceeded at once to Salina Cruz.

We had to wait, as usual, while the Captain dressed himself in his uniform. An attractive looking young fellow who took the dignity of his office with great seriousness, he spent considerable time carefully reading our papers. When he had finished I spent an equal amount of time complimenting him and all the other officials we had met, for the kindness and consideration with which we had been received by them throughout our sojourn in Mexico. I suggested that since we were leaving for Guatemala and there was a faint question in our minds as to how we might be received there, a letter of introduction from him would undoubtedly help us. To save him time, I said, I had prepared such a letter for him to sign. This was always a good idea, for it was easier for the average port official to copy or sign a letter than to compose one. He listened without comment to what I had to say, then called his secretary, and in a voice vibrant with feeling, dictated a letter that would have opened the gates of heaven to us—providing Saint Peter could read Spanish. It was a masterpiece, requesting all civil and governmental authorities to do their utmost in our behalf.

As we left his office, our precious letter and other papers carefully tucked away in their waterproof pouch, we met Gomez, manager of the cable office. News travels fast in Salina Cruz, and he already knew of our visit to the Port Captain. He remarked, when we told him that we had our clearance papers, that he was surprised, for he had not expected the Captain to permit us to leave during the stormy weather. It was a good thing, he concluded, that the Captain did not know the size of the *Vagabunda*.

We had one last fling in Salina Cruz, and spent the rest of the day eating and drinking. When we returned to La Ventosa late in the afternoon neither one of us felt happy. We had eaten too much, and had somehow acquired splitting headaches.

The norther continued all the following week, which gave us time to make some repairs on the canoe and to repaint it. Then we overhauled and renovated our equipment, so that when Don Juan announced quietly, "Tomorrow the wind will die," we were ready to take advantage of the lull.

As soon as he passed the news along to the villagers that we were ready to leave, we heard the clatter of a horse's hoofs. In reply to my questioning look, he said, "He is going to tell your friends in Salina Cruz." We were singularly touched by the affectionate interest that these simple people took in our welfare.

We worked late that night bringing all of our equipment down to the warehouse, preparatory to an early start the following morning. We stowed away in the grub box enough corn, beans, rice, coffee, and tobacco to last us for about three weeks. When everything was in perfect order, we went for a last stroll along the beach. The wind had dropped to a dead calm, and the treacherous gulf was a placid as as lake, its broad expanse dotted with the flickering lights of the torches attached to the bows of the fishing canoes. These people fish day and night during the lulls in the northers, for they may wait a month or more before they have another opportunity. Fish is the staple article of diet and their only item of barter.

Dawn found us transporting the canoe to the water's edge, our friends carrying the other equipment. Then the rattle of the Ford truck announced the arrival of the people from Salina Cruz. The first truck was closely followed by a second. In a few minutes they came streaming across the beach to meet us, loaded down with baskets of food, and carrying their guitars. Since the news could not have reached them until late the preceding night, they had apparently spent the rest of it preparing food and getting to La Ventosa. Here they were, dressed in their best, and loaded down with gifts that a dozen *Vagabundas* could not have carried. Anxious as we were to put to sea, we did not have the heart to leave until after their farewell fiesta. Old Doña Facunda now came down to the beach, bringing a big olla of coffee and some of her famous *pan dulce* for our breakfast. "Getting away is certainly going to be tough," I whispered to Ginger.

People ranged themselves round the canoe, and began singing songs of the sea and of farewell, accompanied by the tinkling guitars. When the fiesta was at its height, the fishing canoes began to come in. The fishermen, clad only in loin cloths, approached us with anxious faces. "Danielito, the wind, *Ya viene el viento*" ("the wind is coming"). A murmur went up from the crowd.

How long would the wind last this time? I asked the fishermen. They were not sure, but it might last a month. However, it did not always blow all the way down the coast, only in the gulf itself. We knew that if we could get out of the gulf before the wind became too strong, we still had a sporting chance; but we must leave immediately.

We hurriedly said good-bye, carried the canoe into the water, and loaded it. As we paddled out beyond the breaker line, we stopped and waved a last farewell before we hoisted sail and started down the coast, hugging the shore line. Our friends still stood on the beach, holding the gifts they had brought us.

The fiesta and the prolonged farewells had taken up most of the morning and it was nearly noon. The wind had increased in strength, and though we reefed and double-reefed the sail, it was almost too rough for sailing before we reached the mouth of the Tehuantepec River which empties into the gulf three miles south of La Ventosa. On reaching the bar at its mouth, we found that we had to go to sea about half a mile to round it. The canoe began to pitch and toss so badly that it was almost impossible to use the sail at all, so we furled and lashed it to the deck. Paddling out round the bar was easy, but getting back inshore was not. The chop was so high that it broke completely over the canoe, and our best efforts at the paddles weren't good enough to make any headway against the wind. Ginger shouted, "We aren't gaining any ground at all."

"Give her all you've got," I shouted back. "We've got to make it." I had visions of the canoe being blown backwards out to sea and hammered to pieces by the pounding waves. There wasn't a chance to swim in such a sea either, for the breakers were short and high and the wind blew the tops off them. Blisters rose on our hands and the paddles grew sticky as they broke. It was impossible to see for the spray that blew in our eyes and blinded us. But we had to make it somehow.

Now I knew why those fishermen had come ashore at the least hint of the norther. If the wind increased, or we broke a paddle . . . ? I could hear Juan say, "And then, my friend?" Deciding it was better to risk a crack-up on the bar than to continue fighting the waves, we changed our course and paddled at an angle towards the bar. We had had a seven-months vacation from fighting storms at sea, and our softened muscles were so tired that we could hardly use them.

It seemed to us that the wind and the ocean were having a mighty tug of war with the frail canoe as the prize. The big breakers that rolled under us carried us but a little distance shoreward before the giant hand of the norther sheared off their white crests and sent them spinning seaward in a cloud of spume. While the wind held us back, the spent wave rolled out from beneath the canoe and continued on towards the beach in a blanket of spray. Nevertheless, the breakers did enable us to maintain a slight headway against the wind. Without them our efforts with the paddles would have been utterly useless. Then for a brief moment the norther eased a bit. Putting every ounce of our remaining strength behind our strokes, we were able to catch a wave and to shoot into shore with it, landing close beside the river's mouth. As though the wind had declared a truce just long enough for us to reach shore, it now charged down upon the gulf with fury.

Sand stung our bodies and filled our eyes and ears as we pulled the canoe high up on the beach and stacked the equipment in the lee of it. We took the guns and harpoon, and ploughed through the sand storm to the shelter of some mangroves that grew along the river banks, where we sat and listened to the wind and wondered what we ought to do. Of course we could return to La Ventosa, but that seemed rather an inglorious climax to our dramatic exit. The alternatives were either to camp near the river, which had dried up to a trickle, or attempt to reach the lagoons, which according to the charts, were at least ten miles inland. Before we could reach a decision, we saw through the fog of blowing sand two figures approaching the canoe. Ginger remained behind in the mangroves, while I went forward to investigate.

The two men were pawing over the equipment when I arrived. Entirely naked except for a bit of dirty rag wrapped round their heads, and carrying wicked-looking spears, they were the toughest-looking fellows I had ever seen. Neither man responded to my greeting, but darted swift, sly glances at me, trying to determine what weapons I carried. I asked them if they spoke Spanish; their reply was a grunt. Another grunt answered my next question as to what tribe they belonged to. I tried again to find out where they lived. "Under the trees," one replied in broken Spanish, and with that the conversation languished. They seated themselves in the lee of the equipment, and I sat down opposite them. Ginger soon joined me, and from then on the four of us just sat and looked at one another. The natives' appearance and behaviour were unlike anything we had previously encountered. Not even the mixed tribes we had fought with in the north seemed so primitive or savage. "This looks like an endurance contest," I said to Ginger, after what seemed hours of waiting. "I wonder who these natives are and what they want."

"I don't know," she replied, "but, judging by appearances, they're probably the wickedest natives we'll see in a long time."

There was nothing to do but wait, and we sat and fidgeted and fingered our gun butts, while the wind whipped sand into our backs. The natives sat with their heads bowed to the wind, saying nothing, doing nothing. Occasionally one of them would glance covertly in our direction. His close-set, cold eyes seemed to be trying to determine the exact moment to strike. Still neither one of them made any overt gesture, and until they did there was nothing for us to do but wait.

In the late afternoon we saw a horseman coming down the beach, his head lowered to the wind, a gun across the pommel of his saddle. A short distance away he jumped off his horse, and came plodding towards the canoe, with his gun ready for action. There was something familiar about his swinging walk. Then he raised himself from his half-crouching position, and we saw his face. It was Juan! But a Juan so angry that we hardly recognized the kind, placid man that we knew so well. *"Afuera!"* ("Get out!") he shouted, and raised his gun and started towards the two natives. They jumped and ran like scared rabbits.

"Juan!" we shouted, and ran after him. He stopped and waited for us.

Then he put his arm round Ginger's shoulder and patted it, as he said, "I was so afraid for you, the wind—it is here again, and so I rode down the beach to see if you had got ashore. You are in great danger here and we must leave at once. This is the territory of the Mareños, who occupy most of the lagoon country south of the Tehuantepec River. On the other side of the river you will be safe, for they do not dare to cross it, but we must get there quickly."

The wind made paddling round the bar impossible; but we had once towed the canoe through shallow water for seven miles along the coast of Baja California near Ensenada, and we could tow it in this emergency. Juan helped us carry it into the water and load it. Then while Ginger and I pulled it through the shallow water across the bar at the river's mouth, he kept a parallel course along the beach. The wind and our blistered hands made progress doubly hard, but at last we managed to get the canoe to a place where Juan considered we would be safe for the night.

We cleared a camp site among the mangroves on the beach, and while Ginger prepared supper, Juan and I sat by the fire and talked. The strange-looking Indians had aroused my curiosity and I urged Juan to tell me all he knew about them. He said that they lived in the vast, little-known lagoon country which extended from the Tehuantepec River to Champerico, Guatemala. I got out the chart of the lagoons, and together we scanned it by the firelight. Juan disagreed with my descriptions of the territory as indicated on the map. "No, no," he said, "it is not like that at all. Those men have not seen it. Many of those lagoons are not connected as they appear to be on your map. They are not open bodies of water, but are waterways that wind in and out among dense mangrove swamps. Perhaps they were different once, when the Spaniards lived in that country, *quien sabe?*"

"No," said Juan in answer to my question, "there are no people living anywhere near these lagoons now, only wild Mareños who are bandits and live by theft. Some of them have guns which they have stolen from travellers who have tried to pass through their country, others are only armed with spears. They build no cities or houses, but live in brush shelters; nor do they plant crops. They are wanderers who live for the most part on the fish they spear, and what they can steal. The Mexican government sent in troops to punish them, but they easily ambushed the soldiers and killed them, and then stole their guns and ammunition. The Mareños had a great advantage over the soldiers because they had canoes and knew the waterways where the soldiers were unable to follow them. Just recently a caravan of traders, who should have known better, went into the country in hopes of trading with them. The Mareños killed the men and stole their women and oxen. I tell you, Danielito, that they are very bad people, and that is why no one knows very much about their country."

Poor Juan had not the slightest idea of the effect that his hair-raising story had on us. The coffee boiled over while Ginger sat wide-eyed and forgetful, listening to his tale. I lit my pipe and tried to appear only mildly interested. "You know, Dan," said Ginger, after a long pause, "there really isn't anything to see along the coast between Salina Cruz and Champerico—just a straight sand beach."

"Uh huh, I was thinking that, too."

"Well?" interrogated Ginger.
"Well, what?" I turned to Juan.
"Juan, how far is it from here to the nearest lagoon?"

He looked at me in surprise. "About ten miles, but there is no road. The nearest lagoon to the ocean is called Punta de Agua at this end, where it is only a narrow channel. Further down the coast where you enter it from the ocean it is very wide and is called Laguna Inferior. But you surely are not thinking of going there—the Mareños would kill you. Also it is not possible to travel through these inland waters to Champerico, for they are closed in many places by *cerrados* (channels overgrown with mangroves) through which you cannot travel even on foot—certainly not in the canoe. Why not wait with us in La Ventosa until the norther goes down, and then continue your journey on the ocean? That would be better."

"Yes," I agreed, "it would be better, and a lot safer, but we want to see this country you've told us about. There should be many things of interest in the waters and on the shores of those lagoons. We'd like to know more about those naked Indians, explore the great swamps, and perhaps visit some of the old Spanish cities. These are the things we like to do. That is why we are making this trip."

He tried to dissuade us by enumerating all the insects, poisonous plants, and reptiles that lived in the country. We agreed that they were probably pretty bad, but if they were not there many men would have gone into the country before us, and by now it would be no more exciting than the Isthmus. He finally gave up with a shrug and a smile, and promised before he left that he would arrange for oxcarts to come for the canoe and the equipment in the morning. With a parting admonition to keep a sharp lookout for Mareños, he mounted his horse and rode away.

We discussed the problem of Mexico for a few minutes before we went to sleep in the canoe. It was easy to see why the Spaniards had never actually conquered the country, and why successive Mexican governments had failed to produce order and stability throughout the Republic. It was possible to succeed in the valley of Mexico, but the mountains of Sonora, the deserts of Baja California, the highlands of Southern Mexico, and the steaming swamps and jungles of the *tierra caliente* were another matter. In addition to the climate and geographical handicaps, thousands of belligerent Indians who lived in these areas liked nothing better than a good fight, and were prepared to go to any lengths to keep out invaders. Some of them, like the Huicholes and the Zapotecs whom we had met, were susceptible to a high degree of culture, such as they had once enjoyed. Others, like the mixed tribes further north and the Mareños, were savages pure and simple.

About midnight I awoke with an uneasy feeling that some one was approaching the canoe. I cautiously peeked over the gunwale just in time to see several Mareños coming up the beach. I waited quietly as they drew nearer. Then pulling the sheet over my head I slowly rose to my feet, and with the barrel of the Luger, lifted it as high above my head as I could reach. The thud of pounding feet on the sand indicated the effect of this manœuvre on our visitors. I waited a moment and then peeked out from under the sheet. They were far down the beach and still running. Ginger chuckled. "We'll probably be full of such little tricks before we're through with the Mareño country."

Nothing happened throughout the rest of the night, and soon after daylight we awakened to see oxcarts coming down the beach with Juan in the lead. After a hurried breakfast, we placed the canoe on a bed of tules to protect it from injury, and loading the equipment on the other cart, started back for La Ventosa. Our arrival there provided our friends with a fine opportunity for much good-natured joking and a grand excuse for another fiesta.

The real difficulty started when we tried to find cartmen to make the trip to Punta de Agua. Part of the way lay through the unfamiliar Mareño country, and their fear of these Indians was genuine. They presented us with a variety of reasons why it was imperative for them to remain in La Ventosa. Illness was rampant in their families; there were other important matters pending which demanded their constant presence in the village. Finally we found two that half-way consented; and perhaps emboldened by the bracing effects of *tequila*, they at last reluctantly agreed to make the trip.

For the second time the entire village turned out to see us off as we left La Ventosa at daylight on the morning of December 8, 1935, bound for the lagoons. Our party consisted of the two slightly swacked cartmen, Ginger and I, and Juan, who was to accompany us to Punta de Agua. We had taken extra precautions to insure the safety of the canoe on what was certain to be a rough journey. It was lashed securely to the springless *carreta*, where it rode on a thick, soft bed of cornstalks, its bow just missing the oxen, and its stern hanging over the rear of the cart. The second cart carried the equipment.

We travelled along the beach for two miles before the road turned inland to follow an old trade route which roughly paralleled the course of the Tehuantepec River. Where the road turned there was a small wayside shrine. At Juan's request we accompanied him to it while he asked for a safe journey for us. Then we continued in the wake of the creaking carts as they wound in and out among the stands of heavy timber, and across the hot sands of dry lake beds. At ten o'clock we met a picturesque caravan of oxcarts bound for Salina Cruz. We stopped to take pictures, and to ask for directions. When the drivers learnt that we were going into the Mareño country, they were loud in their fears for our safety. They pointed out, however, a pass that led through the hills on the other side of the Tehuantepec River, which they said would take us to Punta de Agua.

We crossed the river, and followed a faint roadway which led inland for half a mile through heavy brush. Many trails made by the woodcutters branched off from it, but none of them led any distance from the river. The road ended at a small abandoned ranch, and from then on Juan and I scouted the route through the brush, cutting a trail wide enough for the oxcarts to follow. This was a slow, tedious task, since it was necessary to cut a serpentine course round the many obstacles over which the cumbersome carts could not pass. In addition, we had to assist them over fallen logs, and work the canoe under limbs of trees that were too big for us to cut. After a short halt for lunch we continued on through the dense growth in the general direction of the pass. Then we came to a deep ditch. "What in the world is this?" I asked Juan.

His eyes lighted. "That is an old road made by the Spaniards. Perhaps it will lead us to Punta de Agua. Let us follow it."

With considerable difficulty we eased the oxcarts down into the ditch. The roadway was so narrow that often the hubs of the carts rubbed against the vertical banks, but the cutting was easier and we made better time. It led through the pass in the hills, and far ahead we could see the glimmer of water. Our hopes rose as we pushed on through the sultry heat. Even the patient, tired oxen seemed to take a new interest in life. The road entered heavily wooded country, where it paralleled the course of a small stream. Through the trees we sighted the ruins of a large building, and Ginger and I stopped to explore it while the oxcarts went on ahead. It had probably been built in the time of the Conquistadors, for its massive masonry was similar to Cortez' lighthouse in La Ventosa. The great stone ruins had at one time probably been the hacienda of some Spanish Don who dominated the surrounding country. This area had been extensively developed by the Spanish after the Conquest, and there is enough fertile land in this one section alone to support half of Mexico. Today its hundreds of square miles of rich soil are uncultivated, and practically uninhabited. After a hasty survey we hurried on to rejoin the carts.

The ancient roadway led us directly to Punta de Agua which we reached towards sundown. The great inland sea, its muddy waters whipped into foam by the stiff norther, caused us considerable misgiving. The oxen were driven close to the water's edge while the canoe was unloaded and launched. As we transferred our things from the cart to the canoe, we sank nearly to our knees in the mud of its oozy bottom. After we finished loading, we anchored the canoe to a paddle stuck in the mud and waded ashore to say good-bye to Juan and the cartmen. It was hard to find words which would adequately express our gratitude for all Juan had done for us, but I think he knew how grateful we were. We waded back to the canoe, washed the mud off our legs, and climbed in, while Juan and the cart boys stood on the beach and waved good-bye.

Pushing with our paddles on the muddy bottom, we skirted the shore line in the dusk. The wind made it impossible to travel any distance away from the slight protection it offered. The muddy water splashed over us, and the force of the blasts often made it necessary to stick the paddles deep in the mud to keep from being blown backward. But this was the life we liked. Let the wind blow! We enjoyed being alone; and we enjoyed the sensation of facing the unknown and the unpredictable. Some people, I suppose, are so constituted that hazards are incidental to a special kind of pleasure to be found only under such circumstances. It is difficult to say truthfully why this is so. Perhaps it is the necessity for fast action, or never quite knowing in advance the course of events, that lends such a fascination to these ventures.

A small shell beach in the shelter of dense mangroves offered a landing. We tied the canoe securely to a log, and waded ashore with our supper—dried fish and tortillas. The stories of the Mareños had got under our skins, and though we had seen no evidences of them, we had an uneasy feeling that they were watching us. Our guns were swung low on our hips, and our trigger fingers were decidedly nervous. Lighting a fire might attract unwelcome attention, so we ate the cold food, and just wished for hot coffee. After the meal we sat on the tiny shell beach and wondered what our next move would be. To cross the *pampa* (the local name for a body of water) was impossible in the norther, and the mudflats made it equally difficult to cruise near the shore. Since there was no immediate solution, and nothing else to do, we waded out to the canoe, curled up in the cockpit, and went to sleep.

At midnight I awakened with the feeling that something unusual had happened. There was a profound silence. Then I knew—the wind had gone down. "Come on, Ginger," I said, "we're going to travel." She mumbled something about being sleepy, squirmed round a bit, and went back to sleep. I got the canoe under way and started out across the wide *pampa*. Soon the canoe grounded on a mudflat, and I got out and pushed. Then Ginger waked up and wanted to know what was the matter, and did I see any Indians? Assured that when I did see Indians she would hear the Luger, she went back to sleep. The whole lagoon seemed to be a series of mudflats, and I alternately pushed and paddled the way across. About 4 A.M. I could see mangroves ahead, and then the canoe grounded for the hundredth time on another mudflat. Pushing did no good, for the ooze was so deep that the canoe stuck fast, so I anchored it to a paddle shoved in the mud, washed my feet, and curled up in the cockpit.

The scream of the wind wakened us shortly before daylight. The tide had come in and the canoe was afloat about a quarter of a mile off shore. Even though we were in the lee of the shore it was difficult to make headway. Shallow water and mudflats prevented us from getting close enough to the beach to make a landing. However, there is nothing like the thought of a hot meal after having walked, pushed, and paddled the better part of

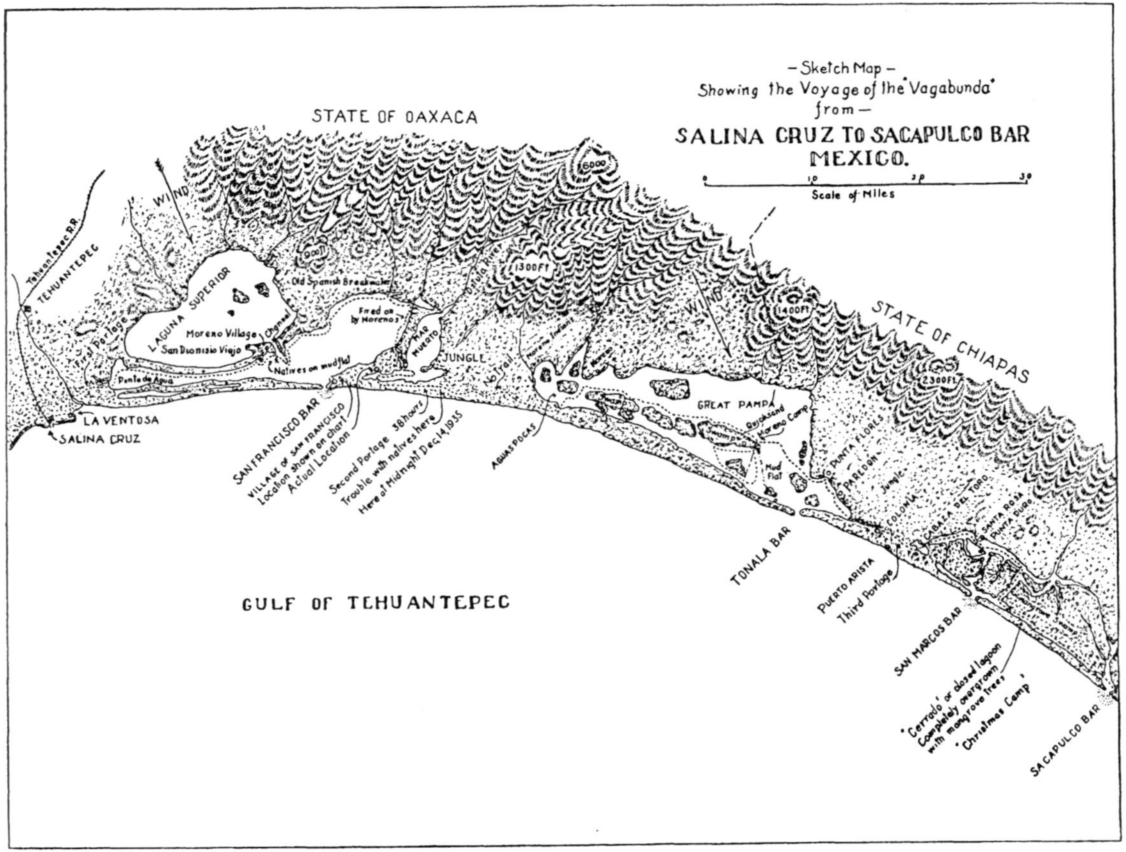
– Sketch Map –
Showing the Voyage of the "Vagabunda"
from –
SALINA CRUZ TO SACAPULCO BAR
MEXICO.
0
10
20
30
Scale of Miles
STATE OF OAXACA
STATE OF CHIAPAS
WIND
WIND
Tehuantepec R.R.
TEHUANTEPEC
First Portage
LAGUNA SUPERIOR
Moreno Village
San Dionisio Viejo
Punta de Agua
Natives on mudflat
Old Spanish Breakwater
Fired on by Morenos
MAR MUERTO
JUNGLE
1300 Ft
1400 Ft
2300 Ft
6000
GREAT PAMPA
Mud Flat
LA VENTOSA
SALINA CRUZ
SAN FRANCISCO BAR
VILLAGE OF SAN FRANCISCO
Location shown on chart
Actual Location
Second Portage 38 hours
Trouble with natives here
Here at Midnight Dec. 14, 1935
AGUAS POCAS
TONALA BAR
PUERTO ARISTA
Third Portage
PUNTA FLORES
PAREDON
Jungle
COLOMA
SAN MARCOS BAR
SANTA ROSA
PUNTA DURO
"Cerrado" or closed lagoon
Completely overgrown
with mangrove trees
"Christmas Camp"
SACAPULCO BAR
GULF OF TEHUANTEPEC

twenty-four hours since the last one, to stimulate one's efforts. So we got out and pulled the *Vagabunda* until we came to a small channel where we could drag it close into shore. We lost no time in hurrying to the beach with the grub box and cooking equipment, where we found shelter under a mangrove.

Restored by cups of hot, bitter, black, strong coffee and hot food, we went for a hike along the beach after breakfast, hoping to find game. A small ravine led to the top of a low ridge from which we had an excellent view of the surrounding country. In front of us stretched the huge expanse of Laguna Superior, its muddy waters beaten to a froth by the wind that almost swept us off the ridge. The high, choppy seas breaking on its beaches would pound a small boat to pieces, and we were glad to be on the lee shore of the smaller body of water. The two lagoons were separated by a narrow strip of low, brush-covered sand hills not more than fifty yards wide. We stood silently looking at this lost world of wind and water, fringed with gnarled mangrove thickets. The norther lashed the waters with squalls of hurricane violence, and tried to wrench the trees from their stubborn grip upon the ooze. Further along the ridge we saw two deer and a few rabbits, and knew that fresh water must be near-by. We found a clear, sweet spring where we filled our canteens before going back to the canoe. Then we continued on down the lagoon.

Late in the afternoon we came to a deep bay at whose upper end the sand spit widened out and terminated in a mountainous cape. It took all our strength to hold the canoe against the wind that raged unchecked down the wide expanse of Laguna Inferior. Near the head of the bay it was possible to progress only by walking along the shore with each of us holding on to the doubled anchor line tied to the bow of the canoe. While beating our way up the beach we saw two natives dodge into the brush on the opposite side of the bay. We stopped long enough to get out extra ammunition and clips and to loosen our guns in their holsters. From then on, between watching the brush and keeping an eye on the canoe, we almost wore out our necks. But the natives did not reappear.

Burnt by the wind and pelted by sand and flying pebbles, we at last rounded the bay, where, sheltered by the lee of the mountain, we could paddle along the shore. Towards sundown we discovered a little cove. After anchoring the canoe some distance from the beach—in case we had to leave in a hurry—we enjoyed a leisurely swim and a hot supper. For safety's sake we slept in the canoe again, anchoring as far out in the lagoon as we could go without being carried off by the wind. There was little to see, for great clouds of spray blotted out the landscape in all directions.

Daylight found us ashore eating breakfast. After preparing a lunch to take with us, we continued on down the coast. Our precautions of the day before had not been unwise, for as we rounded the point of the cove, we saw ahead a great stone fort, set among a grove of palm trees. Near it on the beach were native dugouts and groups of naked Indians. The chart called the place San Dionisio Viejo. While we were fairly itching to examine the ancient citadel, it seemed unwise to disturb its present occupants. By detouring as far from shore as possible we hoped to sneak by them unnoticed. The old stronghold had probably been built by the Conquistadors to guard the entrance channel to Laguna Superior, a half mile above the village. Our hopes of being allowed to pass unmolested were soon dissipated. As we passed beyond the village Ginger said, "Two canoes just shoved off the beach and are coming our way." I looked quickly round. They were coming—and fast—with several men paddling each dugout.

For the moment the *Vagabunda* was in deep water, but directly ahead of us lay a shallow expanse of lagoon, flanked by the shore on one side and a dry mudflat on the other. Beyond the broad stretch of chocolate-coloured mud and water, we could see the deeper blue of the open channel. A hasty glance convinced us that an attempt to skirt the barrier by making a right angle turn towards the centre of the *pampa* would force us to pass in front of the bows of the oncoming dugouts. To get within range of the Indians' old muzzle-loaders, bad marksmen as they were, was out of the question. Our only course lay straight across the shallow water.

Now we were in the shoals, and although we pushed mightily with our paddles against the soft bottom, the canoe grounded a short distance from deeper water. There was no time to lose; we immediately jumped out and began pulling, wading up to our knees in the muck. The natives were a good hundred yards behind, and since their dugouts drew more water than the canoe, I had a feeling that they might have trouble on their own account if they kept on following us. Within a few minutes we heard their shouts of rage as they tried to drag the grounded dugouts through the mud. Not that it stopped them, for they kept right on coming. It was evident that these gentlemen meant business. We were almost on the edge of the channel when I noticed something that made me laugh.

"Well, what's so funny?" Ginger demanded.

"Look behind you," I answered, "and then look at the channel."

"I've looked behind," she answered after a moment, "and it isn't funny —they're gaining on us. There's nothing ahead but deep water and wind."

"Which way is the tide going?" I asked.

"Out. But what does that spell?" she puzzled. Then she laughed as she noticed the fast-running streams pouring off the shoal into the channel. "Oh, yes, now I see."

Fate had provided us with an opportunity too good to miss. We decided that we were entitled to a little fun. The tide was rapidly receding, and in a few minutes the mudflat would be as dry as a bone. The heavy dugouts could be floated with the next tide, but not before. In the meantime, our welcoming committee would have many hours in which to meditate. So we put on a heart-rending spectacle for their enjoyment. The canoe became suddenly immovable. We tugged and strained and groaned aloud. Since the Indians had no way of knowing that our light craft weighed less than their heavy dugouts, they figuratively threw up their hats for joy at this supposed misfortune. By now we had the canoe in open water, but we kept pulling and straining at the astonished *Vagabunda* just the same. Without further ado they abandoned their dugouts, waving their guns and shouting, as they wallowed through the deep mud towards us. One old fellow in the lead could hardly restrain his enthusiasm. He stopped and raised his gun, then decided that the distance was too great and the risk of wasting his precious ammunition unnecessary. We delayed climbing into the canoe until they were almost within gunshot range. Then I allowed myself the luxury of a little boy's trick—the classic gesture of thumbing the nose. But this to my regret was wasted, for it brought no response from the Mareños. The unexpected sight of the moving canoe brought plenty, however. They screamed with rage and disappointment as we paddled away from the mudflat. It was too bad, but it was one of those situations that could not have had a happy ending for both the Mareños and ourselves.

It was an out-of-the-frying-pan-into-the-fire triumph, for as soon as we lost the shelter of the hill we were in the full force of the norther. The narrow channel between the lagoons formed a funnel through which the wind blew us sideways faster than we could paddle ahead. The short high seas slapped the *Vagabunda's* thin sides with such violence that she shook as though she were about to break in two. The cockpit soon filled with water, and we rode so low that each wave broke over us. Half-way across the channel we sighted a sand bar running out from the point on its opposite side. This was good news, because it meant that we could run before the wind towards the end of the bar, and if we could round it, could then work our way towards the protecting shelter of the lee shore of Laguna Inferior.

As we ran before the wind, the seas boiled over the canoe's stern where I perched precariously. Ginger knelt in the water-filled cockpit, paddling as though the devil were after her. We shot round the end of the sand bar, where we still had the wind but not the seas. But the norther seemed determined to prevent us from landing. For a few minutes there was every likelihood of being blown out into the open *pampa* and pounded to pieces in short order. Each painful gain of a few feet was cancelled in the twinkling of an eye by the wind. A slight lull eventually gave us the chance we needed. Gaining the bar, we rested a few minutes, and bailed out the cockpit before continuing on towards the hills, towing the canoe close inshore.

After a long, weary walk we gained the shelter of the hills and found respite from the wind in a tiny cove where we stopped for a bite to eat. As we sat in the sparse shade of a dwarf tree and relaxed our tired muscles, we gazed at the muddy, wind-swept lagoon. Ahead of us we could see no land in any direction. Nothing broke the monotony of the hills on our side of the landscape except a few purple patches of some flowering vine which grew on otherwise barren slopes. The whole outlook was bleak and depressing, and unfriendly beyond anything that we had imagined. Ginger sighed as she suggested that we had better move on. We were still too near the Mareño encampment to make the cove a healthy place in which to spend the night.

Before resuming the journey, we got out the charts and studied the route by which we hoped to travel from one lagoon to another. A channel appeared to connect our present lagoon with the one due south, Mar Muerto. But there was no waterway shown connecting Mar Muerto with the big lagoon called Great Pampa which lay twenty miles beyond it. If we could not find a way across, we might have to come back and try to secure oxcarts with which to make the portage from the village of San Francisco del Mar, located on the map near the lagoon's sea entrance. The idea of going to San Francisco del Mar for the night occurred to us, but sailing across the lagoon in the norther was out of the question, and to get there we would have to circumnavigate the great bay. We decided to take a chance and go on to Mar Muerto. There might be an unmapped native village on its shores.

The canoe made good time under double-reefed sail. Near the head of the bay we came to what had been at one time a deep estuary at the mouth of a tidal river, with an extensive breakwater of ancient Spanish masonry across it. The narrow channel was so filled with silt that it soon became too shallow even to float the canoe. We turned back, tied up the canoe, and waded out to inspect the breakwater. It was a substantial piece of work about ten feet wide and nearly two hundred feet long. Probably a port had once existed near-by, and the sand bars which had converted the open ocean into lagoons had been formed at a later date. Somewhere, undoubtedly, there are written records of the Spaniards' activities in this country which ought to make a fascinating story. We speculated about those far-off days, and wondered who had built the cities which no longer existed, and why they had been abandoned. The old fort, the breakwater, and other evidences of the Spanish occupation were thrilling examples of their enterprise and daring. We recommend this strip of country to historical novelists in search of a brand-new setting.

Since we could discover no navigable channel, we looked round for fresh water for our nearly empty canteens. I began to dig a shallow well on the river bank. Frequently, by digging a few feet down we would find water that, though brackish, could be used. I had just started when Ginger came running up from the beach where she had been prospecting for clams. "Dan, Mareños!"

We washed the mud off our hands and started back towards the canoe as two naked natives approached it from the beach. Their long hair was bound by a dirty rag tied round their heads. Both of them carried single-bladed spears. They looked over the canoe and the gear with an air of insolent ownership, and merely grunted in response to my greeting of "*Buenos tardes.*" I then asked, "Do you speak Spanish?"

"A little," one man replied.

I told them that we were seeking a passage to Mar Muerto, and asked for directions. This was met by, "I do not understand," and a demand for a cigarette. A vague motion towards the back country answered my question as to where we might find fresh water. Other inquiries produced only further demands for cigarettes, food, fishline, and other things. Their incessant begging became irritating. I finally offered to give them some of the things they wanted, if in return they would show us the passage. They could talk well enough when it suited their purpose, and one man answered, "We cannot tell you, but we can show you the way."

"That's fine," I said. "Let's go."

Then they became full of excuses. "We cannot go now. Stay with us, and in the morning we will go with you." This was accompanied by a rapid exchange of glances between them.

Ginger, who had hung back, came a little nearer. She was dressed in her travelling shorts, and I didn't care in the least for the way both men stared at her. I took a position beside the canoe where I could keep an eye on the brush back of the beach. One Indian fingered the harpoon line. "I want this," he said. The other fingered his spear.

"You'll get a hell of a lot more than that," I muttered to myself. "Come on, Ginger, let's get out of here." She came down and climbed into the canoe. I pulled the paddle out of the mud and untied the painter.

"No," said one Indian, stepping closer to us.

"*Porque?*" ("Why?") I asked.

"This is our country. Stay with us," he commanded.

"Please be careful, Dan. Don't let's have any trouble with them," Ginger urged. "If we do, they'll pass the word on ahead and we'll have every Mareño on the lagoon looking for us, and we've got a long ways to go in this country."

It was sound advice. "Listen," I said to the men, "we are going out to fish, and will return here tonight. Tomorrow you may show us the passage to the other lagoon."

"Give me a cigarette first," one man demanded. We had no cigarettes, but I compromised by giving them each a leaf of raw tobacco, and before they could argue further, we were off. They stood watching us for a moment, their faces full of hatred and disgust. Then muttering, they turned and walked up the beach.

Back in La Ventosa we had been anxious to meet the Mareños. Perhaps we had anticipated a little of our usual good luck in dealing with natives, for Ginger had a way with the women, and I managed well enough with the men. But these sons of Cain made the Seris and other reputedly savage

Indians, seem like nice people. We hoped to be able to give them a wide berth in the future.

Paddling very close to shore, we kept a sharp lookout for a passage into Mar Muerto. Once we thought we'd found it. Upon landing, we discovered that although there was another lagoon, separated from Laguna Inferior only by a narrow strip of sand, it was so shallow and full of trees that travelling on it would be almost impossible. We paddled along for another five miles without further incident. Then we saw a group of Mareños running on the beach, dodging behind sand dunes. We slowed down a bit to observe them. Soon they were way ahead of us, sprinting for dear life down the sand towards a grove of palm trees some distance ahead. "More fun," I said. "Wonder what those devils are up to?"

"They probably intend to hide in that grove until we come along, and then try to hit us. They have guns or they wouldn't be trying a stunt like that," Ginger answered.

The wind was at our backs, so we shook out a reef in the sail and skimmed along the beach. As we neared the clump of palms we changed our course to get further away from shore and out of range. Ginger meanwhile got out the clips of ammunition. I was certain that we were out of range of their muzzle-loaders, but if by any chance they had got hold of rifles, we might be hit. Ginger was philosophical. "We've been shot at before without being hit."

"If they have rifles, we'll open up on them," I said as we drew opposite the grove. Now the Mareños came running down to the beach—five men and a boy, and three of them carried guns. At the water's edge, they raised the guns and fired. Puffs of black powder smoke blotted out their figures. Half-way between the canoe and the beach, the water was splattered with shot.

We roared with laughter. "You'd better be careful," I yelled to them in Spanish, "or you'll shoot off your toes."

Ginger settled herself in the cockpit. "Just sit there and enjoy the show," I said, swinging the canoe back in towards the beach. The natives had momentarily disappeared, but we knew that they had by no means abandoned the hunt. I swung inshore as close as I dared.

"Here they come," said Ginger. They were a hundred yards behind, and were running in back of the sand dunes towards some other ambush. To tease them, I spilled some of the wind from the sail by edging a shade nearer the shore, and slowed down a bit. When they were nearly abreast of us, we turned out from shore and ran before the wind. "I think you're mean, Dan," said Ginger, as I alternately raised and lowered their hopes by zigzagging down the beach. Each time the canoe got too far ahead, we slowed down and waited for them. They were seemingly tireless, running on mile after mile. It was obvious that sooner or later we were going to have trouble, for they were quite capable of dogging our trail until they

The Land of Primitive Men

did catch up. I felt it was about time to make them realize that we could do more than play, and swung the canoe back in towards the beach. "Now what are you up to?"

"Let's give them a good scare," I answered. "We'll try to coax them to come out on the beach. Then while you tear up the sand to the right of them, I'll tear it up to the left. When they see what a modern gun can do, maybe they'll be discouraged. We'll give them a chance to get ahead of us and to reload their guns."

They passed us, but when we drew up opposite the place where we'd last seen them, they were nowhere in sight. A careful examination of the shore line revealed no trace of them. Ginger suggested that perhaps we had tired them out and they had quit, but I had a feeling that they were not so easily discouraged. We should have settled with them sooner. It was late in the afternoon and we had yet to find water and a place in which to spend the night.

Ahead of us, a point of land extended out some distance into the lagoon. I shaped the course to round it, and settled down to the business of sailing. As we neared it, something told me to give the place a wide berth. I swung further out into the *pampa*, and then noticed that just off the point a big mudflat extended out into the bay, with a channel between the two. It would take at least a half hour to sail round the flat. "How about it?" I asked Ginger. "Shall we take a chance on the channel?"

"It's pretty close to shore," she demurred, "but let's try it." We swung into the channel, hugging the seaward side to put as much distance between ourselves and the point as possible. Too late, we saw that the channel was narrower than it had appeared at a distance.

"I don't like the look of this at all," I said, and began laying out extra clips. Ginger crouched in the cockpit beside me. We were not a moment too soon. As we drew abreast of the point, the Mareños came running out on the beach. We were well within their range. "Let them have it," I shouted. We placed our shots as close on each side of them as we dared, and they started dancing as though the sand had become red hot. They streaked for the shelter of the sand dunes. We contented ourselves with kicking up sand from the tops of the dunes for a minute or two before scooting out of the channel.

Laying our hot guns in the cockpit to cool, we collected and reloaded the empty clips. "You know, Dan, I used to think we were romanticizing a bit back home when we spent hours practising to do these things in a hurry," Ginger commented.

In retrospect, I could see the two of us down in the arbour by the fish pond back in Santa Ana, loading clips and firing at targets for all we were worth. My mother sometimes came to watch us, and I could hear her say, "Children, it's time for lunch. Don't you think you've done shooting enough for one day?" Long ago and a world away seemed that pleasant garden in Southern California.

A string of mangroves threading their way inland revived our hopes of finding a channel to Mar Muerto. This might be the passage. Upon investigation it turned out to be a deep channel, perhaps a hundred yards wide, which wound in and out among the mangroves in the general direction of the lagoon that we were seeking. We pulled the canoe across the shallow water at its mouth and started down the passage. The sun was low on the horizon, and both of us had a feeling that it was wise to make haste. To be caught by the Mareños in the channel after dark might have unpleasant consequences. We were within range from either shore, and as we advanced the waterway narrowed. Dense walls of vegetation pressed close upon it, throwing long shadows over the constricted stream. Then ahead of us as we rounded a bend, we saw two natives in a canoe just disappearing round another bend. We stopped, looked at each other, and took counsel. "I'm afraid it's run or fight," I said.

"If you're game to go ahead, I am," Ginger answered.

We continued down the winding ribbon of dark water, carefully scanning both shore lines. Every nerve and muscle tensed as we approached each possible ambuscade. But nothing rewarded our straining eyes and ears until, while negotiating a sharp bend in the channel, we heard a loud crash in the brush. Instantly I started firing in that direction. "Hold it!" Ginger shouted above the fusillade. "That was just an alligator."

I felt sheepish. "I don't know what policy to adopt. Should we shoot first, and then look, or look first and then shoot?"

At last we emerged from the channel to see before us the wide expanse of Mar Muerto (sometimes called Laguna Cerro Blanco). Weariness and depression followed quickly our relief from tension. What were we going to do? Now that we were here, where could we go? The great landlocked lagoon looked like a dead sea. Its black shore line offered slight hope of sanctuary, and perhaps concealed a multitude of unknown dangers. How were we going to get the canoe over the twenty miles of jungle that lay between this and the next lagoon? If we had to go back through the narrow channel and down the shores of Laguna Inferior to San Francisco del Mar, would our good luck hold? At that moment we had no reserves with which to face the future. We needed hot coffee and a hot meal, but they weren't worth a battle with the Mareños, so we decided to anchor for the night on the *pampa*. The norther had gone down and the surface of the water was like a polished obsidian mirror as we paddled towards the centre of the lagoon.

"Dan, look shorewards!" I turned quickly at Ginger's urgent tone. A paddle flashed faintly in the slanting rays of the sun.

"Oh, Lord!" I said; "if we're going to have more trouble let's get it over with before dark. We'd better go to them, before they come to us."

With that we started inshore at an angle, trying to overtake the canoe. As we approached it we could see that some one on the stern was poling, and some one else paddling at the bow. They were making good time, and as we drew nearer, they speeded up. In spite of our efforts, the distance remained about even. Then they pulled out into the full rays of the setting sun. Ginger stopped paddling, and said that she was either seeing things, or the men in the dugout wore clothes. We redoubled our efforts to catch them, but they seemed equally determined not to be caught. Finally they began to slow down, and the distance between us narrowed. We passed on the western shore the white limestone headland that gave the lagoon the name by which it is sometimes called, Cerro Blanco (White Hill). The dugout ahead of us entered a wide channel lined with mangroves. The men were poling and paddling frantically, but they were having difficulty of some kind, for their pace grew slower and slower. We gained on them rapidly. Soon we were near enough to see that they were trying to work through a dense growth of swamp grass, which extended across the wide arm of water towards which they were travelling. Seemingly badly frightened by our efforts to catch them, they would look occasionally in our direction, and then renew their desperate efforts to force a way through the entangling growths. As soon as we came within hailing distance, I shouted reassuringly, "*Hola, amigos!*" They stopped poling in open-mouthed surprise. We, too, had difficulty when we struck the grass and tried to work the canoe closer to them. The dugout poled back to meet us, and we saw that it contained an old man and a boy.

"Oh," said the old fellow in a relieved voice, "we were afraid that you were Mareños."

We confessed that we also feared them for the same reason. After telling them who we were and what we were doing in the lagoon, we asked them if they knew of a safe place near-by in which to spend the night.

"We are going to the village of San Francisco del Mar," said the old man, "and if you will follow, we will lead you to it."

Since our chart showed the village to be at the sea entrance of Laguna Inferior, I was puzzled. But the old man stoutly affirmed that the chart was wrong and that San Francisco del Mar was just round the bend on Mar Muerto. He started poling through the tangled grass with the *Vagabunda* on his heels. We finally emerged, and after rounding a small tree-covered point, came upon a number of canoes tied to poles stuck in the mud. Above the beach, said the old man, lay the village of San Francisco del Mar.

Long before we reached the mooring place of the native dugouts, the lagoon became so shallow that it was necessary for us to get out and wade through the soft mud, pulling the canoe after us. We dragged it within twenty-five yards of the shore before anchoring it to a paddle stuck in the ooze, but the old man was forced to leave his heavier craft further away.

While we waited for him to join us, we looked for signs of life from the village, which lay silent and concealed behind a grove of trees. No one came near the beach; and there were none of the usual small sounds of an Indian village at dusk—the clatter of cooking pots, and the voices of women busy about their fires. This might mean anything, but it generally meant trouble. The old man reached our side and explained that the absence of the villagers was probably due to the fact that they were frightened by the approach of strangers, who never came to San Francisco del Mar. He would go on ahead and assure them that we meant no harm. He plodded away through the mud towards the beach. While giving our ambassador time to precede us, we got out a supply of fishhooks and needles for gifts, and stuffed extra clips of ammunition in our pockets. Thus prepared for the quality of our reception, we waited until we heard the old fellow shouting and a babel of answering voices. "Come on," I said, "let's make the acquaintance of San Francisco del Mar."

Half-way up the beach we were met by a procession of natives led by the old man, the women holding their dresses high above their knees as they splashed through the muck. "I have told them of your strange boat," he said when we came abreast, "and they are anxious to see it."

Back to the canoe we went, with a crowd of at least fifty chattering natives at our heels. They thumped the *Vagabunda's* canvas deck with their knuckles, and asked innumerable questions in a mixture of very bad Spanish and some unknown native tongue. Our Spanish seemed equally unintelligible to them. This was partly due to the fact that the Spanish language undergoes strange transformations at the hands of the Indians. Such a word, for example, as *pampa*, which means a body of water when used by the Indians of the Isthmus, comes to mean a grassy plain as one travels further south. Our conversational difficulty was solved when a young fellow who had just arrived stepped up and said, "Perhaps I can help you. I am from Tonala, and speak good Spanish." We explained to him that we were en route from Salina Cruz to Champerico, that we had come from the North, and so forth. He translated to the crowd, who buzzed with excitement. After he had finished, he said, "My name is Enrique. I am the village storekeeper. Come to my house and we will have supper and talk."

We had been up before dawn, and every minute of the long day had been filled with excitement and hard physical labour. The thought of hot food lent strength to our tired limbs as we plodded after him to his house, which was also the store, where we were greeted by his plump, pretty bride, Teresa. They were both youngsters, neither one of them looking over eighteen. While Teresa went to the communal kitchen to prepare the food—several families shared the same kitchen because of the scarcity of firewood—Enrique produced some crude trestles for seats. These could also be converted into beds, he said, by spreading a bamboo pole mat across them. Then he lighted a smudge to keep off the mosquitoes, who were *"muy bravo"* according to Enrique.

He then told us about the village. It was very old and the graveyard was very big. This did not mean that the place was unhealthy, he said. On the contrary, it was very *sano*, but the graveyard had been there for many years. The dry wind of the norther swept across the country incessantly, and kept the climate good and the air free from insects, which could not live in its blasts. Of course this did not mean the mosquitoes, who could live any place.

Then Teresa produced what seemed a banquet to us, and what we found out later was indeed a banquet for San Francisco del Mar. The meal consisted of eggs, stewed in a sauce of tomatoes and chili, tortillas, fried rice, fried beans, and good hot coffee. We ate it with keen appreciation.

During the meal we could hear voices outside the hut, and by the time we had finished a big crowd had collected. Enrique said that they had never before seen white people. They were particularly fascinated by the colour of Ginger's hair, which the sun had bleached to a straw yellow, and they marvelled at its short length. The youngsters would come up solemnly, touch her, and as solemnly move away to make room for the next youngster. Finally she went outside the hut to give her audience a better chance to look at her, since they could not all crowd in. Soon I heard shouts of laughter from among the women, and went out to investigate. One old woman, whose name was Carmen, and who looked like the traditional witch, had the centre of the stage. She was the spokeswoman for the group, and she had asked Ginger why she liked Mexico. Ginger replied, because she liked the warm climate, the *"tierra del sol"* (land of the sun). This had produced the volleys of laughter. Old Carmen announced that in their native language *sol* meant pig!

At last, pleading our very real weariness, we went back to the canoe, accompanied by Enrique and about fifteen others. Streams of people had evidently been going out to the boat all evening, for a deep channel had been cut through the mud, and we were forced to make a wide detour to reach it. Everything on deck had been examined, but nothing taken. We spread out the bag in the cockpit and lay down, but we were not to be rid of our audience so easily. One group departed only to make room for a new contingent. This went on until about eleven o'clock, when things quieted down.

Ginger had fallen asleep and I was dozing, when I heard more splashing. I peeked over the cockpit to see three men, armed with machetes and shotguns, approaching the canoe as quietly as was possible through the sucking ooze. I picked up the Luger and held it under the railing, aimed at them. When they were quite near, I sat up and said, *"Buenos noches."*

"Buenos noches," they replied. "We want to see your commission."

I replied that we had no commission, and that I did not know what they meant. Ginger began wiggling. I nudged her to be quiet. "Señores, you have made a mistake," I said. "We are travellers and nothing else."

"Oh, yes, you *have* a commission, and we want to see it," they repeated. "Just why would you come to San Francisco del Mar if you have no commission? Tell us that!" they persisted. The men were becoming ugly, fingering their machetes in a suggestive manner. I could think of no other answer to give them, except to repeat my denial that we had come to the village for any ulterior purpose. "Señor, it is useless to deny that you have a commission, and we are here to see it. *En que forma viene?*" ("In what form do you come?") the spokesman repeated.

"Señores," I said, "please believe me when I tell you that we come only as friends, and to receive your protection against the Mareños. From whom should we receive a commission?"

"The government, of course," they replied. "Who else?"

We argued back and forth for an hour. Then I delivered, what was to them, the crucial argument. "Do you think," I said, "that if we had a commission, we would sleep in this canoe? Of course not. We would sleep in the best house in the village." Since the "servants of the people" are no more modest in Mexico than elsewhere in demanding the best of everything for themselves, this was conclusive proof (as indeed it ought to be) that we were simply tourists.

Then everybody laughed, and we all shook hands. They explained that a "commission" meant a tax collector, or some one who had come to spy on the churches, to see whether the priests were holding secret masses. We parted friends, and they marched off through the mud. Once again we settled down for some much-needed sleep.

Fortunately we had gone to sleep with our clothes on, for daylight brought a new procession of visitors, who began arriving in the midst of my morning shave. They were entranced by my soap-covered jaws, and the shiny thing with which I scraped my face. I suppose it did look strange to the scant-bearded Indians. We finished our toilettes under the scrutiny of fifty pairs of curious eyes. Then we found ourselves unable to leave the canoe because of the churned-up mud. This was explained to the audience, who with much laughter dragged the canoe to a new anchorage, where the mud was firmer.

The news that we were without "commissions" had apparently gone the rounds, for the people were even friendlier than they had been the previous evening. We waded with our escort up to the beach, where Enrique was waiting for us with an invitation to breakfast. Then we were deluged with invitations to breakfast, but we accompanied Enrique to his house, where, according to the standards of San Francisco del Mar, Teresa had prepared a lavish meal. This consisted of a dried fish apiece, which had been broiled over the coals, an egg, and a large toasted tortilla. Here eggs and corn are a luxury, since there is very little land suitable for farming. The main dish consists of fish, eaten regularly three times a day.

While we were at breakfast, trading started in Enrique's little store. I saw no money change hands, dried fish and fish roe being the only medium of exchange. All the supplies for the village had to be hauled from Juchitán, we were told, six days distant by oxcart. Though it was only two days' travel by water, the natives preferred the longer haul over the awful roads to running the gauntlet of Mareños, who patrolled the waterways, constantly on the lookout for the unwary traveller.

After breakfast we went for a stroll through the village. It was a curious place of perhaps fifty huts, each one crowning a rather high mound. These mounds are all that are left of the ancient buildings erected by the Spaniards. In the centre of the village was a ruined church, with two of its arches still in place. Water was obtained from an old well of Spanish masonry, near the church. All over the village, especially near the higher mounds, we found pieces of broken pottery. Some of it was of recent origin, but most of it was of a thin, dark type, different from any now in use. No one could tell us how old the village really was, but we gained some idea by going to the graveyard. It was immense for the size of the village, and many of the older monuments were of Spanish design and workmanship. Some of them had deep recesses, in which a tiny altar could be set up and candles lighted, safe from the blasts of the wind. The wind-driven sand had eroded most of the dates from the earlier stones, but we did find one dated 1702 which was still legible. There were a few trees, their branches growing only on the south side, evidence of the *norte* which blows continuously. Since there was little else to see in the village, we returned to Enrique's, with the curious crowd still at our heels.

We had a whole day before us, and decided to spend it trying to find out something of the lagoon country ahead of us. But no two people had the same story to tell. Some said that it was only two miles to the next lagoon, Great Pampa, and that there was a trail all the way. Others were sure that it was much further, that there was no trail, and that the jungle was impassable. Still others doubted the existence of the lagoon at all! I suggested to Enrique that we go and see the *Presidente*, who might be better informed; but alas, he was away fishing and was not expected to return until the following day.

Ginger then suggested that it might be a good idea to find out something for ourselves by climbing to the top of the limestone headland, Cerro Blanca. Teresa fixed a lunch for us and we were off. The norther was nothing more than a stiff breeze when we started paddling to the west side of the lagoon. On the way over, we changed into our travelling shorts to preserve our shore clothes against the wear and tear of climbing rocks. Then the sky to the north began to darken, and another wind was on its way.

Anchoring the canoe some distance from shore, we waded towards the towering mass of limestone blocks. We had to hack a way through the jungle before we could begin the ascent. On the lagoon side, the great stone slabs offered no foothold, so we cut a trail to the seaward side of the hill. Here, with caution, the rock could be climbed. Half-way up its broken surface the wind began to roar On the lee side we still had some protection from the blasts; but as we neared the crest, and worked our way round to the east side where we could see the canoe, the wind became so strong that we dared not leave the shelter of the big boulders. The canoe was riding on a lake of white foam. Whirling clouds of spray danced in the grip of the wind, to dissolve at last into needle-fine mist as they dashed against the western foreshore. Even high up in our eagle's aerie, the rocks and our faces were wet with spume. But we were unable to gain a complete view of the country unless we climbed a pinnacle peak which blocked the horizon to the south. It was a mad and dangerous scramble up the steep incline, with each blast of the wind trying to dislodge us. At last we gained the shelter of a ledge from which the vast panorama could be seen in its entirety. Between Mar Muerto and Great Pampa stretched an immense tree-covered plain. It appeared to be an impenetrable barrier to our passage, unless we could prevail upon some one to transport the canoe and equipment the intervening distance. But who in the village would dare to venture into Mareño country? One glance seaward at the rough waters of the gulf was enough to discourage any thought of travel by sea. The great inland bays through which we had come since leaving La Ventosa were equally perilous, and in reality offered no retreat, since there was no way of transporting the canoe from Agua Punta to the coast.

We made our way down the lee side of the hill in silence. As we pushed out of the dense growth and stepped on to the beach, the blasts of wind almost drove us back into the shrubbery again. To walk, let alone paddle, was all but impossible. "How in the world," asked Ginger, "are we ever going to get back to the village?"

I had no immediate solution to offer, but led the way, while Ginger pushed me from behind, towards the canoe. She climbed in, and I managed to pull the paddles out of the mud. Before I had a chance to join her, a heavy gust struck the canoe and it veered quickly round to one side. I grabbed and tried to hold it with the anchor line, but a wind-driven wave slapped me in the pants and down I went, the canoe dragging me through the slimy, matted grass and water. Somehow I managed to dig in my heels, and stop the wildly curvetting *Vagabunda*. A second wave deposited a chaplet of swamp grass on my head, and festooned a lei of the stuff round my neck. Ginger, who had struggled with her merriment over the first mishap, made no effort to conceal her hysterical laughter over my appearance.

"Quit laughing, and get out and shove!" I shouted.

With a noble effort she restrained her mirth, and after unstrapping her gun, joined me in the muddy water. My precious Luger, which was as plastered with mud as I was, I also placed in the canoe. Together we fought our way across the shallow lagoon. I tugged the canoe from the bow, while Ginger shoved it from the stern. Every so often, a sea higher than the rest would knock me down, and the boat would swing broadside to the waves, dragging us both through the liquid mud until we could regain our footing. The smaller waves were content to break on my stomach, which became sore from their pounding. After what seemed hours, we reached the lee shore and calmer water. We beached the canoe and went in for a swim to wash off the mud. Then Ginger took a kettle of water and her shore clothes into the seclusion of the bushes, and soon emerged spick and span. I followed her example.

We climbed back into the canoe and serenely paddled close inshore to San Francisco del Mar, where a crowd of natives awaited our arrival on the beach. The crowd began to murmur as we came ashore. "Impossible," they kept repeating in Spanish, as they stared at us, wonder and a sort of awe written large on their faces. They followed, but at a respectful distance, as we made our way to Enrique's house. "Now what do you suppose?" asked Ginger. I shook my head—there was no accounting for the vagaries of these people.

Our escort hurled comments in their native tongue at Enrique, who came out of the store to greet us. He looked at us for a moment, then laughed. "You have some explaining to do," he said. "These people want to know how you crossed the *pampa* in the *norte*, without being affected by the wind and water."

I looked at Ginger's neatly combed hair and spotless shore dress and grinned. Evidently our dramatic crossing and subsequent rehabilitation had not been observed from the village. As I started to explain, a native pushed his way through the crowd and said to me, "Señor, the *Presidente* has returned and wishes to see you at once."

We had left our official papers at Enrique's house, and after picking them up, we followed the messenger to the *agencia*, a thatched hut with mud walls, where *El Presidente*, surrounded by his secretary and a group of village dignitaries, awaited us. After the usual greetings, I immediately presented our papers, and asked the *Presidente* if he would favour us by putting his signature and seal upon them. We had learnt through experience that it was always wise to do this at once, as though it were a matter of routine procedure with which all village officials were familiar. If we asked an official's permission to remain, and so forth, before getting our papers signed, it gave him time to ponder over their legality, and whether we should be allowed to stay at all.

The *Presidente* started hunting for his seal before he even looked at the papers. After a good deal of searching about his dark cubby-hole, he found it. Then he spread out the papers, one by one, on the side of the broken dugout that served him for a desk. He drew his brows together over the importance of what he was about to do, and with a grand flourish stamped each paper with his seal, scrawling a row of zigzag lines beneath each stamp. I whispered to Enrique, who stood beside me, "Doesn't the *Presidente* read papers before he signs them?"

"He can't read," he whispered back.

We were going to need *El Presidente's* help if we ever expected to get to Great Pampa, and I thought a recital of our virtues and importance, as described by the Port Captain of Salina Cruz, might help. So I fished the letter out, and asked Enrique to read it. As he declaimed its grandiloquent phrases, the group listened intently, and when he had finished, they broke into the clipped staccato of their native tongue. In a few minutes the room became quiet. The small, dignified *Presidente* took his place behind the official dugout desk. He looked very solemn as he donned a pair of old-fashioned spectacles—the Lord only knows where he got them—and cleared his throat in an impressive manner. The other people ranged themselves round the walls. The place took on the air of a court room and I knew something was about to happen. I looked pleadingly at Enrique, but he only shrugged. After all he was not a native of the village, and it was apparent that he knew as little as we did. We might have broken a dozen local tabus without his knowing it. Then my name was called.

I felt a little shaky as I strode up in front of the *Presidente* and faced him. He looked over his glasses, as he asked in an inquisitorial tone, "Are you an engineer?" This information he had gained from the letter which Enrique had read to him. I nodded, yes, I was an engineer. Then he sprang a bombshell. "Do you understand making maps?" Shades of Magdalena Bay! Were we going to be held in this God-forsaken little village on charges of spying? Before I could answer, another question, equally disturbing, was on its way. "Do you," asked *El Presidente*, "understand photography?" My face got red. Now I *knew* we were to be accused of spying. I glanced over at Ginger to see how she was taking it. She looked frightened, too.

"Just what would you like to know?" I stammered.

But we were not to be put out of our misery so soon. The *Presidente* carefully examined his hands. The room held its breath—and so did we! Then he said, choosing his words, "My people say strange things of you. You crossed the *pampa* against the *norte* today, which no man can face, yet not a drop of water touched your clothes, nor did the wind displace a hair on your heads. You came safely through the Mareño country. It is reported that you have sailed your boat on the *mar viva*" (the ocean). His voice rose with excitement—we could feel the hysteria in the room—as he finished. "These are strange things. We think you possess strange powers."

To be accused of possessing supernatural powers was a dangerous business, and we knew it. If these natives believed in the tradition, imported by the Spanish, of *Ojos de Diablo*, we were in for a lot of trouble. Unpleasant things happened to people who had the "evil eye." Something must be done and done quickly. I began to talk in a quiet, reassuring voice. "Some men," I said, "have the ability to understand things which are a mystery to others. These men find pleasure in doing things that other men say cannot be done. They learn to do these things by study, hard work, and the attainment of knowledge. Such men are not *Ojos de Diablo*, they are *Amigos de Dios* (the friends of God). They are your best friends, if you are friends to them. I hope that we may be your friends."

This speech was greeted by silence. The *Presidente* stared at me with a bewildered expression. Apparently he had something else, and not the "evil eye" in mind. After a long pause he said, "We realize that you are such a man, and we have called this meeting to ask a favour of you. Can you bring back to life that which is dead?"

Ginger smiled at me reassuringly, as I pondered the proper reply. It seemed best to invite a little more detail before I confessed to such power. "What is it that you wish me to do?" I asked.

"I will show you," answered the *Presidente*. From an old chest in one corner of the hut, he fished out an ancient copper tube, green with verdigris. It was a chart tube, and might have seen service on some Spanish galleon. He removed its cap with difficulty, and pulled out a parchment, yellow and brittle with age. With the help of several others I carefully unrolled it. A masterpiece of fine penmanship, it bore the insignia of the eagle and the serpent beautifully drawn with pen and ink, and in the lower right-hand corner, the bold signature "Cortez."* It was the original charter for the Port of San Francisco del Mar. I could hardly believe my eyes. There was a certain irony in the fact that the preservation of this memento of vanished sovereignty was of no concern to any one who might have had a sense of identity, through race or inheritance, with what it had once signified. It is hard to say precisely what it meant to its present custodians, who watched my face with grave anxiety, while I carefully examined it. In some indefinable way, it represented a link with a past more glamorous than the present; and its preservation to these descendants of those whom it had despoiled was a matter of gravest import. Though it was dry and brittle, and part of its border had been eaten away by termites, I believed that it might be restored.

The *Presidente* beamed as I said, "Yes, I can bring it back to life, and I will be glad to do so if you will help me."

Still beaming, he addressed the others in their native tongue. Then he turned to me, and asked in Spanish, "What is it that we can do for you?"

"As you know," I said, "we are on our way to Champerico. We wish to reach the next water south. To do this we will need two oxcarts and two men." That started the argument of how far, and so forth, it was to the next lagoon. Everyone talked at once, and there was no agreement.

I finally interrupted the discussion. "Today," I said, "we climbed to the top of Cerro Blanco, and saw the country to the south. We have made

---

* Probably a descendant of the conqueror of Mexico, who had, besides his legitimate children, several natural children who were given land grants in this country.

portages by oxcart before. I know there are men in this village who have been to the next lagoon. Let us talk to those men. It is useless to listen to those who do not know the country. We will remain here tomorrow, and I will work upon your document. For the work I will need a large piece of cloth, finely woven; a large, smooth piece of wood, bigger than the paper, and a quantity of the poison that you use to kill fish. And," I added with a smile, "two oxcarts and two drivers."

The *Presidente's* face was a study in perplexity. He wanted his charter "brought back to life," but it was obvious that he knew of no one who would take us to the lagoon. That was his problem, though, and I had a feeling he would make an effort to arrange it somehow.

With that, we carefully put the charter back in its container, and followed Enrique to his house.

The next morning when we arrived at the *agencia*, the *Presidente* was there with all the materials I had asked for. Ginger made some paste out of flour we had brought with us from Salina Cruz, into which I stirred the poison, *mata pescado*. The cloth I stretched over the slab of wood, gave it a thorough coating of paste, and placed the charter upon it. When the old vellum adhered firmly to its new cloth backing, we covered it with a second piece of cloth, and weighted it down with bricks salvaged from the ruined church. There was a good chance that the liberal dosage of poison in the paste might discourage the termites' future activities. After allowing sufficient time for the paste to dry partially, we removed the bricks, set the board in the sun, and took several photographs of the relic. We promised the *Presidente* that if the pictures could be developed in Champerico, we would send him one—perhaps a large one if it could be arranged—so that if anything happened to his charter, he would always have its likeness. We then replaced the bricks and set the document away to dry thoroughly.

Our part of the bargain was completed, now what about the oxcarts? We looked at *El Presidente* inquiringly. He smiled and motioned into the room two men who were loafing outside the entrance. Their names were Pedro and José, the *Presidente* said, and they were experienced cartmen thoroughly familiar with the lagoon country. Both of them looked tough enough to cope with anything, including the Mareños. Neither man, however, seemed anxious to make the trip, and each began the usual recital of reasons why he could not go: there was a road, but it led only a short distance; one of them had a sick wife; there was the danger from Mareños; the trip would require four days. And finally, they had turned their oxen loose and did not know where to find them!

Then I had an idea. I said to Pedro, the elder of the two, a tough-looking *hombre* with shifty eyes and a hard, straight mouth. "If I can make your wife well, will you both go with us?"

He brightened. "*Si*, Señor." We closed the deal and followed Pedro off to his hut, with José, the smaller and less aggressive of the two, trailing dispiritedly in our wake.

Pedro's hut was a miserable affair on the outskirts of the village. His sick wife lay in a dilapidated hammock under a sleazy palm roof. She complained of a bad headache and fever. From her symptoms it was easy to diagnose her illness as a light malarial attack. I went to the canoe to get the medicine kit, while Ginger prepared some *atole* for the sick woman. I gave her a stiff shot of quinine, followed by two aspirins, and told her to drink nothing but boiled water, and eat nothing but *atole* for the next week.

While we were doctoring the sick woman quite a crowd collected to watch the proceedings. As we turned to leave, one of the natives hobbled up and pointed to his foot, which was badly infected. "Can you make this well, too?" he asked.

Then I realized that we were getting into deep water. In our anxiety to persuade the cartmen to make the trip, we had overstepped the authority of the local medicine man or woman. This was a serious breach of etiquette. Poor as their local resources might be, it was all the natives had once we were gone and sometimes their medicine men had considerable skill. I tried to look very grave. "In our travels," I said, "we have learned many things, but we are powerless to help you without the aid of your own doctor."

The crowd talked among themselves for a few minutes. Finally an old woman hobbled up and announced that she was the local midwife and "*doctora*." "Come," I said to her, "let us talk to the *Presidente*."

The crowd scattered off to spread the news, while we secured the *Presidente's* permission to teach the old woman some of the things we knew about medicine. Then we went with her to her hut, a short distance from Enrique's store. On the way over I explained to her the necessity for cleanliness, for I had a strong hunch we would have to clean up her hut before we could administer to the rapidly growing number of patients. Her hut was cleaner than we had anticipated, but a little antiseptic treatment wouldn't do it any harm, especially since the old woman was in the mood to learn what she could. She was a pleasant and an intelligent native with a likable personality. Her clothes were old and faded, but they were clean; and her sparse grey hair was neatly tied at the nape of her neck.

Ginger organized the hospital force by soliciting the additional services of Teresa and old Carmen. The *Presidente* came along in the rôle of generalissimo. We barred the door against the prying eyes of the crowd and went to work. While Ginger superintended the work of making the hut sanitary by the unlimited use of boiling water and much scrubbing, I showed the *Presidente* and the old midwife how to sterilize needles, knife blades, and cloth. Then I arranged with the midwife the procedure to be followed in treating the patients. I would do the work, but she was to stand by and tell me how to do it—after first observing very carefully what it was that I meant to do. If she did not understand, I would ask her a leading question, to which she was always to reply "yes." We went over the business until I was sure that she thoroughly comprehended the arrangement. The *doctora* was no fool, and she knew quite well that this teamwork would increase her prestige with the natives for miles around.

We opened the door and admitted our first patient, the man with the infected foot. Out of hearing of the patient, I explained to the *doctora* what was to be done. First, she was to instruct me to scrub the foot thoroughly in hot water; then to open and drain the wound with the aid of sterilized needles and a broken piece of razor blade, which I had furnished. Next, we were to remove the source of the infection (in this case a thorn which had broken off in his foot), and finally we were to bandage the wound with sterile bandages. The needles and the razor blade were to be always sterilized by washing them in permanganate of potash before we used them. She nodded, and we went to work on the patient.

We got along famously together, treating one patient after another for infections, malaria, dysentery, bad cuts, and *nigua* bites. She had a nice sense of humour, for her eyes twinkled as we went into a professional huddle over what was to be done for "Tomas' sore toe," and for the "spirits" that were causing Conchita's stomach to behave in a most peculiar fashion. Our clinic was a curious blending of traditional lore and modern medicine. Our patients had not been spoiled by reading accounts, written for the layman, on "how to diagnose your own case," and they never questioned our treatment. The combination of tribal authority and gringo medication was unbeatable.

By the time our last patient had gone, the old *doctora* was famous. Her fame would be lasting, for we had used neither implements nor medicine which she could not procure after we were gone. There were many things in our medicine kit better suited to the purpose than the things we used, but to have introduced them to this isolated village would have been more detrimental than helpful. There was no easily available source from which the natives could secure hospital gauze such as we used for our own bandages. Had we instructed them in its use, instead of showing them how to sterilize their own handwoven cloth, they might have traded for it, for a time, in Tonala or Juchitán, but most likely they would have quickly reverted to the use of a dirty rag.

Two weeks of intensive effort in a village, working through the right authorities, and using a terminology comprehensible to the native mind, would do more to stamp out unsound practices than a number of trained doctors turned loose in the same village. For instance, "bad" spirits like to live in dirty water, unclean bandages, open cesspools; but only "good" spirits inhabit sterile needles, scalded ollas, and so forth. It is surprising how quickly the local shamans get the idea. Their fame and prestige depends upon curing the sick; and they speedily adopt any measures to that end, once they are pointed out to them.

Late in the afternoon of that day, the *Presidente* came to see us. We knew by his lugubrious face that something had gone amiss. Yes, he said, something was very wrong. The cartmen had just paid him a visit, and flatly announced that they had reconsidered, and would not make the trip. I was furious. They had both faithfully promised that if I cured Pedro's wife they would go. We made tracks for Pedro's hut. The quinine and aspirin had done their work fairly well. Mrs. Pedro was busy over the *metate* grinding corn, while Pedro lay asleep in her hammock. I awoke him without ceremony. "What do you mean by breaking your promise?" I demanded.

Pedro lazily opened one eye. "Why should I go?" he said. "She is now able to cook." I delivered a scorching denunciation of people who broke promises, but Pedro simply turned over and ended all discussion by going back to sleep. I was to wish later that I had twisted the hammock round his neck then and there, and hung him from his own roof beam.

With Enrique we canvassed the entire village for another driver. We were warmly greeted, but our offer coolly declined. There were no other drivers—and that was that!

Enrique was sympathetic, but unfortunately that was not enough to produce a cartman. He tried to console us with a recital of what bad characters Pedro and José were. They were not natives of the village, but lived there because they were the only people able to drive an oxcart through Mareño territory and live to tell the story. The other drivers had all been killed off. They made a good living, judged by village standards, since they had no competitors. Enrique suspected that this was true only because the men were Mareños themselves, who had adopted village life and married village women. In any event, they were bad actors and we were well rid of them. This was interesting, but it didn't help the situation. Then I had a bright idea, and went back to Pedro's hut.

Pedro was still in the hammock, and by now mightily bored by my insistence that a promise was a promise. "Very well, Pedro," I said, "I promised you I'd cure your wife, and kept my word. But now that you've broken your promise, I shall break mine. Tomorrow your wife will be sick again." This statement was based on the chance that his wife had recurrent malaria. If so, she would have another attack of fever in the morning. Pedro leered and said nothing eloquently. He was a sceptic of the first order. Since there was nothing to be gained by further argument, I left with as much dignity as was possible under the circumstances, returning to Enrique's house.

Here a collection of the village notables were assembled, busily planning for a big fiesta to take place that night. My late assistant, the *doctora*, the *Presidente*, Teresa, and old Carmen, with the face of a grinning gargoyle, were the principal masters of ceremony. They had thoroughly organized the village: every woman was to prepare some dish; other villagers were to dance, or sing, or play guitars. It was a big evening, with everyone present except Pedro, José, and their families.

We returned to the canoe about midnight. The mud, as usual, was so churned up that we had to circle round it until we had located the anchor line and dragged the boat to a new anchorage before going aboard. We lay in the sleeping bag, looking at the stars, and listening to the wind overhead. How were we going to get out of San Francisco del Mar? The only solution seemed to be to retrace our steps to Laguna Inferior, go out the sea entrance into the Gulf of Tehuantepec, and down the gulf to the sea entrance of Great Pampa. Closer acquaintance with the norther had enormously increased our respect for its potency, but there seemed to be no other way for us to reach the next lagoon.

The following morning we were up at daylight. After dragging the canoe as close to the beach as we could, we unloaded the equipment and spread it out to dry. To neglect this chore was to invite disaster, for in the humid heat everything moulded or rusted in a day. Ginger smiled as we went about our tasks. "Something tells me," she said, "that today tells the story. It's the thirteenth, too. Wonder where we'll be by Christmas?" I unrolled the tent, wondering just where we would be by Christmas. Whether somewhere to the south in the lagoon country, or in Davy Jones's locker (via the Gulf of Tehuantepec) depended for the moment on who had been fooled—Pedro or myself.

We were still at work when that precious pair, Pedro and José, came down to the beach—full of questions and hostility. Pedro fired the opening gun. "Are you well armed?"

"We are always well armed," I answered significantly.

"How much are your possessions worth?" he asked in the tone of an assessor putting the bee on a reluctant taxpayer.

"Less than nothing to any one else," I retorted. "Each piece is stamped with a magic sign." I pointed to the monogram stamped or painted on each piece of equipment. "No one may use the things so stamped except ourselves, without incurring the wrath of the spirits."

They fidgeted, fussed, and asked impertinent questions, but we worked on as though they were not there. Pedro began demanding additional guarantees of payment over what the *Presidente* had already promised. José sidled over to me and whispered that Pedro's wife was "very sick." Pedro stood on one foot and then the other. Finally, he said, "What work is it that you are doing now?"

"We are going back to Laguna Inferior, and sail down the *mar viva* to the entrance of Great Pampa," I replied. At this evidence that we were prepared to do without him, his face darkened, and without a word he turned and walked off the beach. José cast a greedy look at the equipment spread on the sand and followed him.

"I don't know, Dan, but I have a hunch," Ginger remarked thoughtfully, while we were repacking the dry equipment, "that it would be just as safe, and much smarter, to tackle the gulf, norther or no norther, than to trust ourselves to the tender mercies of that couple."

"Oh, well," I said reassuringly, "they can't do much. Men without guns, with oxteams on their hands, won't be much of a menace."

While we were eating breakfast at Enrique's, the old *doctora* appeared. I told her about Pedro's and José's little visit. She gave me a sly wink. "I will be back soon," she said, and trotted off. She returned shortly, and smiled as she said through her toothless gums, "Pedro's wife is very sick; and I told them both that she would not get well until you were *safely delivered* at Aguas Pocas."

Aguas Pocas (little waters) was the name given to the big bay at the northern end of Great Pampa. According to Pedro it was a distance of twelve leagues, which meant absolutely nothing, since a league in this country can mean from two to five miles. On the map, providing it was accurate, Aguas Pocas looked about twenty miles away from San Francisco del Mar.

Then Pedro arrived, all smiles. "When will you be ready to start?" he beamed.

We were ready whenever he was, I replied. He pointed to the place where the sun would be at about two o'clock that afternoon, and said that at that time he would be at our service. We agreed to meet on the opposite side of the lagoon, near the base of Cerro Blanco, since it was impossible for loaded carts to cross the soft mud. He also promised to cut a sufficient number of palm branches to provide a bed for the canoe to ride on. Even though we knew the reason for his going, there was still something else behind his excessive amiability. A reluctant Pedro would have reassured us, but a Pedro anxious to be off was something else again.

I wrapped up half our supply of quinine in a piece of paper, and handed it to the medicine woman. "*Doctora*, see that Pedro's wife becomes well as soon as we leave." She flashed again that toothless grin, more eloquent than words.

By one o'clock we were ready for the trail. We had donned our blue jeans and shirts. Our guns were well oiled and loaded, the machete razor-edged. Teresa and the other women had prepared a lunch for us, more than sufficient for the journey.

After the usual prolonged good-byes, we started off in the canoe with a considerable portion of the villagers wading across the shallow waters of the lagoon as an escort. Further up the lagoon the oxcarts were crossing, with the balance of the population in their wake. "They wish to help you load," I was informed. I groaned inwardly. What a mess that would be!

The oxcarts came into the water to meet us, and the oxen promptly succumbed to the jitters, as the crowd milled, shouted, and splashed round them. Ginger and I sat tight in the canoe waiting for the tumult to die down. Then all the village children clambered aboard the canoe, and almost sank it before we could make them understand that it wouldn't hold an army. The *Presidente* finally put in an appearance, and we pleaded with him to quiet the crowd and tell them that we preferred to do our own loading. That was all right as far as the equipment went. There, the natives were willing to concede that we might know best. But the problem of loading the canoe was another matter. Individually and collectively they pressed forward with advice and suggestions. Stern first . . . bow first . . . upside down . . . forward . . . on end . . . In the middle of the discussion they began to tear the cart to pieces—the wheels should be nearer the front.

In desperation, I yelled to the *Presidente* please to stop them—the canon could never stand the strain of riding as they wished to place it. That gallant soul waded into the mud, churned to liquid by now, and waving his arms, announced to the crowd, that he—and nobody else—from now on was going to superintend the loading of the canoe.

We replaced the wheels on the cart where they belonged. Then I informed the two dozen men waiting to lay hands on the *Vagabunda*, that only myself and the *Presidente* were going to lift it into the cart. The shock of this pronouncement kept them silent for a minute or two. I took the bow and the *Presidente* the stern, and together we began to lift. A buzz went up. "*No pueden*" ("They can't do it"). It was incomprehensible to the crowd that the decked-over canoe should weigh less than a dugout, and that two men could lift it, since it took eight men to lift a dugout. As the canoe slid into place, the crowd began to cheer. The *Presidente* stepped back and threw out his chest. The oxen, scared to death by the noise, plunged off through the mud, the canoe cart headed one way, the equipment cart another. The crowd stampeded; some of them tried to get out of the way of the oxen, others floundered through the mud, trying to stop them.

At last order of a kind was restored. Everybody, including ourselves, was splattered with mud. At first Ginger and I congratulated ourselves that we had fared better than the others—but not for long. By the time we had received the "familiar farewell" from one hundred muddy arms encircling our shoulders, we looked as though we had been dragged the length and breadth of the lagoon. The men begged us to stay. The women cried. The *Presidente* made a speech. And we were off! As long as we remained in sight, they stood in the mud, waving, and calling "Adios."

Chapter Twenty-two

THE SECOND PORTAGE

TROUBLE with Pedro developed at the outset of the second portage, when I insisted that he climb down from the bow of the canoe, where he had perched himself. I carefully explained why he could not ride there; that the boat was too frail to stand his weight—but this, of course, did not matter to Pedro. He made a few angry and caustic remarks about gringos who rode on equipment carts, while better men walked. "All right," I said, "we'll all walk." He stamped on ahead of his oxen, and we fell in behind the enveloping cloud of dust, listening to José's incessant chatter. He soon began to talk about guns.

"Rifles," said José, "are of little use in shooting small game, but a shotgun with many bullets—that is a gun that gives a man a chance."

There was food for thought in this chance remark. "And a pistol, José?" I queried.

"Oh, with a pistol such as yours—but they are worthless. One has to be very, *very* close to a man to kill him, and as for game, that, of course, is impossible."

"Oho," Ginger said, and continued in English. "Do you hear it, too? A little jubilant it seems to me, to be setting off on a long journey through bad country with only a couple of popguns to protect them. It might be a good idea to impress those fellows."

The road led for a distance along the lagoon, and as we came out on the open shore, I noticed a flock of water-birds nearby. "José," I asked, "could you hit one of those birds with a rifle?"

He smiled pityingly at my naïveté. "No," he replied. "Impossible."

It was an easy shot, since the birds were all bunched together, and I dropped two. Then a large, slow-flying crane, startled by the firing, sailed overhead. I took careful aim at its neck, made a direct hit, and the great bird crashed to earth a short distance from us.

The oxen snorted and started to run. When he had them under control, Pedro came running back to us. The men exchanged glances. "She, too," blurted Pedro, pointing to Ginger. She was a much better shot, I assured him—her feats of marksmanship were legendary. Again the men looked at one another. "But," protested Pedro, "you shot twice without reloading." Apparently neither man had ever heard of an automatic pistol, so I told them that both our guns would fire as many shots as we wished them to.

Pedro looked at me through narrowed eyes, turned on his heel and stalked ahead to rejoin his oxen.

Ginger flashed me a muddy smile, and assured me that our exhibition had probably settled any future doubts about guns. I wasn't so sure. Pedro had a good opinion of himself, and would try to outsmart us yet—if he got the chance. I urged Ginger to keep her distance from their machetes, for a native can wield one with uncanny speed and precision; and to keep her gun swung low and her eyes open. As we walked along in the dust behind the carts we went over every possible trick that the men might try, working out a counter-offensive to each situation, until we had covered all the possibilities that occurred to us.

Throughout the long, hot afternoon the deeply rutted trail meandered through low dense scrub, around tangled thorn thickets, and across flats of thick, razor-edged buffalo grass. But as roads go in this country, it was fairly good. Towering stands of flower-tipped cacti and flowering trees added an occasional colour note to the otherwise unattractive landscape. But nothing else broke the monotony of the journey as we plodded on, hour after hour. The sun grew low and sank below the horizon. It became more difficult to avoid the thorns and spiked vegetation, for the moon would not rise until late. Still nothing was said by either Pedro or José about finding a place to rest.

About eight o'clock Pedro called a halt, but he only wanted to trade places with José. Then, instead of walking at the head of his team, he dropped behind to walk with us. I was decidedly suspicious of this manœuvre, for it was too dark to detect and nip in the bud any sudden move he might make. Ginger suggested that we walk ahead of the carts for a while. So we cut round them, keeping just far enough in advance of the lead cart to keep an eye on José. We were desperately hungry and tired; but Pedro was calling the turn, and we could continue if he could.

At nine o'clock the road emerged on a grass-covered plain, where José called to us to stop—it was time to eat. The men had brought little food and no water. Our four gallons, all that our canteens would hold, had to last us until we reached the lagoon, and perhaps for a time after that. The men sat down and munched their tortillas and fish without enthusiasm, eyeing our food covetously, although we were eating the same fare. "Water!" Pedro demanded peremptorily. I handed him one of our canteens, and he drank from it greedily. Both camps ate in silence. When the brief meal was finished, the march was resumed.

Three more hours we stumbled along in the darkness, until Pedro called another halt at midnight. This time we were to rest, while the tired oxen were turned loose to graze. The moon was due to rise shortly, and we would continue on by its light. The men spread out some rags and lay down. Pedro insisted that we, too, sleep for a while. We spread out our canvas on the opposite side of the cart, but in a position from which we could keep a watchful eye on our fellow travellers. Needless to say, we had no intention of sleeping, but even rest was impossible. Our clothes felt as if they were full of hot needles, although an examination of our arms and shoulders disclosed nothing. Later, when the moon rose and we could see by its light, we found that our bodies and clothes were alive with *pinolillos*. While the cartmen pretended to sleep, we spent the time beating our clothes and trying to pick off the ticks. It was soon apparent that unless we could reach water and scrub them off before they had a chance to dig in, we would be covered with nasty sores that would take a month or more to heal.

I routed out Pedro and José. Pedro was surly and ill-tempered. The oxen were nowhere in sight, but we soon found their tracks going back down the trail. Pedro suddenly became all animation. He would go and get them, he announced, and started off at a jog trot. I said to Ginger in English, "There's something funny here. Pedro's too anxious to get those oxen, and I'm going to follow him. Stay here and watch José, and stay within shooting distance. If he gets funny, make him say 'Uncle.'"

I followed Pedro, making no noise and keeping well concealed. A half mile down the trail, I caught up with him. The oxen were just ahead, and as he came up to them he threw his arms in the air and gave a low hiss, which is the signal for oxen to "Gee up!" Since the beasts were being driven homeward they responded with a will. Furious at this evidence of his duplicity, I yelled, "If you don't catch those oxen, I'll blow your ears off." He started ducking for the brush, but I cut off his retreat. He wilted at sight of the gun, and started off to circle the oxen and turn them back towards the carts—with the Luger right behind him. On the return trip, Pedro drove the oxen, and I drove Pedro.

Once more we walked behind the carts, our clothing chafing the *pinolillos* which had already dug into our skins until the itching almost drove us crazy. But there was nothing we could do about it. Pedro stopped the oxen and began to spank his clothes with a small switch. José also attempted to free himself from the ticks. "From here on there are many *pinolillos*," he said. I laughed. The threat of encountering more of the pests didn't mean much, since we were already completely covered with them.

At 3 A.M. Pedro called another halt. He quieted the oxen and came back to us. "We have arrived," he announced. In answer to my query about just where we had "arrived," he blandly replied, "At our destination."

"Our destination is Agua Pocas," Ginger interrupted.

Something had been planned for this small grassy clearing that he had chosen for his "destination," and we knew it. His own explanation that from here on he did not know the way, was, of course, nonsense. "I think we'd better keep on travelling, Pedro," I said slowly and with emphasis.

He was silent for a moment, and then began talking with José in their native tongue. His tone was nasty, and I watched him carefully.

Pedro's machete arm was hanging close by his side. The moonlight gleamed on the sharp blade. Without a second's warning, the blade flashed up and out, directly at my head. I ducked and lashed out with my gun. The Luger jumped and spat flame as it thudded against Pedro's head. I was as much surprised at its accidental discharge as he was. He dropped to the ground moaning, thoroughly convinced that he had been shot through the head. The leading oxen started off on a wild stampede through the clearing into the jungle.

Ginger had stepped back and was covering José. "Is Pedro dead?" she asked in a shaky voice.

"No such luck; just scared," I answered. "When I slapped him with the gun, the pressure of my hand and the jar pulled the trigger. He thinks he's dead, though."

"Come on, there," I said to Pedro, "get up." I slapped him on the rear with his machete, and walked back to where I could cover both men. "I'll have your machete, too, José."

Pedro slowly got to his feet, feeling his head to see if it were still there. It was—not even the skin had been broken. With both men walking ahead of us, we ran down the oxen, disentangling them from the growth where they had sought refuge. José was tractable and agreed to drive his team without further difficulty; but Pedro flatly refused. "You do not understand them—and I will not drive," he said sullenly.

"All right, my friend, you walk ten feet ahead of me. If you walk faster than that, I'll shoot." After tossing his machete into the cockpit of the canoe, and relieving him of his *picadura* (a stick with a pointed bit of metal on the end shaped like an arrowhead, used for guiding and prodding the oxen), I gave the team the signal to move on.

The technique of driving an oxteam lies in the driver's knowledge of what to do with the *picadura*. This was what Pedro hoped we did not understand. The method of driving them differs slightly throughout the country, but it essentially concerns the use of the goad. To start the team, the stick is raised over their heads, with the barb pointing towards the rear. Experience has taught them that if they do not start moving immediately, their hindquarters will feel the barb. To stop them, the stick is rapped against the yoke—the implication being that the rapping will be transferred almost instantly to their heads. To make a sharp turn, the stick is held above the head of the off ox. This encourages him to hurry up and walk round his partner. At night, when it is too dark for the off ox to see, the prod is placed on his horns—its point menacing his rear—and he hurries ahead and makes the turn. The only oral sound used is a long-drawn-out hiss, which generally has to be accompanied by a sharp jab from the goad before it is taken seriously. Comprehension of these few simple directions, plus the fact that from calfhood the ox is accustomed to having his horns tied to those of his partner, constitutes his entire fund of knowledge. The old adage, "As dumb as an ox," is quite true.

Pedro stamped on ahead, time after time trying to lead us astray through the heavy brush. Only a certain kind of patience that one learns to use in dealing with childish people saved him from the beating that he richly deserved. This, and perhaps a sort of macabre humour about the situation that persisted in spite of the *pinolillos*, the weariness, and the danger: the angry *Indio*, balked in his designs against our goods and persons, stalking ahead in the throes of a tantrum that a spoiled child might envy; the wheedling voice of José, now all sweetness and amiability, warning Ginger of every little obstacle on the trail—as he preceded ten paces in advance of her gun trained on his spine. I could hear him with the gallantry of a Sir Walter Raleigh, "*Cuidado*, Señora, here is a thorn bush." Then again, "Be careful, Señora, to miss this stone—just a little to the right." It was hard to determine whether his concern was for her or for himself—in case she should stumble and shoot him inadvertently.

Overhead a pale moon threw weird shadows across the path and dappled the backs of the tired, straining oxen. Our legs and arms had long since become automatons that moved without any effort of will. The excitement of dealing with these graceless scoundrels intent on murder, theft, or worse, had carried us, for the moment, beyond the state where fatigue imposes limitations.

This was a situation that would have intrigued writers of the old-fashioned school of melodrama, I thought as we went along. The setting was perfect, and it had everything, including the lady and the double-dyed villain. Its principal victims to date, however, were the poor oxen. It was a shame that they had to be deprived of their proper rest, food, and water to make a Roman holiday for Pedro. However, it was unwise to stop even long enough to let them graze on the dew-soaked grass, which would have helped their parched throats; and there was no time to look for water holes. They were so tired that only continual prodding kept them moving at all, for they had been on the march fourteen hours.

Then I heard Ginger speaking sharply to José. "I'm sorry, but you're not going to leave the trail—for anything!"

"But, Señora, I tell you I must—I *must*!" came José's answer in a rising wail. Further pleas and promises of good behaviour brought a reiterated refusal.

"What's going on back there?" I called back, and stopped the team. Pedro, ahead, seized the interruption to fall on his knees and groan.

"José wants to make a little detour," Ginger called back in a voice muffled with laughter.

I called to José, "Come on up here. I thought you were too damned mean to be modest." Pedro was hauled out of the grass, protesting, and the pair of them marched to one side of the trail.

When we returned, Ginger said to Pedro, who had sworn that he would rather die than walk further, "Are you the man who can make the five-day cart trip to Juchitán? I don't believe it, for that man would be ashamed to let a woman out-travel him after only fourteen hours of walking."

Without a word Pedro found his legs and started ahead. I called him back, and lined up the pair of them. "Listen carefully, my friends, for I have something to tell you. You have suddenly become a great nuisance to us, and for the cost of only two bullets, we can relieve ourselves of the difficulty—and save for ourselves the water you are drinking. We are familiar with the handling of oxen in this country. Would it not be easier for us to put you out of the way and continue on alone? We have every reason to do this, for you have tried to kill me and take the canoe and our things for yourselves. Surely no one would blame us. Are we not doing you a favour in taking you with us? Now listen, this is your last chance. We are going to Aguas Pocas whether you aid us or not. If you help us, we will reward you. And heaven help you if you don't!"

Pedro then protested that he did not know the way. José thought it was more to the east. "No matter," I said. "We shall follow the open country until daylight."

On and on we followed the exhausted oxen, winding in and out among the heavy growth in an effort to keep in the clearings. It seemed that daylight would never come. Finally we could go no further, for we were completely hemmed in by the jungle. I called a halt and unhitched the tired beasts. Pedro was prevented just in time from turning them loose. "Tie them to the cart," I ordered. Grumbling, he obeyed.

The oxen apparently safely tied, and Pedro and José stretched out within range of our eyes, we lay down for a brief respite. Within a few minutes Ginger nudged me. Pedro was wriggling towards the oxen. He had tied them so loosely that it was only the work of a second before the freed animals started off, making tracks for home and water. My patience exhausted, I raised the Luger, with every intention of killing him. Ginger grabbed my arm, and José ran up and pleaded, "Please, Señor, I will bring back the oxen." In spite of Ginger's doubts, I let him go alone. For a wonder he was to be trusted, and returned shortly with the beasts. This time they were securely tied under my supervision.

The two men returned to their ragged blankets; and we climbed on the equipment cart to escape the *pinolillos*. The ticks were digging in and the itching was almost unbearable. Every time I looked at the Indian, eyeing me from his dirty blanket, I had to stifle the almost irresistible impulse to kill him, for he was as venomous as any reptile. Our arms ached from the constant strain of holding the guns trained on the men. I wondered dully why we didn't use them once and for all, and then put them away in our

The Second Portage

holsters, and give our arms a rest. Ginger and I went over our plans once again for dealing with the situation, while the east paled and the sun came over the mountains. After sunrise, we could see a dense haze to the east—and that meant water!

Since there was little use in further waiting, Ginger got out some food, and I took part of it, together with the canteen the men had used to drink from, and went down and wakened them. After the meal, José and I hitched up the oxen, and skirted the growth until we found an opening in the iron wall through which the carts could pass. Pedro was put to breaking trail in front. I was not at all sure that he had learnt anything by the events of the last eighteen hours, but José was thoroughly cowed. He had been under the strain of marching all night in front of a woman with a gun.

The heat was terrific. Not a breath of wind stirred. Our bodies glistened with sweat. The *pinolillos* dug in with increased energy, until it seemed as though we were bathed in fire. On and on we went, the sun pounding our heads with a molten club. From time to time Pedro complained that we were killing his oxen by travelling through the heat of the day. Then Ginger would call to him and ask sweetly if he was worrying about "poor Pedro, or the *Presidente's* oxen?" This always shut him up for a few minutes—seldom longer.

It was hard on the poor beasts and we hated to do it; but the idea of spending another night in the jungle with Pedro was nothing to look forward to. Besides, we had to have water and lots of it. In addition to the *pinolillos*—as if they were not enough—we were covered with an inch-thick deposit of sweat and dust. To lie and float in cool water, with the *Vagabunda* riding nearby—that would be heaven. So we kept on, always in the direction of the beckoning haze.

One thing that José and I discovered while cutting a path through the brush was that the ticks were only to be found in the shade. To avoid them, we made many detours in the sun.

José was overjoyed to be trusted to the extent of having his machete returned to him, and he cut the brush when necessary with a good will. A native deprived of his machete is a man without honour; he feels as naked without it as a white man might feel stripped of his clothes and turned loose on some busy metropolitan street. Ginger always kept Pedro well covered while we were away; and never failed to praise José's magnificent courage and stamina when we returned to the carts.

Towards sundown the oxen pricked up their ears and took a new lease on life. A light breeze brought us the smell of water. To the left the growth became thicker and greener. Even Pedro ceased complaining, and for the first time since he had been put to breaking trail picked out the best route. He announced, as though it were due to his efforts, and as if he had completed a hard task uncomplainingly and was now about to receive a just reward, "Señor, we have arrived. This is Aguas Pocas. May I go ahead and see if I can find a trail to the water?" I nodded. "But, of course, I shall need my machete," he added.

"Aw, Pedro," I said, "we're too tired for any monkey business. If the growth is so thick that you need a machete, how are we going to get the carts through? Didn't you say you were going to look for a trail? Run along, and remember we're not in the mood for one of your little surprises." Pedro started off, showing his second burst of speed on the trip.

As we trudged wearily along, Ginger called to me, "Aren't you taking a long chance, Dan? He may have something up his sleeve."

"I don't think so," I replied. "Maybe he's been converted. Outside of going after the oxen, this is the first initiative he's shown on the trip; perhaps he sees the error of his ways—it's about time to dish out a few fishhooks. How are you coming along back there?"

"Pretty good," she replied, "except that my arm aches from holding the gun on José. And don't forget the other time that Pedro got ambitious."

I marvelled at her endurance. My own arms ached from the weight of the heavy Luger, and the continual use of the goad. My legs ached from the weight of the heavy gun belt, and from the ceaseless tramp, tramp—one foot after the other—through grass and brush, over sticks and logs, hour after hour. Vines and creepers held our feet in a viselike grip, while thorny branches scratched every exposed inch of our bodies. And in addition to the heat, lack of sleep, *pinolillos*, and scanty rations of food and water, there was the nervous strain of watching and waiting. Yet Ginger had managed, somehow, in spite of her slight physique, to withstand these things for thirty hours.

We went on for another mile or two without a sign of Pedro. I kept a sharp lookout, and was careful not to get too close to any dense growth. Since he was unarmed, there was little he could do; but thirty hours of Pedro had convinced us that there was little he wouldn't try. He had a genius for mischief, and a profound belief in his own capacity that no amount of failure could diminish. Then we heard a shout, and he came running back, all smiles, to inform us that he had found an easy trail down to the water. Said Pedro, with his most ingratiating voice, "Señor, your long journey is over."

But something in the quality of his tone made us feel that Pedro had a longer journey in mind than Aguas Pocas. He insisted politely that Ginger and I should precede the carts, and that he and José should follow. "Perhaps you're right—this time, Pedro. Perhaps the Señora and I will take your advice and go on ahead. Possibly, who knows," I suggested, "we may find something to shoot at?"

We knew that once away from the noise of the carts our hearing would be keener. So we started off, keeping carefully to the trail Pedro had found. Ginger examined the growth to the left, and I to the right. We were following an old cart road. A half mile ahead of the carts, a slight movement

The Second Portage

in the brush sent the Luger jumping in my hand. Ginger fired at a similar disturbance on her side of the trail. As the sound of the guns died away, a frantic crashing through the brush indicated that something, or some one, was leaving in a hurry.

Within a few minutes we came out upon a small sand beach where the mirrorlike expanse of Aguas Pocas spread out before us. We arrived in time to see a dugout manned by Indians disappear round a bend in the shoreline. I sent up a geyser of water close beside them.

"Don't you think we'd better go back and assure Pedro that the way is clear—sort of put his mind at ease?" asked Ginger.

Just then we heard the voices of the men urging the spent oxen forward. We stepped back and waited until Pedro came into view. His face wore the look of a man who, through sheer perseverance, has at last triumphed over seemingly insurmountable circumstances—a gay, relaxed, at peace with the world expression. We almost hated to disturb his colossal satisfaction. When he was almost abreast of us, I hailed him. "Come on, Pedro, everything's fine. Come right down to the water," I commanded.

The oxen needed no inducements, but plunged into the brackish water and began to drink. Pedro and José stared. But we had no further time to waste on Pedro; and while he was still in his trance, we hurriedly slid the canoe into the water, and loaded the equipment into it. Then I called to José, who waded out to the canoe, closely followed by Pedro, to come and get the six fishhooks which I held out to him. José beamed his thanks, but Pedro had the audacity to whine over his failure to receive a parting gift. "No fishhooks," he moaned, "and we are hungry, and we want hot coffee and some food. We need water and provisions for the long trip home."

"That's just too bad," I returned. "You drank up all of one canteen on the way down. We had only one gallon left for ourselves, but I wouldn't deny even a rattlesnake a drink of water. Here." I handed him the canteen, and together they finished the last of our fresh water. Then Ginger decided that we might as well do a good job of it, so she gave them the balance of the food that Teresa had prepared.

We were still too near shore for the canoe to float with our weight in it; and we pushed off further before I stuck Pedro's machete in the mud, and called good-bye to José. We suspected he was rather the victim of the stronger and more aggressive Pedro's machinations, than of his own evil impulses.

Chapter Twenty-three

SWAMP GRASS, QUICKSAND, AND A FEW MAREÑOS

For days the problem of reaching Aguas Pocas had been our chief preoccupation. The great lagoon, in theory at least, had promised easy transport down the coast. Its many islands, which spanned its length like links in a chain, offered additional protection against the norther. We could sail snugly between them and the land to seaward. Rivers emptied into these tidal lagoons, and though the water was brackish, animals could drink it. There would be game to supplement our food supply. But as we now gazed upon its broad expanse, it seemed that the effort expended in getting here had won for us only a Pyrrhic victory.

We spent the first few minutes after our arrival in giving our *pinolillo*-blackened bodies a vigorous scrubdown with sand. We rolled over and over in the shallow water in an effort to dislodge them. This gave only temporary respite, since hundreds of them had burrowed under the skin, and would have to be dug out. Then, refreshed by the brief bath and clean clothes, we searched for a place to set up camp.

As far as the eye could see in all directions there were birds: herons, cranes, flamingos, ducks, and multitudes of tiny sandpipers wading ankle-deep in the shallow lagoon. Great piled-up clouds, stained with the flame of the setting sun, cast a rosy glow over the tranquil water. A hundred square miles of it, lovely to look at—and only six inches deep. To the west, and out towards the centre of the lagoon, there appeared to be an island, perhaps three miles away. This, with the exception of the mainland we had left, was the nearest land in sight.

Since the lagoon was too shallow to float the canoe with our weight in it, we had to drag it. Only the thought of a hot meal, and a long, uninterrupted sleep in the tent gave us the strength to do this. To force ourselves over those three long miles to the island was slow torture. Also there were many places where the water was too shallow to float even the empty boat. Then we had to stop and hunt until we found a deeper channel.

At nine o'clock when we finally reached the shore of the island our bubble burst. Gone were our hopes of a dry camp, a hot meal; and the longed-for opportunity to rid ourselves of the *pinolillos*. For the island was only a ring of mangrove roots surrounding a boggy swamp. There was no alternative but to look further on. We continued to drag the canoe along the shore of the swamp, always hoping to find a bit of dry land. And the ticks continued to raise merry hell. When we could find a spot of water two feet deep, we lay down in it. But even this momentary relief was denied to us—swarms of malarial mosquitoes stung our unprotected faces.

The lagoon was now deep enough to float the canoe. I urged Ginger to lie down in the cockpit and cover herself with canvas for protection against the mosquitoes, while I paddled on to another island that loomed ahead. The point of land as I paddled towards it took on the quality of a mirage, now retreating, now advancing. I wondered vaguely if we should ever reach it. We were lost in an aqueous world of swamps, mangroves, *pinolillos*, and mosquitoes. I repeated the words soundlessly, for there was nothing else left in all creation. All the other tangible, concrete things had disappeared—had been dissolved, transmuted, changed into brackish water and mud . . . swamps . . . mosquitoes . . . mangroves . . . mosquitoes.

I dimly realized that I was becoming light-headed. Things began to march in columns of fours. Then ahead I saw a moving spot of white at the base of the point. What was it? I strained my eyes towards the island. Yes, now I knew—it was a canoe. I strapped on the Luger. No, it wasn't a canoe. A sand beach? But there weren't any sand beaches. There was nothing left in the world but swamps. I had it! We were coming into port. Ginger must wake up. Had to get the ship's papers—captain would want to see them. Would he keep us under quarantine . . . *pinolillos*? Yes, we'd be quarantined for *pinolillos*.

Hours later it seemed, the *Vagabunda* ground her nose on a tiny white shell beach. I stepped out into the shallow water and tried to lift Ginger out of the cockpit, but couldn't make it. She spilled over the side of the canoe and lay down in the water, muttering something about Mareños. I lay down beside her. Splashing water over our faces restored us to consciousness. We looked round. A swamp fringed with mangroves, and a narrow beach of shell, perhaps thirty feet across. Under ordinary circumstances no camper's paradise, but a veritable Eden to us.

We unloaded the canoe, and stacked the equipment on the beach. Ginger rummaged round in the grub box and finally brought out a small package. "I've been saving this for Christmas, but I think we need it now," she said. unwrapping a bar of medicated soap that she had secured in Salina Cruz. We made scrubbing wads of the dry swamp grass that lined the beach, and gave ourselves the most thorough scouring I think either one of us ever had. The soap and friction set the bites to burning until we danced with the torment of them. But what a joy to scrub out those burrowing black devils! The preliminary de-ticking was done by moonlight. Then we built a big fire and finished the job. The heat of the flames on our tortured skins gave the sensation of scratching. It felt good.

I built another fire higher on the beach, and put the still on. Examining our possessions by firelight, we found everything full of *pinolillos* except the inside of the tent. While I put that up, Ginger prepared some food.

At three o'clock on the morning of December 16, 1935, we sat in the smoke of the fire and enjoyed what I will always believe to be one of Ginger's gastronomic triumphs: black coffee, dried fish, and toasted tortillas.

As in the *taleje* camp, we slept in relays. I took the first watch, and tired as I was, Ginger kept me alert and busy. I held her hands when she moaned, and tried to scratch, and released them as soon as she quieted down. At daylight she awoke, and guarded me. We alternated until the heat in the tent became unbearable. But it was the only way to avoid the nasty running sores caused by skin abrasions in the tropics.

The mosquitoes were waiting for us as we emerged from the tent. One look and we ran for the water. "Am I glad mosquitoes can't dive!" said Ginger as she rolled round in the shallow lagoon, ducking her head each time a squadron landed on her face. But they could do everything else, I reminded her.

Our shorts were the only clothes we had that were free from ticks, and the mosquitoes were making the most of that circumstance. It occurred to me to take the long-legged jeans and long-sleeved shirts that we had worn on the portage, and submerge them in the lagoon while we ate breakfast. They were black with *pinolillos*, but I knew a cure for that—we'd drown them. How little, despite a long and close acquaintance, did I know my *pinolillos*!

Breakfast was an ordeal—and a relay race—as we dashed from the smoke of the fire to the greater safety of the water. After the meal I hopefully retrieved the clothes. Surely by now they were free from ticks. Not a chance. The ticks were still very much alive. Their immersion seemed to have revived them, and they crawled about energetically looking for a host.

It was the ticks or us. We'd boil them. All the pots and the five-gallon still-cans were filled with water and set over the fire. We scoured the beach looking for wood. The termites had found most of it first, but we burnt it anyway—including the termites.

As the clothes began to boil, we stood in the smoke and with profound satisfaction watched our late tormenters rise to the surface and float in the foam. Then we poured scalding water over everything that was too big to boil. The tent, sleeping bag, boxes, everything that water wouldn't ruin, got a scalding. The canvas deck and cockpit were soused—myriads of ticks clung to them, scraped off by the canoe's passage through the brush.

We could hardly wait for the clothes to cool before putting them on. But blue denim didn't mean a thing to those Mexican swamp mosquitoes. They were all equipped with the latest model pneumatic drills. We flew to the shelter of the tent, and stayed there until sundown.

In sober truth it is hard to exaggerate the danger of these tropical insects. The only parallel in the North might be the periodic grasshopper and locust inundations. The reader can readily imagine the result to animals and men, if these insects were carnivorous. There is nothing periodic or intermittent about the insects who live south of the tropic of Cancer. And most of them are flesh-eaters. Far more remarkable to us than Cortez' conquest of the Aztecs, was the ability of Pedro de Alvarado and others to take large bodies of men, unused to the climate and wearing European clothes, long distances through the jungle and swampy lowlands, where not one step can be taken without encountering hordes of these voracious man-killers.

Soon after daybreak of the second day we were loaded up and under way. We had by no means recovered from our bites; and our bodies were stiff and sore, and covered with small running ulcers. It would take days of rest to eliminate the poison and repair the damage of the long, forced march. Eighteen hours on the shell beach had exhausted the firewood—but not the mosquitoes. Drugged and weary, we started off to look for some Elysian Field where there was a flowing spring of clear water, food in abundance—and no bugs! This paradise we hoped to find sometime before Christmas—nine days away.

We paddled along the winding channels among the many islands of the *estero*. The lagoon was the breeding place of countless thousands of wading birds, but the low-lying, swampy islands offered no subsistence for other animals. After travelling about six miles, Aguas Pocas opened out into Great Pampa. The water here was also shallow, most of it two feet or less; and in many places the swamp grass was so thick that travelling became difficult. One of us had to perch on the bow and push the mass of grass to one side as it piled up in front of the canoe. A light breeze came up and we hoisted sail, but even with the aid of the wind it was hard to pass through the miniature Sargasso Sea. Finally we became completely entangled.

I was on the bow trying to work the stuff to one side, when Ginger gave her peculiar little squeal that meant danger. I hastily looked round to see a canoe with three *Indios* coming towards us from the rear. Frantically I tore the grass away. It seemed to multiply under my fingers. We pushed against the soft mud, which yielded and gave no purchase. The oncoming dugout moved easily along the cleared path that we had made. Then Ginger shouted, "They're going to shoot!" A man stood in the bow, raised his gun, and fired.

"Thank God," I said, "it's a muzzle-loader." The shot fell short. But a second man stood up and waved a gun, which looked like a carbine or an army rifle. They could plug all day long with a muzzle-loader—but a carbine was another story. I grabbed the Luger, aimed it at the side of the dugout, and let go. The Mareños ducked like well-trained snipers as I placed a second and a third shot close to their heads. To keep them down, I began splintering the wooden platform where the stern poler stands. Not an Indian put his head above the gunwale.

"Shall I begin shooting, too?" asked Ginger, while I waited for a head to show. I told her to knock splinters off the stern at regular intervals.

This would keep them flattened out against the bottom of the dugout, and give me a chance to free the canoe.

A breeze came up while I pulled and pushed at the packed grass. Ginger kept firing as I worked. The sky was like an inverted oven, and I could have screamed as the perspiration and the heat bit into the hundreds of *pinolillo* punctures. Were we never going to get the canoe out of the damned grass? A gust of wind swept down across the *pampa*. It hit the sail and swung the canoe broadside, nearly overturning us. I got the boat stern to the wind, and close-hauled the sheet as another blast struck us. Held in the grip of the grass, we were certain that the mast would break with the strain. The little sailboat hung poised for flight. Again the wind slapped the sail. This time the canoe lifted her stern, shuddered, and shot out of the densest tangle of weeds into water dotted with scattered clumps of grass.

As the *Vagabunda* skimmed along, we looked back at the apparently empty dugout idly floating with the current. I skippered while Ginger sat in the cockpit and watched. In a short time we were out of the weeds entirely. The canoe raced along making the spray fly. After a long interval, Ginger said softly, "For the love of Mike, they're *still* down! Why, we'll be back in Santa Ana before they come up for air. I'd certainly like to see their faces, when they do pop up and find us gone."

It was blowing up so we headed for the lee of an island in the distance. The lagoon was so shallow that when small breakers rolled up, we hit bottom. The norther tearing down the *pampa* lashed it into foam, and the canoe raced directly before the wind. Soon we swung into the lee, where the mangroves let in just enough wind to make good sailing, and the lee shore gave us smooth water. The island terminated in a shell point. Before us lay the great, wind-swept *pampa*, the other side of which we could not see. Since it would be suicidal to attempt to cross it in the norther, we decided to make camp on the beach. On the opposite side of it we found the remains of a large Mareño camp, consisting of several crude racks for drying fish and some tumbledown brush shelters. The beach was about twenty feet wide and a hundred feet long, with a swamp at one end and the *pampa* at the other. We chose a fairly open place on the lee side of the island, hoping to foil the mosquitoes by placing the camp site in the sweep of the wind.

"We're certainly asking for trouble," Ginger said, as we unloaded the canoe. I agreed that the place looked like the old home town of all the Mareños who lived on the lagoon, but at least we could thank them for providing us with firewood. "And only luck to thank for getting us out of that mess in the grass," she commented briefly.

Any one who has never tried setting up camp in a good stiff wind has a treat in store for them. Eventually Ginger built her fire, and I put the tent up. These preliminaries over, we began to think about food. We were as hungry as bears, and anything we could secure with hook, spear, or gun would be the menu for supper. So we paddled to the calmer water on the lee of the island, and started looking about.

I took a position on the bow, with the spear poised, while Ginger managed the boat. The water was muddy, and my only target was a swirl in the water. But before we could fish I had to spear the bait. I pegged at a large swirl and hit, and from the way the spear shaft flew through the water, I had taken a big fellow—perhaps we had our supper. I pulled in the line, grabbed the shaft, and started to lift our catch into the cockpit; but decided against it when I saw the creature impaled on the spear's prongs. It was a large sting ray of a variety new to us. Three wicked looking, bony spines protruded from the mid-section of its slender tail; its round, flat body was black and shiny. In the muddy water of the lagoon, the creature had been invisible.

"Whew! What ugly wounds you'd get from that fellow," said Ginger. "Well, anyway, it's good for bait." We cut off a portion of its flesh, and paddling out from shore as far as we could without getting into the full force of the norther, dropped the anchor. Here, after a stiff tussle, we landed two large fish, also of a type new to us—possibly catfish. At any rate they were good to eat, and we soon had them sizzling over the fire.

By the time the meal was ready, the wind was so strong that we had to retreat to the shelter of the tent to eat it. During the meal, Ginger asked my plans for the night. "Sleep," I answered, "and plenty of it. We're behind on our schedule." That brought up the question of the possible return of the Mareños, and how both of us could sleep at once without scratching the *pinolillo* bites. There was little likelihood of the Mareños returning during the norther. As long as the wind blew we were safe. But to make certain that we were not taken by surprise, I would devise an alarm that would waken us instantly if any one approached the tent. The danger of scratching could be eliminated by making "boxing gloves" out of our clothes, and tying them securely round our hands. This last idea amused Ginger immensely; she laughed heartily. "You'll see," I said confidently. "It will work. At least we can't dig in with our fingernails." But like so many bright ideas, it had one fatal and unpredictable flaw—it worked too well!

My Mareño alarm was a minor masterpiece. I entirely encircled the camp with a line, and tied one end to a slipknot from which were suspended two of Ginger's kettles. Anything coming in contact with the line would drop the kettles close beside my head. Whereupon I would seize my trusty Luger and prepare to meet the foe.

We worked long and diligently at the job of encasing our hands, and were rather proud of our ability to do it without outside aid. The last knot on Ginger's right hand had been tied by using a slipknot and pulling with our teeth.

I went to sleep feeling both virtuous and secure. The two stumbling-blocks to a good night's rest had been settled to my satisfaction. Some time towards morning I awakened to the sound of falling metal, and jumped for my gun. But my gun hand was wrapped up in my shorts. I tried the other hand, but, wrapped in the folds of my shirt, it, too, was useless. "Do something!" I cried to Ginger. "There are Mareños out there, and I've got to use my gun." She motioned towards my bound hands and helplessly waved her own. I began biting at the knot on her right hand—the slipknot that we had so cleverly tied. It loosened a bit. She giggled, as I frantically tugged with my teeth, and finally removed the makeshift glove from her hand. She grabbed her gun, unzipped the tent, and looked out on the moon-bathed camp site. Then she howled with laughter as she reported that the wind had tipped over the still can. My burglar alarm was still intact.

The next morning, coping with the wind taxed our ingenuity. We awoke to a blast that almost carried the tent from its moorings, and crawled out into heavy gusts that would have whipped it to pieces in another hour. We immediately untied the ridge rope and let the tent down, piling logs on it to keep the wind from snatching it from beneath our fingers. The gale increased while we worked. It pelted our faces with spray picked up from the *pampa*, where black clouds of spume gyrated like small cyclones. How to cook, build a fire, or distil water in the face of a wind that we could hardly stand against was an issue that had to be met. We went to work cutting brush for a windbreak. By noon we had constructed a substantial, three-sided stockade out of brush, and poles salvaged from the Mareño camp. The enclosure was large enough to contain the tent and the fireplace. To build a big enough fire to distil water, we dug a hole close to the windbreak, and lined it with mud from the swamp. This served its purpose admirably, and the still can soon whistled.

After lunch we strapped on our guns and started out to see what a swamp looked like. Its beginning was within twenty feet of our camp. Since travelling through it seemed impossible, we skirted a narrow strip of sand to the east, keeping an eye out for game. The wind lashed the mangroves and whipped their branches on our heads and into our faces, so that to travel at all we had to cut through the trees and enter the swamp. Here, hundreds of lagoon birds had taken refuge from the norther that roared overhead. Rather than face its blasts, they almost refused to fly, huddling disconsolately behind any available shelter.

Now well within the confines of the swamp, we stopped and looked about us. It was a strange and curiously fascinating place. The turgid black water, covered with slime and full of rotting vegetation, seemed to belong to some remote geologic age—the earth before the advent of mammals. Mosses and other parasitic growths hung in wraithlike festoons from the dark trees. In the perpetual twilight and hot steaming vapours of the swamp there was a commingling of the elements, as there had been in the beginning. No sound, except the soughing of the wind and the ceaseless murmur of the waters, broke the stillness.

The silence was shattered by an explosive report. Startled, we turned quickly to see a large alligator swim off. It had slid unseen down the incline of a log and smacked the water. Skimming along like an aquaplane, its body seemed hardly to touch the surface, and its feet thrashed the water like paddle wheels.

"What do you say we go into the swamp? I'd like to explore one."

"I suppose if we're ever going to know anything about one at first hand, we'll have to go into it," Ginger answered. "But we're sure to get wet and dirty—it looks deep."

We plunged off into the ooze, and were soon waist-deep in slime and water that was full of living matter. Leeches fastened themselves on our legs, and our feet began to itch with *sabañones*, a fungus which lives in the mud and attacks the feet. It was difficult to make headway because of the tangled, rotting vegetation. Each step was a gamble. We had often wondered whether a human being could traverse a tropical swamp, and what his sensations would be once in one. Now we were finding out. In many places we sank to our armpits in the ooze, holding our gun belts and machetes high above our heads. Snakes slithered into the water, and clouds of mosquitoes swarmed in the gloom. At last we emerged on to firmer ground.

We began to follow the firmer ground back to camp, crawling through dense mangrove thickets, until we came to a large open stretch of sand, perhaps five hundred feet long. Its surface was unbroken except for a little tide drift, and it was as flat as a billiard table. "This is surely a break for us," I said. "Wish we had this kind of travelling all the way back." Tall, straight mangrove trees fringed the sand island, and though there was nothing obviously wrong about it, I began to have an uneasy feeling as we approached it. For some unknown reason I shuddered and stopped.

"What's the matter?" Ginger asked.

"I don't know, unless I've got the jitters from the swamp. Or maybe the wind's gone down and some Mareños are on their way to play with us. Let's go." I shook off the premonition and led the way across the sand.

About thirty feet further on, another sharp premonition of danger swept over me. "Come on, Ginger, let's go back to the mangroves. There's trouble here."

"I feel that way myself." Ginger was puzzled. "But what about? I can't see anything wrong."

Nevertheless, it seemed best to play the hunch, so we started back the way we had come. Then it happened. Without an instant's warning, I broke through the surface of the sand and went down to my knees. A circle of water appeared on the sand round me. "Run, Ginger!" I shouted. She ran for the mangroves, water appearing in each footstep as she sped towards the trees.

Now I had sunk in the quicksand to above my knees. Struggling would only make me sink the faster. My mind raced helplessly over the few alternatives for action. A few seconds delay might be gained by distributing my weight over as big an area as possible, so I threw my body forward. Ginger was lopping off branches as fast as she could; but it was evident that by the time she could cut enough to make a path in and out, I'd be under. Furthermore, I couldn't climb out of my sandy tomb without the aid of heavy pieces of wood to use as hoists. It was doubtful if she could drag them across the semi-fluid surface without getting sucked in herself, even if she had time to procure them.

The sand was now creeping round my waist. I looked at the sky. The tall trees silhouetted against it gave me one last forlorn hope. I called to Ginger, "Try cutting down that tall tree nearest me, and fell it this way." She quickly attacked it with swift strokes of her machete. The sand had reached my armpits. The scheme was hopeless; she couldn't get the tree down in time. Her sobs mingled with the ring of the machete as she cast quick glances in my direction, and then redoubled the fury of her attack upon the hard mangrove wood. What would become of her? How could she ever get out of the country alone? Black panic seized me. We had often told ourselves that death was only a moment of acute discomfort, and soon over. But this other thing? We were a team, reinforcing each other physically and morally; we could face together any contingency, but alone . . . I didn't know.

My arms were raised and the sand had crept up round my shoulders, when Ginger looked again. With a cry of horror she slashed at the tree from another angle. Then a thrill of joy shot up from my toes. With only my head and forearms above the sand, I had hit bottom. I sent up a prayer of thankfulness; and turned to shout the good news to Ginger. But at that moment she turned. Seeing just my head above the surface of the sand, she dropped her machete, and ran for the small stack of branches she had piled near the edge of the quagmire. I knew what was in her mind. She was going to pick up that futile bunch of branches and run out to me with them. And she, too, would be caught in the treacherous sand. Nothing I could say would stop her if she thought I was simply trying to prevent her from taking the risk. But she must be stopped. Some word, some counter suggestion of danger equally imperative that she would respond to automatically. I had it! I shouted with all the emphasis and fear that I could put into it, "Ginger! Quick—Mareños!"

She whirled, dropping the branches and reaching for her gun. Then quietly, in a matter-of-fact voice, I said, "Listen, I've struck bottom. The danger is over."

"What did you say?" she asked in a dazed, uncomprehending voice. I repeated the news. "But the Mareños?" she questioned. I explained. At last she understood and went back to tree-cutting.

I had instructed her to fell the tree in my direction. It not only fell "in" but on. I saw it coming, closed my eyes, and ducked down in the sandy ooze. The sand shivered and shook with the impact. I tried to get my head above the surface, bumping it against the trunk. At last I was out in the air again, but could neither see nor breathe. Sand plastered my eyes and plugged my nose and mouth. Although my arms were above the surface, they were caught in the branches and I couldn't use them. Then Ginger was there, doing the job for me. After she cleaned my face, I opened my eyes and stared up into her tear-stained face, trying to smile reassuringly. "Well, so far so good, but how am I going to get out of here? I'm stuck fast."

We tried using various arrangements of branches, but I could secure no leverage with any of them. Exerting pressure on anything placed upon the surface of the quicksand simply caused it to yield. Then we had a new idea. Ginger cut and trimmed a limb close to the crotch, so that it formed a hook with an eight foot handle. We worked this down beside my leg, and with a great deal of wriggling, I finally managed to get my foot in the stirrup. After considerable manœuvring I bent my knee into a walking position. With the aid of my crutch, and by pulling myself along on the overhead branches, I could move forward an inch or two at a time. Quicksand is easy to get into, but it's hell to get out of; and it was an hour before we scrambled over the fallen tree, and at last sat down on terra firma. And it takes quicksand to make you appreciate what that phrase means!

I took the sand-clogged Lugger from its holster and looked at it ruefully. "Well, there's no use doing any more hunting today," I said. "We might as well go back to camp."

The norther blew itself out sometime during the night, and soon after sunup we pulled away from the little shell beach. Approaching the southern terminus of the island, we found our way blocked by a long sand bar extending out from the point of the island due west to the faint shore line that separated the gulf from the lagoon. It was a matted tangle of brush, stumps, and tide drift, so we went back to the island and portaged across our old camp site to the opposite side of the *pampa*. Once again we embarked, our goal an estuary leading into the next series of waterways.

It was a beautiful tropical morning. The air was as soft and as bland as cream. There was no wind, and the great inland sea was like a burnished mirror. No wind meant we should have to paddle. It would take us all day to reach the shore line, but neither one of us cared. In the clear air, the *pampa* to the east merged into the high mountains of Chiapas. The whole world was a symphony in blue. Mountains, sea, and sky were infinite gradations of azure, turquoise, and soft hazy blue-greys that melted into each other. After yesterday's experience, it seemed to me that I could never get enough of simply looking at great, unfilled spaces. Yet there was a fly in the ointment of this perfection—a vague sense of uneasiness. Something about the venture was ill-timed. I tried to localize it without success. This was the only calm weather we had had in weeks. There was no sign of wind anywhere. On the surface, conditions were ideal.

We paddled along in silence. Perhaps this premonitory feeling was only the ebb tide of the continuous excitement to which we had been subjected. In postponement, and in returning to camp would lie the real danger. The Mareños would be out fishing in their canoes during this calm. The smoke from our campfire must have been seen. Once again I scrutinized the horizon. The high mountains to the east still wore their halos of grey-blue haze, to us an unmistakable sign of good weather.

Perplexed and rather shamefaced, I turned to Ginger. "I've got another hunch, though heaven knows why——"

"So have I," she interrupted. "We'd better go back."

Since we were only a half mile from shore, we decided to stay there and enjoy a leisurely swim while awaiting further developments. We splashed round in the warm water, keeping an eye out for sharks, and then stretched out on deck to let the sunshine soak in. A half hour passed in which nothing unusual occurred. "Damn!" I said. "I'll bet we won't have another chance to cross this *pampa* for two weeks."

"That may be true," Ginger answered, "but nevertheless, I don't think it's wise to go off in the face of this hunch—or whatever it is."

"We're always between the devil and the deep blue sea," I grumbled. "If we were back in camp with the wind down, the mosquitoes would eat us alive. And if we don't get out of here, every naked devil on the lagoon will be out in his canoe, looking for something to shoot at. The only time we're free from mosquitoes and Mareños is when it's worth our life to travel."

We played round for a half hour, and were going over the side for another dip when I saw a phenomenon to the north that riveted my attention—a hard black line that looked as though it were drawn in India ink. We both looked at it. "I wonder what it means?" puzzled Ginger. "I've never seen anything like it before."

"I don't know," I answered. "Say, look at the mountains!" White clouds rolled over their crests, skimming down their sides as though a giant were pouring milk over them. Then I knew. We were watching the inception of the dread hurricane, whose local name is Tehuantepecer, a norther in its most destructive aspect.

There was no time to lose. We grabbed the paddles and struck out for shore. Mareños and mosquitoes be damned. That shell beach was our only place of refuge. As we sped shoreward, the black line widened, and its lower edge turned to white. We knew what that creeping line of white meant. The wind was rolling up the *pampa* into a wall of foaming water, which rushed across the lagoon like an avalanche. In its resistless force it was overwhelming. Great clouds torn loose from their mountain moorings scudded across the darkening sky.

The canoe skidded underneath the mangroves and shot into the beach. Not for us, this time, a careful, calculated handling of our equipment. We threw the boxes on the beach. The canoe must be gotten out of harm's way before that rushing wall of water engulfed it and smashed it to kindling wood. While we worked, short choppy seas began pounding the shore. At last we and our possessions were out of the water, but by no means safe yet from the gale. Battling against a wind that knocked us on our haunches, we dragged our things and rolled the canoe into the shelter of the windbreak. And thanked our lucky stars that it was ready for our use, and that we were there to use it. We were drenched in spray from the great clouds of vapour that roared across the *pampa* to dash themselves against the mangroves. The air seemed to be full of the shrieks of ten thousand fire engines. Black columns of water, with whitened crests, spun about like whirling dervishes.

Safe behind the sheltering windbreak, Ginger unrolled the sleeping bag and stretched out on it. "Imagine being out in that," she said. "Dan, from now on, as long as we live, let's play our hunches."

"Listen," I answered. "It's more dangerous to get a fixed idea in our minds about hunches than to disregard them. We don't know anything about them, really. Suppose we refused to act unless we had a 'hunch.' First thing you know, all our decisions would be based on feeling instead of logic and reason. I think it's bad business to form conclusions about things when we only know part of the story."

"What about the quicksand? What about this storm?" Ginger argued. "How could we reason either situation out from the data we had? This morning this camp, full of mosquitoes and potential Mareños, was all wrong. The calm, peaceful *pampa* was right. Now this is right and the other wrong."

"You're answering your own argument," I said. "Nothing's inherently right or wrong in either situation. The circumstances changed, and consequently we reversed our position. We have to shift with the times. Nature does it, nothing there follows a straight line. The water birds aren't on the lagoon now, or in the air, they're in the mangroves. Remember, most of our premonitions have to do with weather. The explanation is probably exceedingly simple. The norther blowing up would have some effect on the area just ahead of it, naturally. It may have increased the air pressure. This would in turn affect our ears, and our subconscious mind would transfer it into a warning. Or it may have caused a change in the electrical content of the air, which might have some effect on us. Yesterday we walked across ground that probably vibrated beneath our feet—and we were too tired to notice. But that doesn't mean that because our conscious faculties sometimes fail to report things that we must necessarily remain unaware of them. There may be a special kind of hyper-sensitivity that operates in moments of extreme danger. These are matters, however, that we can't be too sure of, and it's highly doubtful that they are wholly dependable. See what I mean?"

"You're probably right," Ginger conceded. "It's the middle way between the two extremes that we have to follow. I'm glad we talked this over. I'd begun to take our hunches a little too seriously."

I was also glad that we had talked it over, for there had been a rather remarkable series of coincidences of this nature during our months of travel. It was becoming increasingly easy to rely on premonitions rather than on ourselves. And that I felt, was a highly dangerous procedure. Eventually it would undermine our common sense. As I had observed it, there was a variability about life and the operation of natural laws that precluded hasty generalizations based on limited data and ill-digested facts. The human mind is too prone to incorporate scanty knowledge into systems, interpretations, and formulas. Or it seizes an idea advanced as a pure speculation only, and decks it out in the mantle of indisputable fact.

There is a tree that grows in the tropics, all of whose seeds look alike. However, they are not alike. True, they grow in the same pod, fall to the ground at the same time, and in every way—but one—exactly resemble each other. Some of the seeds germinate immediately. Others must remain two or three years before they sprout. Still others, under certain conditions, may remain dormant for fifty years or more before they send forth shoots. It certainly would be difficult to formulate an axiom about this tree from hasty observation. Its delayed germination refutes the general belief that fertile seed of the same species in combination with sun, suitable soil, and water always produces new growth within a given period. Indeed, from watching only this one tree, you could make a new rule: Trees of the same species germinate under conditions not wholly dependent on soil, moisture and climate; some unknown factor, determines the time of germination.

After our discussion we began to think about food. If we were to be marooned for any length of time, it might be well to work our way through the mangroves to the lee side of the island and try our luck at fishing. The storm would have driven the fish to the calmer waters of the lee. With luck we might pick up something. Armed with the harpoon and our guns, we waded along the shallow water looking for bait. We soon came upon some odd-looking little fish which stuck their heads out just above the surface of the water. They were all right for bait but too small to harpoon. "How are we ever going to catch them?" I said.

"Shoot them" Ginger answered, drawing a bead on one. Her bullet stunned the fish, and I ran and picked it up—the oddest marine animal we had yet seen. It was perhaps six inches long and was shaped like a catfish.

"Dan, it has four eyes," Ginger exclaimed. It had—two perfect pairs of eyes, one pair set above the other. With its upper set, it could see everything above the surface. The other pair informed it of underwater events. We shot enough of them for bait, and began fishing.

The dinner of broiled fish over, we went to work checking our equipment. We took good care of it each day, but there were always things that went unnoticed until they received the closest scrutiny. Ginger found weak points in the tent and in the sail which she carefully reinforced. I polished, oiled, and sharpened every piece of metal that had a cutting edge. Each tiny spot of rust was a potential menace that had to be eradicated.

The tent in particular had to be safeguarded from rough or careless handling, since it was the only real protection we had against the insects. The ground was always swept clean of even the tiniest twig or stone before we set it up. If the ground was rough, we first covered it with palm branches, leaves, or leaf mould as a cushion for the fragile fabric. We never even walked or sat on the tent floor.

Ginger took care of all the fabric, including our clothes, the sail, sleeping bag, grub sacks—anything made of cloth. In addition to this, she took care of the grub box and all it contained: the mess kit, food, and so on. She also attended to her gun and hunting knife. My job was to care for the canoe, all the ropes, lines, and wooden articles of the equipment, including the paddles and the mast; the harpoon; the equipment box and its contents, which included the camera and films, diaries, first-aid kit, fishing gear, and so on.

At the beginning of the trip I used to tease Ginger about her extreme fussiness. She never touched a grub sack or any article of her domestic equipment if her hands were the least bit soiled. After every meal she scoured and scrubbed each mess pan until it shone. Her reply to my comments was that she liked doing it. In time I also grew to like the task of caring for my tools; quite as much for the satisfaction of knowing that my knives were sharp enough to cut paper, as for the necessity of having them sharp.

The wind went down about seven o'clock. We talked of starting out that night, but decided it would be better to wait until just before daylight. Most of our gear we packed, and moved the canoe down to the beach, so that we could set off early the next morning.

The absence of wind increased the likelihood of Mareños. To guard against a surprise visit, we built a large fire in camp to indicate that we were still there, and then quietly made our bed in the canoe. If the Mareños did come to the island, they would confine their attentions to the camp at first. As under other similar circumstances, we took turns standing watch.

I was on watch about 2 A.M. when I began to feel apprehensive. The sensation of being the target for invisible eyes grew until I could stand it no longer. I wakened Ginger. "Better get up, something's wrong," I whispered. She rubbed the sleep out of her eyes and sat up.

We quietly slipped over the side, and made our way to the lee side of the lagoon. There was nothing to be seen there. The water reflected only the light of the stars; not a ripple disturbed its smooth expanse. But I still felt unsatisfied. Leaving Ginger on watch, I stole through the trees and began to encircle the camp. This was productive of nothing unusual. I went back to the beach where I had left Ginger.

"I'm sure I just saw a canoe," she whispered. "I even heard the splash of the poles. It landed in that clump of mangroves behind camp. We'd better pack up the rest of our things and get out of here."

We crept through the trees, quickly transported the balance of the equipment to the beach, and slid the canoe down into the water. As we were stowing away the last of the boxes, a spurt of flame from the camp illumined the darkness, and was followed by the throaty roar of a muzzle-loader. Buckshot rattled through the foliage round us. Ginger ducked behind a tree and sprayed the brush with bullets, while I pushed the canoe into deeper water. There were no answering volleys from shore. The canoe afloat, I pumped shots, while Ginger left her tree and raced for the cockpit. I followed her. We broke all records for swinging the paddles.

Well out of range, we stopped and looked back at our hurriedly vacated shell beach. There was no sight or sound of a native. We wondered why we had been the recipients of only one load of buckshot, finally concluding that our attackers had only one gun, and neither time nor opportunity to reload. With heart-felt sighs of relief, we bent to the paddles and started across the dark *pampa*.

After sunrise the whole lagoon became covered with mirages. They were similar to the familiar desert phenomena, except that they were much more vivid and detailed. The water forms a smoother plane for the strata of air to settle upon than the rough contours of the desert. These air strata of different densities bend the light rays passing through them, and act as mirrors. We had seen mirages before, but nothing so weird and beautiful as these distorted, inverted, and elevated landscapes wrought in silver and gold through which we travelled. Only when the sun is near the horizon, in the early morning and late afternoon, are the brilliant golden lights reflected in the mirage. We paddled through an unreal, fantastic world in which nothing was recognizable except the water surrounding the canoe. The optical illusion of a world transformed by the Midas touch was aesthetically satisfying, but hard to navigate in. There were no landmarks to guide us, and we could only keep on paddling in the general direction of the southern shore. We sailed through clumps of golden mangroves, across islands that vanished with our passage.

About ten o'clock the images began to assume grotesque shapes, as though reflected in a distorting mirror, and we knew that the wind was rising. With the memory of yesterday's norther still fresh in our minds, we hoped to be spared another while in the centre of the *pampa*. A light breeze coming from the north rippled the water, and the mirages vanished. Hoisting sail, we settled down to the business of getting to the nearest shore, which now appeared in the far distance.

We finally did reach the shelter of a point of land on the opposite shore, but not before the oncoming norther had given us one of the most hectic hours in our long career of sailing. A good blow on the ocean was a tame experience compared to the battering of the short, high seas in the shallow lagoon. Time after time the gusts stopped just short of snapping the mast, and ripping the sail to shreds. And we were not yet in the full force of the gale.

As we huddled down in the cockpit behind a clump of sheltering mangroves, Ginger said, "Well, we have the Mareños to thank for saving our necks this time. If we had left at five o'clock as we intended to, we'd have been in the middle of that rumpus by now." We had reached the trees with about two minutes to spare.

After an hour's wait, when the first mad rush of the wind was over, we felt that we could safely travel close inshore. The Mareños kept pretty much to the lagoons we had left, and we looked forward to a release from the necessity of subordinating everything else to guarding against them. The calmer water in the channel was alive with fish which, like ourselves, had come to it for protection against the churning waters of the *pampa*. We got out the bone jigs and started trolling. Ginger pulled in one fish after another. They were fine fat beauties that looked like bass, and weighed from one to three pounds. With our dinner flopping round in the bottom of the cockpit, we rounded a small point and found a well-sheltered little cove where we stopped to broil them.

At peace with the world after a meal of the succulent fish, we went for a stroll along the beach. On the sand were the tracks of sandals that had been cut from automobile tires. "Hurray!" Ginger shouted. "Now I know we're out of Mareño country." The evidence pointed to a village somewhere near-by where the natives had contact with civilization. We hurried on to find it before dark.

As we sailed down the channel looking for the village we continued fishing, for no villager ever spurns a fish. Our only concern was that we might not reach the village soon enough, for unless kept in the shade, the fish would spoil within an hour. In this climate death and dissolution are almost simultaneous.

Then ahead of us we saw a canoe. The poler wore a shirt. There could be no further question but that we were out of the Mareño country, for nothing could be more distasteful to a Mareño—unless it were a traveller—than the thought of wearing clothes. The canoe disappeared round a point, the *Vagabunda* hot on its heels. A little fishing village, perched on a white sand beach in a tiny cove, lay behind the point. We zigzagged our way among the long rows of upright poles on which the fishermen dried their nets. As we drew near, a crowd gathered on the beach and several canoes pushed out to meet us, their crews shouting a welcome. Surrounded by the laughing, friendly, excited villagers, we came on shore.

An old woman sidled up to Ginger, and Ginger promptly invited her to help herself to the fish. She took three, Ginger two more, and the pair of them started off to the old woman's hut. Thus are friendships cemented and matters arranged in Indian villages in Mexico. I called for the headman, and found that he was the man to whom I was talking. To him was turned over the business of dividing the fish. While he passed them out, I washed out the cockpit and tied the canoe to a mooring mast. Together we walked to the old woman's hut, followed by the crowd.

Ginger was sitting in the shade of the thatched shelter. Plans for a banquet had been arranged, she informed us. Local resources for the event were to be supplemented from our stores. This was the Mexico that we knew and loved, simple, friendly, and unostentatious. In these little villages we were almost immediately caught up in a current of good feeling. The natives gave us whatever they had that they thought we needed, or wanted; and we returned the compliment. Sometimes only one or two people in a village spoke a Spanish of sorts, but that was seldom a bar to communication. Men's needs are similar the world over. We smiled, gestured, and did our share of the work. The entente cordiale was established.

While the women prepared the meal, I squatted in the shade with the men, who began asking questions. That we had come from Salina Cruz was accepted as a matter of course. They easily understood how we had managed to travel through the dry stretches; how we had ducked the northers. But our escape from the Mareños was another matter. That was incomprehensible.

"Those *Indios*," they said, "are very bad. We suffer much from them. Often they rob us. Many of our people have met death at their hands. They sometimes come to our village and leave a woman who is with child. We are forced to take care of her, until she and her child are able to travel."

The men said the Mareños left their women at night while the village lay asleep. Failure on the villagers' part to take her in would be followed, of course, by swift retaliation. A baby had died in a village where a woman had been left. The Mareños killed the entire family who had taken care of its mother. Families in outlying districts were frequently forced to support Mareños, who quartered themselves upon them for months at a time. The government occasionally sent in troops to punish the wild *Indios*, but it did little good, for the soldiers were helpless in the lagoon country.

The name of this village was Punta Flores, they said. Further on, connected with it by a trail, was another village called Paredón. These were the only two villages on the great *pampa*. A cart road connected Paredón and the inland city of Tonala, where both villages traded their fish for other goods. Here again we found both our Mexican map and the United States hydrographic chart to be in error. The village of Paredón was shown to be some distance inland—not on the lagoon at all. Also Great Pampa, which we had just traversed, was mapped as a long, narrow body of water, instead of a great inland sea with a maze of lagoons leading far inland.

Since their livelihood depended upon fishing, the villagers were keenly interested in finding out how we caught so many fish. I let them examine our fishing outfit, and instructed them in the method of making and using bone jigs. Everywhere the people were interested in knowing how to improve their simple techniques in securing food.

The next morning we sailed away from the hospitable little cove and reached Paredón at noon. Sight of the village from the lagoon was obscured by the long lines of drying nets strung along poles set in the water. The nets are strung up by the returning fishermen before they beach their canoes, which simplifies handling. As we worked our way through the nets, we heard sounds of a great to-do on shore. Natives ran up and down on the beach; and several canoes, loaded with women and children dressed in their Sunday best, shoved off to meet us.

"What's going on here, *amigos?*" I asked, when the leading canoe drew near. "Are you having a fiesta?"

"No, Señor, it is because you are arriving. We have been waiting for you a long time."

"How did you know that we were coming?"

"One of our people heard of you in Tonala. He has a friend there, who is the son of Don Juan and Doña Facunda of La Ventosa."

We were certainly due for a warm welcome if Doña Facunda had press-agented our coming. As we approached the beach it became increasingly evident that she had done a good job of it. A marimba started playing in the little market place; and the crowd almost carried us, canoe and all, out of the water. The *Presidente*, decked in his best, and surrounded by villagers, equally resplendent, read us an impressive speech of welcome. (He may not have read it, but he held a piece of paper in his hand.) Still in our old, dirty blue jeans, we felt a little self-conscious in the midst of all this elegance.

We thanked them for their fine reception. And settled the matter of whose guests we were going to be by a compromise; we would all dine together in the *mercado*. Here the women brought broiled fish, stacks of tortillas, and an array of ollas filled with beans, fried rice, and fish *mole*. We ate and talked to the tune of a marimba played by five young men.

After the banquet was over everyone was either sleepy or stupid from the copious draughts of native brew that had been passed round, and we prepared to leave. A shout of protest went up at this, but we were anxious to be on our way. Inquiries as to the best route to the nearest lagoon as usual, received a dozen contradictory answers. Finally, two of the men said that they knew the passage, and were going there that night to hunt alligators. They invited us to go with them.

We gratefully accepted their offer; asked the *Presidente* to sign our papers; said good-bye all the way round; and took our leave. It was like trying to break away from a party that has just started. Then followed the business of tactfully refusing the enormous amounts of food that they pressed upon us. But at last we left the village, with its hospitable and friendly people, to follow our guides across the *pampa*.

The boats in this district are called *pangas*. Like other native boats they are dugout canoes, but are propelled only by poles. The *panga* has a flat platform protruding over the stern on which the men stand to cast their nets, and while poling. The waters of the lagoon are so shallow that paddles would be useless—in fact the natives did not know what a paddle was, or how they were used.

At first the wind was too strong for us to leave the protection of the lee shore. Later, when it quieted a bit, we hoisted sail and ran before it, after tossing a tow rope to our friends in the *panga*. This was a new experience for them, and they were exorbitantly pleased. These Indians, like pre-Columbian natives, knew nothing of the sail. This was the first time they had ever ridden in a boat not propelled by man power! As we raced along across the *pampa*, they shouted compliments on the speed of the canoe, and enjoyed themselves thoroughly. But when we reached water too shallow for sailing, our rôles were reversed. They shot ahead, while we panted after them. We tried using our paddles as they used their poles, but in spite of our best efforts, the heavier dugout kept the lead. Finally they took pity on us. Since they had two poles, and we still had a long way to go, one of the men offered to change places with me. I climbed in the *panga*, while he took his place on the *Vagabunda's* stern. Then we did make time.

This was the first opportunity I had ever had to see our canoe in action. There was a real thrill in watching the graceful, speedy little boat cleave through the water. Soon Ginger and her gondolier shot round us, both of them smiling broadly at our slow progress in the heavier dugout. While the *Vagabunda* skimmed along, the fellow on her stern kept shouting, "*Muy facil, muy facil.*" It was—for an expert.

But the lagoon soon grew too shallow to float even the *Vagabunda*, and we dragged the boats over a wide stretch of inch-deep water before we came to an almost concealed opening in the dense vegetation that walled the shore line. I went back to our canoe, and followed the natives along the deep, crooked, winding channel that tunnelled through the overhanging mangroves. We had reason to congratulate ourselves on our guides, for without them we would never have found the passage; or, if we had found it, suspected that it led to any place in particular.

As we followed the natives in the gathering dusk, strange noises came from the great swamps on either side of the channel—the beating of wings, the hoarse croaking of birds seeking their roosts; the splashing of alligators wakening from their day-long torpor to begin their nightly quest for food. Creatures of the day hurried by, seeking safety and security for the long, dark hours. Creatures of the night emerged from their sunless, underwater caverns. Owls and bats began to reconnoitre. Crickets rasped and sang in unison against the contrapuntal booming of the deep-voiced frogs. Fireflies flashed their tiny beams so brightly that it looked like starshine on the water. Somewhere on the higher terrain a jaguar screamed. Night closed down; that swift dramatic black-out that terminates the brief twilight hour of the tropic day.

We paddled along in the soft inky darkness for an hour, our only guide the murmuring voices of the moving shadows ahead. Then the natives ceased poling. Apparently we had reached the end of our journey. A dozen dugouts were drawn up on the bank near-by. "We have arrived," our guides announced. When I asked where, they said, "At the end of the water, of course."

They knew nothing about a further passage to the south, beyond the fact, "It is a long ways from here." I did find out that the owners of the *pangas* drawn up on the bank lived in a little village "up the trail." No, they were not going to the village, they said. They had come to hunt alligators. Would we like to go hunting with them? Later, we promised, we would return and hunt, but first we must go to the village. "*Bueno*," they said. "We will be along the *estero* not far from here."

We started up the pitch-dark trail, feeling our way along the jungle walls, laughing and stumbling along in the darkness; and wondering what kind of a reception awaited us. A host of dogs began barking, then we saw the flickering lights of the cooking fires. Some one shouted, "*Buenos noches.*" We shouted back a hearty response.

As we entered the small clearing where a dozen huts nestled under great trees, a husky boy ran to meet us. He took us at once to the headman, who graciously welcomed us, and invited us to enter his house. This was the usual native establishment. A thatched roof set on poles, with latticed sides, was the living room. It was furnished with several tables, low benches, and hammocks. A smaller room, roofed and sided, the family's sleeping quarters, adjoined it. The kitchen was a thatched roof without sides.

After the introductions were over, I asked about a passage to the next lagoon. It was ten miles away, and the portage would have to be made by oxcart, our host informed me. He also politely mentioned the fee—six pesos—for the trip.

We were more than anxious to get in on the alligator hunt, so after dinner we excused ourselves, promising to return the next day, and returned down the trail to the canoe. Our search for the hunters was short. One fellow had fastened a carbide light to his hat, and stood in the bow of the *panga*, with his harpoon in his hand, searching the banks with the beam of light. The line fastened to the harpoon head was very heavy.

Ginger paddled, while I made our harpoon ready. Not to be outdone, I fastened the anchor line to its head, since one apparently had to have heavy tackle to catch alligators. Quietly we manœuvred the canoe close behind the hunters, trying to be as silent as they were.

We all sat motionless until the carbide's beam steadied on two points of light down the *estero*. Then slowly, noiselessly, we glided ahead. The *panga* moved inches at a time; and it seemed hours before we were close enough to see the alligator's great head. It was back in among the mangrove roots, and still too far away to harpoon. Carefully, inch by inch, we crept under the overhanging branches, working our way round the roots, until we were within easy range.

Then for some unknown reason the natives stopped and waited. At first we were puzzled by the delay. Then we could see that the animal was facing us. The head and back of an alligator is armoured with a thick, tough hide which it is almost impossible to penetrate with a harpoon. The natives were waiting for it to turn sideways, so that they could strike at the softer flesh just back of the foreleg.

There was a movement of the dark body among the mangroves. The light flickered as the man on the bow hurled his harpoon. Sounds of a tremendous commotion, that drowned out all the other night noises, came from the roots. The light went out, and then a match flared. The men in the dugout had changed places, and the man with the carbide was trying to relight it. The *panga* rocked violently. The match went out. He cursed and lit another.

We backed away to give them room to fight. Something slapped our canoe so hard that it nearly threw us out. The light flared. The alligator was now between the two boats. It repeatedly dived and came to the surface. Each time it emerged it thrashed the water with its huge tail until we were wet with spray. Ginger and I grabbed our guns and blazed away at its head. Then the roar of a muzzle-loader drowned out the bark of our pistols. How we failed to shoot each other was a miracle! The alligator's struggles grew weaker, and the native hauled in on the harpoon line. This time we delivered a volley into its head that ended the rumpus. It took the combined efforts of all four of us to drag the big beast into the *panga*. It measured fourteen feet long.

The natives said they received one peso per foot for alligator hides. With the proceeds of their night's work they could now go on a glorious two weeks' vacation. True, they had just come from a vacation, they admitted; but they were again men of property, worth all of seven pesos each. Such men did not work. They attended fiestas, cockfights; drank *tequila*; perhaps visited with other men so fortunately situated; or just sat in the sun—and rested. Surely Fortune did not smile upon a man for the purpose of keeping his nose to the grindstone. They had heard, they said, of men who continued to slave after having accumulated a tidy sum—say ten pesos—but for themselves it seemed so useless, so avaricious. Two weeks was long enough to plan ahead. *Quien sabe*, who knows what tomorrow will bring? They fairly tore through the water, so anxious were they to return to Paredón and the sophisticated life open to a man with seven pesos.

We paddled back to the head of the channel, anchored the canoe in midstream, and settled down for the night. Several million assorted gnats, mosquitoes, *mosco cabezones*, and *jenjenes* tried to settle with us. A veritable London pea-soup fog of insects—we hardly dared open our mouths to speak.

Long before daylight there were sounds of great activity round us. All the canoes were out in the water, their crews shrimping. The natives catch the shrimps by poling slowly along while a man on the bow throws his circular net. This net is about twelve feet in diameter, and is weighted with stones round the circumference. It is draped over the arm and thrown in such a way that when it strikes the water it spreads out in a perfect circle. The weights quickly carry it to the bottom, where it imprisons the shrimps. Then the fisherman closes the net and hauls it in by pulling with a jerking motion on lines which are threaded round the circumference and attached to the centre. They make these nets themselves, and it takes about three weeks to complete one. The canoes travelled abreast of each other up and down the channel in groups of four or five, so that when the men cast their nets they covered the width of the water. Most of the canoes were propelled by youngsters, some of them not more than six years old.

At daylight we walked up to the village. The headman ran to meet us as we entered the clearing, and with *"mucho gusto"* ushered us into his house. His wife was busily preparing breakfast, "for you," she announced. Several old men gathered round. Pancho, the headman, all smiles, inquired how soon we wanted to start on the portage. I reminded him that we had not yet settled on the price. He waved away the thought of payment. "Oh, no," he said, "there will be no charge. I did not know last night that you were the *Vagabundos*. We are anxious to help you in any way we can."

We never knew the exact details of how this grapevine telegraph worked, but that the natives had some means of communicating with each other was frequently demonstrated.

Three o'clock was set as the time for our departure, for then the sun would be well past the meridian. The natives dislike travelling during the heat of the day.

This business settled, the old men plied us with questions about the lagoon country until the meal was ready. We sat down to a good breakfast of eggs cooked in chili sauce, shrimps, and *gorditas*. The *gordita* is a small, thick corn cake made from meal prepared as for tortillas, but about three inches in diameter and three-quarters of an inch thick. Nowhere else, except in part of the lagoon country, did we see them.

This little village, we learned, was La Colonia. One *legua* away, on the Gulf of Tehuantepec, was another village, Puerta Arista. While in Salina Cruz we had met a customs official who was to have charge of Puerta Arista, and who expected to have assumed his post by the time we arrived. We had promised to stop and see him, for our plans at that time were to sail down the coast. Since we had some hours to spend before three o'clock, we decided to pay him a visit.

Dressed in our white shore clothes, we started on the four-mile walk to the port. Puerta Arista consisted of a lighthouse and several thatched huts clustered together on a straight beach, where a very heavy surf broke. Why the place was ever called a port is one of the mysteries of Mexico. No boat could possibly land through the surf—even if the norther gave it a chance. There was no one in sight, so we went to the lighthouse and routed out the keeper, who was asleep in a hammock. He made us welcome and promised to go in search of our friend. He soon returned with Don Nancho in tow, who immediately welcomed us to Puerta Arista and invited us to his house.

The worthy Don said that he had long ago given us up, believing we had been lost at sea. When I informed him that we had come through the lagoons, he was highly incredulous, and questioned us closely about the country. "*Caramba!*" he exclaimed. "You actually came through the Mareño country?" He shook his head, and added the Spanish equivalent of "It just isn't done." "Why," said he, "when I was younger, I led an army through that country. I know it, and I know the Mareños. They will kill you for nothing. I do not understand how you could do it." Except for our knowledge of its geography, we should never have convinced him.

Don Nancho was sixty-five, and very young and active for his age. This —along with his successful marriage to a woman forty years his junior— he attributed to his lifelong habit of drinking curdled milk. This milk was prepared from a culture "of worms," which he said he had used for twenty-five years. I have no idea what Don Nancho's "worms" really were, but he swore by them. They were put in fresh milk and allowed to stand over night. The following day the milk was strained and drunk. The "worms," said he, would cure anything . . . restore the vigour of youth . . . he offered to lend me some of his culture . . . I would soon see for myself whether they were overrated or not . . . I hastily declined his kind offer. Then, Doña Felicia, his fat young wife, brought in his mid-morning tipple. He drank it down with great gusto, and a mighty smacking of his lips.

Swamp Grass, Quicksand, and a Few Mareños 319

Doña Felicia smiled broadly. Yes, she said, it was a remarkable antidote for the ravages of time.

After an excellent lunch of chicken *mole*, quite the best we had ever eaten, we started back up the dusty trail. Half-way we were met by a horseman, who said he had been sent to look for us, since Pancho was afraid that we might have lost our way.

The oxcarts were ready and waiting in the village. While loading the canoe, one of the men called my attention to a bullet hole in the stern. I called Ginger, pointing to the place just below the gunwale. "Oh," she gasped. "I was standing by the stern when they fired."

We said *Adios*, and started down the road. As we passed each house the family came running out and handed us gifts of food. They gave us *yuca*, bananas, plantains, coco-nuts, and breadstuffs. The cockpit was half full by the time we left the village. A hundred yards past the last house, we heard a child screaming. We turned round to see a little girl running towards us, waving her arms and yelling. The carts went on ahead while we waited for her. Ginger picked her up, and with the tears streaming down her dusty face she sobbed, "I was so afraid you would go away before I could give you this." Clenched in one dirty little fist, was an egg!

The third portage passed without incident. Again we made our way along the intricate waterways that meandered in and out of mangrove thickets, swamps, and shallow lagoons. At a little village called Cabezo del Toro, friendly Indians guided us through a difficult maze to the next open water. This country was mapped on the charts as dry land. And after pushing the canoe for a distance of ten miles through barely wet mud, we were not disposed to quarrel with the map makers.

The second day out from La Colonia, we were cruising down a shallow *estero*, wondering when we would find enough water to bathe and to wash our muddy clothes in. This was the dry season, and all the tributary streams were dry, too. We were caked with mud from head to toe. On the *estero* we met two fishermen, who told us that at the base of the next hill ahead we would find a village.

We paddled on, hoping to find a place where we could clean up a bit before going on to the village. But within a short distance a canoe came to meet us, filled with men and women in their fiesta clothes. They were very cordial and insistent that we come at once to the village. Ginger protested that we were too dirty, and urged them to go on ahead. We would follow when we had made ourselves presentable.

"No, no," laughed a young fellow who had invited us to be his guests. "It is perfectly natural that you should be dirty after such a trip. You must come to our house. There you can bathe with fresh water and soap."

We beamed at each other. "Fresh water and soap." This would be the first luxury of the sort we had had since leaving Salina Cruz.

As we made our way up the *estero* we could see that this was not the poor, sandy country we had left. The sloping hills were covered with rich, cultivated fields of corn and cane, and groves of coco-nut palms, oranges, and bananas. Santa Rosa was also the largest settlement we had visited since leaving Salina Cruz. But unlike the usual Mexican village, it was not built round a central square or plaza; its two hundred thatched huts were strung along a single street.

We followed our host, Roberto, to a coco-nut grove, where he filled a large wooden trough with water from a near-by well. This was his bathroom. He presented us with some hard native soap and retired, leaving us to the privacy of our bath. The native soap was black, hard, and full of grit, but it made a good lather. After thoroughly removing the successive layers of mud, we dressed ourselves in our white shore clothes, stuffed our dirty native costumes into the clothes bag, and started back towards the hut.

When we again presented ourselves to the natives, we noticed a decided change in their manner. Where before they had chatted away with easy informality, now they became reserved and excessively polite. They no longer addressed us in the familiar language, but used the formal pronouns reserved for strangers. They offered us food and drink with the greatest courtesy. Their house was ours, they said. But we were not fooled. With our European clothes we had become *gringos*—strangers. We did our best to bridge the awkward, constrained silences. Ginger looked at me, as though to say, "Something must be done about this."

Then she had an inspiration. "We are very sorry that we have to wear these clothes in your village," she smiled. "We only wear them in the ports and large cities, for they are not comfortable, and we prefer our native clothes. But now those are dirty, and we have only these."

I followed through with the story of our sorry appearance in Salina Cruz, and how everyone laughed at my white pants with blue flowers. This helped a bit, but it took more than a good story to make them forget that we were gringos.

While we were talking a crowd of natives gathered outside Roberto's hut, where they kept their distance, and just stared. Ginger stood it as long as she could. Finally she said, "Come on, let's put on our native clothes; dirty or not, it will be better than this."

Excusing ourselves, we beat a retreat to the coco-nut grove, where we pounded as much of the dirt off our mud-encrusted blue jeans as we could before putting them on. Ginger began carefully packing away our good clothes. "This will be the last time," she said grimly, "we'll wear these clothes in Mexico." I laughed. She was fairly safe in her pronouncement, since our next port of call of any size would be Champerico, Guatemala.

Although our hosts were appreciative of our efforts to please them by wearing native clothes, they were still quite conscious that they were entertaining gringos. It was not until we were out in the street on our way to the *Presidencia*, where we laughed and talked with natives who had not seen us dressed in our finery, that we became at ease again.

The *Presidente's* official signature affixed to our documents, we strolled back up the long street towards Roberto's house, where we had promised to return for dinner. On the way we stopped in at a Chinese store—the only store in the village—to do a little trading. Its proprietor said business was bad, because people in this town seldom bought manufactured articles. Everything was much cheaper than in Matias Romero and Salina Cruz, where we had purchased our last supplies. *Panela*, native sugar, was one cent a pound (American money) as against three cents a pound on the Isthmus. After a little dickering, we traded eight fishhooks and ten .22 shells for twenty pounds of *panela*, a dozen large onions, a pound of lard, and some cacao beans.

After dinner, we presented Roberto and his mother with fishhooks and needles, thanked them for their hospitality, and returned to the canoe. We declined invitations to stay over for a day or two, for we were anxious to reach an uninhabited section of the lagoon, where we could celebrate Christmas in our own manner.

The usual quest for information had been unproductive in Santa Rosa. No one knew anything about the country ahead beyond the fact that past the next village, called Punta Duro, four miles south, the lagoons were closed. We started off for Punta Duro. The country between the two villages was dotted with coco-nut groves and banana plantations. The water was full of fish and shrimps. Everywhere there was an abundance unknown to such villages as San Francisco del Mar.

When we pulled in at the little *embarcadero* of Punta Duro, the *Presidente* was there to meet us. The village, smaller than Santa Rosa, was charming. The thatched huts, each with its own well, were set among groves of coco palms and spreading shade trees. It was late in the afternoon, and the villagers, dressed in spotless white homespun and fresh from the siesta hour, strolled along the little street, or in their gardens. Not since leaving Tehuantepec had we seen so many flowers. Each hut was surrounded with brilliant tropical shrubs and flowering vines. Hibiscus, bougainvillaea, *cresta de gallo*, and many others grew in profusion.

Machineless men, dwelling outside the currents of time and change, the faces of the villagers of Punta Duro reflected the peace and contentment that came from being presented with no problem beyond their capacity to solve. Close to the earth, they drew their sustenance from it without question. They needed no philosophers to prove to them that this was the best of all possible worlds. They knew it. They smiled and nodded as we passed, and called out greetings in their soft, unhurried voices.

In Punta Duro we consulted the usual authorities about the country to the south. There were no roads or trails, and the lagoons were closed, they said. One old man vouchsafed the information that many miles down the lagoon there was a village called La Barra. This sounded as though it were located on some bar, or sea entrance; and so I asked him how big the village was. "Oh," he said, "it is no longer there. Once it was a large *pueblo*, but everyone died of malaria."

Well used to such contradictory statements by now, I patiently kept on asking questions. A village called Ocos was next suggested. This, I knew, was two hundred miles to the south, on the border between Mexico and Guatemala. Nothing of further interest could be obtained beyond one suggestion: several miles past this village, at the end of the *estero*, lived a man who made his living hunting alligators. He was an authority on the lagoon country, and perhaps he might be able to help us. Encouraged by this prospect, we said good-bye and started off in search of him.

As we paddled down the narrow channel in the dusk, the children ran along the bank shouting *"Adios, que la vaya bien."* When we could no longer see them, their voices drifted down to us in the still twilight, a long drawn out, faint *"adio-os."* Night caught us two miles down the *estero*. Since it was too dark to navigate among the mangrove roots, we tied the canoe to a limb and turned in.

We awoke at daylight in a hazy, misty world from which all sense of direction had fled. The lagoon at this point was only ten feet wide. The night before I had tied the canoe to an overhanging limb in the centre of the waterway, and now could not remember which way the bow had pointed. Sunrise would be no help, since we frequently paddled north to go south in these labyrinthine channels. The current had turned the canoe round several times and the line was kinked and twisted. In an effort to determine the direction, I studied the current. Small twigs floated by. As frequently happens, the study of one problem solves another. "Look," I called to Ginger, "see these twigs; they're moving too rapidly for this to be a closed channel. Somewhere, not far off, the tide is coming in. It's not likely to be as far south as Sacapulco Bar."

We started down the crooked channel that wound through a big mangrove swamp, paddling against the current. At ten o'clock we arrived at the little *ranchito* of the alligator hunter. He was not at home, but his fat old wife and his three young daughters were. They were so astonished at the sight of two gringos in this isolated country, that at first they were speechless. The old lady hurried off to prepare a warm meal for us when she found out that we had not had one since leaving Punta Duro. Then her husband arrived. He was a fine-looking, elderly man, who claimed to know every channel in the vast lagoon country.

Twenty-five years ago, he said, there was a passage leading all the way to the Ocos River in Guatemala. Since then the mangroves had blocked the channel. Mud and silt had collected round their roots, and as soon as they cut off the current, other trees took root. Not only were the channels blocked by the mangrove roots, but during the wind storms, trees had also blown across them. He had made many attempts, he said, to get through to hunt, but without success. There were no roads, for no one ever went into the country to the south. The *estero* that we had paddled down wound in a great circle towards the ocean, where it joined many other channels. Where they met, there was a bar opening out into the ocean. This was our only route, for all the lagoons were closed a few miles south of his house. There was one little difficulty, he added, in attempting to reach the *mar viva*— the breakers at the mouth of the channel were too high to get through.

We thanked him and took our leave, sailing on down the little waterway towards the coast. Three miles brought us to a fairly large *estero* running north and south. Towards the west, we could hear the boom of heavy surf.

We stopped and took counsel. The country to the south sounded interesting. It might be impassable, and then again, it might be penetrated with effort. We had learned to discount stories as to whether country could be travelled or not. So little was really known about these great areas that it seemed worth the effort to find out more. This sea entrance to the lagoons that we had discovered was unmapped. No entrance from the ocean was charted nearer than Sacapulco Bar, sixty miles due south. There was always the alternative: if we couldn't whack our way through the *cerrado* (closed lagoon) we could return and try the bar. Ginger made the decision. "Let's head south," she said. "If we don't like it we can turn back. There's six hours of daylight left. Let's see how far we can get before dark."

The *estero* ran due south for four miles, where it became so narrow that we touched the trees on both sides as we passed. It finally ended in a small *pampa* from which there seemed to be no outlet. A second careful skirting of the trees revealed a slight current coming out from beneath the trees opposite the channel. Such as it was, this was the passage.

We turned the canoe round and backed it into the mangroves. Ginger placed herself on the bow so that she could propel the canoe by pulling on the mangroves, while I knelt on the stern to clear a passage by slashing the growth with the machete. Within a few feet of the little *pampa*, we were in a different world.

This was a land of roots: a topsy-turvy world of grotesque, unreal forms; of perpetual twilight. Overhead a green canopy of interwoven leaves and branches reached down to the water below. They crossed and crisscrossed in a tangled network of breather-roots, suckers, branches, and fallen trees. The mangrove is one of Nature's oddest specializations. Its overhead roots, exposed at low tide, enable the tree to breathe. Its seeds germinate while still attached to the parent tree. A mangrove swamp looks like an inverted forest, whose roots have changed places with the tree tops. The illusion is further heightened by its reflection in the water. We looked round at this tangled maze of roots, and then at each other. Never had anything looked more difficult than cutting through that barrier.

"It's a question," I said, "whether we want to tackle this thing or not.

If we don't want to, then we'd better go back to the bar, make our Christmas camp there, and after that go down to Champerico along the coast. I don't know where we'll find a place to build a camp in this swamp."

Ginger laughed. "We could build a tree house somewhere, and play Swiss Family Robinson."

"Are you trying to say that you want to go in?" I asked.

She said she was willing to try it, if I was. That settled the matter. How, or when, we'd get out of the *cerrado* neither one of us knew. I started slashing at the mangroves.

Chapter Twenty-four

HOLIDAY IN THE *CERRADO*

WHEN two people, of their own volition, go into country as difficult and heartbreaking to traverse as a mangrove *cerrado* in Southern Mexico, I suppose they ought to furnish the reader with a good reason for doing so; or else keep still about the hardships they encounter. The truth of the matter is, probably, that there seldom is a "good reason" for going to hazardous places. Men go because it promises adventure, excitement, a release from humdrum life, the thrill of being a trail breaker. Sometimes men go with the accolade of a scientific mission to lend verisimilitude to their claim that they do these things for "science," but much of this, I suspect, is "protective colouration." Man likes to think of himself as a rational creature—and uses a little artifice to substantiate his claim. Otherwise he is apt to feel foolish in his own eyes and, moreover, leave himself open to attack by cautious mortals who never leave the house on cloudy days without their umbrellas, as being a man of indifferent sense. Our alibis were simple: we had an insatiable curiosity about any place that no one else had been to; and we liked proving to ourselves that we were equal to the handicap presented by a new environment.

The *cerrado* certainly offers a challenge to any one's ability to take a beating and like it. We had one piece of good fortune, though, when we found that the mangrove's aerial roots were not attached to the mud—as we at first thought. The possibility of snagging the canoe's canvas hull as it passed over the stumps had worried us. But to my surprise, the severed roots sank from sight when I slashed through them. However, we had to be constantly on the lookout for the limbs of submerged logs that might puncture the frail canvas in some unguarded moment.

As we progressed further into this wild country, the birds and the aquatic life grew more abundant. There were many water snakes, small alligators, and strange, snakelike fishes—perhaps eels. Wading birds were everywhere: pink flamingos, great white swans, pelicans, scarlet ibises, egrets, blue and white herons, and many varieties of brown marsh birds. There were five or more varieties of iguanas.

Since there was no dry land on which to make camp, we ate the cold victuals and fruit that had been given to us at Santa Rosa, and slept in the canoe. But Christmas was just a day away, and we hated to give up our cherished plan of finding some place in which to celebrate it. Ginger, I knew, had planned on making this third Christmas away from home something of an occasion. We had spent our first Christmas on the poverty-stricken beach at Turtle Inlet in Magdalena Bay. Last year at this time we were convalescing from malaria in Puerto Escondido. This year it seemed likely that the day would be spent somewhere in a swamp in Chiapas—dining off an uncooked plantain. It was not an hilarious prospect.

By now we were becoming increasingly grateful for the few open spaces where, for fifty yards or more, we could paddle. Most of the time we were tunnelling through mangrove roots, or encountering submerged logs which had to be hacked away to a sufficient depth to permit our passage. Both of us were a mess, and the canoe was no better. We were covered with mud, leaves, spider webs, ants, and insect bites; the canoe was full of bark, twigs, bugs, and dirt. Ginger's hands were blistered from pulling on the mangrove roots to propel the canoe; and mine from gripping the machete hour after hour, while I slashed at logs and roots that seemed made of iron. Still, there was just one way to find dry land, and that was to go ahead.

In the afternoon of our second day in the *cerrado*—the day before Christmas—we saw what appeared to be palm boles on the ocean side of the swamp. Ginger tried vainly to suppress her excitement. "If those are palms, that means high ground and a place to camp."

We tied the canoe as near as possible to the place where we had sighted the trees, and began scrambling over fallen logs and roots. The growth was heavier outside the narrow confines of the channel. Once I fell from a log into the mud, half expecting to sink out of sight, but to my surprise the ground beneath the muddy surface was fairly firm. The mangroves thinned out, so that I could cut a trail through the brush. Then we saw the feathery tops of the palms. The wild life for miles must have been frightened and dismayed at our war whoops. We were going to have a dry camp for Christmas!

We decided to go no further, but to return at once to the canoe and pick up what equipment we needed for the night before it grew too dark. The trail we had cut from the mangroves was easy to follow, but when we reached its end, we realized that in our excitement we had failed to blaze a way over the roots. This was a pretty situation, for neither one of us was certain which direction we had taken from the canoe. Disheartened, Ginger started in one direction, I in another, after we had agreed to keep in touch by shouting back and forth; to fire three shots if we got into difficulty, one shot if we found the canoe.

I had spent Christmas Eve in many strange ports and places, but that hunting a lost canoe in an equatorial swamp about capped the climax. After an hour's search, the staccato crack of Ginger's twenty-two announced that the quest was ended. Both of us had passed close to the canoe several times before, but in the gathering dusk we had failed to see it.

This time, after securing the tent, sleeping bag, and what food we needed for the night, we were careful to blaze a trail that a blind man could follow. Again we set out for the palms.

The grove was an ideal camp site with two exceptions: the ground was full of ants—with mandibles like red-hot pincers; and the undergrowth was like a barbed-wire barricade. There wasn't room to spread a handkerchief, let alone set up a tent. To make the place habitable would be a tremendous job, but we had set our hearts on having a Christmas celebration, and we were determined to have it.

I cleared away a small spot in the centre, and built a fire by the light of which we surveyed the scene. We were hemmed in by a welter of fallen branches, logs, ants, and undergrowth. Nothing could be thrown out, but it could be burnt. We started piling the debris on the flames, working from the centre, so that the cleared space formed a firebreak. The heat of the fire, added to the humidity of the tropic night, soon had us simmering; and sometimes a sudden flare-up singed us. But the results were well worth it, for in an hour's time we had burnt a room forty feet square.

When the fire burnt down to coals, we raked them over the entire camp site with forked sticks, so that the heat would bake out the ants and other insects inhabiting the soil. After allowing sufficient time for the heat to kill the bugs, we raked the coals to the room's circumference, and swept away with palm-leaf brooms the remaining ashes and debris right down to the clean, white sand. Then we surveyed our handiwork with pardonable pride.

At midnight we sat down to the first warm meal we had eaten since leaving the alligator hunter's *ranchito*. Tonight we would sleep in the tent, the first night's sleep, outside the crowded confines of the canoe, since leaving the Mareño country. Out of such things as these do wayfarers in the wilderness find cause for rejoicing.

We both slept like logs and waked up full of spirit. "Just think! No trail to start on. No natives—not even nice ones. Plenty of food. A place we can spend a week in if we want to. And it's Christmas!"

Out in the sunlight, we were surprised at the beauty of our camp site, for the palm enclosure was one of the prettiest places we had ever made camp in. Our good luck in finding it amazed us.

After breakfast, when the rest of the equipment had been brought from the canoe, came the real business of the day—Christmas dinner. Ginger needed, she said, just three things: plenty of wood, fresh meat, and water.

"All right," I promised, "you start the dinner and I'll take care of the rest." The jungle was full of wood. I could either dig a shallow well, or start the still with salt water from the ocean. And the country looked like game. I collected the wood, and then began cutting a trail towards the ocean. In a few minutes I came back empty-handed.

Ginger looked up from her work in surprise. "What brings you back? Isn't there any game in this country?"

Enjoying my private joke, I said, "I just thought I'd come back and find out what you wanted for Christmas dinner."

"Anything you can get will be fine," she answered amiably.

"You name it," I said. "There's chicken, turkey, wild pigeon, doves, coon, deer, and iguana."

"Well, considering the occasion, suppose you bring in a turkey."

To any one who has never seen wild life in countries uninhabited by men, its prodigality is amazing. I wondered how many animals there were for the many that I saw. At each stroke of the machete they fled before me, and I could hear more of them than I could see; the whir of wings and the snapping of twigs sounded as they scuttled to cover. Within a few feet of camp I saw my turkey sitting in a tree top, and shot it, but it remained fast in the branches. Ginger came running out. "What's the matter? You're shooting so close to camp."

"How are we going to get it down?" I asked. The obvious answer, "Shake the tree," isn't such a good one in the tropics, where each tree is laced to a dozen others by stout aerial cables of tough vines. We slashed at such lianas as were within reach, and pushed against the trunk, but the bird remained fast in its perch. Then Ginger gave a vicious yank to a vine attached to the tree top, and down came our big fat Christmas turkey.

When I came back to camp with the dressed bird, ready for roasting, Ginger made a hurried movement towards the grub box. "Go away," she commanded. "You're not supposed to see this yet."

So while she worked on the dinner, I dug a well, using our bailing can for a shovel. About five feet down I struck water, sweet and cold. Ginger took time out to celebrate the event. For months we had used fresh water with the greatest economy. Now, waxing extravagant, we had a water fight and poured the precious liquid over each other, grateful for its coolness against our wind-roughened, sun-scorched skins. The day was perfect.

There was just one thing more that I wanted—a Christmas tree—and I started off towards the ocean in search of one. En route I discovered some coco-nut palms, and cut down a small one, collecting the nuts, both green and ripe, and the heart or terminal bud. We would have milk and salad as well as turkey for our feast. But nowhere could I find a little tree that in any way resembled the pointed firs of home.

As I cut my way through a thorny maguey thicket towards the beach, I could hear the roar of the surf, but not even its thunder prepared me for the size of the breakers; they were gigantic, towering forty feet before they crashed, throwing spray seventy-five feet into the air. The boat has never been built that could go through such surf. Just how would we get to Champerico, I wondered?

The beach was lined with beautiful, multi-coloured shells. I picked up all I could carry in addition to the coco-nuts and palm heart.

Ginger was pleased with my offerings. We had lots of sugar, and now that we had the nuts we could add coco-nut candy to our list of good things for the day. Since she seemed anxious to have me leave camp, I started out once more to find a tree.

It's strange how the mind fastens on certain symbols. At home I doubt if I should have concerned myself unduly over a Christmas tree, but out here that symbol became a link with the past, which seemed farther away than time. After a vain search through the humid jungle, disconsolate and a little home-sick, I returned to camp.

"After all," Ginger reminded me, "this is the tropics. What's the matter with that palm?"

I cleared a space round it, and then went out and collected some bright-coloured berries. Together we trimmed the little tree. Punching holes in the shells that I had brought from the beach, we tied them to its branches with palm fibre and when our job was finished the tree looked very gay. On the white sand beneath it, we placed the mysterious packages that we had bought in Matias Romero.

Then Ginger announced, "Dinner is served," and placed it on the green palm fronds that I'd spread over the sand in lieu of a table. And such a dinner! There was broiled turkey with coco-nut stuffing, cheese *enchiladas*, fried onions, hearts of palm salad, baked plantain, and parched corn.

I seated myself.

"Wait a minute," she said. "Close your eyes and promise you won't peek."

I heard her open the grub box, and set something down before me.

"You can look now," she said. I looked—and looked again. My eyes were certainly playing me tricks, for there sat a three-layer chocolate coco-nut cake! Of course, I knew that she had been up to something, but that she could produce such a miracle as this in the jungle seemed impossible. The flour and baking powder, she confessed, she had obtained in Salina Cruz and had husbanded for just this purpose.

It was a great day.

After dinner we made candy. Then towards dusk I remarked that it would be fun if we had candles so that we could light the tree. "We can," Ginger assured me. "We have six candles to last us until we reach Champerico; two of them cut into short lengths will be plenty for the tree." Soon the little palm gleamed with six tiny candles that cast dancing lights on the jungle walls.

"It's time for Santa," Ginger reminded. So we sat side by side under the palm and unwrapped our presents. Silk underthings for Ginger, and I had also remodelled a piece of good machete steel into a hunting knife for her. Ginger's present to me was a fine new shirt—which I needed—and a package of my favourite pipe tobacco.

Our Christmas party lasted until midnight. We sat beneath the tree and sang songs—and felt more than a little home-sick. Two years of roaming, and all of it fun; but tonight, our own people and the old remote life seemed suddenly very desirable.

The next morning, rested and refreshed by our holiday, we started out to explore the surrounding country. Many of the forest creatures exhibited no fear of us, and we were able to approach them closely by quiet stalking. Sudden noises frightened them, but they did not seem particularly disturbed by the man scent. One of the tree dwellers, a little animal about the size of a raccoon, and looking like a miniature bear, was new to us. We thought that it was probably a sloth. Also there were many iguanas in variegated colourings that we had not seen before, and a large black bird, about the size of a turkey, with a feathered crest, that Ginger shot for eating.

We spent several days at "Christmas Camp," resting and preparing for the long jump ahead. The jungle provided us with ample raw materials, which we converted into cooked foodstuffs that could be taken with us. My dulled machete was put in shape to cut the iron mangroves. Our clothes were cleaned and such equipment as needed it was overhauled. At last everything was shipshape, but we were reluctant to go. We would come back, we told ourselves, and spend months here. For we never tired of exploring the jungle. Nor was one piece of jungle like another. There was infinite difference between this stretch of country and the forests of Oaxaca, or those of Guerrero and Nayarit.

Once again we cut our way through the *cerrado*. Mangrove swamps alternated with stretches of higher ground covered with great trees; it was as difficult travelling through one as the other. In the swamps a way had to be cleared through a solid wall of roots. Where the channel wound through the forest we had great hardwood logs to contend with; many of them were just below the surface, and years of submergence had hardened them almost to the consistency of stone. The machete began to look more like a saw than a knife. By both of us standing on the same end of a log, we were sometimes able to sink it deep enough to drag the canoe over without unloading. But it was more often necessary to unload and stack the equipment on some ant-infested tree trunk. Sometimes logs lay across the channel. Then we unloaded the canoe, filled the cockpit with water, and shoved it under the obstacle. Whenever the canoe went over or under these logs, I removed every snag and branch that I could see; but in spite of these precautions the canvas hull became bruised and much paint was scraped off.

One of the most difficult things to do was to keep in the channel where it traversed the swamps. At times there was almost no way of knowing that there was a channel except by taking repeated soundings.

Strange fish swirled in these black waters, whose grotesque heads were huge in comparison with their small bodies; one creature looked half fish and half alligator. Unfamiliar birds and butterflies circled round us. The dank, humid atmosphere and rotting vegetation made a perfect incubator for insects, and they, too, were everywhere. There seemed to be a hundred varieties of stinging flies, and ants without end. But more annoying than these scourges were the caterpillars; wherever they touched our bodies a red rash broke out that burnt like fire. It was due apparently to a poisonous substance in the tiny hairs, which looked like spun glass. The water also contained an element, or an organism, that felt like hydrochloric acid on the skin; to wade in it was sheer torture. We had believed that the country could offer us no new surprises in the way of pain, but that was before we hit the caterpillar-infested growth. It took all the grit we had just to keep going.

We were travelling through a forested section of the *cerrado* when we noticed that the sky to the north had become hazy; while we watched it great clouds of black smoke rose in the air. For a moment we were puzzled. What could it be? Then we realized that we were in the path of a forest fire. There was a strong wind from the north, and the flames would sweep across the dry tindery ground on both sides of us, setting fire to all the logs and branches in the channel above the water line. Our only safety lay in reaching the swamp ahead, and to that end we worked like mad. In our haste we ran into snag after snag. Soon the air was filled with cinders. Our lungs ached from the acrid smoke; the heat became terrific. Behind us we could see the red tongues of flame, and hear the crash of giant trees. Our muscles hurt with the strain of slashing and pulling.

We had a hundred yards to go. Animals all round us were running for their lives. Birds tore by overhead; spotted jungle cats and deer raced side by side, indifferent to our presence as to each other, plunged into the water towards the safety of the swamp.

Just as we reached the fringe of the mangroves, the flames swept across the open space behind us, spanning the channel with a bridge of fire. We slashed at the roots that barred the way until we had sufficient water and green growth between us and the flames, then paused exhausted to rest.

How the fire started we had no idea. There had been no lightning; and as far as we knew there were no natives living near-by. Our own fires were always carefully doused with water or covered with earth before we left a camp site. We could only believe that it had originated through spontaneous combustion in some pile of mouldering vegetation or grass heaped up by the wind.

Towards sundown the channel emerged into open country and turned towards the beach. The fire had swept along the shore, burning off the grass and undergrowth for miles. We raked away the hot ashes from beneath some palms, and set up the tent. Tired and sore from the long day's grind, we wanted nothing more than a bite to eat and a long sleep.

The next day's journey led through a dense growth of fresh-water plants that blocked the channel where a river emptied into the lagoon. We cut long poles, and laid them down on each side of the canoe. By stepping on the poles our weight sank the plants, and the canoe could then be dragged for a few feet, after which we repeated the process.

Eventually we got through the growth, only to have the channel turn once more into a mangrove swamp. My hands were blistered, and I was very tired. Somehow, in slashing a root, the machete glanced and slipped from my grasp into the water. This was the last straw. We had just taken a sounding and knew the water was eight feet deep. We looked at each other in consternation. Without the knife we were helpless. Retreat along the way we had come was impossible. There was nothing that ingenuity could devise that would take the place of the knife.

"There's only one thing to do, and that's to dive for it," I said.

Since it was torture to wade in the water, how could I dive in it? Ginger asked. "Try feeling round with the harpoon, and see if you can locate the knife."

But the harpoon failed to reveal any trace of the elusive machete. Finally I unstrapped my gun belt, and lowered myself into the water—wondering just how many of those strange fish were going to sample my hide. I was up to my waist when my foot came in contact with a slimy log. Standing on one foot, I felt round with the other; it came in contact with an interwoven mass of roots. Diving was impossible.

Ginger manœuvred the canoe, while I hung on to the gunwale, with just my nose sticking out of the water, exploring the ooze below with my feet. A thousand leeches seemed to be boring their way into my skin. And then something bit my toes! I yanked my foot out of the water to see what damage had been done and discovered not a bite, but a long cut. The machete was located. Now I carefully lowered both feet into the hole where I had been "bitten," and found that the knife had fallen handle end first. How to grip that blade—which I kept sharp enough to cut paper—between my feet without slicing off a toe occupied all our attention for the next few minutes. It was a ticklish business, but at last I felt the smooth blade between my feet. With Ginger's aid I hoisted myself up on to the gunwale. She leaned over and retrieved the machete.

It was necessary then to remove the hordes of parasites that clung to my hide—a dozen varieties of leeches, many small crawling worms that had already started burrowing beneath the skin, and an insect that looked like a tick. It took over half an hour to get them all.

Late in the afternoon we left the *cerrado* behind us, and entered the channel that led to Sacapulco Bar and the ocean. Turning the canoe round, we took up our old positions at the paddles. It was great to have the *Vagabunda* back in her natural element. We made a ceremony of stowing the machete away.

The roar of the surf sounded good to our ears that night as we made camp on the sand bar between the lagoon and the sea. We had been swamp sailors so long that we were hungry for the sight of open water. And so after supper, when Ginger suggested that we go down to the ocean and see a ship, we trotted off across the dunes. To our delighted surprise we did see one. It was a long way offshore, but we watched its twinkling lights until they faded from view as it sailed northward. We saw it go with a faint nostalgia.

"I wonder if you're thinking what I'm thinking?" Ginger queried.

I laughed. "Yes, I'm thinking that the surf isn't too high for a swim."

We waded out into the clean, salt water that had so long been a luxury; its bite soothed the intolerable itching of our skins. Then we lolled in the shallows while the breakers tumbled over us, and finished off the evening with a brisk run up the beach to relieve our cramped leg muscles. At last we returned to camp, dog-tired, out of breath, and ready for a long sleep.

After the dirt and insects of the *cerrado*, the fine clean sand looked good to me, and I proposed that we stay on the beach for several days. The canoe was in none too good shape and needed a coat of shark-oil paint. But to my astonishment Ginger wasn't quite satisfied with the place.

"What's the matter?" I asked. "I don't know what better camp site any one could ask than this."

"It is a fine place," she agreed, "but there are no coco-nut palms here."

"Just what are you driving at?" I demanded.

Had I forgotten that tonight was New Year's Eve? Why not a New Year's party? Of course, you had to have something with which to celebrate such an occasion. It took about four hours to ferment coco-nut sap. If you put the sap in the still . . . it was the same procedure as making fresh water.

A great light broke over me. "Oh, that's it! Let's go."

But where to find a coco-nut grove? Two miles down the lagoon we sighted a village. Approaching closer, we could see that it was deserted. We beached the canoe and wandered among the tumbledown huts. Off to one side there was a large graveyard which contained nearly two hundred graves of approximately the same age. The huts indicated that the village had had a population of perhaps two hundred people. Then I remembered the story that the old man at Punta Duro had told us. This must be the village of La Barra whose inhabitants had died of malaria. We left it in a hurry.

Six miles south of La Barra we found the ideal site for our second holiday camp. A beautiful grove of coco-nut trees grew on a grass-covered beach on the ocean side of the blue lagoon. While Ginger prepared the midday meal, I cut down a large palm—felling it in such a way that the butt end of the bole was higher than the top; then I trimmed off its branches, and cut a square hole in its trunk just below the heart. The sap began to drain immediately into the cavity.

After lunch we went back to the tree with our mess kettles. The hole was completely filled with foaming sap which we dipped out into the pots and set in the sun. In an hour we had two gallons of the fluid. We poured this into the five-gallon still can, added a little sugar, and hung the can over the cooking fire out of reach of the ants. While waiting for it to ferment, we cut a trail to the beach and enjoyed another long swim. At four o'clock we returned to camp, and while Ginger started dinner I rigged up the still and built a good fire under it. As soon as the liquid in the can became hot, I raked away most of the coals so that it would just simmer, then began pouring cold lagoon water over the condensing can. Alcohol will not condense at as high a temperature as does water. When more sap collected in the palm bole, I added it to the quantity already in the still.

Dinner over, we made additional preparations for the party by constructing small bombs out of powder from .22 shells.

At ten o'clock we were ready to celebrate New Year's Eve in the traditional fashion. It must have been a grand party, but we both had a little difficulty remembering some of the evening's finer details the next morning. I remember sitting on the bank in the moonlight and toasting the New Year, the Adventurer's Trail, Mexico and the Mexican people, the fallen palm that had produced this magic brew, and even the mosquitoes that buzzed round our ears—it was that kind of a party. We exploded the bombs at midnight, but were disappointed in the amount of noise they made. By then nothing short of a cannon would have been entirely satisfactory. However, there was nothing ineffective about the liquid dynamite that we had concocted; it was an outstanding success.

The next morning, after a few simple restoratives, a swim in the ocean and a *very light* breakfast, we packed our things and sailed on down the lagoon. At ten o'clock we arrived at the little village of Zapotal.

As we swung in towards the shore, the natives ran up and down the beach screaming and shouting, *"Viva Ano Nueva—Feliz Ano Nueva."* The village had been waiting for us all morning, the *Presidente* informed us, and had prepared a New Year's fiesta in our honour. How they could possibly have known of our arrival we have no idea. We got only smiles in answer to our questions. After the *Presidente* gave us the "familiar embrace" the crowd almost tore us to pieces, overwhelming us with offers of food and drink. A marimba began playing, and everyone started to dance. It was a perfect bedlam as the roar of home-made fireworks mingled with the music and the shouts and laughter of the hilarious natives.

To our relief, things quieted down a bit after lunch when the siesta hour claimed some of the celebrants. The *pampa* was wide at this point, and since there was a fair breeze, I suggested to the *Presidente* that we take him out for a sail. As usual when the villagers got wind of what we meant to do, they all tried to clamber aboard. Only the *Presidente's* authority saved the canoe from foundering on the spot. To preserve peace I promised to take the crowd in relays later. Most of the afternoon consequently passed in treating the Indians to a ride—four at a time. None had

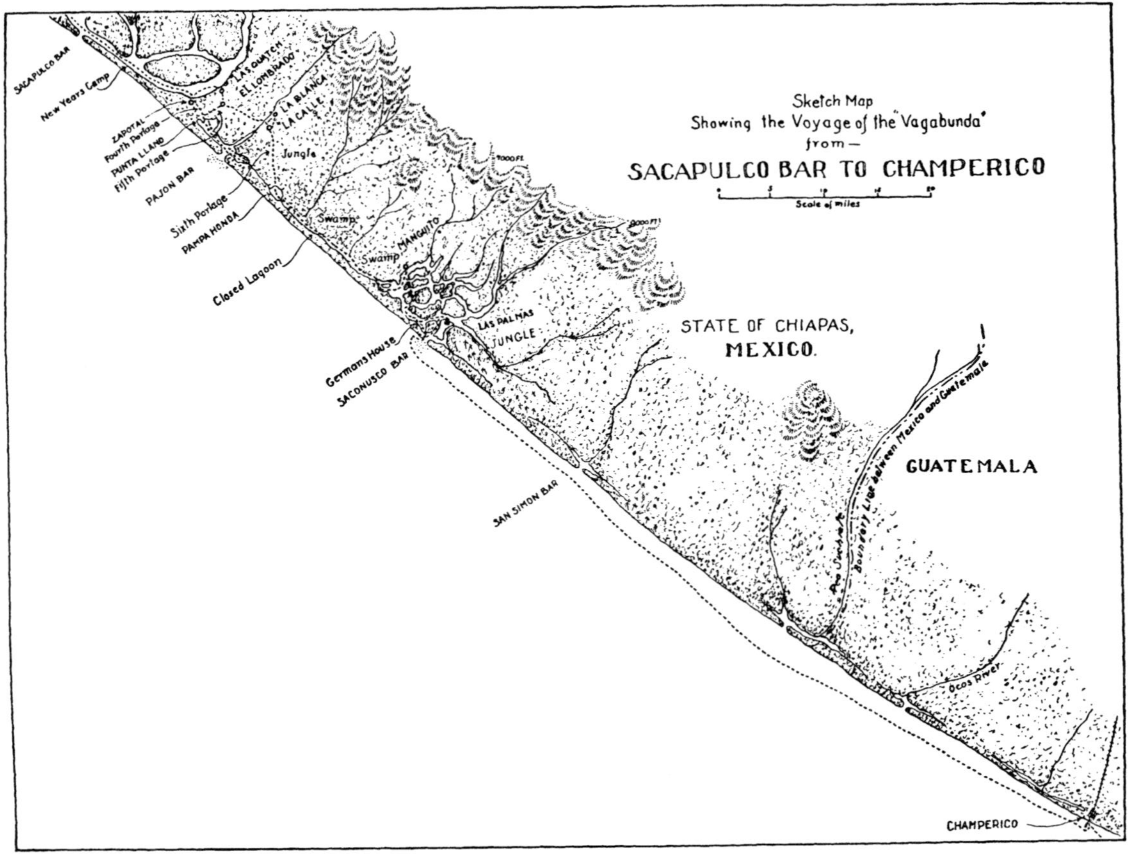
Sketch Map
Showing the Voyage of the "Vagabunda"
from—
SACAPULCO BAR TO CHAMPERICO
Scale of miles
SACAPULCO BAR
New Years Camp
ZAPOTAL
Fourth Portage
PUNTA LLANO
Fifth Portage
PAJON BAR
Sixth Portage
PAMPA HONDA
Closed Lagoon
LAS QUATCH
EL LOMBRADO
LA BLANCA
LA CALLE
Jungle
Swamp
Swamp
MANGUITO
9000 Ft.
9000 Ft.
LAS PALMAS
JUNGLE
Germans House
SACONUSCO BAR
STATE OF CHIAPAS,
MEXICO.
SAN SIMON BAR
GUATEMALA
Boundary Line between Mexico and Guatemala
Ocos River
CHAMPERICO

ever been in a sailboat before, and they almost fell overboard in their excitement.

When it came the children's turn, they were so excited that we could hardly control them. Little Indians are ordinarily the best-behaved children in the world, but these youngsters were beside themselves. A dozen or more would try to climb into the canoe at once—we could carry only eight. They squealed and waved their arms to their friends on shore. Occasionally a child would try to stand upright on deck.

Finally the last boatload had been safely returned to their anxious mothers, and we sighed with relief. Now, we thought, we can join their parents or rest a bit. But there was no way to rid ourselves of the children; they clung to our garments, all of them talking at once and clamouring for attention.

"How about teaching them some games?" Ginger suggested.

After securing the *Presidente's* permission, Ginger took the little girls to a near-by clearing, where she taught them "Blindman's buff," "Drop the handkerchief," and "In and out the window." I started the boys playing "Dare base." In a few minutes some of the younger men broke away from the dancing and joined us.

One attractive young man by the name of Emiliano, introducing himself to me, asked me to teach the games to him, so that he could continue to instruct the village children after our departure. I showed him Indian wrestling, "cock fight" and similar games, which he in turn taught to the other young men. By sundown a regular field meet was in progress, with nearly the entire contingent of able-bodied villagers participating. A "tug of war" wound up the festivities.

Emiliano owned the only oxcart in the village, and he was also the only person who seemed to know anything about the country to the south. The lagoon on which Zapotal was located turned inland, he said, and the next lagoon that was parallel to the coast lay six miles beyond it. There were no connecting waterways. The portage would have to be made by oxcart. He readily agreed to transport us to the next *pampa* the following afternoon.

Emiliano was as good as his word, and left us at a village called Punta Llano. From there on for the next two weeks everything went wrong.

Leaving Punta Llano, we sailed on down the lagoon, hoping by some hook or crook to reach the *pampa* below it. Natives whom we met en route assured us that the way was entirely blocked by dense growths of freshwater plants such as we had fought our way through farther back. Once was enough; so, disappointed, we retraced our steps to an uncharted bar we had discovered.

We sat round for several days on the sand dunes, waiting for the high seas to subside; and had just about made up our minds to risk the surf and continue on down the coast, when a horseman brought word that the *Presi-*

dente of Zapotal was waiting for us at Punta Llano. He wished to see us, said the messenger, because he had heard that we were marooned at the bar; and he wanted to tell us about another *estero* that would lead us to the lagoons further south. This puzzled us, because the *Presidente* had apparently been unaware of such a passage only a few days before. But you never knew with natives, we told ourselves.

Back in Punta Llano I searched for the *Presidente* in vain. "No, Señor, he is not here, nor has he been here," said the villagers. I left Ginger, borrowed a horse, and rode to Zapotal; but the elusive *Presidente* was not there. Perhaps, said the natives, he might be found in Las Quatch, one of the three little villages under his authority. I borrowed a dugout and went to Las Quatch, where I finally caught up with him in the store that he owned.

"No, Señor," he admitted under questioning, "there are no other *esteros*. But it is very dangerous for you to attempt to sail on the ocean, and I thought if we could bring you back you might be persuaded to make the journey to Manguito by oxcart. I will arrange for the carts."

This sounded fine, and I gratefully accepted his offer. Manguito was ten *leguas*, roughly thirty miles, due south. With the exception of one small lagoon, the country between Punta Llano and Manguito seemed impassable except by oxcart.

Back in Zapotal, I hunted up Emiliano, and arranged with him to transport the canoe to the village of El Lombrado, where the *Presidente* had promised to have the carts. El Lombrado, Zapotal, and Las Quatch were the three *pueblos* over which the *Presidente* presided. El Lombrado was nearest to Punta Llano, only a mile away. Emiliano agreed to be in Punta Llano early the next morning.

Well pleased with the results of my trip, I hurried to Punta Llano to tell Ginger the good news.

We were up at daylight, ready and waiting for Emiliano, but noon came and he failed to appear. About three o'clock I became uneasy, and again borrowed a horse and started back to Zapotal in search of him. According to the arrangements I had made with the *Presidente*, we should have left El Lombrado hours ago.

On the way I met the cart. Emiliano was riding a horse and importantly shouting orders to a very drunk native by the name of Pancho, who was driving the oxen. I had made Pancho's acquaintance during the New Year's festivities in Zapotal; and he had been drunk and quarrelsome on that occasion. The day after, still drunk, he had accompanied us on horseback to Punta Llano, and had fallen off his horse. I was anything but pleased to see Pancho.

In Punta Llano we finally loaded the canoe and equipment on the cart, but not before Pancho had driven us almost as crazy as Pedro of Aguas Pocas fame had done. He backed the oxen into the brush, got tangled up in the harpoon, dropped the equipment box in the mud, and finally insisted on riding on the canoe.

When we reached El Lombrado there were no carts waiting for us as promised. The *Presidente's secretario* finally put in an appearance. Tomorrow there would be carts, he said. In the meantime, he had arranged for us to stay in the village overnight. The teams would arrive at daylight.

At nine o'clock the next morning one cart did arrive. The other cart would arrive at noon, we were told. Late in the afternoon we learnt that the cart would arrive in the morning.

We were up before daylight of the second morning, all packed and ready to go. At ten o'clock the *secretario* started out to find the missing cart. He returned in triumph with it, but announced that its driver refused to make the trip. At the *secretario's* suggestion we began loading the canoe on the driverless cart; he assured us that before we had finished, he would have secured a driver. To say the least, this was optimism on his part. When the canoe was finally loaded, he reappeared with the good news that the first cartman had reconsidered and now refused to make the trip.

"Contain yourself, Señor," said the *secretario* soothingly, "I go now to find drivers—it will be very simple." Everything would be fine, he said, if we would exercise patience. Just then Pancho, quite sober, put in an appearance, and volunteered his services. We thanked him, but told the *secretario* privately that under no circumstances would we consider Pancho. No, no, if we didn't want Pancho that was quite all right, the *secretario* said; it was a simple matter to get drivers. Nothing could disturb his serenity. He hurried off.

At last the drivers were secured, and everything looked rosy. At that point the *secretario* handed me a letter. This letter, he said, was to the *Presidente* of La Calle, a village half-way between El Lombrado and Manguito: it requested him to furnish us with oxcarts and men for the rest of the trip, since the drivers from this village did not know the way past La Calle.

Any such scheme as this was just asking for trouble and we knew it. No, I said, we'd give up the idea of making the portage and take our chances with the ocean. How did we know that we could get oxcarts in La Calle? Why, said the *secretario* and the *Presidente*, it would be just as easy to get oxcarts in La Calle as it had been in El Lombrado. That statement alone should have warned us.

We were all ready to leave when we noticed Pancho standing by the oxen of the canoe cart. Ginger asked the *Presidente* if Pancho were making the trip. No, he answered, just walking a little ways—the driver was an especial friend of Pancho's. We started off, Pancho walking beside the lead cart, while I walked beside the second cart on which Ginger rode.

On the outskirts of town, the driver of the lead cart said that he had forgotten something in the village and must go back and get it; in just a few minutes he would rejoin the carts, but we were not to wait. Then he ran past us in a great hurry. And that was the last we were to see of him. The driver of the second cart had difficulty in starting his team, so some time elapsed before we again came in sight of Pancho, who was riding astride the canoe. I hauled him down in a hurry.

Right then and there we should have gone back to El Lombrado—and saved ourselves a lot of trouble. Pancho, I found out, couldn't drive an ox team; but for some unknown reason he had made up his mind to go with us. Porfirio, the driver of the second cart, was an experienced man; and so we compromised by giving him the lead cart, and making Pancho drive the second cart—after a fashion.

The road led through dense jungle, and was uneven and full of roots. There were swarms of mosquitoes, and flies of a particularly dangerous species, which bit us behind the ears. These flies deposit their eggs beneath the skin of a living host; and if the eggs are not removed before they have had time to hatch, the maggots burrow deeper into the flesh. The natives say the flies cause blindness. While travelling through an extremely dense section of growth both ox teams plunged off the road and into the brush. Porfirio explained that the bite of a certain fly, which inhabits this heavy undergrowth, drives the animals crazy; and that whenever they begin to annoy the beasts, the oxen become uncontrollable.

In the late afternoon we passed through a lovely stretch of country, and I wanted to take a picture of it, including myself and the oxen. We stopped the teams, while I went on ahead to set the camera and start the automatic device. Then I sprinted back towards the carts. This frightened the oxen, who took to the brush. But I finally got their pictures and my own by roping their horns to a tree. These oxen, I might mention—the natives have a weakness for fancy names—were called *Grano de Oro* (Grain of Gold), Noble, *Diamonte* and Rosita! The names were without exception inappropriate—particularly *Grano de Oro* and Noble, for that precious pair were neither golden nor noble.

Arrived at La Calle soon after sundown, Pancho said he was on the verge of collapse; even though he had ridden on the equipment cart for hours while I led his team. We learnt, furthermore, that the *Presidente* was not in La Calle. The villagers thought he could be found in La Blanca, about a mile away. We tried to induce Pancho to stay behind and rest while we went in search of him; but in this, as in everything else, Pancho was contrary; if we went to La Blanca, he, Pancho, would go to La Blanca—even if it killed him. He moaned and groaned as we toiled up the steep trail.

We finally ran the *Presidente* to earth in La Blanca. He was sorry, he said, but there were no oxcarts in the village. Oxen, yes, but no carts. We retraced our steps to La Calle. Yes, there were carts, but no oxen, said the villagers. "My God," I groaned to Ginger, "the truth isn't in them. How are we going to get to water?"

"Let's unhitch the oxen and let them feed and rest while we have our own supper," she suggested. "Maybe we'll have an inspiration."

Pancho refused to eat, and sat sulking throughout the meal. Both he and Porfirio were all for unloading their carts and returning at once to El Lombrado, leaving us to get out of our mess as best we could. This I refused to let them do; and this was the reason for Pancho's refusal to eat. Then I made Porfirio a tempting offer—one whole box of fishhooks for himself if he would take us to Manguito. Yes, he would gladly do so, but he did not know the road. Pancho, hearing this, set up a wail, "*Hasta Manguito?*" ("As far as Manguito?")

We spent the intervening hours until midnight trying to find some one who knew the road. There were natives who knew it, but none that we could induce to go with us. Then the *Presidente* put in an appearance. In the morning there would be carts, but they would take us only to the next *rancho*, he said. Of course, we could easily secure fresh teams at the *rancho*. "Nothing doing," I said to Ginger. "I've heard all the 'in the morning' stuff I ever want to listen to. There's just one thing to do—forget Manguito and try to get to Pampa Hondo. It's only six miles away."

Porfirio had never been to Pampa Hondo either. Surely the Señor did not mean to go that night? The Señor and Señora most emphatically did mean to go, I assured him. Pancho had said that the *Presidente* would be very angry if the oxen were not returned, at the latest, by the following day, and Porfirio had confirmed this. There was the possibility that he might ride over, or send some one to bring them back, by morning. Nevertheless, I ordered Porfirio to hitch the beasts to the carts. Then Pancho wailed that he and the oxen were too tired to make the trip. Personally, we hoped that he would stay in La Calle, I told him. After that he pulled himself together, and insisted that he be allowed to go to Pampa Hondo.

No two people agreed on the route, so I started off on a road which led in the general direction of the lagoon and let Porfirio follow with the equipment cart. It was bright moonlight, and the road was not difficult to follow. At the first *rancho* we stopped and woke up the rancher and asked for directions. We were on the right road. Pancho folded up once more and rode the balance of the way with Ginger on the equipment cart. At 3 A.M. we arrived at another *rancho*. The road had dwindled to a cart track by now, so the rancher's son saddled a horse to escort us the balance of the way. The brush was full of *pinolillos*, and our bodies became covered with them.

We arrived at Pampa Hondo at six o'clock in the morning, had breakfast, and immediately the men set out for La Calle. The next four hours Ginger and I spent in removing the *pinolillos*. These insects were a particularly vicious variety with hooked heads; when they were pulled out, the hooks remained underneath the skin and left a wicked sore. Ginger had picked up fewer of them because she had ridden most of the way on the cart, but my body was so swollen that I could hardly move.

The next seven days were a nightmare. I have often wondered since just how we managed to live through them. We assuredly would never have survived were it not that we had gradually built up an immunity to poisons, heat, thirst, hunger, and fatigue.

Pampa Hondo was a small body of water just a mile and a half long, and its only outlet was a narrow channel running through a *cerrado* that made our two previous mangrove swamps seem child's play. Day after day we cut our way through a ring of iron roots. There was not an inch of dry land on which to set up camp. Since we had no opportunity to distil water we carefully rationed out what we had—a pint a day apiece. The growth was full of ants, spiders, and caterpillars, and these, added to the mosquitoes, made our lives miserable. Our bodies were a solid mass of sores, welts, bruises, and insect bites. The pain was intense.

On the seventh day the channel led through a particularly heavy grove of young mangroves. We were entirely out of food and water, and so weakened by hunger, thirst, and pain that each bodily movement was a separate act of sheer will. Slowly we crept forward, a few feet at a time, tunnelling our way through the barricade. How much longer we could keep it up was only a matter of hours. The charts gave our position as a few miles north of a considerable body of open water, but distances measured in miles meant nothing and the charts might not be accurate. We had been averaging less than four miles a day.

Then at sundown we reached the lagoon. Our relief was so great that we could hardly contain ourselves; it was a new lease on life. Ginger scooped up a handful of water and tasted it; it was clean and salt. Piling over the side of the canoe, we let it cleanse and soothe our tired, burning bodies.

We beached and unloaded near a coco-nut grove. Since my body was too swollen and sore to allow me to climb a tree, we both worked at chopping one down. Then we feasted on the crisp white palm heart, and drank the cool, refreshing milk.

After a night and a day of alternately resting, eating, drinking, and soaking ourselves in the lagoon, we started off in search of the village of Manguito. It was located, we knew, on one of the dozens of channels that threaded the numerous islands, but which one was a problem. We paddled for hours through the maze of lagoons; and had just about decided to give up the search for the time being when we saw a faint glimmer of light ahead. A little farther on the glow of cooking fires came into view.

Our arrival occasioned a great deal of excitement. The natives had heard of us, via the grapevine telegraph, and knew that we were attempting to pass through the *cerrado*, but that we should have succeeded seemed to them—as it did to us—in the nature of a miracle. The frightful condition of our bodies, more than anything we said, convinced them.

One of the women took Ginger in her arms. "Poor little one, you are very tired. Come with me."

She took us to her hut, which was one of the largest in the village. Here we rested, while the good Señora Lencha prepared the evening meal, the first hot food we had eaten in eight days. Never had food tasted so good. For dessert we were given a hard, brown confection that looked like a cookie and was delicious. They were called *tureletas*, and were made with corn, eggs, and *panela*. Possibly they were a village specialty, for we found them nowhere else.

After the meal the natives kept talking among themselves about a bath and soap. Since we had spent most of the preceding night and half the day soaking in the lagoon, we were puzzled; our clothes and our persons were clean. Then they explained that they were worried about the multitude of little caterpillar hairs that still stuck to our skins. If the "hairs of the little worms" were not promptly removed, they said, our skins would rot away, and we would die. They never entered the *cerrado* because of these worms; no, not even for one hundred pesos would they go ten feet. They finally proposed that we allow them to give us a bath.

The women led Ginger in one direction, while the men took me to another part of the lagoon. Then with a great deal of merriment (not shared by us) they proceeded to give us a scrubdown that we will remember to the end of our days. A tar-and-feathering would be preferable any day. But this was not all. There was more whispered conversation. Several natives dashed away and returned, after which an old man motioned me to follow him.

He led me to a hut where an olla filled with some peculiar, evil-smelling liquid simmered over the fire and asked me to remove my clothes. "Oh, Lord," I groaned, "what's coming now?" Dipping his hands in the olla, he smeared me from head to toe with the mess, which seemed to be a mixture of coco-nut oil and herbs; he even rubbed the stuff in my hair. I smelled like ten thousand polecats. When he had finished I reached for my clothes, but he shook his head. Washing was not enough, he said, the clothes had to be boiled to remove the hairs. He handed me a large sheet of handwoven cloth, which I wrapped round me as best I could. Draped in my Roman toga, I followed him back to Lencha's hut.

Ginger soon arrived outfitted in a similar rig. Without further delay we were ushered into a smaller hut and put to bed on a palm-leaf cot. For the first time in over a week we were free from the intolerable itching that had tormented us both night and day. Almost instantly we dropped off to sleep.

When we awakened the next morning the swelling had gone down, the itching had subsided, and we were fairly comfortable. Clean native clothes were laid out beside the cot. For the second time we owed our lives, perhaps, to native care and medication.

Our presence was a fine excuse for a fiesta; and we spent the day in a round of feasting, drinking, and conversation. We were infinitely in the villagers' debt, yet they never made us feel the slightest trace of obligation. One of the women had a few yards of blue cloth, and wanted Ginger to show her how to make a dress for her seven-year-old daughter "such as the little girls in your country wear." Ginger was, of course, delighted to be of some service. The garment when finished had a full skirt gathered on to a short yoke, with puffed sleeves, and made an enormous hit.

In the course of the day I made the usual inquiries about the country to the south, and was relieved to find that the open lagoon extended down to Soconusco Bar. Near the bar, they said, was the great house of a wealthy German, a very rich man, who owned a boat with an engine in it. I asked what his business was, and why he lived there, but was told that he had no business; he was just a very rich man who had come to this country and built a great house with many rooms in it. He was a very good friend to all the natives in the district. "By all means," they told me, "you should stop for a few days and visit this man; he will be very glad to see you." From the natives' description of the German's establishment, we had visions of a castle among palm trees, set between the lagoon and the sea; a romantic retreat for some man who wanted to get away from the world.

The next day we left the village, eager to meet the *El Señor Alemán* of whom the natives talked so much. Discovering that the fifteen different directions we had been given for reaching his place were all of them hopelessly wrong, we stopped at a small *rancheria* for further guidance. Yes, certainly the *Alemán* lived near by. You took three turns to the right, and two to the left, and ——

"We'd better follow our noses," I said to Ginger when we had thanked our informants.

We came to an old fifteen-foot cabin cruiser, sans bottom, lying on a mud bank; the engine sat forlornly to one side. Further on there was a landing made from a flattened palm bole, with several dugouts drawn up near by. Behind the beach there was a large, thatched house and many outbuildings. Everything looked neat and in exceptionally good order, and I suggested that we might be able to learn the German's whereabouts from these people. But Ginger believed that this might be his establishment.

"Why, it isn't anything like the place described to us," I objected. "What makes you think so?"

"Because the thatching is trimmed even at the lower edges. Did you ever see a native's house with a trimmed thatch?"

As a matter of fact I never had, but this was far from the sort of place I had been led to expect. Then we saw a man and a woman strolling down the palm-lined path towards the beach. We pulled in at the landing. It wouldn't do any harm to wait and inquire the way from them. As they came nearer we saw that they were dressed in native clothes. The woman was barefoot, her thick, blue-black hair bound round her head in a coronet. She was handsome and well-groomed, but indisputably a native. The tall thin man at her side, clad in home-made blue jeans, was also dark; his skin was a shade less swarthy perhaps, but this in itself was not unusual, since the native complexion varies from black to pale cream.

We exchanged greetings in Spanish. The man cocked his head to one side, surveying us with a quizzical expression for a moment or two, before he said in excellent English, "Hello, Vagabonds, it seems to me you ought to be able to speak English." We looked at him, speechless. Then we laughed and he laughed. "Come ashore," he invited, "you look hot and tired."

We introduced ourselves. He had heard of us through the natives, he said. His name was Sebastiano, and he presented his wife, Elena. Just who he was, we were not certain, but he evidently was not the *El Señor Alemán* that we had started out to find. Since it seemed less than tactful to bombard him with questions about some one else the moment we arrived, we postponed inquiries about the German for the time being.

Our host directed us to a tin sink with faucets, where we washed ourselves, then seated us in comfortable chairs made from saplings and woven rawhide on the wide veranda. His wife appeared with big glasses of cool lemonade.

Sebastiano appeared to be perhaps forty-five; his manners were attractive and he was obviously a gentleman. Since he seemed interested in our journey, we told him something of its adventures; and how much we had grown to like Mexico. He also loved it, he said; and had made his home in Mexico since leaving Germany. So he was *El Señor Alemán*. Somehow we had pictured the elusive German as being big and blond.

We stayed with Sebastiano and Elena for two weeks; but we never learnt the story—if there was a story—of why he had come to this far country to lose himself among the lagoons of Chiapas. He had certainly picked an ideal spot and he had made the most of it. His home was built on a narrow arm of land with the ocean and the lagoon on the east and west, the jungle on the north and south.

The main building was two hundred feet in length (little wonder that it had seemed immense to the natives), and was divided into two parts by a wide corridor. One half of the house Sebastiano retained for his own use. In this enormous room, he kept his books and personal belongings; it was furnished with a big table, a desk, two beds of woven rawhide on frames, and chairs; and in addition it contained an altar and a much prized hand-cranked sewing machine. The other side of the house was partitioned off by cloth screens into four small guest rooms; these were furnished with a few shelves, chairs, and beds of woven rawhide. The floors were made of hand-hewn planks; and the sides of the house were partially boarded to a height of eight feet; above the boards, the walls were of lattice work to insure ventilation. Everything was in spotless order.

The kitchen and dining room, in a separate building, were equipped with several stoves, one for the making of tortillas only, and a round mud oven, about four feet high. The entire establishment was a unique combination of native tools and methods and European ingenuity. There were many labour-saving devices, also comfortable worktables, shelves, screened coolers, a sink with running water, and a big dining table and benches.

The water was supplied from a deep, rocked-in well equipped with a hand winch for bringing up the buckets. Above the well was a large tank, which Sebastiano filled with water every morning with the aid of a hand pump. This tank provided the running water for the house and the kitchen. Near the well, there was a small outbuilding containing a shower bath and a wooden laundry tub.

With German thoroughness Sebastiano had constructed another building which was sometimes used as a guest house, but whose real purpose was to provide them with shelter in the event that the big house should burn, or be shaken down by an earthquake. He also had a fine workshop with a forge, a lathe, many tools, and other equipment.

He had by no means "gone native," even though he had married a native woman and in all probability had no contacts with Europeans from one year to the next. He was clean shaven, and dressed himself in fresh clothes each afternoon. During the cooler part of the day he was busy. Round noon he took a short siesta.

He had a few cattle, and owned a salt works, worked by his wife's brother. There was a well-kept vegetable garden, sufficient for their own use, and a fine grove of coco-nut palms and banana trees. He said the near-by jungle was full of game, and the lagoon of fish. A few miles away, on the same lagoon, at the village of Las Palmas, supplies not produced on his own place could be obtained in exchange for salt, coco-nuts, and cattle. Sebastiano had certainly chosen well.

During our stay here we took advantage of the place's facilities to put our badly damaged equipment in shape. Sebastiano helped me paint and repair the canoe. He also went with me to Las Palmas to have our papers signed.

Elena, who was a wonderful cook, taught Ginger many of her famed recipes and Ginger in return gave her some "helpful household hints." One thing I remember with amusement was Ginger's attempt to instruct Elena in the rudiments of geography. "The world is round," said Ginger. Elena was polite, but dubious; and intimated that such an equivocal statement should be backed up by proof. So Ginger made some drawings of a sphere. These left Elena unmoved. All the evidence pointed to the fact that it was flat, she said.

When Ginger told Sebastiano of the incident he shrugged and laughed. "Ach," he said, "I have tried many times and it is hopeless, but perhaps it is just as well. Elena knows the things that are necessary to make her a good and happy woman; for her it is enough. I doubt if our kind of knowledge would be of any use to her. I no longer try to change her views. For intellectual companionship I have my books."

As the time neared for us to leave, Sebastiano tried to dissuade us. He was childless, and there was no one to inherit his possessions. Why not remain? We could all be happy, and there was enough for everyone. Eventually, all that he had would be ours. We regretfully refused, for we had set our minds on going to Panama.

But it was easier to make the decision to leave than to execute it. Day after day we tried without success to go through the breakers. Everything seemed against us. A storm blew up. The change of the moon came, and the ground swells were huge. Then the tides were wrong. We wanted to reach Champerico, Guatemala, in one day's jump by taking off at daylight. Eventually we decided to leave at low tide no matter what the hour. Each day the weather permitted we took the canoe out to the breaker line; and each day we would spill, come back, unload, and wait for the next day.

The day before my birthday we packed up as usual and went out into the surf. The breakers were high, but we hoped to get out during the calm spell. We were riding close to the beach, gradually edging out into the foaming water, while we waited for the opportunity to get through. Sebastiano was in swimming. He had taken hold of the canoe's stern, preparatory to shoving us off. Suddenly he was torn loose. Ginger looked back and saw him swimming inshore. Again we focussed our attention seaward, watching the breakers. Then we saw Sebastiano sweep past us, carried out by the rip tide, his face white and strained. We worked the canoe over to him and he clutched at its slippery side, but there was no place for him to take hold; and before we could throw him a rope, a descending sea washed him away. Again we paddled out to him. This time, he grabbed my paddle, and in so doing swung the canoe round broadside to a crashing sea; the paddle was jerked loose from his hand by the breaker that hurled the *Vagabunda* shoreward. By what miracle the boat failed to capsize, spilling us both into the rip tide, I will never know.

After what seemed an infinity, we straightened out the canoe, and again started towards him. He was almost exhausted. For ten minutes we fought to reach each other, and each time that we seemed on the verge of success, we'd lose him. His stamina and nerve in the face of death were wonderful; his presence of mind never failed him. At last we got him round to the stern, where he had some protection against the swirling waters, and headed for shore as fast as we could. Twice again the breakers washed him off before we made the beach. His only comment, as he staggered shorewards through the shallow water, was a beautifully guttural "Ach!"

But Elena, who had been having hysterics on the beach all this while, made up for Sebastiano's lack of emotional display; she alternately hugged and kissed all three of us. "*Gracias a Dios! Maria Santissima,*" she exclaimed over and over. Her thanks to heaven were quickly followed by "*Voy hacer una fiesta.*" ("I am going to have a fiesta.")

The wind had increased and, needless to say, we had lost all desire for any more travelling that day. So we followed Elena and Sebastiano back to the house, where Elena went to work at once on her preparations for a fiesta. Her party was to serve two purposes, she said: the first, to celebrate Sebastiano's escape; the other, my birthday. She immediately dispatched her brother to Las Palmas for supplies, and to invite the populace. Gallons of corn for the making of tortillas and tamales were put on to boil.

At 3 A.M. the next morning Elena, her sister-in-law, Consuelo, and Ginger began the business of grinding corn on the *metate* into *masa* for the tamales.

These tamales were not like the so-called tamale with which Americans regale themselves. The American version is made with corn meal—ground dried corn. The Mexican tamale is prepared from corn that has first been boiled in strong lye water to remove the husks, and ground while moist; this is called *masa*, and is different both in texture and flavour from corn meal. Tamales, made as the Mexicans make them, require time and skill, and are not a common article of diet, but are served to celebrate extraordinary occasions.

While the *masa* was being ground, Elena went to work on the tamale filling, which she prepared from finely chopped meat, cloves, garlic, chilis and marjoram, boiled and thickened with a little *masa*. Then the rest of the ground *masa* was mixed with turtle oil and made into a soft dough. The women placed a handful of this dough on a banana leaf held in their left hand and pressed it with their right hand into a flattened ball, with a depression in its centre for the filling. The banana leaf was then rolled lengthwise (like a jelly roll) and the ends turned back. The finished tamales were placed, folded side down, in huge ollas, and these in turn were set on tripods of rocks, with a small fire underneath each one, to steam slowly for hours.

By the time the tamales were finished, several women arrived from Las Palmas and set to work making a punch called *mistela*. Into a large olla they poured a powerful native liquor made from sugar cane; to this they added a syrup made from *panela*, a very strong cinnamon tea, and anise flavouring. The result was good—and potent.

These details I learnt from Ginger, who volunteered the further information that as the women compounded the brew, Elena frequently sampled it, and long before the party officially opened she had gotten off to a flying start. Elena was a big woman, full of fun and vitality.

While the women were engaged in the kitchen, we were busy in the yard. Water was sprinkled over the ground to lay the dust. Benches were brought out; and bunches of bananas hung up within easy reach. Quantities of drinking coco-nuts were cut down, and piled beside a cutting block, with a machete near-by for the convenience of the thirsty.

In the afternoon boatloads of people began arriving from Las Palmas and neighbouring *ranchitos*. They laughed, chatted, and felicitated me. Was it not my birthday—*my Dia de Santo?*

Suddenly a shout went up—"*Ya viene! Ya viene!*" Everybody ran down to the shore. "*Ya viene la marimba!*—Here comes the marimba!" A big dugout poled to the landing. A dozen pairs of hands carefully brought the big wooden instrument ashore. No fiesta in this part of Mexico would be complete without this one-piece, four-man orchestra. When it had been set up in the corridor of the house the musicians struck up a lively tune and everyone shouted, "*Viva* Danielito! *Viva* Sebastiano!"

While this was going on, Elena took Ginger to the big house, where they arranged the altar. "*Quando viene el Santo,*" Elena kept saying. ("Wait until the Saint comes.") She laughed mysteriously when Ginger questioned her. "Wait and see," she said. On a table beside the altar she laid out many tall, home-made candles, and placed beside them a box of long, thin, hand-made cigarettes.

It was now dusk. The women's household tasks finished, they dressed themselves in their fiesta clothes and joined the party. There were at least a hundred people present; and never have I seen such a display of joyous, carefree spirit. Suddenly a shout went up from the strollers nearest the beach. "*Ya viene! Ya viene!*" Elena gathered the women together, and to each of them she gave a candle. We all hurried down to the water.

There, I saw one of the prettiest sights I can remember. Five canoes, filled with natives holding lighted candles, floated silently down the palm-lined lagoon. Then the occupants of the canoes began to sing a haunting, minor melody and the crowd on shore quieted. Now the boats drew nearer. We could see that the largest canoe, flanked on either side by two small canoes, was the most brilliantly illuminated. The candles seemed to surround some object amidship.

A profound hush fell over the crowd as the canoes approached the landing, their crews still singing in muted voices. "Ah, ah," the waiting people breathed, "*El Santo.*" A glass box, wreathed in flowers, was carefully and reverently handed ashore; it contained a picture. Then the women, holding lighted candles high above their heads, formed a procession behind it. It was a never-to-be-forgotten sight—those graceful, barefoot women walking like queens behind their Santo, their full skirts swaying, their brown faces illuminated by the flickering candlelight.

The men took no part in the procession, nor did they enter the house, where the *Santo* was placed before the altar. Ginger, of course, was in the procession; and from her I learnt what took place there.

The *Santo*, she said, was called the *Corazon de Jesús* (Heart of Jesus) and was intended to typify on this occasion the "brave hearts" of Sebastiano and the rescue party. After it had been placed before the altar, the candles were blown out; and Elena passed around the cigarettes. While the women sat and smoked in silence, the marimba played a chantlike melody. Then tiny *jicaras* containing a few drops of the *mistela* were handed about. The women sipped the drinks, finished the cigarettes, and rejoined the men. With that, Elena announced, the fiesta was officially opened.

Now the marimba swung into a faster beat, and dancing became general. Ginger and I stood on the side lines for a few minutes, watching. Picturesque is an overworked word, but it was never used with more justification than to describe the scene before us. The fire lit the dark foliage and the dancing figures. From time to time, her white teeth gleaming, her full skirts swirling, some girl overcome with the intoxication of the music would break away from her partner's arms in a breath-taking solo. And above the indescribable lilt of the marimba, we could hear the boom of the surf.

By eleven o'clock everyone was hilarious and Elena decided that it was time to serve supper. Banana leaves were cut into squares for use as plates; and on these were placed the delicious tamales, fried rice, fried beans, baked plantains, and other foods. We ate in the kitchen with Sebastiano and a few of his personal friends, sharing a bottle of liquor he had saved for his own consumption, and for his supper guests.

Round four in the morning Sebastiano, Ginger, and I decided we could do with some sleep; it had been twenty-five hours since we had last been to bed. Ginger and I turned into the canoe—just in case some playful native should decide to launch it. But with people coming and going, it was difficult to sleep, and at seven o'clock we went back to the house. The party was still going strong; thirty or more of the hardier guests remained. Elena, who had been up and busy since three o'clock the preceding day, was still the liveliest and gayest of the lot.

Finally just the four of us were left. During breakfast we congratulated Elena on her party, and invited a good, old-fashioned razzing. Said Elena, "Frail people, these gringos. A few drinks, a little dancing, and they are finished—they must sleep. Of what use is it to give them a party? They will not be there to enjoy it." She thoroughly enjoyed herself teasing us. And not until siesta time did she stop cleaning and restoring the house to order; then she slept for several hours. What a woman! She was middle-aged, and we could only wonder what she must have been like at twenty. We asked Sebastiano, who just smiled reminiscently. Elena had been a fine girl, he said.

The following day we took the canoe over to the lagoon side, and loaded it, preparatory to sailing down to Soconusco Bar, two miles south. It seemed barely possible that we might have better luck getting out the bar than we had had trying to go through the breakers on the open ocean.

Sebastiano and Elena stood on the beach and waved good-bye. We left them as we had first seen them—standing together under the palms. Not only because we were parting from friends were we heavy-hearted—we were leaving Mexico as well. We had long since overstayed our leave. Two gay, colourful, exciting and adventurous years had slipped by; and now that they were gone, how short they seemed! Mexico had become another homeland, and some day we hoped to return to its warm, friendly, and hospitable people.

"*Adios, amigos, que le vaya bien. Viva Mexico!*"

Chapter Twenty-five

GUATEMALA TO COSTA RICA

THE port of Champerico is a roadstead: it has no protected harbour. Boats wishing to take on or discharge cargo at this port must anchor off the end of a heavy pier built out into the ocean, well beyond the breaker line. Lighters ferry the cargo between the ships and the pier, where it is transferred to and from the lighters by travelling cranes.

A small freighter was anchored off the port when we arrived. We circled round the vessel, the *Salvador*, one of the British-owned Pacific Steam Navigation Company's boats. Its crew waved to us, and we returned their gay greetings. Later on the presence of the *Salvador* turned out to be a piece of real luck for us.

We paddled over to the pier, more than a little anxious about our reception. With the exception of our Seaman's Protection Certificates, we had no papers for Guatemala or for any of the countries south of Mexico. We hoisted a "protest" flag, a white rag on the end of the harpoon shaft stuck in the mast seat. According to maritime law, a ship in need of supplies, or repairs, may by hoisting a "protest" flag, enter any port without the payment of port charges. However, when a ship does enter under "protest," the decision as to what shall be done with the vessel rests with the Port Captain. Though he cannot refuse a ship water, food, or emergency repairs, he can refuse to permit the crew to go ashore.

We pulled up beside a lighter unloading cargo and informed the superintendent of the pier that we wished to speak to the Port Captain. After an hour's wait, a delegation of officials arrived. The two dozen soldiers who were guarding the pier snapped to attention. The officials began shouting to us, but we were unable to understand them because of the roar of the ground swells that churned about the pilings. The Port Captain finally grew tired of shouting. A crane swung over our heads which lowered him down to the lighter in a passenger chair. All passengers embarking or disembarking at Champerico must use the chair to gain the pier or the lighter. He stumbled his way across the lighter and glared at us. "What is it that you want?" he demanded.

"We wish to enter your port," I answered politely.

"You have papers?"

"Of course, Señor *Capitán*," I replied, handing him the papers we had used when travelling down the coast of Mexico. Actually, these papers weren't worth anything in Guatemala except as identification, still you never could tell. Many of the port officials who had been unable to read had nevertheless been highly impressed by the official seals and stamps on the documents. This fellow could read, however, and he read every word of every paper. When he had finished, without further speech, he walked to his travelling chair, climbed in, and was hoisted up to the pier.

Ginger gave me a sickly grin. "Now we are stuck. That fellow's taken all our papers."

The boom swung out and the chair was lowered again, this time with two uniformed guards as passengers. They came over and one of them started to step into the canoe. "Wait a minute," I protested. "What's the idea?"

"You two," he said brusquely, "are to go up on the pier. I am detailed to guard your boat."

We climbed into the chair and were hoisted up on the pier. The guard untied the *Vagabunda* and started paddling toward one of the lighters. When we stepped out of the chair, two guards ranged themselves on each side of us, informing us that we were under arrest. The Captain and his friends had departed.

One of the guards tugged at our shore clothes bag, which Ginger held firmly clasped under one arm. "What have you there?" he growled. Ginger meekly explained. "I must see them," he insisted. To her great embarrassment he drew out every single item of her clothing and mine, and subjected each piece to the closest scrutiny. Luckily, we had left our cigarette lighters in the canoe, for they are contraband in Guatemala, where matches are a government monopoly. After considerable persuasion on our part, and stubborn resistance on theirs, we were finally allowed to seclude ourselves for a few minutes in a small room to one side of the pier, where we changed into our shore clothes.

We waited on that pier all day. No one except the guards and the foreman of the pier came near us. Pedro Jauriqui, the foreman, seemed to be the only friend we had in the whole of Guatemala; he divided his lunch with us, and found a Guatemalan magazine for us to read. About three o'clock I got "riled," and demanded to see the Port Captain. A guard, dispatched to his office, soon returned with the good news that the Captain was asleep. He pointed out that of course it was out of the question to disturb His Excellency's siesta, because of two forgotten gringos cooking in the Guatemalan sun.

About five o'clock things began to pick up a bit. An officer made two trips to the *Salvador* and back. When he returned from the second trip, he stopped by the lighter and took the canoe in tow. The poor guard, who had been assigned to watch it, had also been allowed to simmer in the hot sun all day; but he wore a broad grin as the canoe was pulled up alongside of the lighter below the pier.

To our unspeakable delight the lieutenant in charge informed us that the captain of the *Salvador* had asked the Port Captain's permission, which had been granted, to take us aboard his ship for the night. We were as pleased as children as we paddled the *Vagabunda* towards the freighter, whose crew received us with open arms.

The officers and crew of the *Salvador* were a noteworthy exception to many crews aboard small boats. An air of amiability and friendliness from the Captain down pervaded the ship; it was apparent that they liked each other and their jobs. Smart, clean-cut young Britishers, they did their work efficiently, and without friction. The *Salvador* was a combined passenger and cargo boat, touching at all the Central American ports between Cristóbal, C.Z., and Champerico. She was a trim little craft with all her paint work clean and her bright work polished.

Everyone took a great interest in our trip and in the canoe, and suggested that the *Vagabunda* be hoisted aboard for a closer inspection. When they saw the condition of the little craft—for we had had some tough sailing after leaving Sebastiano's—the whole gang immediately set to work repairing and painting her. Two coats of quick-drying paint that night, and one the following morning, did wonders for her weatherbeaten canvas.

Well-fed, rested, and with our morale miraculously restored, we paddled back to the pier the following morning. There we found that the Grace Line representative, Mr. F. C. B. Close, had also come to our rescue, and that we were to be allowed to go ashore and see the Port Captain. Since the Grace Line owns most of Champerico, Mr. Close's word carried weight with the Guatemalan officials. We had no idea as to what lay in store for us as we followed a uniformed guard, lugging a gun several sizes too big for him, to the Captain's office. The Captain greeted us cordially, and invited us into the living quarters adjacent to his office. After presenting his wife, official formalities were dropped, and for the duration of our stay in Champerico we were treated with courtesy by the authorities.

The Captain explained the reason for our cool reception. It seems that most of the people who start out to see the world in small boats, and to live the life of Riley in the tropics, manage to run out of money and everything else by the time they hit the Central American ports. A few days before our arrival, a small ship had entered under "protest," and had demanded food, water, and even ice, which the crew had no money to pay for. There are also a number of tramps sailing along the coast, who attempt to beg supplies at every port they enter. Little wonder that the port authorities are slightly reluctant to welcome small boats. The *Salvador* captain's explanation that we had money to pay for anything we needed changed our status at once. When we were ready to leave, we were given a letter to the officials of San José, Guatemala.

San José is one of the larger West Coast tourist ports where the American tourist has the reputation of being a sucker. The moment we went

Guatemala to Costa Rica

into a restaurant, prices were boosted; coffee automatically became worth ten cents a cup, and rolls five cents each; in contrast to the regular price of four cups of coffee and all the bread you want for three cents gold (American money).

However, when one considers what the natives have to put up with from the tourists, the charges do not seem half enough. The British Consul's wife, Mrs. Summerhayes, told Ginger of a typical experience she had with a group of travelling Americans. She had gone to market with her Guatemalan maid. The maid placed the big market basket under a tree beside her mistress, while she went off to buy meat. Meanwhile a party of American tourists came along who were "doing" the market. They were not only rude, but unobservant as well, for Mrs. Summerhayes is tall, slender, and definitely English. The tourists stopped and looked at her. "She looks fairly clean, but you never can tell, perhaps it's only on the outside," one of them commented. "Yes," agreed another, "she may be dreadfully dirty underneath." All this time they were poking about among the contents of her market basket, with never a "by your leave"—no doubt acquiring material for a club paper on "Life in Guatemala." The Consul's wife was so dumbfounded that she lost her voice and just stood there. At that moment the Grace Line factor came by, and guessing from Mrs. Summerhayes' outraged expression what was happening, broke through the ring of tourists, picked up the market basket, and asked after her health and that of the British Consul. That finished the snoopers; they melted away very quickly, but without a word of apology. Imagine the effect of such a manœuvre on a Guatemalan lady, who might quite as easily have been the victim of their rudeness as Mrs. Summerhayes. It would take more than the pronouncement of the head of the United States to make her feel that North Americans were "good neighbours"—or good for anything!

Another incident was related to us by an American, who owns a ranch some distance out of San José. Guatemala is his home and he has adapted himself to the country, dressing in native costume when among the natives. He comes into town once a week to visit the Summerhaye's, the Grace Line factor, and other Europeans. He always rides into town wearing his *vaquero* dress, and changes later into European clothes. He came in one day for his usual week-end while a tourist boat was in port. A picturesque figure in his *vaquero* costume, he immediately attracted the attention of the visitors, who gathered round him, and through their interpreter, asked permission to take his picture. The interpreter spoke to the young man in Spanish, who replied in the same language, "*Si, como no*" ("Sure, why not"). During the business of focussing the cameras, posing the subject, and so forth, the camera clickers talked among themselves. One woman protested to another, why waste time in taking a picture of the "dirty greaser"? An animal lover among them was sure that he must be cruel to his horses, she had "heard . . ." Some one else was sure that he wasn't too clean. (Cleanliness seems to be a pathological obsession with the tourists—and their only standard of virtue.)

When the American had had enough of it, he spoke to the interpreter, who in turn informed the crowd that the Guatemalan cowboy would like to borrow one of their cameras. A roar of protest went up at this. What did he want to borrow a camera for? The tanned young "cowboy" grinned as he answered his interrogators in good Americanese, "Oh, I'd just like to take a picture of the biggest bunch of goddamned fools I've ever seen!"

In the course of the next few weeks we travelled down the coast from port to port along the straight sand beaches of Guatemala, El Salvador, and Nicaragua. The breakers were huge and travelling was difficult. In the ports we missed the easy informality and cordiality that characterized life in Mexico. The smaller the country, the more soldiers were in evidence. All the piers were patrolled by heavily armed guards. In all the towns there were large garrisons of soldiers, and it was impossible to walk along the streets without seeing many of them. One felt that martial law was in force. Many of the soldiers carried machine guns or automatic rifles, and their officers were weighted down with heavy forty-fives. The officials were sticklers for regulations, and exceedingly suspicious of travellers. In most places the authorities were civil, but seldom cordial.

En route to Corinto, Nicaragua, we ran into a storm; the wind was almost hurricane strength, and the canoe took an awful beating. By the time we reached Cardon Channel outside Corinto, she was badly battered and leaking. Pulling in behind Cardon Island, which forms one side of Corinto harbour, we washed and changed into our shore clothes before paddling on to the dock at Corinto. The canoe was in bad shape, so we hoisted both our "protest" and quarantine flags. Officers soon arrived, who motioned us away from the pier. We waited half an hour for the Port Captain, who instructed us to come round to the landing. We pulled round to the small bay back of the dock, but as we started to land, the Captain motioned us away from the steps.

Eventually an officer came down the steps, and asked to see our papers. After much hesitation and conferring among themselves, the port officials finally decided that we should be given permission to land, although they were anything but enthusiastic.

American adventurers are no novelty in Corinto. The town was long occupied by the United States marines, and most of the natives speak a few words of English. Americans seem to be generally disliked; and from the town's attitude towards us we might have been poison. Whether this attitude is entirely due to contact with American military forces is hard to say. The average native reminded us of a stick of dynamite, walking round while waiting to explode.

We spent ten days in Corinto repairing the boat. At first we were unable to find a place to stay; the Nicaraguans would have none of us, and we camped on the edge of the jungle. Then we passed by a sailboat under construction on the beach; and being interested in small boats, went over to look at it. A big, rawboned white man was working away. We introduced ourselves. He was a Dane named Charley Neilson, who was engaged in the boat-building business. He lived with his father and one unmarried brother in a wing of the ramshackle marine barracks. When we told him about the condition of the *Vagabunda*, he at once offered us his tools and such materials as we needed. The old barracks was all but uninhabitable, so he suggested that we use a twenty-foot sloop that was pulled up on the beach, resting on stilts.

We had tried to purchase paint and other materials in Corinto, but they were either not to be had, or we were asked to pay about ten times the usual price for them. Consequently we were more than glad to offer the Neilsons payment for the things we needed, but they would not accept money. Then Ginger found that they had been eating in a restaurant where they got nothing but corn, beans, and rice. From then on she took charge of the culinary arrangements. Every day she went to the market for fresh fruits and vegetables, which she converted into some of the delicious recipes that she had developed on the trail. The men were delighted.

At first Ginger had a difficult time in the *mercado*. All the natives were out to skin the whites, and prices bounded sky-high the moment she appeared. But a big, fat woman, invariably dressed in black despite the heat, took a liking to her, and helped her out with the buying. Ginger would tell her what she wanted, and the woman would go round to the various vendors, haggling until she brought the price down to its customary level. But on the day the tourist boats appeared most of the natives went down to the pier with their produce; and then no one in Corinto could buy avocados and other fruit except at gringo tourist prices. Ginger went down to the dock on one occasion, hoping to buy some avocados, since none remained in the *mercado*. There she found the native women that she knew selling them on the sidewalk. She asked the price of the fruit. They were twenty-five *centavos* (ten cents gold) today, she was informed. "But," she protested, "you sell them to me every day for three or four *centavos*." Yes, and they sold them to her gladly at that price, the women answered; but today the tourist boat was in, and the price was what the tourists would pay—twenty-five *centavos*.

The *Salvador* came into port while we were in Corinto, and we had a reunion with Captain Grant and the crew that lasted nearly all night. Then the Port Captain decided that we might be nice people, so he gave a cocktail party for us at which we met and really got to know the officials. They stretched a point and permitted us to stay in port after the boat was repaired until the weather became calm enough to travel. The long jump from Corinto to San Juan del Sur worried us considerably, for the wind and weather had been consistently bad for days.

At last our preparations were complete. We left at three c'clock one afternoon, hoping with luck, to arrive at our destination round eleven o'clock the next day. If the weather ran true to form it would give us an all-night sail with a following wind. The high wind generally died down to a stiff breeze round six or seven o'clock in the evening. We were willing to battle heavy seas during the late afternoon to gain additional headway.

The start was not auspicious. To save about three miles, we took a short cut out of the harbour, going out what is known as False Channel. The tide was going out and the current was strong. Occasional whirlpools, and the breakers which extended almost completely across the narrow channel, nearly threw us on the rocks several times.

We reached the ocean and faced the heavier seas with a feeling of apprehension. This section of coast, between Corinto and Cape Elena to the south of San Juan del Sur, is occasionally visited by strong gales, known locally as *papagayos*. They are similar to the "chubascos" of the Gulf of California, but of longer duration. Away from the land, the wind was blowing directly up the coast, with very short, capping seas. We were soon wet with spray, and the cockpit had to be continually bailed out. Before sundown the seas were so high that it was impossible to open the cockpit to get at the canteens and food. The salt spray made us very thirsty.

By sundown we had made only eight miles, and the wind, instead of decreasing, was increasing. We debated the situation. Should we return to Corinto, while we could still see to navigate the channel; or take a chance on the wind going down, as it had every day for the past two weeks? We decided to stick it out a while longer.

But as the sun disappeared, the wind increased in fury. Our retreat cut off, there was nothing to do but go on. We were still hopeful that the wind was having one last fling before settling down as usual. But by eight o'clock it was stronger than ever. The *Vagabunda* reeled under the impact of the pounding seas; we could feel her bottom spring each time a big wave smacked us; several times she almost turned over. We took a double reef in the sail, and rigged life lines. Then to forestall being swept away by the furious seas, we lashed ourselves down. Nothing in our long battle with storms—not even the storm off Cape San Lucas—had prepared us for the fury of this one. A great wave would pick us up, toss the canoe high into the air, and before she had time to hit the water, another sea would come up to meet her, with such a tremendous smack that we could feel her bottom buckle. These seas were so high that we could not see the lighthouse behind us.

At nine o'clock the wind was blowing a gale, and there was nothing we could do to meet it. It was impossible to point into the wind, because the canoe would ride out over the seas to crash down with tremendous force

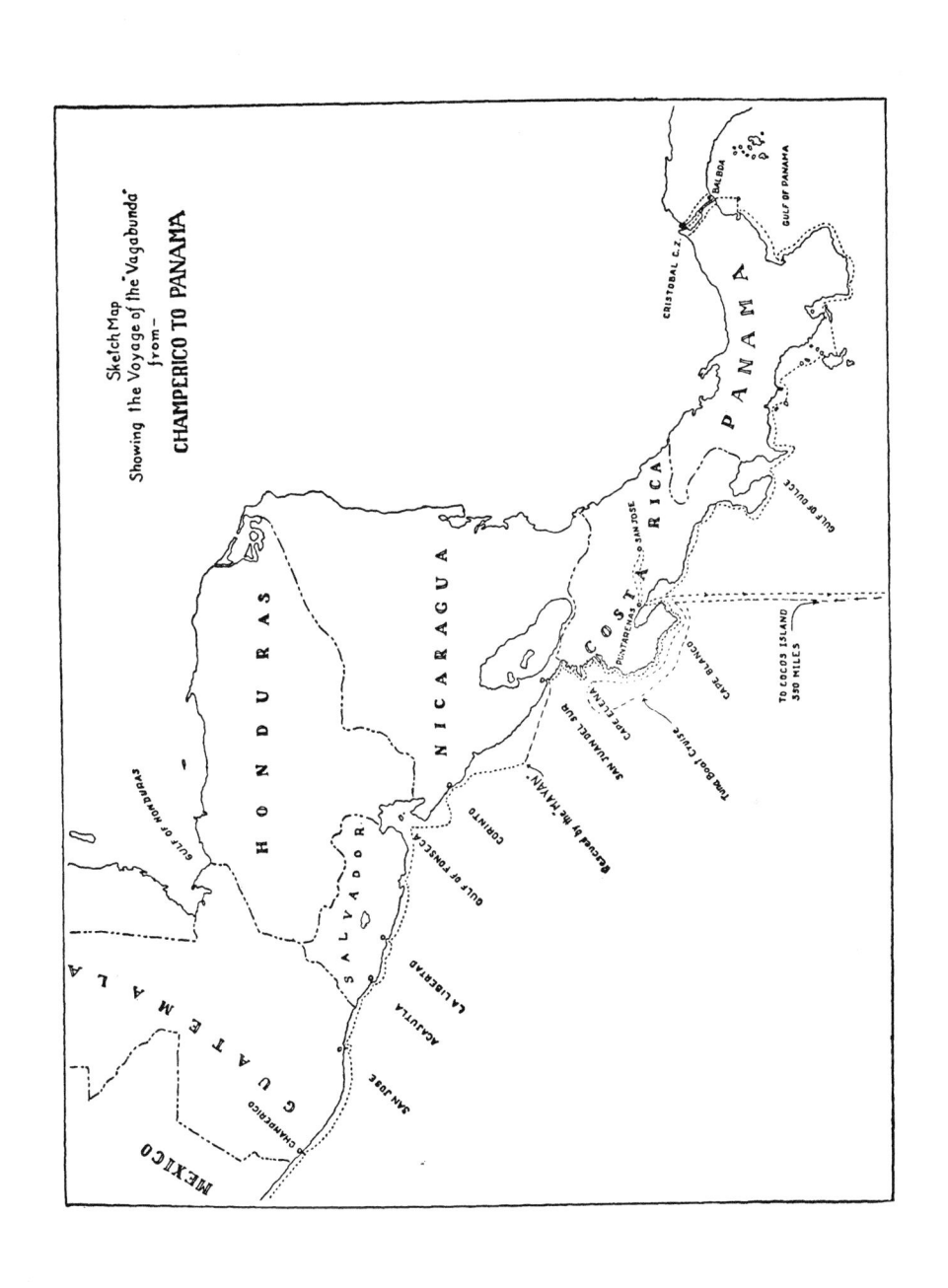

into the trough; nor was it possible to ease off, because seas hitting us on the beam would turn the boat over. Then great, black, monstrous waves began rolling in towards us. We managed to get past the first one safely, but as the second caught us, and the canoe rode high on its crest, its cap hit her so hard that it threw her into the air. She smacked the water with a terrific wallop; we could hear the crackle of splintering wood. A third sea struck her; again that ominous rending sound.

To get to shore while we still had something to ride on was our only purpose now. An attempt to turn towards the coast proved disastrous; the great waves tossed the canoe high into the air; the following seas hit her on the beam. We skidded sideways and only saved ourselves from capsizing by leaning far over on the windward gunwale. It took all my strength on the steering oar to keep the canoe going straight. We couldn't even shape a course that would permit us to pile up in the breakers. Since we couldn't sail against the wind, and couldn't run before it, we had to fight it out. Another series of big seas came along; and again the canoe took a beating to the tune of splintering wood. Then came the most hair-raising sound of all—ripping canvas. "There goes the bottom," Ginger shouted. "We're going to sink."

"Stay with the boat," I shouted back. "Our still cans will keep us afloat."

Another hissing roller struck the canoe, and part of the gunwale gave way. The deck sagged and buckled under the impact of the following wave. Again we heard the sound of splintering wood and ripping canvas. The *Vagabunda* was at last done for—and so were we.

"Dan!" Ginger screamed. "Look out!" I turned to see a great, black hull almost on top of us; its knife-edge headed straight for the middle of the canoe. High above us, lights were swinging in an arc; and for a moment I thought they were signalling to us, but the boat plunged steadily on. We swung round in a desperate attempt to get away from that bow. The wind struck the sail and ripped it from the mast. Ginger fought to get the whipping canvas under control, while I fought to swing the water-logged canoe round. The irony of being sunk by the one thing that could save us, I thought, as Ginger grabbed a paddle and aided in our frantic efforts to escape that charging mass of steel. A wave curled over our heads, smothering us in foam; the canoe grated and twisted from the impact.

Then from somewhere above us, a voice boomed through the scream of the wind, "For Chris' sake, quit playing tag and come aboard." A line arched over the *Vagabunda's* battered deck, and a searchlight bathed us in its ghostly glare. I grabbed the line and fastened it to the painter. We smacked against the lee side of the ship, out of the wind. A rope ladder rolled down her side, and as the canoe lifted on a wave, Ginger grabbed the ladder's ropes, and scrambled up the side. Willing hands pulled her over the rail. More ropes thudded on the canoe's deck, and I hurriedly fastened them to the ring bolts on the bow and stern. The canoe rose to another swell, and then hung suspended in the air, as a dozen men strained on the ropes that slowly lifted her up the side of the ship.

I scrambled up the ladder and joined Ginger on deck. She stamped her wet feet on the solid steel. "How does that feel?"

"Never felt anything better in my life," I said with hearty emphasis.

The crew surrounded us, all talking at once. Passengers lined the promenade decks above our heads. We seemed to be in a swirling world of voices. But neither one of us could say more than a few words in answer to the bombardment of questions. Then an officer came to our rescue and took us both by the arm. We trotted along meekly as he escorted us to first-class cabin Number 2. The door closed behind us. Bankrupt of energy and resource, we stood there in our dripping clothes, looking at each other. A steward entered with dry clothes, and a stiff drink of whisky apiece. He asked if we were hungry. We had both been ravenous round seven o'clock, but now the thought of food was nauseating; we shook our heads. He suggested tea. Ginger nodded vaguely. But we were sufficiently revived by the whisky, a hot shower, and clean clothes to enjoy the tea and sandwiches when they arrived.

After the meal we felt like new people. Our rapid recovery surprised us both, for it was not usual. It had often taken us days to overcome entirely the effects of some near-catastrophe. The difference this time was that we were not alone in some God-forsaken wilderness trying to pull ourselves together, but among hundreds of people. In the midst of our discussion there came a rap on the door. "Captain wants to see you," said a voice.

Up on the bridge we were met by a big, stern-faced, broad-shouldered man, who gruffly invited us to step into his cabin. I was well aware that we had undoubtedly been a considerable nuisance to the Captain of the *Mayan*, but I was hardly prepared for his unfriendly, brusque, accusing manner. "Do you know who that is?" he demanded, pointing to a picture standing on his desk.

My eyes followed his pointing finger, and looked into the smiling pictured face of a sweetheart of my high school and college days. "Why that's Marie Carruthers," I stammered, so flabbergasted I could hardly talk.

"No," corrected the Captain, "that is Marie Fischer, my wife." He grinned.

Then I remembered. I had heard that Marie had married the first officer of the ship that had taken her to New York about the time that Ginger and I were preparing for our trip. The first officer had evidently been promoted to captain. I held out my hand to meet Captain Fischer's and the three of us stood smiling at each other.

"I have been looking for you all along the coast," he said. "Marie and

I make our home in Panama; and every time I return to my home port, Cristóbal, she asks if I have seen you. Lucky we met tonight, wasn't it?"

We found out that the meeting was not as accidental as it had seemed at first. The *Mayan* had put in at Corinto, where Captain Fischer had learnt of our departure only a few hours previously. When he put to sea, he had posted extra lookouts. During the manœuvring of his ship, which had given us such a scare, he had been attempting to place the bow of his vessel between us and the wind, so that he could pick us up without stopping the boat. If he had stopped his engines in a storm of such magnitude, the ship would have swung round in the trough of the seas. This might have caused considerable damage aboard, besides endangering the passengers. The rescue could have been effected more easily had we not tried to get out of the *Mayan's* way.

Before turning in that night, we spread our soaked equipment out to dry in the engine room hatch, and then took a turn round the promenade deck to have a look at the weather. The ship was making slow progress against the gale. When the monstrous waves hit the *Mayan's* bow, the vessel would quiver from stem to stern and stand still. Recovering from the onslaught, she would shake herself free and plunge forward to meet the next charge. For our peace of mind, we tried hard not to think of what would have happened if Captain Fischer had not turned up in the nick of time.

The next morning the storm was still raging; and the ship was making very poor time. After breakfast we examined the canoe. Our fears of the preceding night had not been exaggerated; the *Vagabunda* looked like a total wreck. Six of her ribs were broken; one whole section directly forward of the cockpit was staved in; the gunwale on the starboard side was broken and torn loose; the stem had worked loose from its fastenings; and the siding was broken in a dozen places. The keel had sprung loose from her bottom. While we were wondering how to go about repairing the damage, the ship's carpenter worked his way through the crowd surrounding the canoe. Captain Fischer had instructed him to lend a hand, he said. With the aid of the carpenter and members of the crew, we began to replace the broken timbers.

The *Mayan* was due to arrive at San Juan del Sur at one-thirty that afternoon, five hours behind schedule. We were worried as to whether our presence aboard might not involve the Captain in difficulties, and suggested that he put us overside before the ship arrived in port. That was impossible, he said, until the wind went down, which might not happen for several days. He suggested instead that we accompany him to Panama and "cut out this damn gallivanting round in an eggshell." But from San Juan del Sur south, the coast is again a series of bays and inlets, and we wanted to explore them. The Captain then proposed that we remain aboard until the *Mayan* left San Juan del Sur; by then the canoe would be in fair shape.

The port officials who came aboard and examined our papers at San Juan del Sur were very friendly, and extended the facilities of the port to us for making further repairs on the canoe. By five o'clock the *Vagabunda* had been repaired sufficiently not to leak, and as the *Mayan* prepared to sail, we lowered her over the side.

We went to say good-bye to the carpenter, and found him busy in his shop laying out material. "I have gone over your canoe thoroughly," he said, "and here are the things you will need for a complete repair job." He had assembled paint, glue, screws, canvas, and wood—things that we might not be able to secure in San Juan del Sur.

In addition to the food and clothing that Captain Fischer and the crew thoughtfully provided, many of the passengers presented Ginger with gifts. The *Vagabunda* was well loaded when we paddled away from the *Mayan*.

After the *Mayan's* departure, we set out towards the pier, but the wind was so strong that finally a launch came out to assist us. Señor Carranza, manager of the All America Cable office, met us at the landing, and cordially invited us to be his guests while in San Juan del Sur.

A week later, when the canoe was again seaworthy, we loaded up and sailed south in high anticipation of what the coast of Costa Rica had in store for us. The *Vagabunda*, however, was never her old self again. She was warped and twisted out of shape, her trim lines gone for ever.

Our trip down the coast was all we anticipated—and more. We ran in and out of storms in the Gulf of Papagayo; explored islands, bays and inlets; visited great haciendas and small native villages. We hunted and camped along the "rich coast" that is Costa Rica. Looking back over our diaries, we find them replete with a hundred incidents of exciting days, kindly people, wind, and stormy weather.

Now the big moment was about to arrive. We were going to cross the Gulf of Nicoya to Puntarenas, Costa Rica. Puntarenas had been our principal destination since leaving Salina Cruz. We had planned to reach it the preceding year, and had instructed our families to send mail there. By now there should be enough letters to keep us busy for days. The weather was not auspicious, but we were in a predicament. This was Holy Week, and we either had to get to Puntarenas today or postpone our arrival until the following Monday. Tomorrow would be Good Friday; and besides the fact that the offices would be closed, it is considered extremely bad taste to travel on Good Friday. The observance of such matters may not seem important in Protestant countries, but they mean a lot in Catholic Central America.

Half-way across the gulf we stopped at Alcatraz Island to prepare for our entrance into port. Ginger went over our shore clothes; and we cleaned, dried, and oiled the gear. When everything was shipshape, we cut each other's hair, and otherwise made ourselves presentable. We planned on staying several days at least in Puntarenas, where we hoped to secure permission to visit Cocos Island. With our official papers handy, and our shore clothes ready to put on quickly, we set out attired in shorts for the crossing to the mainland.

The *Pilot Guide* warned against tide rips in the gulf, especially at the change of tide. The crossing gave us no reason to doubt the accuracy of this invaluable mariner's guide, for we encountered tide rips, wind, rocks, shoals, and breakers. Part of the way, the wind and current carried us along at a dangerous speed; the canoe became all but unmanageable, and we had to balance it much as one rides a surfboard. Finally we got across a bad stretch of shoal water, and could see Puntarenas ahead. We fairly flew towards the pier, the wind whistling as it blew us along. There seemed to be no place for us to land, for boats anchored out from the end of the pier were pitching with such violence that we could not tie up to any of them.

On the end of the pier a man signalled wildly to us, and then we could see that the pier was in the shape of an L. We sailed round it, entering the shelter behind the sea wall. The small crowd who had gathered to watch our landing found it hard to believe that we had crossed the gulf in the squall. For that matter, we did too, when we looked back at the pitching white water.

I looked up and down the pier for some sign of the customs guards who had been so conspicuous in all the other Central American ports, but none were in sight. "Where are your customs men?" I inquired.

"I am the customs man," answered a young fellow dressed in European clothes and a sea-going cap. "Come up on the pier," he invited.

"Not until we present our papers," I returned. "We are entering this port under 'protest.'"

"Oh, that won't be necessary," he said. "Tie up your boat near the ladder, and I'll take you to the Port Captain."

"What's this?" asked Ginger in English. "Some kind of a game? Every other place they've had a dozen guards ready and waiting until they could find a good excuse to throw us into gaol. It's mighty funny that there isn't anybody here but that fellow in the cap."

Then we saw a policeman, neatly attired in a spick-and-span uniform, leisurely approaching. As he drew near, I shouted up to him, "We have just come down the coast from Nicaragua, and we want to enter port. Where is the Port Captain?"

"Well, why don't you come ahead and enter, Señor? The Port Captain is in his office," the policeman replied.

We fully expected to be thrown into the local gaol for such a breach of etiquette as going ashore without a permit, but apparently we had to take the chance. This was an unprecedented reception for Central America, and we still suspected a trick. It would have taken the entire resources of the State Department plus presidential intervention to have gotten us out of the jam that would have resulted in Guatemala, Nicaragua, or El Salvador had we done such a thing.

The young fellow in the cap instructed the policeman to watch the canoe and see that it did not bump against the pilings, and then we started off to the Port Captain's office. On the way Ginger asked permission for us to step inside somewhere and change into our shore clothes. "Why not?" said the customs man. "You have your clothes in that bag?" We nodded, too thunderstruck for words—customs officials who hadn't searched us from stem to stern, shaken us upside down, and put us through the third degree! He showed us a little building on the pier. "You will find everything that you need, Señora—a wash basin, towels," he said amiably.

Having changed our clothes we followed our guide past the customs house on the end of the pier and up the street for several blocks to a green building. He ushered us into a room that looked like anything but a Port Captain's office to us. There were no soldiers at the door to snap to attention and salute, nor any officials dressed in gold braid and packing forty-fives. In the center of the pleasantly furnished room there was a large table, with big easy chairs placed round it. A smiling, middle-aged man in shirt-sleeves came forward, extending his hand. "Won't you be seated—and what will you have to drink?" he said in excellent English.

"Listen, Señor," I said, slightly irritated by my inability to get the so necessary formalities over with, "we have been trying for the last half hour to present our papers to the port officials." I went on to tell him that we hadn't passed quarantine; we had no shore permit; we had no . . .

"Don't worry about it," he laughed. "I am the Port Captain. We know all about you in Puntarenas—we have been hearing about you for over a year. If I remember rightly you were supposed to arrive here some time last year. And your papers—we won't bother about them just now. Welcome to Puntarenas and to Costa Rica. The country is yours, and we hope that you can remain with us for a long visit."

We had been hearing all the way down the coast that Costa Rica was a friendly country, and now we believed it. Some of our past troubles we told the Captain. He explained the difference by saying that Costa Rica was not a country torn by internal strife; there was no necessity for soldiers parading the streets. Costa Rica's pride was her efficient police force. He hoped we'd stop by their headquarters on our way down town. Certainly we should hear their Saturday night concert in the plaza—it was well worth listening to.

"How about going up to San José?" I questioned. "Will we need a permit to go that far inland?" No, it was not necessary, he replied—everybody knew who we were. While it was true that Costa Rica was strict about permitting foreigners to remain in the country, still there was no necessity for putting visitors through a lot of red tape.

We finally prevailed upon him to sign our papers—for the record—but instead of walking all over town to get clearances from the immigration, the customs, and other officials, the Captain merely telephoned them, announcing the *Vagabunda's* arrival. He informed us that when we were in the neighbourhood of the various offices—and had time to spare—they would be glad to fix up any papers. And that was our introduction to official Costa Rica. When he had finished telephoning, the Captain suggested that we go to the cable office and meet the manager, Mr. Cotter, who had a pile of letters for us.

We walked down the wide cement walk that paralleled the water front, and into the well-kept yard of the All America Cable office, where Mr. Cotter greeted us with a smile. He had received cablegrams about us from several offices along the coast. He also had a stack of mail for us. Mr. Cotter's family had moved inland for the duration of the rainy season, which was due; and since he had more room than he knew what to do with, he invited us to make our home with him at the cable office.

He detailed his man to help us. The Port Captain also sent down a couple of men to help us unload the canoe, which was brought round in front of the cable office. In a short time, we were comfortably installed in a lovely room and the *Vagabunda* stowed away in the backyard. During the process of unloading, newspaper reporters and camera men appeared. They wanted to know so much that we told them to come back in half an hour when our work was finished and then we'd try to answer all their questions.

After that was over, we went for a walk round the town. Puntarenas is built on a long, low sand spit of the same name, Punta Arenas, which runs out into the gulf. During the spring tides, half the town is under water, and boats are used to traverse the flooded sections. There are many trees, but few flowers, for the salt in the sandy soil prevents their growth. Most of the buildings in the main part of town are well-built adobe or wood. Puntarenas boasts a club, which is built out over the bay. For an admission charge of about eight cents (gold) any one may use its private bathing beach, which is enclosed with a stout wire fence to keep out sharks. An esplanade, lined with shade trees, benches, and soft drink stands, runs along the beach.

Everywhere we went people spoke to us and were friendly. Their difference from other Central Americans was marked; in Costa Rica the population is predominantly white, blondes are not uncommon. And the women are beautiful! Unlike most Latin American women, they keep their figures after thirty.

We wanted to go to Cocos Island, a Costa Rican possession, but to get there we had first to secure official permission. Captain Pinel, Chief of the

National Boats, said that if we went to the capital, San José, to see the President, we could undoubtedly secure the necessary permit. The following Tuesday we were up early for the trip. The train that was to take us looked like a beautiful little Christmas toy in comparison to the big, black monsters that mean locomotives to a North American. There is nothing inefficient, however, about the neat, clean, narrow-gauge railway system of Costa Rica. We left Puntarenas on time, and were soon headed for the capital.

Our train stopped at every little village on the way. The scenery was magnificent—great, well-wooded valleys and mountains, and little cleared farms as neat as a pin. We climbed steadily, and soon noticed the change in temperature.

At noon we stopped for lunch at a tiny village where women came through the train carrying trays loaded with good things to eat. They had nearly everything imaginable in the way of tropical produce. There were vendors with delicious fried chicken, hard-boiled eggs, tortillas, fruit drinks, coffee, avocados, candy, and so on.

In the afternoon we wound up a huge canyon, cut by a deep gorge, through which flowed a tempestuous, tawny river, its colour indicative that the rainy season had already started inland. We crossed over a great bridge to the other side of the canyon, and passed the flume that carries water to Puntarenas. At two o'clock the train pulled in at San José de Costa Rica.

A big reception committee waited for us on the platform, but when we heard "Where are the canoeists?" we ducked through the train and out the station's side entrance. For some reason panic always seized us at such times; and we could never think of anything to say. But some one saw us and shouted, "There they are," so, as gracefully as we knew how, we went back, answered questions, and shook everybody's hand.

We went to the Hotel Europa, where we had planned to meet Señor Carranza, our host in San Juan del Sur, only to find that he had had to leave the day before. When the clerk informed us of the tariff, we too left. The rate was twenty *colones* ($3.00 gold) per day. For us, that was out of the question. We found an excellent room, with board, in a private family for four *colones* (60c) per day. It was modern, clean and comfortable; and the family was charming.

The events of the four days that we spent in San José run together in our memories like colours on a piece of cloth. For almost twenty-four hours a day, we were either going places or being entertained.

The American Minister to Costa Rica, Mr. Sacks, invited us to tea, but we had to send our regrets because we had no suitable clothes. We could manage well enough in the ports, but our clothes were out of place in San José, which is four thousand feet above sea level, and very cool. People in San José wore dark, formal clothes. My white pants and shirt and Ginger's print dress were hardly the thing. We explained in our note of regret why we did not feel able to come—since we had to have some reason for refusing. Within the hour we received another note, worded in such a way that a refusal would have been the height of bad manners, inviting us to tea the following day. We really wanted to go, but we felt conspicuous enough without turning up at a tea party in tennis shoes. The papers had printed our pictures all over the front pages, and every time we went on the street, people turned and stared. "Ah-h-h, *los señores de la canoa!*"

The following day at tea time, we presented ourselves at the spacious two-storey American legation, and were ushered through big rooms, with winding staircases and beautiful furnishings, out into the walled garden, where Mr. and Mrs. Sacks, with their legation staff, awaited us. We stopped, and for a moment could hardly believe our eyes. Every person present was dressed as we were! The men wore white pants, with their shirt sleeves rolled up; and the women wore print dresses. It was a gesture that we will never forget.

For both of us the afternoon was perfect. The garden itself was beautiful, with orchids and myriads of other brilliant tropical flowers. Two gorgeous macaws had the run of things. Their special delight was to climb on the arm of your chair, and deftly relieve you of the sandwich that you were about to eat.

When we were ready to leave, Mr. and Mrs. Sacks walked back to the door with us. The late afternoon was turning chill, and when they observed that we had come without wraps, they promptly produced warm coats for us to use during our stay in San José.

The President of Costa Rica received us graciously, gave us permission to go to Cocos, and presented us with an autographed, hand-painted seal of Costa Rica. The German colony entertained us royally at the German club and we were given a luncheon in the block-long *mercado*, where everything from harness to shoes is sold. Then we visited the big German brewery, where they broke open a keg of beer and produced pretzels. Thus, when we finally got on the train for Puntarenas, we were dizzy with the excitement of those four days.

Chapter Twenty-six

THE LAST ADVENTURE—COCOS ISLAND

EVER since either one of us was old enough to read books of adventure, Cocos Island, with its rich legendary background of pirate treasure, bold bad men, shipwrecked sailors, treasure seekers, and bloodshed had seemed the ultimate in adventure and romance. I remember a particularly bad session I had one time with a Mr. Nealley, my instructor in philosophy, for drawing a sketch map of the island during one of his lectures. I had picked up an old parchment map (showing the location of the treasure, of course), and I could always escape the boredom of the class room on drowsy, summer afternoons by reproducing from memory its fascinating outlines. I doubted if Mr. Nealley would quite understand this, so I made no effort to explain the immeasurable attractions of Cocos for a restless boy as against the charms of Mr. J. S. Mill and Herbert Spencer. Primarily, I suppose, the matter went deeper than that. My behaviour pattern and my personal philosophy were grounded in action, objectivity. I needed to discover truth and wisdom for myself through trial and error. I wanted tactual, as well as mental contacts with life. This also happened to be Ginger's set-up, so we drew sailing ships on the margins of our school books, while we waited for the day when we would at last be free, and could "go places and do things." Cocos became a symbol—for years we never heard the word or saw it in print without a thrill. Now we had permission from the Costa Rican government to go there. How we would get there, as yet we had no idea.

Cocos Island lies in latitude 5° 32′ North, and longitude 87° 00′ West, and is approximately three hundred and fifty miles off the Costa Rican coast. The latest hydrographic charts of the island showed that a great part of it was still unexplored; even part of its coast line was not exactly known, for it was merely indicated with a dotted line. The centre of the island, with the exception of two peaks, was blank.

Perhaps it is in order to give a short résumé of the island's fascinating history for those readers who are not familiar with it. This extraordinary little speck of land in the Pacific has had a hold upon the imaginations of men since its discovery in the seventeenth century. Almost invariably there has been bloodshed and trouble for everybody in any wise concerned with it—including the Lambs.

The English discovered Cocos, or at any rate they are the first to mention the island. Half a dozen Central and South American countries have claimed it; Ecuador and Colombia fought a pitched battle over it in the '80's. A buccaneer captain, John Eaton, master of the *Nicholas*, was the first to visit the island in 1685. According to the captain, it was "all but inaccessible except at the N.E. end, where there is a small but secure harbour and a fine brook of fresh water runs into the sea there." This harbour was named by the next visitor of record, Lionel Wafer, who arrived fourteen years later, in 1699, and called it "Wafer Bay."

It was Wafer who started the story of a lake somewhere in the interior of the island. He said, "There is a steep hill in the middle of the island thick set with coco-nut trees, but a great many clear springs of clear and sweet water rising to the top of a hill are there gathered as in a large basin or pond, and the water, having no channel, it overflows the verge of its basin in several places, and runs trickling down in pleasant streams." (We later had reason to suspect that this was guesswork on Wafer's part, for he apparently never explored "the middle of the island set thick with coco-nut trees.") He goes on to relate how his crew relished the coco-nut milk, and how it affected them. He says, "We did not spare the coco-nuts. One day, some of our men minded to make themselves merry, went ashore and cut down a great many coco-nut trees, from which they gathered the fruit, and drew about twenty gallons of the milk. They then sat down and drank the healths of the king and queen, and drank an excessive quantity, yet it did not end in drunkenness; but this liquor so chilled and benumbed their nerves that they could neither go nor stand, nor could they return on board without the help of those who had not partaken of the frolic. Nor did they recover in four or five days' time." (We often experienced the peculiar numbing effects of an excess of coco-nut milk—rather like too much aspirin.)

Lieutenant Colnett of the Royal British Navy is the next person who tells us of Cocos. He arrived in Wafer Bay in 1793 aboard the British merchantman *Rattler*. ". . . we left Hogs and Goats and sowed every kind of garden seed," he writes in his log. He also left ". . . a bottle with a letter in." The weather was just as villainous then as later visitors reported it. Says Colnett (the *Rattler* was anchored in Wafer Bay), "At Noon, heavy rain, no sight of land. P.M. and night. Light winds and variable seldom any intermission of heavy rain and at times thunder and lightning." He mentions the lake. ". . . in a beautiful valley at the head of this bay, in which there are cocoanutts innumerable, and also a run of water 18-20 feet broad supplied from a Bason about a mile distant where the officers and people went by turns to bathe." But notwithstanding the beauty of Cocos it had its difficulties, according to the Lieutenant. "The greatest inconveniences we experience in this Isle (Cocos) were the continual rains frequently accompanied by thunder and lightning, and the rains are so heavy as to obscure for hours together the Jibb Boom, but perhaps it may not be so at all seasons. The woolen Cloaths of all who were on shoar were flyblown in large spots and covered with maggots. Should any vessel repair to this island to land their sick or to water, they might soon destroy the flies by kindling of fires, and as tents would not keep the water out, I would recommend building a house. There is wood at hand and plenty of cocoanutt leaves to thatch with."

Captain George Vancouver went to Cocos two years after the *Rattler's* visit. He found the "bottle with a letter in," but he couldn't find the "bason" or lake. That seems to be the history of Cocos both past and present; the features of its landscape shift every other week or so.

Legend says that in 1819 or thereabouts a certain Captain Thompson, entrusted by the Spanish merchants of Lima, Peru, with $12,000,000 in gold bullion, jewels, and plate for safekeeping (". . . because his ship flew the British Ensign"), disabused their trust, and ran away in his ship, the *Mary Dear*, from the harbour of Callao, and buried the loot in a cave on Cocos. This happened during the wars of independence when the Peruvian liberator, Bolivar, was challenging the power of Spain, and wealthy Spaniards and the Church fathers were trying desperately to conceal their wealth from his insurgent armies. It was the beginning of Cocos' fame as a treasure cache.

Now comes the era of map making, and gullible treasure hunters by the boat load. Captain Thompson (of course) made a chart showing the treasure's location. This chart eventually fell into the hands of two sailors named Keating and Bogue. They organized a treasure hunt which set out from Newfoundland in 1845 or 1846. They found the cache, or so the story goes, but the crew mutinied, and the survivors sailed home empty-handed.

In 1896 a British Admiral named Palliser landed a crew of bluejackets on Cocos and tore up the landscape with dynamite (for which he was sharply reprimanded by the British Admiralty), but his luck was no better nor worse than that of his predecessors. He found nothing, but he became bitten with the Cocos' treasure bug; and after his retirement from the Navy helped organize another expedition to the island. Palliser's and his partner Hacking's hopes were founded on maps which they obtained from Keating's daughter. The net result of this foray was also exactly nothing.

In addition to the Thompson loot, Cocos is also supposed to contain eleven million dollars or so hidden by the pirate, Benito Bonito, who stole it in a sensational exploit near Acapulco, Mexico. After quelling a mutiny on Cocos in which fifteen of his crew were killed, Bonito divided the treasure into four parts among the survivors. Bonito buried his in a cave, and the officers and men cached theirs in different places among the island's many fastnesses.

Within the last fifty years dozens of expeditions have been financed and outfitted in London, New York, Canada, and elsewhere to seek the untold riches cached on Cocos. But the most picturesque and interesting figure associated with the island's recent history was a German, August Gissler, who lived on Cocos for eighteen years, having arrived in 1884. He had a concession from the Costa Rican government for exclusive treasure rights, and watched, with equanimity, expedition after expedition come and go. An impressive figure, the bearded German was six feet four inches in height. He always greeted the intruders on his little domain with a pleasant smile. Yes, there was gold aplenty, he used to tell them—but you had first to find it! He said that he knew where the treasure was hidden, but it was now covered by a landslide, and would require capital, machinery, and time to recover it. Gissler frequently found in the underbrush, he said, the bones of the pirates who had been slain in Benito Bonito's mutiny, and in other sanguinary battles over treasure. But as far as any one knows, that is all he ever did find.

The history of Cocos is replete with stories of old gentlemen who, repenting on their deathbeds for the sins of their youth, have pressed into the hands of sympathetic bystanders an old, worm-eaten chart of Cocos, showing the *exact* location of at least sixty million dollars worth of plate, doubloons, gold ingots, jewels, a solid gold Madonna—". . . a weight for ten or fifteen men," says one chronicler who claimed to have seen it—bar silver, jewel-studded swords, and so on. Everybody connected with the pirates, Captain Thompson, Bonito, Keating, and Bogue, left myriads of descendants—all outfitted with maps. These in turn found funds and organizers for trips to Cocos.

Is it any wonder that we wanted to go too? We were following in distinguished company. British admirals, noted explorers, Sir Malcolm Campbell of racing fame, dozens of the great and near-great had been to Cocos. Some of them went for the fun of it, and others with serious intent to bring back that odd sixty million. For our part, we were not interested in treasure hunting; we wanted to see the place that, two hundred and fifty years after its discovery, no one really knew anything about.

Captain Pinel, of the Costa Rican Coast Guard Patrol, was a mine of information on the island's recent history. He had seen a dozen expeditions come and go. Most of them left a record behind them of quarrels and troubles of all sorts. One of the main dissatisfactions, bitterly complained of, was the weather—it rained every day. Captain Pinel said that the weather had not been exaggerated; the sun seldom shone for any length of time during the rainy season, now beginning. He said that mould and mildew covered everything in a day's time. It was impossible to keep fresh food, even coffee, from spoiling almost immediately. There was very little food on Cocos—that is, wild fruit and vegetables; and it would be necessary for us to take a six months' supply of canned goods, or else not eat. We could afford no such outlay, and I told him so. Three weeks', or a month's supply at the most, was the best we could do. "But we can take seeds and plant a garden," I said.

"That won't do you any good," said Pinel. "It's been tried. The seeds grow, but the plants all go to leafage, because of the rich soil and incessant rain. Food isn't the only thing to consider either. Boats seldom call at Cocos—perhaps once a year some one puts in for fresh water. Suppose one of you gets sick, or is injured, what are you going to do? There's no way to get help. Have you thought of that, and have you given it enough consideration?"

I talked the matter over with Ginger. Cocos seemed to be a "tropical hell," from all accounts. I told her that Pinel said that as long as he could remember, everyone who went to the island swore on returning to the mainland that they never wanted to hear its name mentioned again. But Ginger was not particularly perturbed. Since we couldn't travel down the coast during the rainy season, and we had to stay somewhere, why not Cocos? At the end of the rainy season we could come back to Puntarenas, go on down the coast to Panama as we intended, and from there take a steamer home.

"We're becoming awfully optimistic, it seems to me," I said, "when we start talking about going to Cocos; about how long we're going to stay; and just when we're coming back. I haven't the foggiest notion of how we're going to get there in the first place. We can't sail in the *Vagabunda*—at least we know that. And if we do get there, we'll have to trust our luck as to when we're coming back."

"Well, if we do get there," Ginger replied, "Cocos ought to put the finishing touches on our potential careers as adventurers. We've tried our hand at living where it only rains once in eight years or so, and if we can survive where it rains every day, that ought to prove something. Let's go ahead with our plans—just as though we knew the answers—and see what happens. The first thing is the grub list—what shall we take?"

We had very little money, over and above our passage home, so the list was limited. The absolute minimum was a three weeks' food supply, ten packages of garden seeds, fishhooks, a small roll of wire for fencing, permanganate of potash, and bandages. Ginger also wanted a few yards of bright-coloured cloth for clothes, something to counteract the effect of the rain. Anyway, we'd look gay.

Our living expenses in Puntarenas were very low. We spent about a hundred *centimos* each day for food (15c U.S. currency). We were very fond of avocados, which cost forty *centimos* (6c) per dozen. Our breakfast of bread and coffee could be purchased at the *mercado* or any number of little eating stands for fifteen *centimos*, a little more than two cents. Other prices were in proportion. For one dollar a day (gold, i.e., U.S. currency) one could live handsomely in Costa Rica. We found that we could purchase the supplies that we needed without dipping into our passage money.

Captain Pinel thoroughly disapproved of the proposed Cocos trip, and among other things which he gave us to read (which he hoped would

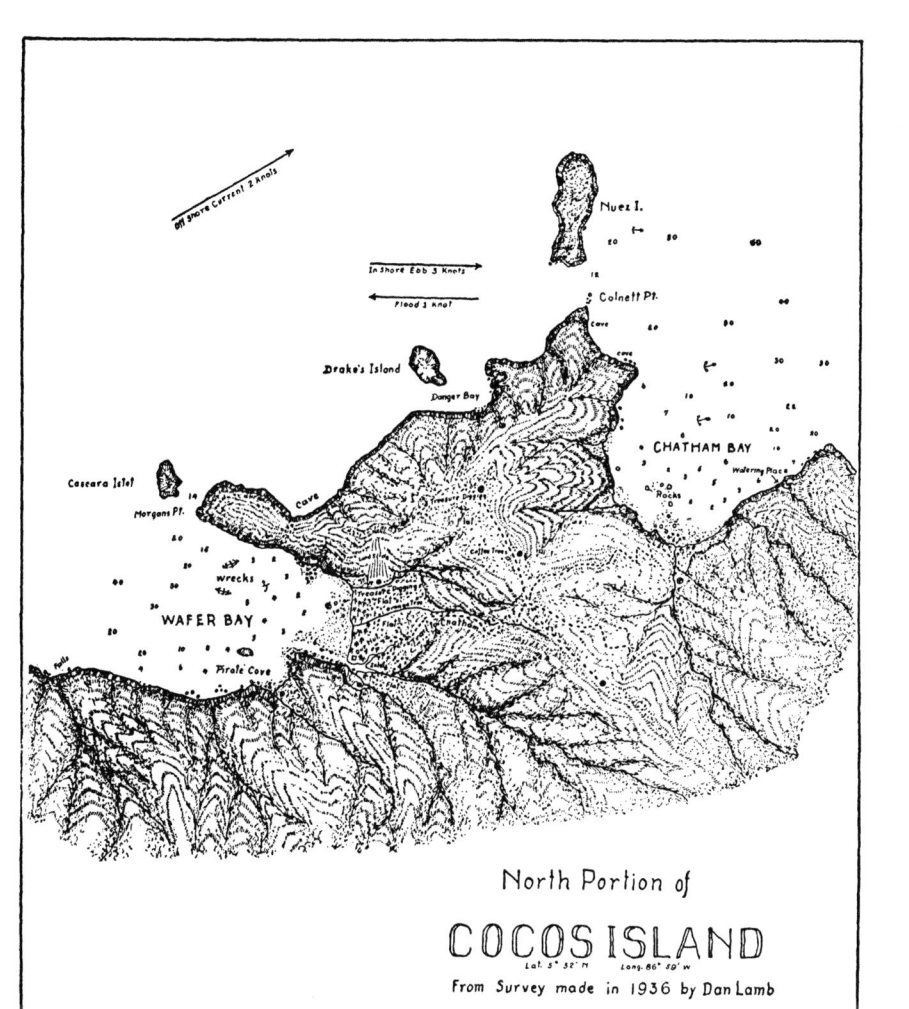

North Portion of
COCOS ISLAND
Lat. 5° 32' N   Long. 86° 59' W
From Survey made in 1936 by Dan Lamb

⊕ Treasure Locations   ----- Old Trails

Scale ·· 4" = 1 mile

quench any lingering fires of enthusiasm for Cocos) was a copy of the *American Magazine* for February 1932. This article contained a vivid account of three men who had spent six months on the island. They had had a terrible time. Their durance vile on Cocos was unintentional. While attempting to careen their boat for repairs, they had beached it on the island at what they assumed to be high tide. The tide had continued to rise for two hours, and the waves had pounded the small boat to pieces. They salvaged their stores and equipment from the craft, and fixed up a deserted shack on the beach. The list of salvaged equipment sounded munificent to us. They had tick mattresses, clothes, an ax, two hatchets, three jack-knives, three razors, three rifles, a pistol, three hundred rounds of ammunition, a stove, a gallon of gasoline, and matches. Their food supply was scant: flour, a few dried beans, and some tinned stuff—sardines, soup, cocoa and milk. This had not bothered them at first, for they knew that in the tropics things grew on trees—you simply picked them off when you were hungry. But this proved to be an illusion; the paradisiacal fruits of this tropic Eden turned out to be pigs and coco-nuts. They soon grew extremely bored with a diet of boiled pig, and it took all their time to chop down coco-nut trees with their dull ax.

"Why on earth didn't they roast the pig, or pickle it in brine and smoke it?" asked Ginger.

"I dunno," I answered, and kept on reading aloud the story of their misadventures. Little things drove you crazy when you were cast away on a desert island where it rained all the time, they said. The monotony, the muggy weather, the limited diet, the close and unavoidable association with the same people day after day—these things got on your nerves. Finally they took their guns apart to avoid "accidents"; they had begun to talk of shooting each other.

"If they took their guns apart, how did they kill the pigs?" asked Ginger inquisitively.

"Maybe they declared an armistice during pig-killing time—the article doesn't say," I answered.

They were not very active apparently, and grew fat on the coco-nuts, but the fat didn't mean much. Eventually it took two men to bring in a pig, and required frequent intervals of rest; they grew tired easily. Once by some lucky fluke they chopped down a coco-nut tree which fell across the top of another tree and broke it off. Two trees in one day! That gave them all the next day for a holiday.

Ginger snorted. "What they needed was work—not a day off."

"You're forgetting," I said, "that work isn't fun for most people. Sure, those fellows would have been a lot better off, and had a much better time, if they'd even exercised a little legitimate curiosity about the island, instead of spending most of their time sitting round feeling sorry for themselves. One of the men slept in his bunk for a whole month before he inadvertently discovered a box of dynamite beneath it. They never mention trying to make the shack habitable, and it's apparent that they didn't, or they'd have found the dynamite."

They didn't think much of old Crusoe either. They were sure that if he had been on Cocos, he would have been running round in a gee string, eating boiled pig and coco-nuts as they did. They were also dubious about his reception of Friday; he'd have probably killed him in a week, because he didn't like the colour of Friday's skin, or for some other trifling reason. I wasn't so sure. The character in Defoe's immortal tale had a lot of spunk, sense, curiosity, ingenuity, and imagination—and plenty of energy. Juan Fernández, the island where Alexander Selkirk, the British sailor on whose memoirs Defoe partially built his story, was marooned, probably hadn't a whole lot on Cocos.

"Well, do you still want to go?" I asked Ginger when I'd finished reading the article.

"Certainly. I think Cocos would be a swell place to try out our theories. Just how much does environment control your thinking? It ought to be an interesting experiment. There's one thing I'm not sure about, though. We're both restless, and Cocos isn't very big. How will we react to the rain and the solitude once, to use your expression, we 'get things under control'? Before then, we'll both be busy and interested, but after that——?"

"I don't know the answer to that either," I said.

Just then some one rapped on the door. A man from the coast guard patrol stood outside. "Captain Pinel wants to see you at once," he said.

"Well," said Pinel, as we hurried into his office, "what did you think of the castaways' experiences on Cocos? Still want to go?"

"Yes!" we answered in unison.

He cleared his throat. "Hm-m, you'll be interested to know that the coast guard patrol boat *Santa Rosa* is leaving for the island in a day or two, and will probably make another trip to Cocos in November."

"Can you take us?" we demanded in high excitement.

Pinel grinned. "I wouldn't be a bit surprised if you obtained permission." He said that the exact date of sailing had not been decided. He had yet to receive word from the *Administrador* of the Coast Guard Patrol. It might be a day or two—a week perhaps.

It was evident that we had some one to thank for arranging matters so conveniently; particularly in view of the Costa Rican government's opposition to any one's attempting to live on the island. Many of the ill-starred expeditions had put the Government to no little trouble and expense, and it was becoming increasingly difficult, we were told, to secure official permission—to say nothing of Government aid—to go there.

We returned to the cable office, and proceeded at once to put our equipment in shape for the long sojourn on "Treasure Island."

The next morning we were awakened at an unholy hour by some one

The Last Adventure—Cocos Island

pounding on the door. I sleepily opened it, and accepted the letter handed to me. It was from Pinel. "At two o'clock tomorrow," it said, "the *Santa Rosa* will leave for Cocos." I glanced at the date, the letter had been written the day before.

"When did Pinel give you this letter?" I asked.

"Yesterday," answered the stolid messenger.

"Holy smoke!" I yelled. "We're leaving this afternoon and we haven't bought a thing, and nothing's ready."

We hurried into our clothes and dashed down to Pinel's office. He was out, but his assistant confirmed the sailing date, and showed us the telegram from the *Administrador* received the day before.

Out of Pinel's office and down to the *mercado* we sprinted at top speed. So many things to do, and such a short time to do them in! The shop keepers must have thought we were crazy. At last the goods were bought, the bills paid, and the merchants instructed to deliver our purchases to the *Muellecito*, the little pier, where the *Santa Rosa* docked.

Then Ginger went off to do some personal shopping, and I went to the post office to arrange to have our mail held; and made the rounds of the customs house, the immigration office, and so on, to get the necessary clearance papers for Cocos. These things done, I went back to the cable office, where I met Ginger.

With the help of the neighbours we got the canoe down to the beach, where we loaded it. Then I paddled round to the dock where the *Santa Rosa* lay, while Ginger dashed off to make some last minute purchases.

The *Santa Rosa*, a sturdy little boat built for Coast Guard work, was Pinel's pride and joy, for he had designed her and superintended her building. She was fifty feet long, twenty feet wide, and powered with a Diesel engine. In view of what we'd experienced of the old Pacific's humours along this section of the coast, the *Santa Rosa* needed to be sturdy.

At one o'clock, out of breath and ready to drop, we rushed into Pinel's office. "You Americans, how you rush round," he said.

"But you said two o'clock," Ginger gasped.

"Two o'clock is the time we should like to start," Pinel said with a twinkle in his eye. "But if you were not ready, of course, the boat would wait for you."

"There's just one thing more that I think we ought to have." Ginger hesitated and looked at me. I knew what she wanted, for she had been hinting about it for some days. Since I was far from sold on the idea, my face took on a "please don't bring that up again" expression. Pinel grinned. A married man himself, he was apparently well acquainted with this domestic byplay. Ginger wanted a dog. All the way down the coast she had stopped to pat every mangy dog in every Indian village that we came to. We both like animals, but it had been obviously impossible to care for a dog on a trip like ours. But now that we were going to Cocos—well, how about a dog?

"Wait a minute," I protested. "If it's going to be as hard to feed ourselves as everyone says it is, how are we going to feed a dog?"

"Don't you think we could manage, if it were a little dog?" Ginger's face wore a very pleading look, and eventually I gave in—not too gracefully and with misgivings. "But remember, it's got to be a little dog, and you've got to teach it to eat fish."

Pinel winked at Ginger and left the office without a word. I had a faint suspicion that I'd been jobbed. There was still half an hour until sailing time, so Ginger and I went out to look over the assortment of dogs running up and down the street. She didn't seem to care for any of the available dogs, however, and suggested that since she had not spent all the money which I had given her, it might be a good idea to spend it on one real meal. We went into a restaurant and ordered nearly everything on the bill of fare. On the way back to the dock we made a few additional purchases: paper for diaries, extra leads for pencils, and a can of white lead for repairing the canoe.

The boat was a beehive of activity when we returned. Mrs. Pinel and several other men's wives had come to say good-bye to their husbands, who were undertaking, they believed, a hazardous voyage. No one in this part of the world likes to see a member of his family go to sea during the rainy season, with its fierce attendant storms.

Mrs. Pinel had over her arm a market bag made of fibre. At a nod from Captain Pinel, she reached into it and handed something to Ginger. It was a tiny ball of black fur. Pinel and his wife laughed at the expression on Ginger's face as she gazed at the tiny creature. "Is this a dog?" she exclaimed.

"It certainly is," said Pinel. "And according to specifications, too." The little thing just fitted into the palm of Ginger's hand. "Furthermore," he continued, "it is a very fine dog. Its father was imported from England, and on its mother's side it is related to all the breeds of Costa Rica—and that's a distinguished pedigree."

It lifted its solemn little face to Ginger, and then nuzzled down in her hand. "Do you suppose it's old enough to eat?" I asked, trying to put a little enthusiasm into my voice. Pinel had certainly put over a fast one.

"Oh, sure," he said. "See, its eyes are open."

On the spot Ginger named it Coco; and more than made up for my lack of interest, profusely thanking Captain and Mrs. Pinel for their gift.

After a half hour of confusion and shouted orders, the lines were cast off, and then some one shouted, "Where is the Señora?" Since there was only one "señora" going on this trip, I looked round. She was nowhere in sight. Then racing down the pier to accompanying cheers came Ginger. She took off in a wild leap, cleared the distance between the ship and the dock, and landed in a heap with two of the crew who had been standing by to help her.

The *Santa Rosa's* engines began to swing us round, and we chugged off into the gulf. When we were under way, I turned to Ginger and asked, "Where in hell were you?" Well, Coco was little, and it was a long way to the island; in the meantime, Coco had to eat. So she'd gone to a drug store, where she knew the proprietress, and had gotten a bottle of milk. Once on the island, Coco would learn to drink coco-nut milk, but she couldn't let a little dog go that length of time without food—even if she did take a chance on missing the boat.

After sunset Ginger and I sat on the stern, gazing at the lights of Puntarenas, just visible on the horizon, and taking our last look at civilization for months to come. Ginger shivered a bit. "Cold?" I asked.

"No," she answered. "Just thrilled and excited. We've talked so much about this trip, and now that we're on our way, I can hardly believe it. Did you honestly ever think we'd actually go to Cocos?"

"I don't exactly know," I answered. "Cocos was part of a dream—a dream I suppose that everyone has at sometime in his life. It was one of those places about which you say to yourself, 'Some day I'll go there,' without ever quite knowing how it's to be done."

Pinel sauntered up as we passed Cape Blanco light. "I have just set the course for the island," he said. "This is the last time you will see the mainland, or any other land, for three days, for we're heading straight out into the Pacific."

"This is a familiar run to you, is it not, Captain?" I asked. "How many trips have you made to Cocos?"

"More than I like to think of," he answered. "When treasure hunters were on the island, it was necessary for us to run out about every two months."

"Tell us something about them," Ginger urged. "Did they take the business of treasure hunting seriously, or was it just a sham on the part of the people who had organized the companies to satisfy their investors?"

Pinel laughed. "There's been every conceivable type of human among them," he said. "Some of them were honest men who believed that they had information of real value as to the treasure's location, and confidently expected to retrieve a fortune for themselves and their backers. Others," Pinel shrugged, "were obvious tricksters. Well-known geophysical engineers have visited the island. Several companies came equipped with electrical locators and adequate machinery for digging. One outfit brought a medium. The locators and the medium were of about equal value—neither one found anything. Some simple souls thought all they had to do was to bring a pick and a map, and if they came on Saturday they expected to be off by Monday with the loot. I have seen a great many of their charts, and seldom are any two of them in agreement. On some of the maps the treasure is located under a cliff on Wafer Bay; others show it to be located on the west side of Chatham Bay; still others place it upstream from Wafer Bay. Sometimes it is hidden in a cave, and sometimes it's buried beneath a sand bar. Many of these so-called copies of the old charts show plainly that they have been copied from the modern hydrographic maps of the island, which show it to be almost round; the earlier maps depict it as long and narrow." Pinel chuckled. "You'd be surprised at the number of charts that turn up which plainly indicate that whoever made them never saw Cocos—and didn't even bother to copy anybody's map. Of course, there isn't the slightest shred of proof that there ever was anything of value buried on Cocos, but that doesn't seem to affect the treasure seekers in the slightest."

While we sat talking, the beam from the light grew fainter and fainter until we could barely see it through the mist. "It's a funny thing about that island," Pinel mused—"what it does to people. No one has ever lived there any length of time but Gissler. It's a long way off the beaten track, and there isn't much arable land, and it's hard to grow things because of the incessant rains; but there's more to it than that. Something about the place seems to turn men into devils; they quarrel, hate, and often kill each other. Maybe that's what the gold lust always does to men. I don't know." He sighed and threw up his hands, as though the whole complicated problem of human behaviour was too much for him. "Let's have some coffee," he said.

For four days we ploughed through the restless, squall-swept sea. The crew spent most of the time in their bunks, especially when it rained, but Ginger and I were too excited to remain still very long. Much of our time we were in the pilot house with Pinel, making observations, a difficult task, to say the least, for the sun shone through the clouds only at intervals. Often at night Ginger would steer the ship, while I lounged in a corner with the helmsman and talked, listening to the patter of the rain and the hissing of the seas as they splashed over the bow.

During the brief intervals of sunlight, the ocean about us presented an ever changing panorama. Huge clouds, their upper surfaces flooded with light, scudded across the horizon; below them, black streaks of rain descended in torrents into the sea. The effect of the white-capped clouds alternating with the black bands of rain, the contrast of the foam-crested, wind-lashed waves and the dark valleys between them, made a never-to-be-forgotten sight. I counted seven rain squalls in our immediate vicinity during one interval of clear weather. When the squalls rushed down upon us, the little ship would shiver from the impact of the furious waves, shake herself, and plough ahead in the pelting rain that cut down the visibility to a bare fifty feet. Lieutenant Colnett hadn't exaggerated when he said, ". . . and the rains were so heavy as to obscure for hours together the Jibb Boom."

Finding Cocos after you get to the proper latitude is no easy matter sometimes. It is quite possible to sail within a mile of the island and never see it, since it is almost continually shrouded in clouds. And when the visibility is poor, it is impossible to see it from a distance of half a mile off shore. Colnett records in his log that he couldn't see land while anchored in Wafer Bay. There are also very strong currents along this section of coast, between the mainland and the island, and they are very irregular. These currents may set a boat fifty or even a hundred miles off her course, either up or down the coast.

At noon of the fourth day we took an observation. The island could not be far off, but no land was visible through the heavy mist. Captain Pinel cut the engines to half speed, and the *Santa Rosa* ploughed cautiously through the misty seas. We had hoped that the weather would clear, and that sometime during the daylight hours Cocos would loom directly before us. But it was not until midnight that we reached the correct latitude.

At 1 A.M. the Captain, Ginger, and I were on the bow watching a school of porpoises streak through the phosphorescent water. Nothing else was to be seen through the heavy mist. Fifteen minutes later a flash of lightning directly ahead showed us a high, dark outline rising out of the enveloping fog. As we drew nearer it grew more distinct. Flashes of lightning played round the summits of its peaks, and we could see the palm trees silhouetted against the skyline. There it was, silent, mysterious lonely. We could hear the seas beating against its rocky shores—Cocos Island.

"Damn my hide," said Pinel, "are we north or south of Chatham Bay? Well, we'll just have to cruise until we find it, even if we have to circumnavigate the island."

"Now, Captain," remonstrated Ginger, "you can't fool us. Chatham Bay is on the north side—and you know north from south."

Pinel grinned. "Young lady, you're a better navigator than your husband—he didn't let out a peep."

"Why don't we steam into Chatham Bay round that little island ahead?" I asked. "I haven't gazed at a map of Cocos all these years for nothing. Besides, you should be ashamed of yourself, missing your course by a whole half mile on a three-hundred-and-fifty-mile run."

Pinel laughed. He hadn't gotten away with a thing. "That's your fault," he said. "You helped with that last observation. Anyway, we're mighty lucky. One time I missed the island, and spent six days hunting for it. Well, here we are."

The crew came forward and stood by the anchor while we inched our way past the dark shadow of Nuez Island into Chatham Bay. Captain Pinel had no time for joking now, for this was a dangerous anchorage. A strong current swept between Nuez Island and Colnett Point, making navigation difficult. The head of Chatham Bay is foul ground, and a ship must not approach too close to shore.

At Pinel's command, the anchor splashed into the water. We had arrived. "We really are here," Ginger said with a tremor in her voice. The rest of the crew turned in, but Ginger and I sat on the hatch holding hands, and gazing at the black, rugged landscape about us.

The east paled; the black cliffs turned to deep purple, which changed to blue; then "the dawn came up like thunder." Outlined against the sun stood the mysterious peaks of Cocos, their summits crowned with verdure. The emerald waters of the bay were bounded on the east by red-brown cliffs over which tumbled sparkling waterfalls; and on the west by rank, tropical growth that grew down to the water's edge. Between the arms of the bay was a small valley fringed with palms. The scene was so lovely—beyond anything that we had dreamed of—that words failed us.

Captain Pinel came on deck. "After breakfast we'll take you round and put you off at Wafer Bay; it's more beautiful than Chatham, though that's hard to believe," he said.

We were both too excited to eat. As the *Santa Rosa* steamed round the point of Nuez Island, and past another small island, Ginger and I stood on the bow, scarcely believing that the scene we looked at was real. Then before us opened out the beautiful expanse of Wafer Bay. On its south side a silvery ribbon of water tumbled down a high cliff, cascading nearly a thousand feet into the green foliage below. This was the waterfall described by Wafer. ". . . the water pours down in a cataract so as to leave a dry place under the spout, and form a kind of arch of water. The freshness which the falling water gives in the air in this hot climate makes this a charming place." Pirate Cove came into view. It looked as we had imagined it—the way a pirate cove ought to look. As we glided further into the bay, we could see the white sand beach with its background of slender coco palms. Behind the beach rose rugged hills covered with huge trees, many palms, and giant ferns.

The north side of Wafer Bay is bounded by high brown cliffs. Midway between the head of the bay and the point, the sea pounds through a great tunnel to the blue waters of the other side.

Captain Pinel ordered the anchor dropped well offshore, explaining that the bay was full of wrecks and rocks; and that at low tide one of the wrecks, close inshore, was visible.

We lost no time in getting the canoe over the side and loaded up. Since we had more supplies than we could carry in one trip, Pinel ordered the dinghy launched to transport the surplus baggage, climbing in himself to accompany us. "It's high tide now," he said, "and we can row in through a channel and land on the south end of the sand beach where the stream enters the bay."

He led the way in the dinghy. As we approached the channel, he pointed

The Last Adventure—Cocos Island

out the dangerous rocks to be avoided. There were only a few small breakers on the bar, and we were soon in the deep water of the stream. We landed on a steep sand bank shaded by coco-nut palms.

Walking beneath the palms where other men had lived, we gazed at the wreckage that littered the grove, the sad remains of their occupation: trash, cans, parts of things that had served them, broken machinery, bottles, worn-out batteries, mildewed pieces of cloth, a broken oar, rusted iron, pieces of radio locators, and so on. We made our way through the wreckage to three rickety sheet-iron huts, with piles of trash beside them. They were filthy.

In one of the huts there was an old rusted stove, now useless. Outside the window, from which the screen had rotted away, was a pile of rotting refuse. All the garbage had been dumped out of the window. Bones of fish and pigs showed white where the rain had washed the other filth away. Beyond the piles of trash, we could see the fallen boles of coco palms. The whole place stank, but not only because of the decaying rubbish. There was a psychic stench about the place as well from the unloveliness of the men's characters who could make such a pestilential hole out of this beautiful tropical island. Ginger kicked half-heartedly at a rusted can; it rolled across the ground to keep company with a rotten coco-nut someone had tossed out of the door after drinking its milk. Swarms of house flies buzzed in our faces. The waves pounding on the clean white sand seemed to be vainly trying to reach this abomination, as though eager to wash away a stain on the landscape.

That afternoon the *Santa Rosa* sailed away, leaving us alone upon the island of our dreams. But what a rude awakening! We felt sick. The boat's crew had come ashore and picked up everything that might be of use to them. We were glad to see them take it, for we wanted none of it. Even the broken stove was dismantled and carted away. We stood on the beach and waved until Pinel and the crew were out of sight, and then walked slowly down the white strip of sand between the coco-nut grove and the bay. It was long past mealtime, but the filth that lay over everything had killed any desire we might have had for food.

The very air seemed charged with every ugly phase of human behaviour. One felt that for the most part the men who had come here had left all the decencies behind; the overwhelming desire for gold had stripped them of every consideration—even of intelligent self-interest—until nothing remained but the forces of disintegration. The fact that the men who had recently been here were the representatives of a civilized social order, and had brought with them the tools of its progress, only made the case more damning. To the best of their ability they had converted Cocos into a physical and moral slum; not even the degenerate Indians of Tiburon could have done a better job.

We returned to the filthy camp, and set up temporary headquarters among the palm trees—as far from its disorder as we could get. Round the campfire that night we talked over our plans. When we awakened the next morning it was raining. All day the rain fell from the grey, leaden skies, that steady, remorseless drip-drip, pat-pat on the palm fronds, the reiterated single note on the corrugated iron roofs, that had driven men mad. In the half light the place looked indescribably lonely and desolate.

The first thing on the program was to rid the place of the refuse. We found and repaired an old scow that had been left behind by some treasure outfit, and with this we ferried the rubbish out to sea and dumped it. Each time the tide was high enough to permit us to cross the bar, we took a load of trash to Davy Jones's locker. There was a certain almost vicious pleasure to be had out of destroying the unlovely mementos of Cocos' former inhabitants.

We cleaned, scrubbed, and repaired the most suitable of the three buildings, using parts of the other two for repair materials. Ginger scoured and scrubbed every square inch of the inside. Then, after salvaging the materials we could use, such as lumber and nails, we tore down the two shacks, carted them out to sea, and dumped them.

We made our camp by a pool while we were engaged in cleaning up the place. During the days when it did not rain, we made frequent trips to the stream to wash off the accumulation of filth. On other days the rain, of course, kept us clean.

At the end of the first week, the camp was fairly well rid of its accumulated litter. We cut away the weeds, made rakes, raked the weeds and other refuse on the ground into piles, and dumped this in the bay too.

Meanwhile we had begun experimenting with the seeds. Some we placed in a little patch of rich soil; others where the ground was half soil and half sand. Near the beach, where it was nearly all sand, we planted beans.

Then we began a tour of the area round our part of the island. Along the banks of a large stream that flowed down from the centre of the island and past our camp, we discovered a plant similar to watercress, and in the stream bed we found crawfish. On a flat back of the coco-nut grove, where August Gissler had built his hut, were several lemon trees and an orange tree. The lemons tasted like a cross between a lemon and a lime, and were delicious. There were also a number of almond trees, and two varieties of guava trees. A few papaya trees grew among the palms just back of the beach. On the ridge, between Wafer and Chatham bays, we found coffee and mango trees. There were many trails made by the pigs, descendants of Lieutenant Colnett's "hogs."

In addition to the coco-nuts, fruits, and pig, we had plenty of fish, lobsters, and birds' eggs. Since there was ample food for any able-bodied person who was willing to look for it, we became increasingly sceptical of those high-powered yarns we had read about castaways starving on Cocos. Conditions hadn't changed to suit our convenience either, for Lieutenant

Colnett, writing one hundred and forty-two years ago, hadn't noticed any scarcity. He says, ". . . as we neared the Island, Boobies, Egg Birds, and Man of War Hawks, fin back Whale, Grampasses, with Bonnetta and Albecores innumerable . . . fish were in great abundance . . . eels and toad fish were in plenty, plump and very large size. Shell fish were scarce. A new kind of large limpets . . ."

We spent about two weeks constructing our hut, meanwhile continuing to live in the tent. We built the hut near the stream among a clump of coco palms, and set it up off the ground on palm-log pilings. It was twenty feet square, and was divided into two rooms. The sides and roof were made of palm thatch. Ginger's kitchen occupied one corner; here she had a stove made from an oil drum, a worktable, and shelves. Over the stove was a row of bars on which to hang food and articles of clothing and equipment, where the heat would dry them out, preventing spoilage from mildew and mould. In another corner we built a small bunk, and cushioned it with a thick layer of feathery palm leaves.

The repaired shack was converted into a workshop, where we made tools from scraps of iron salvaged from the wreckage. A hacksaw blade from our own equipment served as a saw. I made a hammer and an ax out of pieces of rusted metal. To make the ax I first built a forge, using the red adobe mud from the hill back of camp. A tanned pigskin made an excellent pair of bellows, and a large block of iron that we had saved for possible use as an anchor served for an anvil. The most difficult thing to obtain was charcoal, for most of the wood on the island was always damp, and the kiln had to be continually rekindled. We really did need an ax, and to my delight it finally took shape. I was also pleased to find upon tempering it that it was steel. The surface was polished with my carborundum stone until it was bright and shining, and then sharpened to a razor edge.

With these tools, plus a square and a pair of dividers made from wood, we constructed the furnishings for our hut out of the salvaged lumber and nails. This part of the job was pure fun, though we put in about sixteen hours a day of hard work. Most of the time it rained, but we were so busy that we hardly noticed. Only when the tropical squalls were so strong that we could not stand against them did we seek the shelter of the hut, and, barring the door against the blasts, set to work on the inside.

The hut's furniture consisted of a table, two chairs, a writing desk, a comfortable lounge built along one wall, a tiny ship's bunk for Coco, and numerous handy little gadgets for use about the house. We became so enthusiastic over the job of creating a home atmosphere that we cut away one wall and built a fireplace. Although it was actually too warm to enjoy the fire, we spent many pleasant evenings in the light of the small blaze, making objets d'art for the house. They really weren't bad either. We made a lamp in which we could burn coco-nut oil from a carved coco-nut shell; and we also made ash trays, flower vases, salt shakers, and fruit bowls out of coco-nut shells; and fancy tableware from hardwood which we collected upstream. Ginger wove mats, made curtains, and cut doilies out of palm fibre, which she used for a luncheon set. These looked very pretty on the clean white boards of our dining table.

In an open space back of the coco-nut grove we put up a drying rack for meat and fish, and built a small smokehouse for curing ham and bacon.

Down by the stream we constructed a table for cleaning fish, and another for washing dishes. We also fixed up a little place in which to do the laundry. The water in the stream was very soft, for it was nothing more than rain water, and it was perceptibly colder than ocean water. Water on Cocos is in a state of perpetual motion. Sea water evaporates and forms clouds, which immediately come to Cocos to drop their moisture. The rain runs down the steep sides into the creeks and streams and out into the ocean, whereupon the process repeats itself.

One of the secrets of living successfully in such a restricted area as Cocos, is to be able to change the scene of your activities. A little alcove among the coco-nut palms suggested rustic benches where we could sit and enjoy fresh coco-nut milk. A palm stump in the centre served as a chopping block for opening the nuts. It was a pleasant retreat during the heat of the day.

On the bank beside the stream Ginger built an aquarium. On our foraging tours she was always on the lookout for some little fish or crab to add to her collection. Adjoining the aquarium she made a rock garden with ferns and flowers. While she was busy with these projects, I built fish and lobster traps.

We dug a sizable garden plot, after constructing a rustic fence to keep the deer and pigs out. In it we planted corn, beans, carrots, peppers, and tomatoes. Melons, *chiotes*, and more beans were planted in various other open spots. While we were cleaning up the camp, we found some potato plants that had probably sprung up from discarded peelings. When transplanted, they grew exceptionally well. Experiments with seeds proved that they grew best where the soil was not too rich—that is, they produced something else beside leafage. So to retard their leafy growth we mixed beach sand with the rich humus.

There was seldom an idle hour during the daytime, and often we worked far into the night. When we were not making something for the house, we were foraging in the back country, or working in the garden, or fishing, or diving for lobsters, or paddling out to the islands offshore to collect birds' eggs; or hunting wild pigs, tanning their hides, and rendering out lard. A successful pig hunt meant a lot of work. The smokehouse fire had to be tended while the meat was cured into ham and bacon, though sometimes we pickled it in brine, and used it as corned pork.

Climbing coco-nut trees was made difficult by the great number of small red ants and the parasitic growths on the palm boles. We made a long pole

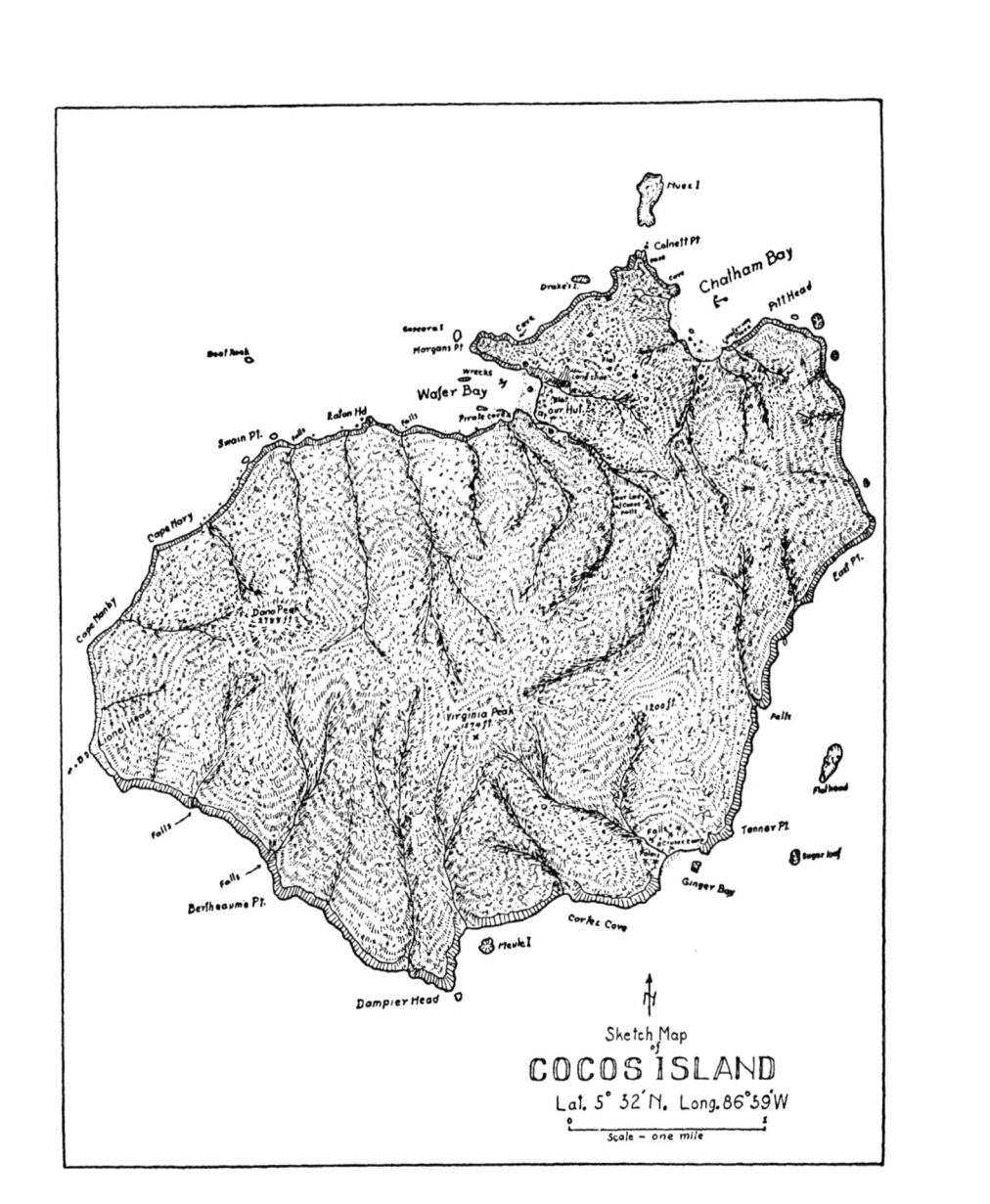

Sketch Map of
COCOS ISLAND
Lat. 5° 32′ N. Long. 86° 59′ W
Scale – one mile

with a hook attached to the end, and by manipulating it together we could detach the nuts. The use of this contraption was not without its minor casualties—to get out of the way of the falling nuts required fast foot work, and sometimes we weren't fast enough.

We were fond of palm-heart salad, so I occasionally felled a small tree that grew in a clump which needed thinning out. Ginger made delicious salads from the crisp white flesh, garnishing them with hard-boiled birds' eggs and watercress. Sometimes she fried the heart, which cooks to the consistency of fried onions, and is very good to eat.

The deer often came into camp, trying to nip off the tender tops of the growing vegetables by reaching over the fence. To prevent them from doing this, we placed little tidbits out for them, such as a bit of corn, coconut meat, or palm heart when we had it. Finally they became so tame that they ate out of our hands. One old buck decided that he liked to have his head scratched. Every day he came in, accepted his little tidbit, and then turned his head on one side for us to scratch just below the ear. When that side had been scratched to his satisfaction, he would turn his head to the other side. If we did not immediately comply with his wishes, he would butt us gently with his horns. These deer had been placed on the island by the Costa Rican Government, and in consequence were not completely wild.

Once the filth was cleared away, and all the breeding places filled in, the flies soon vanished. The thousands of cockroaches also disappeared when there was nothing left for them to eat. We disposed of every scrap of refuse by dumping it into the stream immediately after the daily deluge, when the high water would carry it out to sea. The refuse from cleaning fish was used to bait the lobster and fish traps, or, if we did not need it, disposed of in the sea. Ginger, who scrubbed and scoured the hut each day until it shone, kept me busy making soap out of ashes and coco-nut oil.

She made some gay clothes for herself out of the cloth we had bought in Puntarenas. One bright, flowered piece became a South Sea island wrap-around skirt with a triangular bodice. My clothes consisted of the briefest of shorts. And since it rained every day, and we were almost always wet, either from swimming or being out in the rain, the fewer clothes we wore the better.

One night while we sat in front of the fire making charcoal sketches of sailing ships for wall decorations, Ginger said, "We seem to have about everything in our new civilization but a golf course." She laughed.

"All right," I said, "if you want to go in for society sports we'll make one tomorrow. If you'll weave a golf bag out of palm fibre, I'll make the clubs and whittle out some hardwood balls; and then we'll lay out a course."

Two days later we began playing golf on the beach. The fairway was along the strip of white sand, and the rough was either in the water or back in the brush that fringed the beach. At first we had difficulty with

Coco, who insisted on chasing the balls, but we soon trained her to chase them only when they went into the rough.

Coco was a very smart dog, and we devoted time each day to her training. But she had one bad habit—she bolted her food, especially meat, gobbling it down as though she thought it might be taken from her. We cured her of this habit by stuffing her. Ginger cooked a big pot of fish and another of pork. After Coco had eaten all the fish she could hold we gave her the meat; this, too, she gulped down as though she were famished. When her appetite began to lag we fed her one piece at a time. She would take one end of the strip that we held out to her in her mouth, and hold it there, glaring at us if we threatened to take it away. The poor pup swelled up like a balloon, and we both felt so sorry for her that we were ready to cry, but it was a case of kill or cure. Finally poor Coco could no longer swallow—she couldn't even walk—and we carried her outside the hut. By now she was a sick dog. She remained in her bunk until noon the next day. But after that she ate her food as a sensible dog should.

After a time it became increasingly difficult to find absorbing things to do and make. I carved a rustic sign "Broadway," and nailed it to a coconut tree in front of the hut. Attracted by the hammering Ginger came out to see what was going on. "The final touch," I said. "Every town has a Broadway. Here it is."

For the moment there seemed to be no more worlds to conquer on Cocos. We began to feel constricted. In a small way the same thing was happening to us that happens to society at large when its activities reach a stalemate. During our busy creative period we had been happy. In theory, we should have been happy in the enjoyment of the things that we had created, since all the world agrees that leisure plus security is the *summum bonum*, the ultimate aim of human activity. Well, we had it, and by all the rules we should have been happy. That we were not was not altogether due to the conditions of life on Cocos. Happiness is an active principle; it comes from the harmonious exercise of all the faculties. It seems that the stream of life turns back upon the man who fails to use it. Freedom from life's uncertainties and hazards wasn't the "good life" at all, we found.

We went into the hut one day, and sat down upon the lounge to talk it over. We were both suffering from the same illness; we were restless and bored. "Well, let's try exploring next month," Ginger suggested. "The island has never been accurately mapped and thoroughly explored—authorities say it can't be done because the cliffs are unscalable. I'd like to see if there is a lake in the unexplored interior."

The accounts of this lake always had a mythological flavour that had filled us with the greatest scepticism. One of the hoards of pirate gold is supposed to be cached on its shores. How this could be done, in view of the fact that empty-handed men have been unable to scale the cliffs, has never been satisfactorily explained. One tale that recounts how two shipwrecked sailors found the lake, built a thatched hut on its shores, and made a dugout in which they hunted ducks, is one of the minor masterpieces of Cocos' fiction. Why two shipwrecked sailors would travel inland to set up housekeeping on the shores of a tiny lake was never made clear. For ducks to fly three hundred and fifty miles across storm-tossed waters to take up residence upon a lake on a little island only four miles in diameter was an added touch that would discredit even a duck's intelligence.

We laid in a good supply of food so that we should not have to spend so much time foraging, and on the first clear day started up the stream which ran beside the hut. It cascaded down the rugged, jungle-covered mountains that formed the canyon through which it coursed.

For a mile we followed what had once been a trail probably used by treasure hunters, but now so overgrown that we had to cut our way. The stream's banks were lined with a dense growth of vines, ferns, and tall trees. The ferns were infested with red fire ants, an exceptionally vicious variety. They do not raise welts, as do many kinds of jungle ants, but cause a painful rash. By carefully cutting a trail wide enough to avoid brushing against the ferns we managed to escape most of these pests.

These ants, and a little gnat that made its appearance in great swarms at each full moon, were the only insects that ever troubled us on the island. There are no snakes and we found only one variety of spider. It was large, sometimes three inches in diameter, but harmless. We could seldom get close to one; if we touched it with a twig, it would run.

The only other mammals besides the deer and the pigs were cats and rats. The cats were of the domestic variety gone wild, and would not prey upon the rats, eating instead the young pigs and birds. At low tide there are a number of round stones exposed on the beach, and often at dawn or just after sunset, we would see one of these stones come to life in a wild leap upon some unsuspecting bird. The cats curled up among the stones until a bird approached within leaping distance; then the cat unwound like a coiled steel spring and brought it down.

Colnett said, "The common ratts were in great abundance, as we found many of their nests on the tops of trees we cut down." They were still in "great abundance" during our sojourn on the island. They lived for the most part on coco-nuts. They climbed the trees, gnawed off the nuts, chewed a hole through the husk, and ate the meat. When the hole was large enough they crawled inside and finished the job.

Our greatest difficulty with the rats was to prevent them from gnawing holes in our pillows to get at the seeds of the tree cotton with which they were stuffed. Ginger made several attractive pillows for the lounge and the rats soon discovered them. We trapped them, but we had to use a different kind of trap each time to fool them. Once a rat was caught in one type of trap, all the others gave it a wide berth. We kept them out of the garden by hanging the captured rats at the points where the others entered.

Another Cocos legend is the size and ferocity of the land crabs. But even this is under dispute. One treasure hunter, who lived on the island during the expedition of 1932-33, says that he never saw a land crab during all that time. Another one-time resident of Cocos says they meet you on the beach, and almost "bite your toes off." Colnett reported ". . . and common land crabs in great plenty." And Colnett was right. The island is infested with crabs, but they are harmless to man. It is sometimes reported that they climb the coco-nut trees, gnaw off the nuts, and open them as do the rats. With this we do not agree. While we sometimes found crabs in the trees, we doubt that they go there for nuts. We tried feeding the crabs in Ginger's aquarium coco-nut meat, but they wouldn't touch it; their preference was for green vegetables—tender growing plants.

The most notable things on Cocos were the ferns. They came in every type, size, and variety imaginable, from giant tree ferns to tiny parasitic ferns that grew on the trunks of trees. An elephant-eared variety grew occasionally on the boles of palms.

About two miles up the stream from camp, we heard the roar of a waterfall. Scrambling up over the boulders that filled the narrow gorge, we came upon the most beautiful cascade that we had ever seen—lovelier than any in the Great Plateau country. It was set in a deep box canyon as in a picture frame. A great log wreathed in ferns had fallen across the head of the gorge, and ferns lined the steep canyon walls. The waterfall tumbled down into a deep emerald pool fringed with peridot-coloured mosses and ferns. It was not high—perhaps a hundred feet—but its beauty lay in its perfection rather than in the spectacular nature of its descent.

Ginger tugged at my arm. "Dan, do you see it? Look, there's a lovely woman." Puzzled, I turned. "No, no," Ginger said, "in the falls. Look towards the top, and you can see her face and shoulders sculptured in the rock; the lacy sprays of the water form her tresses and skirt." Then, I, too, could see her, her face turned towards the top of the falls. "Our Lady of Cocos," Ginger named her.

I sat down on a rock, and on the map of the island that I was making inserted the legend, "Our Lady of Cocos Falls."

The next morning we paddled out of the channel, formed where the bay and the river merge at high tide, and started towards Morgan's Point. We were going to explore Chatham Bay—and way points.

This was Coco's first canoe ride. Since it would not in all probability be her last, Ginger set her on the deck so that she could get used to it. She had grown a little, but she was still a clumsy pup. She would walk along the edge of the deck and step over the gunwale with one foot, sprawl half over the side, and then look at us to find out what to do next. Her little face looked so funny and solemn each time her foot came in contact with the unsubstantial air, that we both roared with laughter. Coco was our daily comic strip. And, of course, each time that she came near to falling in, Ginger would rescue her. "Let her go," I urged, "and see what she will do. It's better to let her fall in once, and get it over with, than to be always watching her to see that she doesn't. As soon as she finds out that riding in the canoe is easier than swimming, we won't have to worry about her."

Finally Coco fell in with a splash. Over Ginger's protests, I let the canoe drift on ahead, and then waited until Coco had done all the swimming that she wanted to do for a while. Ginger picked her up and began commiserating with her. Personally, I felt that I had done Coco a service.

The wrecks of many ships were scattered offshore along the coasts adjacent to the island, and the chart located several in Wafer Bay. Lying on deck over a spot where the chart showed a sunken ship, our heads hanging over the side, we looked through the crystal clear waters to the white sand and rocks below. We took bearings and found that there was no wreck at the place indicated on the chart. The canoe was allowed to drift towards the cliffs on the north side of the bay. Fifty yards further on we found the sunken hulk, partially covered by drifting sand. Rough, stormy seas had broken the wreck apart and scattered it over an area of many square yards. Another sunken vessel lay not far away. At extreme low tide, its bow, pointing shoreward, was visible.

On our way out to Morgan's Point, we passed by the great tunnel that extends all the way through the cliff to the cove on the other side. The seas were not rough and the water looked deep, so we cautiously paddled into the entrance, just to get a good look at the place. Then we kept right on going. The cave's average width is about eight feet, and its height approximately twenty. The water was smooth enough until we reached the centre of the channel, where the waves coming in from both directions met. They tossed the canoe high into the air, and it took all our skill with the paddles to keep from being dashed against the sheer rock sides of the tunnel. We were glad to emerge with whole skins into the quiet waters of the bay on the other side.

We paddled along the black, precipitous cliffs towards a small, white, cone-shaped island of sedimentary formation. Here we paused to make a sketch of the bay, and to take compass bearings in order to chart the coast line. When we were leaving, Ginger said that we ought to name the island and the little cove inshore. She suggested that since many of the landmarks of Cocos had been named for famous explorers, and since Drake's name appeared nowhere on the map, that we call them Drake's Island and Drake's Cove.

When we reached the channel between Colnett Point and Nuez Island, the water became very choppy, with a strong current running. At ebb tide the current sets west at about three knots, and on the flood tide it sets east with a speed of one knot. The current would probably be much swifter during the spring or neap tides. We found the current offshore Nuez Island travelled at a rate of two knots in a north-westerly direction.

Nuez Island is bold, high, and topped with brilliant green vegetation. There is a fairly large cove on the inshore side. Some of the legends say that treasure is buried in this cave.

When we got to Chatham Bay we found it to be even more beautiful in the daylight than it had seemed in the dawn, when we first saw it from the *Santa Rosa's* decks. But it still did not have the gorgeous setting of Wafer Bay. Two canyons open on to the beach, forming two heavily-wooded flats. Tumbling down the cliffs on the west side of the bay are two beautiful waterfalls. The most westerly tumbles from a sheer ledge into deep water; it is reported that from this fall the pirates of old secured their fresh water. To the east of the larger canyon is a high hogback covered with razor grass, with what appears to be a zigzag trail leading down over the top of the ridge. The water in Chatham Bay is clearer than it is in Wafer Bay, and full of fish. On the boulders that lined the beach we could see the names of many ships. Most of them bore the names of modern yachts and tuna boats, but some were marked with the names of famous old ships, long lost in time. The earliest decipherable date was 1710, but there were weather-worn, unreadable dates that might have been earlier than this.

We landed the *Vagabunda* on the sand beach and started to explore. Back among the palms, we found a pathetic shelter probably made by the victim of a shipwreck. Walking up the stream, we entered a beautiful deep canyon shaded by huge trees. A mile further on was a second shelter—a log enclosure about four feet high. Scattered about was every conceivable thing that one might salvage from a shipwreck. There were tin cans, pieces of life preservers, rusted lanterns, clothing, milk bottles, two water casks, rotted line, wire and gear, and cooking utensils. Filth and debris were piled two feet deep round the place. Ginger shuddered as I began looking round to see if I could find anything we could use. "Dan, I don't think we want anything from this mess, even though we could use it. I'd rather not have it round our camp."

"All right," I agreed, and threw away a piece of iron I had picked up.

"I wonder why they ever came up here to build a hut in the first place," Ginger speculated, "when they could have built it down on the beach where it is drier? There, they could at least have kept it cleaner by dumping their refuse into the bay for the tide to take."

"I'm sure I don't know," I answered. "Think of the things that people do that can't be figured out on the basis of common sense; they do them without thinking, I suppose. Let's get out of here, the place gives me the creeps."

We cut over to the east side of the stream on the return journey. Just before we arrived on the beach, we came across the trail we had seen from the bay, leading up to the hogback. It was completely overgrown with tough, sharp, razor grass, and in places had been washed away by the rain. We abandoned the attempt to follow it, and zigzagged our own way to the crest. On its flat top was a great yawning hole, where some one had dug for treasure. There was a magnificent view of Chatham Bay from the point, and I took bearings for the chart. The balance of the day was spent in charting the bay between Colnett Point and Pitt Head.

The next day we hiked along the beach of our own bay to Pirate Cove. The cove itself is merely an indentation in the coast line between two cliffs, but directly in back of the cove is an extensive flat which tallies with the description of the site of the mythical millions buried by Captain Thompson, after he decamped with the Peruvian treasure. The Captain's map, the reader may remember, fell into the hands of two Newfoundland sailors, Keating and Bogue. Bogue was murdered, or "fell into the surf and was drowned," his pockets loaded with loot, while he was trying to get back to his ship to quell the mutineers. Keating always refused to tell any one where they had discovered this bonanza, but his second wife said that "it is in a bay with a little beach shaped like a crescent, with black rocks on either side and hidden from the open sea."

The flat was so thickly overgrown that progress was difficult. As I stepped forward to cut a path, the earth seemed to open up under my feet, and I just had time to toss my machete to one side before I started falling through the vines to fetch up on the bottom of a pit ten feet below. "Damn those treasure hunters," I yelled in response to Ginger's laughter.

Ginger hadn't laughed at my tumble, she said, but at the speed and celerity with which I rid myself of the machete when I started to fall. I reminded her that practice makes perfect; and she reminded me that long ago in Wilderness Camp I had said that if one became sufficiently expert in using a machete, his chance of falling on it was about one in a million. Then she said soberly, "If I were you I think I'd be mighty careful from now on; if the law of averages works out, the percentage is now against you." I agreed that from now on I'd treat the machete as though it were a stick of dynamite.

We gave Pirate Cove a thorough examination, finding about a dozen treasure pits. Over against the south wall of the cove, the large boulders had been blasted apart with dynamite. Judging from the amount of rock blown up, approximately a ton of powder had been used in this one location.

Our next expedition was across the ridge that divides Wafer and Chatham bays. On the crest of the ridge we found an extensive flat covered with great trees. Deep pits here and there indicated that it had been the scene of treasure hunts. This ridge led back towards the interior of the island; we followed it two-thirds of the way across.

On the peninsula between Wafer and Chatham bays, the treasure hunters' trails led everywhere. There were large clearings in many places. Some of them had evidently been made by Gissler for his garden, for coffee and mango trees grew there. In other places the brush had been chopped off and piled to one side, with the stumps left standing.

We cut down the steep slope on the eastern side of the ridge and followed the course of a little stream back to our own flat. All along the stream's banks were tunnels. Why treasure seekers ever picked out this particular spot to dig tunnels in will always remain a mystery; it must have seemed a good idea at the time.

Two weeks were spent in exploring the interior of the island. We climbed the two highest peaks, which we named for ourselves. Dana Peak is 2788 feet high, and Virginia Peak 1574 feet. From these vantage points we made plane table maps of the island, charting the various watercourses and ridges.

There is no lake or "Bason" in the centre of Cocos. Colnett got the idea from the many streams and waterfalls that run into the sea, assuming their source to be a lake. Nor were there any ducks.

We had finished exploring the island on foot, and were preparing to circumnavigate it in order to map its coast line accurately, when I decided to climb the high ridge to the south of Wafer Bay. I wanted to make observations for the starting point of our chart. Climbing was difficult, because most of the way had to be negotiated on hands and knees. Reaching the top, some distance back from the bay, I walked along the hogback to where I could look down upon the bay below. It was raining, and I fooled round awhile waiting for it to stop, so that I could work on the chart. It began to grow late, and I knew that if I waited much longer Ginger would worry. I started back along the hogback, looking for a short cut to camp. It became increasingly difficult to walk at all, for the rain had turned the red adobe into slippery mud. Several times I slipped and fell, as I started the descent down the steep slopes. And each time I fell into the ferns I collected hordes of fire ants. My whole body tingled and burnt from their stings. Cutting a trail was almost impossible because of the many rocks, which would damage the machete's blade beyond repair.

I stood looking at the steep incline, wondering whether I could make it or not, when for no reason at all my feet slipped out from under me, and I crashed to the ground. A sharp pain shot up the nerves of my arm. I rolled over and looked at my right hand; the first and second fingers were almost cut off; bright arterial blood spurted from the long diagonal slashes. At last the law of averages had caught up with me—I had fallen on the machete.

I jerked loose the leather thongs with which I tied the gun holster round my leg in rough country, and tied them tightly round each finger to form a tourniquet. The now useless machete I hid at the base of a tree. Dizzy and nauseated, I faced the long descent to camp. Never before had I realized how difficult it is to travel without cutting a trail; the leathery vines and clinging growths wrapped themselves round my legs and arms. Most of the way all I could do was slide—and sliding through fern brakes lined with fire ants is no joke. I could see nothing ahead, and only hoped that I couldn't slide over the edge of the cliff on to the rocks below.

After what seemed hours, I reached the creek, covered with mud, blood, and ants. As I began wading across the stream to camp, I saw Ginger hurrying up the trail which I had taken earlier in the day. "Hey," I shouted, "where are you going?"

"Oh," said Ginger, running towards me, "I was just starting out to look for you. Are you hurt?"

I dissembled a little. "It's nothing. I just fell on that damned machete."

But Ginger's face went white when she saw the condition of my fingers; they were crooked and lopped over to one side, the wide, deep gashes filled with clotted blood. She helped me wash off the mud, ants, and blood in the stream, and then we went into the hut to dress the fingers. We straightened them out, bound splints round them, and, when they continued to bleed after removing the tourniquets, wrapped them securely in bandages soaked in a mild solution of permanganate. When the dressing was completed, Ginger made a sling for my arm. After that I began pacing the floor and cussing. It was not only the pain, which was bad enough, but the idea that I would be laid up and useless for weeks made me mad. My trigger finger would probably be numb and useless from now on, for the machete had cut through the nerves and almost through the bone. Of course I might learn to shoot with my left hand, and already I was fairly proficient with the machete in that hand.

Ginger was patient, and let me pace and cuss to my heart's content. She set the table for dinner, and when I showed no interest, sat down and nibbled at her own. I was too provoked and nauseated to think of eating.

We are both extremely susceptible to each other's moods and misfortunes. Ginger told me afterwards that she had had a very queer feeling about me that day. She knew that something was wrong, so that when I failed to show up she had started out to hunt for me.

The experience taught us both a lesson. For the next week I was idle for the first time since we had landed on Cocos. I became cross, dissatisfied, careless about my appearance, and generally miserable. Everything Ginger said or did irritated me. Finally one night at supper, she balked. "Dan, I think there's something we ought to talk over."

"I know; I'm crabby, lazy, and selfish."

"You know why, too, don't you?" she said. "You're feeling sorry for yourself. Tomorrow let's begin the day with a game of golf, both of us using only our left hands. And how about a swimming race, holding our right hands out of the water?"

From then on I went ahead with my regular duties, finding that I could manage almost as well, allowing for more time, with one hand as with two. I even managed to chop wood.

Then one evening, while were were sitting at the supper table, we heard the sound of a ship's bell. We jumped up from the table and ran out of the hut, but there was no ship in the bay.

That night we were awakened by the sound of something crashing against the roof of the hut. We scouted round in the darkness, but could discover no cause for the noise. The next day we found that a coco-nut had fallen from a near-by tree and landed on the roof.

A few days later, while we were pulling weeds from the garden, something thumped to the ground beside us. Ginger ran over. "Ye gods!" she exclaimed, "it's raining fish!" We stared at it in amazement, and then looked at the sky, but there was nothing to be seen except the clouds that sent down a light drizzle of rain. We knew that man-of-war birds, fighting over the spoils, had probably dropped that fish. But for the moment, we didn't want to accept any factual explanation for it—we wanted it to be mysterious. Everything else about the island had a haunted quality. Why not a rain of fishes?

Then we heard the roar of a motor boat out in the bay—but there was no boat there. It was, obviously, the echo and re-echo of a squall on its way; the sounds of wind-lashed water out to sea carried in and deflected on the stone faces of the cliffs. But this, too, seemed to warrant some mysterious explanation.

We talked the matter over that night. Bit by bit we were beginning to lose our common sense. As we reviewed the last two weeks, contrasting them with the ones that had gone before, it was easy to see what was happening. We had done nothing since my injury, except to play or putter about. Ginger had written my diary for me while my hand was sore, but that night I did it myself. My fingers were still stiff and numb, but I managed after a fashion.

The next day we began making preparations for the trip round the island. Even Coco sensed the change. She frisked about so much that we thought she'd wear herself out long before we started. She ran to the beach and barked at the sandpipers on the shore. Then she barked at the rats in the coco-nut trees. She even teased old Spike, our pet deer, until he put her in her place with a slap of his hoof. When we put on her home-made harness, she became almost delirious with excitement, for she knew that this meant a canoe trip. One of the breeds of Costa Rica from which Coco was descended must have been the seal, for she loved the water. She often entirely submerged her head in the creek, trying to fish out some bright-coloured stone or leaf lying on the bottom.

Just as we were ready to leave the following morning we did hear the roar of a motor boat—there was no doubt about it this time—and we ran down to the beach. A mahogany motor boat, her bright work glistening, was speeding across the bay. As she came in close to the beach, we waded out to meet her. The boat's occupants were as surprised to see us as we were to see them; they had not expected to find any one living upon the island. They said that when they first sighted our hut, they half expected to find pirates or savages living there, and so came in cautiously. Such is the fame of Cocos.

The motor-boat party had come round from Chatham Bay, where their yacht was anchored, to do some fishing in Wafer Bay. We invited them ashore. While Ginger entertained those who were interested in our hut and the things we had made, I took several of the men hunting. They wanted to shoot a deer, but I convinced them that since there were only six adult deer and a couple of fawns on the island, it might be a good idea to wait and give the deer a chance.

When the yacht was ready to leave Chatham Bay, the owner offered to take us back to the States. We refused the invitation, although we were, and we admitted it, a little homesick. But this was a test trip, and we wanted to be quite sure that we were qualified adventurers before returning home.

The yacht carried away the accumulation of letters that we had written since coming to the island, and several rolls of exposed film. We were particularly glad to have the pictures developed before sweating ruined them, as it had all the ones we took in the "Forbidden Land." But Cocos seemed twice as lonely after the yacht's departure.

We then made the planned exploration trip round the island. In recharting the coast we found the maps in use were far from accurate. The southern side of Cocos consists of sheer cliffs that rise precipitously from the water's edge. Many little streams cascade over their faces. Rounding Dampier Head we came upon an indentation of the coast line which was filled with coco palms, and just west of it, where the map showed only a dotted line, we found a beautiful little cove, which we named Cortez Cove. Still further west on the island we found a headland that had not been charted, and this we called Lamb's Head. North of Lamb's Head is a wide gorge with many palm trees, the cliffs on each side of it forming a small bay. Ginger went into raptures over its beauty, so I marked Ginger's Bay upon our own chart. Due to the rough seas and heavy rain squalls, the trip was difficult, so that, our charting done, we were more than glad to get back to Wafer Bay.

My fingers by this time had limbered up enough to be of some use, although they were still numb. Whenever I picked up anything I had to identify the object by glancing at it, for there was no sense of touch in my finger tips.

Our next plan was to emulate Robinson Crusoe. We had often wondered how far any one would get using the equipment that Defoe gave his famous castaway. We intended to repair the old scow, rig up a leg-of-mutton sail, and make a pair of big oars to propel it in case we had no wind; then to go aboard with the machete, our home-made hammer, a few nails, a sheath knife, and our mess kit. The idea was to sail the scow round to one of the coves on the southern side of the island, wreck it, and from then on see how it felt to play Robinson Crusoe.

We stowed the canoe in the hut, reinforced the fence round the garden, and carefully packed away the rest of the equipment where it would be safe from the weather.

On the morning of July 3, 1935, with Coco acting as mascot and figurehead, we worked our cumbersome craft out of the little channel and started across Wafer Bay. Half-way across a squall struck us. We certainly fought to manage that unwieldy scow, but could make no headway against the wind. As her bottom grated on the shore at the north side of the bay, a breaker struck her and piled us up on the beach.

"If this is what you call playing Robinson Crusoe," said Ginger as she grabbed Coco and waded for shore, "how about going back to camp and cooking something to eat? I'm beginning to miss my little cookstove already."

We unloaded the scow, dragged it as high on shore as we could get it, and then walked back to camp, bending our heads before the torrents of rain sweeping in from the open sea. "Every cloud in the Pacific apparently makes a detour to drop its moisture on Cocos," Ginger remarked, streams of water running off the tip of her nose. And it's true. The island seems to attract the storms and the wind as though it were a magnet.

Back in camp we came to the conclusion that it was probably a good thing that we hadn't been able to start on the trip. The next day was the Fourth, and we hadn't celebrated it for two years. We had a fine time, and so did Coco, who went into ecstasies over the home-made firecrackers. The day's program consisted of a golf tournament, a track meet, and aquatic events. We sat down that night to a dinner table gaily decorated with small American flags, which Ginger had made from notebook paper.

Two days later we set sail in the repaired scow, getting out of Wafer Bay without further difficulty. As we rounded Cascara Island, the current caught us and carried us down through the channel between Colnett Point and Nuez Island. We tried to work the clumsy craft closer inshore to get out of the strong current, but as it swept us past Pitt Head, we had to battle simply to keep from being carried out to sea.

No Robinson Crusoe ever had a wilder voyage than we made in that old scow. It was without benefit of a centreboard, and it made almost as good time sideways as it did ahead. A squall came up that carried us round East Point. From then on we had our hands full keeping off the rocks. We missed piling up on Flathead Island by an eyelash. It was no part of our plan to be blown on some bird rock, with a stretch of shark-infested water between ourselves and the mainland. The rain descended in torrents, blotting out all visibility past a range of fifty feet. We could only guess at our relationship to the coast, for there was no way of knowing. Ginger bailed continually with the mess kettle, but the water poured in faster than she could bail it out. As the boat sank lower in the water, Coco, who had taken shelter under the seat in the bow, began to whine. When the boat pitched, and the water surged forward in the bow, she was forced to swim. She'd paddle round in the water, looking pleadingly at us, but there was nothing we could do to relieve her misery. We dared not put her on one of the seats, because she would most certainly be washed or blown overboard. Right then and there we ceased being heroes to Coco. We had failed her miserably. But we had our own troubles.

Without any warning the bottom under our feet heaved up with a splintering crash. A wave caught the boat, and spilled us into the seas. The scow was aground. We frantically grabbed our equipment. As Ginger picked up Coco and the mess kettle, a wave slapped her on the back and sent her sprawling. Coco, scared out of her wits, swam for shore, yowling mournfully, Ginger stumbling after her.

I ran up to the beach with the gear I had rescued, and then started back to the scow which was fast being ground to pieces by the breakers. "Where are you going?" Ginger shouted.

"To get the rest of the equipment," I yelled back.

"But we have everything," she protested. I turned and walked back to where she stood, and looked at the little pile on the rocks—machete, hammer, and mess kit. Ginger wore the sheath knife on her belt. The only thing missing was the nails, and then I remembered that they were in the mess kit. It was rather a shock to realize that this was all the equipment we had. Then we heard a grinding crash, and turned in time to see the last of the scow as a giant comber flattened it out on a rock.

We picked our way across the boulders to the beach. The rain had subsided enough so that it was at least possible to see our surroundings. "Oh," shouted Ginger, "we're in Ginger's Bay." This was a break, for it was one of the few spots on the island that we were eager to explore. We walked back in among the coco-nut trees, and up along the little stream. Further back in the canyon, a waterfall tumbled down over sheer cliffs. Ginger's Bay was even lovelier than Wafer Bay. Climbing to a little flat beside the stream, we found that we were not the first to have discovered this gorge. There were ax marks on the trees, but they were very old. To one side lay a rotten coco-nut log split in half. We decided to make our camp here. When we cleaned the camp site, we found an old boarding spike, a rusted sword hilt, and an odd-looking eating fork with only two prongs.

A crude palm shelter and a dinner of coco-nuts served us for the first night. The next day we salvaged what lumber and nails remained from the wreckage of the scow.

But following in old Crusoe's footsteps wasn't too bad. We built a small, comfortable hut, equipped it with rustic furniture, and out of mud and rocks made an altar stove such as the natives use. Light cord braided from coco-nut fibre, and nails hammered into fishhooks, provided us with fishing outfits. A spear fashioned out of nails enabled us to add crawfish to our menu. We made a crude catamaran out of balsa logs, and by paddling out to the small islets offshore secured plenty of birds' eggs. Ginger brought back a small bird from one of these expeditions which she christened "Peep," because, unless it was stuffed so full of fish that it could hardly move, it chirped constantly. We made clothes from coco-nut fibre. Ginger fashioned a nobby creation for herself—a hula skirt. Any one who thinks that Crusoe lived a life of leisure ought to try it sometime. We were busy every minute of the daylight hours.

Eventually we started homeward across the island. It took us two days to travel the four miles to Wafer Bay. Not only was travelling through the dense growth difficult, but we had to carry Coco, who couldn't scale peaks.

When we reached camp we found out what a tropical climate can do in one month. Every single piece of equipment was either rusted or mildewed. Most of the food was spoiled. Even the tent which we had so carefully dried and packed away was mildewed. Mould and fungus growths were all over the hut. The heavy squalls sweeping in across the bay had wrecked the garden, and the pigs had rooted up the fence and finished the job. The only vegetables left were the beans which grew high on the fence, and the *chiotes* which had climbed the trees.

It took a week to make the camp habitable. After that we turned our attention to treasure hunting. It was not an occupation that we took very seriously. We had, like everyone else who comes to Cocos, a treasure map. Ours, also, was supposed to be the original Thompson chart. There are several versions of this chart, but it really doesn't make much difference which you use, because they all give directions that you can't follow.

On the north side of Wafer Bay is a place which at one time must have been a high cliff accessible from the beach, but which is now covered by a landslide. In this small area the ground is pitted with treasure seekers' excavations. They have also dug many caves into the landslide, but none of them that we investigated were deep enough to have penetrated into the original surface of the cliff. The boulders strewn about the flat near this site have been dug under; some of them have markings carved upon their surfaces. This is the place that Gissler believed to be the location of one of the pirates' caches. According to the story, the pirates rowed ashore eleven boatloads of treasure at high tide. After the tide fell they hauled the gold to the foot of a cliff. They rigged up a derrick by sinking an eyebolt into the crest of the cliff, and hoisting the treasure on to a ledge. Above the ledge the land rises fifty yards or so to a ridge of rock. Beyond the ridge was a flat, two acres in extent. The pirates hoisted the treasure up the slope with running tackle. It was then thrown into a natural crack in the rock, and covered with earth and stones.

Another location is out towards the point on the north side of Wafer Bay. Here the treasure hunters have blasted the soil and scenery sky high.

We were well acquainted with most of the legendary cache sites on the island, but the pirates who buried the gold were apparently better men than the treasure seekers who came after them. The job of digging where they are supposed to have cached their loot is herculean. One such place is under a rock which is only exposed at very low tide. The directions for finding this rock are simple. One walks along Wafer Bay to a point where the farthermost rock on Morgan Point coincides with the southern face of Cascara Islet. Keeping these objects lined up, you walk directly towards the water until you come to a large flat boulder—under the boulder lie seven tons of buried gold! Finding the rock was easy, but digging under it was something else again. We dug down until we struck heavy boulders. The next day when we investigated the hole, we found that the tide had completely filled it with sand. How the pirates ever dug a hole beneath that rock big enough to hold seven tons of gold, with the tide covering the excavation every six and a half hours, we'd like to know.

There is a story that an old sea captain living in New York does very well for himself making fake charts of Cocos treasure caches. I think he must have made ours, for we came to the conclusion that whoever drew it had never been to Cocos at all.

Even an authentic treasure chart would be of little value except to the man who drew it. It would be intended to refresh his memory, which is not the same thing as disclosing a secret to some uninitiated treasure seeker. None of the charts state definitely that either Chatham or Wafer Bay is the actual location of the supposed horde. If we were doing any digging, our choice would be Ginger's Bay. To hunt for it there would require a crew of fifty men and a couple of steam shovels. Radio locators are of little use on Cocos because of the extreme humidity, black sand strata, and the saturated soil. The physical characteristics of the island are also constantly changing because of the frequent landslides and the fast-growing vegetation. The treasure seekers themselves haven't helped matters any on the northern side of Cocos. The southern side has largely escaped their attention, but they have blasted and dug in Chatham and Wafer bays until the landmarks have become unrecognizable, if the older descriptions are to be believed.

The month we were devoting to the treasure was about half over when we came upon our most promising find. While scouting along a sedimentary cliff on the south side of a canyon, we saw a large slab of rock set into its face. It looked like a sealed doorway, half buried by the deposits which had swept down from the cliff above. We cleared away the tangled growth, and discovered in the centre of the doorway a round hole about an inch in diameter. This corresponded to all the accounts of a treasure cache in a cave, except that in some of the stories the hole was supposed to be square.

This is the account given by Admiral Palliser, who heard the story from an old Newfoundland fisherman named Fitzgerald, who in turn heard the story from Keating. Keating's authority was Captain Thompson himself. Thompson told him to go up the bed of a "stream flowing inland" (this would be at high tide). Here he was to measure seventy paces west by south. Then, against the skyline, he would see a gap in the hills. From any other point the gap is invisible. The directions from this point were to turn north and walk to a stream where he would see a rock with a smooth face rising sheer like a cliff. At the height of a man's shoulder from the ground there was a hole big enough in which to insert your thumb. By thrusting an iron bar into the cavity the door would swing outward—behind it lay the treasure! This is the cave which Bogue and Keating are supposed to have rediscovered.

The cave—this is Keating's story—was fifteen by twelve feet, and contained bars of gold bearing the stamp of Peru; also a quantity of coins, sacks of silver, and a solid gold statue of the Madonna. Needless to say, we were elated by this find, and planned to return the next day armed with our home-made pick and shovel. For once we were almost sold on Cocos' treasure. But the following morning I was awakened before daylight by an intense pain on the right side of my abdomen. I lay in bed until dawn, when Ginger wakened. By that time there was no doubt as to the nature of my ailment—appendicitis. The possibilities of this affliction staggered us. But what to do?

At noon my temperature was 101, and my heart action had noticeably increased. Part of this I attributed to my mental condition, for the nearest aid was three hundred and fifty miles away, and if . . . well, we would have a job on our hands. Neither of us talked about it. Talking only made the situation seem worse—and it was bad enough.

I took two boards, salvaged from the wreckage of the huts, placed them together, and painted a large sign in white letters, "Help. Wafer Bay." I was too sick to make the trip, but Ginger hiked up the tortuous trail to Chatham Bay, where she nailed the sign to a palm tree. There was just a bare chance that some boat putting in for water might see it in time.

After she had gone, I began making a set of operating instruments. I broke two razor blades in half, lengthwise, and fastened them to wooden handles, then fashioned flesh clamps out of fishhooks. There was no use acquainting Ginger with my plans as yet, because I wasn't sure that the instruments would work.

That night, when the pain became so intense that sleep was out of the question, I crawled round the floor on my hands and knees, and gained

The Last Adventure—Cocos Island

some relief. Our only medicines were iodine, quinine, and permanganate of potash. There was no benefit to be derived from any one of them.

Things were pretty bad the second day. Ginger made a bowl of *atole*, the thin rice gruel that the Indians swear by, and I drank a little of it. Then I told her that I was going to take a walk along the beach; the exercise might help. She wanted to go along, but I dissuaded her. There was something I wanted to find out, and I wanted to be alone. Taking my gun, I left the house.

Within sight of the hut, I walked slowly down towards the lower end of the beach, then I cut back to one of our hunting trails. The small pigs went unmolested this time. A big pig was needed. An old sow came along, and I shot her. Ginger would hear the gun, but I could always say that I had missed the target. The operation was successful with one exception— I couldn't find the pig's appendix. The instruments only required a few slight changes, however, to be quite efficient.

When I laboured into the hut, empty-handed, Ginger looked at me questioningly, but I said nothing.

That night we faced the grim situation. The poison was permeating my system, and the appendix might burst at any time. I showed Ginger the instruments that I had made, and we put them on to boil in a solution of permanganate. Ginger gave me three of her largest needles which I heated in the fire before flattening them out and grinding them to a sharp cutting edge. One was bent into a half arc, another into a half circle, the third I left straight. We made thread out of the tender palm fibres, which was the only thing that we could think of that would dissolve like catgut. We might have used catgut or the intestines of pigs, but we were afraid of infection, due to the minute spores of mould that found their way into all animal matter almost immediately. We worked until late that night making preparations for the next day's operation. We had decided the sooner the better. Every hour's delay increased the danger of a rupture.

Our work finished, we sat down to talk it over. Ginger had had her appendix out some time previously, and from her scar we had an approximate idea of where to look. I began making sketches to illustrate how she was to go about the business, but every time I mentioned the word "operation" her face turned dead white. Suddenly she covered her face with her hands. "I can't . . . I can't do it."

"Well," I said, "we've either got to do this . . . or you're going to play gravedigger, so take your choice. Of course you can do it." But game as she was, she couldn't steel herself to the task. She could do it, she said, if it were possible to give me a local anaesthetic; even if we had enough aspirin to dull the pain. I thought of making some palm wine; but if I stupefied myself with liquor and something went wrong, I couldn't help her.

Finally we concluded that I should begin the operation. When I reached the point where I needed help, she would assist me. We made every preparation that we could think of. We cut ropes for lashing my legs down, and fastened a handle to her tiny mirror so that she could hold it in a position for me to work by.

Neither of us slept that night. The leaden-footed hours passed while we lay there wide-eyed and unwilling to talk, trying to suppress our fears. All ordinary channels of escape seemed closed. When tomorrow came would we have the courage to act?

In the morning Ginger got up white and shaken. I suppose I was in the same state. We couldn't eat—and we didn't try. This was August 20, 1935. We grimly went about the task of laying out the paraphernalia. Ginger made swabs and sponges out of bandage gauze. We mixed a solution of potassium permanganate, and threaded the needles. We were ready. All we needed now was nerve enough to tackle the job. The operation was to be performed at noon when the light was best. It was now about eleven-thirty.

Ginger stepped outside the hut to compose herself. Then I heard her scream. I hobbled to the door and looked out. She was running towards the beach, wildly flinging her arms about. Suddenly she turned round and ran back towards the canoe shed, tore the canvas covering from the cockpit, and again headed for the beach, frenziedly waving the canvas. Out to sea I could discern the dim outlines of a small ship through the haze. I grabbed some burning sticks out of the stove and made my way to the beach, where I built a smoky fire. But the boat sailed on by and soon disappeared from sight.

We returned to the hut, discouraged and shaken. To see a boat and then have it fail to see our signals was worse than having no hope of help.

I lay down, and Ginger knelt beside me. "Do you think we dare wait another day?" she questioned. It was possible, I said, but pointed out that each day's delay increased the inflammation. "Please, let's wait until tomorrow," she pleaded. I agreed.

Twenty-four hours more of uncertainty to live through! We were both drugged and weary from fatigue and the prolonged nervous tension. One o'clock came and went. Outside there was a thin drizzle of rain, and the wind sobbed and sighed in the palms. After an infinity I looked at my watch. Two o'clock. Ginger sat silent, her face bowed in her hands.

I must have fallen asleep, for when I first heard the sound I thought that it was part of a dream.

At three o'clock the bay echoed and re-echoed with the blast of a ship's whistle. We looked out to see a large tuna boat steaming round Morgan Point, ploughing into Wafer Bay at full speed. Before she even dropped her hook, a small boat was overside and speeding shoreward.

The grimy crew of the tuna clipper raced up the beach towards the hut. Their pockets were stuffed with soap and towels. While fishing in the

The Last Adventure—Cocos Island

vicinity, they had decided to put into Chatham Bay and take a fresh-water bath, and going ashore they had seen our sign asking for help. . . .

Forty-five minutes later all of our equipment was loaded on the clipper; Ginger, Coco and I were aboard, and I was packed in ice. We were steaming full speed ahead towards Puntarenas.

To Captain W. R. Dobbs and the crew of the tuna clipper *Fisherman II* I owe my life. The famous boat that once belonged to Zane Grey had again performed an act of mercy on the high seas.

Chapter Twenty-seven

THE END OF THE TRAIL—PANAMA

AFTER the rescue we suffered for days from the kick-back of emotional strain; we were weak and exhausted. Captain Dobbs and his crew did everything that they possibly could for us. The Captain even offered if necessary to give up the chance of a ten-thousand-dollar tuna catch in order to rush me to medical aid. During the three days we steamed toward the mainland I began to feel better, though I darn near froze to death, because the ice in which I was packed was made from brine. The pain subsided and my temperature went down—it was 103 the day I was rescued.

Radiograms from our parents and friends, and from all parts of the United States poured in. We even garnered that immediate reward of temporary fame—or notoriety: an offer from the movies. Needless to say, we were not anxious to commemorate the horrors of the Cocos predicament on celluloid—we wanted to forget it as fast as we could.

At Cape Blanco we learnt that there was no hospital in Puntarenas, and that I would have to be transferred to San José. Captain Dobbs then suggested that as long as the ice-pack treatment seemed to be helping the appendix it might be a good idea to remain on board. He had read somewhere, he said, that packing in ice sometimes cured an attack of appendicitis. So we cruised along the coast of Costa Rica for the next ten days. By the end of that time I felt much better. On the return trip south the pain disappeared completely, and we felt like travelling again.

Despite the Captain's protests, we loaded the *Vagabunda* overside, but before leaving we gave Captain Dobbs a letter absolving him from all responsibility for anything that might happen to us. Then we started down the coast towards Panama. On the way we left Coco with a kindly native family who had never seen a trained dog before and were amazed and delighted when she responded to our commands. Although we hated to give her up, we dared not take her into the Canal Zone. The quarantine regulations were very strict.

When we finally put into the Canal Zone, it seemed that we were going to have serious difficulty with the port officials. While in Corinto we had written a letter to the Port Captain, stating that we had travelled all the way down the coast as a regular ship, carrying the same ship's papers that a ten-thousand-ton freighter would carry, and if possible we wanted to transit the Canal with the same status. We said that we had read the

Canal Zone regulations, but would he please make two exceptions: Would he instruct the boarding party of five men to board us one at a time? And since the rules called for a "pilot aboard at all times" would he please pick a small, thin one?

As we pulled into the harbour of Panama word was sent out to proceed to a position between piers 18 and 19 in front of the Pacific Terminal Building, where the offices of the Port Captain, etc., were located, and to hoist our quarantine flag and stand by. We obeyed. But earlier that day we had fought a tropical storm in the Gulf of Panama, and the *Vagabunda* had threatened to go to pieces like the one hoss shay. The mast split; the boom pulled off; the zipper round the cockpit parted at the fabric. The *Vagabunda* was clearly on her last legs, and it seemed doubtful if she could make port. We got her in, but it was a dilapidated pair of adventurers in a badly battered craft that paddled between the two long docks and stood by. Our quarantine flag was a yellow rag tied to the harpoon shaft, stuck in the mast seat.

While we waited for official recognition, crowds lined the docks, cameras clicked, and plenty of good-natured ribbing floated to us across the water. Then a delegation of port officials, dressed in gold-braided white uniforms motioned us in. They were stern faced and most businesslike. "Let me see your clearance papers for this port," one said curtly. "I will examine your bills of health," said another. A third began asking questions and filling in a form. "Any explosives aboard? Any stowaways? When were you last fumigated? What is your fuel consumption per hour? Number of passenger accommodations?" And so on. Everyone was as sober as a judge about to pronounce sentence. We were scared to death.

The quarantine officer looked over our bills of health. "H-m-m, you have called at more ports than any ship that has ever gone through the Canal," he said. "It is going to take two forms to list them, and there will be an extra charge for that."

The Port Captain interrupted, "While we're talking about charges, do you know what it costs to transit the Canal?"

"No, sir," I answered meekly.

He cleared his throat and looked at us sternly. "Some ships pay toll charges of as much as thirty thousand dollars, and it's just as much work to put your little sixteen-foot craft through the locks as it is to put through a big freighter. We have to open and close the gates just the same, fill the chambers with water, and all the rest of it. Do you have any idea of what that's going to cost you?"

Ginger and I groaned. This was something that neither of us had thought about. Then the admeasurer stepped forward, whose job it is to figure the displacement of the ship about to transit the Canal. He stood on the dock, looking down at our tiny cockpit, and then stepped gingerly into it. He was a big broad-shouldered chap, and the canoe sank about six inches under his weight. He got down on his hands and knees, working his big body into the confines of the cockpit; unreeled about ten inches of his hundred-yard tapeline, and started measuring the *Vagabunda's* draught. His shoulders began to shake; he sputtered and gulped, and finally abandoned all efforts to suppress his mirth. "Ha, ha, ha!" he roared. We looked up at the dock. All the other officials were shaking with laughter, too.

Now they jerked us up on the dock, and began to congratulate us. When the crowd surged in, almost pushing us back into the water, the Canal Zone Police rushed to our rescue, and to protect the canoe from the usual vandals who had come armed with pocketknives, intent upon souvenirs. Then amid the cranking of cameras and the shouts of the bystanders the police broke a trail to the main dock for us—a bedraggled, salt-encrusted, bewildered pair.

Aboard the U.S. army transport *Château Thierry*, we were given the stateroom reserved for high army officials. Stewards came and went. Soap, towels, and clean clothes were laid out. After we had made ourselves presentable we went down to the officers' mess, where a big table groaned under all the dishes that we especially like and had missed for three years.

While we were eating, port officials and officers crowded round us with questions. Their curiosity was legitimate. Any one who would come from San Diego in a sixteen-foot canoe must be crazy, and they wanted to see for themselves just how cracked we were.

Then in came the Port Captain, his face wreathed in smiles as he extended the courtesy of the Panama Canal Zone to the crew of the *Vagabunda*. The admeasurer appeared, wearing a long face and carrying several pieces of paper covered with figures.

"Are you ready for the sad news?" he inquired. "Feel strong enough to take it?"

"We might just as well get it over with," I answered.

He looked as though he would like to smile—but he didn't. Instead he scowled. "It's been a big job to figure out your toll charges. And the best I can do for you, young man, is—*seventy-five cents*. When do you want to start?"

"Tomorrow." And right then and there we paid out seventy-five cents to the Canal Zone Administration. But we didn't begin the transit of the Canal for several days.

That night Commander Brown, U.S.N., entertained us at his residence. Some one poured Ginger into an evening gown whose long skirt she had an awful time managing after three years of shorts. I had on borrowed plumage, too—a white suit that fitted very well. Later, after the party was over, we shut the door of our bedroom and surveyed our lovely surroundings. Ginger walked over and felt the bed.

"It's three years," she reminisced, "since we've slept between linen sheets on a spring mattress. Won't it be swell?"

The End of the Trail—Panama

And how we would sleep, I thought.

But the next morning when our host failed to waken us by tapping on the door, he peeked in. We were sound asleep on the floor. After lying on hard surfaces for three years, we couldn't adjust ourselves to the soft mattress in one night.

As guests of the Army we spent a full day of sightseeing, ending with a night at Fort Clayton. Then for our last day and night in Panama City, the Navy again took us in tow. Luncheon, a cocktail party, and tea were followed by a dinner party which Admiral Williams gave for us aboard his flagship, the U.S.S.S. *Memphis*. After dinner came Ginger's crowning moment. As she stepped on deck with Mrs. Williams, feeling very elegant in her long evening gown, the assembled sailors snapped to salute. We were then taken to see our first motion picture in three years.

The next day we started through the Canal. As we entered the chamber of the first lock, behind a big ship, we were surprised at the number of people who had gathered to watch the smallest vessel ever to transit the Panama Canal officially. The locks began to fill, and the *Vagabunda* slowly rose, as millions of gallons of water poured into the chamber. When we reached the level, the gates ahead of us opened, and we followed the steamer into the second lock. Men had the canoe by ropes, but big ships are taken through the locks by means of electric donkeys.

Now the gates of the second chamber closed behind us. Again we rose, this time to the level of Miraflores Lake, which is fifty feet above the sea. The Canal Zone "mosquito fleet" met us in the lake, and escorted us with great merriment to the third lock, Pedro Miguel Lock, which is on the Pacific side. The "fleet" comprised every conceivable kind of small craft: kayaks, motor boats, rowboats, and so on. The Pedro Miguel Sea Scouts were also out to convoy us. The boys had planned a potluck dinner in their club house, they said. Would we be their guests? We had to go through the locks on schedule, but promised that we would break our journey after passing through Pedro Miguel Lock. We did, and had a fine time.

Paddling through the Canal was fun all round. Every ship that passed whistled a salute. Pilots and officers waved. In Culebra Cut, we stopped to see the great dredgers at work, and we visited the Darien Naval Radio Station, where there was another grand party. We've never been able to make up our minds as to which takes the most stamina: a round of fiestas, à la Elena, or transiting the Panama Canal in a canoe. You have to be good to do either.

We crossed Gatun Lake, the largest man-made lake in the world, on a squally day, and did not arrive at Gatun Locks until well after dark—wet, bedraggled and tired. The next morning we made the descent through the locks to Limon Bay, which is accomplished in three steps. As the canoe zigzagged her way through the chambers that lowered her to sea level, we were feeling as weary and battered as our outfit looked. At Cristobal we moored the canoe to a dock, and, while waiting for Captain and Marie Fischer to arrive, took one last picture of the *Vagabunda* before we lifted her from the water for the last time.

There she sat, her hull weatherbeaten, scarred, and twisted out of shape, the names of a hundred ports of call carved in the railing of her cockpit. For her a life of adventure had ended.

We spent a week in Cristobal. Then the *Vagabunda* was loaded aboard a passenger vessel and we three transited the Canal to the Pacific, retracing in seven days the route which had taken us three years to cover. We had arrived in Cristobal on October 9, 1936, three years to the day after leaving San Diego.

The question most frequently asked us since our return is: "How does it feel to be back?" That is not an easy question to answer.

We left the United States at the height of the depression, and returned to find things booming—some things. Progress along scientific and mechanical lines can be taken for granted. But what of social relationships, the things that really count?

I am afraid that we no longer fit into the picture. While we were a p. of organized society much that we now see went unnoticed: the increasing reluctance and inability of large groups to solve their own problems; people's growing distaste for economic, social, and political freedom, if it entails personal responsibility; their willingness to barter these things for some one's promise of a "larger life," with a minimum of effort on the part of the individual; the tendency of more and more people to regard governmental relief agencies as a "career"; their naïve belief that a political messiah or an economic formula can do for them the things that all men must do for themselves or perish.

Another disadvantage to living in a civilized society is that there is no time left for playing. About the grimmest thing we've seen since our return is the "hot spot," where everybody tries so damned hard to relax—and boredom, like prosperity, is just round the corner. I wonder if one had a million dollars to spend, and combed the United States for the guest list, whether it would be possible to throw one of Elena's parties and get the same joyous response?

When the natives work, they work hard; and conversely—when they play, they play. Having no passion for getting ahead, the fact that they are behind the Joneses in no wise disturbs them. In this they are decidedly realistic, and it is we who are foolish and impractical. They love life and live it while they are able. The theory that it is desirable to forego pleasure in the present that you may in some mythical future enjoy the provisions stored up for the rainy day would leave any intelligent *Indio* cold. Furthermore, he isn't interested in exercising power through the possession of things—he suspects that you can't take them with you, and at best the tenure is brief.

The End of the Trail—Panama

Since most of what he needs he produces, he naturally doesn't have to cope with the problems that beset highly organized, interdependent societies. Paris may decree shorter skirts for women, and the edict will affect the lives and fortunes of millions who never heard of Schiaparelli or Captain Molyneux. The native grower only knows that for some inexplicable reason his product—cotton, wool, silk—has become a drug on the market. For him, it is a major calamity.

Of course, a few smart people in an organized society exercise their foresight and escape—but most of us aren't smart. There's a chance to beat a malarial mosquito, because Nature gives her creatures a break. When you fight disease, you aren't fighting something you are totally unequipped to face. The problems Nature presents you with can for the most part be met by intelligence, work, discipline, and knowledge. And there is something else to be said for wresting a livelihood from natural resources: there is the priceless satisfaction of knowing that you've taken nothing from any one; that your place in the sun isn't contingent upon crowding your fellows into outer darkness.

To live the "simple life" isn't easy; it's hard—if you hate work. But Nature is just, or so it seems to us. The results of your efforts are concrete. If you fail in an enterprise, there is nothing mysterious about it; and there is always something that you can do to prevent its recurrence. Cause and effect are not obscured through a hundred intermediaries. Thank God, there is nothing indefinite about natural law; if you live in accordance with it, study its inexorable rules, it will reward you—and the slicker can't beat it. Personally, we prefer to take our chances with its hazards rather than attempt to fit ourselves into the confused pattern of the modern social order. Physical injuries and hardships may damage you, but they are soon forgotten. The psychic injuries of a competitive life are too high a price to pay—for us—in exchange for its dubious benefits.

Our trip was made for purely personal reasons. At the outset, we had no particular belief in its interest or value to any one else. That perhaps is the written record's greatest flaw. Many things of general interest that we might have learnt and reported are obscured by the personal. Primarily, we wanted to find out something about ourselves and our capacities; whether our romantic daydreams of a fuller and more colourful life could stand up against the actualities. For us, these questions are answered. For whoever reads this book, who knows?

Some of the other titles in the Adventure Travel Classic series published by The Long Riders' Guild Press. We are constantly adding to our collection, so for an up-to-date list please visit our website:
www.thelongridersguild.com

The Rob Roy on the Jordan	John MacGregor
In the Forbidden Land	Henry Savage Landor
From Paris to New York by Land	Harry de Windt
My Life as an Explorer	Sven Hedin
Elephant Bill	Lt.-Col. J. H. Williams
Fifty Years below Zero	Charles Brower
Quest for the Lost City	Dana and Ginger Lamb
Enchanted Vagabonds	Dana Lamb
Seven League Boots	Richard Halliburton
The Flying Carpet	Richard Halliburton
New Worlds to Conquer	Richard Halliburton
The Glorious Adventure	Richard Halliburton
The Royal Road to Romance	Richard Halliburton
My Khyber Marriage	Morag Murray Abdullah
Khyber Caravan	Gordon Sinclair
Servant of Sahibs	Rassul Galwan
Beyond Khyber Pass	Lowell Thomas
True Stories of Modern Explorers	B. Webster Smith
Call to Adventure	Robert Spiers Benjamin
Heroes of Modern Adventure	T. C. Bridges
Death by Moonlight	Robert Henriques
To Lhasa in Disguise	William McGovern
The Lives of a Bengal Lancer	Francis Yeats-Brown
Twenty Thousand Miles in a Flying Boat	Sir Alan Cobham
The Secret of the Sahara: Kufara	Rosita Forbes
Forbidden Road: Kabul to Samarkand	Rosita Forbes
I Married Adventure	Osa Johnson
Grey Maiden	Arthur Howden Smith
Sufferings in Africa	Captain James Riley
Tex O'Reilly – Born to Raise Hell	Tex O'Reilly and Lowell Thomas

The Long Riders' Guild
The world's leading source of information regarding equestrian exploration!
www.thelongridersguild.com